MW00577177

This book comes with access to more content online.

Quiz yourself, track your progress,
and score high on test day!

Register your book or ebook at
www.dummies.com/go/getaccess.

Select your product, and then follow the prompts
to validate your purchase.

You'll receive an email with your PIN and instructions.

Series 7 Exam 2024-2025

by Steven M. Rice

A Wiley Brand

Series 7 Exam 2024-2025 For Dummies®

Published by: **John Wiley & Sons, Inc.,** 111 River Street, Hoboken, NJ 07030-5774, www.wiley.com

Copyright © 2023 by John Wiley & Sons, Inc., Hoboken, New Jersey

Media and software compilation copyright © 2023 by John Wiley & Sons, Inc. All rights reserved.

Published simultaneously in Canada

For general information on our other products and services, please contact our Customer Care Department within the U.S. at 877-762-2974, outside the U.S. at 317-572-3993, or fax 317-572-4002. For technical support, please visit https://hub.wiley.com/community/support/dummies.

Wiley publishes in a variety of print and electronic formats and by print-on-demand. Some material included with standard print versions of this book may not be included in e-books or in print-on-demand. If this book refers to media such as a CD or DVD that is not included in the version you purchased, you may download this material at http://booksupport.wiley.com. For more information about Wiley products, visit www.wiley.com.

Library of Congress Control Number: 2023935193

ISBN 978-1-394-18703-4 (pbk); ISBN 978-1-394-18699-0 (ePDF); ISBN 978-1-394-18698-3 (epub)

Printed and bound by CPI Group (UK) Ltd, Croydon, CR0 4YY

C9781394187034_280423

Contents at a Glance

Table of Contents

Introduction

S o you want to be a stockbroker (registered representative)? The good news is that a career in the securities field can be extremely lucrative and rewarding. The not-so-good news is that anyone who plans to become a stockbroker and sell securities in any of the 50 states must first pass the Series 7 exam (Series 7 Top-Off Exam), which is no joke. And to accomplish this, you have to commit time and effort.

I passed the Series 7 exam (back when 250 questions counted toward your score) the first time with a very high score, but it required weeks of study and sacrifice. Those who aren't totally prepared on exam day are in for an unpleasant wake-up call. I always had a few students in every class who enrolled after they already failed the exam the first (or second) time they took it. Most of them initially expected the same easy ride that they'd experienced in high school or college. Not only were they wrong, but they also had to pay hundreds of dollars to reregister for the exam and wait another 30 days (a mandatory FINRA rule) before they could retake the exam. For those unlucky (or unprepared) enough to fail the exam three times, there is a 180-day waiting period.

Back to the good news again. You're obviously interested in doing well, so you probably won't be one of those people. This book can help you pass the Series 7 and achieve your goal.

About This Book

This book has all you need to pass the exam, although I certainly encourage you to view other materials and take whatever exams you can get your hands on.

I cover the topics that appear on the test, offer formulas, provide definitions, and go over the foundational information you need to know. I also include lots of tips and a few memory tricks. But the real benefit of this book is finding out how to study and think through problems as well as you possibly can. That's why I help you choose a study program, explain how to handle specific question types, warn you about common mistakes, connect concepts, and show you how to pull questions apart and get to the bottom of what's being asked. You then get to apply this knowledge in two full-length practice tests that appear in this book and online, as well as four additional online tests, so you get a taste of the Series 7 experience. (To find instructions for accessing the online practice exams, see the upcoming section, "Beyond the Book.")

This is a reference book, and most sections are self-contained. In other words, you can read a section and understand it without looking over the text that comes before it. When some background information is helpful, I give cross-references to related topics. Therefore, you can pretty much jump in and out whenever you find topics you like (and when you find those you don't). And like all good tour guides, I also point you to some other sites of interest — topics you can explore further on your own.

I've scattered sample questions throughout this book so you can test your understanding of new info and get a feel for Series 7 exam questions. I've also added a quiz and detailed answer explanations at the end of each chapter in Parts 2, 3, and 4 (which cover the subject matter of the exam). And of course, for those sections that don't include questions, remember that the practice tests that come with this book deal with all kinds of subjects.

I also use the language and lingo of FINRA. That means you see official names (like the Federal Reserve Board), nicknames (the Fed), and acronyms galore (like the FRB). That way, during the test, understanding the POPs, YTMs, TEYs, NAVs, EPSs, ADRs, LMVs, DRs, and so on, shouldn't be too much of a hassle.

If you're short on time, you can skip the sidebars, which are those little gray boxes that contain interesting but nonessential information.

Foolish Assumptions

While writing this book, I made a few assumptions about you and why you picked up this book. For starters, I assume that you're looking for a no-nonsense study guide that provides you with the meat and potatoes you need to pass the Series 7 along with a ton of example questions and some sample exams. Well, look no further! Whether you're preparing to take the test for the first time, retaking the test after a less-than-stellar performance, or looking for a refresher before you recertify, this is the book for you!

Icons Used in This Book

To make this book easier to read and use, I include some icons to help you find and fathom key ideas and information.

This icon highlights example Series 7 test questions (which I follow with helpful answer explanations).

This icon is attached to shortcuts and insider advice for studying for and passing the Series 7 exam.

This icon points to information that's especially important to remember in order to do well on the test.

This icon warns you away from actions that can harm your work and drop your score.

Beyond the Book

In addition to what you're reading right now, this book comes with a free access-anywhere Cheat Sheet that includes tips to help you prepare for the Series 7. To get this Cheat Sheet, simply go to www.dummies.com and type **Series 7 For Dummies Cheat Sheet** in the Search box.

I also include an appendix of some important figures and formulas on the publisher's website. To get this appendix, go to the following web address:

www.dummies.com/go/series7exam2024-2025fd

Remember: You can't take these resources into the exam center, so you need to memorize the information ahead of time.

You also get access to six full-length online practice exams. To gain access to the online practice exams, all you have to do is register. Just follow these simple steps:

1. **Register your book or ebook at Dummies.com to get your PIN. Go to** www.dummies.com/go/getaccess.

2. **Select your product from the dropdown list on that page.**

3. **Follow the prompts to validate your product, and then check your email for a confirmation message that includes your PIN and instructions for logging in.**

If you do not receive this email within two hours, please check your spam folder before contacting us through our Technical Support website at http://support.wiley.com or by phone at 877-762-2974.

Now you're ready to go! You can come back to the practice material as often as you want — simply log on with the username and password you created during your initial login. No need to enter the access code a second time.

Your registration is good for one year from the day you activate your PIN.

Where to Go from Here

Although you can read this book from start to finish, you can certainly work your way through in more creative ways. Where you start is up to you, though please, please don't start with the tests! Give yourself a good grounding in the content here, and then use the tests to evaluate your understanding and show you where to focus your studies. You can flip to the topics you think you understand fairly well to boost your confidence or skip directly to whatever's giving you trouble — let the index and the table of contents be your guides. If you have a good understanding of how to take the Series 7 exam, from how it's structured to how to tackle questions, then you can go directly to the chapters in Parts 2 or 3, which address types of securities. If you're feeling shaky on the legal aspects, check out the FINRA rules and regulations in Part 4. Everyone, however, can probably benefit from Part 1's test-taking basics and info on study plans. Wherever you go, feel free to take detours to your textbooks, flash cards, FINRA websites, and any other resources for more information. Just remember to come back so you don't miss anything here!

1

Gearing Up for the Series 7 Exam

IN THIS PART . . .

Review the computerized exam format and the procedures for registering to take the Series 7 exam.

Select the right study course and materials to prepare yourself for exam day.

Understand how to organize your study time efficiently and effectively.

Learn test-taking tips to improve your chances of scoring well.

Discover what to expect on test day.

» Taking a look at companion tests

» Getting a sponsor and registering to take the exam

» Uncovering topics tested on the Series 7

» Mastering the computerized exam format

Chapter **1**

Introducing the Series 7 Exam

Congratulations on your interest in becoming a stockbroker (or registered representative, to use the parlance of our times). But before you can lose yourself in the energy of the office, the eager voices of your clients, and the warm glow of success, you have to face the Series 7. In this chapter, I give you an overview of the Series 7 exam, including its purpose, structure, format, scoring, and some helpful tips to guide you through the registration procedure. By this point, you've probably already taken and passed the co-requisite Securities Industry Essentials (SIE) exam, so you should be somewhat familiar with the effort taken to pass a securities exam. If you studied for the SIE exam using *The Securities Industry Essentials Exam For Dummies,* much of the first four chapters of this book regarding how to take the exam, study procedures, test-taking tips, and so on will look familiar. If so, please feel free to gloss over the information you have a handle on.

What Is the Series 7 Exam, Anyway?

The Series 7 exam (Series 7 top-off exam) qualifies you to hold the title General Securities Registered Representative (stockbroker), to sell many different types of securities, and to hopefully make stacks of money for your clients (and a bit for yourself). Individuals who earn their license by passing the Series 7 exam are qualified to solicit, purchase, and/or sell securities products, including

» Corporate stocks and bonds

» Municipal bonds

» U.S. government bonds

>> Options

>> Direct participation programs (limited partnerships)

>> Investment-company securities

>> Variable contracts

The exam's purpose is to protect the investing public by ensuring that the registered reps who sell securities have mastered the skills and general knowledge that competent practicing stockbrokers need to have.

The Series 7 itself is a computer-based exam given at Prometric (www.prometric.com/finra) test centers throughout the United States. The 125-question exam, administered by the Financial Industry Regulatory Authority (FINRA), is three hours and 45 minutes in duration. A score of 72 percent or better gets candidates a passing grade and puts big smiles on their faces.

The sections later in this chapter explain the setup of the Series 7 and give a rundown of how to register for the exam. If you have other questions, contact the FINRA Support Team at 240-386-4040 or visit www.finra.org/industry/qualification-exams.

Profiling the Series 7 Exam-Taker

The Series 7 exam is for people who want to

>> Enter the securities industry

>> Become registered representatives

>> Work for a securities broker-dealer

Although some less-prestigious exams (for example, the Series 6 - Series 6 Top-Off Exam) can qualify you to sell some securities, most broker-dealers want their rising stars (that's you) to have the Series 7 license. That way, you can work with almost the whole kit and caboodle — corporate stocks and bonds, municipal and U.S. government bonds, options, direct participation programs, investment companies, variable contracts, and so on.

People who have a long and sordid history of embezzlement, forgery, and fraud are generally disqualified and precluded from taking the exam. Candidates must disclose any prior criminal records, and FINRA reviews each application on a case-by-case basis.

One's Not Enough: Tackling the Series 63 or Series 66

As of October 1, 2018, FINRA upset the applecart by dividing the Series 7 into the Securities Industry Essentials exam and the Series 7 (Series 7 top-off) exam. Because you don't need a sponsor to take the Securities Industry Essentials exam, you've probably already taken it. So, after tackling the Securities Industry Essential and Series 7 exams, you'll have to take one of the state licensing exams. You'll need to pass the Series 63 or Series 66 to be able to work in the securities industry because these exams and the Series 7 are co-requisites in most states. You can take the Series 63 or 66 either before or after you take the Series 7, but most people start studying for the Series 63 or 66 and register to take it right after passing the Series 7.

Note: Even if you live in a state that doesn't require either of these licenses, you still need to obtain one if you want to sell securities to someone who lives in a state that does require it. Just figure that your firm will require you to obtain the 63 or 66 to sell securities — your firm should tell you which one to take. The following sections explain what the two state-licensing exams cover.

Series 63: Uniform Securities Agent State Law Exam

The Series 63 is a 65-question test that the North American Securities Administrator Association (NASAA) developed, and it's designed to qualify candidates as securities agents. The Series 63 exam covers state securities regulation rules as well as rules prohibiting unethical and dishonest business practices (not that you'd do anything like that). The Series 63 used to be the most common test taken along with the Series 7 and SIE. Judging by class sizes, however, now, many more students are taking the Series 66 as compared to the Series 63.

Series 66: Uniform Combined State Law Exam

The Series 66 is a 100-question NASAA exam that combines the Series 63 and the Series 65 (Uniform Investment Adviser). The Series 66 is designed to qualify candidates as both securities agents and investment adviser representatives (IARs). The Series 65 portion of the Series 66 allows you to collect a fee for just giving investment advice. This license was implemented several years ago, and it'll most likely be required if you work for one of the bigger broker-dealers. More and more firms are requiring the Series 66 because it gives their registered reps an additional service to provide for their clients and an additional way for you (and your firm) to make money.

Securing Sponsorship and Signing Up

Unlike the SIE, all candidates (that's you) must have a sponsoring brokerage firm in order to register for the Series 7 exam. After passing the exam, your license will be in your own name; however, you have to be working for a firm in order for your license to be active. Generally, a firm hires you and then acts as your sponsor.

The following sections explain the basic exam requirements and help you navigate your way through the exam registration process.

Filling out an application to enroll

For you to obtain admission to the Series 7, your sponsoring firm has to file an application form (called a *U-4*) and pay the required processing fees with the Central Registration Depository (CRD). The U-4 is an annoying little form with about a gazillion pages that requires you to remember where you were ten years ago. You're also required to submit your fingerprints, and you have to complete this step through an approved facility. Your firm will likely recommend the place it uses — often the local police precinct. (Be advised that your sponsoring firm will probably frown upon your fingerprints if they're attached to your mug shot.)

If you want to see a preview of the U-4 registration form that you're responsible for filling out and that your firm has to submit, go to www.finra.org/sites/default/files/form-u4.pdf.

It's a date! Scheduling your exam

After your firm files the application with the Central Registration Depository and receives your enrollment notification, you can schedule an appointment to take the exam by contacting the Prometric Testing Center. Locate the test center nearest you by calling the Prometric center (800-578-6273) during business hours. Or you can visit www.prometric.com/test-takers/search/1finra to schedule to take your exam at a Prometric testing center or to schedule for online delivery to take the test at your location (click the link "Option 2: Schedule your exam for online delivery").

REMEMBER

Online testing at your desired location became increasingly popular during the pandemic when many of the testing centers were closed. At the end of this chapter, I discuss what you need to do to take the exam online. Check out the sidebar "Can You Take the Test at Your Location?"

Your Series 7 exam enrollment is valid for 120 days — you have to take the exam within this time frame. When scheduling your exam appointment, be ready to provide the exam administrators with

>> Your name and Social Security number and/or FINRA number

>> The name of your firm

>> A telephone contact to reach you and your employer

>> The name of the securities exam you're registering to take

>> Your desired test date

Getting an appointment usually takes about one to two weeks, depending on the time of year (you may wait longer in the summer than around Christmastime). Prometric will confirm your appointment on the phone or via email.

TIP

I suggest putting pressure on yourself and scheduling the exam a little sooner than you think you may be ready to take it; you can always move the test date back. (There will be a charge if you cancel within ten business days of your test date.) You know yourself best, but I think most students study better when they have a target test date.

You have a choice of locations to take the exam. If you don't mind traveling, you may want to schedule your exam at a location far away (maybe even in a different state) to get the test date that you want.

After you have your test date set, you may find that you're ready sooner or will be ready later than your scheduled appointment. The exam center administrators are usually pretty accommodating about changing appointments and/or locations as long as you call before noon at least two business days before your test date, but there may be a fee involved.

You can get an extension from the 120-day enrollment only if you call within ten days of your enrollment expiration and if no earlier test dates are available.

Planning ahead for special accommodations

If you require special accommodations when taking your Series 7 exam, you can't schedule your exam online. You have to contact the FINRA Special Conditions Team at 800-999-6647 or fill out the special-accommodations form at www.finra.org/sites/default/files/SA-Eligibility-Questionairre.pdf. Read on for info on what the test administrators can do if you have a disability or if English isn't your first language.

WARNING

Depending on your testing center, you may have to receive authorization to bring medical devices and supplies — such as insulin pumps, eye drops, and inhalers — into the testing room. If you need authorization, call your local Prometric testing center, and they'll be able to guide you on the approval process.

Americans with Disabilities Act (ADA) candidates

If you're disabled or learning impaired, FINRA provides testing modifications and aids in compliance with the provisions of the Americans with Disabilities Act (ADA). To qualify for ADA provisions, your disabilities have to permanently limit a major life activity, such as learning, speech, hearing, or vision.

To apply for special accommodations, you need to submit documentation from your physician or licensed healthcare professional to FINRA, along with a letter from your sponsoring firm requesting the special arrangements. Additionally, you have to submit the FINRA Special Accommodations Eligibility Questionnaire and Special Accommodations Verification Request Form for all special arrangement requests. (You can find links to the forms at `www.finra.org/industry/ special-accommodations`.)

You may request the accommodations you want approved; possible aids include but are not limited to

>> Extra time
>> A reader, writer, or recorder
>> A private testing room
>> A large-print exam booklet
>> Wheelchair-accessible locations

FINRA reserves the right to make all final decisions about accommodations on a case-by-case basis.

English as a second language (ESL) candidates

If English is your second language, you can request additional time to take the exam when you schedule your SIE test date. If FINRA approves, you receive a little extra time to complete the exam. In general, it gives an extra 30 minutes for exams less than two hours and an extra hour for exams over two hours.

To qualify for extra time due to English being your second language (LEP — Limited English Proficiency), fill out the form at `www.finra.org/sites/default/files/LEP-request-form.pdf`.

Just in case: Cancelling as an option

If something comes up or if you feel you're just not ready, you can cancel your appointment to take the Series 7 exam without penalty if you do so at least ten business days before the exam date. If a holiday falls within the cancellation period, you have to cancel an additional business day earlier. For example, if you're scheduled to take the exam on a Wednesday, you have to cancel on Tuesday two weeks before your exam date. If a holiday falls between those dates, you have to cancel on Monday two weeks before your exam date. For more information, you can visit `www. finra.org/industry/reschedule-or-cancel-your-appointment`.

WARNING

If you cancel after the proscribed deadline, if you don't show up to take the exam, or if you show up too late to take the exam, you will be charged a cancellation fee equal to the Series 7 exam fee paid by your firm, and there is no hardship policy. I'm sure the old "I forgot" excuse has been tried, but I've never heard of it being effective.

Taking a Peek at the Tested Topics

As a practical exam, the Series 7 requires you to master vocabulary, handle customer accounts, understand the rules and regulations that govern the securities industry, and yes, work with some math formulas. For ease of use (and because humans have a limited life span), this book focuses on the most commonly tested topics on the Series 7 exam. Here's an overview of what to expect:

>> The underwriting process (how new securities come to market) (Chapter 5)

>> Common and preferred stock (Chapter 6)

>> Corporate bonds and U.S. government securities (Chapter 7)

>> Securities issued by local governments (municipal bonds) (Chapter 8)

>> Margin accounts (using money borrowed from broker-dealers to purchase securities) (Chapter 9)

>> Investment companies (including mutual and closed-end funds) (Chapter 10)

>> Direct participation programs (limited partnerships) (Chapter 11)

>> Options (Chapter 12)

>> Analyzing the benefits and risks associated with investments; making appropriate recommendations to customers (Chapter 13)

>> Following how new securities are brought to the market and how existing securities are traded in the market (Chapter 14)

>> Income-tax implications that stock market investors face as well as a look at certain retirement plans (Chapter 15)

>> Rules and regulations governing the purchase and sale of securities and the registered representative's responsibility for maintaining accurate record keeping (Chapter 16)

FINRA has released a listing of the distribution of questions on the Series 7 exam. See Table 1-1 for the number of questions devoted to each activity that a registered rep performs.

TABLE 1-1 **Distribution of Series 7 Exam Questions**

Activity Performed by a Registered Rep	Number of Questions	Percent of Exam
Seeks business for the broker-dealer from customers and potential customers	9	7%
Opens accounts after obtaining and evaluating customers' financial profile and investment objectives	11	9%
Provides customers with information about investments, makes suitable recommendations, transfers assets, and maintains appropriate records	91	73%
Obtains and verifies customers' purchase and sale instructions and agreements; processes, completes, and confirms transactions	14	11%
Total	**125**	**100%**

Each of these activities falls under multiple areas of study. For example, to correctly answer questions that address the topic of handling customer accounts, you have to know enough about different types of stocks, bonds, and so on, to be able to guide your customers, including which investments are more beneficial to retirees and which work better for investors who are just entering the workforce.

A LITTLE TESTING INFO FROM FINRA

The FINRA website (www.finra.org) is certainly worth checking out. It contains all the nitty-gritty details about the Series 7 and related exams. Use this website for the following:

- **FINRA Current Uniform Registration Forms for Electronic Filing In WEB CRD:** This page includes the U-4 Series 7 registration forms and a link to the Uniform Forms Reference Guide, with contact numbers and other explanatory information for filers.

- **FINRA Test Center Rules of Conduct:** Just in case you're unable to distinguish the Series 7 test center from that third-period algebra class you had back in high school, FINRA gives you the rules and regulations for taking the Series 7 (do not hide a list of equations under the brim of your baseball cap, do not roam the halls during your restroom break, and do not pass notes, no matter how bored you are).

- **FINRA Registration and Exam Requirements:** This section gives a comprehensive list of the categories of securities representatives and the exam requirements.

- **FINRA Appointments and Enrollment:** Here you find FINRA tips for scheduling appointments to take the Series 7 exam, info about obtaining extensions, and the exam cancellation policy.

- **FINRA Registration Exam Fee Schedule:** Check out this page to see the fees for registering for the Series 7 Exam.

Although Table 1-1 shows the outline of the exam, I (and most other study material providers) break the chapters down by similar content to keep you from having to jump back and forth through your study material.

Understanding the Exam Format and Other Exam Details

To make sure you don't walk into the testing center, take one look at the computer screen, go into shock, and start drooling on the keyboard, I use the next few sections to cover some of the testing details for the Series 7 exam.

Exam basics

The Series 7 exam is a computerized, closed book (in other words, no book), three-hour and 45 minute exam. The exam consists of 135 multiple-choice questions (although only 125 of them count toward your score — see the next section).

You can take restroom breaks at any time, but the clock continues to tick away, so you may want to reconsider drinking a mega-jumbo iced latte the morning right before your test.

For information on the types of questions to expect, see Chapter 3. Flip to Chapter 4 for an overview of how your exam day may progress.

Ten additional trial questions

To ensure that new questions to be introduced in future exams meet acceptable standards prior to inclusion, you answer ten additional, unidentified questions that don't count toward your score. In other words, you get 135 questions to answer, but only 125 are scored.

If you see a question on the Series 7 that doesn't seem even remotely similar to anything that you've studied (or even heard about), it may very likely be an experimental question.

The computerized format and features

Although you don't need any previous computer experience to do well on the exam, you don't want your first encounter with a computerized exam to be on the date of the Series 7. Being familiar with the way the questions and answer choices will appear on the screen is essential. FINRA has been nice enough to provide a convenient tutorial for taking their qualification exams such as the Series 7 at the following link:

```
https://www.finra.org/sites/default/files/external_apps/proctor_tutorial.
swf.html.
```

A friendly exam-center employee will give you an introductory lesson to familiarize you with how to operate the computer before the exam session begins. Although the computer randomly selects the specific questions from each category, the operating system tracks the difficulty of each question and controls the selection criteria to ensure that your exam isn't ridiculously easier or harder than anyone else's. As a matter of fact, FINRA has recently started weighting the questions so that some will be worth a little more than average and some will be worth a little less depending on FINRA's feeling about how difficult the question is. To get you to a possible score of 100, the questions will average out at 0.8 points each.

The following list describes some important computer exam features:

» Scroll bars for moving the questions on the screen

» A time-remaining clock to help you track how much time you have left during each part (if the clock is driving you batty, you can hide it with a click of the mouse)

» A confirmation box that requires you to approve your answer choice before the computer proceeds to the next question

» An indication of which question you're currently on

» A choice of answering the questions by

- Holding down the <CTRL> and <ALT> buttons and typing in the letter for the correct answer on the keyboard

- Using the mouse to point and click on the correct answer

» The capability of changing your answers or marking questions that you're unsure of for later review, which allows you to go back and answer them at any time during that particular part. The "Mark for Review" button appears at the bottom of the screen after you select an answer. There is also a "Previous" button that allows you to go to the previous question if you want to change an answer.

» Both "Calculator" and "Notepad" buttons are available on the top-left of the screen for you to use if necessary to help you answer the questions. Whatever you type in the notepad will be available the whole time you're taking the test.

» If during the test you forget how any of the test features work, you can always click on the "Help" button in the upper-left corner for instructions.

» After you have completed the exam, you can click on the "Exit Exam" button in the upper-left corner. At that point, you can review questions or continue exiting the exam.

TIP

Although you can review and change all your answers at the end, don't. Your brain is going to feel like it went through a blender by the time you get there. Review only your *marked* questions and change the answers only if you're 100 percent sure that you made a mistake. As an instructor, I know that people change a right answer to a wrong one five times more often than they change a wrong one to a right one.

You can review your questions at any time during the test by clicking on the "Review Questions" button on the bottom of the screen. At that point, you will see a highlighted list of all of the questions that you've answered, and the ones marked for review will have a green flag next to them. Just click on the number to review questions you want to see again. You can remove a "Marked for Review" flag by clicking the "Mark for Review" button again. Click on the "Return to Test" button at the top of the screen to get out of the review section.

Exhibits

Some of the questions may require you to look at an exhibit such as an income statement, or balance sheet to answer a question. Back when I took the exam, each candidate was given an exhibit book, and the question told you which exhibit you needed to look at in the book. Now, the exhibits are right on the screen next to the questions that need them. You will be instructed to refer to the exhibit to extract the information you need to answer the question. If a question requires more than one exhibit, the thumbnails of the exhibits appear on the right. Just click on each one of them to open them up.

Receiving and Evaluating Your Score

Remember having to wait days or weeks for a standardized test score, hovering somewhere between eagerness and dread? Those days are gone. At the end of the Series 7, the system calculates your score and displays a grade result on the computer screen. Although the wait for your grade to pop up may feel like an eternity, it really takes only a few seconds to see your grade. When you sign out, the test center administrator will tackle you (well, approach you) and give you a printed exam report with your grade and the diagnostic score results with your performance in the specific topics tested on your exam.

Each question on the Series 7 exam is worth an average of 0.8 points (some are worth more and some are worth less depending on FINRA's feeling of how difficult a question is), and candidates need a score of 72 or better to achieve a passing grade. This percentage translates to 90 questions out of 125 that you have to answer correctly. The scores are rounded down, so a grade of 71.6 is scored as 71 on the Series 7. When I took the exam, back when the passing grade was 70, one of the other students from my class got a 69.6 (which was rounded down to a 69), and he had the NASD (now called FINRA) review his exam to try and get him the extra point. Needless to say, they ruled against him, and he had to take the exam again.

You passed! Now what?

After you pass the SIE, Series 7, Series 63, and/or Series 66 exam, FINRA will send your firm confirmation that you passed. At that point, you can buy and sell securities for your customers in accordance with your firm's customary procedures.

To continue working as a registered rep, you'll need to fulfill FINRA's continuing education requirements. Within 120 days after your second anniversary as a registered rep, and every three years thereafter, you have to take a computer-based exam covering regulatory elements such as compliance, regulatory, and ethical and sales practice standards at the Prometric exam center. In addition, there is a requirement (called a brokerage firm element) which requires broker-dealers to keep their registered representatives updated on job and product-related topics.

So you need a do-over: Retaking the exam

Sorry to end this chapter on a negative note; although the Series 7 isn't the mountain it used to be, it's still a difficult exam, and certainly a lot of people need a do-over.

If you fail the Series 7, your firm has to request a new test date and pay for you to retake the test. Your sponsors can send in one page of the U-4 requesting a new exam, or they can apply online through the Central Registration Depository (CRD) system. You should reapply immediately, though you have to schedule the new test date for at least 30 days after the day you failed (that's 30 days of prime studying time!). If you fail the exam three times, you're required to wait six months before you can retake the exam.

Use the time between exams to understand what went wrong and fix it. Here are some of the reasons people fail the Series 7 exam and some of the steps you can take to be successful:

» **Lack of preparation:** You have to follow, and stick to, a well-constructed plan of study. You have your diagnostic printout after you take the exam, and you can use that to focus on the areas of study where you fell short.

  Prep courses can help you identify and focus on the most commonly tested topics and provide valuable tips for mastering difficult math problems. Also, consider tutoring sessions tailored to accommodate your busy schedule and pinpoint the areas of study where you need the most help.

» **Nerves won out:** Some people are just very nervous test-takers, and they need to go through the process to get comfortable in unfamiliar situations. Next time around, they know what to expect and pass with flying colors.

  The people who are the most nervous about taking the exam tend to be the ones who haven't prepared properly. Make sure that you're passing practice exams on a consistent basis with grades in at least the high 70s before you attempt to take the real exam.

» **Insufficient practice exams:** You need to take enough practice exams before you take the real test. I think getting used to the question formats and figuring out how to work through them is as important as learning the material to begin with.

Check out Chapter 2 for info on setting up a study schedule and making the most of your practice exams.

CAN YOU TAKE THE TEST AT YOUR LOCATION?

Although all of the testing center locations have opened back up at full capacity, the online testing option is up and running. Obviously, there are some things you need (or need to know) prior to setting up to take the test at your location. I suggest that you go through the complete list here:

  www.prometric.com/sites/default/files/2020-04/PrometricProUserGuide_3.1_1.pdf

This site lists requirements for your computer (speakers, microphone, movable camera) and operating system. There are also downloading instructions and explanations of ID requirements, what a readiness agent is, and who will be watching you.

Chapter **2**
Preparing for the Series 7 Exam

When you're preparing for the Series 7 exam, a good cup of java and an all-nighter just aren't gonna cut it. Neither will a frantic two-week study session like the ones that used to work miracles when you were taking college finals. Even though it's not the 250-question beast it used to be, the Series 7 is not to be taken lightly, so you need to train for it both mentally and physically.

In this chapter, I discuss your options for studying to take the Series 7 exam. If you plan to enroll in a Series 7 exam prep course, I cover what to look for when selecting a course. I also help you organize your study time efficiently and effectively — even when your preparation time is limited.

Courses and Training Materials: Determining the Best Way to Study

When deciding how to go about studying for the Series 7 exam, your first mission is to identify the training mode that best suits your needs. If you're likely to benefit from a structured environment, you may be better off in a classroom setting. A prep course can also give you emotional guidance and support from your instructors and others in your class who are forging through this stressful ordeal with you. On the other hand, if you're the type of person who can initiate and follow a committed study schedule on your own every day, you may be able to pass the Series 7 exam without a prep course, and you can save the money you would have spent for classes. The following sections help you evaluate these options in more detail.

Back to school: Attending a prep course

People who learn best by listening to an instructor and interacting with other students benefit from attending prep courses. Unfortunately, not all Series 7 exam prep courses and training materials are created equally. Unlike high school or college courses, the content of Series 7 prep courses and the qualifications of the instructors who teach them aren't regulated by your state's Department of Education, the Securities and Exchange Commission (SEC), the Financial Industry Regulatory Authority (FINRA), or any other government agency. Do some research to locate the Series 7 training course that works best for you.

The following sections explain some things to consider and questions to ask before enrolling. Take a look at the info you gather and trust your gut. Is the primary function of the prep course to train students to be successful on the Series 7 exam, as it should be? Or do you suspect it's the brainchild of a broker-dealer who's looking for extra revenue to supplement her failing stockbroker business? (Run away!)

Training school background

To find information about a program you're considering, browse the training school's website or contact the school's offices. Find out how many years the training school has been in business and check with the Better Business Bureau or the Department of Consumer Affairs to see whether anyone has filed any complaints. Look for a school that has stayed in business at least five years. This staying power is generally a sign that the school is getting referral business from students who took the course and passed the Series 7.

Try to get recommendations from others who took the course. Word of mouth is an essential source of referrals for most businesses, and stockbroker training schools are no different. The stockbroker firm you're affiliated with (or will be affiliated with) should be able to recommend training schools.

Courses offered through a local high school's continuing education program can be just as effective as those offered through an accredited university or a company that focuses solely on test prep, as long as the right instructors are teaching them. Read on.

Qualifications of the course instructor(s)

The instructor's qualifications and teaching style are even more important than the history of the company running the course (see the preceding section). An instructor should be not only knowledgeable but also energetic and entertaining enough to keep you awake during the not-so-exciting (all right, *boring*) parts.

When looking for a course, find out whether the teacher has taken — and passed — the Series 7 exam. If so, the instructor probably knows the kinds of questions you'll be asked and can help you focus on the relevant exam material. The instructor is also likely to have developed good test-taking skills that she can share with her students.

Whether the instructor is a part-timer or full-timer may be important. For example, a full-time instructor who teaches 30 classes a year probably has a better grasp on the material than a part-time instructor who teaches 4 classes a year. By the same token, an instructor who owns the school that offers the course probably has greater interest in the success of the students than someone who's paid to teach the class by the hour. Use your best judgment.

TIP

Before you register, ask whether you can monitor a class for an hour or so with the instructor who would be training you. If the company says no, I suggest finding another course because that course provider may have something to hide. While you're at it, make sure the classroom is comfortable, clean, and conducive to learning.

Texts, course content, and extra help

To really benefit from a course, you need good resources — in terms of not only the actual training material but also the people in the classroom. These elements affect how the class shapes up and what you actually learn:

>> **Training material:** Will you have a textbook to study from or just some handouts? The instructor should provide you with textbooks that include sample exams, and a prep course should be loaded with in-class questions for you to work on. The course should also provide you with chapter exams that you can work on at night before the next session (yes, homework is a good thing). Remember, the more questions you see and answer, the better.

>> **In-class practice tests:** You want a prep course that includes test sessions where the instructor grades your exams, identifies incorrect answers, and reviews the correct answers.

>> **Instructor availability:** Ask whether the course instructors will be available to answer your questions after the class is over — not only at the end of the day but also during the weeks after you've completed the course and are preparing for the Series 7.

The practical details

The perfect course can't do you any good if you never show up for class. Here are some issues to consider about the course offering:

>> **Days and times:** Make sure the class fits your schedule. If getting there on time is too stressful or you can't attend often enough to justify the expense, you won't benefit from registering to take the course.

>> **Class size:** If more than 30 to 35 people are in the class, the instructor may not be able to give you the individual attention you need.

>> **Cost:** Obviously, cost is a major concern, but it definitely shouldn't be your only consideration. Choosing a course because it's the least expensive one you can find may be a costly mistake if the course doesn't properly prepare you. You end up wasting your time and spending more money to retake the exam. You can expect to pay anywhere from $300 to $600 for a standard Series 7 prep course, including training materials (textbooks and final exams).

Quite a few people don't pass the first time around, so find out whether the school charges a fee for retaking the prep course if you don't pass the Series 7 exam or even if you feel that you're not quite ready to take the test.

Selecting prep material to study on your own

If you're the type of person who can follow a committed study schedule on your own every day, you may be able to pass the Series 7 exam without a prep course. Many different types of study aids are available to help you prepare.

REMEMBER

No matter what your learning style is, I'm a firm believer in using a textbook as a primary training aid. You can use online courses, online testing programs, CDs, apps, and flashcards as supplements to your textbook, but give your textbook the starring role. By virtue of its portability and ease of use (you don't have to turn it on, plug it in, or have access to the Internet, and it can never, ever run out of batteries), the textbook is simply the most efficient and effective choice.

My personal favorites are the Empire Stockbroker Training Institute's *Series 7 Coursebook* and its companion, *Series 7 Final Exams* (www.empirestockbroker.com). The textbook focuses on the relevant exam topics, is easy to read and understand, and includes plenty of practice questions and detailed explanations. A lot of the better Series 7 course textbooks are available online rather than in bookstores. Unfortunately, from what I've seen, some of the Series 7 textbooks, even from some of the more reputable companies, have a great deal of information in their books that is not in the FINRA Series 7 outline. In addition to this book, consider investing in one or more of the following popular study aids:

>> **Online testing:** I'm all for online testing. Certainly, the more exams you take, the better. If the practice exam simulates the real test, it's even more valuable. With this study aid, you have access 24 hours a day, 7 days a week, and can pace yourself to take the exams at your leisure. Fortunately, this book gives you access to six online tests, which include online versions of the two that appear in this book. (For help accessing the online test bank, refer to the Introduction of this book.) If you need more questions, select a program (for example, www.empirestockbroker.com always has the most current, updated simulated exams) with a couple thousand questions or more, along with answers and explanations.

>> **Audio CDs:** You may still be able to find audio CDs or audio courses to help you prepare for the Series 7. This form of training can be beneficial as a review for people who already have a decent understanding of the course material. You can listen to recorded material while on the go or in your home.

TIP

Personally, I think recording your own notes — especially on topics you're having trouble with — is a wise use of your time. Putting the info in your own words, saying ideas out loud, and listening to the recordings can really help reinforce the concepts.

>> **Flashcards:** For those who already have a grasp on the subject matter, flashcards are good because you can tuck them in your pocket and look at them anytime you want. Commercial cards may be confusing and long-winded. You're better off making cards that focus on the areas that are most problematic for you.

TAKING A COURSE ONLINE

Remember that not all classes take place in brick-and-mortar buildings. For people who want to take a course but have scheduling constraints or lack a vehicle for commuting, instructor-led virtual classrooms may be an option. Students interact through online chats, email, message boards, and/or phone conferences. Classes may be scheduled at specific times, or you may work on your own time at your own pace. Before purchasing an online course, find out whether you can monitor one for an hour or so to see whether it meets your needs.

Note: Some so-called "online courses" may consist solely of a packet of study materials without any outside instruction. Make sure the course you sign up for has the features you want.

Outlining Your Series 7 Study Strategy

This section is designed to help you set up a plan based on how much time you have left to study. You can just wing it, but I've found that most successful students have at the very least a basic plan to help themselves get to the goal line as easily as possible. The following subsections describe what you should do based on the amount of time you have (or have left) to study. This is a guideline, of course, and if you have a way that you believe would work better for you, go for it.

Sharpening your skills when you have 8 weeks to prepare

If you have eight weeks to prepare to take the Series 7 Exam, you may feel like you're cruising on Easy Street. However, that doesn't mean that you should wait until your exam date gets closer to start studying. And of course, I don't know if you're working three jobs or have a spouse and kids that will be taking up a lot of your time. You may also already be working for a firm doing contact calling.

Start by looking at your schedule and coming up with times you can put aside for studying. Once you have that set, you can get going:

>> **Read the book start to finish.** You've most likely taken the Securities Industry Essentials Exam already, so much of the information will look somewhat familiar. Since you have such a long time before your actual exam, I suggest that you refrain from taking the chapter exams and final exams until you get closer to your test date so that you'll get a better handle on whether you're ready or not and not just remembering the questions because you've seen them before. I feel in most cases, it's best to start taking questions after you have a pretty good grasp on the material. After you've been through the book at least once, you can start making flashcards.

>> **Make your own flashcards.** I know that there are some companies out there that provide flashcards, but you'll get more out of the experience if you make them yourself. Go through chapters 5 through 16, and make flashcards for anything you find difficult to understand or remember. As an alternative, you can use sticky notes to affix notes right next to the material in the book you have trouble with.

>> **Bring your book and/or flashcards with you.** You don't know when you can sneak in a few extra minutes of studying. If you have your book or flashcards with you, you can get in some "unplanned" extra studying when you're on break at work or sitting in your car while your significant other is shopping.

>> **Gradually whittle down.** When going through your book or flashcards, start reducing the amount of things you need to really focus on. This doesn't mean that you can forget everything else because certainly everything in the book is important. However, you can start putting flashcards aside (or removing sticky notes) when you feel you have a really good grasp of a certain concept. This will allow you to really focus on the info you still need to work to understand.

Remember, you can always move your test date up. If you feel that you're extremely comfortable knowing that you're going to go in and ace the exam, move your test date up. Certainly if you're doing some contact calling, it would be nice to be licensed and starting to open accounts for yourself instead helping a colleague build their book.

Hitting your stride with 4 weeks till exam day

Most students take about four weeks to study. If you have more time than that, it's a good thing. If you have four weeks till exam day and just started studying, please review the bullet-pointed list in the preceding section, "Sharpening your skills when you have 8 weeks to prepare," because I'm going to suggest you do all of the things on that bullet-pointed list. However, I'm adding one thing at this point: Start taking the chapter quizzes and practice exams in the book. Besides reading the material and making and reviewing flashcards, you need to start getting a feel for Series 7 practice questions.

When you take a chapter quiz or practice exam, circle any questions you have difficulty with. Then, after you complete the quiz or exam, you have to thoroughly review. You should spend way more time reviewing the questions than you do taking the quiz or exam. Especially spend a lot of time reviewing the questions you got wrong or circled. You probably will guess correctly on some of the questions you don't understand, and you likely will make some careless mistakes. Now is the time to make those careless mistakes so that you can make sure you don't do it again. Reviewing an exam also means rereading chapters or sections of chapters until you have a solid grasp on the information.

If you take the practice exams in the book for the first time and you get 80s or better, you may want to consider moving your test date up. Wiley and I provide you with an online test bank of questions. To get the most out of these practice questions, I recommend that you take them as close as possible to your test date, preferably no more than two weeks prior.

Getting down to the wire . . . 2 weeks left to study

Hopefully if you're reading this, you've already been studying for a couple of weeks and only have two weeks left to go. However, if you have two weeks left to go and you just started studying, you really need to buckle down. I suggest that you clear the decks and carve out as much study time as you're able to. The bulleted list in the previous section, "Sharpening your skills when you have 8 weeks to prepare," provides a good start.

Since you only have two weeks left to prepare, I also suggest that you plan on taking all the exams in the book and the online ones. Remember, do not take another practice exam until you have thoroughly reviewed the last one you took, as described in the preceding section, "Hitting your stride with 4 weeks till exam day." The idea is to get better each practice exam, not to keep making the same mistakes over and over. If you're hankering for additional test questions to take, you can ask people at your firm if they have any practice exams or you can purchase some online exams such as the ones on the empirestockbroker.com website.

Feeling extra pressure when you only have 1 week left to study

So, you're down to the wire now. If you haven't started studying yet, I hope you have nothing else to do but study and take practice exams up until your exam. If you've just started, see the bulleted list in the previous section, "Sharpening your skills when you have 8 weeks to prepare," which will help head you in the right direction. However, since there is only 1 week left, you need to take a lot of practice questions. Take and review all the quizzes at the end of each chapter, take and review the two practice exams contained in Part 5 of this book, and take and review the practice exams provided in the online test bank that accompanies this book.

If you've been studying previously and this is your last week before the test, it should be smooth sailing. A majority of your studying at this point should revolve around taking practice questions like the ones in the book and online. Feel free to take questions from other books or online sources. If you see some odd questions from other sources, don't worry about it. I have covered what you need to pass the exam as quickly and efficiently as possible. Always make sure that you spend more time reviewing than taking exams. If you get tired of taking exams, review your flashcards (all of them) or reread each of the chapters in the book. Remember, you're looking to score at least in the 80s on the first time you take a practice exam. Good luck.

Managing Your Study Time Wisely

Unless you're a direct descendent of Albert Einstein, you probably need to allow yourself as much time as possible to prepare for the Series 7 exam. Even though the Series 7 exam is only 125 questions, the amount of material you have to study to be prepared to answer those 125 questions out of their universe of questions is quite extensive.

Get your affairs in order. Go to the dentist and get that sore tooth filled, pay your bills, get your flu shot, visit your friends and relatives, finish any critical home improvement projects — basically, clear the decks as best you can so you can concentrate on your studies. The following sections can help you establish a study plan.

Blocking out some time to study

You have to use your time efficiently, and to accomplish this, you need to grab every spare moment and channel it into study time. If you're attending a Series 7 prep course, your instructors should help you (and your classmates) set up a study schedule for before, during, and after you complete the course.

If you're in charge of carving out your study time, then plan on putting in around 30 to 40 hours per week. You know yourself best, but most students require 150 to 200 hours of studying, which means that 4 to 6 weeks would work well for most people. (For advice on how to study well, please look at "Exploring Study Strategies" later in the chapter. The following section discusses setting up an actual schedule.)

Especially for those of you who continue to work at your full-time job, now may be the time to have a heart-to-heart with your boss to negotiate some extra study time. After all, you need to work this out only for the next few weeks. Can you take vacation time? Will your boss allow you flex time (where you agree to work two hours later each day for four days and have the fifth day off)? Can you arrange a quiet place at work to study during breaks and lunchtime?

TIP

Set aside a consistent time to study on a daily basis. If possible, schedule your study time around your internal clock. For example, if you're the type who needs a brass band to wake you up and get your mind functioning first thing in the morning but you're wide awake and ready to go at midnight, you may be better off with a study schedule that begins later in the day and lasts into the night. By contrast, if you're leaping out of bed like a jack-in-the-box at the crack of dawn but are dead on your feet by 10 p.m., a morning study schedule would be more favorable.

TIP

You never know when extra time to study will present itself, so carry your textbooks or some flashcards with you whenever you leave home. You can read or drill yourself whenever you find some spare time — on the train, waiting in line, and yes, even during your trips to the restroom.

It's a plan: Getting into a study routine

Establishing and sticking to a study routine is essential. Many people find the Series 7 exam to be difficult because they have to absorb so much material in a relatively short time span. Furthermore, most of the information on the test is easy to forget because it's not info you use every day. Therefore, you have to reinforce your knowledge on a daily basis by constantly reviewing and revisiting the old information while learning new material. You'll continue to follow this routine over and over and over again.

Organizing yourself to cover all the topics you'll be tested on is crucial. If you're taking a prep course or home study course, a huge benefit is that during the course, the time necessary to learn and review all the subject matter will be allotted for you.

TIP

If you're trying to study on your own, get yourself a course textbook and divide the pages by the number of days you have available for studying. Be sure to allow yourself an extra week or two for practice exams. Review each chapter and complete each chapter exam until you have a firm grasp on a majority of the information. Take notes, highlight, and review the material you're having problems with until you feel comfortable with the concepts. Initially, you'll spend a majority of your time on new material; after that, you'll spend your time reviewing and taking chapter quizzes.

During the last one to two weeks leading up to the exam, take as many practice exams as possible. Remember to review each exam thoroughly before moving onto the next one. For more helpful tips, check out the section "Exploring Study Strategies" later in this chapter.

Give it a rest: Taking short breaks

If you find yourself reading the same words over and over and wondering what the heck you just read, it's probably time to take a break. Taking short (5- to 10-minute) breaks can help you process and absorb information without confusing new ideas with the old.

SETTING UP SHOP: FINDING AN IDEAL PLACE TO STUDY

When you're first learning new material, set yourself up in a place where you have as few distractions as possible — the local library, a separate room, even the bathtub. One of my students used to retreat to his car in the driveway after dinner while his wife put their young kids to bed.

The exam room, with its small cubicles, places you in proximity with other people who are taking the exam at the same time. If clicks of the mouse, taps on the keyboard, the scratch of pencil on paper, and the frustrated sighs of less-prepared test-takers are likely to distract you, you may want to use earplugs, which are available at most exam centers. If, however, you don't want to use earplugs, you can prepare for the worst by subjecting yourself to a somewhat noisy study environment somewhere along the line. (When I was taking my exam before earplugs were permitted, construction crews were working in the next room. Luckily, I'd studied in noisy settings; otherwise, the sound of screw guns and workmen talking would have driven me to distraction!) Go to a coffee shop (or any populated establishment) during lunch hour, or turn on a fan or a radio to familiarize yourself with background noise while you're taking your practice exams. Obviously, if you're taking the exam at home, you have more control over your environment.

When you reach your saturation point and really start zoning out, you can practice a bit of productive procrastination — walk the dog, shower, do some sit-ups and/or push-ups, grab a meal or a snack, or do anything else that lets you move around or take care of the little things that have to get done. A little human contact can go a long way too, provided you have the discipline to hit the books again.

Sometimes, taking a break from one study method can be as good as taking a break from studying altogether. Use multiple types of study material (textbooks, class notes, flashcards, and so on). If, for example, you get sick of looking at a textbook, try reviewing your notes, flipping through or creating some flashcards, or taking some online practice exams.

Staying focused from day to day

Passing the Series 7 exam is a rite of passage. It's your ticket to wealth, fame, and fortune (or at least a decent job). If you put the time and effort into studying for the Series 7, you'll be rewarded. If not, you'll have to relive the nightmare over and over again until you reach your objective. To reap your reward as quickly as possible, make a resolution: Until you pass the Series 7, commit to limiting your social life, and devoting most of your waking hours to one purpose — studying for the exam. Repeat after me: "This is my life for now."

If you find that you really need to take a mental health day off at some point, make sure that you don't separate yourself from your textbooks for more than one day — jump right back into the Series 7 fire the next day.

WARNING

Under no circumstances (except in the case of a family emergency) should you stop studying for more than one day within a two-week period. I've had students who were doing quite well come back to take another prep class because their test dates were too far off, and they'd put the books down for a while. The next thing they knew, they'd forgotten half of what they'd learned. Fortunately, the information comes back faster the second time around.

TIP

To keep focused on your studies without permanently forgetting about otherwise important life activities, prepare a file folder labeled "To do after I pass the Series 7." If anything comes up while you're studying, instead of interrupting your study time or stressing about things that need to be done, write down the task or event on a piece of paper, place it in your to-do file, and put it out of your mind.

Devoting time to practice tests

Certainly, when you're first going over new material, you should spend most of your time learning the information and taking chapter quizzes. After you feel like you have a good handle on the material, you should start taking full practice exams to see where you stand. (This book includes questions throughout Parts 2–4, followed by two full-length 125-question practice exams with answers and explanations in Part 5.) The last week or two before the exam should be almost entirely devoted to taking practice exams and reviewing them.

After you move into the practice-test phase, continue to use your textbook not only to reference material you don't understand but also to ensure you don't forget what you've learned. Too many people rely solely on the tests and forget to read their textbooks now and then. Figure on rereading one to two chapters per day. After taking a practice exam, always completely review it before you move on to the next one. And don't listen to the people who say you have to take three or four practice exams a day; you're better off taking one exam per day and spending twice as long reviewing it as you spent taking it. This method helps to ensure that you know the subject matter and that you won't make the same mistakes twice.

Practice exams can help you gauge whether you're ready for the real Series 7. See "Knowing When You're Ready" at the end of this chapter for details.

If you run out of exams to take, it's better to purchase more or see whether someone else in your firm has a different book with tests you can borrow than to take the same exams over and over again.

Avoiding study groups

Unless your study group includes your instructor, I recommend that you avoid a study group like the plague. The problem with study groups is that everyone wants to study the information that they're having problems with, and chances are, not everyone is struggling with the same thing. And if everyone *is* having the same problem, who can help you? I strongly feel that your time is better spent studying on your own.

If you really feel you'd benefit from studying with someone else, try to arrange a tutoring session with a Series 7 instructor.

Staying in shape

Ignoring the importance of physical fitness when you prepare to take the Series 7 exam is a big mistake. The exam itself (and the prep time you put into your study schedule) is not only mentally exhausting but physically demanding as well. You have to be able to stay alert and concentrate on difficult questions for a full three hours and 45 minutes. In the weeks leading up to the test, any exercise you can do to keep yourself physically fit — including cardiovascular exercise such as jogging or bike riding — can help out. A workout also gives you a great reason to take a study break.

Exploring Study Strategies

The more ways you work with a piece of information, the better able you'll be to recall it. Here are some study strategies to supplement your routine of reading your textbook and taking practice exams:

>> **Aim to understand concepts and relationships, not just formulas and definitions.** Having a good grasp of how ideas are related can provide a safety net for when rote memory fails; you may be able to make educated guesses, re-create formulas, or come up with something to jog your memory. When you see an equation, try to figure out where the numbers come from and what the formula really tells you.

>> **Create an outline of your notes or write flashcards.** Using your own words, try to put the more difficult areas of study into an outline or on flashcards. The whole process of condensing large mountains of information into your own abbreviated outline helps you process and absorb difficult concepts.

>> **Mark up your textbook.** You don't have to return your textbook to the library, so use the margins to rephrase ideas, draw diagrams, repeat formulas or equations, and highlight unfamiliar words.

>> **Record yourself reading your notes and then play back the tape at night while you're falling sleep or when you're driving.** Although the play-it-at-night technique has been known to give some people nightmares, this temporary condition usually clears up after the exam. I've also heard some people proclaim the nighttime playback is "as soothing as Sominex." (If it prevents you from falling asleep, turn off the tape and opt for getting some rest.)

Note: While you're sleeping, the brain may process ideas you learned during your waking hours; however, you generally have to be paying attention to remember something new. The main benefit comes from making the initial recording and letting study material be the last thing you hear before you fall asleep.

>> **Use sticky notes to flag difficult topics or concepts.** As you study, put a sticky note on a section or page in the book where you need more work. After you've filled your book(s) with stickies, concentrate your study on those difficult areas (where the stickies are). After you feel that you have a good grasp on this information, remove the note from the book. As you learn more and more, you'll whittle down the number of pages with stickies until you've removed them all from the textbook.

Developing Solid Test-Taking Skills

To be successful on the Series 7, developing your test-taking skills is just as important as mastering the concepts that form the basis of the questions. The best way to develop test-taking skills is to take practice tests, such as the ones in this book. Following are some tips that can also help you polish up your skills.

Read the question carefully

Don't be fooled. Exam creators love to trip you up by making you jump ahead and answer the question — incorrectly — before you read the entire problem. Often one of the last words in the call (specific inquiry) of the question is worded in the negative, like "all of the following are true *except*," or "which of the following is the *least* likely to," and so on. When reviewing the answers to a practice test, these questions cause some students to groan or slap themselves in the head when they realize their mistake. Don't worry — this common reaction usually goes away after you start getting better at taking exams.

Look for phrases that lead to the topic tested

Try to identify the specific category that the question is testing you on. If you study for the number of hours that I recommend (see "Blocking out some time to study"), you'll most likely cover the material the question references at some point, and you'll be able to identify the topic that the question applies to. After you know the topic, your brain can retrieve the information you need from its mental file cabinet, making it easier for you to focus on the applicable rule, equation, or concept so you can answer the question correctly.

Work with what you have

If possible, work with the facts — and only the facts — in the question. Too often, students add their own interpretation to the question and turn a straightforward problem into a mess. Use the facts that are given, dump the garbage information that isn't necessary to answer the question, and don't make the question more difficult or assume that there's more to the question than what appears.

Adding irrelevant information into a question seems to be a very common practice for students (for example, they ask, "Yeah, but what if she were married?"). My standard answer is, "Did it say that in the question?" to which the response is *no*. Don't make your life more difficult by adding your own speculations into the question; just answer the question that's given to you.

Don't obsess; mark for review

If you experience brain freeze while taking the exam, don't panic or waste valuable time on one question. Eliminate any answer(s) you know must be wrong (if any), take your best guess, and *mark the question for review* so that you can easily return to it later. The question may even resolve itself. For example, another question may trigger your memory as you continue to take the exam, and the correct answer to the earlier question may become clear.

Keep track of time

Time yourself so you're always aware of how much time you have left to complete the exam. One way to do so is to figure out which question you need to be up to at the end; use that as a benchmark to keep track of your progress. In your session, you have three hours and 45 minutes to complete the exam. You have to answer a total of 135 questions (10 don't count toward your score). This gives you 1.38 minutes (or 1 minute and 22.8 seconds) to answer each question.

Translating these numbers to half-hour benchmarks gets you the results shown in Table 2-1.

TABLE 2-1 **The Series 7 Exam in 30-Minute Increments**

Time	Number of Questions Completed
30 minutes	18
1 hour	36
1.5 hours	54
2 hours	72
2.5 hours	90
3 hours	108
3.5 hours	126
3.75 hours	135

TIP

Memorize these benchmarks, write them on your scrap paper (or dry erase board) as soon as the exam administrators allow you to begin, and keep referring to your watch or the clock on the computer screen to track your progress in relation to the benchmark. If you find yourself falling behind, pick up your pace. If you're really falling behind, mark the lengthier, more difficult questions for review and spend your time answering the easier questions. Even though the more difficult questions (at least in their estimation) may be worth a little more, you can't afford to be bogged down for too long on one question.

Most students don't have a problem finishing the Series 7 exam on time. If you easily and consistently finish 125-question Series 7 practice exams in less than three and a half hours or so, you should be okay on the real Series 7.

TIP

When you are taking the Series 7 exam at the test center, if you find yourself obsessing over the clock on the computer to the point that you can't concentrate on the question in front of you, you can hide or make the clock appear by clicking on the lower-left corner of the computer screen.

Master the process of elimination

The Series 7 exam is a standardized exam. This format makes it similar to other practical exams of this type: The best way to find the correct answer may be to eliminate the incorrect answers one at a time. I help you develop this crucial skill as you tackle the topic-specific questions throughout this book.

Maintain your concentration

To maintain your concentration, read the *stem* of the question (the last sentence before the answer choices) first to keep yourself focused on what the question is asking. Next, read through the entire problem (including the stem) to get a grip on the facts you have to consider to select the correct answer. You can then anticipate the correct answer and read all the answer choices to see whether your anticipated answer is there. If you don't see your answer and none of the other choices seem to fit, reread the stem to see whether you missed an important fact. Check out Chapter 3 for more detailed test-taking tips.

You can also take care to keep yourself physically alert. The last hour or so is usually the most difficult. I recommend eating a small protein bar prior to starting the test to help keep your levels of energy and concentration high. Forget high-sugar/high-carb foods; leave them for after the exam. These foods boost your sugar level temporarily, but when the level drops, your energy and concentration levels sink like a lead balloon.

Low energy levels can lead to sloppy mistakes. If you feel yourself fading, do whatever it takes to stay alert and focused: Get up and get a drink of water, splash some water on your face, stretch, or dig your fingernails into the palms of your hands.

Think carefully before changing your answers

In general, if you select an answer and you can't really explain why, maybe it was just a *gut* answer. You're five times more likely to change to a wrong answer than to the right one, so change your answer only if

>> You didn't read the question correctly the first time and missed a major point that changes the answer choice (for example, you didn't see the word *except* at the end of the question).

>> You're absolutely sure you made a mistake.

Use the scrap paper wisely

In addition to the "Notes" button in the upper-left corner of the computer screen, if taking the test at a testing location, you will receive a few pieces of letter-sized scrap paper (or a dry erase board), all of which will be collected — so restrain yourself from writing any obscenities about the exam or its creators. Here are some more productive ways to use this valuable resource:

>> **Mark dubious questions for review.** You have to answer each question before you can go to the next, so if you're not sure of the correct answer, eliminate the wrong answers, take your

best guess, and mark the question for review later. On your scrap paper, write down the numbers of any questions you want to check before the end of the session.

- » **Eliminate wrong answers.** You can't write on the computer screen, so for each question, you may find it helpful to write *A, B, C,* and *D* on your scrap paper (in a column) as they appear on the screen and eliminate answers directly on your paper.

- » **Do a brain dump.** After the exam begins and before your brain gets cluttered with Series 7 exam questions, use your scrap paper or dry erase board to jot down the formulas you've memorized or topic matters that tend to give you problems so that you can refresh your memory during the exam. Your scrap paper or dry erase board will be collected at the end of the session.

TIP

When doing a brain dump, write only the things that you're really having problems with. You know — the ones that you still feel the need to study the morning of the test. Don't worry about cataloguing things you already know and feel comfortable with, because it's a waste of your time (and paper). Those items should come to the surface of your brain as soon as you need them.

- » **Time yourself.** Write down your half-hour benchmarks (prepared for you in the "Keep track of time" section earlier in this chapter) on your scrap paper and check periodically to make sure you stay on track.

- » **Perform calculations and draw diagrams.** Use the scrap paper to work out math problems, create seesaws, or make any other diagrams that help you rack up points.

Knowing When You're Ready

Your goal is to consistently score 80 to 85 percent on the sample tests that you take to ensure that you're ready for the real exam.

REMEMBER

To determine your readiness, consider your scores on the practice exams the *first time* you take them. In other words, don't convince yourself that you're ready if you score 85 percent on an exam that you've already taken three times. If you take a practice exam more than once, you may just be remembering the answers. I'm not against taking the same exams more than once, but don't use exams you've taken before to gauge how prepared you are.

My company and some other companies sell an exam as a final benchmark to test a student's readiness to take the Series 7 exam. We call ours The Annihilator: a 125-question exam designed to be four to six points harder than the real exam. Students who pass with a 72 or better are most likely ready to take the Series 7.

IN THIS CHAPTER

» Exploring the composition of Series 7 exam questions

» Analyzing the purpose and intent of a question

» Identifying the correct answer

» Mastering the process of elimination

Chapter **3**

Examining and Mastering Question Types

Yes, I know, I know: "Why can't they just ask regular questions?" This problem has perplexed Series 7 test-takers throughout the ages (all right, maybe not, but it does bug me). The test designers have riddled the old pick-the-best-answer questions with all kinds of pitfalls. The people in charge want you to choose combinations of correct answers and pick out exceptions; they expect you to pull numbers from balance sheets and apply complex formulas; and, as if you don't have enough to worry about, they even give you extraneous information to try to trip you up. Sheesh!

In this chapter, I introduce you to the types of questions to expect on the Series 7 exam, and I show you how to analyze the facts in the questions and identify what the examiners are *really* testing you on. I also show you how to use the process of elimination to find the right answer and, if all else fails, how to logically guess the best answer.

The Series 7 tends to have more exhibit questions than the SIE. However, if you've already taken the SIE exam, you're somewhat familiar with the question types.

TIP

You should also be aware that in its effort to make securities exams more fair to all test-takers, FINRA has decided to weight the questions according to levels of difficulty. What this means to you is that for the most part, easier questions (or what FINRA deems to be easier questions) will be worth less than the average question and more difficult ones will be worth more than average.

Familiarizing Yourself with Question Formats

Even though there are only 125 questions (135 if you're including the 10 that don't count), there are a massive number of questions that could be asked. The Series 7 exam is a challenging test that poses questions in many different ways and shouldn't be taken lightly. You have to deal with multitiered Roman numeral nightmares, open- and closed-ended sentences, and killers like *except* and *not.* In this section, I show you how the examiners phrase the questions and how they can trip you up if you aren't careful.

Working with the straight shooters: The straightforward types

Straightforward question types include a group of sentences with the facts followed by a question or incomplete sentence; you then get four answer choices, one of which correctly answers the question or completes the idea.

Closed-stem questions

As with other FINRA exams, you'll find more closed-stem questions than any other question type on the Series 7 exam, so you'd better get a handle on answering these babies, for sure. Thankfully, closed-stem questions are fairly run-of-the mill. They begin with one or more sentences containing information and end with a question (and, appropriately enough, a question mark). The question mark is what makes closed-stem questions different from open-stem questions, which I discuss in the next section. Your answer choices, lettered (A) through (D), may be complete or incomplete sentences. Here's a basic closed-stem question.

EXAMPLE

Mr. Bearishnikoff is a conservative investor. Which of the following investments would you recommend to him?

(A) Buying put options

(B) Buying long-term income adjustment bonds

(C) Buying common stock of an aggressive growth company

(D) Buying Treasury notes

The right answer is Choice (D). The first sentence tells you that Mr. Bearishnikoff is a conservative investor. This detail is all the information you need to answer the question correctly, because you know that conservative investors aren't looking to take a lot of investment risks and that U.S. government securities such as Treasury notes (T-notes) are considered the safest of all securities — they're backed by the fact that the government can always print more money to pay off the securities that it issues.

Of course, sometimes the phrasing of the answer choices can help you immediately cut down the number of feasible answer choices. For instance, Mr. Bearishnikoff would probably balk at investing in an *aggressive growth* company, which certainly doesn't sound stable or safe. Check out the section titled "Picking up clues when you're virtually clueless: The process of elimination" for details on raising your odds of answering questions correctly.

By the way, the *you* in the question refers to you on your good days, when you're considerate and rational and have had a sufficient amount of sleep. Mr. Bearishnikoff probably wouldn't appreciate any rogue-elephant investing, even if you think he should be more daring. The question also assumes normal market conditions, so don't recommend a different investment because you think the government is going to collapse and T-notes are going to take a dive. Just accept the conditions the problem presents to you.

TIP

Be careful to focus only on the information you need to answer the question. The Series 7 exam creators have an annoying tendency to include extra details in the question (such as the maturity date, coupon rate, investor's age, and so on) that you may not need. See "Focusing on key information," later in this chapter, for some tips on zeroing in on the necessary info.

Open-stem questions

An open-stem question poses the problem as an incomplete sentence, and your mission, should you choose to accept it, is to complete the sentence with the correct answer. The following example shows how you can skillfully finish other people's thoughts.

EXAMPLE

The initial maturity on a standard option is

(A) three months

(B) six months

(C) nine months

(D) one year

The answer you want is Choice (C). *Options* give the purchaser the right to buy or sell securities at a fixed price (see Chapter 12). Options are considered *derivatives* (securities that derive their value from another security) because they're linked to an underlying security. Standard options have an initial maturity of nine months. On the other hand, Long-Term Equity AnticiPation Securities (LEAPS) may have initial maturities of up to three years. But this example question asks about a standard option; therefore, you don't assume that it's a LEAP.

The preceding example is quite easy. Anyone who has been studying for the Series 7 exam should know the answer. However, what makes the Series 7 so difficult is that the exam is loaded with so many date-oriented details. Not only do you have to memorize the initial maturities of all the different securities, but unfortunately (and believe me, I feel your pain), you also have to remember a truckload of time frames (for example, accounts are frozen for 90 days, new securities can't be purchased on margin for 30 days, an options account agreement must be returned within 15 days after the account is approved, and so on).

TIP

Date-oriented details are excellent material to include in your flashcards. See Chapter 2 for more study suggestions.

Encountering quirky questions with qualifiers

To answer questions with qualifiers, you have to find the "best answer" to the question. The qualifier keeps all answer choices from being correct because only one answer rises above the rest.

Working with extremes: Most, least, best

Recognizing the qualifier in the question stem and carefully reading every single answer choice are very important. Check out the following example.

EXAMPLE

Which of the following companies would be MOST affected by interest rate fluctuations?

(A) SKNK Perfume Corp.

(B) Bulb Utility Co.

(C) Crapco Vitamin Supplements, Inc.

(D) LQD Water Bottling Co.

The answer is Choice (B). Although all companies may be somewhat affected by interest rate fluctuations, the question uses the word *most*. If interest rates increase, companies have to issue bonds with higher coupon (interest) rates. This higher rate, in turn, greatly affects the companies' bottom lines. Therefore, you're looking for a company that issues a lot of bonds. Utility companies are most affected by interest rate fluctuations because they're *highly leveraged* (issue a lot of bonds).

Making exceptions: Except or not

When a question includes the word *except* or *not*, you're looking for the answer that's *the exception* to the rule stated in the stem of the question. In other words, the correct answer is always the *false* answer. The question can be open (as it is in the next example) or closed.

WARNING

Right off the bat, look for an *except* or *not* in the stem of every question on the Series 7. Many students who really know their material accidentally pick the wrong answer on a few questions because they carelessly miss the *except* or *not*.

Take a look at the following exception problem.

EXAMPLE

A stockholder owns 800 shares of WHY common stock. WHY stockholders were given cumulative voting rights. If there are three vacancies on the board of directors, stockholders can cast any of the following votes EXCEPT

(A) 800 for one candidate

(B) 800 for each candidate

(C) 2,400 for one candidate

(D) 900 for each candidate

The answer you're looking for is Choice (D). Cumulative voting rights give smaller stockholders (not height-wise, but in terms of the number of shares they own) an easier chance to gain representation on the board of directors because a stockholder may combine his total voting rights and vote the cumulative total in any way he wants. Here, the stockholder has a total of 2,400 votes to cast (800 shares × 3 vacancies = 2,400 votes).

In this example, you may be tempted to select Choices (A), (B), or (C), any of which would be correct if you were asked for the number of votes this stockholder *could* cast. For example, the stockholder can use 800 shares to vote for only one candidate (Choice A) — he doesn't have to use all 2,400 votes. Choice (B) is another possible voting arrangement because nobody said the stockholder has to use all his votes for one candidate. Choice (C) is an option because the stockholder has a total of 2,400 votes to cast. In this question, however, you're looking for the number of votes the stockholder *can't* cast because the word *except* in the question stem requires you to find a false answer. Therefore, Choice (D) is the correct answer because in order to cast 900 votes for each candidate, the stockholder would need a total of 2,700 votes (900 × 3).

REMEMBER

If you're one of the unlucky people who get an "all of the following are false except" question, you have to find the *true* answer. Don't forget, two negatives in a sentence make a positive statement. You may want to try rephrasing the question so you know whether you're looking for a true or false answer.

Roman hell: Complex multiple choice

Yes, the Series 7 exam creators even sneak complex (two-tiered) Roman numeral questions in on you. They can pose the question by asking you to put something in order, or they can ask you to find the best combination in a series of answer choices. To make things even more enjoyable, sometimes they even add *except* and *not* to the question (see the preceding section).

Imposing order: Ranking questions

To answer a ranking question, you have to choose the answer that places the information in the correct order — for example, first to last, last to first, highest to lowest, lowest to highest, and so on. Check out the following example.

EXAMPLE

In which order, from first to last, are the following actions taken when opening a new options account?

I. Send the customer an ODD.

II. Have the ROP approve the account.

III. Execute the transaction.

IV. Have the customer send in an OAA.

(A) I, II, III, IV

(B) II, I, IV, III

(C) III, I, II, IV

(D) I, III, II, IV

The correct answer is Choice (A). Wasn't it nice of me to arrange all the answers in order for you? Because option transactions are so risky, the customer has to receive an options risk disclosure document (ODD) prior to opening the account. Statement I has to come first, so you can immediately eliminate Choices (B) and (C), giving you a 50 percent chance of answering correctly. After the client receives the ODD, the registered options principal (ROP) needs to approve the account before any transactions can be executed; II has to come before III, so you can finish the problem here — the answer is Choice (A). Last but not least, the customer signs and returns an options account agreement (OAA) within 15 days after the account is approved by the ROP.

Taking two at a time

The Roman numeral format also appears on the Series 7 with questions that offer two answer choices as the correct response. In these types of questions, you choose the responses that best answer the question.

EXAMPLE

Which TWO of the following are the minimum financial requirements for an investor to be considered accredited?

I. An individual with a net worth of $500,000 excluding primary residence

II. An individual with a net worth of $1,000,000 excluding primary residence

III. An individual who earned $200,000 per year in the most recent two years and has a reasonable expectation of reaching that same level in the current year

IV. An individual who earned $300,000 per year in the most recent 3 years and has a reasonable expectation of reaching that same level in the current year

(A) I and III

(B) I and IV

(C) II and III

(D) II and IV

The correct answer is Choice (C). Statements I and II both deal with net worth; III and IV deal with earnings. Therefore, you're dealing with two questions in one; to be accredited, the answer to at least one of these two questions must be satisfactory:

>> What is the individual's minimum net worth?

>> What is the individual's minimum income?

To be considered an accredited (sophisticated) investor, the minimum financial requirement is a net worth of $1,000,000 excluding primary residence and/or a yearly income of $200,000 in the most recent two years, with a reasonable expectation of reaching that same level in the current year. If the word *minimum* were not used in the question, answer IV would also be correct. The list of who or what would be considered an accredited investor has greatly expanded to include: financial institutions; insiders of the private placement of the issuer; corporations, partnerships, or organizations with a net worth of at least $5 million; reps registered and in good standing with the SEC, FINRA, and/or at least one state who have passed the Series 7, Series 65, Series 66, and/or the Series 82 exams; knowledgeable employees of private funds; rural business investment companies; LLCs with more than $5 million in assets, and family offices with at least $5 million in assets under management.

A little mystery: Dealing with an unknown number of correct statements

In the preceding section, the question states that only two responses can be correct. The following question may have one, three, or four correct answers. You can recognize this type of question simply by glancing at your answer choices. To make the problem more difficult (don't hate me, now), I add an *except* because I'm feeling really good about you, and I just know you're up to it.

EXAMPLE

All of the following are considered violations EXCEPT

    I. rehypothecation

    II. commingling

    III. odd lot transactions

    IV. forward pricing

(A) I only

(B) II only

(C) I, III, and IV only

(D) I, II, III, and IV

The correct answer is Choice (C). The only violation among the choices listed is commingling. *Commingling* occurs when a broker-dealer combines a customer's account with his own or combines a customer's fully paid securities with margined securities. (Chapter 16 fills you in on rules and regulations.)

You're looking for the choices that are *not* violations, so you want to identify the actions that are allowed. If you eliminate commingling, Roman numeral II, your choices are A (I only) or C (I, III, and IV only). You know that I is correct because it's in both answer choices, so you need to evaluate only III and IV. (You have to check only one of these because you know that if III is correct, IV must be as well; if III is false, so is IV.) Odd lot transactions (III) are ones for fewer than 100 shares (a round lot) and are okay. Forward pricing (IV) is what mutual funds do with orders placed by investors, allowing them to purchase or sell at the next price (usually at the end of the day), which is also okay. Choice (C) is correct because it's the only one that lists all three correct choices (I, III, and IV).

Looking at exhibits: Series 7 diagram questions

The Series 7 exam also gives some exhibit questions. The exhibits will be shown on the computer screen next to the question. These exhibits may include newspaper clippings, option prices, bond prices, trading patterns, a specialist's book, income statements, balance sheets, and so on. Out of the exhibit questions you get, some of them just require you to find the correct information; others require a little calculating. I wouldn't be too concerned about them if I were you, because most of them are quite easy.

Take a look at the following problem.

GHI Corporation Balance Sheet at 12-31-XX
(In Thousands)

Assets		Liabilities	
Cash and cash equivalents	$8,000	Accounts payable	$1,000
Receivables (net)	$1,000	Wages payable	$800
Inventory	+$3,000	Taxes payable	$700
Total current assets	**$12,000**	Interest payable	+ $500
		Total current liabilities	$3,000
Notes receivable due after		Long-term debt 8%	+$4,000
one year	$1,000	**Total liabilities**	**$7,000**
Property, plant, and			
equipment (net)	$4,000	**Stockholder's Equity**	
Goodwill	+$1,000	Preferred stock $100 par 9%	$2,000
Total long-term assets	**$6,000**	Common stock $1 par	$2,000
		Paid-in capital	$4,000
Total assets	**$18,000**	Retained earnings	+$3,000
		Total stockholder's equity	**$11,000**
		Total liabilities and	
		stockholder's equity	**$18,000**

© John Wiley & Sons, Inc.

What is the working capital of GHI Corp.?

(A) $7,000

(B) $7,000,000

(C) $9,000

(D) $9,000,000

The answer you're looking for is Choice (D). This example accurately portrays the difficulty level of most of the exhibit questions on the Series 7 exam. After you remember the formula for working capital (see Chapter 13), you simply have to find the information you need — the current assets and current liabilities — on the balance sheet so you can answer the question:

>> working capital = current assets − current liabilities

>> = $12,000,000 − $3,000,000

>> = $9,000,000

You may wonder why the answer is in millions instead of thousands. Notice that the top of the balance sheet says "in thousands," which tells you that you have to multiply the numbers in the balance sheet by 1,000.

WARNING

When you answer exhibit questions, take care not to miss labels like "in thousands" in headings or scales on a graph that would change your answer. Almost nothing is worse than missing a question that you know how to figure out because you carelessly overlook something right in front of you.

The following question has you locate information on call options.

Option			Calls		Puts	
CDE	**Strike Price**	**Expiration**	**Vol**	**Last**	**Vol**	**Last**
68.50	65	Aug	10	3.75	90	0.10
68.50	65	Sep	40	4.50	120	0.80
68.50	65	Nov	20	6.75	4	1.80
68.50	65	Feb	21	7.00	—	—
68.50	70	Aug	140	0.40	5	2.00
68.50	70	Sep	155	1.70	1	3.00
68.50	70	Nov	28	3.00	30	4.35
68.50	75	Feb	40	2.60	—	—
68.50	80	Nov	70	0.65	—	—

© John Wiley & Sons, Inc.

EXAMPLE

What is the time value of a CDE Nov 65 call?

(A) 4.00

(B) 3.25

(C) 3.00

(D) 2.40

The right answer is Choice (B). This question involves options (see Chapter 12 for calculations and more information). The first step is to find the premium for the CDE Nov 65 call in the exhibit. To accomplish this, line up the 65 strike price with the Nov expiration month; you find it in the third row of data. Follow that row over to the fifth column to get the premium for the Nov 65 call. In this case, it's 6.75. Next, use the following formula: P = I + T, where P = premium, I = intrinsic value (the in-the-money amount), and T = time value (how long an investor has to use the option).

First, enter the premium into the equation. Next, you have to determine the intrinsic value (how much the option is in-the-money). Call options go in-the-money when the price of the stock is above the strike price. The stock price is 68.50 (left column) and the strike price is 65, so the option is 3.50 in-the-money (68.50 – 65 = 3.50). After placing those two numbers (6.75 and 3.50) in the equation, you see that the time value has to be 3.25:

$$P = I + T$$

$$6.75 = 3.50 + T$$

$$T = 3.25$$

Shredding the Questions: Tips and Tricks

In Chapter 2, I give you general exam proficiency tips. In this section, I show you how to improve your analysis of topic-specific Series 7 questions. I also provide you with more sample exam questions to further demonstrate the art of choosing the correct answers.

Focusing on key information

The Series 7 exam questions can be particularly difficult if you rush through the exam and miss details that change the meaning of the question.

TIP

When you first start taking practice exams, read through the question to determine what's being asked; then go back to the beginning of the problem to identify the key facts and underline or highlight them. Marking the questions may seem time-consuming when you first begin to study, but if you get into the habit of picking out key words in each question, zoning in on the important information should be second nature by the time you take the test. Of course, you can't underline items on the computer screen at the testing center (the test center administrators may get upset if you write on the computer screen). So instead, if you find yourself getting distracted by useless information, use the scrap paper or dry erase board to write down the information you do need.

This example zeroes in on the essential information.

EXAMPLE

A 55-year-old investor purchases a <u>6 percent</u> DEF convertible mortgage bond at 90 with 10 years until maturity. If the bond is currently trading at <u>97</u>, what is the <u>current yield</u>?

(A) 5.72%

(B) 6.00%

(C) 6.19%

(D) 6.67%

The correct answer is Choice (C). When determining the current yield of a bond, all you need is the market price of the bond and the coupon (interest) rate (see Chapter 7). The fact that the investor is 55 years old or that the bond is a convertible mortgage bond that was purchased at $900 (90 percent of $1,000 par) with 10 years until maturity means nothing in terms of determining the answer. Underline or highlight what you do need (6 percent, 97, current yield) so you don't get distracted.

To determine the current yield, divide the annual interest by the market price. The annual interest is $60 (6 percent of $1,000 par) and the market price is $970 (97 percent of $1,000 par):

$$\text{current yield} = \frac{\text{annual interest}}{\text{market price}} = \frac{\$60}{\$970} = 6.19\%$$

TIP

To avoid confusion when faced with a math problem, read the stem of the question to determine what's being asked; before you consider the rest of the question, jot down the formula you need to calculate your answer.

Answer me this: Picking the correct answer

The Series 7 exam is a practical, multiple-choice exam. The correct answer has to be one of the choices. This setup means you don't have to *provide* the correct answer; you just have to *recognize* it when you see it.

Picking up clues when you're virtually clueless: The process of elimination

When you don't straight-out know an answer, your approach can definitely make the difference between passing and failing the exam. Your best strategy may be eliminating the wrong answers. In theory, you should be able to eliminate, one by one, three incorrect answers for each question.

Even if you can't eliminate three incorrect answers, you'll certainly be able to eliminate one or two answers that are definitely wrong. Don't try to guess the right answer until you've axed as many wrong answers as you can. Obviously, if you can get the choices down to two potential answers, you have a 50-50 chance of answering correctly.

REMEMBER

For an answer choice to be correct, every aspect has to be correct, and the selection has to specifically answer the question that's asked. As a rule of thumb on the Series 7 exam, a more-precise answer is correct more often than a less-precise answer, and a longer answer usually (but not always) prevails over a short answer.

If a response is potentially correct, write *T* for *true* next to the answer in your practice exam, and if a response is wrong, eliminate it by writing *F* for *false* next to the answer. If you do this step correctly, you should end up with three Fs and one T, with T indicating the correct answer. Or, if the question is looking for a false answer, you should end up with three Ts and one F (see the earlier section "Making exceptions: Except or not" for more info on this scenario). On the actual test, you can write the letters A through D on your scrap paper or dry erase board and mark the answer choices appropriately.

TIP

Always look to eliminate any wrong answers that you can. Pay attention to the wording, and get rid of choices that simply sound wrong or make statements that are too broad or absolute. If you're still undecided, use your scrap paper or dry erase board to write down the question number and the answer choices that remain. Take your best guess and mark the answer for review. When you review, look at your scrap paper or dry erase board to help you zone in on your potential answers. Change your answer only if you're sure you made a mistake.

Stop opposing me: Dealing with opposite answers

If you see two opposing answer choices, only one can be right. Traditionally, in practical exams like the Series 7, when you see two answer choices that are complete opposites, the exam creators are trying to test your knowledge of the correct rule, procedure, or law, so one of those opposing choices is most likely the correct answer. Take a look at the following example.

EXAMPLE

Which of the following is TRUE of UGMA accounts?

(A) There can be only one minor and one custodian per account.

(B) There can be more than one minor and one custodian per account.

(C) Securities can only be purchased on margin.

(D) They must be set up for children who have reached the age of majority.

The answer you want is Choice (A). Notice that Choices (A) and (B) oppose each other. If you have two opposing answers, in almost all cases, one of them is the right answer. Therefore, you can ignore Choices (C) and (D), which gives you a 50 percent chance of getting the answer right. Uniform Gifts to Minors Act (UGMA) accounts are set up for minors who are too young to have their own accounts. Each account is limited to one minor and one custodian. (See Chapter 16 for details on custodial accounts.)

GETTING DOWN WITH NUMBERS: ELIMINATING SOME MATH

The process of elimination can get you out of some messy calculations. When dealing with math, look at the answer choices before you begin working out the problem. You may be able to get the answer without doing any calculations at all. For instance, if you have a forward stock split, you know that the number of shares has to increase and that the price of the stock has to decrease (see Chapter 6). If three of the answers fail to meet these conditions, you have your answer right off the bat.

Facing Roman numerals: Not as hard as you think

Complex (two-tiered) multiple-choice questions, with both Roman numerals and letters, can be really frustrating because they usually signal the test-taker (you) that you need more than one correct answer. Well, today's your lucky day, because I show you a shortcut that can help you blow these questions right out of the water.

Traditionally, the first tier of these types of questions gives you several statements preceded by Roman numerals; the second tier (preceded by letters) provides you with choices about which of those statements are correct. Fifteen different combinations of I, II, III, and IV are possible (16 if you count "none of the above," which is almost never correct), but each problem can list only four of them in the answer choices. Because of the limited answer choices, you may not have to evaluate every statement — certain combinations of Roman numerals may be logically impossible.

TIP

Read the question carefully, and then mark *T* for *true* or *F* for *false* next to the Roman numerals to indicate whether they're correct answers to the question. If a Roman-numeral statement is correct, circle that number in the choices that follow the letters in the second tier. If the Roman-numeral statement is false, all the letter answers that include that numeral must also be false, and you can cross them out. If you're really lucky, three of the Roman numerals can be eliminated right away, leaving you with one answer choice.

Look over this Roman numeral question.

EXAMPLE

Which of the following is TRUE of the 5% Markup Policy?

   I. It covers commissions charged to customers when executing trades on an agency basis.

   II. It covers markups on stock sold to customers from inventory.

   III. It covers markdowns on stock purchased from customers for inventory.

   IV. Riskless and simultaneous transactions are covered.

   (A) I and IV only

   (B) IV only

   (C) II and III only

   (D) I, II, III, and IV

The correct answer is Choice (D). The 5% Markup Policy applies to nonexempt securities sold to or purchased from customers. This situation is one where you should look at the Roman-numeral statements and pick out those that you know answer the question. For example, if you know statement I is right (which it is), put a T (for true) next to it. Next, look at Choices (A), (B), (C), and (D) and eliminate Choices (B) and (C), because neither one includes the Roman numeral I. Because both answers that remain, (A) and (D), include the Roman numerals I and IV, you don't even have to bother reading statement IV — it's in both remaining answers, so you know it has to be true. Write T next to the Roman numeral IV. If you know that either statement II or III is correct (which they both are), the answer has to be Choice (D) because it's the only one that lists all the correct choices.

Don't make the same mistake twice

When studying for the Series 7 exam, the practice exams can help you pinpoint your weaker areas of knowledge. The questions you answer incorrectly can be your best learning tools if you thoroughly review the explanations for each wrong answer.

WARNING

You may be tempted to jump from one practice exam to the next without taking adequate time to review your wrong answers. Don't do it! If you put the effort into finding out why your choices are wrong when you're practicing, you're less likely to repeat the same mistake on the Series 7 exam, when it really counts.

Chapter **4**
Surviving Test Day

Y ou've done your homework, taken practice exams, and completed your self-study and/ or prep course, and now the day of reckoning is upon you. You're ready to exchange the gazillion hours of study and hard work for your Series 7 license. The last hurdle awaits you at the test center.

In this chapter, I give you a snapshot of the Series 7 exam experience when taking the exam at the Prometric testing center, so you know the procedure before, during, and after you take the exam and can hit the ground running.

Note: This chapter relates mostly to individuals taking the exam at a testing center. In mid 2020, during the Covid-19 pandemic, FINRA along with Prometrics added an option that allows you to take the test at your location. Even though we're a few years after the start of the pandemic, taking the test at your location remains an alternative. If you're taking the test at your location, see the end of Chapter 1 for more information.

Composing Yourself the Day Before

On the day before the exam, review the information that you're still having problems with until noon; then call it a day. Get away from the books, go out to dinner (maybe skip the spicy foods and alcohol), go to a movie. Rest your mind. If you've put the required time and effort into study- ing up to now, you'll benefit more from a good night's rest than anything you can learn in the final hours the night before your exam. Taking the evening off can help prevent brain fatigue and make zoning into exam mode easier tomorrow, when it counts most.

REMEMBER

Before you go to sleep, gather the items you need to take with you to the exam. If you prepare yourself the night before, you'll be more relaxed on exam day. Here are some activities to com- plete the night before the exam to finalize your preparations for the big day:

>> Make sure you have the proper government-issued ID bearing your name, signature, and a recent photo. The name on your ID must identically match the name on the Web CRD

registration form. An expired ID won't be accepted. Official (primary) identification can be in the form of a valid passport, a driver's license, or a military ID card. A current (unexpired) State ID is acceptable in lieu of a driver's license, as long as it includes the person's full name as it appears on the Web CRD registration form, an expiration date, the student's signature, and a current photograph.

If you use a military ID that doesn't have a signature, you need to bring a secondary form of ID with a signature. Secondary ID can be a valid credit card, a bank automatic-teller machine (ATM) card, a library card, a U.S. Social Security card, an employee ID/work badge, or a school ID.

>> Pack earplugs (if allowed — ask when you schedule your exam).

>> Pack a snack with the rest of your stuff.

>> Bring study materials — including the topics and/or math formulas you're having trouble with — for a final review before you enter the test center.

>> Have your watch ready to make sure you're on time.

>> Lay out your clothes (dress in layers in case the test center feels like either your refrigerator or your oven).

>> Review the directions to the exam site. Make sure you have a charged cellphone and the test center number in case you get lost.

Additionally, you have to bring at least one finger with you, preferably yours, so that the exam administrators can take a fingerprint (though you probably have that packed already).

REMEMBER

You can't bring study material, textbooks, briefcases, purses, electronic devices, cellphones, notes of any kind, or your really smart friend with you into the testing room. Calculators, pencils, and scrap paper or a dry erase board will be provided for you at the exam center, and the exam administrators will collect the calculators, pencils, and all scrap paper (used and unused) or dry erase board at the end of each session.

Making the Most of the Morning

Now the big day is here. Certainly, you don't have to dress up for the pictures the Series 7 administrator takes, but you should at least do what you need to do to feel awake and alive and good about yourself (do some push-ups, take a quick walk, take a shower, shave, whatever).

Be sure to eat at least a light breakfast. You may feel like you're too nervous to eat, but if you're hungry when you take the exam, you won't be able to concentrate. And if you overeat, you'll be wasting valuable energy (and blood flow!) digesting the meal — energy your brain needs to sustain you. To avoid an energy crash, I suggest a protein bar, fruit, and/or veggies rather than sugar or carbs.

Grab everything you packed up the night before (see the preceding section) and head out the door.

TIP

Leave your home in time to arrive at the test center at least 30 minutes before your scheduled exam so you have time to check in. I recommend that you arrive at the test center 1½ hours before the exam so you have 1 hour to review the topics and/or math formulas that give you the most trouble and a half-hour to check in.

Arriving on the Scene

The Series 7 exams are administered by Prometric, and you can contact the center for additional information. In this section, I cover the steps to take upon your arrival at the exam center.

In Chapter 1, I discuss the availability of special accommodations if you're disabled or learning impaired or if English is your second language. If you require special accommodations, contact the FINRA Special Conditions Team at (800) 999-6647 for information about registration and for instructions about arriving at the exam center.

Taking advantage of one last chance to cram

The information you review just before the exam will be on the surface of your mind. When you arrive at the exam center (or even during your commute if you take public transportation), do some last-minute cramming. Review the topics or math formulas you're having trouble with.

Each Series 7 exam center is set up differently; you may find areas in the building where you can study, or you may have to study outside in your car, on a bench, or at a nearby coffee shop. When you're ready to enter the exam center (30 minutes before the exam) you can leave your books in your vehicle if the exam center doesn't have lockers (see the section "Getting seated").

Signing in

To enter the Series 7 exam center, you have to provide the administrators with valid ID. (See "Composing Yourself the Day Before" for what constitutes "valid.") After you're inside the test center, you have to sign in and get photographed and fingerprinted. In addition, before you begin the exam, you have to read a form called the Rules of Conduct and agree to the terms. A preview of the Rules of Conduct is available on the FINRA website (`www.finra.org/industry/test-center-rules-conduct`).

Getting seated

Basically, the only things you may bring into the testing room are your own sweet self and possibly a set of earplugs. You can store all other personal property in a locker at the exam center. (All new testing sites are supposed to have lockers, but some older sites may have been grandfathered without them. You can ask when you make your appointment.) For a list of the (mostly) medical items you can bring into the exam room, including which ones need inspection or preauthorization, please call your testing center.

Some exam centers have cafeterias and/or vending machines with snacks and drinks, but you can't even bring chewing gum into the exam room. I don't know why — maybe because of the noise, or maybe so the exam staff doesn't have to scrape gum wads off computer screens.

The exam administrators escort you to the exam room. In the testing room, you receive scrap paper (or a dry erase board), a pencil, and a basic calculator. You'll have to return the paper, pencil, and calculator to the exam center administrators at the end of the session (yes, even the unused scrap paper). You can't bring anything else into the cubicle where you take the exam.

Taking the Exam

Take a deep breath, crack your knuckles, and get ready to make things count — this Series 7 exam is the genuine article. The exam is three hours and 45 minutes long, and you're graded on a total of 125 questions. The test designers have even prepared a bonus for you: To ensure that new questions to be introduced in future exams meet acceptable standards, you also answer 10 additional, unidentified questions that don't count toward your score. Lucky you! This means that you answer 135 questions, but only 125 really count toward your score.

REMEMBER

Most test centers offer the inspirational creature comforts of the office: You take your Series 7 in a cubicle (approximately 4 feet wide) with a computer and a small desk area. You may leave your cubicle for restroom breaks at any time, if necessary. The clock continues to run, however, so try to limit your intake of fluids before your session.

Just before you begin your exam, a member of the test center staff will walk you through the steps of how to use the computerized system. Don't worry — you don't need any previous computer experience to understand the way the computer operates (it's that easy). If you do have any tech problems during the test, you can use the help button or summon the exam administrators. A link that shows a picture of how a question appears on the computer screen is in Chapter 1.

As the test begins, you're ready to put all those test-taking skills to use (check out Chapter 2 for a rundown of what those skills are). Right off the bat, write down everything you think you're likely to forget. Keep track of time. Mark questions for review. Concentrate on the facts in question, and look for key words that can give you clues. Use your amazing powers of elimination to identify wrong answer choices. Work your magic with specific question types (see Chapter 3). You've done your homework, so be confident.

REMEMBER

Before your session ends, double-check the questions you marked for review. Don't change any answers unless you're certain your initial answer is wrong.

TIP

If you're one of those speed demons (and I hope you're not) who finishes the test in an hour and are tempted to review all your answers, don't do it. Go over only the questions you marked for review. If you try to review all the questions, not only will you drive yourself bonkers, but you'll also do more harm than good by second-guessing your right answers.

STAYING RELAXED, FOCUSED, AND CONSCIOUS

Here are some ways to keep stress at bay and make sure you're giving the test the attention it deserves:

- If you feel tense, take a few slow, deep breaths and give yourself a mini-massage.

- If you find yourself growing tired, stretch, sit up straight, or go to the restroom just for a chance to walk around.

- Give your eyes a rest from the computer screen by looking away from the computer every so often.

- Avoid looking at someone else's computer screen — it's not only frowned upon but will get you ejected.

- If you have trouble focusing, write down significant details from the question. If you're stuck on a multipart question, break down the question into segments. Try drawing diagrams. If you're still having trouble, choose a tentative answer and mark the question for review.

- Don't lose track of your mission here — now is not the time to let up. Visualize success and hang in there!

Getting the Results: Drum Roll Please . . .

You've completed many hours of studying. You've deprived yourself of weekend parties and long afternoons of leisure. Your social life has been almost nonexistent, and if you're the type who becomes unpleasant when in a stressful state of being, you may have alienated the people who used to hang out with you.

After surviving three hours and 45 minutes of mental abuse from taking the Series 7 exam, you're ready to push the button that reveals your score and can change your life.

The time may seem much longer, but in reality, you have to wait only a little while before your score is revealed. Your grade and the word *passed* or *failed* appear on the computer screen. If your grade is 72 or better, you pass the exam. (Please remember that you're now a professional and refrain from doing a victory dance in the middle of the test center.) If your score is less than 72, you don't pass the exam. Don't call your friends and tell them you've decided to become an astronaut or firefighter instead. You can retake the test, so you may still have a future on Wall Street. See Chapter 1 for what to do next.

After you receive your exam score, you can leave your cubicle. Bring your scrap paper or dry erase board, pencil, and calculator with you, and turn them over to the exam center staff.

Regardless of whether you pass or fail the exam, you receive a printout of your grade and the breakdown of your performance on the Series 7 exam topics, which is unfortunately pretty vague. Employers receive a copy of the results in the mail, or, if tied into the FINRA computer system, they can get results online.

2

Mastering Basic Security Investments

Get familiar with basic securities — stocks and bonds, including municipal securities — that form the foundation of an investor's portfolio.

Review the registration procedure that securities go through before they can be sold to the public and find out which securities are exempt from registration.

Distinguish common stock from preferred stock, corporate bonds from U.S. bonds, and municipal bonds from general obligation bonds.

Chapter **5**

Underwriting Securities: Bringing New Issues to Market

All issuers of securities need a starting point, just as all securities need a birth date (just not the kind that's celebrated with funny-looking hats and a cake). Most securities go through a registration procedure before the public can buy them. The Series 7 exam tests your ability to recognize the players and institutions involved in the registration process.

In this chapter, I cover topics related to bringing new issues (securities) to market. You find out about key players, types of security offerings, kinds of securities that don't need to be registered, and other details about the underwriting process. This chapter also includes a few practice questions interspersed throughout the chapter and a quick quiz at the end of the chapter to help you measure how well you understand the topic. You'll also notice that there's an overlap of information tested on the Series 7 and what you learned when taking the Securities Industry Essentials.

Bringing New Issues to the Market

A lot of things need to happen before securities hit the market. Not only do the securities have to be registered, but the issuer has to find a broker-dealer (like your firm) to sell the securities to the public. The Series 7 exam tests your expertise in answering questions about this process.

Starting out: What the issuer does

For an entity to become a corporation, the founders must file a document called a *corporate charter* (bylaws) in the home state of their business. Included in the corporate charter are the names of the founders, the type of business, the place of business, the number of shares that can be issued, and so on. If a corporation wants to sell securities to the public, it has to register with states and the Securities and Exchange Commission (SEC). Read on for info on how the registration process works.

Registering securities with the SEC

Unless the securities are exempt from registration (see "Exempt securities" later in this chapter), when a company wants to go public (sell stock to public investors), it has to file a registration statement and a prospectus with the SEC. (See "Getting the skinny on the issue and issuer: The prospectus" later in this chapter.)

The *registration statement* includes

>> The issuer's name, address, and description of its business

>> The company's articles of incorporation (unless previously supplied)

>> The names and addresses of the underwriter(s) and all commissions or discounts they will receive either directly or indirectly from the sale

>> The expected price at which the security shall be offered to the public

>> The names and addresses of all the company's control persons, such as officers, directors, and anyone owning more than 10 percent of the corporation's securities and how much they hold of the corporation's securities

>> The estimated net proceeds of the sale from the security to be issued and what the proceeds will be used for, including property (if any), or good will (if any), other businesses to be purchased (if any), and if any of the proceeds will be used to pay off outstanding debt

>> The company's capitalization (outstanding long- and short-term debt, authorized and outstanding stock, par value of its stock if any, voting rights, exchange rights, and so on)

>> Complete financial statements (including balance sheets and income statements)

>> Any legal proceedings against the corporation that may have an impact on it

>> Any net proceeds derived from any security sold by the issuer in the previous 2 years along with the underwriter's particulars

>> The names and addresses of the counsel who have passed on the legality of the issue and a copy of their opinion or opinions with regard to legality of the issue

>> Any agreements or indentures which might affect the securities being offered

REMEMBER

The information above regarding the Registration Statement is known as *Schedule A,* and it typically applies to corporations issuing new securities. There is also a *Schedule B,* which applies to local government issues (typically municipal bonds). The information required when a local government issues securities is, as you can imagine, geared toward what a local government would have to supply in its registration statement. Most of the information required is very similar; in fact, you can substitute the word "municipality" for "company" for most of the items required. You need to know the name of the borrowing government or subdivision, what it is raising the money for, the amount of funded debt and the amount of floating debt there will be after the new security is issued, whether the issuer has defaulted on debt in the last 20 years, the names of all people involved (such as counsel, underwriter(s), and so on), commission to be paid to the underwriters, a copy of the agreement(s) made with the underwriter(s), a legal opinion made by the counsel with regard to the legality, possible tax-free nature of the issue, and so on.

Shelving the issue: Shelf registration

Since the registration process to sell securities is a somewhat daunting and costly process for issuers, they may register more securities than they may need to sell now. Shelf registration

(SEC Rule 415) allows the issuer or selling shareholders (insiders) to sell securities on a delayed or continuous basis that were previously registered with the SEC without needing additional permission. Shelf registration allows issuers up to 2 to 3 years (depending on their status) to sell previously registered shares.

Cooling-off period

After the issuer files a registration statement (the filing date) with the SEC, a 20-day cooling-off period begins. During the 20-day (and often longer) cooling-off period, the good old SEC reviews the registration statement. At the end of the cooling-off period, the issue will (hopefully) be cleared for sale to the public (the effective date of registration). In the event that the SEC sees that the registration statement needs to be amended or it needs additional information, it will issue a *deficiency letter* and halt the registration process until it receives the information required. If the SEC (the Commission) finds that the registration statement is misleading because the issuer included untrue statements of material fact or omits a material fact, it issues a *stop order,* which suspends the effectiveness of the registration statement. At this point, the issuer will be required to amend the registration statement and answer any questions posed by the Commission in order to continue the registration process.

REMEMBER

Neither the SEC nor any self-regulatory organization approves an issue. The SEC just clears the issue for sale. The SEC also is not responsible for making sure that the information included in the registration statement is true and accurate. As a matter of fact, it is unlawful to in any way represent that the SEC approved of an issue or issuer.

During the cooling-off period, the underwriter (or underwriters) can obtain indications of interest from investors who may want to purchase the issue. Agents scramble to get indications of interest from prospective purchasers of the securities. Although the underwriters may keep records of indications of interest, they *may not* accept any money in advance of the public offering.

REMEMBER

Indications of interest aren't binding on customers or underwriters. A customer always has the prerogative to change his mind, and underwriters may not have enough shares available to meet everyone's needs.

A *tombstone advertisement* — a newspaper ad that's shaped like, well, a tombstone (typically, it's rectangular with black borders) — is simply an announcement (but not an offer) of a new security for sale. It's the only advertisement allowed during the cooling-off period. They are not required and do not have to be filed with the SEC. These ads contain just a simple statement of facts about the new issue (for example, the name of the issuer, type of security, number of shares or bonds available, underwriters' names, and so on). In addition, tombstone ads often provide investors with information about how to obtain a prospectus. Tombstone ads may or may not include the price of the security being offered. Tombstone ads are the only form of advertisement allowed prior to the effective date, although they may appear after the effective date. They must contain a disclaimer stating that the advertisement is not an offer to sell nor a solicitation of an offer for any of these securities, as this offer is made only through a prospectus.

Underwriters and selling group members use the *preliminary prospectus* to obtain indications of interest from prospective customers. The preliminary prospectus must be made available to all customers who are interested in the new issue during the cooling-off period. I talk more about what that prospectus has to include in the section "Getting the skinny on the issue and issuer: The prospectus" a little later in this chapter.

Due diligence meeting

Toward the end of the cooling-off period, the lead underwriter holds a due diligence meeting. This meeting is required by law. During this meeting, the underwriter provides information about the issue and what the issuer will use the proceeds of the sale for. This meeting is designed to provide such information to syndicate members, selling groups, brokers, analysts, institutions, and so on, and allows them to ask questions.

The last time syndicate members can back out of an underwriting agreement is toward the end of the cooling-off period (around the time of the due diligence meeting). You can assume that if syndicate members are backing out, it's most likely due to negative market conditions.

Blue skies: Registering with the states

All *blue sky laws,* or state laws that apply to security offerings and sales, say that in order to sell a security to a customer, the broker-dealer (brokerage firm), the registered representative, and the security must be registered in the customer's home state. The issuer is responsible for registering the security not only with the U.S. Securities and Exchange Commission (the SEC), but also with the state administrator in each state in which the securities are to be sold. State securities laws are covered under the Uniform Securities Act (USA). Although usually quite similar, all states have their own set of securities laws. Here are the methods of state security registration:

>> **Notification (registration by filing):** Notification is the simplest form of registration for established companies. Companies who have previously sold securities in a state can renew their previous application.

>> **Coordination:** This method involves registering with the SEC and states at the same time. The SEC helps companies meet the blue sky laws by notifying all states in which the securities are to be sold.

>> **Qualification:** Companies use this registration method for securities that are exempt from registration with the SEC but require registration with the state through the State Administrator.

Effective date

The effective date is at the end of the cooling-off period. This is the first day that the security can actually be sold to the public. Just prior to the security going public, the offering price will be determined. At this point, you can call all your customers who expressed indications of interest and ask, "How much do you want?" Remember, all purchasers and potential purchasers must be provided with a copy of the final prospectus, which includes the public offering price. A copy of the final prospectus must be delivered no later than the time the sale is confirmed (see Chapter 16). The final prospectus may be provided either electronically (that is, via email) or through the mail.

Role call: Introducing the team players

The following list explains who's involved in the securities registration and selling process. Registered reps can work for any of these firms:

>> **Investment banking firm:** An *investment banking firm* is an institution (a broker-dealer) that's in the business of helping issuers raise money and helping them abide by securities laws. You can think of investment bankers as the brains of the operation, because they help the issuer decide what securities to issue, how much to issue, a suggested selling price, and so on. Not only do investment bankers advise issuers, but they usually underwrite the issue and may also become the managing underwriter in the offering of new securities.

>> **Underwriter:** The *underwriter* is a broker-dealer that helps the issuer bring new securities to the public. Underwriters purchase the securities from the issuer and sell them to the public for a nice profit (yippee!).

THE SECURITIES ACTS

Registration helps ensure that securities issued to the public adhere to certain regulations (though anti-fraud rules also apply to exempt securities). The following acts are designed to protect investors from unscrupulous issuers, firms, and salespeople (see Chapter 16 for details on other rules and regulations).

The Securities Act of 1933: This act — also called the Truth in Securities Act, the Paper Act, the Full Disclosure Act, the Prospectus Act, and the New Issues Act — regulates new issues of corporate securities. An issuer of corporate securities must provide full and fair disclosure about itself and the offering. Included in this act are rules to prevent fraud and deception. All nonexempt securities are subject to the rules of the Securities Act of 1933.

The Securities Exchange Act of 1934: The Act of 1934, which established the SEC, was enacted to protect investors by regulating the over-the-counter (OTC) market and exchanges, such as the New York Stock Exchange (NYSE). (Chapter 14 can tell you more about markets.) In addition, the Act of 1934 regulates

- The extension of credit in margin accounts (see Chapter 9)

- Transactions by insiders

- Customer accounts

- Trading activities

The Trust Indenture Act of 1939: This act prohibits bond issues valued at over $50 million from being offered to investors without an indenture. The trust indenture is a written agreement that protects investors by disclosing the particulars of the issue (coupon rate, maturity date, any collateral backing the bond, and so on). As part of the Trust Indenture Act of 1939, all companies must hire a trustee who's responsible for protecting the rights of bondholders.

>> **Syndicate:** When an issue is too large for one firm to handle, the syndicate manager (managing underwriter) forms a syndicate to help sell the securities and relieve some of the financial burden on the managing underwriter. Each syndicate member is responsible for selling a portion of the securities to the public (see the upcoming section titled "Agreeing to sell your share: Western versus Eastern accounts" for details). In the event that an issuer is accepting bids for a new issue instead of hiring the underwriter(s) directly, which happens more with municipal securities (see Chapter 8), the syndicate will enter a *syndicate bid,* and the winner will be the one who can sell the securities at the highest price and/or lowest cost to the issuer.

>> **Managing (lead) underwriter:** The managing underwriter (syndicate manager) is the head firm that's responsible for putting together a syndicate and dealing directly with the issuer. The managing underwriter receives financial compensation (buckets-o-bucks) for each and every share sold.

>> **Selling group:** In the event that the syndicate members feel they need more help selling the securities, they can recruit selling group members. These members are brokerage firms that aren't part of the syndicate. Selling group members help distribute shares to the public but don't make a financial commitment (that is, they don't purchase shares from the issuer) and therefore, receive less money per share when selling shares to the public.

Although corporations could use a bidding process to pick the underwriter for new issues, they typically choose the underwriter directly. This type of offering is called a *negotiated offering.* However, because Municipal GO (general obligation) bonds are backed by the taxes of the people living in the community, they will most likely choose a *competitive offering* (bidding process by way of syndicate bids) to insure that they are getting the best deal (highest bond price and/or lowest coupon payment) for taxpayers. (This topic is covered in more detail in Chapter 8.)

Agreement among underwriters

When an issuer hires underwriters (dealers) to help sell its securities to the public, the parties must sign an agreement among underwriters, which is also known as an *Underwriting Agreement* or *syndicate agreement.* The Underwriting Agreement will outline, among other things, the method of distribution (firm commitment, best efforts, or standby).

The Underwriting Agreement is a contract between the issuer of the securities and the managing or lead underwriter. It must be agreed upon and signed prior to any securities being sold to the public. Now, for Series 7 purposes, you don't need to know all the details about the Underwriting Agreement, but you should have a basic understanding of the types of underwritings: firm commitment and best efforts.

Firm commitment

In a firm commitment underwriting, the lead underwriter and syndicate members (other underwriters who may be helping in the sale of the securities) agree to purchase all the securities that remain unsold after the offering. In this case, the underwriters assume all the financial risk.

Another type of firm commitment offering is a standby. A standby underwriter signs an agreement with the issuer to purchase any stock not purchased by the public if or when an issuer has a rights offering (see Chapter 6).

Best efforts

In a best efforts underwriting, the underwriters are agreeing to make their best efforts to sell all the securities to the public. (Hey, that's how they make money.) If, however, they cannot sell all the securities to the public, the issuer has the right to either cancel the offering or take back some of the unsold securities depending on whether it is an all or none offering or a mini-max offering:

>> **All or None (AON):** If the offering is set up as an AON agreement, all the securities must be sold by the deadline or the deal is cancelled and the money must be returned to the investors.

>> **Mini-Max:** A mini-max offering is one in which a specified minimum number of securities must be sold in order for the deal not to be cancelled. If that minimum threshold is reached, more securities may be sold up until the maximum amount is reached. The issuer will take back any securities that remain unsold.

You should be aware that if securities are sold on a best efforts basis, purchasers and potential purchasers must be made aware that the offering has a chance of being cancelled. Purchasers' money is held in an escrow account until the terms are met or the deal is cancelled. Once the specified number of securities are sold, the underwriters release the securities to the purchasers. If, however, the underwriters do not sell enough of the securities by the deadline, the purchasers receive their money back.

Selling group agreement

Similar to the syndicate agreement, selling group members must sign a *selling group agreement.* Although the selling group members aren't making a financial commitment like syndicate members, the selling group agreement provides a likely offering price for the securities, how many securities will be allotted to the selling group members, how much the selling group members will get paid, and so on. Both the underwriting agreement and the selling group agreement must include the price at which the securities are to be sold to the public.

REMEMBER

According to FINRA, "A member, in the conduct of its business, shall observe high standards of commercial honor and just and equitable principles of trade." So, regardless of whether the securities offered during an IPO are sold on a firm commitment or best efforts underwriting, it must be a *bona fide offering* of the securities at the public offering price. Firms cannot hold back securities for themselves, associated persons and their immediate family, industry insiders, portfolio managers, and so on.

Stabilizing bids

Sometimes even though a syndicate has made its best efforts to sell all the securities, the demand for the securities is just not high enough to sell them all. In this case, the syndicate may make a stabilizing bid to purchase the securities at a price at or slightly below the public offering price. Stabilizing bids are instituted to help keep the price of the security from dropping too quickly. This is the only form of securities price manipulation allowed by the SEC.

Who gets what: Distributing the profits

When larger issues come to market, the lead underwriter often has to form a syndicate to help sell the securities. When selling the securities to the public, each entity (the lead underwriter, syndicate members, selling group members, and so on — see the preceding section) receives a different portion of the selling profits.

The *spread* is the difference between the amount the syndicate pays the issuer when purchasing new shares or bonds and the public offering price for each share or bond sold. For example, if the syndicate buys shares from the issuer at $8.00 per share and then turns around and sells them to the public for $9.00 per share, the spread is $1.00 ($9.00 – $8.00). Naturally, you get the following formula:

$$\text{spread} = \text{public offering price} - \text{price paid to the issuer}$$

So the spread is just the initial profit from selling the security; you still have to divvy it up among the salespeople. The syndicate splits the spread into the manager's fee and the takedown, so you get the following equation:

$$\text{spread} = \text{syndicate manager's fee} + \text{takedown}$$

Here's what you need to know about the manager's fee and the takedown:

>> **Takedown:** The *takedown* (total takedown) is the profit that each syndicate member makes when selling shares or bonds to the public. Remember that the syndicate members are the ones taking the financial risk and therefore, deserve the lion's share of the sale's proceeds. You can use the spread formula (spread = syndicate manager's fee + takedown) to calculate this value, rearranging the terms like this: takedown = spread – syndicate manager's fee. For example, if the spread is $1.00 and the manager's fee is $0.15, the takedown is $0.85 ($1.00 – $0.15). The takedown may be further broken down as follows:

- **Selling Group Concession:** The *concession* is the profit that the selling group makes when selling shares or bonds to the public. Selling group members don't step up to the plate financially and therefore, don't receive as much of the sale's proceeds as syndicate members do. The concession is paid out of the takedown. The profit made by syndicate members on shares or bonds sold by the selling group is called the *additional takedown*. The formula looks like this:

  takedown = additional takedown + concession

- **Reallowance:** The portion of the takedown that's available for firms that aren't part of the syndicate or selling group is the *reallowance*. For example, assume ABC Corporation is in the process of issuing new shares. You're a stockbroker, and one of your customers calls to let you know that she's interested in purchasing shares of ABC Corporation from you, but you're not one of the official distributors of the stock. No sweat. You contact the syndicate manager, who gives you a discount off the public offering price (POP). That discount is the reallowance.

» **Syndicate manager's fee:** This part of the spread is the profit the syndicate manager makes on shares or bonds sold by anyone. This fee is usually the smallest of all the listed fees.

The following question tests your knowledge of distribution of profits.

EXAMPLE

Nogo Auto Corp., which specializes in fuel-efficient cars, is in the process of selling new shares of its company to the public. Nogo contacts Thor Broker-Dealer Corp. to underwrite the securities. Thor realizes that the issue is too big to underwrite by itself, so it forms a syndicate. Nogo will receive $15.00 per share for each share issued, and the public offering price will be $16.20. If the manager's fee is $0.25 per share and the concession is $0.40 per share, what is the additional takedown?

(A) $0.55

(B) $0.80

(C) $0.95

(D) $1.20

The correct answer is Choice (A). This question is a little tricky because you have to determine the takedown (the profit syndicate members make) before you can figure out the additional takedown. The additional takedown is the profit syndicate members make on shares sold by the selling group. The spread of $1.20 ($16.20 selling price – $15.00 to Nogo) is made up of the manager's fee of $0.25 and the takedown of $0.95 ($1.20 spread – $0.25 manager's fee). If the syndicate members had sold the shares by themselves, they would have received the takedown of $0.95 per share. However, the selling group sold the shares, receiving a concession of $0.40 per share. The concession is paid out of the takedown; thus, the additional takedown is $0.55 per share ($0.95 – $0.40).

REMEMBER

Under FINRA Rule 5141, during the sale of securities in a fixed offering, no single underwriter, syndicate, nor selling group members may sell the securities being offered at a price lower than the stated public offering price (reduced price). Once the offering is terminated, or if there are still securities left after making a bona fide public offering and the members are unable to sell at the public offering price, the securities may be sold at a lower price.

Agreeing to sell your share: Western versus Eastern accounts

The syndicate agreement, as described earlier in this chapter, is the contract among syndicate members. In addition to the bucks that each member of the syndicate gets when selling shares or bonds, the syndicate agreement lays out each syndicate member's amount of commitment (how many shares or bonds each party will sell).

The syndicate manager can set up underwritings on a Western or Eastern account basis:

TIP

>> **Western (divided) account:** In this securities underwriting, the syndicate agreement states that each syndicate member is responsible only for the shares or bonds originally allocated to it. If a syndicate member commits to selling 500,000 shares and sells them all, the syndicate member doesn't have to sell any more.

To distinguish an Eastern account from a Western account, remember the phrase *wild, wild West,* because back in the day, each man (or *syndicate member* in this case) was for himself.

>> **Eastern (undivided) account:** In this securities underwriting, the syndicate agreement states that each syndicate member is responsible not only for the shares or bonds originally allocated to it but also for a portion of the shares or bonds left unsold by other (apparently less aggressive) members. A syndicate member that's originally responsible for 10 percent of the new issue is responsible for 10 percent of the shares or bonds left unsold by other members as well.

The following question tests your knowledge of Eastern and Western accounts.

EXAMPLE

A syndicate is underwriting $5,000,000 worth of municipal general obligation bonds. There are 10 syndicate members, each with an equal participation. Firm A, which is part of the syndicate, sells its entire allotment. However, $1,000,000 worth of bonds remain unsold by other members of the syndicate. If the syndicate agreement was set up on an Eastern account basis, what is Firm A's responsibility regarding the unsold bonds?

(A) No responsibility

(B) $100,000 worth of bonds

(C) $200,000 worth of bonds

(D) $1,000,000 worth of bonds

The right answer is Choice (B). Your key to this question is that the underwriting was done on an Eastern account basis. On an Eastern account basis, the underwriters (because they're so nice) have to help the slackers sell any shares of unsold bonds. Firm A sold all its bonds, so it has to help sell the remaining bonds that the other syndicate members didn't sell. Firm A's responsibility is in proportion to its original responsibility. Because it was responsible for 10 percent of the original issue (10 syndicate members with equal participation), it's responsible for selling 10 percent of the unsold bonds:

$$10\% \times \$1,000,000 \text{ of unsold bonds} = \$100,000 \text{ worth of bonds}$$

If the underwriting had been on a Western account basis, the correct answer would have been Choice (A).

Getting the skinny on the issue and issuer: The prospectus

The issuer prepares a preliminary prospectus (sometimes with the help of the underwriter) that's sent in with the registration statement. The preliminary prospectus must be available for potential purchasers when the issue is in registration (during the cooling-off period) with the SEC. The preliminary prospectus is abbreviated, but it contains all the essential facts about the issuer and issue except for the final offering price (public offering price, or POP) and the *effective date* (the date that the issue will first be sold). The preliminary prospectus is used to help determine the level of interest in the security.

A preliminary prospectus is sometimes called a *red herring*, not because it smells fishy (or is totally misleading and irrelevant) but because a statement in red lettering on the cover of the preliminary prospectus declares that a registration statement has been filed with the SEC, it's not the final version, and that some items may change in the meantime.

The *final prospectus,* which is prepared toward the end of the cooling-off period, is a legal document that the issuer prepares; it contains material information about the issuer and new issue of securities (a description of the business, what the proceeds will be used for, a history of the business, risks to purchasers, a description of the management, an SEC disclaimer, and so on). The final prospectus has to be available to all potential purchasers of the issue. If the final prospectus has been filed with the SEC and is available on a website, providing the clients with information on how to view the final prospectus online would be equivalent to delivery of the prospectus. The final prospectus includes updated information such as the following:

>> The final offering price

>> The underwriter's spread (the profit the underwriters make per share)

>> The delivery date (when the securities will be available)

REMEMBER

There must be an SEC disclaimer on the front of every prospectus that is clear for all investors to see. The disclaimer must state that the Securities and Exchange Commission or any State Securities Commission *does not* approve or disapprove of the securities. In addition, it must state that the Securities and Exchange Commission or any State Securities Commission has not concluded that the prospectus is accurate or adequate. Remember that the SEC just clears the issue and doesn't make a judgment whether it's a good investment or not. Any claim that the SEC, FINRA, MSRB, and so on, has approved of an issue is a criminal offense.

Note: Because all mutual (open-end) funds constantly issue new securities, they must always have a prospectus available. In addition, many mutual funds also provide a *statement of additional information (SAI),* which provides more detailed information about the fund's operation that may be useful to some investors. A statement of additional information is also known as "Part B" of a fund's registration statement. Mutual funds may also provide a *summary prospectus* to investors, which is covered in more detail in Chapter 10.

REMEMBER

A preliminary or final prospectus may not be altered in any way. You may talk to potential purchasers about certain sections, but you *cannot* underline, highlight, circle, cross out, and so on.

For initial public offerings (IPOs), a final prospectus needs to be available to all purchasers of the IPO for *90 days* after the *effective date* (the first day the security starts trading).

With primary, secondary, or combined offerings, a final prospectus has to be available to all purchasers of the primary offering for *25 days* after the effective date for all issuers whose securities are already listed on an exchange or NASDAQ. If an issuer has already issued securities but not on an exchange or NASDAQ, the final prospectus has to be available for *40 days* after the effective date.

The following question tests your knowledge on the types of offerings, whether new or outstanding.

DEF Corp. is offering 2,000,000 shares of its common stock to the public; 1,500,000 shares are authorized but previously unissued, and insiders of the company are selling the other 500,000 shares. Which of the following are TRUE about this offering?

I. The EPS of DEF will increase.

II. The EPS of DEF will decrease.

III. The number of outstanding shares will increase by 500,000.

IV. The number of outstanding shares will increase by 1,500,000.

(A) I and III

(B) I and IV

(C) II and III

(D) II and IV

The answer you're looking for is Choice (D). This offering is a combined, or split, offering. The 1,500,000 shares that were previously unissued are a primary offering, and the 500,000 shares held by insiders are a secondary offering. Answering this question correctly requires a little bit of deduction on your part. You first have to note that unissued shares aren't considered part of the outstanding shares (because for stockholders, owning the shares before they're even offered would be a pretty impressive feat!). Because 1,500,000 shares were previously unissued (kept by the company for future use), the number of outstanding shares will increase by that amount. When considering whether the earnings per share (EPS) will increase or decrease, you can assume that the company earns the same amount of money. Now, that same amount of money has to be divided among 1,500,000 more shares. Therefore, you deduce that the EPS will decrease, not increase.

Reviewing Exemptions

Certain securities are exempt from registration because of either the type of security or the type of transaction involved. You may find that securities that are exempt because of who's issuing them is a bit easier to recognize. You'll probably have to spend a little more time on the securities that are exempt from registration because of the type of transaction.

Exempt securities

Certain securities are exempt from the registration requirements under the Securities Act of 1933. Either these securities come from issuers that have a high level of creditworthiness, or another government regulatory agency has some sort of jurisdiction over the issuer of the securities. These types of securities include

>> Securities issued by the U.S. government (Treasury bills, Treasury notes, Treasury bonds) or federal agencies

>> Municipal securities (local government notes and bonds)

>> Securities issued by banks, savings institutions, and credit unions

>> Public utility stocks or bonds

>> Securities issued by religious, educational, or nonprofit organizations

>> Notes, bills of exchange, bankers' acceptances, and commercial paper with an initial maturity of 270 days or less

>> Insurance policies and fixed annuities

Fixed annuities are exempt from SEC registration because the issuing insurance company guarantees the payout. However, variable annuities require registration because the payout varies depending on the performance of the securities held in the separate account. For more info on annuities and other packaged securities, see Chapter 10.

Exempt transactions

Some securities that corporations offer may be exempt from the full registration requirements of the Securities Act of 1933, due to the nature of the sale. The following sections cover these exemptions.

Intrastate offerings (Rule 147)

An intrastate offering is, naturally, an offering of securities within one state. For such an offering to be exempt from SEC registration, the company must be incorporated in the state in which it's selling securities, 80 percent of its business has to be within the state, 80 percent of the proceeds raised by the offering are used within the state, and it may sell securities only to residents of the state. The securities still require registration at the state level.

WARNING

Don't confuse *intra*state offerings (securities sold in one state) with *inter*state offerings (securities sold in many states). *Inter*state offerings do need SEC registration. To help you remember, think of an interstate roadway, which continues from one state to the next.

Regulation A+ (Reg A+) offerings

An offering of securities worth $20 million (Tier 1) or $75 million (Tier 2) or less within a 12-month period is Regulation A+. Although these companies may seem large to you, they're relatively small in market terms. Regulation A+ offerings are exempt from the full registration requirements but the issuer still has to file a simplified registration or abbreviated registration statement. In addition, the issuer also has to file an *offering circular* and provide it to potential investors. An offering circular is similar to a prospectus but not quite as extensive.

>> **Tier 1:** Besides the $20 million in 12 months' cap, of the $20 million, no more than $6 million can be sold on behalf of existing stockholders.

>> **Tier 2:** Besides the $75 million in 12 months' cap, of the $75 million, not more than $22.5 million can be sold on behalf of existing stockholders. In addition, Tier 2 investors must be *accredited* (see the definition of accredited under Regulation D offerings) or limited to a maximum of 10 percent of the investor's net income or 10 percent of the investor's net worth, whichever is higher.

Regulation S (Reg S) offerings

An offering of securities by U.S. issuers made outside of the U.S. Regulation S offerings are not subject to registration requirements of securities sold in the U.S. because the sale of these securities takes place in another country.

Regulation D (Reg D) offerings

Also known as a private placement (private securities offering), a Regulation D offering is an offering to no more than 35 unaccredited investors per year. Companies that issue securities through private placement are allowed to raise an unlimited amount of money but are limited in terms of the number of unaccredited investors but not limited in the amount of accredited investors (see below). Sales of Reg D securities are subject to the sales limitations set forth under Rule 144 (see "Rule 144" later).

Investors of private placements must sign a letter (agreement) that they will hold the stock for investment purposes only. Stock purchased through private placement is sometimes called *lettered* or *legend* stock because purchasers must sign the investment letter.

Previously, an *accredited* or *sophisticated* investor meant an insider of the issuer; a Qualified Institutional Buyer (see the paragraph after the following list); or one with a net worth of $1 million or more excluding primary residence or an investor who has had a yearly income of at least $200,000 (for an individual investor) or $300,000 (for joint income with spouse) for the previous two years and is expected to earn at least that much in the current year.

However, under SEC Rule 501, the list of who or what is an accredited investor has recently expanded greatly to also include:

>> Corporations, partnerships, or organizations with a net worth of at least $5 million

>> Reps registered and in good standing with the SEC, FINRA, and/or at least one state who have passed the Series 7, Series 65, Series 66, and/or the Series 82 exams

>> Corporations, partnerships, or organizations with a net worth of at least $5 million

>> Knowledgeable employees of private funds (hedge funds, private equity funds, and so on) that have the ability to raise money privately

>> Rural business investment companies (investment companies that raise money to invest in small rural businesses)

>> Limited Liability Corporations (LLCs) with more than $5 million in assets

>> Family offices with at least $5 million in assets under management

For the purposes of private placements, *Qualified Institutional Buyers (QIBs)* are allowed to purchase private placements in the same way that accredited investors are. QIBs can be a bank, insurance company, employee benefit plan, a trust fund, a business development company, and so on, that owns and invests on a discretionary basis at least $100 million in securities of issuers not affiliated with the entity. Broker-dealers may also be considered QIBs if they own and invest on a discretionary basis at least $10 million in securities of issuers not affiliated with the broker-dealer.

REMEMBER

Private placements aren't for everyone, so there are restrictions placed on firms soliciting or advertising for private placements under SEC Rule 506. Either the company refrains from advertising and solicitation and limits the number of accredited investors to 35 *or* if the company solicits or advertises, it sells only to accredited investors.

Rule 144

This rule covers the sale of restricted, unregistered, and control securities (stock owned by directors, officers, or persons [including holdings of immediate family members] owning 10% or more of the issuer's voting stock). According to Rule 144, sellers of these securities must wait anywhere from 6 months to a year, depending on whether the corporation that issued the securities is subject to the reporting requirements of the Securities Exchange Act of 1934, prior to selling the securities to the public. Additionally, the most an investor can sell at one time is 1 percent of the outstanding shares or the average weekly trading volume for the previous four weeks, whichever is greater.

Rule 144A

This rule allows unregistered domestic and foreign securities to be sold to Qualified Institutional Buyers in the U.S. without a holding period.

The following example tests your ability to answer restricted-stock questions.

EXAMPLE

John Bullini is a control person who purchased shares of restricted stock and wants to sell under Rule 144. John has fully paid for the shares and has held them for over one year. There are 1,500,000 shares outstanding. Form 144 is filed on Monday, May 28, and the weekly trading volume for the restricted stock is as follows:

Week Ending	Trading Volume
May 25	16,000 shares
May 18	15,000 shares
May 11	17,000 shares
May 4	15,000 shares
April 27	18,000 shares

What is the maximum number of shares John can sell with this filing?

(A) 15,000

(B) 15,750

(C) 16,200

(D) 16,250

The right answer is Choice (B). The test-writers often try to trick you on the Series 7 exam by giving you at least one week more than you need to answer the question. Because John has held his restricted stock for over a year, he can sell 1 percent of the outstanding shares or the averaged weekly trading volume for the previous four weeks, whichever is greater:

$$1\% \times 1,500,000 \text{ shares outstanding} = 15,000 \text{ shares}$$

$$\frac{16,000 + 15,000 + 17,000 + 15,000}{4 \text{ weeks}} = \frac{63,000}{4 \text{ weeks}} = 15,750 \text{ shares}$$

WARNING

In this case, the previous four weeks are the top four in the list, but be careful; the examiners are just as likely to use the bottom four to give the table a different look.

Figure out 1 percent of the outstanding shares by multiplying the outstanding shares by 1 percent (easy, right?). In this case, you come up with an answer of 15,000 shares. That's one possible answer. The other possible answer is the average weekly trading volume for the previous four weeks. Add the trading volume for the previous four weeks (the top four in the chart), and divide by 4 to get an answer of 15,750 shares. Because you're looking for the greater number, the answer is Choice (B).

REMEMBER Even securities exempt from registration are subject to antifraud rules. All securities are subject to antifraud provisions of the Securities Act of 1933, which requires issuers to provide accurate information regarding any securities offered to the public.

Testing Your Knowledge

Now that you've reviewed what you need to know about bringing new securities to market (at least as far as the Series 7 exam goes), it's time to attack some questions. Take your time as you work through the following questions so that you don't make any careless mistakes.

1. Which of the following underwriting agreements specify that any unsold securities are retained by the underwriters?

   (A) Best efforts

   (B) AON

   (C) Firm commitment

   (D) Mini-max

2. The cooling-off period for a new issue lasts approximately how many days?

   (A) 20

   (B) 30

   (C) 45

   (D) 90

3. A Regulation D offering is an offering of

   (A) securities only within the issuer's home state

   (B) securities worth $75 million or less in a 12-month period

   (C) securities to no more than 35 unaccredited investors within a 12-month period

   (D) a large block of previously outstanding securities

4. Which of the following are exempt securities?

   I. Municipal bonds

   II. Securities issued by savings institutions

   III. Variable annuities

   IV. Commercial paper with an initial maturity of 365 days or less

   (A) I and II

   (B) I, III, and IV

   (C) II, III, and IV

   (D) I, II, III, and IV

5. An investor has held shares of ABC restricted stock for over one year. ABC has 3,000,000 shares outstanding. The most recently reported weekly trading volumes for ABC are as follows:

Week Ending	Trading Volume
July 31	30,000 shares
July 24	40,000 shares
July 17	25,000 shares
July 10	35,000 shares
July 3	40,000 shares

What is the maximum number of shares the investor can sell under Rule 144?

(A) 30,000

(B) 32,500

(C) 35,000

(D) 40,000

6. If a new issue will be offered to the public at $14.00, all of the following are acceptable stabilization bids EXCEPT

(A) $13.80

(B) $13.90

(C) $14.00

(D) $14.10

7. A final prospectus includes

    I. the offering price

   II. the underwriter's spread

  III. the delivery date

(A) I and II

(B) II and III

(C) I and III

(D) I, II, and III

8. All of the following are types of state registration EXCEPT

(A) filing

(B) coordination

(C) qualification

(D) indemnification

9. According to the Securities Act of 1933, sales of which of the following is an exempt transaction?

(A) U.S. government note

(B) Security issued by a bank

(C) Regulation S offering

(D) Municipal bond

10. A syndicate is underwriting a new stock offering in an undivided account. The offering is 5,000,000 shares, and a member of the syndicate is responsible for selling 500,000 shares. After selling the entire 500,000 shares of the allotment, the manager reports there are 1,500,000 shares left unsold by other members of the syndicate. How many shares is the syndicate member responsible for selling at this point?

(A) 0

(B) 100,000

(C) 150,000

(D) 300,000

Answers and Explanations

Hopefully, you just read the chapter and didn't find any of the questions too difficult. Because there are 10 questions, each one is worth 10 points.

1. **C.** In a firm commitment underwriting, any unsold securities are retained by the underwriters.

2. **A.** It usually takes the SEC about 20 days to review the registration statement of a company.

3. **C.** A Regulation D offering is also known as a private placement. It is an offering to an unlimited amount of accredited investors but only 35 unaccredited (small) investors per year. As such, Regulation D transactions are exempt from the full registration requirements under the Securities Act of 1933.

4. **A.** Exempt securities are securities that don't have to be registered with the SEC before issuance. Out of the choices you were given, municipal bonds and securities issued by savings institutions are exempt securities. Variable annuities are not exempt; fixed annuities are. Commercial paper has to have an initial expiration of 270 days or less to be exempt, not 365.

5. **B.** Because this is restricted stock, the investor may sell the average weekly trading volume for the previous 4 weeks or 1 percent of the outstanding shares, whichever is greater.

$$\frac{30,000 + 40,000 + 25,000 + 35,000}{4} = \frac{130,000}{4} = 32,500$$
$$1\% \times 3,000,000 = 30,000$$

   The average weekly trading volume for the previous 4 weeks (the top 4 numbers) is 32,500 shares, and 1 percent of the outstanding shares is 30,000. Since 32,500 is larger, that's the answer.

6. **D.** Stabilization bids may only be entered at or below the public offering price. Therefore, answer D won't work.

7. **D.** The final prospectus is prepared during the end of the cooling-off period. Among other things, it includes the offering price, delivery date, and the underwriter's spread.

8. **D.** The three types of state registration for securities are coordination, qualification, and notification (filing).

9. **C.** Exempt transactions include Rule 147 offerings, Regulation A, Regulation D, and Regulation S. All of the other choices listed are considered exempt securities, which are securities exempt from registration based on the type of security, not the type of transaction.

10. **C.** If this underwriting were set up on a divided (Western) account basis, the syndicate member would be done since the member sold its entire allotment. However, since this underwriting was set up as an undivided (Eastern) account basis, this syndicate member is responsible for a percentage of the shares left unsold by other members. The syndicate's responsibility is equal to the percentage of the offering the syndicate signed up for. The original offering was for 5,000,000 shares, and this syndicate member signed up to sell 500,000 shares or 10 percent of the offering.

$$\frac{500,000}{5,000,000} = 10 \text{ percent}$$

   Because there are 1,500,000 shares left unsold by other syndicate members, this syndicate member is responsible for selling another 150,000 shares.

   $1,500,000 \text{ unsold shares} \times 10\% = 150,000 \text{ shares}$

Chapter **6**

Corporate Ownership: Equity Securities

E quity securities — such as common and preferred stock — represent ownership interest in the issuing company. All publicly held corporations issue common stock to investors. Investors love these securities because they've historically outperformed most other investments, so an average (or above-average, in your case) stockbroker sells more of these types of securities than any other kind.

The Series 7 exam tests you on your ability to recognize the types of equity securities and on some other basic information. Although you may find that the Series 7 doesn't test you heavily on the info provided here, this chapter forms a strong foundation for many other chapters in the book. I think that you'll find it difficult (if not impossible) to understand what an option or mutual fund is if you don't know what a stock is. Needless to say, even though this chapter is small, don't ignore it or it may come back to bite you.

You've most likely taken the Securities Industry Essential (SIE) exam already. If so, as in other chapters, there's a certain amount of overlap of information. That's good news for you because you should (I hope) have a decent grasp on some of the topics covered in this chapter. Mixed in throughout this chapter, I give you plenty of examples to familiarize you with the types of equities securities questions on the Series 7 exam, and I give you a quick quiz with explanations at the end of the chapter.

Beginning with the Basics: Common Stock

Corporations issue common stock (as well as other securities) to raise business capital. As an equity security, common stock represents ownership of the issuing corporation. If a corporation issues 1 million shares of stock, each share represents a one-millionth ownership of the issuing corporation. The market value of the common stock of a corporation is based on the worth (or perceived worth) of the company, the amount of shares outstanding, supply and demand, and so on.

REMEMBER

Since stockholders are owners of a corporation, they are afforded certain rights: *pre-emptive rights* (first right to buy shares if the company is issuing more stock), the *right to receive dividends* if declared, access to certain *corporate books* (annual financial statements provided by the issuer, not detailed financial records), *voting power,* and the *residual claim on corporate assets.* Since common stock is considered junior to a corporation's debt and preferred stock, common stockholders would be the last to be paid in the event of corporate bankruptcy.

Read on for the ins and outs of common stock.

Understanding a stockholder's voting rights

One of the most basic rights that most common stockholders receive is voting rights — although rarely corporations issue *nonvoting common stock.* Nonvoting stock may be issued by corporations to protect their board of directors, but it's not as attractive to investors who like to have some control over who's running the company. Most preferred stock (covered later in the chapter) is nonvoting.

When investors have voting rights, every so often a corporation may have those investors vote to change members on the board of directors. Although investors may be able to vote on other issues, the Series 7 focuses on voting to change board members.

Because having all stockholders actually attend the annual corporate meeting to vote would be difficult, stockholders usually vote by *proxy,* or absentee ballot.

Statutory (regular) voting

Statutory, or regular, voting is the most common type of voting that corporations offer to their shareholders. This type of voting is quite straightforward. Investors receive one vote for every share that they own multiplied by the number of positions to be filled on the board of directors (or issues to be decided). However, investors have to *split the votes evenly* for each item on the ballot.

For example, if an investor owns 500 shares and there are four positions to be filled on the board of directors, the investor has a total of 2,000 votes (500 shares × 4 candidates), which the investor must split evenly among all open positions (500 each). The investor votes yes or no for each candidate.

Cumulative voting

Cumulative voting is a little different from statutory voting (see the preceding section). Although the investor still gets the same number of overall votes as if the corporation were offering statutory voting, the stockholder can vote the shares in any way she sees fit. Cumulative voting gives smaller shareholders (in terms of shares) an easier chance to gain representation on the board of directors.

For example, if an investor owns 1,000 shares and three positions on the board of directors are open, the investor has a total of 3,000 votes (1,000 shares × 3 candidates), which the investor can use to vote for any candidate(s) in any way she sees fit.

Cumulative voting doesn't give an investor more voting power, just more voting flexibility. The only way to get more voting power is to buy more shares.

The following question tests your ability to answer a cumulative voting question.

Bella Bearishnikoff owns 800 shares of CBA common stock. It is time for CBA to hold its annual shareholders' meeting, and there are four candidates for the board of directors. CBA offers its shareholders cumulative voting. Which of the following are acceptable votes from Bella?

I. 800 votes for each of the four candidates

II. 2,000 votes for one candidate and 400 votes for each of the other candidates

III. 3,200 votes for one candidate

IV. 3,200 votes for each of the candidates

(A) I only

(B) II and III

(C) I, II, and III

(D) I, III, and IV

The correct answer is Choice (C). Ms. Bearishnikoff has a total of 3,200 votes (800 shares × 4 candidates). Because CBA offers cumulative voting, she can vote the 3,200 votes in any way she likes. Statements I, II, and III are all correct because none of those choices require more than 3,200 votes. However, IV would require 12,800 votes. As a side note, if the question had asked about statutory voting, the answer would have been Choice (A).

Categorizing shares corporations can sell

All publicly held corporations have a certain quantity of shares that they can sell based on their corporate charter. These shares are broken down into a few categories depending on whether the issuer or investors hold the shares:

>> **Authorized shares:** Authorized shares are the number of shares of stock that a corporation can issue. The issuer's bylaws or *corporate charter* (a document filed with the state that identifies the names of the founders of the corporation, the company's objectives, and so on) states the number of shares the company is authorized to sell. However, the issuer usually holds back a large percentage of the authorized stock (which it can sell later through a primary offering — see Chapter 5 for details on offerings). In the event that the issuer wishes to sell more shares than were previously authorized, the issuer's corporate charter would have to be updated, which would require a vote by stockholders.

>> **Issued shares:** Issued shares are the portion of authorized shares that the issuer has sold to the public to raise money. Logically, the portion of authorized shares that haven't been issued to the public are called *unissued shares.* Unissued shares do not carry the rights and privileges of issued shares. Shares may be kept unissued for up to 2 or 3 years (shelf registration) for future use.

>> **Outstanding shares:** Outstanding shares are the number of shares that are in investors' hands. This quantity may or may not be the same number as the issued shares. At times, an issuer may decide to repurchase its stock in the market for numerous reasons, including to help increase the demand (and the price) of the stock trading in the market or to avoid a *hostile takeover* (when another company is trying to gain control of the issuer). Stock that the issuer repurchases is called *treasury stock.*

The standard formula for outstanding shares follows:

outstanding = issued − treasury

The following question tests your understanding of outstanding shares.

EXAMPLE

ZZZ Bedding Corp. is authorized to issue 2,000,000 shares of common stock. However, ZZZ issues only 800,000 shares to the public. One year later, ZZZ repurchases 150,000 shares to increase the demand on the outstanding shares. How many shares does ZZZ have outstanding?

(A) 650,000

(B) 800,000

(C) 1,200,000

(D) 1,850,000

The right answer is Choice (A). You probably didn't have too much difficulty with this one. All the question is asking is how many shares are still outstanding in the market. Check out the following equation:

Outstanding = Issued – Treasury
Outstanding = 800,000 – 150,000 = 650,000

Because ZZZ issued only 800,000 shares of the 2,000,000 that it's authorized to issue, the most ZZZ ever had in the market was 800,000. However, a year after issuing those shares, ZZZ repurchased 150,000 shares, giving the company treasury stock. Therefore, the amount of outstanding shares is 650,000.

Considering the par value of common stock

Par value (stated or face value) for common stock is not as important to investors as it is to bondholders and preferred stockholders (see the later section "Considering characteristics of preferred stock"). *Par value* for common stock is more or less a bookkeeping value for the issuer. Although issuers may set the par value at $1 (or $5, $10, or whatever), the selling price is usually much more. A stock's par value has no relation to the market price of the stock.

REMEMBER

The amount over par value that an issuer receives for selling stock is called *additional paid-in capital, paid-in surplus,* or *capital in excess of par.*

The *stated par value* is printed on the stock certificate; it changes if the issuer splits its stock. An issuer can also issue *no par value stock* (stock issued without a stated par value); in this case, the stock has a stated value that the corporation uses for bookkeeping purposes. A lack of par value doesn't affect investors.

REMEMBER

Splitting common stock was covered on the Securities Industry Essentials Exam. So, you won't have to know the math related to splitting common stock on the Series 7. However, you should remember that forward stock splits lower the par value and market value per share as well as increasing the number of shares held by existing stockholders. Reverse splits increase the par value and market value per share while decreasing the number of shares held by existing stockholders.

Sharing corporate profits through dividends

If a corporation is profitable (and the members on the board of directors are in a generous mood), the board of directors may decide to issue a dividend to investors. Dividends are just a way for corporations to distribute cash, stock, product, or whatever, out of its earnings and profits. If and/or when the corporation declares a dividend, each shareholder is entitled to a *pro rata* share of dividends, meaning that every shareholder receives an equal proportion for each share that she owns. The Series 7 exam expects you to know the forms of dividends an investor can receive and how the dividends affect both the market price of the stock and an investor's position. Although the investor can receive dividends in cash, stock, or *property forms* (stock of a subsidiary company or sample products made by the issuer), I focus on cash and stock dividends because those scenarios are much more likely.

REMEMBER

Investors can't vote on dividends; instead, the board of directors decides dividend payouts. You can imagine that if this decision were left in the investors' hands, they'd vote for dividends weekly! For more info on voting, see "Understanding a stockholder's voting rights," earlier in this chapter. Even if the issuing corporation is profitable, it may decide not to pay a cash dividend to investors because it has other plans for the money, such as reinvesting the money for new machinery, expansion, and so on.

Cash dividends

Cash dividends are a way for a corporation to share its profits with shareholders. When an investor receives cash dividends, it's a taxable event. Corporations aren't required to pay dividends; however, dividends provide a good incentive for investors to hold onto stock that isn't experiencing much growth. Although cash dividends are nice, the market price of the stock falls on the *ex-dividend date* (the first day the stock trades without a dividend) to reflect the dividend paid:

$$\text{stock price} - \text{dividend} = \text{price on ex-dividend date}$$

Try your hand at answering a cash dividend question.

EXAMPLE

ABC stock is trading for $49.50 on the day prior to the ex-dividend date. If ABC previously announced a $0.75 dividend, what will be the next day's opening price?

(A) $48.25

(B) $48.75

(C) $49.50

(D) $50.25

The correct answer is Choice (B). Check your work:

$$\$49.50 - .75 = \$48.75$$

The math's as simple as that. Because stocks are now trading in pennies instead of eighths like they used to, calculating the price on the ex-dividend date is a snap.

Stock dividends

Stock dividends are just like forward stock splits in that the investor receives more shares of stock, only the corporation gives a percentage dividend (5 percent, 10 percent, and so on) instead of splitting the stock 2-for-1, 3-for-1, or whatever. Unlike cash dividends, stock dividends aren't taxable to the stockholder because the investor's overall value of investment doesn't change.

The primary reason for a company to give investors a stock dividend is to make the market price more attractive to investors (if the market price gets too high, it limits the number of investors who can purchase the stock), thus adding *liquidity* (ease of trading) to the stock.

The following question tests your expertise in answering stock dividend questions.

EXAMPLE

John Johnson owns 400 shares of WIN common stock at $33 per share. WIN previously declared a 10 percent stock dividend. Assuming no change in the market price of WIN prior to the dividend, what is John's position after the dividend?

(A) 400 shares at $30

(B) 440 shares at $33

(C) 400 shares at $36.30

(D) 440 shares at $30

The answer you want is Choice (D). In this case, you can find the answer without doing any math. Because the number of shares increases, the price of the stock has to decrease. Therefore, the only answer that works is Choice (D). I can't guarantee that you'll get a question where you don't have to do the math, but don't rule it out; scan the answer choices before pulling out your calculator.

Anyway, here's how the numbers work. You have to remember that the investor's overall value of investment doesn't change. John gets a 10 percent stock dividend, so he receives 10 percent more shares. Now John has 440 shares of WIN (400 shares + 40 shares [10 percent of 400]). Next, you need to determine his overall value of investment:

$$400 \text{ shares} \times \$33 = \$13{,}200$$

Because the overall value of investment doesn't change, John needs to have $13,200 worth of

WIN after the dividend:

$$\frac{\$13{,}200}{440 \text{ shares}} = \$30 \text{ per share}$$

John's position after the split is 440 shares at $30 per share.

Corporate spin-off

Corporations sometimes decide to spin off a portion of their company to create two distinct companies. They will typically do this because they feel that the companies will be stronger separated. An example of this is eBay. In 2015, eBay spun off PayPal Holdings, Inc. Investors who are holding shares of the parent company prior to the spin-off would receive shares of the new company equal to their percentage ownership of the parent company.

Consolidations

Consolidation happens when two or more companies combine to form a new company or entity. The idea is for the new company to be able to gain more market share and possibly have more buying power. Some of the additional benefits might be the merging of expertise or technology. Unlike mergers where typically the larger company absorbs the other, consolidations may result in a new company altogether. If this happens, stockholders will receive shares of the new company based off of their (but not in direct proportion to) percentage ownership of one of the companies prior to the consolidation.

Penny stocks

Penny stocks are low-priced equity securities issued by corporations. Penny stocks are non-NASDAQ equity securities that trade OTC (over the counter) at less than $5 per share. Penny stocks are considered extremely speculative in nature and aren't for everyone. Prior to even contacting a client about the purchase of penny stocks, you must determine the investor's suitability based on information about his objectives and financial situation. Cold calling potential customers pushing penny stocks is a no no.

All broker-dealers who trade penny stocks must provide a *penny stock disclosure* document, which outlines the risks of investing in penny stocks (lack of liquidity, quick price changes, and so on) to investors prior to effecting any penny stock transactions. The broker-dealer must receive a signed and dated acknowledgement of receipt of the document from the customer. (Certain established customers are exempt from having to receive and sign the disclosure document.) The broker-dealer must wait at least 2 business days after sending the document to the customer prior to any penny-stock transaction. Broker-dealers must maintain the customer's signed acknowledgement. In addition, if requested by the customer, the broker-dealer must provide the penny stock information provided at the SEC's website at www.sec.gov/investor/pubs/microcapstock.htm.

Compensation

Prior to effecting a transaction in penny stocks, associated persons must disclose (orally or in writing) the amount of cash compensation they will receive as a result of the transaction. In addition, it must be sent to the customer in writing at or prior to the time the confirmation of trade is sent.

Note: Any customer holding penny stocks must receive a *monthly account statement* indicating the market value, number of shares, issuer's name, and so on. (For more on account statements, see Chapter 16.)

Exempt penny-stock transactions

Under SEC Rule 15g-1, the following penny-stock transactions will be exempt:

» Transactions by a broker or dealer whose commissions, markups, markdowns, and commission equivalents from penny stock transactions did not exceed 5 percent of its total commissions in the preceding 3 months and during 11 or more of the preceding 12 months, or the preceding 6 months and who hasn't been a market maker in that particular penny stock in the preceding 12 months.

» Transactions that meet the requirements of Regulation D (covered in Chapter 5).

» Transactions in which the client is an institutional accredited investor.

» Transactions that are not recommended by the broker-dealer.

» Transactions in which the customer is the issuer, officer, general partner, director, and so on of more than 5 percent of any class of equity security of the issuer of the penny stock.

» Any other transaction deemed to be exempt by the SEC that it deems as consistent with the protection of investors and is in the public's interest.

Getting Preferential Treatment: Preferred Stock

Equity securities represent shares of ownership in a company, and debt securities, well, represent debt (see Chapters 7 and 8 for info on debt securities). Although preferred stock (sometimes simply called "preferreds") has some characteristics of both equity and debt securities, preferred stock is an equity security because it represents ownership of the issuing corporation the same way that common stock does.

Considering characteristics of preferred stock

One advantage of purchasing preferred stock over common stock is that preferred shareholders receive money back (if there's any left) before common stockholders do if the issuer declares bankruptcy. However, the main difference between preferred stock and common stock has to do with dividends. Issuers of common stock pay a cash dividend only if the company is in a position to share corporate profits. By contrast, issuers of preferred stock are required to pay consistent cash dividends. Preferred stock generally has a par value of $100 per share (although it could be $50, $25, and so on) and tends to trade in the market somewhere close to that par value. However, like debt securities, the price of preferred stock will increase or decrease based on changes in prevailing interest rates.

Because preferred stock receives (or are supposed to receive) a consistent dividend, they are somewhat like debt securities receiving interest. Because of that similarity, like debt securities (bonds), many preferred stocks are rated by rating agencies such as Moody's, Standard & Poor's, and Fitch. (For more on rating agencies, see Chapter 7.) Some of the drawbacks of investing in preferred stock over common stock are the lack of voting rights, the sometimes higher cost per share, and limited growth. You can assume for Series 7 exam purposes that preferred stockholders don't receive voting rights unless they fail to receive their expected dividends. (A few other exceptions exist, but you don't need to worry about them now.) Also, because most preferred stock pays consistent dividends, the market price will increase or decrease depending on prevailing interest rates similar to debt securities.

REMEMBER

If the issuer can't make a payment because earnings are low, then in most cases, owners of preferred stock are still owed the missing dividend payment(s). The dividend (sharing of profits) that preferred stockholders receive is based on par value. Thus, although par value may be nothing more than a bookkeeping value when you're dealing with common stock, par value is definitely important to preferred stockholders.

To calculate the annual dividend, multiply the percentage of the dividend by the par value. For instance, if a customer owns a preferred stock that pays an 8 percent dividend and the par value is $100, you set up the following equation:

$$8\% \text{ preferred stock} \times \$100 \text{ par} = \$8 \text{ per year in dividends}$$

If the issuer were to pay this dividend quarterly (once every three months), an investor would receive $2 per share every three months.

REMEMBER

When working on a dividend question on preferred stock, you need to look for the par value in the problem. Remember, it's normally $100, but it could be $25, $50, and so on.

Getting familiar with types of preferred stock

You need to be aware of several types of preferred stock for the Series 7. This section gives you a brief explanation of the types and some of their characteristics. Some preferred stock may be a combination of the different types, as in cumulative convertible preferred stock. Here are the distinctions between noncumulative and cumulative preferred stock:

>> **Noncumulative (straight) preferred:** This type of preferred stock is rare. The main feature of preferred stock is that investors receive a consistent cash dividend. In the event that the issuer doesn't pay the dividend, the company usually still owes it to investors. This isn't the case for noncumulative preferred stock. If the preferred stock is noncumulative and the issuer fails to pay a dividend, the issuer doesn't owe it to investors. An investor may choose noncumulative preferred stock over common stock because the company is still supposed to pay a consistent

cash dividend and, in the event of corporate bankruptcy, preferred stockholders still get paid before common stockholders. Noncumulative preferred stock is riskier for investors than cumulative preferred stock, so the issuer typically offers a higher dividend.

>> **Cumulative preferred:** Cumulative preferred stock is more common. If an investor owns cumulative preferred stock and doesn't receive an expected dividend, the issuer still owes that dividend. If the issuer declares a common dividend, the issuer first has to make up all delinquent payments to cumulative preferred stockholders.

The following question tests your understanding of cumulative preferred stock.

EXAMPLE

An investor owns ABC 8 percent cumulative preferred stock ($100 par). In the first year, ABC paid $6 in dividends. In the second year, it paid $4 in dividends. If a common dividend is declared the following year, how much must the preferred shareholders receive?

(A) $6

(B) $8

(C) $12

(D) $14

The right answer is Choice (D). Because ABC is cumulative preferred stock, issuers have to catch up preferred stockholders on all outstanding dividends before common shareholders receive a dividend. In this example, the investor is supposed to receive $8 per year in dividends (8% × $100 par). In the first year, the issuer shorted the investor $2; in the second year, $4. The investor hasn't yet received payment for the following year, so she is owed $8. Add up these debts:

$$(\$8 - \$6) + (\$8 - \$4) + \$8 = \$2 + \$4 + \$8 = \$14$$

All preferred stock has to be either cumulative or noncumulative. Both types may have other features, including the ability to turn into other kinds of stock, offerings of extra dividends, and other VIP treatment. I run through some of these traits in the list that follows:

>> **Convertible preferred:** Convertible preferred stock allows investors to trade their preferred stock for common stock of the same company at any time. Because the issuers are providing investors with another way to make money, investors usually receive a lower dividend payment than with regular preferred stock.

The *conversion price* is the dollar price at which a convertible preferred stock par value can be exchanged into a share of common stock. When the convertible preferred stock is first issued, the conversion price is specified and is based on par value. The *conversion ratio* tells you the number of shares of common stock that an investor receives for converting one share of preferred stock.

You can use the following conversion ratio formula for convertible preferred stock and also for convertible bonds (see Chapter 7 for info on convertible bonds):

$$\text{conversion ratio} = \frac{\text{par value}}{\text{conversion price}}$$

REMEMBER

The conversion ratio helps you determine a *parity price* where the convertible preferred stock and common stock would be trading equally. For example, say you have a convertible preferred stock that's exchangeable for four shares of common stock. If the convertible preferred stock is trading at $100 and the common stock is trading at $25, they're on parity because four shares of stock at $25 equal $100. However, if there's a disparity in the exchange values, converting may be profitable. If the convertible preferred stock is trading at $100 and the common stock is trading at $28, the common stock is trading above parity; converting makes sense because investors are exchanging $100 worth of securities for $112 worth of securities ($28 × 4). Convertible preferred stock typically trades very close to the parity price.

>> **Callable preferred:** Callable preferred stock allows the issuer to buy back the preferred stock at any time at a price on the certificate. This stock is a little riskier for investors because they don't have control over how long they can hold the stock, so corporations usually pay a higher dividend on callable preferred stock than on regular preferred stock. Issuers will issue callable preferred stock with a *sinking fund provision,* which means that the issuer will set aside money in an account (custodial account) to repurchase the shares (if he decides to) sometime in the future. A call feature may be added to other types of preferred stock such as: callable convertible preferred.

>> **Participating preferred:** Although rarely issued, participating preferred stock allows the investors to receive common dividends in addition to the usual preferred dividends up to a certain amount. Most preferred stock is non-participating, meaning that they don't receive common dividends, only preferred dividends.

>> **Prior (senior) preferred:** Preferred stockholders receive compensation before common stockholders in the event of corporate bankruptcy. In this case, senior preferred stockholders receive compensation even before other preferred stockholders. Because of the extra safety factor, senior preferred stock pays a slightly lower dividend than other preferred stock from the same issuer.

>> **Adjustable (variable or floating rate) preferred:** Holders of adjustable preferred stock receive a dividend that's reset every three months to match movements in the prevailing interest rates. Because the dividend adjusts to changing interest rates (usually based off of a certain benchmark, such as the T-bill rate), the stock price remains more stable.

The following example gives you an idea of how to determine the conversion ratio.

EXAMPLE

If ABC preferred stock ($100 par) is convertible into common stock for $25, what is the conversion ratio?

(A) 1 share

(B) 4 shares

(C) 25 shares

(D) 100 shares

The answer you want is Choice (B). This equation is about as simple as the math gets on the Series 7 exam. Because the $100 par value preferred stock is convertible into common stock for $25, it's convertible into four shares:

$$\text{conversion ratio} = \frac{\text{par value}}{\text{conversion price}} = \frac{\$100}{\$25} = 4 \text{ shares}$$

If you'd like to have more fun (and I use that term loosely) with convertible securities, please visit the convertible bond section in Chapter 7.

Securities with a Twist

Some securities fall outside the boundaries of the more normal common and preferred stock, but I still include them in this equities chapter because they involve ownership in a company or the opportunity to get it. This section gives you an overview of those special securities.

Opening national borders: ADRs

American Depositary Receipts (ADRs) are receipts for foreign securities traded in the United States. ADRs are negotiable certificates (they can be sold or transferred to another party) that represent a specific number of shares (usually one to ten) of a foreign stock. ADR investors may or may not have voting privileges. U.S. banks issue them; therefore, investors receive dividends in U.S. dollars. The stock certificates are held in a foreign branch of a U.S. bank (the custodian bank) and, to exchange their ADRs for the actual shares, investors return the ADRs to the bank that's holding the shares. In addition to the risks associated with stock ownership in general, ADR owners are subject to currency risk (the risk that the value of the security may decline because the value of the currency of the issuing corporation may fall in relation to the U.S. dollar). For information on how the strength of the dollar affects the relative prices of goods in the international market, flip to Chapter 13.

Rights: The right to buy new shares at a discount

Corporations offer rights (subscription or preemptive rights) to their common stockholders. To maintain their proportionate ownership of the corporation, *rights* allow existing stockholders to purchase new shares of the corporation *at a discount* directly from the issuer, before the shares are offered to the public. Stockholders receive one right for each share owned. The rights are *short-term* (usually 30 to 45 days). The rights are marketable and may be sold by the stockholders to other investors. If existing stockholders don't purchase all the shares, the issuer offers any unsold shares to a standby underwriter. A *standby underwriter* is a broker-dealer that purchases any stock that wasn't sold in the rights offering and then resells the shares to other investors.

For the Series 7, you can assume that *common* stockholders automatically receive rights.

Because rights allow investors to purchase the shares at a discount, rights have a theoretical value. The board of directors determines that value when they decide how many rights investors need to purchase a share, as well as the discounted price offered to investors. To determine the value of a right, you can use one of two basic formulas: the cum rights formula or the ex-rights formula. Look closely at the question to determine which one you need. The following sections explore each.

Using the cum rights formula

You may have to find the value of a right while shares are still trading with rights attached. To find out how much of a discount each right provides, you can simply take the difference between the market price and the subscription price, divide that by the number of rights, and come up with a nice, round number. But not so fast! On the *ex-date* (the first day the stock trades without rights), the market price will drop by the value of the right. Before the ex-date, you can find the value of a right by using the cum (Latin for *with*) rights formula:

$$\text{Value of a right cum rights} = \frac{M\,(\text{market price}) - S\,(\text{subscription price})}{N\,(\text{number of rights needed to purchase one share}) + 1}$$

The +1 in the denominator accounts for the later drop in the market price. Try out the following rights question.

DEF Corp. is issuing new shares through a rights offering. If a new share costs $16 plus four rights and the stock trades at $20, what is the theoretical value of a right prior to the ex-date?

(A) $0.20

(B) $0.80

(C) $1.00

(D) $1.20

The right answer is Choice (B). The stock is trading with (cum) rights (the words *prior to the ex-date* in the problem tip you off), so you need to use the cum rights formula to figure out the value of a right:

$$\frac{M-S}{N+1}=\frac{\$20-\$16}{4+1}=\frac{\$4}{5}=.80$$

The theoretical value of a right is $0.80.

Using the ex-rights formula

When you calculate the value of a right on the *ex-date* (the first day the stock trades without rights), the market price has already fallen by the value of the right. You simply have to use the new market price and the subscription price to figure out the discount per right. If the stock is trading ex-rights, use the following formula to figure out the value of a right:

$$\text{Value of a right ex-rights} = \frac{M \text{ (market price)} - S \text{ (subscription price)}}{N \text{ (number of rights needed to purchase one share)}}$$

The cum rights and ex-rights formulas are the same except for the +1 in the denominator. Because *ex* means *without*, remember that the ex formula is without the +1.

Warrants: The right to buy stock at a fixed price

Warrants are certificates that entitle the holder to buy a specific amount of stock at a fixed price; they're usually issued along with a new bond or stock offering. Warrant holders have no voting rights and receive no dividends. Bundled bonds and warrants or bundled stock and warrants are called *units*. Unlike rights, they are *long term* and sometimes perpetual (without an expiration date). Warrants may be referred to as *sweeteners* because they're something that the issuer throws into the new offering to make the deal more appealing; however, warrants are marketable securities and can be sold separately on the market. When warrants are originally issued, the warrant's exercise price is set well above the underlying stock's market price.

For example, suppose QRS warrants give investors the right to buy QRS common stock at $20 per share when QRS common stock is trading at $12. Certainly, exercising their warrants to purchase QRS stock at $20 wouldn't make sense for investors when they can buy QRS stock in the market at $12. However, if QRS rises above $20 per share, holders of warrants can exercise their warrants and purchase the stock from the issuer at $20 per share.

When a corporation offers new stock through a rights offering or by issuing warrants, the corporation includes an *anti-dilution agreement* or *anti-dilution provision* in its corporate charter and prospectus. The anti-dilution agreement states that if the issuer offers new securities to the public, it must offer them to its current stockholders first. This allows its existing stockholders to keep the same proportionate ownership of the issuing corporation.

Testing Your Knowledge

Now that you've finished the chapter, it's time to put your hard work to use. Here is a quick quiz with detailed explanations to test your knowledge.

1. Johnny Investor owns 2,000 shares of common stock of a company. The company has four vacancies on the board of directors. If the voting is cumulative, the investor may vote in any of the following ways EXCEPT

   (A) 2,000 votes for each of the four open positions

   (B) 4,000 votes each for two of the four open positions

   (C) 5,000 votes for one of the four open positions and 3,000 votes for another of the open positions

   (D) 3,000 votes for three of the four open positions

2. TUV listed stock closed at $20 on the business day prior to the ex-dividend date. If the TUV previously announced a 55-cent dividend, at what price will the stock open the next day?

   (A) 19.25

   (B) 19.45

   (C) 19.50

   (D) 20.00

3. DEF Corporation has previously issued 4% $100 par cumulative preferred stock. In the first two years, it paid $2 and $3 in dividends respectively. If the company announces a common dividend in the following year, how much does it owe preferred stockholders?

   (A) $3

   (B) $4

   (C) $5

   (D) $7

4. Which of the following are TRUE about both common and preferred stock?

   I. They are equity securities

   II. Dividends are determined by the issuer's board of directors

   III. Holders have the right to vote for members of the board of directors

   (A) I and II

   (B) I and III

   (C) II and III

   (D) I, II, and III

5. Which of the following types of preferred stock would most likely have the highest dividend?

   (A) Participating preferred

   (B) Callable preferred

   (C) Convertible preferred

   (D) Senior preferred

6. All of the following are TRUE of warrants EXCEPT

   (A) They can trade separately

   (B) They are usually issued to make a stock or bond offering more attractive to investors

   (C) They provide holders with a perpetual interest in the underlying security

   (D) None of the above

7. Which TWO of the following best describe ADRs?

   I. They are receipts for foreign securities trading in U.S. markets

   II. They are receipts for U.S. securities trading in foreign markets

   III. They are used to help finance foreign corporations

   IV. They are used to help finance U.S. corporations

   (A) I and III

   (B) I and IV

   (C) II and III

   (D) II and IV

8. The amount of money a corporation receives above its stated par value when issuing stock is known as

   (A) earned surplus

   (B) shareholder's equity

   (C) book value

   (D) additional paid in capital

9. ABC Corporation is issuing new shares through a rights offering. If the stock trades at $30, and it costs $24 plus 12 rights to purchase a new share, what is the theoretical value of a right, ex-rights?

   (A) $0.46

   (B) $0.50

   (C) $0.92

   (D) $1.00

10. Penny stocks are non-Nasdaq stocks trading at _____ or less.

   (A) $0.99

   (B) $1

   (C) $5

   (D) $10

Answers and Explanations

I hope you did fairly well on the quiz. Since there are 10 questions, each one is worth 10 points.

1. **D.** Under cumulative voting rules, this investor would have a total of 8,000 votes (2,000 shares × 4 vacancies), which can be voted in any way he sees fit. Answers A, B, and C are all possible but answer D would require Johnny to have 9,000 votes (3,000 votes × 3 candidates), which he doesn't have.

2. **B.** Remember, the ex-dividend date is the first day that a stock trades without a previously declared dividend. So the stock has to be reduced by the amount of the dividend on the ex-dividend date. Questions like this used to be a little more difficult when stocks traded in fractions instead of pennies. Now, it's simply a matter of subtracting the amount of the dividend from the closing price.

   $$20 - 0.55 = 19.45$$

3. **D.** Because this is cumulative preferred stock, the corporation must make up any preferred dividends owed prior to paying dividends to common stockholders. In this case, they shorted the preferred shareholders $2 per share in the first year ($4 due [4% of $100 par value] and only $2 paid), $1 per share in the second year ($4 due and only $3 paid), plus the $4 due now.

   $$\$2 + \$1 + \$4 = \$7$$

4. **A.** Common and preferred stock are considered equity securities because holders are owners of the corporation. Dividends paid to both common and preferred stockholders are determined by the board of directors. However, only common stockholders have voting rights. The only time preferred stockholders have voting rights is if they don't receive their expected dividends.

5. **B.** Out of the choices listed, callable preferred stock would most likely have the highest dividend because the issuer has the right to call back the preferred stock from the holders. Obviously this is not advantageous to the holders because the issuer would most likely call the stock when interest rates decrease. Thus, investors would likely have to invest in preferred stock with a lower dividend. Since it's a disadvantage to holders of callable preferred stockholders, the issuer has to offer a higher dividend to entice investors.

6. **C.** Warrants are often issued with stock and bond offerings more attractive. (When issued together, they're called a unit.) Warrants give the holders the right to buy stock from the issuer at a specific price. Warrants are marketable securities, meaning they can trade separately. They are long term and sometimes but not always perpetual (no end date), so answer C is the exception.

7. **A.** ADRs (American Depositary Receipts) are receipts for foreign securities trading in U.S. markets. The underlying securities are typically held in a foreign branch of a U.S. bank. The purchasers receive a receipt from that bank saying that they purchased a specific number of shares of the underlying security. These receipts are marketable, meaning they can be traded separately. ADRs help provide financing for foreign corporations by giving those foreign corporations access to U.S. investor's money.

8. **D.** Unless a corporation's stock is issued with no par value, they set a par value (stated par value) of a certain amount ($1, $5, $10, and so on), which is used for bookkeeping purposes. However, even though the par value is set, the issuing corporation typically sells the stock above its stated par value. The amount they receive above that stated par value is called additional paid in capital or capital surplus.

9. **B.** A rights offering occurs when an issuer offers new shares to existing shareholders at a discount prior to offering them to the other investors. Rights have a theoretical value that is determined by the following formula where M equals the market price of the stock, S equals the subscription price (discounted price), and N equals the number of rights needed to purchase one share.

$$\frac{M-S}{N} = \frac{\$30 - \$24}{12} = \frac{\$6}{12} = \$0.50$$

As a reminder, if the question was looking for the theoretical value of a right when the stock trades with (cum) rights, you would've needed to add 1 to the denominator.

10. **C.** Penny stocks are non-Nasdaq stocks that trade at $5 or less. Because of the risk of investing in penny stocks, most customers must receive a penny stock risk disclosure document.

Chapter **7**

Debt Securities: Corporate and U.S. Government Loans

Instead of giving up a portion of their company (via stock certificates), corporations can borrow money from investors by selling bonds. Local governments (through municipal bonds) and the U.S. government also issue bonds. For Series 7 exam purposes, most bonds are considered safer than stocks.

Bondholders aren't owners of a company like stockholders are; they're creditors. Bondholders lend money to an institution for a fixed period of time and receive interest for doing so. This arrangement allows the institution to borrow money on its terms (with its chosen maturity date, scheduled interest payments, interest rate, and so on), which it can't do by borrowing from a lending institution.

The Series 7 exam tests you on your ability to understand the different types of bonds issued, terminology, and yes, some math. This chapter has you covered in topics relating to corporate and U.S. government debt securities. You'll also notice that there is a bit of an overlap of the material that you needed to know for the Securities Industry Essentials exam and the Series 7 exam. As with other chapters, I've included some questions at the end of the chapter to help with your learning experience.

Tackling Bond Terms, Types, and Traits

Before you delve deeper into bonds, make sure you have a good handle on the basics. Understanding the bond basics is a building block that can make all the rest of the bond stuff easier. In this section, I first review basic bond terminology and then move on to some bond characteristics.

Remembering bond terminology

The Series 7 exam designers expect you to know general bond terminology. (And I give it to you here — that's why I get paid the big bucks!) In this section, I help you reinforce the information you should have already learned from taking the Securities Industry Essentials exam. This stuff is basic, but the Series 7 exam does test it:

>> **Maturity date:** All issued bonds have a stated maturity date (for example, 20 years, 30 years, and so on), which is the date bondholders get paid back for the loans they made. At maturity, bondholders receive par value (covered in the next bullet). Investors not looking to tie up their money for a long period of time are more likely to purchase short-term bonds.

>> **Par value:** Par value is the face value or principal of the bond. Although par value isn't significant to common stockholders (whose issuers use it solely for bookkeeping purposes), it's important to bondholders. Although U.S. Treasury securities may trade in smaller denominations, you can assume that the par value for each corporate bond is $1,000 (or in multiples of $1,000) unless otherwise stated in the question.

REMEMBER

Bond prices are quoted as a percentage of par value, often without the percent sign. A bond trading at 100 is trading at 100 percent of $1,000 par. Regardless of whether investors purchase a bond for $850 (85), $1,000 (100), or $1,050 (105), they'll receive par value plus any interest due at the maturity date of the bond, usually with semi-annual interest payments along the way. Corporate bonds are usually quoted in increments of 1/8% (1/8% = 0.00125 or $1.25), so a corporate bond quoted at 99 3⁄8 (99.375%) would be trading at $993.75.

>> **Coupon rate:** Of course, investors aren't lending money to issuers for nothing; investors receive interest for providing loans to the issuer. The coupon rate on the bond tells the investors how much annual interest they'll receive. Although bonds are no longer issued with physical coupons, some bonds previously required investors to detach dated coupons (bearer bonds and partially registered bonds) from their bonds and turn them in to receive their interest payments. Bonds with a set, or fixed, coupon rate are considered fixed-income securities.

The coupon rate is expressed as a percentage of par value. For example, a bond with a coupon rate of 6 percent would pay annual interest of $60 (6% × $1,000 par value). You can assume that bonds pay interest semiannually unless otherwise stated. So in this example, the investor would receive $30 every six months.

REMEMBER

Bondholders receive *interest* (payment for the use of the money loaned), and stockholders receive *dividends* (see Chapter 6).

>> **The bond indenture:** The *indenture* (also known as *deed of trust* or *resolution*) is the legal agreement between the issuer and its bondholders. It's printed on or attached to the bond certificate. All indentures contain basic terms:

- The maturity date

- The par value

- The coupon rate (interest rate) and interest payment dates

- Any collateral securing the bond (see "Comparing secured and unsecured bonds" later in this chapter)

- Any call or conversion features (check out "Contrasting callable and put bonds" and "Popping the top on convertible bonds" later in this chapter)

The bond indenture also includes the name of a trustee. A *trustee* is an organization that administers a bond issue for an institution. It ensures that the bond issuer meets all the terms and conditions associated with the borrowing. Essentially, the trustee tries to make sure that the issuer does the right thing.

The following question tests your knowledge of bond interest.

Ayla Dough purchased 100 AAA rated bonds issued by SSS Corp. Ayla purchased the bonds at 102 percent of par value, and they are currently trading in the market at 101. If the coupon rate is 3½ percent, how much annual interest does Ayla receive?

(A) $17.50

(B) $35.00

(C) $1,750.00

(D) $3,500.00

The correct answer is Choice (D). This is a nice, easy question after you wade through the information that you don't need. You need only the number of bonds and the coupon rate to figure out the answer. Don't let yourself get distracted by the rating, purchase price, or market price. That information is there to confuse you.

Ayla purchased 100 bonds with a par value of $1,000 (remember you can assume $1,000 par) with a coupon rate of 3½ percent, so do the math:

$$100 \text{ bonds} \times \$1,000 \text{ par} \times 3\ 1/2\% = \$3,500.00$$

Choice (C) would have been correct if the question had asked for the semiannual interest.

Comparing secured and unsecured bonds

The assets of the issuer may or may not back bonds. For test purposes, assume that bonds backed by *collateral* (assets that the issuer owns) are considered safer for the investor. *Secured bonds*, or bonds backed by collateral, involve a pledge from the issuer that a specific asset (for instance, property) will be sold to pay off the outstanding debt in the event of default. Obviously, with all else being equal, secured bonds normally have a lower yield than unsecured bonds issued by the same company.

The Series 7 tests your knowledge of several types of *secured bonds*:

>> **Mortgage bonds:** These bonds are backed by property that the issuer owns. In the event of default or bankruptcy, the issuer must liquidate the property to pay off the outstanding bonds. Mortgage bonds may be open- or closed-end. With an *open-end* mortgage bond, the issuer may borrow more money using the same property as collateral. With a *closed-end* mortgage bond, the issuer cannot borrow more money using the same property as collateral.

>> **Equipment trusts:** This type of bond is mainly issued by transportation companies and is backed by equipment they own (for instance, airplanes, railroad cars, trucks, or any other rolling stock). A trustee holds the title to the equipment and if the company defaults on its bonds, the trustee will sell the assets backing the bonds to satisfy the debt.

>> **Collateral trusts:** These bonds are backed by financial assets (stocks and bonds) of other issuers that the issuer owns. A *trustee* (a financial institution the issuer hires) holds the assets and sells them to pay off the bonds in the event of default.

>> **Guaranteed bonds:** Guaranteed bonds are backed by a firm other than the original issuer, usually a parent company. If the issuer defaults, the parent company pays off the interest and/ or principal of the bonds.

Unsecured bonds are the opposite of secured bonds. These bonds are not backed by any assets whatsoever, only by the good faith and credit of the issuer. If a reputable company that has been around for a long time issues the bonds, the bonds aren't considered too risky. If they're issued by a relatively new company or one with a bad credit rating, hold onto your seat! Again, for Series 7 exam purposes, assume that unsecured bonds are riskier than secured bonds. Here's the lineup of unsecured bonds:

>> **Debentures:** These bonds are backed only by the issuer's good word and written agreement (the indenture) stating that the issuer will pay the investor interest when due (usually semiannually) and par value at maturity.

>> **Income (adjustment) bonds:** These bonds are the riskiest of all. The issuer promises to pay par value back at maturity and will make interest payments only if earnings are high enough. Companies in the process of reorganization usually issue these bonds at a deep discount (for example, the bonds sell for $500 and mature at par, or $1,000). For test purposes (and real-world purposes), you shouldn't recommend these bonds to investors who can't afford to take a lot of risk.

REMEMBER

Because secured bonds are considered safer than unsecured bonds, secured bonds normally have lower coupon rates. You can assume that for the Series 7, the more risk an investor takes, the more reward he will receive. Remember the saying "more risk equals more reward." More reward may be in the form of a higher coupon rate or a lower purchase price. Either one — or both — lead to a higher yield for the investor.

Check out the following question for an example of how the Series 7 may test your knowledge of the types of bonds.

EXAMPLE

Jon Bearishnikoff is a 62-year-old investor who has 50 percent of his portfolio invested in common stock of up-and-coming companies. The other 50 percent of his portfolio is invested in a variety of stocks of more secure companies. Jon would like to start investing in bonds. Jon is concerned about the safety of his investment. Which of the following bonds would you LEAST likely recommend?

(A) Collateral trust bonds

(B) Mortgage bonds

(C) Equipment trust bonds

(D) Income bonds

The answer you're looking for is Choice (D). This problem includes a lot of garbage information that you don't need to answer the question. One of your jobs (should you decide to accept it) is to dance your way through the question and cherry-pick the information that you do need. The last sentence is usually the most important one when answering a question. Jon is looking for safety; therefore, you'd least likely recommend income bonds because they're usually issued by companies in the process of reorganizing. As a side note, if you become Jon's broker, he shouldn't have 100 percent of his investments in stock. At his age, Jon should have a decent amount of his portfolio invested in fixed-income securities.

REMEMBER

From the SIE Exam, the secured and unsecured bonds may be in book entry form (most likely), full registered, partially registered, or in bearer form. They can also be series bonds, serial bonds, or term bonds.

Additional bond types

The following bonds may be secured or unsecured, which would be stated in the bond indenture.

Zero-coupon bond

Unlike most other bonds, zero-coupon bonds do not make interest payments but instead are issued at a deep discount and mature at par value. The advantage of zero-coupon bonds is that they require a relatively low investment ($300, $400, and so on) and they mature at par value (usually $1,000) in a number of years. Since these bonds are issued at a discount, the bonds must be accreted, as described in Chapter 15. Zero-coupon bonds are ideal for planning for future events such as college. Because of the deep discount, the current prices of discount bonds fluctuate quite a bit when interest rates change.

Eurodollar bond

Eurodollar bonds are dollar-denominated debt securities issued by foreign corporations, foreign governments, international agencies, and U.S. companies with foreign locations (usually Europe). The bonds are issued outside of the U.S. but may trade in the U.S. after 40 days of issuance. Because they are dollar-denominated bonds, the interest and principal payments are in U.S. dollars. Because these securities are issued in a foreign country, they don't have to be registered with the SEC. Remember, since they're issued outside the U.S., they are subject to currency risk. (For more on investment risks, check out Chapter 13.)

Sovereign bond

Sovereign bonds are debt securities issued by foreign national governments, not corporations. In the case of sovereign bonds, the interest and principal payments are paid in the foreign government's currency (not U.S. dollars). As with Eurodollar bonds, sovereign bonds are subject to currency risk. As you can imagine, sovereign bonds issued by more developed countries are considered safer than those of less developed countries. So, the riskier the sovereign bonds, the higher the yield.

TIP

Because Eurodollar bonds and sovereign bonds are issued outside of the U.S., they may be ideal for certain investors looking to protect themselves in the event of a decline in the value of the U.S. dollar. Both are subject to *currency risk*, which is covered in Chapter 13.

Making Basic Bond Price and Yield Calculations

The Series 7 exam tests your knowledge of bond prices, bond yields, and how to calculate them. In this section, I review the relationship between bond prices and bond yields. I also show you how accrued interest can affect how much customers have to pay for the bond. As you can imagine, outstanding bond prices typically don't remain static. Like other securities, bonds are affected by things like supply and demand, corporate rating change, interest rate changes, whether the bond was purchased at a discount (below par value) or a premium (above par value), and so on.

REMEMBER

The relationship between outstanding bond prices and yields is an inverse one. You can assume for Series 7 exam purposes that if interest rates decrease, outstanding bond prices increase and vice versa. Say, for example, that a company issues bonds with a 4 percent coupon rate for $1,000. After the bonds are on the market, interest rates decrease. The company can now issue bonds with a 3 percent coupon rate. Investors with the 4 percent bonds are then in a very good position and can demand a premium for their bonds. Before I show you how the "seesaw" works, make sure you understand the different yields.

Rates down ⇓ = Prices up ⇑
Rates up ⇑ = Prices down ⇓

Finding bond yields

The following sections review the types of bond yields and how the Series 7 exam tests this topic.

Nominal yield (coupon rate)

The *nominal yield* (NY) is the easiest yield to understand because it's the coupon rate on the face of the bonds. For Series 7 exam purposes, you can assume that the coupon rate will remain fixed for the life of a bond. If you have a 7 percent bond, the bond will pay $70 per year interest (7% × $1,000 par value). When a problem states that a security is a 7 percent (or 6 percent or whatever) bond, it's giving the nominal yield.

Current yield

The *current yield* (CY) is the annual rate of return on a security. The CY of a bond changes when the market price changes; you can determine the CY by dividing the annual interest by the market price:

$$\text{Current yield (CY)} = \frac{\text{annual interest}}{\text{market price}}$$

The following question involves bond yields.

EXAMPLE

Melissa Moneybags purchased one XYZ convertible mortgage bond at 105. Two years later, the bond is trading at 98. If the coupon rate of the bond is 6%, what is the current yield of the bond?

(A) 5.7%

(B) 6.0%

(C) 6.1%

(D) Cannot be determined

The correct answer is Choice (C). Yes, I'm giving you a question with a lot of unnecessary information. All I can tell you is that, unfortunately, you'll have to get used to it. The Series 7 exam creators are notorious for inserting useless (and sometimes misleading) information into the questions to daze and confuse you. In this case, you need only the annual interest and the market price to calculate the answer. Use the following formula to get your answer:

$$CY = \frac{\text{annual interest}}{\text{market price}} = \frac{\$60}{\$980} = 6.1\%$$

The annual interest is $60 (6% coupon rate × $1,000 par value), and the current market price is $980 (98% of $1,000 par). The facts that the bond is convertible (bondholders can trade it for common stock — see "Popping the top on convertible bonds" later in this chapter) or a mortgage bond (backed by the issuer's property) and that it was purchased at 105 ($1,050) are irrelevant.

REMEMBER

"Cannot be determined," as tempting as it may be, is almost never the correct answer on the Series 7 exam.

Yield to maturity (basis)

The *yield to maturity* (YTM) is the yield an investor can expect if holding the bond until maturity. The YTM takes into account not only the market price but also par value, the coupon rate, and the amount of time until maturity. When someone yells to you, "Hey, what's that bond yielding?" (all right, maybe I run in a different circle of friends), he's asking for the YTM. The formula for YTM is as follows:

$$YTM = \frac{\text{annual interest} + \text{annual accretion or} - \text{annual amortization}}{(\text{market price} + \text{par value})/2}$$

$$\text{annual accretion} = \frac{\text{par value} - \text{market price}}{\text{years until maturity}}$$

$$\text{annual amortization} = \frac{\text{market price} - \text{par value}}{\text{years until maturity}}$$

This formula can be difficult to remember. If you have it down, kudos to you. It's tested (although somewhat rarely) on the Series 7 exam, and you may be one of the unlucky individuals who need this formula. For more on accretion and amortization, please visit Chapter 15.

Yield to call

The *yield to call* (YTC) is the amount that the investor receives if the bond is called prior to maturity. The calculations are similar to those for the YTM (see the preceding section), but you substitute the call price for the par value. The chances of needing it on the Series 7 exam are even more remote than needing the YTM calculations.

Yield to worst

To determine the *yield to worst* (YTW), you have to calculate the yield to maturity and yield to call for all the call dates (if there's more than one) and choose the lowest. If you get a question on yield to worst, knowing the definition should be enough to get you by.

Discount yield

This is the yield on securities that are issued at a discount and don't make interest payments, such as T-bills, T-STRIPS, and zero-coupon bonds. To calculate the discount yield, use the following formula:

$$\text{Discount yield} = \frac{\text{par} - \text{purchase price}}{\text{par}} \times \frac{360 \text{ days}}{\text{number of days till maturity}}$$

Don't spend too much time working on the discount yield formula because even though it's in the FINRA outline, I think your chances of having to do calculations using the formula are pretty slim. The most important thing to remember is that T-STRIPS, T-bills, and zero-coupon bonds don't make interest payments and T-bills are issued on a discount yield basis.

Using seesaw calculations for price and yields

In this section, I show you how to use a "seesaw" to help you better visualize the relationship between bond prices and yields. I know this method is a little goofy, but I'll do anything (well, *almost* anything) to help you pass the Series 7 exam.

Higher numbers make the seesaw rise, and lower numbers make it fall. Looking at the following diagram, you can see that if a bond is at par, the seesaw remains level. If the prices decrease, the yields increase, and if the prices increase, the yields decrease. The center support (*n*) represents the nominal yield (coupon rate) of the bond because it remains constant no matter what happens to the prices or other yields. (*Note:* In the seesaw, NY stands for *nominal yield,* CY is *current yield,* YTM is *yield to maturity,* and YTC is *yield to call.*)

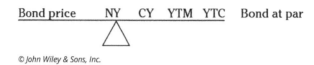

© John Wiley & Sons, Inc.

Check out the following problem and its explanation, which show you how to put the seesaw in motion.

EXAMPLE

Jonathan Bullinski purchased an 8 percent ABC bond yielding 9 percent. He purchased the bond at

(A) a discount

(B) par

(C) a premium

(D) a price that cannot be determined

The correct answer is Choice (A). The question states that the nominal yield is 8 percent and the bond is yielding 9 percent. The 9 percent is the yield to maturity:

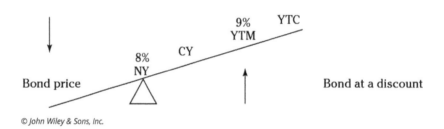

© John Wiley & Sons, Inc.

Because the YTM is greater than the NY, the right side of the seesaw goes up and the left side of the seesaw goes down. This means that the investor paid a price that was at a discount (below par). You can also determine that the current yield (CY) would have to be between 8 and 9 percent and the yield to call (YTC) would have to be greater than 9 percent.

If the YTM were lower than the NY, the seesaw would tip the opposite way, and the price would be at a premium rather than at a discount.

Calculating accrued interest

When investors purchase outstanding bonds in the market, they may have to pay an additional cost besides the market price (and, of course, your commission). The additional cost is called accrued interest. *Accrued interest,* which is due when bonds are purchased between coupon dates, is the portion of the interest still due to the seller. As you may remember, bonds pay interest once every six months. If an investor holds onto a bond for five months out of a six-month period, she is entitled to 5/6 of that next interest payment; that's accrued interest.

When taking the Series 7 exam, you need to be able to calculate the number of days of accrued interest that the buyer owes the seller. Although you can calculate the accrued interest with a few different methods, I'm here to make your life easier by showing you one of the simplest ways.

Accrued interest on corporate and municipal bonds is calculated on a 360-day year and assumes 30-day months. Accrued interest on U.S. government bonds is calculated using the actual days per year and the actual days per month.

The following sample question tests your ability to figure out this prorated amount.

Skippy Skippington III purchased a 6 percent corporate bond on Friday, October 21. The coupon dates are January 1 and July 1. How many days of accrued interest does Skippy owe?

(A) 114

(B) 116

(C) 119

(D) 121

The answer you want is Choice (A). You have to begin your calculations from the settlement date (the date that the issuer records the new owner's name). Corporate and municipal bonds settle in two business days. You're thrown a slight curveball in this question because you have to contend with a weekend.

Accrued interest is calculated from the previous coupon date up to, but not including, the settlement date.

Now you're probably asking yourself, "What the heck does that mean?" I can show you a nice, easy way to calculate the answer. Using the preceding example, assume that the settlement date is October 25. You would write it as 10/25 (tenth month and 25th day). The previous coupon date would be 7/1 (July 1). You can now set up a subtraction problem:

$$
\begin{array}{r}
10/25 \\
-7/1 \\
\hline
3/24
\end{array}
$$

$$(3 \text{ months} \times 30\text{-day months}) + 24 \text{ days} = 114 \text{ days of accrued interest}$$

First subtract the seventh month (July) from the tenth month (October). You end up with three months. Because corporate and municipal bonds calculate accrued interest using 30-day months, you have to multiply three months by 30 days to get an answer of 90 days. Subtract the previous coupon date (1) from the settlement date (25) to get an answer of 24 days. Add the 90 days and 24 days together, and you get 114 days as your answer.

Read carefully. To try to trip you up, the Series 7 exam writers may include the settlement date in the question. If this is the case, you don't need to add days to the trade date.

You can use the same formula to calculate accrued interest on U.S. government securities. (For basic information, see "Exploring U.S. Government Securities" later in the chapter.) However, U.S. government securities settle in one business day, not two. Additionally, U.S. government securities are calculated using actual days per month. The following example shows you how to calculate interest for a U.S. government securities question.

Ayla K. purchased a 5 percent T-bond on Monday, November 18. The coupon dates are January 1 and July 1. How many days of accrued interest does Ayla owe?

(A) 135

(B) 138

(C) 141

(D) 142

The right answer is Choice (C). Take a look at the following calculations:

11/19 The T-bond settled in one business day

−7/1   The previous coupon date

4/18

$(4 \text{ months} \times 30\text{-day months}) + 18 \text{ days} = 138 \text{ days}$

$+ 3 \text{ days for July, August, and October} = 141 \text{ days of accrued interest}$

To get the settlement date, you have to add only one business day. Because the trade date is Monday, November 18, the settlement date is Tuesday, November 19 (11/19). Next, subtract the previous coupon date of July 1 (7/1), and you get an answer of 4 months/18 days. If you multiply the months by 30 as I do in the preceding example and add the days, you end up with 138 days. At this point, you add one day for each of the months that have 31 days (July, August, and October). Your answer is 141 days.

REMEMBER

Your 31-day months are January, March, May, July, August, October, and December. All the rest of the months have 30 days, except for February, which has 28. For February, you subtract two days. I know what you're thinking: "What about leap year?" I haven't heard of anyone getting a leap-year question yet, but if you're that unlucky person, subtract only one day for February.

REMEMBER

Most bonds pay interest every six months. However, occasionally the *dated date* (the first date the bonds start accruing interest) of the bonds doesn't line up exactly six months from the first coupon date. If the first coupon date is more than six months from the dated date, it's called a *long coupon.* And if it's less than six months, it's called a *short coupon.* For newly issued bonds, which haven't made an interest payment yet, accrued interest is calculated from the dated date (the first date a bond starts accruing interest) not the previous coupon date because there isn't one.

Determining the Best Investment: Comparing Bonds

As you grind your way through Series 7 exam questions, you may be asked to determine the best investment for a particular investor. You need to carefully look at the question for clues to help you choose the correct answer. (For instance, is the investor looking for safety? Is the investor close to retirement?) Consider several factors, including credit rating, callable and putable features, and convertible features.

Considering bond credit ratings

The institutions that rate bonds are most interested in the likelihood of *default* (the likelihood that the interest and principal won't be paid when due). For the Series 7 exam, you can assume that the higher the credit rating, the safer the bond and, therefore, the lower the yield.

The two main bond credit rating companies for corporate and municipal bonds are Moody's and Standard & Poor's (S&P). S&P ratings of BB and lower and Moody's ratings of Ba and lower are considered *junk bonds* or *high-yield bonds,* which have a higher likelihood of default, as Table 7-1 explains. (Another credit rating service, called Fitch, uses the same rating symbols as Standard & Poor's.) *Note:* Different sources may show some slight variations in how S&P and Moody's ratings compare; however, the relationships here are the most common.

TABLE 7-1 Bond Credit Ratings (by Quality)

Quality	S&P (Standard & Poor's)	Moody's
Highest	AAA	Aaa
High	AA	Aa
Upper medium	A	A
Lower medium	BBB	Baa
Speculative (junk)	BB	Ba
Speculative (junk): Interest or principal payments missed	B	B
Speculative (junk): No interest being paid	C	Caa
In default	D	D

As if these categories aren't enough, S&P can break down each category even further by adding either a plus (+) or minus (–) sign after the letter category. The plus sign represents the high end of the category, and the minus sign designates the lower end of the category. If you see no plus or minus sign, the bond is in the middle of the category. Moody's can further break down a category by adding a 1, 2, or 3. The number 1 is the highest ranking, 2 represents the middle, and 3 is the lowest. The top four ratings are considered *investment grade,* and the letters below that are considered *junk bonds* or *high-yield bonds.*

TIP

The rating company with the capital letters (S&P) uses all capital letters (AAA, AA, and so on). Additionally, S&P has an ampersand (&) between the "S" and the "P" in its name. Think of the ampersand as being like a plus sign to help you remember that S&P uses pluses and minuses within its categories.

Here's a typical bond-ratings question.

EXAMPLE

Place the following Standard & Poor's bond ratings in order from highest to lowest.

I. A+

II. AA

III. A–

IV. BBB+

(A) I, II, III, IV

(B) I, III, II, IV

(C) IV, I, II, III

(D) II, I, III, IV

The correct answer is Choice (D). When answering this type of question, always look at the letters first. The only time pluses or minuses come into play is when two answers have the same letters, as in Statements I and III. The highest choice is AA, followed by A+ because it's higher than A–, which is even higher than BBB+.

Contrasting callable and put bonds

As you may know, bonds can be issued in callable and put forms. Your mission for the Series 7 exam is to know which is better for investors and when bonds are likely to be called or put.

>> **Callable bonds:** A *callable bond* is a bond that the issuer has the right to buy back from investors at the price stated on the indenture (deed of trust). Callable bonds are riskier for investors because investors can't control how long they can hold onto the bonds. To compensate for this risk, they're usually issued with a higher coupon rate (more risk = more reward).

Most callable bonds are issued with call protection. *Call protection* is the amount of time (usually several years) that an issuer has to wait before being able to call its bonds. Some callable bonds also have a *call premium,* which is an amount over par value that an issuer has to pay if calling its bonds in the year or years immediately following the expiration of the call protection.

If there is a *make whole call provision*, it allows the issuer to call the bonds providing that the issuer makes a lump sum payment to investors that not only includes payment for the bond but also the present value of any future interest payments investors will miss because of the call.

Another type of bond that can be callable is a *step coupon bond*. Also known as stepped coupon bonds or step-up coupon securities, *step coupon bonds* typically start at a low coupon rate, but the coupon rate increases at predetermined intervals, such as every five years. The issuer typically has the right to call the bonds at par value at the time the coupon rate is due to increase.

>> **Put bonds:** *Put bonds* are better for investors. Put bonds allow the investor to "put" the bonds back (redeem them) to the issuer at any time at the price stated on the indenture. Because the investors have the control, put bonds are (of course) rarely issued. Because these bonds provide more flexibility to investors (who have an interest in the bond and stock prices), put bonds usually have a lower coupon rate.

REMEMBER

There's a direct correlation between interest rates and when bonds are called or put. Issuers call bonds when interest rates decrease; investors put bonds when interest rates increase. Check out the following question to see how this works.

EXAMPLE

Issuers would call their bonds when interest rates

(A) increase

(B) decrease

(C) stay the same

(D) are fluctuating

The correct answer is Choice (B). Being adaptable when taking the Series 7 exam can certainly help your cause. In this question, you have to look from the issuer's point of view, not the investor's. An issuer would call bonds when interest rates decrease because he could then redeem the bonds with the higher coupon payments and issue bonds with lower coupon payments to save money. Conversely, investors would put their bonds back to the issuer when interest rates increase so they could invest their money at a higher interest rate.

REMEMBER

You can assume for Series 7 exam purposes that if interest rates increase, bond yields increase.

Popping the top on convertible bonds

Bonds that are convertible into common stock are called *convertible bonds.* Convertible bonds are attractive to investors because investors have an interest in the bond price as well as the price of the underlying stock. The Series 7 exam tests your expertise on whether converting a bond makes sense for an investor. This determination requires you to calculate the parity price of the bond or stock.

Parity occurs when a convertible bond and its underlying stock (the stock it's convertible into) are trading equally (that is, when a bond trading for $1,100 is convertible into $1,100 worth of stock).

When answering Series 7 exam questions relating to convertible bonds, you always need to get the *conversion ratio* (the number of shares that the bond is convertible into). Here's the formula for the conversion ratio:

$$\text{conversion ratio} = \frac{\text{par value}}{\text{conversion price}}$$

You can then use the conversion ratio to calculate the parity price:

parity price of the bond = market price of the stock × conversion ratio

REMEMBER

This same equation appears in Chapter 6 relating to convertible preferred stock.

Use the formula to answer the next example question.

EXAMPLE

Jane Q. Investor purchased a 6 percent DIM convertible bond. Her DIM bond is currently trading at 106, and the underlying stock is trading at 26. If the conversion price is 25, which of the following statements are TRUE?

  I. The stock is trading above parity.

  II. The stock is trading below parity.

  III. Converting the bond would be profitable.

  IV. Converting the bond would not be profitable.

(A) I and III

(B) I and IV

(C) II and III

(D) II and IV

The right answer is Choice (D). You can cross out two answers right away. If the stock is trading above parity, converting is always profitable. And if the stock is trading below parity, converting isn't profitable. Therefore, you can eliminate Choices (B) and (C) right away. You've just increased your odds of getting the question correct from 25 to 50 percent. To increase your odds from 50 to 100 percent, follow these equations:

$$\text{conversion ratio} = \frac{\text{par value}}{\text{conversion price}} = \frac{\$1,000}{\$25} = 40 \text{ shares}$$

parity price of the bond = market price of the stock × conversion ratio

parity price of the bond = $26 × 40 shares = $1,040

Currently, the bond is trading for $1,060 (106 percent of $1,000 par) and is convertible into stock valued at $1,040 (the parity price of the bond). Because the value of the bond is greater than the converted value of the stock, the stock is trading below parity and converting wouldn't be profitable.

Here's another problem that involves parity price.

EXAMPLE

Alyssa purchased a Spanko, Inc., convertible bond at 115 with a conversion ratio of 25. If the common stock for Spanko, Inc., is currently $48 per share, when should Alyssa convert her bond?

(A) Right away

(B) When the common stock falls below $46 per share

(C) When the common stock increases to $50 per share

(D) Never, because bonds are safer investments than stocks

The answer you want is Choice (A). Always assume for test purposes that if the stock is trading above parity, the investor should convert. You don't need to figure out the conversion ratio because it was already given in the question. Here's how to solve the problem:

parity price of the bond = market price of the stock × conversion ratio

parity price of the bond = $48 × 25 shares = $1,200

The bond is currently trading at $1,150 (11.5 percent of $1,000 par) and is convertible into $1,200 worth of stock. It certainly makes sense for the investor to convert at this point. Although you can try to make a point for Choice (C), it's not correct. On the Series 7 exam, if the stock is above parity, convert the bond. Convertible bonds and the underlying stock always seek parity. Even though $50 per share would be better than $48, the bond would also increase in price, and the conversion may not end up being as profitable.

REMEMBER

For the most part, investors will convert their bonds when the value of the convertible bond is trading at a price that is lower than the value of the stock it's convertible into. This is known as an *arbitrage* (taking advantage of a disparity in prices) situation. Sometimes companies force a conversion (called a forced conversion) by calling bonds at a price that's less than parity. In this situation, converting is more advantageous for investors.

Exploring U.S. Government Securities

On the Series 7 exam, you need to know the basic types of U.S. government securities, their initial maturities, and certain characteristics.

As you may already know, the U.S. government also issues bonds. U.S. government bonds are considered the safest of all securities. Yes, you did read that correctly: the *safest of all securities*. I feel it's worth repeating. How can U.S. government securities be so safe when we're running such a large deficit? Guess what — I don't know, and you don't need to know, either. I can only assume that the U.S. government can always print more currency to make payments on its securities if needed. However, even U.S. government securities are subject to certain risks such as interest risk, reinvestment risk, purchasing power risk, and so forth (see Chapter 13).

U.S. government securities are now all issued and held in electronic (book-entry) form. However, because Treasury bonds have maturities of up to 30 years, some are still out there in paper form. U.S. government securities can be purchased directly through a website called Treasury Direct (http://treasurydirect.gov), from broker-dealers, and most commercial banks.

Note: With government bonds, you use some of the same types of calculations you use for corporate bonds. The methods for determining accrued interest, for instance, are very similar. For more information, see "Calculating accrued interest," earlier in this chapter.

Understanding the types and characteristics of U.S. government securities

Table 7-2 gives you an overview of different types of marketable U.S. government securities and their specifics. Memorize all the information in the following chart so you can ace U.S. government securities questions on the Series 7 exam.

TABLE 7-2   U.S. Government Securities and Time until Maturity

Security	Initial Maturity	Characteristics
T-bills (Treasury bills)	4, 8, 13, 17, 26, and 52 weeks	Issued at a discount and mature at par. The difference between the purchase price and par is considered interest even though no interest payments are made. Sold in investment increments of $100.
FRNs (Floating Rate Notes)	2 years	Pay an adjustable rate of interest every 3 months tied to the rate of the most recent discount rate of a 13-week T-bill. Sold in investment increments of $100.
T-notes (Treasury notes)	2, 3, 5, 7, and 10 years	Pay a fixed rate of interest every 6 months. Sold in investment increments of $100.
T-bonds (Treasury bonds)	20 or 30 years	Pay a fixed rate of interest every 6 months. Sold in investment increments of $100.
T-STRIPS (Separate Trading of Registered Interest and Principal of Securities)	6 months to 30 years	Issued at a discount and mature at par. Minimum investment is $100. They are not sold directly by the U.S. Treasury but are sold by financial institutions and government securities broker-dealers. Investors do not receive interest payments. Basically, the principal and all remaining interest payments are stripped from a U.S. Treasury security and sold as separate securities. Purchase price varies.
TIPS* (Treasury Inflation-Protected Securities)	5, 10, and 30 years	Pays a fixed rate of interest every 6 months tied to the adjusted principal amount. The par value and interest payments adjust according to inflation or deflation. Sold in investment increments of $100.

TIPS are tied to the Consumer Price Index (CPI), which measures inflation. The par value changes according to inflation. If inflation is high (prices of goods and services are increasing), the par value increases. If we're in a period of deflation (prices on goods and services are decreasing), the par value decreases. Because investors are getting a percentage of par value as their interest payments, the interest payments vary along with the par value.

TIP

T-bills are sold on a discount-yield basis where the bid is higher than the ask. Typically, you might see the bid and ask prices for a bond as 99.5–99.7, respectively. This means that a person is bidding $995 (99.5% of $1,000 par) to purchase the bond while another person is willing to sell the bond for $997 (99.7% of $1,000 par). However, for T-bills, you might see the bid and ask prices as 2.250–2.150 respectively. The reason that they are quoted like this is that the bidder is bidding for a yield of 2.250, which would represent a lower dollar price than the ask price of 2.150. So if you see the bid number higher than the ask number, it is likely a T-bill quote.

REMEMBER

The previous table covers U.S. Treasury marketable securities, which can be bought and sold from other investors and entities other than the U.S. government. However, the U.S. government also issues non-marketable securities such as Series EE savings bonds and Series I savings bonds. For Series 7 Exam purposes, you should concentrate on the marketable U.S. Treasury securities.

REMEMBER

For the Series 7, remember that the interest received on U.S. government securities is exempt from state and local taxes. The interest received on municipal bonds is exempt from federal taxes (although I get into that a little more in the next chapter). Chapter 15 gives you the scoop on taxes.

The following question concerns various types of bonds and U.S. government securities.

EXAMPLE

One of your new customers calls to tell you that his wife just had a baby. He would like to start saving for the child's higher education. He has $30,000 to invest and seems genuinely concerned about the safety of his investment. Which of the following bonds would you MOST likely recommend to help him meet his goals?

(A) AA-rated corporate bonds with 18 years until maturity

(B) T-STRIPS with 18 years until maturity

(C) T-bonds with 18 years until maturity

(D) High-yielding corporate bonds

The right answer is Choice (B). The question gives you a couple clues. The investor is concerned about safety, so Choice (D) is definitely out. High-yielding corporate bonds are low-rated bonds and are a speculative (risky) investment. Out of the other three choices, (B) makes the most sense. If this customer were to invest $30,000 in the AA-rated corporate bonds or the T-bonds, he'd receive $30,000 at maturity, along with interest payments along the way. However, interest entails risk. T-STRIPS, on the other hand, don't pay interest, so investors can purchase them at a discount. Because the bonds mature in 18 years, perhaps this investor can purchase the T-STRIPS for around $400 each. He could buy 75 bonds with $1,000 par value, which would probably be worth $75,000 in 18 years.

REMEMBER

When you see a question on the Series 7 exam about the best investment when planning for a future event (for instance, college), the right answer will most likely be either zero-coupon bonds or T-STRIPS.

Agency securities

Agency bonds are ones issued by a U.S. government-sponsored agency, or GSEs (government-sponsored entities). The bonds have the implied backing of the U.S. government, but not all are guaranteed by the full faith and credit of the U.S. government (except for GNMA, Government National Mortgage Association, which are directly backed). As such, agency bonds (although almost as safe) are considered riskier than U.S. government bonds and notes such as T-bonds, T-notes, T-bills, and so on.

GSEs include:

>> **GNMA** (Government National Mortgage Association, or Ginnie Mae): GNMAs are the only agency securities backed by the full faith and credit of the U.S. government. GNMAs support the Department of Housing and Urban Development (HUD). Like Treasury securities, the risk of default is almost nonexistent. However, unlike Treasury securities, the interest earned on GNMA securities is taxed on all levels (federal, state, and local). They are often called GNMA *pass-through* certificates because the principal and interest payments pass through to investors. So investors receive *monthly* payments of interest and principal as people pay their mortgages. Over the years as investors pay down their mortgages, the principal amount will decrease. GNMAs are issued with a face value of $25,000 but can be purchased in denominations as low as $1,000. As with other mortgage-backed securities (MBS), they are subject to prepayment and extension risk.

>> **FNMA** (Federal National Mortgage Association, or Fannie Mae): FNMA is a publicly held corporation that is responsible for providing capital for certain mortgages. As such, FNMA may purchase conventional mortgages, VA mortgages, FHA mortgages, and so on. FNMA is

privately owned and publicly held but is still government sponsored (GSE). FNMA issues debentures with maturities ranging from 3 to 25 years and are issued in minimum denominations of $10,000. The longer-term bonds issued by FNMA are pass-through certificates, meaning that the principal and interest are paid monthly. However, FNMA also issues discount notes and benchmark bills, which are shorter-term debt securities available with minimum denominations of $1,000. These shorter-term debt securities are issued at a discount and mature at par, so they don't receive monthly payments. Like GNMAs, they are taxed on all levels. However, unlike GNMAs, they don't have the direct backing of the U.S. government, so the risk of default is a little higher. As you'd expect, because FNMAs are a little riskier, investors receive a higher return.

>> **FHLMC** (Federal Home Loan Mortgage Corporation, or Freddie Mac): As a public corporation, Freddie Mac was designed to create a secondary market for mortgages. Freddie Mac purchases residential mortgages from financial institutions and packages them into mortgage-backed securities, which are sold to investors. Freddie Mac also issues pass-through certificates and the interest is subject to federal, state, and local taxes. Like FNMA securities, FHLMC is not directly backed by the U.S. government.

>> **FFCS** (Federal Farm Credit System): The FFCS consists of lending institutions which provide financing and credit to farmers. It is a government-sponsored agency but is privately owned. The FFCS sells securities through member banks (Federal Farm Credit Banks – FFCBs) to investors and in turn loans the funds raised to farmers. The FFCS is overseen by the FCA (Farm Credit Administration). FFCS issues discount notes and bonds ranging in maturity from 1 day to 30 years. Unlike GNMA, FNMA, and FHLMC securities, the interest received from FCS securities is exempt from state and local taxes but is still subject to federal taxes.

>> **SLMA** (Student Loan Marketing Association): SLMA is not involved in providing mortgages but provides a secondary market for student loans. As such, SLMA purchases student loans and repackages them as short- and medium-term debt securities for sale to investors. Sallie Mae is no longer a government-sponsored enterprise (GSE) but is now a private company. So SLMA also issues stock, which is currently trading on NASDAQ. Interest earned on its debt securities is subject to federal tax but may be exempt from state and local taxes depending on the state.

TIP

Certain mortgage-backed securities have an *average life*, which is shorter than the initial loan term. This is due to investors selling or refinancing their houses. For arguments sake, let's say the average homeowner purchases a 30-year mortgage. However, due to an interest rate drop, he may decide to refinance after 14 years. Therefore, the securities are susceptible to reinvestment risk because many homeowners refinance when interest rates fall (*prepayment risk*). In that case, holders of mortgage backed securities would get paid back sooner than expected and would have to invest at a lower interest rate. In addition, if interest rates stay the same or increase, home-owners will not refinance as often, and holders of mortgage backed securities may end up having to hold their investment for a longer period of time than expected (*extension risk*).

In the tranches: Delving into packaged mortgages (CMOs)

Just when you thought you were going to get out of debt securities relatively unscathed, you have collateralized mortgage obligations (CMOs) thrown at you. *CMOs* are annoying little (or big) debt securities backed by pools of mortgages (GNMA/Ginnie Mae, FNMA/Fannie Mae, FHLMC/Freddie Mac). What makes matters worse is that you probably won't sell one in your entire career. However, CMOs are asset-backed securities covered on the Series 7 exam, and you need to know the basics in order to answer these questions correctly.

As stated in the preceding section, CMOs don't have a set maturity date and are subject to things called *extension risk* and *prepayment risk.* Take a look at these terms:

>> **Average life:** The average amount of time until a mortgage is refinanced or paid off; for example, a 30-year mortgage may have an average life of 17 years.

>> **Prepayment risk:** The risk that a *tranche* (slice or portion) of the loan will be called sooner than expected due to decreasing interest rates; more people refinance when interest rates are low.

>> **Extension risk:** The risk that a tranche will be called later than expected due to a less-than-normal amount of refinancing; extension occurs when interest rates are high.

CMOs are also broken down into tranches (slices) of varying maturity dates. The basic type of CMO has tranches that are paid in a specific sequence. All tranches receive regular interest payments, but only the tranche with the shortest maturity receives principal payments. After the shortest tranche is retired, the second-shortest receives principal payments until that tranche is retired, and then the principal is paid to the next tranche. This type of structure is known as a *plain vanilla* offering. The following list describes other types of CMO tranches:

>> **Planned amortization class (PAC) tranches:** This type of CMO is the most common because it has the most certain prepayment date. The prepayment and extension risk can be somewhat negated by a companion tranche, which assumes a greater degree of the risk. Because of the relative safety of PAC tranches, they usually have the lowest yields.

>> **Targeted amortization class (TAC) tranches:** This CMO is the second-safest. TAC trancheholders have somewhat less-certain principal payments and are more subject to prepayment and extension risk. TAC tranches have yields that are low but not as low as those of PAC tranches.

>> **Companion tranches (support bonds):** Companion tranches are included in every CMO that has PAC or TAC tranches. Companion tranches absorb prepayment risk associated with CMOs. The average life of a companion tranche varies greatly depending on interest rate fluctuations. Because more risk is associated with companion tranches, they have higher yields.

>> **Z-tranches (accrual bonds):** Z-tranches are usually the last tranche (they have longest maturity) in a series of PAC or companion tranches. Z-tranches don't receive interest or principal until all the other tranches in the series have been retired. The market value of Z-tranches can fluctuate widely. Z-tranches are somewhat similar to a zero-coupon bond (which is bought at a discount and does not receive interest along the way).

>> **Principal-only (PO) tranches:** Principal-only tranches are purchased at a price deeply discounted below face value. Investors receive face value through regularly scheduled mortgage payments and prepayments. The market value of a PO increases if interest rates drop and prepayments increase.

>> **Interest-only (IO) tranches:** All CMOs with principal-only tranches also have interest-only tranches. IOs are sold at a deep discount below their expected value based on the principal amount used to calculate the amount of interest due. Contrary to PO tranches, the market value of an IO increases if interest rates increase and prepayments decrease.

>> **Floating rate tranches:** These tranches appear with CMOs in which the interest rates are tied to an interest rate index (for instance, London Interbank Offered Rate/LIBOR). Investors can use these investments to hedge interest rate risk on other investments.

Although I discuss several types of tranches, the most important ones on the Series 7 exam are the PAC, TAC, companion, and Z-tranches.

TIP

The following question tests your understanding of tranches.

EXAMPLE

Companion tranches support

   I. PO tranches

  II. PAC tranches

 III. TAC tranches

 IV. IO tranches

(A) I only

(B) II only

(C) II and III only

(D) II, III, and IV

The answer you're looking for is Choice (C). Companion tranches absorb the prepayment risk associated with CMOs. All PAC and TAC tranches are supported by a companion tranche.

REMEMBER

I know that this information is a lot to take in and may be a little confusing. Remembering the basics can help you get most of the questions correct: PAC tranches are the safest; TAC tranches are the second safest; companion tranches support PAC and TAC tranches; and Z-tranches have the longest maturity.

CMO communications

Retail communications regarding CMOs must include the words "Collateralized Mortgage Obligation"; must not compare CMOs to any other investment vehicle; must disclose that the government agencies backing the CMO are only responsible for face value of the CMO and not any premium paid; and must disclose that the CMOs yield and average life will fluctuate depending on changing interest rates and the rate at which homeowners refinance their loans.

Prior to the sale of a CMO to any investor other than an institutional investor, a member must offer the investor educational material about CMOs. The required educational material must include these items: the characteristics and risks of investing in CMOs (credit quality, prepayment rates, average lives, how interest rates affect prepayment rates, tax considerations, liquidity, minimum investments, and transaction costs). In addition, the educational material must include how CMOs are structured, the different types of tranches and their risks, and the relationship between mortgage securities and mortgage loans. Also, included in the educational material should be questions an investor should ask before investing and a glossary of terms.

If a member is promoting a specific CMO, any communications must include the following: the coupon rate, the specific tranche (number and class), the anticipated yield, the anticipated average life, the final maturity date, and the underlying collateral. In addition, it must include a disclosure statement saying "The yield and average life shown above consider prepayment assumptions that may or may not be met. Changes in payments may significantly affect yield and average life. Please contact your representative for information on CMOs and how they react to different market conditions."

TIP

Remember that retail communication mailed out by any member or member firm must include the firm's name, memberships, address, telephone number, and representative's name.

Radio and television advertisements must include the following statements:

>> "The following is an advertisement for Collateralized Mortgage Obligations. Contact your representative for information on CMOs and how they react to different market conditions."

>> "The yield and average life reflect prepayment assumptions that may or may not be met. Changes in payments may significantly affect yield and average life."

Backed by debt: Collateralized debt obligations (CDOs)

Now that you're a master of CMOs, I figure this is the point at which it makes the most sense to delve into collateralized debt securities (CDOs). The idea behind CDOs is quite similar to collateralized mortgage obligations because they're also broken down into tranches representing differing amounts of risk and/or maturities. Obviously, as with other investments, the more risk, the more reward (or potential reward). The difference with CDOs is that instead of being backed by mortgages, they're backed by a pool of bonds, loans, or other debt instruments. In the event of a shortfall of cash, holders of senior CDOs are paid first. I could break them down into classes for you, but fortunately, I think that would be more than you need to know for the Series 7 exam. Interest received from CDOs is taxable on all levels (federal, state, and local).

CDOs are not ideal investments for most investors. CDOs are complex and often difficult for average investors to understand. Therefore, they are more suitable for sophisticated or institutional investors.

TIP

Playing It Safe: Short-Term Loans or Money Market Instruments

Every Series 7 exam includes a few questions on money market instruments, which are sometimes referred to as *cash equivalents*. *Money market instruments* are relatively safe short-term loans that can be issued by corporations, banks, the U.S. government, and municipalities. Most have maturities of one year or less, and they're usually issued at a discount and mature at par value. The following list reviews some basic characteristics of money market instruments to help you earn an easy point or two on the Series 7 exam:

>> **Federal Funds:** Federal Funds are loans between banks to help meet reserve requirements. Federal Funds are usually overnight loans for which the rates change constantly depending on supply and demand.

Reserve requirements are the percentage of deposits that member banks must hold each night. Banks that aren't able to meet their reserve requirements may borrow from other banks at the Fed Funds rate. For more info on the Fed Funds rate and other tools that the Federal Reserve Board uses to influence money supply, see Chapter 13.

REMEMBER

>> **Corporate commercial paper:** Commercial paper is unsecured corporate debt. Commercial paper is issued at a discount and matures at par value. Commercial paper is issued with an initial maturity of 270 days or less and is exempt from SEC registration.

>> **Brokered (negotiable) certificates of deposit:** Brokered CDs are low-risk investments, which originate from a bank and are outsourced to broker-dealers to sell to investors. Unlike typical CDs, which are purchased directly from a bank, brokered CDs can be traded in the market.

Negotiable certificates of deposit that require a minimum investment of $100,000 are often called *jumbo CDs*.

>> **Bankers' acceptances:** A bankers' acceptance (BA) is a time-draft (short-term credit investment) created by a company whose payment is guaranteed by a bank. Companies use BAs for the importing and exporting of goods.

>> **T-bills:** The U.S. government issues T-bills at a discount, and they have initial maturities of 4, 8, 13, 17, 26, or 52 weeks. T-bills are somewhat unique in that they're sold and quoted on a discount-yield basis (YTM). U.S. government securities — and especially T-bills — are considered the safest of all securities.

Here's what a question on money market instruments may look like.

EXAMPLE

SNK Surfboard Company wants to import boogie boards from an Italian manufacturer in Sicily. SNK would use which of the following money market instruments to finance the importing of the boogie boards?

(A) T-bills

(B) Collateral trust bonds

(C) Repurchase agreements

(D) Banker's acceptances

The correct answer is Choice (D). You can eliminate Choice (B) right away because collateral trust bonds aren't money market instruments; they're secured long-term bonds. A banker's acceptance is like a post-dated check that's used specifically for importing and exporting goods.

TIP

Word association can help you here. If you see *importing, exporting,* or *time draft,* your answer is probably bankers' acceptance (BA).

Structured Products

Structured products are relatively new and have somewhat of a broad definition. However, putting something complex in simple terms, structured products are prepackaged products put together by some other entity (bank, brokerage firm, and so on). Structured products are based on derivatives such as options, which means that the investors don't own the underlying securities directly but have an interest in their performance. The structured product could be based off the performance of an equity index, foreign currencies, a basket of securities, a single security, and so on. Structured products typically require a minimum investment and are fixed-term (such as 12 months, 18 months, 2 years, 3 years, 5 years, and so on). Most structured products are a combination of a note (short-term debt security) and a derivative product. Unless the note is zero-coupon, investors will receive interest payments, and the return at maturity will typically be the face value of the note plus a premium if the derivative portion performs well.

>> **Exchange-traded notes (ETNs):** Exchange-traded notes have characteristics of exchange-traded funds (ETFs) and fixed-income securities. ETNs are unsecured debt securities issued by a bank or financial institution. Their return is usually linked to a particular market index or in some cases commodities or currency. Exchange-traded notes don't receive dividends or coupon payments, so investors receive income at a specified maturity date. Since they are traded on an exchange such as the New York Stock Exchange (NYSE), they may be purchased

on margin or sold short. Investors may trade the ETNs or hold them until maturity. If an investor holds the ETN until the maturity date, the investor will receive a principal amount less any fees based on the performance of the index the note is tracking.

Note: Even though the returns on ETNs are usually linked to the returns on a particular market index, an ETN's value may drop due to a drop in the credit rating of the ETN issuer even if the index has not decreased. Mutual funds represent ownership in a pool of securities; ETNs do not as they simply track the performance of a specified market index. ETNs are typically issued by banks and other financial institutions.

>> **Equity-linked notes:** Unlike exchange-traded notes, equity-linked notes are not traded on an exchange. Equity-linked notes are most often created as bonds. However, instead of having fixed interest payments, the interest payments are variable depending on the return of the underlying equity securities. The return on equity-linked notes may be based off of the return of a single stock, a basket of stocks, or an equity index.

REMEMBER

Structured products are more complex in nature and often require investors to tie money up for a period of several years. Therefore, they are not considered suitable investments for most people.

Testing Your Knowledge

Here's where the rubber hits the road. I've given you the information you need for the Series 7 regarding corporate and U.S. government debt securities, so here's a quick quiz to test your knowledge.

1. Which of the following is TRUE regarding guaranteed bonds:

    (A) They are backed by stocks and bonds owned by the issuing company

    (B) They are mainly issued by transportation companies

    (C) They are backed by the assets of another company

    (D) They are issued by a corporation in bankruptcy

2. A bond is convertible into common stock for $40. What is the conversion ratio?

    (A) 20

    (B) 25

    (C) 30

    (D) 40

3. CMOs purchase all of the following securities EXCEPT

    (A) GNMA

    (B) SLMA

    (C) FHLMC

    (D) FNMA

4. Arrange the following Moody's bond ratings in order from safest to riskiest.

   I. Baa1

   II. Aa2

   III. A3

   IV. Aa1

   (A) I, IV, II, III

   (B) I, IV, III, II

   (C) IV, II, I, III

   (D) IV, II, III, I

5. Which of the following is the only yield found on the indenture of a bond?

   (A) Nominal yield

   (B) Current yield

   (C) Yield to call

   (D) Yield to maturity

6. Ayla is new to investing in bonds and she is very concerned about receiving timely payments of interest and principal. Which of the following types of bonds would be the LEAST suitable for Ayla?

   (A) Debentures

   (B) Equipment trusts

   (C) Collateral trusts

   (D) Income bonds

7. Which TWO of the following are TRUE regarding sovereign bonds?

   I. They are issued by foreign corporations

   II. They are issued by foreign governments

   III. The interest and principal is paid in U.S. dollars

   IV. The interest and principal is paid in the issuer's currency

   (A) I and III

   (B) I and IV

   (C) II and III

   (D) II and IV

8. With everything else being equal, callable bonds would have a _____ yield than/as a non-callable bond.

   (A) higher

   (B) lower

   (C) equal

   (D) more variable

9. Declan K. purchased a 5% ABC Corporate bond on Monday, May 10th with coupon dates January 1st and July 1st. How many days of accrued interest does Declan owe?

(A) 129 days

(B) 130 days

(C) 131 days

(D) 132 days

10. Which of the following CMO tranches is the most common?

(A) PAC

(B) TAC

(C) PO

(D) Z

Answers and Explanations

Here are the answers. Hopefully you didn't find anything too difficult. Since there are 10 questions, each one is worth 10 points each.

1. **C.** Guaranteed bonds are backed by the assets of another company. Guaranteed bonds are mainly backed by the assets of a parent company.

2. **B.** The conversion ratio is the amount of shares that the bond is convertible into. Remember, you can assume that the par value of a bond is $1,000 unless told differently. To determine the conversion ratio, use the following formula:

$$\text{conversion ratio} = \frac{\text{par value}}{\text{conversion price}} = \frac{\$1,000}{\$40} = 25 \text{ shares}$$

3. **B.** CMOs (Collateralized Mortgage Obligations) invest in GNMA (Ginnie Mae), FNMA (Fannie Mae), and FHLMC (Freddie Mac) bonds. CMOs do not purchase SLMA (Sallie Mae) bonds because SLMAs are issued to fund student loans.

4. **D.** Companies like Moody's, Standard & Poor's, and Fitch provide the credit rating of debt securities. Since you are being asked to place these Moody's ratings in order from safest to riskiest, you have to look at the letters first. Out of the choices listed, Aa is higher than A, and Aa1, is higher than Aa2, so you know the order starts with Aa1 and then Aa2. Since A is higher than Baa, the order from highest to lowest is Aa1, Aa2, A3, and finally Baa1.

5. **A.** The only yield found in the indenture of a bond is the nominal yield, which is also known as the coupon rate. The reason that the current yield, yield to maturity, and/or yield to call can't be in the indenture is because all of them change as the market price changes.

6. **D.** Income (Adjustment) bonds are the least suitable because they are issued by companies in financial trouble. These bonds are extremely risky so they're often issued at a deep discount from par value. The issuer is not required to make interest payments unless they can afford it.

7. **D.** Sovereign bonds are ones issued by foreign governments. The principal and interest is paid in the issuer's currency, not U.S. dollars. Since the interest and principal is not paid in U.S. dollars, investors also face currency risk.

8. **A.** When a corporation issues callable bonds, it gives them the right to call (repurchase) the bonds from issuers at a price stated on the indenture. Since this is something that would not be advantageous to investors, the issuer has to sweeten the pot by offering a higher coupon rate than a non-callable bond.

9. **C.** Accrued interest takes place when a bond trades in-between coupon dates. Corporate and municipal bonds assume a 30-day month and a 360-day year. Accrued interest is calculated from the previous coupon date up to, but not including the settlement date. So first, you have to get the settlement date. Since Declan purchased the bond on Monday, May 10th, you don't have a weekend to contend with. Because corporate bonds settle in two business days, the settlement date is Wednesday, May 12th (5/12). Next find the previous coupon date, which is January 1st (1/1). Now set up the equation:

$$\begin{array}{r} 5\,/\,12 \\ -1\,/\,1 \\ \hline 4\,/\,11 \end{array}$$

$$(\,4 \text{ months} \times 30\text{-day months}\,) + 11 \text{ days} = 131 \text{ days of accrued interest}$$

First subtract the fifth month (May) from the first month (January). You end up with four months. Because corporate and municipal bonds calculate accrued interest using 30-day months, you have to multiply four months by 30 days to get an answer of 120 days. Subtract the previous coupon date (1) from the settlement date (12) to get an answer of 11 days. Add the 120 days and 11 days together, and you get 131 days as your answer.

10. **A.** PAC (Planned Amortization Class) tranches are the most common because they have the most certain prepayment date.

Chapter **8**

Municipal Bonds: Local Government Securities

Municipal bonds are securities that state governments, local governments, or U.S. territories issue. The municipality uses the money it borrows from investors to fund and support projects, such as roads, sewer systems, hospitals, and so on. In most cases, the interest received from these bonds is federally tax-free to investors.

Even though you're most likely going to spend a majority of your time selling equity securities (stocks), for some unknown reason, the Series 7 tests heavily on municipal securities. As a matter of fact, municipal bonds are one of the most heavily tested areas on the entire exam. If you've flipped ahead, you may have noticed that this chapter isn't one of the biggest in the book. Why is that? Well, I cover a lot of the bond basics, such as par value, maturity, types of maturities (term, serial, and balloon), the seesaw, and so on, in Chapter 7. Also, you can find some of the underwriting information in Chapter 5.

As with most of the other chapters, you'll find a certain amount of information familiar from what you learned when taking the SIE exam relating to municipal securities.

This chapter and the real exam focus mainly on the differences between GO (general obligation) bonds and revenue bonds. I also give you plenty of example questions for practice plus a chapter test at the end to wrap it all up.

General Obligation Bonds: Backing Bonds with Taxes

Most Series 7 municipal test questions are on general obligation (GO) bonds. The following sections help you prepare.

General characteristics of GOs

REMEMBER

When you're preparing to take the Series 7 exam, you need to recognize and remember a few items that are specific to GO bonds:

>> **They fund nonrevenue producing facilities.** GO bonds are not self-supporting because municipalities issue them to build or support projects that don't bring in enough (or any) money to help pay off the bonds. GOs fund schools, libraries, police departments, fire stations, and so on.

>> **They're backed by the full faith and credit (taxing power) of the municipality.** The taxes of the people living in the municipality back general obligation bonds.

>> **They require voter approval.** Because the generous taxes of the people living in the municipality back the bonds, those same people have the right to vote on the project.

The following question tests your knowledge of GO bonds.

EXAMPLE

Which of the following projects are MORE likely to be financed by general obligation bonds than revenue bonds (discussed later in this chapter)?

I. New municipal hospital

II. Public sports arena

III. New junior high school

IV. New library

(A) I and II only

(B) III and IV only

(C) I and III only

(D) I, III, and IV only

The correct answer is Choice (B). Remember that GO bonds are issued to fund nonrevenue producing projects. A new municipal hospital and a public sports arena will produce income that can back revenue bonds. However, a new junior high school and a new library need the support of taxes to pay off the bonds and, therefore, are more likely to be financed by GO bonds.

Analyzing GO bonds

The Series 7 exam tests your ability to analyze different types of municipal securities and help a customer make a decision that best suits her needs. You should be able to analyze a GO bond like you'd analyze other investments; however, because they're backed by taxes rather than sales of goods and services (like most corporations are), GO bonds have different components to look at when analyzing the marketability and safety of the issue.

Ascertaining marketability

Many different items can affect the marketability of municipal bonds, including the characteristics of the issuer, factors affecting the issuer's ability to pay, and municipal debt ratios. You certainly want to steer investors away from municipal bonds that aren't very marketable, unless those investors are willing to take extra risk. Here's a list of some of the other items that can affect the bonds' marketability:

>> **Quality (rating):** The higher the credit rating, the safer the bond, and therefore the more marketable it is. As with corporate bonds, the three main credit rating agencies are Standard & Poor's, Moody's, and Fitch.

>> **Maturity:** The shorter the maturity, typically the more marketable the bond issue.

>> **Call features:** Callable bonds are less marketable than non-callable bonds.

>> **Interest (coupon) rate:** Everything else being somewhat equal, bonds with higher coupon (interest) rates are more marketable.

>> **Block size:** The larger the block size, the more marketable the bond usually is.

>> **Dollar price:** All else being equal, the lower the dollar price, the more marketable the bond is.

>> **Issuer's name (local or national reputation):** Bonds are more marketable when the issuer has a good reputation for paying off its bonds on time. Also, if they have a national, instead of just local, reputation for paying their debt on time, their debt securities will be more marketable.

>> **Liquidity (ability to sell the bond in the secondary market):** Certainly there are a lot of things that can affect the liquidity (ease of selling the security) of municipal bonds. Investors would have to look at the issuer's name, national interest, the rating of the bonds, the coupon rate, dollar price, maturity, and so on.

>> **Credit and liquidity support:** Municipal securities issued with credit and liquidity support have a bank-issued letter of credit committing to payment of principal and interest in the event that the municipal issuer is unable to do so. Obviously, this adds another level of safety and the issuer would be able to issue securities backed with credit and liquidity support with lower yields.

>> **Denominations:** Unlike corporate bonds, municipal bonds typically have a minimum denomination of $5,000 (although some may be as low as $1,000) and some even impose a higher denomination of $100,000. Certainly municipal bonds with denominations of $5,000 face value will be affordable to many more investors.

>> **Sinking fund:** If the issuer has put money aside to pay the bonds off at maturity, the bonds are more marketable because the default risk is lower.

>> **Credit enhancement:** When the municipal issuer uses credit from another entity to provide additional security to a bond issue, it is considered a *credit enhancement*. A credit enhancement can be bond insurance, bank letters of credit, state or federal government guarantees, and so on. Obviously, a bond with credit enhancement would be more desirable to investors and the issue would have a higher credit rating and lower yield.

REMEMBER

There are many factors that can affect the marketability of municipal bonds. The SEC is now requiring issuers to update the MSRB (Municipal Securities Rulemaking Board) when material changes take place that could affect the marketability of their municipal securities. Any material changes must be disclosed within ten business days of the occurrence of the event. The information will be made available to investors and industry professionals on the MSRB's EMMA (Electronic Municipal Market Access) website (www.emma.msrb.org). The events that must be disclosed include principal and interest payment delinquencies on the securities being offered, unscheduled draws on debt service reserves, unscheduled draws on credit enhancements, substitution of credit or liquidity providers, defeasances, ratings changes, tender offers, bankruptcy, adverse tax opinions that might make the issue taxable, and non-payment-related defaults, bond calls.

Dealing with debt

One factor that influences the safety of a GO bond is the municipality's ability to deal with debt. After you consider the issuer's name, you can look at previous issues that the municipality had and find out whether it was able to pay off the debt in a timely manner.

In addition to the municipality's name (and credit history), you want to look at its current debt. *Net overall debt* includes the debt that the municipality owes directly plus the portion of the overlapping debt that the municipality is responsible for:

>> **Net direct debt:** The debt that the municipality obtained on its own. Net direct debt comes from both GO bonds and short-term municipal notes (see the later section "Don't Forget Municipal Notes!"). Revenue bonds are not included in the net direct debt because they're self-supporting (see "Revenue Bonds: Raising Money for Utilities and Such").

>> **Overlapping debt:** Overlapping debt occurs when several authorities in a geographic area have the ability to tax the same residents. Take, for example, our previous home-away-from-home, Las Vegas. Not only does Las Vegas have its own debt, but because it's part of Clark County, the Las Vegas residents are also responsible for part of Clark County's debt. In addition, because Las Vegas is in Nevada, the residents of Las Vegas are responsible for a portion of Nevada's debt.

To determine the *debt per capita* (per person), which may also be called *per capita debt*, take the debt (overall, direct, or overlapping) and divide it by the number of people in the municipality. Obviously, for an investor, the lower this number is, the better.

Bringing in taxes, fees, and fines

Taxes — one of life's little certainties — are another factor that influence the safety of GO bonds. Property taxes (which local municipalities — not states — collect) and sales taxes are the driving force behind paying back investors. Aided and abetted by traffic fines and licensing fees, taxes put money in the municipal coffers and eventually in investors' hands. The following factors come into play:

>> **Property values:** *Ad valorem* (property) taxes are the largest source of backing for GO bonds. Even though people living in a municipality want their property values to be low (not if they're selling their home but for tax purposes), people investing in municipal bonds want the property values to be high. The higher the assessed value, the more taxes collected and the easier it is for the municipality to pay off its debt.

TIP

When you're dealing with Series 7 questions that ask you to calculate the ad valorem taxes for an individual, always go with the assessed value, not the market value. Quite often you'll find that your assessed house value is out of whack with the market value. Ad valorem taxes are based on mills, or thousandths of a dollar (1 mill = $0.001). To help you remember that a mill equals 0.001, remember that *mills* has two *l*s, so you need to have two zeros after the decimal point.

>> **Population:** Obviously, the more people who live in a municipality and pay taxes to back the bond issue, the better. Also, the population trend is important. Investors prefer to see more people moving into a municipality than moving out.

>> **Tax base:** The tax base is comprised of the number of people living in the municipality, the assessed property values, and how much the average person makes. Larger tax bases are ideal to help support municipal GO bonds.

>> **Sales per capita:** Because sales taxes also support GO bonds, the amount of sales per capita (the amount of goods the average person buys) is also important.

>> **Traffic fines and licensing fees:** You know that $200 speeding ticket that you got last month? The money that you paid in fines helped pay off some of the municipality's debt. I hope that makes you feel better.

REMEMBER

Municipal GO bonds are backed by the huge taxing power of a municipality, so GO bonds usually have higher ratings and lower yields than revenue bonds. Because investors aren't taking as much risk, they don't get as much reward, or *yield*.

Try your hand at a question involving property taxes, an issue that affects the safety of GO bonds.

EXAMPLE

An individual has a house with a market value of $350,000 and an assessed value of $300,000. What is the ad valorem tax if the tax rate is 24 mills?

(A) $720

(B) $840

(C) $7,200

(D) $8,400

The answer you want is Choice (C). First make sure that you start with the assessed value; multiply it by the tax rate and then by 0.001 to get the answer:

$$\$300,000 \times 24 \times 0.001 = \$7,200$$

WARNING

To keep yourself from making a careless mistake, multiply the three numbers separately; the tax rate may be single or double digits. Multiplying by 0.001 means moving a decimal point three places to the left, so 24 mills is $0.024, not $0.0024. In this case, if you multiplied $300,000 by 0.0024 (or 2.4 mills), you got a wrong answer, Choice (A). Although some of you might be lucky enough to live in a municipality where you only pay $720 per year in property taxes, in states like New York, New Jersey, Connecticut, and so on, most of us pay more than that per month.

Bank qualified bonds

Certain issues of GO bonds are considered bank qualified. When municipal bonds are purchased on margin (see Chapter 9), interest expenses associated with purchasing securities are not tax deductible even in the case of municipal bonds. However, if the municipal bonds are bank qualified, commercial banks can purchase the municipal bonds on margin and deduct 80 percent of the margin interest expense on their taxes while still receiving tax-free interest from the municipal bonds. Unfortunately, this big advantage isn't available to investors like you and me.

Revenue Bonds: Raising Money for Utilities and Such

Unlike the tax-backed GO bonds (see the preceding sections), *revenue bonds* are issued to fund municipal facilities that'll generate enough income to support the bonds. These bonds raise money for certain utilities, toll roads, airports, hospitals, student loans, and so on.

A municipality can also issue *industrial development bond(s)* (IDBs) to finance the construction of facilities for corporations that move into that municipality. Remember that even though a municipality issues IDBs, they're actually backed by lease payments made by a corporation. Because the corporation is backing the bonds, the credit rating of the bonds is derived from the credit rating of the corporation.

REMEMBER

Because IDBs are backed by a corporation rather than a municipality, IDBs are generally considered the riskiest municipal bonds. Additionally, because these bonds are issued for the benefit of a corporation and not the municipality, the interest income may not be federally tax-free to investors subject to the alternative minimum tax (AMT). (See Chapter 15 for more information on alternative minimum tax.)

General characteristics of revenue bonds

REMEMBER

Before taking the Series 7 exam, you need to recognize and remember a couple items that are specific to revenue bonds:

>> **They don't need voter approval.** Because revenue bonds fund a revenue-producing facility and therefore aren't backed by taxes, they don't require voter approval. The revenues that the facility generates should be sufficient to pay off the debt.

>> **They require a feasibility study.** Prior to issuing revenue bonds, the municipality hires consultants to prepare a feasibility study. The study basically answers the question, *Does this make sense?* The study includes estimates of revenues that the facility could generate, along with any economic, operating, or engineering aspects of the project that would be of interest to the municipality.

Analyzing revenue bonds

As with any investment, you need to check out the specifics of the security. For instance, when gauging the safety of a revenue bond, you want to see whether it has a credit enhancement (insurance), which provides a certain degree of safety. You also want to look at *call features* (whether the issuer has the right to force investors to redeem their bonds early). You can assume that if a bond is callable, it has a higher yield than a non-callable bond because the investor is taking more risk (the investor doesn't know how long she can hold onto the bond).

For Series 7 exam purposes (and if you ever sell one or more revenue bonds), you also need to be familiar with the revenue-bond-specific items in this section. For instance, municipal revenue bonds involve covenants, wonderful little promises that protect investors by holding the issuer legally accountable. Table 8-1 shows some of the promises that municipalities make on the municipal bond indenture.

TABLE 8-1 **Revenue Bond Covenants**

Type of Covenant	Promises That the Municipality Will . . .
Rate covenant	Charge sufficient fees to people using the facility to be able to pay expenses and the debt service (principal and interest on the bonds)
Maintenance covenant	Adequately take care of the facility and any equipment so the facility continues to earn revenue
Insurance covenant	Adequately insure the facility

If you see the word *covenant* on the Series 7 exam, immediately think of revenue bonds.

Other factors that provide investors with a certain degree of comfort are that municipalities must provide *financial reports* and are subject to *outside audits* for all their revenue bond issues.

Obviously, municipalities don't want to default on their loans. That's why issuers use the *additional bonds test (additional bonds covenant)*, which says that if the municipality is going to issue more bonds backed by the same project, it must prove that the revenues will be sufficient to cover all the bonds. The indenture on the initial bonds may be open-ended or closed-ended. If it's open-ended, additional bonds will have equal claims to the assets. If it's closed-ended, any other bonds issued are subordinate to (in other words, rank lower than) the original issue.

As with GO bonds, revenue bonds are often backed by *credit enhancements*, which will pay the investors in the event that the issuer defaults. Since revenue bonds are backed by a revenue-producing facility, most revenue bond issuers also carry catastrophe insurance. A *catastrophe (calamity) clause* states that if a facility is destroyed due to a catastrophic event such as a flood, hurricane, tornado, or the like, the municipality will use the insurance that it purchased to call the bonds and pay back bondholders.

The flow of funds relates only to revenue bonds. The *flow of funds* tells you what a municipality does with the money collected from the revenue-producing facility that's backing the bonds. Typically, the flow of funds is as follows:

1. **Operation and maintenance:** This item is normally the first that the municipality pays from revenues it receives, which makes sense. If the municipality doesn't adequately maintain the facility and pay its employees, it'll cease to run.

2. **Debt service fund:** Usually the next item paid after operation and maintenance is the *debt service* (principal of maturing or redeemed bonds and interest on the remaining outstanding bonds).

3. **Debt service reserve fund:** After paying the first two items, the municipality puts aside money into the debt service reserve to pay one year's debt service.

4. **Reserve maintenance fund:** This fund helps supplement the general maintenance fund.

5. **Renewal and replacement fund:** This fund is for exactly what you'd expect — renewal projects (updating and modernizing) and replacement of equipment.

6. **Surplus fund:** Municipalities can use this fund for several purposes, such as redeeming bonds, paying for improvements, and so on.

Revenues are normally dispersed as I describe in the preceding list. This system is called a *net revenue pledge* because the *net revenues* (gross revenues minus operation and maintenance) are used to pay the debt service. However, if the municipality pays the debt service before paying the operation and maintenance, it's called a *gross revenue pledge*.

The *debt service coverage ratio* is an indication of the ability of a municipal issuer to meet the debt service payments on its bonds. The higher the debt service coverage ratio, the more likely the issuer is to be able to meet interest and principal payments on time.

The following question tests your debt service coverage ratio knowledge. Use the following formula to answer it.

$$\text{debt service coverage ratio} = \frac{\text{net } or \text{ gross revenues}}{\text{principal} + \text{interest}}$$

EXAMPLE

A municipality generates $10,000,000 in revenues from a facility. It must pay off $6,000,000 in operating and maintenance expenses, $1,500,000 in principal, and $500,000 in interest. Under a net revenue pledge, what is the debt service coverage ratio?

(A) 1 to 1

(B) 1.5 to 1

(C) 2 to 1

(D) 4 to 1

The right answer is Choice (C). Because the question states that the municipality is using a net revenue pledge, you have to calculate the net revenue. First, using the earlier equation, figure the net revenue by subtracting the operation and maintenance expenses ($6,000,000) from the gross revenue ($10,000,000), which gives you $4,000,000. Next, take the $4,000,000 and divide it by the combined principal and interest. The principal is $1,500,000 and the interest is $500,000, which gives you a total of $2,000,000. After dividing the $4,000,000 by $2,000,000, you come up with a ratio of 2 to 1, which means that the municipality brought in two times the amount of money needed to pay the debt service (principal and interest). A debt service coverage ratio of 2 to 1 is considered adequate for a municipality to pay off its debt. A debt service coverage ratio of less than 2 to 1 may indicate that the municipality may have problems meeting its debt obligations.

Here's how your equation should look:

$$\text{debt service coverage ratio} = \frac{\text{net revenues}}{\text{principal} + \text{interest}}$$

$$\text{debt service coverage ratio} = \frac{\$10,000,000 - \$6,000,000}{\$1,500,000 + \$500,000} = \frac{\$4,000,000}{\$2,000,000} = 2 \text{ to } 1$$

TIP

If the question doesn't specifically ask for gross revenues or net revenues, you can assume net because that's the more common way that a municipality pays off its debt.

The Primary Market: Bringing New Municipal Bonds to Market

As you can imagine, like corporations and partnerships, municipalities need help selling their issues. To that end, they can choose their underwriter(s) directly (the way almost all corporations and DPPs do it) or through a competitive (bidding) process.

Note: Whether the new municipal securities are being sold via a competitive or negotiated offering, the SEC requires that the underwriter(s) make sure that the issuer (state or of local government) enters into an agreement to provide required information to the Municipal Securities Rulemaking Board (MSRB). The information required includes annual financial information such as operating data and audited financial statements. In addition, the issuer must provide event notices such as principal and interest payment delinquencies; bond calls or tender offers; ratings changes; unscheduled draws on debt service reserves; bankruptcy; appointment of a successor trustee; defeasances, and so on. Issuers must submit annual disclosures on or before the specified date specified in the *continuing disclosure agreement* or provide a notice of a failure to do so via the Electronic Municipal Market Access (EMMA) website.

Issuers are exempt from providing continuing disclosure if the entire issue is less than $1 million, or the bonds are sold to no more than 35 unaccredited (unsophisticated) investors and sold in units of no less than $100,000, or the bonds are sold in denominations of $100,000 or more and mature in 9 months or less from initial issuance. The bonds were issued prior to July 1995.

>> **Negotiated offering:** This is the type of offering where the issuer chooses the underwriter(s) (a group of underwriters is called a *syndicate*) directly with no competition from other underwriters. Municipalities issuing revenue bonds or IDRs typically choose the underwriter(s) directly, although they have the option of taking bids. Like most corporations, quite often the municipality will already have a relationship with one or more underwriters that it is comfortable working with. Since revenue bonds are not backed by taxing power (like GOs), the issuers are not obligated to get the best price or coupon rate for their bond issue.

>> **Competitive offering:** Because general obligation (GO) bonds are backed by the taxing power of the municipality, the municipal issuers are responsible for getting the best deal for the people living in their municipality. In order to insure the best deal, they will post an advertisement known as a *Notice of Sale* in the *Daily Bond Buyer* (the main source of information about new municipal bonds) saying that they are accepting bids on a new issue of bonds. At this point, interested underwriters will submit a *good faith deposit* (to prove their sincerity) and their bids to the issuer. As you may suspect, the winner of the bid will be the underwriter that presents the lowest cost to the taxpayers backing the bond. The lowest cost could be the result of issuing the bond with a lower coupon rate and/or agreeing to pay more to purchase the bonds. Don't be too concerned about the underwriters who don't win; they'll get their good faith deposit back.

REMEMBER

The Notice of Sale contains all bidding information about new municipal issues. Besides just saying that it is taking bids, the issuer also gives bidding details. It will tell potential underwriters when and where to submit bids, the amount of the good faith deposit, whether it is expecting bids on an NIC (net interest cost) or a TIC (true interest cost) basis, the amount of bonds to be issued, the maturity of bonds to be issued, and so on. It is the responsibility of the underwriters to determine the coupon rate (they'll determine this based on the credit history of the issuer, the amount of outstanding debt, the size of the issue, the tax base, and so on) and selling price of the issue. Remember, the underwriter(s) need to be able to sell the issue and still make a profit. So, the selling price and the coupon rate have to be attractive to investors. You should remember that the difference between the cost the issuer pays for the security and the amount it receives from investors is called the *spread*. For argument's sake, say that the underwriter(s) agrees(s) to purchase the bonds for $990 each from the issuer and then reoffer them to the public for $1,000 each; then the spread is $10 per bond. The underwriter(s)' profit lies within that spread.

>> **Private offering:** A private offering of municipal securities is a primary offering (new issues) where a *placement agent* (municipal securities dealer acting as an agent) sells the new securities directly to the public on an agency basis. In this case, the placement agent is not purchasing the securities from the issuer as in a negotiated or competitive offering but is selling directly for the municipal issuer. There are typically restrictions based on the securities issued through a private offering regarding the resale by investors so they are often required to be provided a *private placement letter* outlining the rules.

>> **Advance refunding:** Advance refunding is when the municipality issues new bonds (refunding issue) to pay off outstanding bonds (refunded issue). In order to meet with tax laws, the refunded issue must remain outstanding for more than 90 days after the issuance of the refunding issue. (Current refunding is when the municipal securities will be redeemed or mature within 90 days or less of the date of issuance of the refunding issue.) Usually, the money received from the sale of the refunding issue is invested in U.S. Treasury securities or U.S. government agency securities. The principal and interest from the U.S. Treasury or U.S. government securities is used to pay principal and interest on the refunded issue.

Note: Another method of advance refunding is called *crossover refunding.* Crossover refunding is when the revenue stream which was originally pledged to pay the debt service on the refunded bonds continues to be used to pay the principal and interest on those bonds until they mature or are called. Once that happens, those pledged revenues crossover and are used to pay principal and interest on the refunding issue and escrowed securities are used to pay the refunded bonds. When both the refunded and refunding bonds are both outstanding, the debt service on the refunding bonds is paid from the interest earnings on the money invested by the municipality from the sale of the refunding issue. Recent rule changes have made it so that advance refundings of municipal bonds will probably go the way of the dodo bird. Rule changes have made it so that the refunding issue cannot be issued as tax-free bonds. Thus, there will be no advantage to municipalities to advance refund their bonds because they'd have to pay interest on the refunding bonds that is much higher than on tax-free bonds. I'm assuming that questions regarding advance refunding will disappear sometime in the future, but as of now, advance refunding is still on the Series 7 outline.

TIP

In some cases, an issuer may offer a *direct exchange* of securities (exchanging the called or matured bonds to the new issue of bonds) to their existing bondholders versus selling new securities. This will help keep costs lower for the issuer because they don't have to market the new securities, pay underwriters, or pay the costs of transferring money or securities.

Escrow requirements

Pre-refunded bonds may be *escrowed to maturity,* meaning that the proceeds of sale from the new issue of bonds is held in an escrow account. Typically the money held in the escrow account is invested in securities with a high credit rating such as U.S. Treasury securities (defeasance). The interest and principal received in the escrow account will be used to make principal and interest payments to the bondholders.

Call features

No matter the type of offering, like corporate bonds, municipal bonds may be issued with call (prepayment) provisions. As such, there are a wide variety of ways municipal bonds can be called.

>> **Par or premium:** Typically bonds are called or redeemed at par or an accreted value (see Chapter 15 for more on accretion and amortization) in the case of original issue discount (OID) bonds or zero-coupon bonds, plus accrued interest up to the redemption date. However, in some cases, they may be called or redeemed above par or accreted value plus accrued interest up to the redemption date, which is called a premium call.

>> **Optional:** This provision gives the holders the right or option to redeem their bonds on or after a specified date determined by the issuer. Typically, that date is set at least ten years from the issue date.

>> **Mandatory:** Mandatory redemptions occur at either on a scheduled basis (in specified amounts or in amounts then on deposit in the sinking fund) or based on when a certain amount of money is available in the sinking fund (sinking fund call).

>> **Partial or in-whole call:** Depending on the terms of the bond contract, the issuer may make an in-whole call, where all the callable bonds of that issue must be redeemed or a partial call where only a portion of the issue must be redeemed.

>> **Sinking fund:** Issuers of callable bonds often set up sinking funds, which are where the issuer puts money aside to pay off the bonds at some future date. Once there is enough money in the sinking fund to redeem the bonds, there will be a mandatory sinking-fund call.

>> **Extraordinary calls:** These are mandatory or optional redemptions due to an extraordinary event such as the loss of a revenue-producing facility backing the bonds. The loss could be due to a hurricane, flooding, fire damage, loss to eminent domain, and so on.

>> **Make whole calls:** This type of call provision allows the issuer to pay off the debt securities early but at a higher expense. In the case of make whole calls, the issuer must make a lump-sum payment based on the net present value of future interest payments that would be due on the bonds that will not be paid due to the bonds being called. Because of the high cost to the municipality, bonds with make whole call provisions are rarely issued.

REMEMBER

Callable bonds are riskier for investors because they aren't sure how long they're going to be able to hold their bonds. And, barring a catastrophe, issuers usually call their bonds when interest rates drop so that they can issue new bonds with a lower coupon rate. So the benefit to issuers is that they won't be stuck making high coupon payments when interest rates fall. The benefit to investors is that they receive a higher coupon rate on callable bonds. Table 8-2 summarizes the benefits and risks.

TABLE 8-2   Callable Bond Benefits and Risks

	Benefit	Risk
Investor	Higher coupon rate	May not be able to keep the bond as long as wanted and if the bond is called, may have to invest at a lower coupon rate if the bonds are called.
Issuer	May call the bonds at a time that's beneficial and can issue new bonds with a lower coupon rate	Making higher coupon payments than non-callable bonds

TIP

Although much more rare, municipal securities may also be issued with *put* or *tender options*. These are much rarer because it puts more control in the hands of investors and takes some of the control away from the issuers. Put options gives the investors the right to require the issuer (or agent of the issuer, tender agent) to purchase their bonds usually at par value at certain specified times prior to the maturity date. Typically, puttable bonds are variable-rate securities (see "Specific types of municipal securities" later in this chapter), with the put option exercisable on dates on which the floating/variable rate changes. Put options give investors more control but usually at the cost of a lower interest rate than a non-puttable security.

Examining Other Types of Municipal Bonds on the Test

Along with standard revenue and GO bonds (see the earlier sections on these topics), you're required to know the specifics of the following bonds:

>> **Special tax bonds:** These bonds are secured by one or more taxes other than ad valorem (property) taxes. The bonds may be backed by sales taxes on fuel, tobacco, alcohol, business licenses, and so on.

>> **Special assessment (special district) bonds:** These bonds are issued to fund the construction of sidewalks, streets, sewers, and so on. Special assessment bonds are backed by taxes only on the properties that benefit from the improvements. In other words, if people who live a few blocks away from you get all new sidewalks, they'll be taxed for it, not you.

>> **Double-barreled bonds:** These bonds are basically a combination of revenue and GO bonds. Municipalities issue these bonds to fund revenue-producing facilities (toll bridges, water and sewer facilities, and so forth), but if the revenues taken in aren't enough to pay off the debt, tax revenues make up the deficiency.

>> **Lease revenue (lease rental) bonds:** These bonds are secured by lease (rental) payments made by the party leasing the facilities financed by the bond issue. Usually lease revenue bonds are used to finance the construction of facilities used by a state or municipality. These facilities include schools and office buildings.

>> **Certificates of participation (COP):** These are similar to a lease revenue bond but instead of the bondholders receiving the interest payments from the municipal issuer, they receive a share in a pledged revenue stream (usually lease payments) paid by the lessor to a trustee who then distributes pro rata shares to each of the bondholders.

>> **Limited-tax general obligation bonds (LTGO):** These bonds are types of general obligation bonds for which the taxes backing the bonds are limited. Limited-tax general obligation bonds are secured by all revenues of the municipality that aren't used to back other bonds. However, the amount of property taxes municipalities can levy to back these bonds is limited. If the bond is backed by an unlimited tax pledge, the municipality can raise property tax rates to make sure the bonds are able to be paid off, which is good for investors but bad for homeowners.

>> **Public housing authority bonds (PHAs):** These bonds are also called new housing authority (NHA) bonds and are issued by local housing authorities to build and improve low-income housing. These bonds are backed by U.S. government subsidies, and if the issuer can't pay off the debt, the U.S. government makes up any shortfalls.

TIP

Because PHAs are backed by the issuer and the U.S. government, they're considered among the safest municipal bonds.

>> **Moral obligation bonds:** These bonds are issued by a municipality but backed by a pledge from the state government to pay off the debt if the municipality can't. Given this additional backing of the state, they're considered safe. Moral obligation bonds need legislative approval to be issued.

REMEMBER

Because they're called moral obligation bonds, the state has a *moral* responsibility — but not a legal obligation — to help pay off the debt if the municipality can't.

The following question tests your ability to answer questions about the safety of municipal bonds:

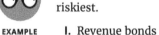

EXAMPLE

From an investor's standpoint, rank the following municipal bonds in order from safest to riskiest.

  I. Revenue bonds

 II. Moral obligation bonds

III. Public housing authority bonds

IV. Industrial development revenue bonds

(A) I, II, III, IV

(B) III, II, I, IV

(C) II, III, IV, I

(D) II, IV, III, I

The correct answer is Choice (B). If you remember that public housing authority bonds are considered the safest of the municipal bonds because they're backed by U.S. government subsidies, this question's easy, because only one answer choice starts with III. Anyway, public housing authority bonds would be the safest; moral obligation bonds, which are also considered very safe because the state government has a moral obligation to help pay off the debt if needed, follow. Next come revenue bonds, which are backed by a revenue-producing facility. Remember that industrial development revenue bonds (IDRs) are considered the riskiest municipal bonds because although they're technically municipal bonds, they're backed only by lease payments made by a corporation.

Municipal bond diversity of maturities

The diversity of maturities hopefully will look familiar to you because it was covered in the Securities Industry Essentials exam. Not only can bond certificates be in different forms, but they can also be scheduled with different types of maturities. Maturity schedules depend on the issuer's needs. Most municipalities issue either term bond or serial bonds. The following list presents an explanation of the types of bond issues and maturity schedules:

>> **Term bonds:** Term bonds are all issued at the same time and have the same maturity date. For example, if a corporation or municipality issues 20 million dollars of term bonds, they may all mature in 20 years. Because of the large payment that's due at maturity, most corporations and municipalities issuing this type of bond have a sinking fund. Corporations typically issue term bonds because they lock in a coupon rate for a long period of time.

   The issuer creates a *sinking fund* when it sets aside money over time in order to retire its debt. Investors like to see that a sinking fund is in place because it lowers the likelihood of *default* (the risk that the issuer can't pay interest or par value back at maturity).

>> **Series bonds:** These bonds are issued in successive years but have only one maturity date. Issuers of series bonds pay interest only on the bonds that they've issued so far. Construction companies that are building developments in several phases issue this type of bond. Because this type of bond is issued mainly by construction companies, they are usually not issued by municipalities.

>> **Serial bonds:** In this type of bond issue, a portion of the outstanding bonds mature at regular intervals (for example, 10 percent of the entire issue matures yearly). Serial bonds are usually issued by corporations and municipalities to fund projects that provide regular income streams. Most municipal (local government) bonds are issued with serial maturity.

   A serial bond that has more bonds maturing on the final maturity date is called a *balloon issue.*

Specific types of municipal securities

Municipalities can certainly offer a wide variety of ways to issue securities. The following list covers the ways that'll be tested on the Series 7. For the most part, the names pretty much explain what they are but you should read on to get a deeper understanding:

>> **Original Issue Discount (OID) bonds:** Actually, the name is pretty self-explanatory. An OID is a bond that was originally issued at a discount from par and matures at par value. The difference between the original purchase price and par value must be adjusted over the life of the bond (see Chapter 7) and is treated as federally tax-free interest. If selling the bond before maturity, you have to take the adjusted book value and compare it to the selling price to determine if there's a gain or loss. OIDs may also receive semiannual interest payments. OIDs that don't receive interest payments are considered zero-coupon bonds.

>> **Zero-coupon bonds:** Zero-coupon bonds are a type of original issue discount bond that receives no interest payments. These bonds are issued at a deep discount and mature at par value. These bonds must be accreted (see Chapter 7) over the life of the bond until reaching face value at maturity. For municipal securities, the annual accretion is considered federally tax-free interest.

>> **Capital-appreciation bonds (CABs):** The issuers of these municipal bonds reinvest the principal amount received from issuing the bonds at a stated compounded rate until maturity. At maturity, investors receive the *maturity value,* which represents the initial principal amount and the total investment return. CABs are different from zero-coupon bonds because the investment return is in the form of compounded interest instead of the accreted original value. CABs are sold at a deeply discounted price with maturity values in multiples of $5,000.

>> **Variable-rate securities:** These securities have interest rates that fluctuate (vary) in response to market movements. Variable-rate securities are also known as *floating-rate securities.* The floating or variable rate is set at specified intervals. As with auction-rate securities, because the interest rate is reset occasionally, the market price of the security tends to remain more stable. Variable-rate securities typically have initial maturities of 10 years or more.

>> **Auction-rate securities:** These are municipal bonds where the interest rate is reset periodically based on a Dutch auction. A Dutch auction is a process by which new securities are sold at the best bid price, which translates to the lowest yield to the issuer (highest selling price and/or lowest coupon rate). Because the coupon rate is reset periodically, the prices of auction-rate securities are more likely to remain stable when interest rates change.

Taxable municipal bonds

Much more often than not, the interest on most municipal bonds is federally tax-free and some-time triple tax-free (the interest is exempt from federal, state, and local taxes). However, some municipal bonds are fully taxable, and some are only taxable to investors who are required to pay alternative minimum taxes (AMT). Issuers create taxable municipal bonds when they can't legally create ones that are tax-exempt because the issue doesn't meet federal tax laws to be tax exempt, such as when the bond issue isn't for public purpose.

There are a couple types that you need to be aware of for the Series 7 that are taxable. These bonds are still issued and backed by a municipality but are still taxable. These bonds were created under the Economic Recovery and Reinvestment Act of 2009 and are called Build America Bonds (BABs). The idea behind the BABs is to help municipalities raise money for infrastructure projects such as tunnels, bridges, roads, and so on. These bonds have either a higher coupon rate than most other municipal bonds because the municipality receives tax credits from the federal government or are more attractive because the investors receive tax credits from the federal government. As such, these municipal bonds become more attractive to all investors, even ones with lower income tax rates. Even though the Build America Bond program expired in 2010, there are still plenty of these bonds out there so, you will be tested on them. The two types of Build America Bonds are:

>> **Tax Credit BABs (Tax Credit Bonds):** Investors of this type of Build America Bonds receive tax credits equal to 35 percent of the coupon rate.

>> **Direct Payment BABs (Direct Pay Subsidy Bonds):** When a municipality issues Direct Payment BABs, it receives reimbursements from the U.S. Treasury equal to 35 percent of the coupon rate. As such, direct payment BABs would tend to have a higher coupon rate than tax credit BABs.

Don't Forget Municipal Notes!

When municipalities need short-term (interim) financing, municipal notes come into play. These notes bring money into the municipality until other revenues are received. Municipal notes typically have maturities of one year or less (usually three to five months) although notes with longer maturities are also issued. Know the different types of municipal notes for the Series 7 exam:

- » **Tax anticipation notes (TANs):** These notes provide financing for current operations in anticipation of future taxes that the municipality will collect, such as ad valorem taxes, which are due at a certain time of the year.

- » **Revenue anticipation notes (RANs):** These bonds provide financing for current operations in anticipation of future revenues that the municipality will collect.

- » **Tax and revenue anticipation notes (TRANs):** These notes are a combination of TANs and RANs.

- » **Grant anticipation notes (GANs):** These bonds provide interim financing for the municipality while it's waiting for a grant from the U.S. government. The notes are paid off from the grant funds once received.

- » **Bond anticipation notes (BANs):** These bonds provide interim financing for the municipality while it's waiting for long-term bonds to be issued.

- » **Construction loan notes (CLNs):** These notes provide interim financing for the construction of multifamily apartment buildings.

- » **Project notes (PNs):** These notes provide interim financing for the building of subsidized housing for low-income families.

- » **Tax-exempt commercial paper (CP):** These short-term bonds are usually issued by organizations such as universities with permission of the government. This debt obligation usually lasts only a few months (within 270 days like corporate commercial paper) to help the organization cover its short-term liabilities.

REMEMBER

AON (all or none) is an order qualifier (fill an entire order at a specific price or not at all) or type of underwriting; it is not a municipal note, no matter how much it looks like one.

Municipal notes are not rated the same as municipal or corporate bonds (AAA, AA, A, and so on). Municipal notes have ratings as follows (from best to worst):

- » **Moody's:** MIG 1, MIG 2, MIG 3, MIG 4

- » **Standard & Poor's:** SP-1, SP-2, SP-3

- » **Fitch:** F-1, F-2, F-3

The following question tests your knowledge of municipal notes.

EXAMPLE

Suffolk County, New York, would like to even out its cash flow. Which of the following municipal notes would Suffolk County MOST likely issue?

(A) RANs

(B) BANs

(C) GANs

(D) TANs

As with other securities, you can also help customers diversify their municipal portfolio. By diversifying with a variety of municipal securities, it adds an extra degree of safety. The ways to diversify in municipals are:

- **Geographical:** By investing in different areas of the country, investors limit their risk that a particular area of the country, a particular state, and/or a particular local municipality may be experiencing trouble making regularly scheduled interest payments. Municipalities may have trouble paying their debt due to poor management, economic downturns, natural disasters, and so on.

- **Type:** Varying the type of municipal securities purchased, such as GO bonds, revenue bonds, municipal notes, short-term and long-term maturities, and so on, provides investors with a certain degree of safety while attempting to take advantage of higher interest rates on riskier investments.

- **Rating:** Investors can also diversify by purchasing bonds with different ratings. Certainly the ones with the higher ratings have the most credit worthiness. However, bonds with higher ratings have lower coupon (interest) rates. Therefore, investors may decide to purchase bonds with different ratings to try to get a higher return on the lower-rated bonds but also provide some safety by purchasing some higher rated bonds.

As with corporate bonds, the main ratings services for municipal bonds are Moody's, Standard & Poor's, and Fitch. Check out Chapter 7 for more info. When a municipality insures its municipal securities, which is known as a credit enhancement, it increases the rating of the bond issue and allows the issuer to offer the securities with a lower coupon rate.

The answer you want is Choice (D). You have to use a little common sense to answer this one. Because the question doesn't state that the municipality is expecting a grant or issuing long-term bonds, you should cross out Choices (B) and (C). Likewise, you can't assume that the municipality will be collecting revenues from some project, so Choice (A) is out. However, municipalities collect property taxes at regular intervals, so (D) is the best choice.

Municipal Fund Securities

Municipal fund securities are similar to investment companies (see Chapter 9) but are exempt from that definition under section 2(b) of the Investment Company Act of 1940. Municipal fund securities are established by municipal governments, municipal agencies, or educational institutions but do not represent loans to the government. Included in municipal fund securities are Section 529 plans, ABLE accounts, and Local Government Investment Pools.

Section 529 plans (529 savings plans)

529 plans are specialized educational savings accounts available to investors. These plans are also known as *qualified tuition plans* (QTPs) because they are designed to allow money to be saved for qualified expenses for higher education (colleges, postsecondary trade and vocational schools, postgraduate programs, and so on). As such, there is an owner (the one who sets up and contributes to the plan, typically a parent but doesn't have to be) and a beneficiary (the one who benefits from the plan, typically a child or relative of the person who set up the plan). Maximum yearly and lifetime contribution limits vary from state-to-state. However, withdrawals of the amount invested plus interest received are tax-free, meaning that the earnings grow on a tax-deferred basis, and there's no tax due if used for qualified educational expenses. Investors must receive an

official statement or offering circular prior to opening the account. You should note the following:

>> Contribution levels vary from state to state.

>> Rollovers are allowed once every 12 months. An investor may roll over the funds from one state's 529 plan to another state's plan or to a Coverdell ESA.

>> The investor may change investment options offered by the plan up to twice a year.

>> There aren't any income limits placed on the investors of a 529 plan.

>> Many investors contribute monthly although not required.

>> Any account balances that are unused (like suppose the beneficiary decides not to go to college or goes to a cheaper local college) can be transferred to another related beneficiary.

>> The assets in the account always remain under control of the owner (donor) even after the beneficiary becomes of legal age (which is 18 in most states).

>> In some cases, plans can be set up as *prepaid tuition plans* (which allows investors to prepay college at a locked-in rate) or a college savings plan, which allows owners to invest as he or she sees fit (aggressively, moderately, or conservatively).

>> As with other securities, there are disclosure requirements. When you're promoting 529 plans, you should discuss the risks and costs associated with different types of plans, recommend that they check out the tax benefits in their home state, and provide a disclaimer stating that the customer should read the disclosure document associated with the investment.

>> If money is withdrawn for a non-qualified reason, the IRS may assess a 10% tax penalty.

Note: Up until Jan 1, 2018, 529 plans were only allowed to be set up for higher education. However, due to the new tax laws, 529 plans may be set up for private, public, or religious kindergarten through 12th grade education. If a 529 plan is set up for K-12 education, the maximum distribution is $10,000 per year per beneficiary but for tuition only.

ABLE accounts

ABLE (Achieving a Better Life Experience) accounts are designed for individuals with provable disabilities and their families. Because of the extra needs and expenses (educational, housing, transportation, health, assistive technology, legal fees, and so on) required for taking care of individuals with disabilities, ABLE accounts allow people to invest after-tax dollars. Any earnings or distributions are tax-free as long as they are used to pay for qualified disability expenses for the beneficiary. ABLE accounts may be opened by the eligible individual, a parent or guardian, or a person granted power of attorney on behalf of the individual with the disability. However, once the account is opened, anyone can contribute. As with college savings plans above, the investments may be conservative, moderate, or aggressive. Many states have annual contribution caps and maximum account balances. ABLE accounts may be opened for the disabled person even if he or she is receiving other benefits such as social security disability, Medicaid, private insurance, and so on. In order to be eligible, the onset of the disability must've been discovered before the individual reached age 26.

Note: Rule G-45 requires dealers underwriting ABLE programs or 529 savings plans (but not LGIPs) to submit information such as plan descriptive information, assets, asset allocation information for each plan available, contributions, performance data, and so on semiannually and performance data annually through the Electronic Municipal Market Access (EMMA) system. MSRB's EMMA system is designed to provide market transparency to help protect market participants.

Local government investment pools

Local government investment pools (LGIPs) are established by states to provide other government entities (cities, counties, school districts, and so on) with a short-term investment vehicle for investing their funds. Since these are set up by state governments for state entities, LGIPs are exempt from SEC registration. As such, there is no prospectus requirement but they do have disclosure documents to cover investment policies, operating procedures, and so on. Although they aren't money market funds, they are similar in the fact that many LGIPs operate similar to one. Like money market funds, the NAV is typically set at $1.00, and normally the money is invested safely, although it doesn't have to be. LGIPs may be sold directly to municipalities or through municipal advisors hired by the municipal issuers.

Municipal fund securities advertisements

As with other securities, there are rules relating to the advertising of municipal fund securities such as 529 plans. Advertisements relating to municipal fund securities must do the following:

>> Remind investors to review the investment objectives, expenses, and risks involved with the particular municipal fund security prior to investing.

>> Disclose that an official statement relating to the municipal fund security will provide additional information. And the official statement should be read and understood prior to investing.

>> Name the firm as an underwriter if it publishes the advertisement and will also supply the official statement.

REMEMBER

The beneficiary of a 529 plan may live in another state. So, advertisements relating to 529 savings plans must tell investors to take into consideration the rules and tax benefits of the beneficiaries' home state also prior to investing.

Understanding the Taxes on Municipal Bonds

Municipal bonds typically have lower yields than most other bonds. You may think that because U.S. government securities (T-bills, T-notes, T-bonds, and so on) are the safest of all securities, they should have the lowest yields. Not necessarily so, because municipal bonds have a tax advantage that U.S. government bonds don't have: The interest received on municipal bonds is federally tax-free.

Comparing municipal and corporate bonds equally

The *taxable equivalent yield* (TEY) tells you what the interest rate of a municipal bond would be if it weren't federally tax-free. You need the following formula to compare municipal bonds and corporate bonds equally:

$$\text{taxable equivalent yield (TEY)} = \frac{\text{municipal yield}}{100\% - \text{investor's tax bracket}}$$

REMEMBER

Because the investor's tax bracket comes into play with municipal bonds, municipal bonds are better suited for investors in higher tax brackets.

The following question tests your ability to answer a TEY question.

EXAMPLE

Alyssa K. is an investor who is in the 30-percent tax bracket. Which of the following securities would provide Alyssa with the BEST after-tax yield?

(A) 5 percent GO bond

(B) 6 percent T-bond

(C) 7 percent equipment trust bond

(D) 7 percent mortgage bond

The right answer is Choice (A). If you were to look at this question straight up without considering any tax advantages, the answer would be either (C) or (D). However, you have to remember that the investor has to pay federal taxes on the interest received from the T-bond, equipment trust bond, and mortgage bond but doesn't have to pay federal taxes on the interest received from the GO municipal bond. So you need to set up the TEY equation to be able to compare all the bonds equally:

$$\text{taxable equivalent yield (TEY)} = \frac{\text{municipal yield}}{100\% - \text{investor's tax bracket}} = \frac{5\%}{100\% - 30\%} = \frac{5\%}{70\%} = 7.14\%$$

Looking into the Series 7 examiners' heads, you have to ask yourself, "Why would they be asking me this question?" Well, because they want to make sure that you know that the interest received on municipal bonds is federally tax-free. Therefore, if you somehow forget the formula, you're still likely to be right if you pick a municipal bond as the answer when you get a question like the preceding one.

Note: Although this situation is less likely, the Series 7 may ask you to determine the *municipal equivalent yield* (MEY), which is the yield on a taxable bond after paying taxes. Once you have that yield, you can compare it to a municipal bond to help determine the best investment for one of your customers. The formula for the municipal equivalent yield is as follows:

$$\text{MEY} = \text{municipal yield} \times (100 - \text{investor's tax bracket})$$

Scot-free! Taking a look at triple tax-free municipal bonds

Bonds that U.S. territories (and federal districts) issue are triple tax-free (the interest is not taxed on the federal, state, or local level). These places include

>> Puerto Rico

>> Guam

>> U.S. Virgin Islands

>> American Samoa

>> Washington, D.C.

Additionally, in most cases (there are a few exceptions), if you buy a municipal bond issued within your own state, the interest will be triple tax-free.

TIP

Unless you see the U.S. territories or Washington, D.C., in a municipal bond question, don't assume that the bonds are triple tax-free. Even if the question states that the investor buys a municipal bond issued within her own state, don't assume that it's triple tax-free unless the question specifically states that it is.

REMEMBER

The tax advantage of municipal bonds applies only to interest received. If investors sell municipal bonds for more than their cost basis, the investors have to pay taxes on the capital gains.

Pricing of municipal securities and other mathematical calculations

You'll find that I cover a lot of this stuff in the previous chapter. Some of the calculations that you'll be responsible for include dollar price, accrued interest (including long or short first coupons also known as odd first coupons), relationship of bond prices to changes in maturity, coupon, current yield, and so on. The following sections describe some of the other pricing and mathematical calculations you'll need to know for the Series 7.

YTC on premium bonds

Remember the seesaw: There is an inverse relationship between interest rates and bond prices. As interest rates increase, outstanding bond prices decrease. When interest rates decrease, outstanding bond prices increase. So when municipal bonds are trading at a premium (above par value), it is usually because interest rates have dropped or the municipality's credit rating increased. Anyway, to the municipal issuer, this means that it can now issue new bonds with a lower coupon rate and save some money. Because it is likely in this scenario that the municipal issuer will call its callable bonds when interest rates decrease, callable bonds trading at a premium must be quoted yield to call (YTC) instead of yield to maturity (YTM). (You can find the calculations for YTC and YTM in Chapter 7.)

Value of a basis point

A basis point (bp) is a unit of measurement used when quoting and comparing yields on all bonds or notes. Basis points are 1/100th of a point. For example, if the yield on a bond increased from 3.25 to 3.27 percent, it is referred to as a two basis point increase.

Bonds in default

Occasionally, an issuer may default on its bonds. This means that the issuer is no longer making interest payments. If a bond is trading in default, there is no way to calculate yields. For bearer (coupon) bonds, all unpaid coupons must be attached in order to be considered good delivery.

Municipal bond quotations

Municipal bonds may be quoted on a yield/basis price or on a dollar price. To figure out the yield/basis (YTM) price, please refer to Chapter 7. For municipal bonds quoted as a dollar price, remember that it is a percentage of dollar price. So a $1,000 par value municipal bond quoted at 98 means that the bond is actually trading at a price of $980 (98% of $1,000 par). However, although some municipal bonds may be available with par values of $1,000, most trade in minimum denominations of $5,000 and many have minimum denominations as high as $25,000 or $100,000 to attract institutional investors.

EXAMPLE

What is the actual dollar price of a $5,000 par value municipal bond trading at 99?

(A) $99

(B) $990

(C) $4,950

(D) $5,000

The answer you want is Choice (C). This question is relatively easy if you remember that the "99" in the question is a percentage of par value, so the $5,000 face value bond is not actually trading at $99. You can use the following equation to get your answer:

$$\$5,000 \text{ face value} \times 99\% = \$4,950$$

Interest rate

Going back to Chapter 7, remember that the interest (coupon) rate is based on a percentage of par value, so an investor with a 4% municipal bond with a par value of $25,000 will receive annual interest of $1,000 (4% × $25,000 par). Since most bonds pay semiannual interest, this investor would receive $500 every 6 months.

REMEMBER

For another calculation, you may be asked to determine the number of days of accrued interest if a bond is traded in-between coupon dates. Accrued interest is paid by the purchaser to the seller. Accrued interest is covered in detail in Chapter 7. However, don't forget that accrued interest on municipal bonds is calculated using *30-day months* instead of actual days.

Following Municipal Bond Rules

Yes, unfortunately, the Series 7 tests you on rules relating to municipal bonds. Rules are a part of life and a part of the Series 7 exam. A lot of the rules relating to municipal securities were already covered on the Securities Industry Essentials exam. This section covers just a few rules that are specific to municipal securities, but if you're itching for more regulations, don't worry. You can see plenty more rules in my favorite (and I use that term loosely) chapter: Chapter 16.

Confirmations

Confirmations are a summary of the details of a trade. Under MSRB rules, all confirmations of trades (MSRB Rule G-15) must be sent or given to customers by the municipal securities dealer at or before the completion of the transaction (settlement date). Municipal securities settle the regular way (two business days after the trade date, or T+2). The following items are included on the confirmation:

» The broker-dealer's name, address, and phone number

» The capacity of the trade (whether the firm acted as a broker or dealer)

» The dollar amount of the commission (if the firm's acting as a broker)

» The customer's name

» Any bond particulars, such as the issuer's name, interest rate, maturity, call features (if any), and so on

» The trade date, time of execution, and the settlement date

» Committee on Uniform Securities Identification Procedures (CUSIP) identification number (if there is one)

» Bond yield and dollar price

» Any accrued interest

>> The registration form (registered as to principal only, book entry, or fully registered)

>> Whether the bonds have been called or pre-refunded

>> Any unusual facts about the security

Advertising and record keeping

A brokerage firm has to keep all advertising for a minimum of three years, and these ads must be easily accessible (not in a bus storage locker) for at least two years.

The Municipal Securities Rulemaking Board (MSRB) requires a principal (manager) to approve all advertising material of the firm prior to its first use. The principal must ensure that the advertising is accurate and true.

REMEMBER

Advertising includes any material designed for use in the public media. Advertising includes offering circulars, market and form letters, summaries of official statements, and so on. However, preliminary and final official statements are not considered advertising because they're prepared by the issuer; therefore, they don't require approval from a principal.

Commissions

Although no particular guideline states what percentage broker-dealers can charge (as with the 5% markup policy — see Chapter 16), all commissions, markups, and markdowns must be *fair and reasonable*, and policies can't discriminate among customers. The items that firms should consider follow:

>> The market value of the securities at the time of the trade.

>> The total dollar amount of the transaction. Although you're going to charge more money for a larger transaction, the percentage charged is usually lower.

>> The difficulty of the trade. If you had to jump through hoops to make sure the trade was completed, you're entitled to charge more.

>> The fact that you and the firm that you work for are entitled to make a profit (which is, of course, the reason you got involved in the business to begin with).

You can't take race, ethnicity, religion, gender, sexual orientation, disability, age, funny accents, or how much you like (or dislike) the client into account.

"G" even more rules

Even though a lot of the "G" rules were covered in the Securities Industry Essential exam, FINRA obviously decided that you should know even more.

TIP

The following list isn't as huge as it could be because many of the rules are already covered throughout this book. However, you're not expected to know the minute details of each rule, just the main idea. Fortunately, many of them just make sense. Also, don't worry about the rule numbers; pay more attention to the rule.

>> **Rules G-8 and G-9** (books and records requirements): All brokers, dealers, and municipal securities dealers must keep records regarding municipal securities business. Among the many items they have to keep are the following:

- Records of original entry (blotters): Itemized daily records of all purchases and sales of municipal securities

- Account records: Account records for each customer account

- Securities records: Separate records showing all municipal securities positions

- Subsidiary records: Records of municipal securities in transfer, municipal securities borrowed or loaned, municipal securities transactions not completed by the settlement date, and so on

- Put options and repurchase agreements

- Records for agency transactions

- Records concerning primary offerings

- Copies of confirmations (for more on confirmations, see Chapter 16)

- Customer account information

- Customer complaints

- Records concerning political contributions

TIP

You aren't expected to remember the entire list. Just get a general feeling for what's required. It looks like the MSRB wants the broker-dealer or municipal securities dealer to maintain records of just about everything.

>> **Rule G-9** (preservation of records): MSRB's record-keeping requirements are very similar to but not exactly the same as FINRA's requirements. Most records have to be kept either four or six years. To keep you from pulling your hair out (this coming from a bald man), look at the record-keeping requirements in Chapter 16, where I note how the MSRB rules and FINRA rules are different.

>> **Rule G-11** (primary offering practices): During the underwriting of new municipal securities, the underwriting syndicate must set up a system for allocation of orders (which orders get filled first). In addition, it must indicate conditions that might change the priority for the allocation of orders.

>> **Rule G-12** (uniform practice): Rule G-12 was established to create a uniform practice between municipal securities broker-dealers in how to handle transactions. Included are settlement dates, good delivery requirements, how to handle mutilated certificates, and so on. Most of this information is covered in more detail in Chapter 16.

>> **Rule G-13** (quotations): According to MSRB rules, all quotations for municipal securities published or distributed by any broker-dealer, municipal securities dealer, or person associated with a broker-dealer or municipal securities dealer must be bona fide (genuine).

>> **Rule G-17** (conduct of municipal securities and municipal advisory activities): Municipal securities broker-dealers, municipal securities dealers, municipal advisors, agents, and so on shall deal fairly with all persons and not engage in dishonest, deceptive, or unfair practices.

>> **Rule G-19** (suitability of recommendations and transactions): As with other securities, brokers, dealers, and municipal securities, prior to recommending municipal securities to a customer, must have a reasonable basis to believe that the recommendation is appropriate for the customer. Brokers or dealers must make sure that the recommendation fits the customer's

investment profile. Included in that profile should be the customer's age, other investments, risk tolerance, tax situation, financial situation, investment experience, time horizon, liquidity needs, and so on.

» **Rule G-21** (advertising): Advertisements by municipal securities dealers, brokers, and dealers can't contain false or misleading statements. Advertisements include published material used in electronic or other public media, promotional literature (written or electronic) made available to customers or the public, circulars, market letters, seminar text, press releases, and so on. However, preliminary official statements, official statements, offering circulars, and so on are not considered advertisements.

» **Rule G-27** (supervision): All firms selling municipal securities must have a designated principal to oversee the firm's representatives. In addition, all firms selling municipal securities must create and update as needed a written supervisory procedures manual. Principals are responsible for approving in writing, the opening of all new customer accounts, each municipal securities transaction, the handling of customer complaints and actions taken, correspondence relating to municipal securities trades.

» **Rule G-28** (transactions with employees and partners of other municipal securities professionals): When an employee of a municipal securities firm opens an account at another municipal securities firm, the municipal securities firm opening the account must notify the employing firm in writing. Besides notifying the employing firm, duplicate confirmations must be sent to the employing firm along with complying with any other requests from the employing firm.

» **Rule G-30** (pricing and commissions): If buying or selling municipal securities for a customer on a principal basis (for or from the dealer's inventory), the aggregate price including the markdown or markup must be *fair and reasonable.* If buying or selling municipal securities on an agency basis for a customer, the broker-dealer is responsible for making a reasonable effort to obtain the best price for the customer and the commission charged must be *fair and reasonable* in relation to prevailing market conditions.

» **Rule G-32** (disclosures in connection with primary offerings): When a client purchases a new issue of municipal securities, the client must receive an Official Statement at or prior to the delivery.

If the municipal underwriting was done on a negotiated basis (where the issuer chose the underwriter directly), the municipal firm must disclose the initial offering price, the spread and/or any fee received as a result of the transaction. If the underwriting was done on a competitive (bidding) basis, the spread does not need to be disclosed.

» **Rule G-34** (CUSIP numbers, new issue and market information requirements): For new issues of municipal bonds (whether negotiated or competitive offerings), the managing underwriters must apply to the Committee on Uniform Security Identification Procedures (CUSIP) to receive identification numbers for the bonds for each maturity, if more than one. For negotiated offerings where the underwriter(s) is/are chosen directly, the managing underwriter must apply prior to the pricing of the new municipal issue. For competitive offerings, the managing underwriter must apply after winning the bid. In the event that the municipal issuer hired an advisor, the municipal advisor must apply no later than the business day after the Notice of Sale is published.

» **Rule G-38** (solicitation of municipal securities business): Brokers, dealers, or municipal securities dealers may not provide or agree to provide payment for solicitation of municipal securities business to any person who is not affiliated with the broker, dealer or municipal securities dealer.

Gathering More Municipal Bond Info

As with other investments, you need to be able to locate information if you're going to sell municipal securities to investors. You may find that information about municipal bonds is not as readily available as it is for most other securities. Some municipal bonds are relatively *thin* issues (not many are sold or traded) or may be of interest only to investors in a particular geographic location. This section reviews some of the information that you have to know to ace the Series 7 exam.

The bond resolution (indenture)

A *bond resolution* (indenture) provides investors with contract terms including the coupon rate, years until maturity, collateral backing the bond (if any), and so on. Although not required by law, almost every municipal bond comes with a bond indenture, which is printed on the face of most municipal bond certificates. It makes the bonds more marketable because the indenture serves as a contract between the municipality and a trustee who's appointed to protect the investors' rights. Included in the indenture are the flow of funds (see "Revenue Bonds: Raising Money for Utilities and Such," earlier in this chapter) and any assets that may be backing the issue.

Legal opinion

Printed on the face of municipal bond certificates, the legal opinion is prepared and signed by a *municipal bond counsel* (attorney). The purpose of the legal opinion is to verify that the issue is legally binding on the issuer and conforms to tax laws. Additionally, the legal opinion may state that interest received from the bonds is tax exempt.

REMEMBER

If a bond is stamped *ex-legal*, it does not contain a legal opinion.

Here are the two types of legal opinions:

>> **Qualified legal opinion:** The bond counsel has some reservations about the issue.

>> **Unqualified legal opinion:** The bond counsel is issuing a legal opinion without reservations.

TIP

Normally, you'd think of *qualified* as a good thing and *unqualified* as a bad thing. For legal opinions, think the opposite!

Official statement (OS)

Municipal bonds don't have a prospectus; instead, municipalities provide an official statement. As with prospectuses, official statements come in *preliminary* and *final versions*. The preliminary version of the statement doesn't include an offering price or coupon rate. The *official statement* is the document that the issuer prepares; it states what the funds will be used for, provides information about the municipality, and details how the funds will be repaid. The official statement also includes

>> The offering terms

>> The underwriting spread (see Chapter 5)

- ❯❯ A description of the bonds

- ❯❯ A description of the issuer

- ❯❯ The offering price

- ❯❯ The coupon rate

- ❯❯ The feasibility statement

- ❯❯ The legal opinion

The Bond Buyer

The Bond Buyer, which is published Monday through Friday every week, is a newspaper that provides information about municipal issues, including new municipal bonds. (You can also find it online at www.bondbuyer.com.) Included in *The Bond Buyer* are the following statistics and information:

- ❯❯ **The visible supply:** The total dollar amount of municipal bonds expected to reach the market within the next 30 days

- ❯❯ **The placement ratio:** The percentage of new issues this week as compared to new issues offered for sale the previous week

- ❯❯ **Official notice of sale:** Municipalities looking to accept underwriting bids for new issues of municipal bonds publish the official notice of sale in *The Bond Buyer;* the official notice of sale includes

  - ● When and where bids can be submitted

  - ● The total amount of the sale

  - ● Amount of the good-faith deposit

  - ● The type of bond being offered (GO or revenue)

  - ● Methods for calculating cost (net interest cost or true interest cost)

  - ● The taxes backing the issue

REMEMBER

  Because GO bonds are backed by taxes paid by people living in the municipality, issuers are more likely to take bids by underwriters for GO bonds than for revenue bonds. The winning bid has the lowest net interest cost to the issuer (the lowest interest rate and/or the highest purchase price).

The Bond Buyer also offers some pretty nifty municipal bond indexes. Here they are:

- ❯❯ **The 20-Bond GO Index:** Also called the *Bond Buyer's Index,* this index measures the average yield of 20 municipal GO bonds with 20 years to maturity; all these bonds have a rating of A or better.

TIP

  To help you remember that *The Bond Buyer's* Index has 20 bonds with 20 years to maturity, remember that two *B*s equals two 20s.

>> **The 11 GO Bond Index:** This index should be a nice, easy one for you to remember because it's the average yield of 11 bonds (of course) from the 20-bond index with a rating of AA or better.

>> **The 25 Revenue Bond Index:** Also called the RevDex, this index is the average yield of 25 revenue bonds with 30 years to maturity rated A or better.

>> **The Municipal Bond Index:** Also called the 40-Bond Index, this index is the average dollar price of 40 highly traded GO and revenue bonds with an average maturity of 20 years and a rating of A or better.

Additional info

Along with *The Bond Buyer* (see the preceding section), investors and registered reps can also find additional information about municipal bonds in public newspapers, dealer offering sheets, EMMA, and RTRS.

EMMA

EMMA (Electronic Municipal Market Access; `https://emma.msrb.org`) is a free comprehensive online source of information about municipal bonds (educational materials, official statements, trade information, 529 plan disclosure documents, market information, credit ratings, and so on) and is designed specifically for retail nonprofessional investors. Once an official statement has been submitted to EMMA, a broker-dealer may disclose to investors or potential investors of the security how to view and print out the official statement obtained from EMMA. In the event that the customer wishes the broker-dealer to send a copy of the official statement, the broker-dealer is obligated to do so.

RTRS

RTRS (Real-time Transaction Reporting System) is a system operated by the MSRB where brokers and dealers can report trades of most municipal securities. As you can see from the name of the system, "real time" means that trades must be reported promptly (within 15 minutes). RTRS is open on business days between the hours of 7:30 a.m. and 6:30 p.m. EST. Trades taking place outside of those hours must be reported within 15 minutes of the opening of RTRS the next business day. Transactions reported to RTRS will be used to disclose market activity, prices, and to assess transaction fees.

The following municipal securities transactions do not have to be disclosed to RTRS:

>> Transactions in securities without assigned CUSIP numbers

>> Transactions in municipal fund securities

>> Inter-dealer transactions for principal movement of securities between dealers that are not inter-dealer transactions eligible for comparison in a clearing agency registered with the commission

Testing Your Knowledge

Now that you've learned what you need to know about municipal securities for the Series 7, it's time to see where you stand. Read the questions carefully so that you don't make any mistakes.

1. A municipal special assessment bond is

   (A) a bond backed by charges on the benefited property

   (B) a bond backed by a private user

   (C) a bond backed by excise taxes

   (D) also known as a LTGO

2. Ayla K. is new to investing in municipal bonds, and she's primarily concerned about the safety of her principal and income. Which of the following bonds would be the best recommendation for Ayla?

   (A) IDB bonds

   (B) Revenue bonds

   (C) PHA bonds

   (D) General Obligation bonds

3. Which of the following municipal securities could have a rating of MIG2?

   (A) IDR

   (B) GO

   (C) PHA

   (D) RAN

4. Which of the following WOULD NOT affect the marketability of an outstanding municipal bond issue?

   (A) The rating

   (B) The dated date

   (C) The maturity

   (D) A sinking fund provision

5. All of the following affect the marketability of an outstanding municipal bond EXCEPT

   (A) the rating

   (B) the dated date

   (C) the maturity

   (D) the issuer's name

6. Which of the following types of municipal bond issues is usually underwritten on a competitive basis?

   (A) General obligation

   (B) Revenue

   (C) IDR

   (D) Equipment trust

7. Which of the following municipal securities could have a rating of MIG 2?

    I. PN

    II. Tax exempt commercial paper

    III. TRAN

    IV. IDR

    (A) I and III

    (B) I, II and III

    (C) I, III and IV

    (D) II, III, and IV

8. Municipal bonds issued by each of the following would be triple tax-free EXCEPT

    (A) Puerto Rico

    (B) Washington D.C.

    (C) Guam

    (D) Hawaii

9. Which of the following IS NOT a type of municipal note?

    (A) AON

    (B) TRAN

    (C) PN

    (D) GAN

10. Municipal bonds settle regular way

    (A) on the same day as the trade date

    (B) one business day after the trade date

    (C) two business days after the trade date

    (D) three business days after the trade date

11. An IDB is

    (A) backed by charges on the benefited property

    (B) backed by a private user

    (C) backed by excise taxes

    (D) a bond that requires legislative approval

12. Which of the following municipal bonds allow the municipality to receive tax credit payments from the U.S. Treasury of 35 percent of the amount of interest paid?

    (A) Tax Credit BABs

    (B) Direct Payment BABs

    (C) COPs

    (D) IDRs

13. Which of the following Bond Buyer indexes measures the average price of a group of bonds instead of the average yield?

(A) Municipal Bond Index

(B) Bond Buyer Index

(C) Revenue Bond Index

(D) 11 Bond Index

14. Which source of information for municipal bonds would provide retail investors with electronic copies of official statements?

(A) FGIC

(B) EMMA

(C) RTRS

(D) TM3

15. Municipal bonds typically have a minimum face value of

(A) $100

(B) $1,000

(C) $5,000

(D) $50,000

Answers and Explanations

I'm hoping you just read the chapter and didn't find any of the questions too difficult. Because there are 15 questions, each one is worth 6.7 points each.

1. **A.** Special assessment bonds are issued to fund projects in which only a certain amount of people in the municipality benefit. These could be issued for projects such as adding new sidewalks, new streetlights, a new or upgraded playground, and so on. As such, only the people living in the properties that benefit from the upgrades are charged higher property taxes to back the bonds issued to pay for the upgrades.

2. **C.** Since Ayla is primarily interested in safety of her principal and interest, an agent should recommend PHA bonds. PHA (Public Housing Authority) bonds are generally considered the safest municipal bonds. PHAs are issued by a municipality but are backed by U.S. government subsidies. In the event that the issuer has difficulty paying off the debt, the U.S. government will make up any shortfalls.

3. **D.** MIG (Moody's Investment Grade) is a rating for municipal notes (short-term municipal debt securities). Municipal notes include RANs (revenue anticipation notes), BANs (bond anticipation notes), TANs (tax anticipation notes), TRANs (tax and revenue anticipation notes), GANs (grant anticipation notes), and tax-exempt commercial paper.

4. **B.** Certainly the rating, the maturity, and a sinking fund provision would affect the marketability of a municipal issue. However, the dated date (the first day the bond starts accruing interest) doesn't matter to investors of outstanding bonds.

5. **B.** How marketable (easy to trade) a security is depends on several factors. Certainly the rating matters because higher-rated bonds are more easily traded. The maturity matters because shorter-term bonds are more actively traded. Also, the issuer's name matters because it is important for investors to know if the issuer has a good reputation for paying interest and principal on time. So out of the choices given, the dated date (the first day a bond starts accruing interest) is not a factor because that only matters on the initial offering.

6. **A.** Competitive offerings are ones in which the municipal issuer takes bids from several underwriters to ensure that they get the lowest interest cost to the taxpayers in the community who are backing the bonds. Out of the choices listed, General Obligation (GO) bonds are the only ones backed by taxes. Therefore, although not a requirement, almost all municipal GO bonds are underwritten on a competitive basis.

7. **B.** "MIG" (Moody's Investment Grade) ratings are for municipal notes (short-term municipal securities). Municipal notes include TANs, RANs, TRANs, GANs, BANs, CLNs, PNs, and tax-exempt commercial paper. IDBs (Industrial Development Bonds) are long-term debt securities issued by a municipality backed by a private user.

8. **D.** U.S. territory bonds and bonds issued by federal districts are triple tax-free (exempt from federal, state, and local tax). However, bonds issued by the state of Hawaii are not. The triple tax-free bonds you should be aware of are the ones issued by Puerto Rico, Guam, U.S. Virgin Islands, American Samoa, and Washington D.C.

9. **A.** Municipal notes are short-term (one year or less) debt securities issued by municipalities to cover a short-term need. These include TANs, RANs, TRANs, GANs, BANs, CLNs, PNs, and tax-exempt commercial paper. AON (all or none) is an order qualifier and not a type of municipal note.

10. **C.** Municipal securities trades settle regular way in 2 business days after the trade date (T+2, which is trade date plus 2 business days).

11. **D.** An IDB (Industrial Development Bond) is issued for the construction of a facility for the benefit of a private user. As such, the bonds are backed by lease payments made by that private user (typically a corporation).

12. **B.** Direct Payment BABs (Build America Bonds) are bonds issued to fund infrastructure projects (such as bridges, roads, tunnels) where municipalities receive tax credits from the U.S. Treasury of 35 percent of interest paid to investors. This allows municipalities to issue the bonds with higher coupon rates than usual. In tax credit BABs, the investors receive the tax credit instead of the issuer.

13. **A.** The Municipal Bond Index (40 Bond Index) measures the average dollar price of 40 highly traded GO and revenue bonds with an average maturity of 20 years and a rating of A or better.

14. **B.** EMMA (Electronic Municipal Market Access) provides retail investors with information about municipal securities. EMMA, which is on the MSRB website, also provides retail time price information and indicates if bonds are pre-refunded where there is enough money in the sinking fund to pay off the debt on the first call date.

15. **C.** Typically municipal bonds are sold with a face value of $5,000 although some may even have a face value of up to $100,000.

3

Delving Deeper into Security Investments

Understand the process by which investors open margin accounts to borrow money for purchasing securities.

Discover the role of investment companies in helping investors diversify their portfolios.

Become versed in limited partnerships — their formation, function, structure, tax advantages, and tax disadvantages.

Get to know options, an investment vehicle that allows investors to buy and sell securities at a fixed price.

IN THIS CHAPTER

» **Understanding the specifics of margin accounts**

» **Zoning in on the initial margin requirements**

» **Calculating with long margin accounts**

» **Summing up short margin accounts**

» **Testing your knowledge**

Chapter **9**

Borrowing Money and Securities: The Long and Short of Margin Accounts

Y ou don't necessarily need cold cash to buy securities. Thanks to the wonder of margin accounts, you can borrow money from a broker-dealer to purchase securities or borrow the securities themselves. Margin accounts allow customers to buy more securities from you (as a registered rep) than they otherwise would, thus leading to more money in your pocket (a greater commission). However, margin accounts are not without an additional degree of risk (which a lot of people found out back in 1929). Margin accounts are great if the securities held in the account are going in the right direction but horrible if they aren't. The Securities Industry Essentials exam barely touches margin accounts, but the Series 7 goes into much more detail.

In this chapter, I cover the Series 7 exam topics relating to short and long margin accounts and show you how to put those math skills to use. And of course, I give you plenty of practice questions.

Practice a lot of these questions, because this stuff is tricky. The biggest mistake students make is mixing up the equations for long and short accounts. By doing the equations over and over again, you can avoid this pitfall. Additionally, the more questions you practice now, the easier the calculations will be for you to recall when you're taking the real exam. Besides the questions within the chapter, I've added a quick quiz at the end of the chapter with answers and explanations to help your study.

Getting the Paperwork Out of the Way

Because purchasing or selling short on margin involves extra risk, not only do the accounts (like all accounts) need to be approved by a principal but all customers must receive a risk disclosure document (Margin Disclosure Statement), which outlines those risks and some of the broker-dealer's rules. Some of the items that must be addressed in the Margin Disclosure Statement include the following:

>> Margin investors may lose more than the amount deposited.

>> Investors are not entitled to additional time to meet a margin call.

>> Firm in-house margin and maintenance requirements may be increased at any time without advance notice.

>> The firm may sell securities in the account to meet an unmet margin or maintenance call without contacting the investor.

>> The investor is not entitled to choose which securities should be sold out of the account to meet an unmet margin or maintenance call.

Besides receiving the margin risk disclosure document, the customer must sign a *margin agreement* before any securities can be purchased or sold short on margin. The margin agreement is broken down into three main sections:

>> **The credit agreement:** Because the investors are borrowing money from the broker-dealer to purchase the securities, they're going to be charged interest on that money. The credit agreement discloses the terms for that borrowing, including the interest rate charged, the broker-dealer's method of computation, and situations under which the interest rate may change. The credit agreement may also be referred to as the *interest rate disclosure document*.

>> **The hypothecation agreement:** This agreement states that all the margined securities must be held in street name (a numbered account in the name of the broker-dealer for the benefit of the customer). In addition, it allows the broker-dealer to use a portion of the customer's margined securities as collateral for a bank loan (*rehypothecation*). The hypothecation agreement also allows the broker-dealer to sell securities from the account in the event that equity falls below a certain level.

>> **The loan consent agreement:** The loan consent agreement (loan consent form) gives permission to the broker-dealer to lend a customer's margined securities to other investors or broker-dealers, typically for the short sale of securities.

REMEMBER

Not all accounts can be approved for margin trading. For example, custodial accounts, IRAs, 401(k)s, 403(b)s, and so on, cannot trade on margin.

Introducing Long and Short Margin Accounts

In margin accounts, investors either borrow some money to buy securities or borrow the securities themselves. As a result, margin accounts come in two varieties: long and short.

As you may remember, *long* means *to buy*. With a *long margin account*, the customer buys securities by coming up with a percentage (typically 50 percent) of the purchase price of the securities and borrowing the balance from the broker-dealer. These optimistic investors are hoping for a bull market, because they want to sell the securities sometime later for a profit.

With a *short margin account,* an investor is borrowing securities to immediately sell in the market. The process sounds a bit backward, but the investor is selling securities he doesn't actually own. Hopefully, for this bearish customer, the price of the security or securities will decrease so the investor can purchase the shares in the market at a lower price and then return them to the lender.

REMEMBER

When a customer buys securities, he can purchase the securities in a cash or margin account, but when a customer sells short securities, the transaction *must* be executed in a margin account.

Playing by the Federal Reserve Board's Rules

The Securities Exchange Act of 1934 gives the Federal Reserve Board (FRB) the authority to regulate the extension of credit to customers in the securities industry. In addition to Regulation T (see the following section), the FRB decides which securities can be purchased on margin.

Regulation T

Regulation T is the Federal Reserve Board rule that covers the credit broker-dealers may extend to customers who are purchasing securities. Currently for margin accounts both long and short, Regulation T (Reg T) requires customers to deposit at least 50 percent of the current market value of the securities purchased on margin, and the balance is borrowed from the broker-dealer.

REMEMBER

Regulation T is currently set at 50 percent; however, firms not willing to take as much risk may increase the house margin requirement to 55 percent, 60 percent, 65 percent, and so on. When you're taking the Series 7 exam, you should assume 50 percent unless the question states a different percentage.

Regulation T applies not only to margin accounts but also to *cash accounts* (see Chapter 16). When customers are purchasing securities in cash accounts, they have a certain number of business days to pay for the trade (one, three, or five). This delay is an extension of credit; therefore, it falls under Regulation T.

Reg T also identifies which securities can be purchased on margin and which ones can't. Securities that may be purchased on margin include

» Exchange-listed securities

» Most NASDAQ securities

» Non-NASDAQ over-the-counter (OTC) securities approved by the Federal Reserve Board

Securities that cannot be purchased on margin and cannot be used as collateral include

» Most option positions

» Rights

» Non-NASDAQ over-the-counter (OTC) securities not approved by the Federal Reserve Board

Securities that cannot be purchased on margin but can be used as collateral after being held for 30 days include

>> Mutual funds

>> Certain new issues

TIP

New securities cannot be purchased on margin for at least 30 days. Since mutual funds are always new issues, they cannot be purchased on margin. However, after holding them for 30 days or more, they can be placed in a margin account and used as collateral.

Note: Treasury securities and municipal bonds are exempt from Regulation T. However, they may be purchased on margin. The margin and maintenance requirement on treasury securities typically ranges somewhere between 1 percent and 6 percent of the market value depending on the number of years until maturity. Municipal bonds can be purchased on margin, and the margin and maintenance requirements are set by the brokerage firms based on the risk.

Margin call

A *margin call* (also known as a *Fed call, federal call,* or *Reg T call*) is the broker-dealer's demand for a customer to deposit money in a margin account when purchasing or shorting (selling short) securities. When customers initiate a margin transaction, they'll receive a margin call for the Regulation T amount (usually 50 percent of the purchase or short sale). This amount must typically be paid by the customer within two to five days, which may vary from one firm to another based on their policies. However, if the amount owed is $1,000 or less, the brokerage firm may choose to just add it to the debit balance. If a customer is buying securities on margin, the customer may deposit fully paid marginable securities in lieu of cash to meet the margin call.

For both long and short margin accounts, the margin call is the dollar amount of securities purchased (or shorted) multiplied by Regulation T (50 percent). So, for example, if an investor purchases $50,000 worth of securities on margin, the margin call would be $25,000. Here's how you figure that:

$$\text{margin call} = \text{the current market value of the securities} \times \text{Reg T}$$

$$\text{margin call} = \$50,000 \times 50\% = \$25,000$$

Opening a Margin Account: The Initial Requirements

The initial margin requirements for short and long accounts apply to the *first* transaction in a margin account only. After the account is established, the investor can purchase or short securities just by depositing Regulation T of the current market value of the securities purchased or shorted.

For an initial purchase in a margin account, customers must deposit a minimum of equity in their margin accounts. Currently, Regulation T calls for a minimum deposit of 50 percent of the current market value of the securities purchased or sold short. However, the Financial Industry Regulatory Authority (FINRA) and the New York Stock Exchange (NYSE) call for a minimum deposit of $2,000 or ask customers to pay for the securities in full. (See the section "Starting long accounts" for more on how this works.)

TIP

When you're taking the Series 7, pay attention to the wording of the question. Phrases like "opens a margin account," "in an initial transaction in a margin account," and so on, indicate that the question is asking for the initial margin requirement rather than a margin call. (See the preceding section for info on margin calls.)

>> **Pattern day trading:** If an investor wants to open a *day trading account,* the initial margin requirement is $25,000, and the investor must keep at least $25,000 in equity (minimum equity) to continue trading. A day trading (pattern day trader) account is one in which the investor buys and sells the same security on the same day or sells short and buys the same security on the same day at least four times in five consecutive business days. (More on pattern day trading accounts in Chapter 16.)

>> **Portfolio margin:** This is another type of margin account for investors who have at least $100,000 invested, although some broker-dealers may require more at their discretion. Portfolio margin looks at the actual risk of the securities held as a whole and adjusts the margin requirement accordingly. So investors who purchase safer securities would have a lower margin requirement. By having a lower margin requirement, investors have more leverage and will have increased profits when the value of the securities held are increasing and greater losses when the value of securities held are decreasing.

Starting long accounts

To open a long margin account, the customer is required to deposit Regulation T or $2,000, whichever is greater. The exception to this rule occurs when a customer is purchasing less than $2,000 worth of securities on margin. In this case, the customer pays for the transaction in full. It certainly wouldn't make sense for a customer to purchase $1,000 of securities on margin and pay $2,000 when he could pay $1,000 if it were purchased in a cash account. Even if the customer pays in full, the account is still considered a margin account because the customer can make future purchases on margin as soon as he has over $2,000 in equity.

Table 9-1 shows you how Regulation T and the FINRA/NYSE requirements affect how much customers have to deposit when opening long margin accounts.

TABLE 9-1 **Deposit Requirements for Long Margin Accounts**

Dollar Amount of Purchase	Regulation T Requirement	FINRA/NYSE Requirement	Amount Customer Must Deposit
$6,000	$3,000	$2,000	$3,000
$3,000	$1,500	$2,000	$2,000
$1,000	$500	$1,000	$1,000

REMEMBER

In short, here's how much an investor has to deposit:

Purchase Price	Amount Owed
Initial purchase < $2,000	Full purchase price
$2,000 ≤ initial purchase ≤ $4,000	$2,000
Initial purchase > $4,000	Reg T (50% of market value)

Opening short accounts

The minimum deposit for short accounts is fairly easy to remember. The $2,000 minimum required by FINRA and the NYSE applies to short margin accounts. Because of the additional risk investors take when selling short securities, the $2,000 minimum always applies, even if the customer is selling short only $300 worth of securities. In this case, the customer must deposit 50 percent of the current market value of the securities or $2,000, whichever is greater. Here's the breakdown:

Purchase Price	Amount Owed
Initial purchase ≤ $4,000	$2,000
Initial purchase > $4,000	Reg T (50% of market value)

Calculating Debit and Equity in Long Margin Accounts

The Series 7 asks you to calculate the numbers in a long margin account, which isn't too difficult if you take it one step at a time. The basic long margin account formula is as follows:

$$LMV - DR = EQ$$

In other words, *long market value minus debit balance equals equity.* The following sections describe the variables of this equation.

Long market value . . .

The *long market value* (LMV) is the current market value of the securities purchased in a margin account. The LMV does not remain fixed; it changes as the market value of the securities changes. Certainly, if an investor is long (owns) the securities, he wants the LMV to increase.

When a customer purchases securities on margin, the margin call (the amount the customer has to come up with) is based on the LMV of the securities. With Regulation T set at 50 percent, an investor has to deposit 50 percent of the value of the securities purchased on margin.

. . . Minus debit balance . . .

DR is the *debit balance* (also called the *debit record* or *debit register*); it's the amount of money that a customer owes a brokerage firm after purchasing securities on margin. The debit balance remains the same unless the customer pays back a portion of the amount borrowed by either selling securities in the account or by adding money to the account through dividends or payments.

Note: Although you aren't as likely to see a question about it on the Series 7 exam, the debit balance may be increased by interest charges imposed by the broker-dealer.

So, for example, if an investor purchases $20,000 worth of securities on margin, the debit balance would be $10,000. First you have to determine the margin call:

$$margin\ call = LMV \times Reg\ T$$

$$margin\ call = \$20,000 \times 50\% = \$10,000$$

Then use the margin call and the following formula to determine the debit balance:

$$DR = LMV - \text{margin call}$$

$$DR = \$20,000 - \$10,000 = \$10,000$$

... Equals equity

The *equity* (EQ) is the investor's portion of the account. When an investor initially opens a margin account, the equity is equal to the margin call. However, the equity changes as the market value of the securities in the account increases or decreases. When an investor has more equity than the Regulation T requirement, he has excess equity; if an investor has less equity than the Regulation T requirement, his account is restricted (see the later section "Checking out restricted accounts").

Note: When an investor has excess equity, he develops a line of credit known as a special memorandum account (SMA) (covered in the section "Let the Good Times Roll: Handling Excess Equity" later in the chapter). Remember that the SMA is built into the equity, not an addition to it. When a customer uses or removes the SMA, the equity decreases and the debit balance increases.

Putting it all together

The following question tests your ability to determine the debit balance in a long margin account.

EXAMPLE

Mr. Downey buys 1,000 shares of DEF common stock at $40 in a margin account. After Mr. Downey meets the margin call, what is the debit balance?

(A) $16,000

(B) $20,000

(C) $24,000

(D) $30,000

The correct answer is Choice (B). I know what you're thinking: "This is too easy." If the Series 7 gods are smiling down on you, you may actually get a question this straightforward. However, even if you don't, you still need a starting point, and this is a good one. First, set up the equation:

$$LMV - DR = EQ$$

Mr. Downey purchased $40,000 worth of stock (1,000 shares × $40 per share), so you need to enter $40,000 under the LMV (long market value). Next, figure out how much he needs to pay. Multiply the $40,000 × 50 percent (Regulation T), and you know that Mr. Downey has to come up with $20,000, which goes under the EQ (the investor's portion of the account). If the LMV is $40,000 and the EQ is $20,000, the DR (debit balance) has to be $20,000:

$$\$40,000 - DR = \$20,000$$

$$DR = \$20,000$$

REMEMBER

Brokerage firms who don't want to take as much risk may increase their house requirement above the Regulation T requirement. In this case, use the house requirement in your calculations. So, for example, let's say the house requirement is 60 percent instead of the Regulation T 50 percent, the investor would have to deposit 60 percent of the purchase, which would go to equity (EQ) and the debit balance (DR) would be 40 percent of the purchase.

Making Short Work of Calculations in Short Margin Accounts

On the Series 7 exam, you may be asked to calculate the numbers in a short margin account. You have to start by setting up the formula correctly. The basic short margin account formula is as follows:

$$SMV + EQ = CR$$

In other words, *short market value plus equity equals the credit balance.* The following sections describe the variables of this equation.

REMEMBER

When a customer purchases securities, he has the choice of whether to pay in full or purchase on margin. When a customer is selling short (borrowed) securities, there is no option: The transactions must be executed in a margin account.

Short market value . . .

The *short market value* (SMV) is the current market value of the securities sold short in a margin account. Just as the LMV in a long account varies (see the earlier "Long market value . . ." section), so does the SMV. The SMV changes as the market value of the securities changes. If an investor is short the securities (selling borrowed securities), he wants the SMV to decrease so the investor can repurchase the security or securities held in the short account at a lower price.

When a customer sells short securities on margin, the margin call (the amount the customer has to come up with) is based on the SMV of the securities. With Regulation T set at 50 percent, an investor has to deposit 50 percent of the value of the securities purchased on margin.

REMEMBER

As with long margin accounts, a brokerage firm may decide to increase the house requirement above the Regulation T requirement.

. . . Plus equity . . .

The *equity* (EQ) is the investor's part of the account. When an investor initially opens a short margin account, the equity is equal to $2,000 or Reg T (50 percent of the market value of the security), whichever is greater.

REMEMBER

In a short margin account, the equity increases when the SMV of the securities decreases; when the SMV of the securities increases, the equity decreases.

When an investor has more equity than the Regulation T requirement, he has excess equity and develops an SMA (see the upcoming section titled "Let the Good Times Roll: Handling Excess Equity"); if an investor has less equity than the Reg T requirement, the account is restricted (see "Checking out restricted accounts," later in this chapter).

. . . Equals the credit balance

There's no debit balance (DR) in a short margin account because investors aren't borrowing money; they're borrowing securities. Instead, short margin accounts have a *credit balance* (also called a *credit record, credit register,* or *CR* for short). The credit balance is initially made up of the amount of money the investor received for selling the stock short (the *short market value*) and the amount that the investor had to deposit into the margin account to pay for the trade (the *equity*). The credit balance remains fixed unless the investor removes excess equity, more securities are shorted, or the investor covers some of his short positions.

For example, say that in an initial transaction in a margin account, an investor sells short $50,000 worth of securities with Reg T at 50 percent. First you determine the margin call:

$$\text{margin call} = \text{SMV} \times \text{Reg T (50\%)}$$

$$\text{margin call} = \$50,000 \times 50\% = \$25,000$$

Then you use the margin call and the following formula to determine the credit balance:

$$\text{CR} = \text{SMV} + \text{margin call}$$

$$\text{CR} = \$50,000 + \$25,000 = \$75,000$$

Putting the equation together

The following question tests your ability to determine the credit balance in a short margin account.

EXAMPLE

In an existing short margin account, Melissa Rice sold short 1,000 shares of HIJ common stock at $30. Prior to this transaction, the short market value of securities in the account was $52,000 and the equity was $25,000. What is Melissa's credit balance after the transaction?

(A) $15,000

(B) $45,000

(C) $77,000

(D) $122,000

The answer you want is Choice (D). This question is a little more difficult because the transaction happened in an existing margin account. Prior to this transaction, Melissa had a short market value (SMV) of $52,000 and an equity of $25,000, which means that the CR was $77,000:

$$\text{SMV} + \text{EQ} = \text{CR}$$
$$\$52,000 + \$25,000 = \text{CR}$$

$$\text{CR} = \$77,000$$

Because you know the existing CR, you only need to determine what happened to it as a result of the new transaction. Melissa shorted another $30,000 worth of stock (1,000 shares × $30 per share), so you need to enter $30,000 under the SMV (short market value). Next, figure out how much she needs to pay. Multiply the $30,000 × 50 percent (Regulation T), and you know that Melissa has to come up with $15,000, which goes under the EQ (the investor's portion of the account). If the SMV increases by $30,000 and the EQ increases by $15,000, the CR (credit balance) has to increase by $45,000:

$$\text{SMV} + \text{EQ} = \text{CR}$$
$$\$30,000 + \$15,000 = \text{CR}$$

$$\text{CR} = \$45,000$$

Because the initial credit balance was $77,000 and it increased by $45,000, the credit balance after the transaction is $122,000.

TIP Not all margin customers have only a short margin account or only a long margin account. If you are one of the unlucky ones who gets a question asking for the combined equity of a customer's long and short margin accounts, you can either work out the equations separately, as if they're two different accounts and add the equity together, or use the following equation:

$$LMV + CR - DR - SMV$$

Let the Good Times Roll: Handling Excess Equity

A special memorandum account (SMA) is a line of credit that a customer can borrow from his margin account or use to purchase more securities on margin. If all is right in the universe and the market goes in the right direction, the customer actually has more equity in the margin account than he needs, which generates an SMA. If a customer removes the SMA, he is borrowing money from the margin account; therefore,

>> The equity is reduced for both long and short margin accounts.

>> The debit balance (the amount owed to the brokerage firm) is increased for long margin accounts.

>> The credit balance is decreased for short margin accounts.

REMEMBER After SMA is generated in a long or short account, it doesn't go away until a customer uses it, even if the account becomes restricted (see "Checking out restricted accounts," later in this chapter, for info on restriction). You can think of developing an SMA as establishing credit; after you establish credit (on a credit card, for example), it remains there until you use it.

SMAs for long margin accounts

When an investor purchases on margin, that customer has a leveraged position, so he has an interest in a larger amount of securities than he would've had if he had paid in full. When a customer has a long margin account, excess equity is created when the value of the securities in the account increases and the equity in the account increases above the margin requirement.

The following question tests your ability to answer a question on excess equity.

EXAMPLE Mrs. Glorious purchased 1,000 shares of DUD Corp. on margin at $50 per share. If DUD is currently trading at $70 per share, what is Mrs. Glorious's excess equity?

(A) $5,000

(B) $7,500

(C) $10,000

(D) $20,000

The answer you're looking for is Choice (C). This question throws you a little curveball because you have to set up a new equation when the market price changes. You first need to find the debit balance. Mrs. Glorious purchased $50,000 worth of securities (1,000 shares × $50 per share), so enter $50,000 under the LMV (long market value). Then Mrs. Glorious had to deposit the

Regulation T amount (50 percent) of the purchase, so enter $25,000 (50% × $50,000) under the EQ (the investor's portion of the account). This means she borrowed $25,000 (the DR) from the broker-dealer:

$$LMV - DR = EQ$$
$$\$50,000 - DR = \$25,000$$

$$DR = \$25,000$$

Now the curveball: The LMV changes to $70,000 ($70 × 1,000 shares). Because the DR (the amount borrowed from the broker-dealer) doesn't change, you bring the $25,000 to your new equation. You find that the EQ has increased to $45,000:

$$LMV - DR = EQ$$
$$\cancel{\$50,000 - \$25,000 = \$25,000}$$
$$\$70,000 - \$25,000 = \$45,000$$

Now multiply the LMV by Regulation T to get the margin requirement, the amount that Mrs. Glorious should have in EQ to be at 50 percent. Take the $35,000 ($70,000 × 50%) and compare it to the EQ. Because Mrs. Glorious has $45,000 in equity, she has $10,000 in excess equity ($10,000 more than she needs):

$$LMV - DR = EQ$$
$$\cancel{\$50,000 - \$25,000 = \$25,000}$$
$$\$70,000 - \$25,000 = \$45,000$$
$$\underline{(50\% \times \$70,000) = \$35,000}$$
$$\$10,000 \text{ excess equity}$$

REMEMBER

The *R* in *DR* should help you remember that the debit balance remains the same as the market price changes.

Some of the margin questions on the Series 7 exam will be related to what happens to SMA during certain events. Remember that when the SMA increases, so does the buying power. Table 9-2 makes it a little easier to see.

TABLE 9-2 **What Happens to SMA?**

Event	SMA	What happens
Deposit of marginable securities	Increases	SMA is increased by the loan value of the securities (usually 50% of the market value).
Receipt of cash dividends or earned interest	Increases	100% of the dividend or interest is added to SMA.
Liquidation of securities in the account	Increases	The investor may take the greater of the excess equity in the account after the sale or 50% of the sale proceeds.
Cash withdrawal	Decreases	SMA decreases by the full amount of the cash withdrawal.
Purchase of marginable securities	Decreases	The margin requirement (usually 50%) of the securities purchased is deducted from the SMA. If the SMA is not sufficient to meet the margin requirement, the investor must deposit cash or fully paid marginable securities to meet the call.

If an investor intends to use or withdraw her SMA, it can only be used to the extent that it won't drop the account below minimum maintenance. (See "Keeping up with minimum maintenance" later in the chapter.)

Loan value

Loan value is the compliment of Regulation T. So, with regulation T set at 50 percent, the loan value is also 50 percent (100% – 50% Regulation T = 50% loan value). Basically, this represents the maximum amount the brokerage firm will lend to a customer based on securities purchased in a margin account. As the value increases (or decreases in a short account), the loan value would increase.

Let's say the customer initially purchased $20,000 of securities on margin; the loan value would be $10,000 (50 percent of $20,000). If the value of the securities increased to $26,000, the loan value would increase to $13,000 (50 percent of $26,000).

Note: As stated earlier in this chapter, you can deposit fully paid marginable securities to meet a margin call. So if you have a margin call of $5,000, you have to deposit fully paid marginable securities with a loan value of $5,000 to meet the margin call. With Regulation T set at 50 percent, the customer would have to deposit $10,000 of fully paid marginable securities to meet the margin call. Because Regulation T is set at 50 percent, 50 percent of the $10,000 in securities would be used to meet the margin call.

SMAs for short margin accounts

Unlike in a long account, an investor with a short margin account earns excess equity when the price of the securities in the margin account decreases. An SMA is a credit line that investors can withdraw as cash or use to help purchase or sell short more securities on margin.

Excess equity is the amount of equity that a customer has in a margin account that's above the Regulation T requirement.

The following question tests your knowledge on determining excess equity for a short account.

Mrs. Rice sold short 1,000 shares of HIJ Corp. on margin at $60 per share. If HIJ is currently trading at $50 per share, what is Mrs. Rice's excess equity?

(A) $5,000

(B) $7,500

(C) $10,000

(D) $15,000

The correct answer is Choice (D). This question has a twist because you have to use a new equation when the market price changes. Start by setting up the equation to find the credit balance. Mrs. Rice sold short $60,000 worth of securities (1,000 shares × $60 per share), so enter $60,000 under the SMV (short market value). Then Mrs. Rice had to deposit the Regulation T amount (50 percent) of the purchase, so enter $30,000 (50% × $60,000) under the EQ (the investor's portion of the account). The credit balance (CR) is $90,000:

$$\text{SMV} + \text{EQ} = \text{CR}$$
$$\$60,000 + \$30,000 = \text{CR}$$

$$\text{CR} = \$90,000$$

Next, the SMV changes to $50,000 ($50 × 1,000 shares), so you need to calculate the investor's current equity. Put that value under the SMV. In a short account, the CR remains the same as the market price changes, so you need to bring the $90,000 straight down from the previous equation. This means that the EQ has increased to $40,000 (the difference between $50,000 and $90,000):

$$\text{SMV} \quad + \quad \text{EQ} \quad = \text{CR}$$
$$\cancel{\$60,000 + \$30,000 = \$90,000}$$
$$\$50,000 + \$40,000 = \$90,000$$

Now multiply the SMV by Regulation T to get the amount that Mrs. Rice should have in equity to be at 50 percent. Compare the margin requirement of $25,000 ($50,000 × 50%) to the current equity. Because Mrs. Rice has $40,000 in equity, she has $15,000 in excess equity ($15,000 more than she needs):

$$\text{SMV} \quad + \quad \text{EQ} \quad = \text{CR}$$
$$\cancel{\$60,000 + \$30,000 = \$90,000}$$
$$\$50,000 + \$40,000 = \$90,000$$
$$\underline{(50\% \times \$50,000) = \$25,000}$$
$$\$15,000 \text{ excess equity}$$

TIP

The *R* in *CR* should help you remember that the credit balance remains the same as the market price changes.

Playing it SMA/RT: Using buying and shorting power for good

Buying power (for long accounts) and *shorting power* (for short accounts) are the dollar amounts of securities a customer can purchase on margin using his excess equity (SMA). You calculate both by dividing the SMA by Reg T:

$$\text{buying } or \text{ shorting power} = \frac{\text{SMA}}{\text{Reg T}}$$

REMEMBER

To help you calculate the buying or shorting power in a margin account, remember the phrase *People who are SMA/RT use their buying (or shorting) power.* This phrase can help you remember that to determine the buying or shorting power, you need to divide the SMA by Regulation T. As long as Regulation T is at 50 percent, you probably don't need this tip because the power will always be double the SMA (for example, $1,000 SMA can purchase $2,000 worth of securities on margin). However, if Regulation T (or house requirements) is anything other than 50 percent, this formula becomes very important.

Try your hand at the following question.

EXAMPLE

Mr. Smith has a long margin account with a market value of $20,000, a debit balance of $5,000, an equity of $15,000, and an SMA of $3,000. If Regulation T is set at 60 percent, what is the buying power?

(A) $3,000

(B) $5,000

(C) $6,000

(D) No buying power

The right answer is Choice (B). Because the question is nice enough to supply you with the SMA, you don't have to figure it on your own. The buying power of a margin account is how much in securities an investor can buy (or sell short) without depositing additional funds. All you need to do is divide the SMA by Regulation T:

$$\text{buying power} = \frac{\text{SMA}}{\text{Reg T}} = \frac{\$3,000}{60\%} = \$5,000$$

Buying power for pattern day trading accounts

With pattern day trading accounts, the minimum maintenance is 25 percent, just like regular customers. However, the buying power is treated a little differently. For pattern day traders, the buying power is four times the maintenance margin excess (equity in the account above the 25 percent minimum requirement). For regular margin accounts, the buying power is two times the SMA.

Note: Pattern day traders are prohibited from using *cross guarantees* and must meet the margin or maintenance requirements of the account independently. In other words, another investor's account (even with a written agreement) or even another account owned by the pattern day trader cannot be used to meet margin requirements.

Looking at Limits When the Market Goes the Wrong Way

Often, securities don't go in the direction customers hope for. When this happens in a margin account, investors lose money at an accelerated rate. If the equity in a margin account drops below the Regulation T (or house) requirement, the account becomes restricted. However, if the equity in a long margin account drops below 25 percent (30 percent for a short account), the situation becomes much more serious. Read on for info on restricted accounts and minimum maintenance.

Checking out restricted accounts

In the previous sections, everything is coming up roses; but what if the market price of the securities held in a long margin account decreases instead of increases? What if the securities in a short margin account show wild success? If this happens, the account becomes restricted. *Restricted accounts* show up when the equity in the account is below the margin requirement. However, a restricted account doesn't mean that investors can't buy (or short) securities in the margin account; investors may still do so by coming up with the margin requirement of the new purchase.

Restricted long margin accounts

A restricted account is calculated the same way as the excess equity (as discussed in the earlier section "Let the Good Times Roll: Handling Excess Equity"), but the investor has less than 50 percent of the long market value (LMV) in equity instead of more than 50 percent. Check out the following example.

EXAMPLE

Macy Bullhorn purchased 500 shares of LMN common stock on margin when LMN was trading at $30 per share. If LMN is currently trading at $25 per share, by how much is Macy's margin account restricted?

(A) $1,250

(B) $2,500

(C) $5,000

(D) $6,250

The correct answer is Choice (A). You may notice the similarities between figuring out excess equity and determining whether an account is restricted. If an account is restricted, the account contains less equity than needed to be at 50 percent of the LMV. First, figure out Macy's debit balance. Macy purchased $15,000 worth of securities (500 shares × $30 per share), so enter $15,000 under the LMV (long market value). Then Macy had to deposit the Reg T amount (50 percent) of the purchase, so enter $7,500 (50% × $15,000) under the EQ (the investor's portion of the account). She borrowed $7,500 (the DR) from the broker-dealer:

$$LMV - DR = EQ$$
$$\$15,000 - DR = \$7,500$$

$$DR = \$7,500$$

Next, find the investor's current equity. The LMV changes to $12,500 ($25 × 500 shares), so enter that under the LMV. Because the DR (the amount borrowed from the broker-dealer) doesn't change, bring the $7,500 straight down from the preceding equation. You find that the EQ has decreased to $5,000 ($12,500 − $7,500):

$$LMV - DR = EQ$$
$$\cancel{\$15,000 - \$7,500 = \$7,500}$$
$$\$12,500 - \$7,500 = \$5,000$$

Now multiply the LMV by Reg T to get the margin requirement, the amount Macy should have in equity to be at 50 percent. Take the $6,250 ($12,500 × 50%) and compare it to the current equity. Because Macy has only $5,000 in equity, her account is restricted by $1,250:

$$LMV - DR = EQ$$
$$\cancel{\$15,000 - \$7,500 = \$7,500}$$
$$\$12,500 - \$7,500 = \$5,000$$
$$\underline{(50\% \times \$12,500) = \$6,250}$$
$$(\$1,250) \text{ restricted}$$

REMEMBER

You can calculate the excess equity (SMA) or determine whether an account is restricted in pretty much the same way. If the investor has more equity than needed, it's an SMA; if the investor has less than needed, the account is restricted.

Restricted short margin accounts

If the market price of the securities held in a short margin account increases instead of decreasing, the situation isn't so great. When this happens, the account becomes restricted. You can figure out whether the account is restricted the same way you figure out the excess equity, only the investor has less than 50 percent of the SMV in equity instead of more than 50 percent.

The following question tests your knowledge of restricted short accounts.

Mr. Willing sold short 400 shares of RST common stock on margin at $40 per share. If RST is currently trading at $44 per share, how much is the account restricted?

(A) $2,400

(B) $6,400

(C) $8,800

(D) $16,000

The answer you want is Choice (A). First, figure out the credit balance. Mr. Willing sold short $16,000 worth of securities (400 shares × $40 per share), so enter $16,000 under the SMV (short market value). Then Mr. Willing had to deposit the Reg T amount (50 percent) of the purchase, so enter $8,000 (50% × $16,000) under the EQ (the investor's portion of the account). You find that the credit balance (CR) is $24,000:

$$\text{SMV} + \text{EQ} = \text{CR}$$
$$\$16,000 + \$8,000 = \text{CR}$$

$$\text{CR} = \$24,000$$

Next, find Mr. Willing's current equity. The SMV changes to $17,600 ($44 × 400 shares), so you need to put that under the SMV in a new equation. In a short account, the CR remains the same as the market price changes, so you need to bring the $24,000 straight down from the preceding equation. You can see that the EQ has decreased to $6,400 (the difference between $17,600 and $24,000):

$$\text{SMV} + \text{EQ} = \text{CR}$$
$$\cancel{\$16,000 + \$8,000 = \$24,000}$$
$$\$17,600 + \$6,400 = \$24,000$$

Now multiply the SMV by Regulation T to get the amount Mr. Willing should have in equity to be at 50 percent. Take the $8,800 ($17,600 × 50%) and compare it to the EQ. Because Mr. Willing has only $6,400 in equity ($2,400 less than the Reg T requirement), his account is restricted by $2,400:

$$\text{SMV} + \text{EQ} = \text{CR}$$
$$\cancel{\$16,000 + \$8,000 = \$24,000}$$
$$\$17,600 + \$6,400 = \$24,000$$
$$(50\% \times 17,600) = \underline{\$8,800}$$
$$(\$2,400) \text{ restricted}$$

Keeping up with minimum maintenance

A margin account can be left restricted, but if a margin account falls below minimum maintenance, the situation is much more serious. Customers then have to deal with a *maintenance call* (or *maintenance margin call* or *Fed call*), which requires investors to deposit money into the margin account immediately, or in stockbroker lingo, *promptly*.

Minimum maintenance on a long account

Minimum maintenance on a long margin account is 25 percent of the long market value. I'm sure that you'll be happy to know that the calculations are the same as for restricted accounts (see the preceding sections) until you get to the last step. Try the following question.

Mark Smithers III purchased 1,000 shares of UVW common stock on margin when UVW was trading at $55 per share. If UVW is currently trading at $35 per share, what is the maintenance call?

(A) $1,250

(B) $7,500

(C) $8,750

(D) $10,000

The right answer is Choice (A). You may notice that the equation looks almost exactly the same as the previous two examples except for the last step. An account may be left restricted, but if it falls below minimum maintenance, the customer must come up with enough money, deposit enough fully paid securities, or sell enough margined securities to bring the account above minimum maintenance right away.

First, use the market value at the time of purchase to determine the debit balance. Mark purchased $55,000 worth of securities (1,000 shares × $55 per share), so enter $55,000 under the LMV (long market value). Then Mark had to deposit the Reg T amount (50 percent) of the purchase, so enter $27,500 (50% × $55,000) under the EQ (the customer's portion of the account). You find that he borrowed $27,500 (the DR) from the broker-dealer:

$$LMV - DR = EQ$$
$$\$55,000 - DR = \$27,500$$

$$DR = \$27,500$$

Then find Mark's current equity. The LMV changed to $35,000 ($35 × 1,000 shares), so you need to put that value under the LMV. Because the DR (the amount borrowed from the broker-dealer) doesn't change, you bring the $27,500 straight down. Therefore, the EQ has decreased to $7,500:

$$LMV - DR = EQ$$
$$\cancel{\$55,000 - \$27,500 = \$27,500}$$
$$\$35,000 - \$27,500 = \$7,500$$

Now multiply the LMV by the 25 percent minimum maintenance requirement to get the amount Mark should have in equity to be at minimum maintenance. Take the $8,750 ($35,000 × 25%) and compare it to the current equity. Because Mark has only $7,500 in equity, he'll receive a maintenance call of $1,250:

$$LMV - DR = EQ$$
$$\cancel{\$55,000 - \$27,500 = \$27,500}$$
$$\$35,000 - \$27,500 = \$7,500$$
$$(25\% \times \$35,000) = \underline{\$8,750}$$
$$(\$1,250) \text{ maintenance call}$$

Minimum maintenance on a short account

As with long margin accounts, short margin accounts can be left restricted, but if a margin account falls below minimum maintenance, the customer gets hit with a maintenance call. Minimum maintenance on a short margin account is 30 percent of the current market value. The rest of the calculations are similar to figuring out the SMA or how much the account is restricted (see "Checking out restricted accounts," earlier in this chapter) until you get to the last step.

Minimum maintenance for a long account is 25 percent of the current market value, and minimum maintenance on a short account is 30 percent of the current market value.

The following question tests your knowledge in determining the maintenance call for short accounts.

Mrs. Martinez sold short 1,000 shares of XYZ common stock on margin at $50 per share. If XYZ is currently trading at $60 per share, what is the maintenance call?

(A) $0

(B) $2,000

(C) $3,000

(D) $8,000

The correct answer is Choice (C). First, find Mrs. Martinez's credit balance. Mrs. Martinez sold short $50,000 worth of securities (1,000 shares × $50 per share), so enter $50,000 under the SMV (short market value). Then Mrs. Martinez had to deposit the Reg T amount (50 percent) of the purchase, so enter $25,000 (50% × $50,000) under the EQ (the investor's portion of the account). The credit balance (CR) is $75,000:

$$\text{SMV} + \text{EQ} = \text{CR}$$
$$\$50,000 + \$25,000 = \text{CR}$$

$$\text{CR} = \$75,000$$

Next, find Mrs. Martinez's current equity. The SMV changed to $60,000 ($60 × 1,000 shares), so you need to put that value under the SMV. In a short account, the CR remains the same as the market price changes, so the CR is $75,000. Therefore, the equity has decreased to $15,000:

$$\text{SMV} + \text{EQ} = \text{CR}$$
$$\cancel{\$50,000 + \$25,000 = \$75,000}$$
$$\$60,000 + \$15,000 = \$75,000$$

Now multiply the SMV by 30 percent to get the amount Mrs. Martinez should have in equity to be at minimum maintenance. Take the $18,000 ($60,000 × 30%) and compare it to the equity. Because Mrs. Martinez has only $15,000 in equity, she'll receive a maintenance call of $3,000:

$$\text{SMV} + \text{EQ} = \text{CR}$$
$$\cancel{\$50,000 + \$25,000 = \$75,000}$$
$$\$60,000 + \$15,000 = \$75,000$$
$$\underline{(30\% \times \$60,000) = \$18,000}$$
$$(\$3,000) \text{ maintenance call}$$

Testing Your Knowledge

So you had a little more math in this chapter. Here are 10 questions to help you in your quest to pass the Series 7. Read them carefully so that you don't make any mistakes.

1. An investor would like to open a margin account by purchasing 100 shares of LMN at $14. How much would the investor have to deposit?

    (A) $700

    (B) $1,400

    (C) $2,000

    (D) $2,800

2. As an initial transaction in a margin account, an investor purchased 1,000 shares of ABC at $40 with Regulation T at 50%. Two months later, ABC increased to $60.What is the investor's equity?

   (A) 10,000

   (B) 20,000

   (C) 30,000

   (D) 40,000

3. An investor has a margin account with $45,000 in securities, a debit balance of $20,000, and equity of $25,000. With Regulation T at 50%, how much does this investor have in excess equity?

   (A) $0

   (B) $2,250

   (C) $2,500

   (D) $5,000

4. Which TWO of the following are TRUE regarding margin accounts?

   I. Minimum maintenance on a long account is 25% of the current market value

   II. Minimum maintenance on a short account is 25% of the current market value

   III. Minimum maintenance on a long account is 30% of the current market value

   IV. Minimum maintenance on a short account is 30% of the current market value

   (A) I and III

   (B) I and IV

   (C) II and III

   (D) II and IV

5. Declan K. would like to open a margin account by selling short 200 shares of OOOP common stock at $7 per share. What is the margin call?

   (A) $700

   (B) $1,400

   (C) $2,000

   (D) Cannot be determined

6. Alyssa has a long margin account with a market value of $30,000, a debit balance of $10,000, an equity of $20,000, and an SMA of $5,000. What is the buying power?

   (A) $2,500

   (B) $5,000

   (C) $10,000

   (D) $20,000

7. Which TWO of the following are TRUE regarding SMA?

    I. 50% of dividends or interest received in a margin account go to SMA

    II. 100% of dividends or interest received in a margin account go to SMA

    III. When an investor withdraws cash from a margin account, the SMA is reduced by 50% of the withdrawal

    IV. When an investor withdraws cash from a margin account, the SMA is reduced by 100% of the withdrawal

    (A) I and III

    (B) I and IV

    (C) II and III

    (D) II and IV

8. With Regulation T at 50%, the loan value is

    (A) 50%

    (B) 100%

    (C) 25%

    (D) 30%

9. Mrs. Rice purchased 500 shares of TUV common stock on margin at $30 per share. If TUV is currently trading at $22 per share, how much is the account restricted?

    (A) $2,000

    (B) $2,500

    (C) $4,000

    (D) $5,500

10. A client opens a margin account by selling short 1,000 shares of DIMCO common stock at $30 per share. Six months later with DIMCO trading at $26 per share, how much does this client have in excess equity?

    (A) $0

    (B) $2,000

    (C) $4,000

    (D) $6,000

Answers and Explanations

If you did well your first time through, kudos to you. Because there are 10 questions, each one is worth 10 points.

1. **B.** If the investor was purchasing the stock in an existing margin account, she would only have to deposit Regulation T (50%) of the amount of stock purchased. However, since she is opening the margin account, she must deposit the full $1,400 (100 shares × $14). If the initial purchase was over $2,000, she would have to deposit the greater of 50% of the purchase, or $2,000. For purchases in a new margin account that are less than $2,000, investors must pay for the purchase in full.

2. **B.** With Regulation T at 50%, the investor would have to deposit 50% of the amount of the securities purchased, which sets up the following equation:

$$\text{LMV} - \text{DR} = \text{EQ}$$
$$\$40{,}000 - \$20{,}000 = \$20{,}000$$

So initially, the investor purchased $40,000 ($40 × 1,000 shares) worth of securities, so the LMV (Long Market Value) is $40,000. With Regulation T set at 50%, the investor had to come up with $20,000 ($40,000 × 50%), which is the investor's EQ (equity). This means that the investor borrowed the other $20,000 from the broker-dealer, which is the DR (debit balance). If the value of the securities increased to $60,000 ($60 × 1,000 shares) change the LMV to $60,000. So with the DR remaining the same, the EQ had to increase to $40,000.

$$\text{LMV} - \text{DR} = \text{EQ}$$
$$\cancel{\$40{,}000 - \$20{,}000 = \$20{,}000}$$
$$\$60{,}000 - \$20{,}000 = \$40{,}000$$

3. **C.** Remember, for this investor to be properly margined, he must have at least 50% of the current market value (CMV) in equity (EQ). That equation looks like this:

$$\text{Margin requirement} = \text{Regulation T} \times \text{CMV}$$
$$\text{Margin requirement} = 50\% \times \$45{,}000 = \$22{,}500$$

Next, to determine the excess equity (SMA – Special Memorandum Account), use the following equation:

$$\text{SMA} = \text{EQ} - \text{Margin requirement}$$
$$\text{SMA} = \$25{,}000 - \$22{,}500 = \$2{,}500$$

Remember, the SMA is excess equity that can be withdrawn or used to purchase additional securities.

4. **B.** Minimum maintenance on a long account is 25% of the current market value (CMV), and minimum maintenance on a short account is 30% of the CMV.

5. **C.** When an investor is opening a margin account by selling short, the investor must deposit $2,000 or Regulation T (usually 50%) or the dollar value of the securities being sold short, whichever is greater. In this case, Declan is only shorting $1,400 (200 shares × $7 per share), so he must deposit $2,000.

6. **C.** Buying power is the amount of securities an investor can purchase or short on margin with their excess equity. This investor has $5,000 in excess equity (SMA – Special Memorandum Account), so this investor can purchase or short another $10,000 worth of securities on margin. The equation looks like this:

$$\text{buying power} = \frac{\text{SMA}}{\text{Reg T}} = \frac{\$5,000}{50\%} = \$10,000$$

Remember, unless told differently, you can assume that Regulation T (Reg T) is 50%.

7. **D.** When receiving dividend or interest on securities held in a margin account, 100% of the dividends and/or interest received goes to the SMA (Special Memorandum Account). Also, when withdrawing cash from a margin account, the SMA is reduced by the full amount of the withdrawal.

8. **A.** The loan value is the amount of money the broker-dealer can lend a customer with a margin account. The loan value is based off of Regulation T or the house requirement if higher than Regulation T. So if Regulation T is set at 50%, the broker-dealer can lend the customer the other 50%.

9. **A.** When securities held in a margin account go the opposite direction of what the investor was anticipating, the account can become restricted. A restricted account just means that the equity (EQ) in the account drops below the Regulation T (Reg T = 50%) requirement. The investor would not be required to deposit any additional money if the account becomes restricted unless the account drops below minimum maintenance. So to see where Mrs. Rice stands, set up the account as follows:

$$\text{LMV} - \text{DR} = \text{EQ}$$
$$\cancel{\$15,000 - \$7,500 = \$7,500}$$
$$\$11,000 - \$7,500 = \$3,500$$
$$(\$11,000 \times 50\%) = \underline{\$5,500}$$
$$(\$2,000) \text{ restricted}$$

Initially, Mrs. Rice purchased $15,000 (500 shares at $30) worth of securities on margin, which means that the LMV (Long Market Value) is $15,000. With Reg T at 50%, she had to deposit $7,500 ($15,000 × 50%) to meet the margin call. This means that the equity (EQ) is $7,500. This also means that she had to borrow $7,500 (the DR) from the broker-dealer. Next, the long market value dropped to $11,000 (500 shares × $22 per share). The DR remains the same, so the EQ had to drop to $3,500. Next, multiply the LMV by 50% to see what the EQ should be for Mrs. Rice to be at the 50% margin requirement. To be at 50% of the LMV, Mrs. Rice should have $5,500 in EQ. Since she only has $3,500, the account is restricted by $2,000 ($5,500 – $3,500).

10. **D.** This client would have to deposit 50% (the Regulation T requirement) of the amount of securities shorted. Because the investor is shorting $30,000 ($30 × 1,000) shares, she would have to deposit $15,000 ($30,000 × 50%) to meet the call. Start by setting up the equation like this:

$$\text{SMV} + \text{EQ} = \text{CR}$$
$$\$30,000 + \$15,000 = \$45,000$$

The SMV (short market value) is $30,000. The EQ (Equity) is the 50% that the investor had to deposit as a result of shorting the securities. The CR (credit balance) is the total when adding the SMV + EQ.

$$\begin{array}{ccccc} \text{SMV} & + & \text{EQ} & = & \text{CR} \\ \cancel{\$30,000} & + & \cancel{\$15,000} & = & \cancel{\$45,000} \\ \$26,000 & + & \$19,000 & = & \$45,000 \end{array}$$

$$(\$26,000 \times 50\%) = \underline{\$13,000}$$

$$\$6,000 \text{ excess equity}$$

The stock price dropped to $26, so you have to change the SMV to $26,000 ($26 × $1,000). Because the CR remains the same as the SMV changes, the EQ had to increase to $19,000 ($45,000 − $26,000) to make the equation balance. Next, take the $26,000 SMV and multiply it by 50% and you'll see that the investor only needs to have $13,000 in EQ to be at 50% of the SMV. Since the EQ is $19,000, the investor has $6,000 in excess equity (SMA), which can be withdrawn as cash or used to purchase or short more securities.

IN THIS CHAPTER

» **Taking advantage of management investment companies**

» **Understanding face-amount certificate companies and UITs**

» **Reviewing REITs**

» **Looking at annuities**

» **Examining life insurance**

» **Reviewing investment company rules**

» **Testing your knowledge**

Chapter **10**

Packaged Securities: Open- and Closed-End Funds and Such

Diversification is key when you're helping customers set up a portfolio of securities, and it's fairly easy for customers who have a good deal of money to invest. But what about investors who have limited resources? Certainly, such investors can't afford to buy several different securities, and you don't want to limit your customer to only one (heaven forbid it should go belly up). Packaged securities to the rescue! These securities, such as open-end funds, closed-end funds, face-amount certificate companies, UITs, real estate investment trusts (REITs), and annuities, offer variety within one security by investing a customer's money in a diversified pool of securities . . . for a cost, of course. A bit of profit-driven teamwork can ensure your customers' investments are much safer than, say, the blackjack tables in Vegas or daily scratching of lottery cards.

In this chapter, I cover topics relating to investment companies, REITs, and annuities. Open-end (mutual) funds and closed investment funds are only the beginning. I also discuss face-amount certificate companies and trusts like unit investment trusts (UITs). The "Investment Company Rules" section at the end of this chapter can help you round out your studies, and the practice questions in this chapter may put you in that question-answering mood. You'll notice, as with other chapters, that there is a bit of an overlap between the information you learned when taking the Securities Industry Essentials exam and the information you'll see in this chapter. At the end of the chapter, I put together a quick little quiz with detailed explanations to test your knowledge.

Diversifying through Management Investment Companies

The Investment Company Act of 1940 divides investment companies into three main types: management investment companies, face-amount certificate companies, and unit investment trusts. This section focuses on management investment companies, which the Series 7 tests more than the other types. I cover the other types in the aptly named "Considering Other Investment Company Options" section later on.

Management investment companies are either open-end or closed-end funds. Management companies are, by far, the most familiar type of investment company. The securities held by the management companies are actively managed by portfolio managers.

Comparing open- and closed-end funds

Management companies have to be either open-end or closed-end funds. Make sure you know the difference between the two.

Open-end (mutual) funds

An open-end fund is more commonly known as a mutual fund. As with closed-end funds, *mutual funds* invest in many different securities to provide diversification for investors. The key difference is that mutual funds are constantly issuing and redeeming shares, which provides liquidity for investors. Because open-end fund shares are continuous offerings of new shares, a mutual fund prospectus must always be available. You need to understand the makings of the net asset value and the public offering price when taking the Series 7 exam:

>> **Net asset value (NAV):** Fortunately, the net asset value or net asset value per share is determined the same way for both open- and closed-end funds — by dividing the value of the securities held by the fund by the number of shares outstanding; however, with open-end funds, the NAV is the bid price. When investors redeem shares of a mutual fund, they receive the NAV. Mutual funds can't ever trade below the NAV. Most open-end funds calculate the NAV at the end of the trading day.

>> **Public offering price (POP):** For mutual funds, the public offering price (the ask price) is the NAV plus a sales charge.

If a mutual fund doesn't charge a sales charge, it's called a *no-load fund*.

REMEMBER

Because mutual funds are new issues, investors must receive a prospectus (for more on what a prospectus is, see Chapter 5) and/or a *summary prospectus*. Certainly prospectuses for mutual funds include their holdings, investment strategy, fees, expenses, graphs of the fund's performance, and so on. Every prospectus for every security must contain a disclosure stating that the SEC does not approve of the issue. I assume that this is the SEC's way of not being sued if investors lose money. The SEC just clears the issue.

If the fund provides a summary prospectus, it must include items like the fund's name and ticker symbol, the class of shares, the fund's investment strategies, investment objectives, costs of investing, investment advisors, financial compensation, risks, performance, and so on. The summary prospectus may include an application that investors can use to purchase shares. Potential investors can also request a full prospectus prior to investing. If an investor purchases via a summary prospectus, he must either receive or be provided online access to a full prospectus.

On an ongoing basis, funds must include in their prospectus annual report graphs comparing the performance of the fund to a proper index (S&P 500, NASDAQ composite, and so on), items and/ or strategies that may have affected the performance in the past year, and the name of the fund's manager.

Note: Expenses of a mutual fund include salaries for the board of directors; management (investment advisor) fees for the person or persons making the investment decisions for the fund; custodial fees for the safeguarding of assets (cash, securities, and so on) held by the fund; transfer agent fees for keeping track of investors, sending distributions, and sending proxies; and 12b-1 fees if any 12b-1 fees are fees paid by a mutual fund out of the fund assets to cover promotional expenses such as advertising, printing, and mailing of prospectuses to new investors, and so on. If there are 12b-1 fees, they must be included in the prospectus.

In addition to a prospectus, mutual fund investors may request a *Statement of Additional Information* (SAI). The SAI provides more detail about the fund and its investment risks and investment policies. The SAI is not sent automatically. However, if requested, the SAI must be delivered within 3 business days.

Closed-end funds

Unlike open-end funds, closed-end funds have a fixed number of shares outstanding (hence the word *closed*). Closed-end funds act more like common stock than open-end funds because they issue new shares to the public, and after that, the shares are bought and sold in the market. Because they trade in the market, they're often called *publicly traded funds*. Although the net asset value of closed-end and open-end funds is calculated the same, the public offering price is determined a little differently:

>> **Net asset value (NAV):** The net asset value or net asset value per share is the parity price where the fund should be trading. You determine it by taking all of the assets owned by the fund, subtracting the liabilities, and dividing it by the number of shares outstanding. Closed-end funds may trade at a discount or premium compared to the NAV based on supply and demand.

>> **Public offering price (POP):** For closed-end funds, after the initial public offering (IPO) the public offering price (the ask price) depends not only on the NAV but also supply and demand for the issue. Investors of closed-end funds pay the POP (current market price) *plus* a broker's commission in an agency transaction.

Note: Although closed-end funds are not purchased from and redeemed with the issuer, most offer a high degree of liquidity, based on the number of outstanding shares. After the initial offering, they can be purchased or sold either on an exchange (called *exchange-traded funds*, or ETFs) or over-the-counter (OTC).

Some closed-end funds are set up as *interval funds*. This type of fund allows investors to sell back a stated portion of their shares to the issuer at preset intervals (typically quarterly, semiannually, or annually). It is up to individual shareholders whether they decide to sell their shares or not.

Open and closed: Focusing on their differences

You can expect at least a few of the Series 7 questions relating to investment companies to test you on the differences between open-end and closed-end funds. Table 10-1 should help you zone in on the major distinctions.

TABLE 10-1 **Comparing Open-End and Closed-End Funds**

Category	Closed-End	Open-End
Capitalization	One-time offering of securities at the IPO (Initial Public Offering) price (fixed number of shares outstanding).	Continuous offering of new shares (no fixed number of shares outstanding).
Pricing the fund	Investors purchase at the current market value (public offering price, or POP) plus a commission.	Investors purchase at the next computed net asset value (NAV) plus a sales charge. See "Forward pricing" in the next section.
Issues	Common stock, preferred stock, and debt securities.	Common stock only.
Shares purchased	Shares can be purchased in full only.	Shares can be purchased in full or fractions (up to three decimal places).
Purchased and sold	Initial public offerings go through underwriters; after that, investors purchase and sell shares either over-the-counter or on an exchange (no redemption).	Shares are sold and redeemed by the fund only. See the next section, "Forward pricing."
Exchange privileges	No exchange privileges.	Shares may be exchanged (converted) within the family of funds. For argument's sake, a customer may wish to exchange his Fidelity Mid-Cap Growth Fund for a Fidelity Intermediate-Term Bond Fund.
Withdrawal plans	After the initial public offering, the securities are sold in the market and therefore, the issuer cannot set up a withdrawal plan for investors.	Mutual funds allow systematic withdrawal plans which allow investors to automatically receive a specific amount from the fund each month as the issuer automatically redeems the shares necessary (see the next item).
Automatic reinvestment of dividends and capital gains	This is not available for closed-end funds.	Mutual funds allow investors to choose whether they wish to receive capital gains and dividends or to automatically reinvest the gains and dividends to purchase more shares.

Forward pricing

Because open-end funds hold a basket of securities that are purchased from and redeemed by the issuer, there is no current NAV. Any purchases or sales that take place during the trading day are held until the close of the market until the next NAV can be computed. All redemptions of mutual fund shares are completed at the next computed NAV (the redemption price).

REMEMBER

The key difference between open-end and closed-end funds is the method of capitalization. An open-end (mutual) fund is a continuous offering of new securities, whereas a closed-end fund is a one-time offering of new securities.

Systematic withdrawal plans

As an extra service, many mutual funds offer systematic withdrawal plans as a way of redeeming shares. This type of plan is ideal for someone who's at the retirement age and is looking for a little extra cash each month while still keeping the balance invested. Systematic withdrawal plans can be set up as a fixed dollar amount periodically, a fixed share amount redeemed periodically, or a fixed amount of time (for example, redeeming all the shares over a 10-year period).

Not all mutual funds offer systematic withdrawal plans, but if they do, as a registered rep, you must disclose the risks involved to your client. Some of the risks, which must be disclosed to customers, is that they can run out of money, and there's no guaranteed rate of return.

Regulated investment companies (RIC): Regulated under Subchapter M

For an investment company to avoid being taxed as a corporation, it must distribute (pass-through) at least *90 percent* of their *net investment income* to shareholders. Net investment income is the amount received in dividends and interest less expenses. In the event that it distributes 90 percent or better, the investment company is only taxed on the amount of net investment income not distributed to shareholders.

Diversified investment company

For an investment company to be considered diversified, it must meet the 75-5-10 test. (The 75, 5, and 10 represent percentages.) So for an investment company to claim it's diversified, no more than 5 percent of the 75 percent can be invested in one company. In addition, out of the 75 percent portion, the investment company cannot own more than 10 percent of the outstanding shares of any company. The remaining 25 percent can be invested in any way. If an investment company doesn't meet the 75-5-10 test, it is considered non-diversified.

Keeping your customer's investment objectives in mind

Unlike investors in face-amount certificate companies and unit investment trusts (see "Considering Other Investment Company Options," later in this chapter), investors of open-end and closed-end funds have many choices available. Investors may be looking for safety, growth, a combination, and so on. This section gives you a glimpse into those investment choices.

Types of mutual funds

Mutual funds come in many types and flavors depending on your client's needs. Mutual funds can specialize in holding stocks, preferred stocks, short-term bonds, intermediate-term bonds, long-term bonds, or any combination of those. Here are some types of mutual funds:

- **»** **Money market fund:** This fund (as you've probably guessed) invests in money market instruments (short-term debt securities). You need to know the specifics of this fund more than other types of funds. Here are the key points:

  - It usually provides a check-writing feature (you're given a checkbook) as a way of redeeming shares.

  - It's always no-load (there's no sales charge).

  - It computes dividends daily and credits them monthly.

  - There's no penalty for early redemption.

- **»** **Equity (stock) fund:** The primary objectives of equity funds are to provide growth and/or income for investors. Equity funds invest primarily in stocks but may hold a small amount of cash or cash equivalents such as money-market securities. Equity funds can be further broken down by investment objectives such as growth, aggressive growth, value, international, dividends, and so on.

- **»** **Fixed-income (bond) fund:** Like an income fund, the objective of a fixed-income fund is to provide current revenue to investors. The difference is that fixed-income funds only invest in debt securities, not common stock or preferred stock.

Volatility ratings

There are companies that provide *volatility ratings for bond mutual funds*. The volatility ratings typically take into account the credit rating of the bonds held, sensitivity to market conditions and general economy, the market price volatility of the portfolio, the fund's performance, interest rate risk, prepayment risk, currency risk, and so on. If these volatility ratings are going to be used in retail communications, there are certain FINRA rules that must be followed:

>> The volatility rating cannot be described as a "risk" rating.

>> The ratings must be the most recent ones (the most recently completed calendar quarter).

>> The ratings must be clear, concise, and understandable and based exclusively on objective, quantifiable factors.

>> The ratings must include the method used to determine the volatility.

>> A toll-free telephone number and/or a website must be provided for the rating company.

Fund objectives

The single most important consideration for customers who invest in packaged securities is the fund's investment objectives. This feature surpasses even the sales charge or management fees. As a registered rep, one of your primary jobs will be to help investors decide which type of fund would be best for them. The test-designers want to know you can handle that job. Comparing like-type funds is secondary. I list funds based on their investment objectives below:

>> **Income fund:** The primary objective of an income fund is to provide current revenue (not growth) for investors. This type of fund invests most of its assets in a diversified portfolio of debt securities that pay interest and in preferred and common stock of companies that are known to pay consistent dividends in cash.

Income funds are considered much safer (more conservative) investments than growth funds. You can assume for Series 7 exam (and real-life) purposes that income funds are better investment choices for retirees and investors who are looking for a steady cash flow without much risk.

>> **Balanced fund:** A balanced fund is a combination of a growth fund and an income fund. Balanced funds invest in common stocks, preferred stocks, long-term bonds, and short-term bonds, aiming to provide both income and capital appreciation while minimizing risk. These funds don't get hammered too badly when the market is bearish but usually underperform when the market is bullish.

>> **Growth fund:** This fund is exactly what you'd expect it to be; growth funds invest most of their assets in a diversified portfolio of the common stock of relatively new companies, looking for big increases in the stock prices. Growth funds offer a higher potential for growth but usually at a higher risk for the investor. This type of fund is ideal for an investor who's looking for long-term capital appreciation potential.

Because of the inherent risk of investing in growth funds, they're better for younger investors who can take the risk because they have more time to recover their losses.

Some growth funds are labeled as *aggressive growth funds* because the securities they invest in are even riskier than that of a standard growth fund.

>> **Value fund:** A value fund invests in stocks that are considered undervalued based on fundamentals. The stocks purchased by this type of fund are ones that the fundamental analysts believe should be and will be trading at a higher price based on things such as the earnings of the company and comparisons to other companies.

- » **Specialized (sector) fund:** A specialized or sector fund is a type of fund that invests primarily in the securities of a single industry or geographical area. A specialized fund may invest only in financial services, healthcare, automotive stocks, Japanese securities, and so on. Because specialized funds are limited in their investments, you can assume that in many cases, they're a little riskier (more volatile) than the average fund.

- » **International or global fund:** An international fund invests in companies based anywhere outside of the investor's home country. A global fund invests in securities located anywhere in the world, including the investor's home country. Although international and global funds may be good to round out a portfolio, they aren't without their risks. Along with the risk that investors face by just investing in securities in general, holders of international and global funds also face currency risk, which is the risk that the currency exchange rate between the U.S. and foreign issuers will hurt investors. There's also the additional risk that politics in a particular country will harm the value of the fund.

- » **Index fund:** This type of fund invests in securities that are similar to a particular stock or bond index. These types of funds are not actively managed so investors can expect lower or no management fees. Investors can expect that the NAV of the fund will increase or decrease based on the movement of the benchmark index (S&P 500, DJIA, and so on) the fund mimics.

Fund performance

Funds must disclose their average annual returns to help investors, representatives, investment advisers, and so on, be able to compare like funds quickly. Securities laws require each fund to disclose the returns for 1-, 5-, and 10-year periods. If the fund hasn't been in existence for 10 years, it must disclose the returns since inception. The performance (showing annual returns taking into account the load) as well as being online is also disclosed in the fund's prospectus.

Life-cycle funds: Understanding the basics

Life-cycle funds are also called *targeted-date* or *age-based* funds. The idea behind life-cycle funds is to automatically adjust the composition of the fund so that investors take less risk as they get older. Typically, younger investors can afford to take more financial risk and therefore invest a larger percentage of their portfolio in equity securities and a lesser percentage in fixed-income securities. As investors get older, the percentages should change so that a larger percentage of the portfolio is in fixed-income securities and a lesser percentage is in equity securities.

Life-cycle funds are set up with targeted retirement dates. Investors choose the life-cycle fund that matches their retirement date, and the fund adjusts its fund holdings occasionally so that equity funds gradually decrease and funds that invest in fixed-income securities gradually increase. Instead of purchasing and selling individual securities, life-cycle funds may also be set up as funds of funds (discussed in the aptly named "Fund of a fund" sidebar).

FUND OF A FUND

Many funds are actually funds of funds (FOF), which are also known as *multi-manager investments*. These FOFs don't purchase individual securities like other funds but invest in a pool of other types of funds. As such, the management fees end up being higher for investors because the investor is not only paying the management fee for each individual fund held but also the management fee of the manager of the FOF. FOFs typically purchase other mutual funds, ETFs or hedge funds. This type of fund provides investors with both a chance to invest in funds that may be out of their price range as well as an extreme amount of diversification to help lower risk and volatility. There are certainly many funds set up as FOFs including many life-cycle funds and some hedge funds.

Hedge funds: What are they?

You've probably heard about hedge funds but aren't exactly sure what they are. For the Series 7 exam, you do need to know a little bit about them. Because they aren't open- or closed-end funds, unit investment trusts, or face amount certificate companies, they are an exception to the standard definition of investment company under the Investment Company Act of 1940. In addition, because they are considered *private* investment companies (sold privately under Regulation D) and are *only* open to sophisticated (accredited) investors, they are *exempt from SEC registration*. As such, many hedge funds have limited available information. Hedge funds often require a very high initial investment — sometimes $500,000 or more and therefore have *limited or no liquidity*. In addition, many have *lock-up provisions*, which means that investors will not be able to redeem or sell shares during that time.

Hedge funds hold a pool of investments and are professionally managed like mutual (open-end) funds but have a lot more flexibility. Hedge funds have a wide array of investment styles, models, and vehicles. Some are even *blind pool/blank check* investments where there's no stated goal. Hedge funds are typically much *more aggressive* in nature and may buy securities on margin, sell securities short, purchase or sell options, and so on in an attempt to maximize gains. I guess you can almost think of them as a "whatever it takes to make money" type of fund.

The fees, costs, and expenses for investing in a hedge fund are typically around 2 percent of assets under management per year for a management fee. In addition, many hedge funds charge as much as 20 percent of the profits made after a certain goal is reached. (This is sometimes referred to as two and twenty, or 2 and 20.) In recent years, some hedge funds have lowered their fees.

Taxation on hedge funds is similar to that of direct participation programs because they are set up as pass-through entities. So the fund itself is free of taxes, and the gains and losses are passed through to the investors who are taxed at the individual level.

REMEMBER

Some hedge funds are set up as a *fund of funds*. So instead of an investor investing in one particular hedge fund, she is investing in a fund that pools many hedge funds together as a way of mitigating the risk of investing in one fund. The fees of investing in a fund of hedge funds are typically higher than investing in just a single hedge fund. In addition, there may be a longer lock-up period.

TIP

Don't let the variety of funds distract you too much. So many different funds are out there that the choices could drive you crazy. I list the main types, but funds can invest by objective (as previously listed) or composition, such as with foreign stock funds (which invest in foreign securities), tax-exempt funds (which invest in municipal bonds), U.S. government funds, and so on. The composition of the fund should help you match it with your customer's objectives. For instance, a customer looking for safety and income may invest in a U.S. government bond fund.

Dealing with discounts and methods of investing

Investors who have the extra funds available may be able to receive a reduced sales charge for large dollar purchases. Breakpoints and the letter of intent are available to investors of open-end funds and unit investment trusts. Because closed-end funds, after the initial offering, are traded in the market, investors do not receive breakpoints. Dollar cost averaging and fixed share averaging are most often used for open-end fund purchases but may apply to other investments as well.

Breakpoints

Funds have an investment adviser (portfolio manager) who gets paid a percentage of the value of the securities held in the fund. Therefore, one way to entice investors to spend more is to reduce the sales charge when they invest a certain minimum amount of money. That's where the breakpoint comes in.

Management investment companies divide purchase amounts into different tiers. Within a certain range, investors all pay the same sales charge percentage. But when investors invest enough to put them in the next tier (when they hit the *breakpoint*), they get a reduced sales charge. Breakpoints have no set schedule, so they vary from fund to fund.

Here are a few key points for you to remember for the Series 7 exam:

>> Breakpoints must be disclosed in the prospectus.

>> Breakpoints are not available to partnerships or *investment clubs* (several people pooling money together to receive reduced sales charges).

>> Breakpoints are generally available to individual investors, joint accounts with family members, and corporations.

EXAMPLE

Here's a hypothetical example of breakpoints for fictional ABCDE Growth Fund (summarized in Table 10-2). For this fund, persons investing less than $25,000 would pay a sales charge of 5 percent, persons investing between $25,000 and $99,999.99 would pay a sales charge of 3 percent, persons investing between $100,000 and $999,999.99 would pay a sales charge of 1.5 percent, and persons investing $1,000,000 or more would pay a 0 percent sales charge.

TABLE 10-2   ## Breakpoints for ABCDE Growth Fund

Purchase Amount	Sales Charge
$1–$24,999.99	5%
$25,000–$99,999.99	3%
$100,000–$999,999.99	1.5%
$1,000,000 and up	0%

Another discount, *rights of accumulation*, allows shareholders to receive a reduced sales charge when the amount of the funds held plus the amount purchased is enough to reach a breakpoint. So using Table 10-2, if the investor initially purchased $18,000 worth of ABCDE Growth Fund, she would pay a sales charge of 5 percent. Let's say that the market has been quite bullish and the NAV of the shares purchased has increased $23,000 and she decides to purchase an additional $7,000 of the fund. Under rights of accumulation, her sales charge on the $7,000 purchase would only be 3 percent because adding the NAV of $23,000 and the purchase of $7,000 would bring the investment to more than $25,000. There is no time limit for rights of accumulation.

Letters of intent

A *letter of intent* (LOI) signed by an investor allows her to receive a breakpoint (quantity discount) right away with the initial purchase, even if the investor hasn't yet deposited enough money to achieve the breakpoint. This document states that as long as the investor deposits enough within a 13-month period, she will receive the discounted sales charge right away.

Here are a few specifics about the letter of intent that you need to know for the Series 7:

>> The investor has *13 months* after the first deposit to live up to the terms of the letter of intent in order to maintain the reduced sales charge.

>> The LOI may be *backdated for up to 90 days,* meaning that it may apply to a previous purchase. However, remember that if the LOI applies to a previous purchase, the 13-month period starts from the date of that previous transaction.

>> While the investor is under the letter of intent, shares are held in escrow to pay for the difference in the sales charge. If the investor doesn't live up to the terms of the obligation, the fund sells the shares held in escrow.

Here's how a letter of intent may work. Suppose, for instance, that Mr. Smith purchased $10,000 worth of ABCDE Growth Fund two months ago and has another $10,000 to invest in the fund right now. Mr. Smith believes that he'll keep investing in ABCDE Growth Fund and would like to get a reduced sales charge for investments of $25,000 and up. (See Table 10-2 for the breakpoints.)

Mr. Smith signs a letter of intent and wants to apply it to his previous purchase. Because his previous purchase was two months ago, Mr. Smith has only another 11 months to invest the remaining $5,000 into ABCDE Growth Fund. Mr. Smith will receive the 3 percent sales charge on his $10,000 investment right now, which will be reduced by the overage he paid on the previous investment of $10,000. In other words, he'll pay only $100 sales charge on the current investment ($300 for this transaction minus the $200 overpaid from the previous investment) when he invests the $10,000. As long as Mr. Smith deposits the additional $5,000 by the end of the letter of intent's time frame, he'll pay the 3 percent sales charge. However, if Mr. Smith doesn't live up to the terms of the agreement, ABCDE Growth Fund will sell the shares held in escrow to pay for the difference in the sales charge.

Investors may redeem their shares at any time, even if they're under a letter of intent.

Dollar cost averaging

If an investor is employing the *dollar-cost-averaging* formula, she is investing the same dollar amount into the same investment periodically (for example, $200 per month). Although dollar cost averaging is primarily used for mutual funds, people can use it for other investments as well. Dollar cost averaging benefits the investor when the price of the security is fluctuating. The investor ends up buying more shares when the price is low and fewer shares when the price is high by depositing the same amount of money each time she makes a purchase.

Dollar cost averaging results in an *average cost per share* that is *lower than the average price per share* if the price of the fund fluctuates.

The following question tests your understanding of dollar cost averaging.

Mrs. Johnson deposits $1,000 into DEF growth fund in four separate months. The purchase prices of the fund are as follows:

>> **Month 1:** $40

>> **Month 2:** $50

>> **Month 3:** $50

>> **Month 4:** $40

What is the average cost per share for Mrs. Johnson?

(A) $40.00

(B) $44.44

(C) $45.00

(D) $48.35

The correct answer is Choice (B). On the surface, this question may look very easy to you and you may jump to Choice (C), but Choice (C) is the average price per share, not the average cost. Remember that because Mrs. Johnson is investing the same amount of money each month, she's able to buy more shares when the price is low and less when the price is high. In the first and fourth months, when the price was $40 per share, she was able to buy 25 shares each time. In the second and third months, she was able to buy only 20 shares each time:

$$\text{1st and 4th months} = \frac{\$1,000 \text{ invested}}{\$40 \text{ per share}} = 25 \text{ shares per month}$$

$$\text{2nd and 3rd months} = \frac{\$1,000 \text{ invested}}{\$50 \text{ per share}} = 20 \text{ shares per month}$$

Over the four months, Mrs. Johnson invested a total of $4,000 and purchased a total of 90 shares (25 + 20 + 20 + 25). The average cost per share is $44.44:

$$\text{average cost per share} = \frac{\text{total amount invested}}{\text{no. of shares purchased}} = \frac{\$4,000}{90 \text{ shares}} = \$44.44$$

TIP

If you use your sense of logic and watch for ways to eliminate answer choices, you may get away with doing very little math. Here, you can answer the question by finding the average price per share, which is *not* what the question is looking for. With dollar cost averaging, buying more when the price is low drives the average cost down; therefore, the average cost per share has to be between the minimum price per share ($40) and the average price per share ($45). The only number that fits these criteria is $44.44, or Choice (B).

You should be prepared to calculate the average cost per share, the average price per share ($45), and the amount saved per share ($0.56).

Figuring the sales charge and public offering price of open-end funds

You need to know two basic formulas to determine the sales charge and public offering price of open-end funds. Yes, every chapter seems to have more formulas, but these formulas are pretty straightforward and shouldn't cause you too many sleepless nights.

Sales charge percent

The sales charge, which is set at a maximum of 8½ percent, is part of the public offering price (POP), or ask price, not something tacked on afterward like a sales tax. One of the tricks for calculating the sales charge for open-end funds is remembering that the POP equals 100 percent. Therefore, if the sales charge is 8 percent, the net asset value (NAV) is 92 percent of the POP. The formula for determining the sales charge percent is as follows:

$$\text{sales charge} \% = \frac{\text{ask} - \text{bid}}{\text{ask}} = \frac{\text{POP} - \text{NAV}}{\text{POP}}$$

The following question tests your expertise in calculating the sales charge of a mutual fund.

AylDec Aggressive Growth Fund has a net asset value of $9.20 and a public offering price of $10.00. What is the sales charge percent?

(A) 6.8 percent

(B) 7.5 percent

(C) 8 percent

(D) 8.7 percent

The right answer is Choice (C). The first thing that you have to do is set up the equation. Start with the POP of $10.00 and subtract the NAV of $9.20 to get $0.80. Next, divide the $0.80 by the POP of $10.00 to get the sales charge of 8 percent:

$$\text{sales charge } \% = \frac{\text{POP} - \text{NAV}}{\text{POP}} = \frac{\$10.00 - \$9.20}{\$10.00} = \frac{\$0.80}{\$10.00} = 8\%$$

To help you remember that the ask (offer) price of a fund is the same as the POP, remember to ask your POP about it.

Public offering price (POP)

When taking the Series 7 exam, you may be asked to figure out the public offering price of a mutual fund when you're given only the sales charge percent and the NAV.

Remember, the sales charge is already a part of the POP, so the sales charge is *not* equal to the sales charge percent times the NAV. Use the following formula to figure out how much an investor has to pay to buy shares of the fund when you know only the NAV and the sales charge percent:

$$\text{public offering price} = \frac{\text{net asset value}}{100\% - \text{sales charge } \%}$$

The following question tests your ability to answer a POP question.

DEF Aggressive Growth Fund has a NAV of $9.12 and a POP of $9.91. If there is a 5 percent sales charge for investments of $30,000 and up, how many shares can an investor who is depositing $50,000 purchase?

(A) 5,045.409 shares

(B) 5,208.333 shares

(C) 5,219.207 shares

(D) 5,482.456 shares

The answer you want is Choice (B). Don't let the decimals throw you off; mutual funds can sell fractional shares. This investor isn't going to be paying the POP of $9.91 per share because she's receiving a breakpoint for a large dollar purchase (see "Breakpoints," earlier in this chapter). To figure out the POP for this investor, set up the formula:

$$\text{POP} = \frac{\text{NAV}}{100\% - \text{sales charge } \%} = \frac{\$9.12}{100\% - 5\%} = \frac{\$9.12}{95\%} = \$9.60 \text{ per share}$$

After working out the formula, you see that the investor is paying $9.60 per share instead of $9.91. Next, determine the number of shares the investor can purchase by dividing the amount of the investment by the cost per share:

$$\frac{\$50,000 \text{ invested}}{\$9.60 \text{ per share}} = 5,208.333 \text{ shares}$$

This investor is able to purchase 5,208.333 shares because of the breakpoint. Without the breakpoint, the investor would have been able to purchase only 5,045.409 shares.

Loads

As I explained earlier in this chapter, most mutual funds charge a sales charge (also known as a *load*) that's built into the public offering price (POP). However, most charge up front, some charge constantly, some charge when redeeming, and some don't charge a load at all. Depending on how investors are charged, mutual funds are broken down into classes:

>> **Class A (front-end load):** The investor pays the load when purchasing shares of the fund. Quite often, Class A shares will impose a sales charge based on the assets held. The asset-based sales charge is often around 1/4 percent per year. However, Class B and C shares often charge closer to 1 percent per year. *Note:* Asset-based sales charges are not paid by investors directly but are taken out of the assets held by the fund to compensate brokers, pay for advertisements, pay for prospectuses,12b-1 fees, and so on.

>> **Class B (back-end load):** In addition to having higher asset-based sales charges than Class A shares, investors pay a load when redeeming shares of the fund, which is also known as a *contingent deferred sales charge* (CDSC). The CDSC is usually not charged if the investor holds the shares for enough years (typically around 6). Typically in about 2 years after the CDSC is eliminated, the Class B shares are converted into Class A shares and the yearly asset-based sales charge is lowered accordingly. Very few mutual fund companies now offer class B shares.

>> **Class C (level load):** Investors do not pay a front-end sales charge but pay an annual asset-based sales charge similar to what Class B shares pay for the first several years. The difference is that Class C shares typically do not convert to Class A shares so the annual asset-based sales charges remain at the same high level no matter how long the shares are held. If shares are held for a long period of time, Class C shares end up costing investors more.

>> **Class D (no load):** Investors don't pay a sales charge but may be charged some sort of transaction fee. Class D shares are not typically available to all investors. Class D shares are only available to certain retirement plans and brokerage firms.

Expense ratio

Something else that investors should be concerned about is a fund's expense ratio. To determine a fund's expense ratio, you have to divide the fund's expenses (management fees and operating costs) by the fund's average net assets. So if the expense ratio of a fund is 2 percent, that means that the fund is charging $2 for every $100 invested. The higher the expense ratio, the more the fund is eating into your profits.

TIP

You can definitely expect a question or two relating to taxes on mutual funds. This is covered in detail in Chapter 15.

Considering Other Investment Company Options

A couple of other types of investment companies — face-amount certificate companies and unit investment trusts (UITs) — aren't as popular as they used to be. Unfortunately, even though you may never sell any, you do need to know them for the Series 7 exam. You probably won't see more than a question or two on these topics. However, exchange-traded funds (ETFs) are becoming increasingly popular, and your chance of having a question on ETFs and/or inverse ETFs is around 100 percent.

Face-amount certificate companies

A *face-amount certificate* is a type of packaged security that's similar to a zero-coupon bond (see Chapter 7); investors make either a lump-sum payment or periodic payments in return for a larger future payment. The issuer of a face-amount certificate guarantees payment of the face amount (a fixed sum) to the investor at a preset date. Very few face-amount certificate companies are around today.

Unit investment trusts (UITs)

A *unit investment trust* (UIT) is a registered investment company that purchases a fixed (unmanaged) portfolio of income-producing securities (typically bonds) and holds them in trust, which means that a UIT acts as a holding company for its investors. Then the company issues redeemable shares (units) that represent investors' interest in the trust. Unlike mutual funds, UITs are set up for a specific period of time and have a set termination date. Any capital gains, interest, and/or dividends are passed on to shareholders at regular intervals.

UITs have a finite number of shares outstanding and are distributed in the primary market at the initial public offering (IPO) price. Because a limited number of shares are outstanding and they must be redeemed with the issuer or sponsor, liquidity is very limited.

Like mutual (open-end) funds, UITs can be purchased by type, such as growth, income, balanced, international, and so forth.

Here are the two main categories of these trusts:

>> **Fixed investment trusts:** These companies invest in a portfolio of debt securities, and the trust terminates when all the bonds in the portfolio mature.

>> **Participating trusts:** These companies invest in shares of mutual funds. The mutual funds that the trust holds don't change, but the securities held by the underlying mutual funds do.

REMEMBER

Because the portfolio of securities is fixed, UITs don't employ investment advisers and therefore have no investment adviser fees during the life of the trust. Nice break!

Exchange-Traded Funds (ETFs)

Exchange-traded funds, or ETFs, are closed-end funds, which passively track an index or other benchmark, or are actively managed. ETFs, as the name implies are actively traded on an exchange. ETFs provide investors with diversification along with ease of trading, the ability to sell short, and purchase shares on margin. Although ETFs can include investments across many asset classes, their main focus is on stocks (equity funds) and bonds (bond funds).

Inverse ETFs (also known as *Short ETFs* or *Bear ETFs*) are exchange-traded funds that are designed using many derivative products, such as options to attempt to profit from a decline in the value of the underlying index (for example, the S&P 500). Inverse ETFs can be used to profit from a decline in a broad market index or in a specific sector, such as the energy or financial sectors.

When compared to mutual funds, ETFs have some distinct advantages, including the ability to purchase shares on margin, ease of trading (mutual funds have forward pricing but ETFs can be traded any time throughout the day at the current bid or ask price), and lower operating costs.

There are a couple of disadvantages when comparing ETFs to mutual funds: Investors are typically charged commissions when buying and selling and because they are so easy to trade, investors are more likely to trade excessively instead of holding their positions. There are some commission-free ETFs but they usually have higher expense ratios.

Reducing Real Estate Risk with REITs

A *real-estate investment trust* (REIT) is a trust that invests in real-estate-related projects such as properties, mortgage loans, and construction loans. REITs pool the capital of many investors to manage property and/or purchase mortgage loans. As with other trusts, they issue shares to investors representing their interest in the trust. REITs may be listed on an exchange or can trade over-the-counter (OTC). (See Chapter 14 for more info on markets.) They also provide real-estate diversification and liquidity for investors.

REITs are distributed in the primary market at the IPO price. Unlike mutual funds, which are redeemed with the issuer, REITs are traded (bought and sold) in the secondary market to other investors. In addition, REITs have a finite number of shares outstanding, like closed-end funds. Because REITs are traded in the secondary market, their price may be at a discount or premium to the NAV, depending on investor sentiment.

Equity REITs take equity positions in real-estate properties; the income is derived from rent collected or profits made when the properties are sold. Equity REITs typically hold income-producing properties like apartments, shopping malls, vacation resorts, and so on. *Mortgage REITs* purchase construction loans and mortgages. The trust receives the interest paid on the loans and in turn passes it on to the owners of the trust (the investors). *Hybrid REITs* are a combination of equity and mortgage REITs. Hybrid REITs generate income derived from rent and capital gains (like an equity REIT) and interest (like a mortgage REIT).

REITs can *avoid* being taxed like a corporation if

>> At least 75 percent of the income comes from real-estate-related activities

>> At least 75 percent of the REIT's assets are in real estate, government securities, and/or cash

>> At least 90 percent of the net income received is distributed to shareholders (who pay taxes on the income)

WARNING

Don't get REITs confused with real-estate limited partnerships (which I cover in Chapter 11). Limited partnerships pass on (the industry term is *pass through*) income and write-offs to investors to claim on their own personal tax return; REITs pass only income through to investors.

Don't kill yourself worrying too much about REITs (not that you would); you won't get more than one or two questions on the Series 7 exam relating to REITs.

REITs typically offer investors stable dividends based on the income the REIT receives. Unlike other equity securities, dividends received from REITs are not qualified, meaning that the tax rate due cannot be reduced based on the holding period and investor's tax bracket (See Chapter 15 for more on qualified dividends). However, dividends from REITs do receive a special tax benefit, which is 20 percent of the income distributed is deductible (tax-free). If the REIT distributes income based on the sale of a property, it will pass through either short- or long-term capital gains to the investor based on the holding period of the property sold. If investors decide to sell their REITs, they may have a gain or loss depending on their cost basis and the selling price. In addition, the gain or loss may be long- or short-term depending on the investor's holding period.

REMEMBER

Dividends declared by a REIT in the fourth quarter (October, November, and December) made payable to shareholders up through January of the following year shall be deemed to have been received by shareholders during the year it was declared.

Adding Annuities to a Portfolio

Annuities are similar to mutual funds, except annuities are designed to provide supplemental retirement income for investors. Life insurance companies issue annuities, and these investments provide guaranteed payments for the life of the holder. The Series 7 exam tests you on the two basic types of annuities: fixed and variable. Because variable annuities are considered securities and fixed annuities are not (because of the guaranteed payout by the insurance company), most of the annuity questions on the Series 7 exam are about variable annuities.

REMEMBER

Gather very specific information about your client before making recommendations. Annuities have been under the watchful eye of state insurance commissions and the SEC due to inappropriate recommendations from some brokers. Annuities typically aren't recommended for younger clients (most annuity purchasers are over the age of 50), for clients older than 75, or for a client's entire investment portfolio. For information on portfolio and securities analysis, see Chapter 13.

Looking at fixed annuities

The main thing for you to remember about *fixed annuities* is that they have fixed rates of return that the issuer guarantees. Investors pay money into fixed annuities, and the money is deposited into the insurance company's general *account*. After the investor starts receiving payments from the fixed annuity (usually monthly), the payments remain the same for the remainder of the investor's life. Because of the guaranteed payout, fixed annuities are *not* considered securities and therefore are exempt from SEC registration requirements under the Investment Company Act of 1940. Therefore, sellers of fixed annuities must have an appropriate insurance license, but a securities license is not required.

REMEMBER

Because the payouts associated with a fixed annuity remain the same, they're subject to *purchasing power risk* (the risk that the investment won't keep up with inflation). An investor who received payments of $1,000 per month in the 1970s may have been able to survive; however, that amount today is not even likely to pay your monthly grocery bill.

Checking out variable annuities

Insurance companies introduced variable annuities as a way for investors to keep pace with (or hopefully exceed) inflation. In a fixed annuity, the insurance company bears the investment risk; however, in a variable annuity, the investment risk is borne by the investor. Because the investors assume the investment risk, variable annuities are considered securities and must be registered with the SEC. All variable annuities have to be sold with a prospectus, and only individuals who hold appropriate securities and insurance licenses can sell them.

It will be your job as a registered representative to make sure that variable annuities are right for your clients prior to recommending them. You should have a "reasonable basis" to believe that your client would benefit from adding variable annuities to her portfolio. To do so, you should analyze whether the client would benefit from the tax-deferral, annuitization, living, and/or death benefits, provided by variable annuities.

Separate account

The money that investors deposit is held in a professionally-managed *separate account* (separate from the insurance company's other business) because the money is invested differently. The separate account is invested in securities such as common stock, bonds, mutual funds, and so on, with the hope that the investments will keep pace with or exceed the inflation rate. The insurance company will provide investment choices for their variable annuity holders such as growth, income, or growth and income. Separate accounts must be registered with the SEC as investment companies. Income and capital gains generated are credited to the separate account. Also, if the investments in the separate account lose money, it is charged to the separate account. The separate account is unaffected by the insurance company's other business.

Assumed interest rate

The *assumed interest rate* (AIR) is a projection of the performance of the securities in the separate account over the life of the variable annuity contract. If the assumed interest rate is 4 percent and the performance of the securities in the separate account is equal to 4 percent, the investor receives the payouts that she expects. However, if the securities outperform the AIR, the investor receives higher payouts than expected. And unfortunately, if the securities held in the separate account underperform the AIR, the investor gets lower payouts than expected.

Putting money into (and receiving money from) annuities

Investors have choices when purchasing annuities and getting distributions. During the accumulation phase, investors will decide how to allocate their investment options. For example, investors may decide to put 30 percent into a particular bond fund, 50 percent into a U.S. stock fund, and 20 percent into an international stock fund. Investors may also choose a lump-sum payment or multiple payments (monthly, quarterly, or annually), depending on their needs. Investors also have a choice regarding how they want to get their distributions at retirement.

Fees

Insurance companies aren't setting up annuities for investors just because they like to help people out; they receive money for doing so. Even though the initial sales loads might be minimal or non-existent for investors purchasing annuities, they will get charged pretty heavy sales charges *(surrender charges)* if they close out the annuity early. The insurance company makes additional money on management fees and other expenses. Some additional charges that investors should be aware of depending on the variable annuity offered could be charges for stepped-up benefits, guaranteed minimum income benefits, and long-term care insurance. All the applicable charges would be found in the variable annuity prospectus.

Looking at the pay-in phase

Payments into both fixed and variable annuities are made from after-tax dollars, meaning that the investor can't write the payments off on her taxes. However, payments into both fixed and variable annuities grow on a tax-deferred basis (they aren't taxed until the money is withdrawn).

If an investor has contributed $80,000 into a variable annuity that's now worth $120,000, the investor is taxed only on the $40,000 difference because she has already paid taxes on the contribution. If an annuitant dies during the pay-in phase, most annuity contracts require a *death benefit* to be paid to the annuitant's beneficiary. The death benefit is typically the greater of all the money in the account or some guaranteed minimum.

Note: During the pay-in phase, an investor of a variable annuity purchases *accumulation units.* These units are similar to shares of a mutual fund.

Investors have a few payment options to select when purchasing fixed or variable annuities. Here's the rundown of options:

>> **Single payment deferred annuity:** An investor purchases the annuity with a lump-sum payment, and the payouts are delayed until some predetermined date.

>> **Periodic payment deferred annuity:** An investor makes periodic payments (usually monthly) into the annuity, and the payouts are delayed until some predetermined date; this is the most common type of annuity.

>> **Immediate annuity:** An investor purchases the annuity with a large sum, and the payouts begin within a couple months.

REMEMBER

Most annuities in which investors are making scheduled deposits provide a *waiver of premium* during the pay-in phase if the annuitant becomes disabled or is confined to long-term care.

Getting the payout

Investors of both fixed and variable annuities have several payout options. These options may cover just the *annuitant* (investor) or the annuitant and a survivor. No matter what type of payout option the investor chooses, she will be taxed on the amount above the contribution. The earnings grow on a tax-deferred basis, and the investor is not taxed on the earnings until withdrawal at retirement.

Note: During the payout phase of a variable annuity, accumulation units are converted into a fixed number of *annuity or annuitization units.* Investors receive a fixed number of annuity units periodically (usually monthly) with a variable value, depending on the performance of the securities in the separate account.

When an investor purchases an annuity, she has to decide which of the following payout options works best for her:

>> **Life annuity (straight life):** This type of payment option provides income for the life of the *annuitant* (the individual covered by the annuity); however, after the annuitant dies, the insurance company stops making payments. This type of annuity is riskiest for the investor because if the annuitant dies earlier than expected, the insurance company gets to keep the leftover annuity money. Because it's the riskiest type of annuity for the annuitant, it has the highest payouts of all the options.

>> **Life annuity with period certain:** This payout option guarantees payment to the annuitant for a minimum number of years (10, 20, and so on). For example, if the annuitant were to purchase an annuity with a 20-year guarantee and die after 7 years, a named beneficiary would receive the payments for the remaining 13 years.

>> **Joint life with last survivor annuity:** This option guarantees payments over the lives of two individuals. As you can imagine, this type of annuity is typically set up for a husband and wife. If the wife dies first, the husband receives payments until his death. If the husband dies first, his wife receives payments until her death. Because this type of annuity covers the life spans of two individuals, it has the lowest payouts.

REMEMBER

All annuities have a *mortality guarantee*. This guarantee means that the investor receives payments as long as she lives, even if it's beyond her life expectancy. This is a risk for the insurance company so it typically charges a small percentage to each account (around 1.25 percent per year) to cover that risk.

Early withdrawal penalty

As with most other retirement plans, annuity investors are hit with a 10 percent early withdrawal penalty if they withdraw the money prior to age 59½. Yes, that's correct — the 10 percent penalty is added to the investor's tax bracket. Typically, retirement plans include a waiver of the 10 percent penalty in cases such as the purchase of a first home, age 55 and separated from work, death, or disability.

As of January 1, 2024, The Secure Act 2.0 allows for penalty-free early withdrawals for certain emergency expenses. The limit is $1,000 per year. According to section 115 of the Secure Act 2.0, an emergency expense is defined as "unforeseeable or immediate financial need relating to necessary personal or family emergency expenses."

Death benefit

If the annuity holder dies before the insurer has started making payments, the beneficiary is guaranteed to receive a specified amount. That specified amount is typically at least the amount that was paid into the annuity even if the account value is less than the guaranteed amount. However, that amount could be lowered if withdrawals have been made from the account. The death benefit is a common option. Investors should understand that additional benefits cost additional money.

Surrender value

The surrender value or *cash surrender value* of an annuity comes into play when an annuity is voluntarily terminated (cashed in) before its maturity. In that case, the annuity holder will receive the cash value less surrender fees. Quite often, the cash surrender value will be less than what the annuity holder has paid in premiums. Typically the surrender fees, which are a percentage of the cash value, decrease the longer the policy is kept in force.

TIP

Investors are usually better off maximizing other investment vehicles such as IRAs and 401(k)s prior to investing in variable annuities.

Exploring Variable Life and Variable Universal Life Insurance

You may wonder what life insurance is doing in the SIE, which is mainly about investments. Well, the answer is that unlike term insurance, certain life insurance products, specifically, *variable life* (VL) and *variable universal life* (VUL), have an investment component. Like variable annuities, variable life and variable universal life insurance policies have a separate account for investing.

That separate account is kept separate from the insurance company's general fund. You won't need to know too much about the aforementioned insurance products, so I'll keep it brief.

REMEMBER

Persons selling variable annuities, variable life insurance, and variable universal life insurance must have not only an appropriate securities license but also an insurance license. Prior to recommending any of the previously mentioned products, you should do an analysis of the client's needs and make appropriate recommendations.

Variable life

Variable life policies have a fixed premium. As with variable annuities, the investor chooses the investments held in a separate account. The death benefit (face amount) on the policy is fixed to a minimum but not to a maximum. Funds covering the minimum death benefit are kept in the insurance company's general fund. The death benefit may increase depending on the performance of the securities held in the separate account. If the separate account performs poorly, there may be limited or no cash value built up. Policyholders may borrow up to 75 percent of the cash value.

Variable universal life

Unlike variable life policies, variable universal life policies do not have fixed premiums. As such, they are sometimes called *flexible premium* variable life policies. As with variable life policies, the investors can pick the securities held in the separate account. In this case, since the premium is not fixed and the securities held in the separate account may perform poorly, the minimum death benefit and cash value are not guaranteed.

REMEMBER

Part of your job is to clearly define specific securities to investors. FINRA has specific guidelines relating to the description of variable life insurance and variable annuities. The following bulleted list focuses on those guidelines:

>> You must make sure that your customers clearly understand the difference between variable annuities and variable life insurance and which one you're recommending.

>> You must not imply that the variable life insurance or variable annuity is not a mutual fund.

>> You must make sure that your customers understand that they are not liquid investments, and there may be severe tax and/or early redemption penalties. Also, with variable life insurance, you must discuss loans and withdrawals and how they would affect the cash value and death benefits.

>> Variable life insurance policies and variable annuities provide holders with certain guarantees, which should not be overemphasized. There should be no representation or implication of a guarantee about the return of principal or investment return of the separate account.

>> You may show historical data of how a fund would've performed had it been an investment option in a variable annuity or variable life insurance policy. However, that information may only be used if there was no significant change to the fund during the period being shown or discussed. You may also compare investment choices and rankings.

>> For variable life insurance communications, you may use a hypothetical assumed interest rate only to demonstrate how the policy operates and how it will affect the cash value and death benefit. However, your customer must clearly understand that it is hypothetical and is not a prediction of investment results.

Because variable life policies have an investment component (the separate account), investors must receive a prospectus at or before the time of solicitation.

1035 tax-free exchange

Investors may find that it is advantageous for them to switch life insurance policies or annuities. Under Section 1035 of the Internal Revenue Code, individuals may exchange an insurance policy for another insurance policy or annuity insuring the same person without having to pay taxes on the income and investment gains in the original contract. Investors are also allowed to switch from an existing variable annuity contract to another. However, investors cannot switch from an annuity to life insurance policy without having to pay taxes.

Investment Company Rules

Besides all the other investment company stuff you need to know prior to taking the Series 7, there are some additional investment company rules you'll need to touch base with. I've done my best to cover most of the rules prior to this section, but, alas, there are some more. I condensed the rules to just the most important info for your reading pleasure.

Investment company sales literature

It's illegal for any person to use misleading sales literature (whether written or electronic) in connection with the offer or sale of investment company securities. Sales literature is considered misleading if it contains a statement of material fact which is untrue, or it omits a statement of material fact which would be necessary to make a statement not misleading.

Advertisements by an investment company (section 10)

Under section 10, the following information must be included with investment company advertisements:

» A statement that investors should consider the risks, investment objectives, charges, and expenses carefully before investing; a statement that investors can find additional information about the investment company in the prospectus (and summary prospectus if available); it must identify how investors can obtain a prospectus (and summary prospectus if available); and that the prospectus (and summary prospectus if available) should be read thoroughly before investing.

» Advertisements used prior to the effectiveness of the investment company's registration statement or the determination of the public offering price (POP) must include a "subject to completion" legend.

» Advertisements relating to open-end investment companies that include performance data must include a statement that you've probably heard a variation of hundreds of times. It goes something like this: "Past performance does not guarantee future results." Or "People can and do lose money." And so on. It must also disclose that investment return and principal value will fluctuate, so when an investor redeems her shares, they may be worth more or less than the original cost, and current performance may be higher or lower than the performance data quoted. The legend should also include a toll-free contact number or web address where investor can obtain the most recent performance data. In addition, if any non-recurring fee such as a sales load is charged, the maximum load or fee must be reflected.

Investment company rankings in retail communication

Under FINRA rules, members may only use investment company rankings in retail communications if the rankings were created and published by a *Ranking Entity* (any independent [independent of the investment company and its affiliates] that provides general information about investment companies to the public and whose services are not procured by the investment company or any of its affiliates to assign the investment company a ranking) or created by an investment company or investment company affiliate that were based off of the performance measurements of a Ranking Entity.

If ranking data is to be used in retail communications, there must not be a statement that implies that an investment company or investment company family is the best performer in a category unless it actually is top ranked.

In addition, the communication with the ranking information must include the name of the category (growth, balanced, international, and so on); the number of investment companies in the category; the name of the Ranking Entity; the length of the period for the ranking; criteria on which the ranking is based; and the normal disclosures (such as "past performance is no guarantee of future results").

Even more rules

The following rules are taken from the Investment Company Act of 1940:

» **Section 10:** The board of director of an investment company must be made up of no more than 60 percent insiders (those who have affiliation with the company that issued the fund). Having this rule allows investors to gain some representation on the board of directors through voting. Although up to 60 percent is the rule, many investment companies have a board of directors that is made up of around 25 percent insiders.

» **Section 12(a):** Registered investment companies may not (1) purchase securities on margin, except as deemed necessary for the clearance of transactions, or (2) participate in a joint trading account in securities unless in connection of an underwriting of securities in which the registered investment company is a participant, or (3) sell securities short except in connection with an underwriting of securities in which the registered investment company is a participant.

» **Section 13(a):** Unless voted on by a majority of its outstanding voting securities, registered investment companies may not (1) change its title of subclassification from a diversified to a non-diversified company, or (2) issue senior securities, borrow money, underwrite securities issued by other companies, buy or sell real estate, buy or sell commodities, or make loans to other persons unless such provisions are contained in the registration statement, or (3) deviate from its investment policy with regards to concentration of investments, deviate from any policy in its registration statement, or change its business in a way so it ceases to be an investment company.

- » **Section 15(a):** A person may not serve as an investment adviser of a registered investment company unless there's a written contract with the investment company and the investment adviser has been approved by a vote by a majority of the outstanding voting securities. The contract must (1) describe how the investment adviser is to be paid, and (2) remain in effect for a period of more than two years from the date of execution with at least an annual approval from the majority of the outstanding voting securities and the board of directors, and (3) provide for the termination of the investment adviser contract (without penalty) with a vote of a majority of the outstanding voting securities and the board of directors, and (4) provide for an automatic termination in the event of its assignment.

- » **Section 16(a):** Persons holding a seat on the board of directors of a registered investment company must be voted into the office by the holders of the outstanding voting securities of the company at an annual or special meeting called for that purpose. In the event a vacancy occurs in-between voting meetings, the seat may be filled at least temporarily by a vote of at least two-thirds of the board of directors who've been voted into office.

- » **Section 19:** Dividends paid out by a registered investment company must (1) come from undistributed net income from profits or losses realized on the sale of securities or other properties, or (2) from another source as long as the dividend payment is accompanied by a written statement adequately disclosing the source of the payment. In addition, registered investment companies may not distribute long-term (over one year) capital gains more than once every 12 months.

- » **Section 30:** Registered investment companies must file annual reports with the SEC. In addition, registered investment companies must transmit to their stockholders, at least semiannually, balance sheets, income statements, and so on.

- » **Section 35:** It is unlawful for any person issuing or selling registered investment company securities to represent or imply that the security or investment company (1) has been sponsored, recommended, or guaranteed by the United States or any of its agencies, or (2) has been insured by the Federal Deposit Insurance Corporation (FDIC), or is guaranteed by or is an obligation of any bank or insured depository institution. If the securities are sold through a bank, the bank shall prominently disclose that it is not FDIC insured or insured by any other government agency.

- » **Section 36:** The SEC has the authority to bring action against persons acting as (1) an officer, director, member of an advisory board, investment adviser, or depositor, or (2) a principal underwriter for a registered open-end investment company, unit investment trust, or face-amount certificate company. The SEC may bring action if, within the last five years, the person has engaged in an act or is about to engage in an act breaching fiduciary duty involving personal misconduct.

- » **Section 37:** Persons convicted of stealing, unlawfully abstracting, unlawfully and willfully converting to his own use or the use of another, or embezzling moneys, funds, securities credits, property, or any other asset of an investment company shall be subject to the penalties provided under section 49 of the Investment Company Act of 1940 (maximum $10,000 fine and/or 5 years of imprisonment).

Testing Your Knowledge

Now that you've learned what you need to know about for the Series 7 about packaged securities, it's time to test your memory. Read the questions carefully to avoid careless mistakes.

1. Which of the following types of management companies has a fixed number of shares outstanding?

    (A) Open-end investment companies

    (B) Closed-end investment companies

    (C) Unit investment trusts

    (D) Variable annuities

2. Which of the following is exempt from the registration requirements under the Investment Company Act of 1940?

    (A) Mutual funds

    (B) Closed-end funds

    (C) Variable annuities

    (D) Fixed annuities

3. Breakpoints investors receive when purchasing a mutual fund are based on

    (A) the number of shares purchased

    (B) the amount of money invested

    (C) the type of securities the mutual fund is issuing

    (D) the amount of purchasers of the fund

4. Which of the following are classifications of real estate investment trusts?

    I. Combination
    II. Hybrid
    III. Equity
    IV. Mortgage

    (A) I and II

    (B) I, III, and IV

    (C) II and III

    (D) II, III, and IV

5. Ayla K. is employing a dollar cost averaging program for purchasing shares of Decco aggressive growth fund. She has been purchasing $440 per month of the fund for the past 4 months. The first month, she purchased the fund at $20.00 per share; the second month, $22.00 per share; the third month, $22.00 per share; the fourth month $20.00 per share. What is Ayla's average cost per share?

    (A) $20.00

    (B) $20.95

    (C) $21.00

    (D) $21.07

6. All of the following are TRUE of a Letter of Intent (LOI) EXCEPT

   (A) It is valid for 13 months

   (B) It may be backdated for up to 60 days

   (C) Investors receive breakpoints as soon as the Letter of Intent is signed

   (D) Shares may be held in escrow in case the full payment is not made

7. Open-end funds may issue

   I. common stock

   II. preferred stock

   III. debt securities

   (A) I only

   (B) I and II

   (C) I and III

   (D) I, II and III

8. A mutual fund has a net asset value of $9.40 and a sales charge of 6 percent. What is the public offering price?

   (A) $9.34

   (B) $9.46

   (C) $10.00

   (D) $10.27

9. Which of the following types of annuity payout options provides the investor with the highest periodic returns?

   (A) Life annuity

   (B) Life annuity with period certain annuity

   (C) Joint and last survivor annuity

   (D) None of the above

10. Which of the following types of life insurance policies has/have no investment component?

    (A) Term

    (B) Variable

    (C) Variable universal

    (D) Both (B) and (C)

Answers and Explanations

This chapter was probably a little more difficult than some of the others. Since there are 10 questions, each one is worth 10 points.

1. **B.** Both open- and closed-end funds are considered management companies. Open-end funds have a continuous offering of new securities while closed-end funds have a fixed number of shares outstanding.

2. **D.** Since the payouts are guaranteed by the issuer, fixed annuities are not considered investment companies and are exempt from the registration requirements under the Investment Company Act of 1940.

3. **B.** Breakpoints (discounted sales charges) are based on the amount of money invested.

4. **D.** The three classifications of real estate investment trusts (REITs) are equity REITs, which take equity positions in real estate; mortgage REITs, which provide loans and mortgages; and hybrid REITs, which are a combination of equity and mortgage REITs.

5. **B.** Dollar cost averaging brings the average dollar price per share down when the fund is fluctuating in value. Dollar cost averaging, which is investing the same dollar amount periodically, allows the investor to purchase more shares when the price is low and less when the price is high. Now, you might think that since Ayla purchased shares at $22 and $20, that she paid an average of $21 per share. However, since she was able to purchase more shares when the price was lower, her average cost per share is less than $21. She was able to purchase 22 shares per month when the price was low and 20 shares per month when the price was higher.

$$\text{1st and 4th months} = \frac{\$440 \text{ invested}}{\$20 \text{ per share}} = 22 \text{ shares per month}$$

$$\text{2nd and 3rd months} = \frac{\$440 \text{ invested}}{\$22 \text{ per share}} = 20 \text{ shares per month}$$

Over the four months, Ayla invested a total of $1,760 ($440 × 4) and purchased a total of 84 shares (22 + 20 + 20 + 22). The average cost per share is $20.95:

$$\text{average cost per share} = \frac{\text{total amount invested}}{\text{no. of shares purchased}} = \frac{\$1,760}{84 \text{ shares}} = \$20.95$$

6. **B.** When investors sign a Letter of Intent (LOI), it allows investors to receive a breakpoint (discounted sales charge) right away even if they haven't deposited enough money to receive a breakpoint. LOIs can be backdated up to 90 days, not 60, meaning they can apply the discount to a previous purchase. They are valid for 13 months, meaning that investors have up to 13 months to deposit enough to receive a discounted sales charge. The issuer may hold shares in escrow in the event that the full payment isn't made.

7. **A.** Unlike closed-end funds, open-end (mutual) funds may only issue common stock. Closed-end funds may issue common stock, preferred stock, and debt securities (bonds).

8. **C.** One of the things about a mutual fund is that the public offering price (POP) includes the sales charge, so it doesn't work if you just take the sales charge percent of the net asset value (NAV) and add it to the NAV. Use the following formula to get the correct answer:

$$POP = \frac{NAV}{100\% - \text{sales charge }\%} = \frac{\$9.40}{100\% - 6\%} = \frac{\$9.40}{94\%} = \$10.00 \text{ per share}$$

9. **A.** Life annuities provide the highest periodic payments because once the investor dies, the insurance company is off the hook and doesn't have to pay any other person. Because it's riskiest for the investor, it pays the highest periodic payment.

10. **A.** Term life insurance policies, unlike variable and variable universal life insurance policies, have no investment component.

Chapter **11**

Direct Participation Programs: Partnerships

irect participation programs (DPPs) can raise money to invest in real estate, oil and gas, equipment leasing, and so on. More commonly known as limited partnerships, these businesses are somewhat similar to corporations (stockholder-owned companies). However, limited partnerships have some specific tax advantages (and disadvantages) that a lot of other investments don't have. According to tax laws, limited partnerships are not taxed directly; the income, gains, and losses are passed directly through to the investors.

DPPs were once known as tax shelters because of the tax benefits to investors; however, tax law changes have taken away a lot of these advantages. As a result, DPPs have somewhat fallen out of favor for investors (though not entirely for the Series 7 designers).

In this chapter, I explain the differences between limited and general partners as well as the types of partnerships, their particular risks, and potential rewards. The info here can help you examine those risks and rewards and determine the suitability of DPPs for investors. I also explain two inevitable facts of life as they apply to partnerships: the filing of paperwork and the payment of taxes. As with just about every chapter, you will see some overlap between the information covered on the Securities Industry Essentials exam and the Series 7. As always, I give you some practice questions to go along with the rest of the questions in this book. At the very end, I test your knowledge with a quick chapter quiz.

Searching for Identity: What DPPs Are (and Aren't)

Just as stockholders are owners of a corporation, limited (and general) partners are owners of a *direct participation program* (DPP). The key difference for people investing in DPPs is that they're illiquid, so investors can expect that their investment dollars will be tied up for a long period of time, though they receive tax advantages for doing so. Most DPPs are set up for real-estate projects, oil and gas projects, or equipment leasing.

REMEMBER

The IRS determines whether an enterprise is a corporation or a limited partnership. For a limited partnership to actually be considered (and taxed) as a limited partnership, it has to *avoid* at least two of the following corporate characteristics (usually the last two):

>> **Having a centralized management:** Corporations have management in one place. The challenges of managing a limited partnership from several locations make this corporate trait quite difficult for a partnership to avoid.

>> **Providing limited liability:** Corporate shareholders have limited liability; well, so do limited partners. The liability of corporate shareholders is limited to the amount invested, and the liability of limited partners is limited to the amount invested plus a portion of any recourse loans taken out by the partnership (if any). Providing limited liability is pretty much unavoidable.

>> **Having perpetual (never-ending) life:** Unlike corporations, which hope to last forever, limited partnerships are set up for a definite period of time. Limited partnerships are dissolved at a predetermined time — for example, when its goals are met or after a set number of years.

>> **Having free transferability of partnership interest:** DPPs are difficult to get in and out of. Unlike shares of stock, which can be freely bought and sold by anyone, limited partners not only have to pass the scrutiny of a registered rep, but they also require approval of the general partner. DPP investors (limited partners) must show that they have enough money to invest initially, plus have liquidity in other investments in the event that the partnership needs a loan.

REMEMBER

For Series 7 exam purposes, you need to remember that the easiest corporate characteristics for a partnership to avoid are perpetual life (continuity of life) and having free transferability of shares; the most difficult to avoid are providing limited liability and having a centralized management.

The DPP Characters: General and Limited Partners

By law, limited partnerships require at least one limited partner and one general partner. Limited partners are the investors, and general partners are the managers. When you're looking at general and limited partners, you want to focus on *who can and can't do what.*

General partners are responsible for the day-to-day decision making (overseeing operations, deciding when to buy or sell, choosing what to invest in, and so on) for the partnership. Limited partners (the investors) provide the bulk of the money for the partnership but, unlike general partners, can't make any of the partnership's investment decisions. Table 11-1 lays out the key things to remember about general and limited partners for the Series 7.

TABLE 11-1 **Comparing General and Limited Partners**

Category	General Partners	Limited Partners
Decision making	Are legally bound to make decisions in the best interests of the partnership; make all the partnership's day-to-day decisions	Have voting rights but can't make decisions for the partnership
Tasks	Buy and sell property for the partnership; manage the partnership's assets	Provide capital; vote; can keep general partners in check by reviewing books
Liability and litigation	Have unlimited liability (can be sued and held personally liable for all partnership debts and losses)	Have limited liability (limited to the amount invested and a proportionate share of any recourse loans taken by the partnership); can inspect *all* the partnership books; can sue the general partner or can sue to dissolve the partnership
Financial involvement	Maintain a financial interest in the partnership	Provide money contributed to the partnership, recourse debt of the partnership, and nonrecourse debt for real-estate DPPs
Financial rewards	Receive compensation for managing the partnership	Receive their proportion of profits and losses
Conflicts of interest	Can't borrow money from the partnership; can't compete against the partnership (for example, they can't manage two buildings for two different partnerships in close proximity to each other)	None; can invest in competing partnerships

Pushing through Partnership Paperwork

For the Series 7, you need to know about certain paperwork that's specific to limited partnerships. In the following sections, I discuss the three required documents necessary for a limited partnership to exist.

Partnership agreement

The *partnership agreement* is a document that includes the rights and responsibilities of the limited and general partners. Included in the agreement are basics that you would probably guess such as the name of the partnership, the location of the partnership, the name(s) of the general partner(s), and so on. In addition, the partnership agreement addresses the general partner's rights to

>> Charge a management fee for making decisions for the partnership.

>> Enter the partnership into contracts.

>> Decide whether cash distributions will be made to the limited partners.

>> Accept or decline limited partners.

Certificate of limited partnership

The *certificate of limited partnership* is the legal agreement between the general and limited partners, which is filed with the SEC (for public offerings) and Secretary of State in the home state of the partnership. The certificate of limited partnership includes basic information such as the name of the partnership and its primary place of business, the names and addresses of the limited and general partner(s), and the following items:

>> The objectives (goals) of the partnership and how long the partnership is expected to last

>> The amount contributed by each partner, plus future expected investments

>> How the profits are to be distributed

>> The roles of the participants

>> How the partnership can be dissolved

>> Whether a limited partner can sell or assign his interest in the partnership

If any significant changes are made to the partnership, such as adding new limited partners, the certificate of limited partnership must be amended accordingly.

Subscription agreement

The *subscription agreement* is an application form that potential limited partners have to complete. The general partner uses this agreement to determine whether an investor is suitable to become a limited partner. The general partner has to sign the subscription agreement to officially accept an investor into the DPP.

One of your jobs as a registered rep is to prescreen the potential limited partner to make sure that the partnership is a good fit for the individual. Consider the following questions:

>> Does the investor have enough money to invest (net worth and annual income)?

>> Does the investor have enough cash or liquidity in other investments in case the partnership needs more money?

>> Is he okay with tying up his money for a long period of time?

>> Can he handle the risks, including the risk of losing his entire investment?

Also, you need to review the agreement to ensure (to the best of your ability) that the information the investor provides is complete and accurate. Besides the investor's payment, the subscription agreement has to include items such as the investor's net worth and annual income, a statement explaining the risks of investing in the partnership, and a power of attorney that allows the general partner to make partnership investment decisions for the limited partner.

The following question tests your ability to answer questions about DPP paperwork:

EXAMPLE

All of the following statements are TRUE regarding the subscription agreement EXCEPT

(A) A general partner must sign the agreement to officially accept a limited partner.

(B) A registered rep must first examine the subscription agreement to make sure that the investor has provided accurate information.

(C) After the general partner has signed the subscription agreement, it gives the limited partner power of attorney to conduct business on behalf of the partnership.

(D) The subscription agreement is usually sent to the general partner with some form of payment.

The answer is Choice (C). The test designers want to know that you understand what this document is and that you have a grasp of who does what. The subscription agreement is a form that the potential limited partner fills out; then the registered rep reviews the document before sending it (with the investor's payment) to the general partner, who signs to accept the terms. Choice (B) shows where the registered rep (that's you!) comes in. Here, you assume that the "investor" is the potential limited partner, so Choice (B) checks out.

Because this is an *except* question, the correct answer is Choice (C); the subscription agreement gives the *general partner,* not the limited partner, power of attorney to make decisions for the partnership. If you remember that limited partners don't really do much in the way of decision making (as I explain earlier in "The DPP Characters: General and Limited Partners"), you can spot the false answer right away.

Types of DPP Offerings

As with many other securities, DPPs can be sold privately through private placements or through public offerings. It's up to the *syndicator* (underwriter) to help determine which type of offering makes the most sense.

Private placements

If a DPP is to be sold privately, the syndicator helps to find several accredited investors, who will become limited partners, to contribute large sums of money. These accredited investors are persons who can afford to take the financial risk and typically have a lot of investment experience. A private placement of DPPs is made through an offering memorandum (private placement memorandum). Private placements of DPPs are exempt from SEC registration under Regulation D of the Securities Act of 1933. For more on private placements, please refer to Chapter 5.

Public offerings

Unless the transaction is exempt, as in private placements, all non-exempt securities transactions must be registered with the SEC. Public offerings of DPPs are no exception. So, in a public offering, not only do investors need to be prescreened, but they also must receive a prospectus. When there's a public offering of a DPP, there will be a lot more investors, and the initial capital contribution will generally be much smaller than in a private placement. In some cases, investors may become a limited partner with an initial contribution as low as $1,000.

Passive Income and Losses: Looking at Taxes on Partnerships

DPPs used to be called *tax shelters* because DPPs flow through (or *pass through*) not only income but also losses to investors (corporations only flow through income). Prior to 1986, investors could write off these losses against income from other investments. Then, the IRS stepped in because it felt that this write-off was too much of an advantage for investors (or the IRS wasn't making enough money) and decided to give DPPs their own tax category. Now, because investors are not actively involved in earning the income, taxes on DPPs are classified as *passive income* and *passive losses.* (See Chapter 15 for more info on taxes and types of income.) So basically, DPPs are like corporations that have a tax pass-through exemption from the IRS. However, unlike corporations that are taxed on the corporate level, prior to distributing dividends to investors, DPPs pass through untaxed income to investors.

REMEMBER

The key thing to remember for Series 7 purposes is that investors can write off passive losses only against passive income from other DPP investments.

Evaluating Direct Participation Programs

Direct participation programs can be offered publicly or privately. Public offerings of DPPs must be registered with the Securities and Exchange Commission (SEC), whereas private offerings (offerings to mostly wealthy investors) are not. Typically, publicly offered DPPs have a lower unit (buy-in) cost than that of privately offered DPPs.

Certainly direct participation programs do provide some advantages, but they also have additional risks that investors don't face with other types of investments, such as having to loan additional money to the partnership if needed. Therefore, when evaluating whether an investment in a DPP may be right for one of your clients, not only do you need to determine whether investing in a partnership is wise for that client, but you also need to consider the following items:

>> The economic soundness of the program

>> The expertise of the general partner

>> The basic objectives of the program

>> The start-up costs involved

>> Leverage and other revenue considerations

Types of Partnerships

Certainly partnerships can be formed to run any sort of business that you can imagine, including business development companies (BDCs), small-cap debt and equity, and so on. However, the Series 7 exam focuses on the big three: real estate, equipment leasing, and oil and gas. You need to be able to identify the risks and potential rewards for each of the following types of partnerships.

REMEMBER

Because of the risks associated with some of the different types of DPPs, investors should have the ability to tie up their money for a long period of time and be able to recover from a loss of all the money invested in case the partnership never becomes profitable.

Real-estate partnership info

Real-estate partnerships include programs that invest in raw land, new construction, existing properties, or government-assisted housing. You need to know the differences among the types of programs, along with their risks and potential rewards. Here are the types of real-estate DPPs, from safest to riskiest:

» **Public housing (government-assisted housing programs):** This type of real-estate DPP develops low-income and retirement housing. The focus of this type of DPP is to earn consistent income and receive tax credits. The U.S. government (through U.S. government subsidies), via the department of Housing and Urban Development (HUD), makes up any deficient rent payments. Appreciation potential is low and maintenance costs can be high, but the DPP does benefit from a little government security. Public housing DPPs are backed by the U.S. government and, therefore, are considered the safest real-estate DPP. One of the major benefits of public housing DPPs is that they qualify for tax credits (LIHTC, or Low-Income Housing Tax Credits). These tax credits or tax incentives are built into the IRS code to encourage developers to create affordable housing. The biggest risks for public housing DPPs is their lack of appreciation potential and the risk of having to foreclose on non-payers.

» **Existing properties:** This type of DPP purchases existing commercial properties and apartments, and the intent is to generate a regular stream of rental income. Because the properties already exist, this DPP generates immediate cash flow. The risk with this type of DPP is that the maintenance or repair expenses will eat into the profit or that tenants won't renew their leases. The properties already exist and are producing income, so the risk for this type of DPP is relatively low.

» **New construction:** This type of DPP purchases property for the purpose of building. After completing the construction, the partnership's goal is to sell the property and structure at a profit after all expenses. Building costs may be more than expected, and the partnership doesn't receive income until the property is sold, but the DPP can benefit from appreciation on both the land and the structure. Although this investment is speculative due to potential increases in building costs, economic downturns, changes in tax laws, competing projects, and so on, it's not as risky as a raw land DPP.

» **Raw land:** This type of DPP invests in undeveloped land in anticipation of long-term capital appreciation; raw land DPPs don't build on or rent out the property. The partnership hopes the property purchased will appreciate in value so that the DPP can sell the property for more than the purchase price plus all expenses. Until that hopefully happens, investors have the cost of principal and interest of borrowed money plus carrying costs (taxes). In the event that the land held by the DPP isn't sold in a reasonable amount of time, investors may have to provide additional funds to cover expenses.

REMEMBER

Raw land DPPs are considered the riskiest real-estate DPP because the partnership doesn't have any cash flow (no rental or sales income), and the value of the land may not increase — it may actually decrease. In addition, investors cannot claim depreciation deductions because land cannot be depreciated.

» **Blind Pool:** This type of DPP gives the general partner wide discretion as to the types of investments that the DPP makes. A blind-pool DPP may have a stated goal of growth, income, and so on, but the investment choices are left to the general partner.

TIP

One of the advantages for real-estate DPPs that invest in existing properties, such as public housing DPPs and existing property DPPs, is real estate *depreciation*, which means you can write off the value of an asset (in this case homes or buildings) over its useful life. I know it sounds strange, but investors can actually write off the value of a house or building (land is not depreciable) over a set number of years (such as 10, 20, 25, and so on). At the end of that period, you've written off enough so that, according to the IRS, your home or building is worth nothing (even though it's most likely appreciated in value), and you can't take additional depreciation write-offs. Although things like equipment can be depreciated on an accelerated basis, real-estate DPPs can only depreciate on a straight-line basis (writing off an equal amount each year).

The following question tests your understanding of real-estate DPPs.

Which of the following types of real-estate DPPs have the fewest write-offs?

(A) Raw land

(B) New construction

(C) Existing properties

(D) Public housing

The correct answer is Choice (A). DPPs that invest in raw land are buying property and sitting on it with the hope that it'll be worth more in the future. Because the DPP isn't spending money on improving the property and land can't be depreciated, raw land DPPs have the fewest write-offs.

Equipment leasing

Although you will be tested on equipment leasing programs on the Series 7 exam, it's the least-tested type of DPP. Equipment leasing programs purchase equipment (trucks, heavy machinery, airplanes, railroad cars, computers . . . you name it) and lease it out to other businesses. The objective is to obtain a steady cash flow and *depreciation* write-offs. The two types of leasing arrangements you need to be aware of are the operating lease and the full payout lease:

>> **Operating lease:** This type of equipment leasing program purchases equipment and leases it out for a short period of time. The DPP doesn't receive the full value of the equipment during the first lease. This type of arrangement allows the DPP to lease out the equipment several times during the life of the machinery.

>> **Full payout lease:** This type of equipment leasing program purchases the equipment and leases it out for a long period of time. The DPP receives enough income from the first lease to cover the cost of the equipment and any financing costs. Usually, the initial lease lasts for the useful life of the equipment.

The main thing to remember about equipment leasing is that the operating lease is riskier because the equipment becomes less valuable or outdated over time and, therefore, less rentable — in other words, no appreciation potential. However, equipment leasing programs, unlike real estate programs, may qualify for accelerated depreciation (being able to write off more in the early years and less in the later years).

Oil and gas

Oil and gas partnerships include programs that produce income, are speculative in nature, or are a combination of the two. You need to know how the types of programs differ, along with their risks and potential rewards. Oil and gas partnerships also have certain tax advantages that are unique:

>> **Intangible drilling costs (IDCs):** IDCs are write-offs for drilling expenses. The word *intangible* is your clue that you're not talking about actual equipment. These costs include wages for employees, fuel, repairs, hauling of equipment, insurance, and so on. IDCs are usually completely deductible in the tax year in which the intangible costs occur. IDC deductions are only for the drilling and preparing of a well for the production of oil and gas. Therefore, when a well is producing, IDC write-offs are not allowed. IDCs provide a tax advantage to exploratory programs.

>> **Tangible drilling costs (TDCs):** TDCs are write-offs on items purchased that have salvage value (items that can be resold). All oil and gas DPPs have TDCs, which include costs for

purchasing items such as storage tanks, well equipment, and so on. These costs are not immediately written off but are *depreciated* (deducted) over seven years. Depreciation may be claimed on either a straight-line basis (writing off an equal amount each year) or an accelerated basis (writing off more in the early years and less in the later years).

REMEMBER

IDCs are fully deductible in the current year; TDCs are depreciated (deductible) over several years.

>> **Depletion:** Depletion is a tax deduction that allows partnerships that deal with natural resources (such as oil and gas) to take a deduction for the decreasing supply of the resource. Partnerships can claim depletion deductions only on the amount of natural resources sold (not extracted and put in storage for future sale).

REMEMBER

Depletion deductions are only for DPPs that deal with natural resources. On the Series 7 exam, the only DPP with depletion deductions that you need to be concerned with is oil and gas.

When investing in oil, partnerships can pioneer new territory, drill near existing wells, buy producing wells, or try a combination of those methods. For Series 7 exam purposes, exploratory programs are the riskiest oil and gas DPPs because oil may never be found, and income programs are the safest oil and gas DPPs. To make your life easier (hopefully), I've composed a DPP comparison chart (see Table 11-2) to help you focus on the main points of each type of oil and gas DPP.

TABLE 11-2 **Advantages and Risks of Various Oil and Gas DPPs**

Type	Objective	Advantages	Risks
Exploratory (wildcatting) programs	To locate and drill for oil in unproven, undiscovered areas	Long-term capital appreciation potential; high returns for discovery of new oil or gas reserves	Riskiest oil and gas DPP because new oil reserves may never be found; high IDCs because the DPP isn't working with producing wells
Developmental programs	To drill near producing wells (in proven areas) with the hope of finding new reserves	Long-term capital appreciation potential (not as much as an exploratory program) with less risk than exploratory programs; oil will likely be found	The property's expensive; the drilling costs may be higher than expected; the risk of dry holes (non-producing wells) is still somewhat high; medium level of IDCs
Income programs	To provide immediate income by purchasing producing wells	The partnership generates immediate cash flow; the least risky of the oil and gas DPPs; no IDCs	High initial costs; the well could dry up; gas prices could go down
Combination (balanced) programs	To provide income to help pay for the cost of finding new oil reserves	The ability to offset the costs of drilling new wells by using income generated by existing wells	Carries the risks of all the programs combined

The following question concerns different DPP investments.

EXAMPLE

Ayla K. has money invested in a limited partnership that's expecting to have a significant amount of income over the next one to two years. Which of the following programs would BEST help Ayla shelter the MOST of that income?

(A) Oil and gas exploratory

(B) Raw land purchasing

(C) Equipment leasing

(D) Existing real-estate property

The answer you want is Choice (A). Oil and gas exploratory programs spend a lot of money attempting to find and drill for oil. These programs have high IDCs (intangible drilling costs), which are fully tax-deductible when the drilling occurs. Therefore, the oil and gas exploratory programs have the largest write-offs in the early years, which could help Ayla offset some or all of her passive income from the other limited partnership.

Testing Your Knowledge

If you've recently taken the SIE exam, you probably noticed that what you learned for that exam isn't all that different compared to this one, which is a great bonus. That being said, I hope this chapter was more of a review. As always, read the following questions carefully.

1. When making a public offering, which of the following documents is a limited partnership required to file with the SEC?

   (A) Certificate of limited partnership

   (B) Agreement of limited partnership

   (C) Subscription agreement

   (D) Both (A) and (B)

2. Passive income can be written off against?

   (A) Passive losses

   (B) Capital losses

   (C) Both (A) and (B)

   (D) Neither (A) nor (B)

3. Which of the following documents must be signed by a general partner to accept a new limited partner?

   (A) Certificate of limited partnership

   (B) Agreement of limited partnership

   (C) Subscription agreement

   (D) Partnership welcome form

4. Which TWO of the following corporate characteristics are the easiest for a limited partnership to avoid?

   I. Having perpetual life

   II. Providing limited liability

   III. Having a centralized management

   IV. Having free transferability

   (A) I and III

   (B) I and IV

   (C) II and III

   (D) II and IV

5. Which of the following partnership documents includes the rights and responsibilities of the general and limited partners?

(A) Certificate of limited partnership

(B) Subscription agreement

(C) Partnership agreement

(D) Both (A) and (C)

6. Depletion deductions may be claimed for

(A) exploratory oil and gas programs

(B) raw land real estate programs

(C) equipment leasing programs

(D) income oil and gas programs

7. Which of the following types of oil and gas programs are considered the safest for investment for the limited partners?

(A) Exploratory

(B) Combination

(C) Income

(D) Developmental

8. Which of the following type of equipment leasing programs is the riskiest for investors?

(A) Operating lease

(B) Full payout lease

(C) Value lease

(D) Partial pay lease

9. Which of the following is a benefit of investing in a direct participation program?

(A) Limited liability

(B) Pass through of income and losses

(C) Professional management

(D) All of the above

10. Which of the following types of oil and gas partnerships are the riskiest?

(A) Wildcatting

(B) Developmental

(C) Income

(D) Combination

Answers and Explanations

This was a relatively small chapter, and I hope you found the questions easy. There are 10 questions, so each one is worth 10 points.

1. **A.** A limited partnership must file a Certificate of Limited Partnership with the SEC prior to making a public offering.

2. **A.** Passive income is income received from a limited partnership. Passive income can only be written off against passive losses, not capital losses.

3. **C.** In order to officially accept a new limited partner to the partnership, a general partner must sign the subscription agreement.

4. **B.** In order for a partnership to not be taxed as a corporation, it must avoid at least two corporate characteristics. The easiest corporate characteristic for a partnership to avoid is having a perpetual life (partnerships are set up for a finite period of time) and having free transferability to partnership interest. Because of the approval process, limited partnerships are some of the most difficult investments to get in and out of.

5. **C.** The partnership agreement lays out the rights and responsibilities of the limited and general partner(s).

6. **D.** In order to be able to claim depletion deductions, the partnership has to be depleting a natural resource. Out of the choices given, only oil and gas programs deal with a natural resource. Exploratory programs (ones in which they're looking for oil) do not have depletion deductions until they actually hit oil and start pulling it from the ground like income programs.

7. **C.** Income producing programs are considered the safest oil and gas DPPs because the investors are purchasing oil producing wells.

8. **A.** An operating lease is when the equipment is only leased for a short period of time, so it is riskier for investors. As equipment gets older and possibly outdated, it becomes less desirable for companies to lease. A full payout lease is best for investors because the equipment is leased out for a long enough period of time to recoup the cost of the equipment purchased. Answers (C) and (D) are made-up answers.

9. **D.** All of the choices listed are benefits of investing in a limited partnership. Investors are certainly getting (or hoping for) professional management by way of a general partner. Also, since a partnership is not taxed as a corporation, the gains and losses are passed through to investors. In addition, limited partners' losses are limited to the amount invested plus any recourse loans (for real-estate DPPs only).

10. **A.** Wildcatting (exploratory) programs are the riskiest because the partnership is drilling in unproven areas trying to find oil. This goes back to more risk = more reward. For this type of program, the risks are the greatest, but if the partnership finds oil, the rewards should be much higher than other oil and gas programs.

Chapter **12**

Options: The Right to Buy or Sell at a Fixed Price

Welcome to the wonderful world of options. I'm sure you've heard stories about the difficulty of options. Put your mind at ease — I'm here to make your life easier. Maybe I'm a little warped, but options are my favorite part of the Series 7 exam! Options are considered *derivative securities* because their value is derived from the value of the underlying stock, index, currency, and so on. Options are one of the more heavily tested areas on the Series 7. Options can be trades on individual stocks, stock market indexes, foreign currency, interest rates, or bonds. And options can be traded on exchanges such as the Chicago Board Options Exchange (CBOE).

Some option info was already covered when taking the Securities Industry Essentials (SIE) exam, so a little bit of this chapter will look familiar. However, the Series 7 digs a lot deeper than the SIE. A lot of the questions are simple calculations, so in this chapter, I show you how to put numbers into an options chart to make even the more difficult calculations simple. I give you plenty of example questions and a semi-quick 30-question quiz at the end so you can put those math skills to good use. I also give you a general tour of the options basics — calls and puts, in- and out-of-the-money, and so on — and introduce you to the unique LEAPS and capped options.

Brushing Up on Option Basics

Options are just another investment vehicle that (hopefully) more-savvy investors can use. An owner of an *option* has the right, but not the obligation, to buy or sell an underlying security (stock, bond, and so on) at a fixed price for, or at, a given period of time; as derivatives, options draw their value from that underlying security. Investors may either *exercise* the option (buy or sell the security at the fixed price), trade the option in the market, or let it expire.

All option strategies (whether simple or sophisticated), when broken down, are made up of simple call and/or put options. After going over how to read an option, I explain a basic call option and help you figure out how to work with that before moving on to a put option. Next, I discuss options that are in-, at-, or out-of-the-money, and the cost of options. After you've sufficiently mastered the basics, the rest (the more difficult strategies later in this chapter) becomes easier.

Reading an option

To answer Series 7 questions relating to options, you have to be able to read an option. The following example shows you how an option may appear on the Series 7:

Buy 1 XYZ Apr 60 call at 5

Here are the seven elements of the option order ticket and how they apply to the example:

1. **Whether the investor is buying or selling the option: Buy**

   When an investor buys (or *longs, holds,* or *owns*) an option, she is in a position of power; by paying the premium, that investor controls the option and decides whether and when to exercise the option. If an investor is selling (*shorting* or *writing*) an option, she is obligated to live up to the terms of the contract and must either purchase or sell the underlying stock if the holder exercises the option.

2. **The contract size: 1**

   You can assume that one option contract is for *100 shares* of the underlying stock. Although this idea isn't as heavily tested on the Series 7 exam, an investor may buy or sell multiple options (for example, five) if she's interested in having a position in more shares of stock. If an investor owns five option contracts, she's interested in 500 shares of stock (check out "Off the charts: Multiple option contracts" later in the chapter for more information on this topic).

   Note: There are such things as mini options, which cover 10 shares of the underlying security and situations such as stock splits which affect the amount of shares per option. However, for test purposes, you can assume 100 shares per option unless told differently.

3. **The name of the security: XYZ**

   In this case, XYZ is the underlying stock that the investor has a right to purchase at a fixed price.

4. **The expiration month for the options: Apr**

   All options are owned for a fixed period of time. Initially, the expiration for new options was *9 months* from the issue date. Now investors can also purchase options with weekly and quarterly maturities as well as long-term options (LEAPS). In the preceding example, the option will expire in April. Options expire on the third Friday of the expiration month.

5. **The strike (exercise) price of the option: 60** When the holder (purchaser or owner) *exercises* the option, she uses the option contract to make the seller of the option buy or sell the underlying stock at the strike price (see the next step for info on determining whether the seller is obligated to buy or sell). In this case, if the holder were to exercise the option, the holder of the option would be able to purchase 100 shares of XYZ at $60 per share.

6. **The type of option: call**

   An investor can buy or sell a call option, or buy or sell a put option. Calls give holders the right to buy the underlying security at a set price; puts give holders the right to sell. So in the example scenario, the holder has the right to buy the underlying security at the price stated in the preceding step.

7. **The premium: 5**

   Of course, an option investor doesn't get to have the option for nothing. An investor buys the option at the premium. In this case, the premium is 5, so a purchaser would have to pay $500 (5 × 100 shares per option).

Looking at call options: The right to buy

REMEMBER

A *call option* gives the holder (owner) the right, but not the obligation, to buy 100 shares of a security at a fixed price and the seller the obligation to sell the stock at the fixed price. Owners of call options are bullish (picture a bull charging forward) because the investors want the price of the stock to increase. If the price of the stock increases above the strike price, holders can either exercise the option (buy the stock at a good price) or sell the option for a profit. By contrast, sellers of call options are neutral or bearish (imagine a bear hibernating for the winter) because they want the price of the stock to either stay the same or decrease.

For example, assume that Ms. Smith buys 1 DEF October 40 call option. Ms. Smith bought the right to purchase 100 shares of DEF at 40. If the price of DEF increases to over $40 per share, this option becomes very valuable to Ms. Smith, because she can purchase the stock at $40 per share and sell it at the market price or sell the option at a higher price.

If DEF never eclipses the 40 strike (exercise) price, then the option doesn't work out for poor Ms. Smith and she doesn't exercise the option. However, it does work out for the seller of the option, because the seller receives a premium for selling the option, and the seller gets to pocket that premium.

Checking out put options: The right to sell

REMEMBER

You can think of a put option as being the opposite of a call option (see the preceding section). The holder of a *put option* has the right to sell 100 shares of a security at a fixed price, and the writer (seller) of a put option has the obligation to buy the stock if exercised. Owners of put options are bearish because the investors want the price of the stock to decrease (so they can buy the stock at market price and immediately sell it at the higher strike price or sell their option at a higher premium). However, sellers of put options are bullish (they want the price of the stock to increase), because that would keep the option from going in-the-money (see the next section) and allow them to keep the premiums they received.

For example, assume that Mr. Jones buys 1 ABC October 60 put option. Mr. Jones is buying the right to sell 100 shares of ABC at 60. If the price of ABC decreases to less than $60 per share, this option becomes very valuable to Mr. Jones. If you were in Mr. Jones's shoes and ABC were to drop to $50 per share, you could purchase the stock in the market and exercise (use) the option to sell the stock at $60 per share, which would make you (the new Mr. Jones) very happy.

If ABC never drops below the 60 strike (exercise) price, then the option doesn't work out for Mr. Jones and he doesn't exercise the option. However, it does work out for the seller of the option, because the seller receives a premium for selling the option that she gets to keep.

Getting your money back: Options in-, at-, or out-of-the-money

To determine whether an option is in- or out-of-the-money, you have to figure out whether the investor would be able to get at least some of his or her premium money back if the option were exercised.

REMEMBER

You can figure out how much an option is in-the-money or out-of-the-money by finding the difference between the market value and the strike price. Here's how you know where-in-the-money an option is:

» When an option is *in-the-money,* exercising the option lets investors sell a security for more than its current market value or purchase it for less — a pretty good deal.

The *intrinsic value* of an option is the amount that the option is in-the-money; if an option is out-of-the-money or at-the-money, the intrinsic value is zero.

» When an option is *out-of-the-money,* exercising the option means investors can't get the best prices; they'd have to buy the security for more than its market value or sell it for less. Obviously, holders of options that are out-of-the-money don't exercise them.

» When the strike price is the same as the market price, the option is *at-the-money;* this is true whether the option is a call or a put.

Call options — the right to buy — go in-the-money when the price of the stock is above the strike price. Suppose, for instance, that an investor buys a DEF 60 call option and that DEF is trading at 62. In this case, the option would be in-the-money by two points (the option's intrinsic value). If that same investor were to buy that DEF 60 call option when DEF was trading at 55, the option would be out-of-the-money by five points (with an intrinsic value of zero).

A put option — the right to sell — goes in-the-money when the price of the stock drops below the strike price. For example, a TUV 80 call option is in-the-money when the price of TUV drops below 80. The reverse holds as well: If a put option is in-the-money when the price of the stock is below the strike price, it must be out-of-the-money when the price of the stock is above the strike price.

WARNING

Don't take the cost of the option (the premium) into consideration when determining whether an option is in-the-money or out-of-the-money. Having an option that's in-the-money is not the same as making a profit. (See the next section for info on premiums.)

TIP

Use the phrases *call up* and *put down* to recall when an option goes in-the-money. *Call up* can help you remember that a *call* option is in-the-money when the market price is *up,* or above the strike price. *Put down* can help you remember that a *put* option is in-the-money when the market price is *down,* or below the strike price.

The following question tests your knowledge of options being in- or out-of-the-money.

EXAMPLE

Which TWO of the following options are in-the-money if ABC is trading at 62 and DEF is trading at 44?

   I. An ABC Oct 60 call option

   II. An ABC Oct 70 call option

   III. A DEF May 40 put option

   IV. A DEF May 50 put option

   (A) I and III

   (B) I and IV

   (C) II and III

   (D) II and IV

The correct answer is Choice (B). Start with the strike (exercise) prices. You're *calling up* or *putting down* from the strike prices, not from the market prices. Because call options go in-the-money when the market price is above the strike price, Statement I is the only one that works for ABC. An ABC 60 call option would be in-the-money when the price of ABC is above 60. ABC is currently trading at 62, so that 60 call option is in-the-money. For the ABC 70 call option to be in-the-money, ABC would have to be trading higher than 70. Next, use *put down* for the DEF put options, because put options go in-the-money when the price of the stock goes below the strike price. Therefore, Statement IV makes sense because DEF is trading at 44, and that's below the DEF 50 put strike price but not the 40 put strike price.

REMEMBER

When someone purchases an option, it is said that he is *long* the option. An investor who is long an option paid the premium for the option so he needs the option to go in-the-money (the price of the underlying security to go in the correct direction) enough for him to not only recoup his premium but also make a few bucks.

When someone is *short* an option, it means that he sold the option. This person is on the opposite side of the transaction than the person who is long the option. In this case, the seller received a premium for selling the option. So someone who is short an option is doing so for income and is hoping that the option expires out-of-the-money so that he gets to keep the premium.

Paying the premium: The cost of an option

The *premium* of an option is the amount that the purchaser pays for the option. The premium may increase or decrease depending on whether an option goes in- or out-of-the-money, gets closer to expiration, and so on. The premium is made up of many different factors, including

» Whether the option is in-the-money (see the preceding section)

» The amount of time until the option expires

» The volatility of the underlying security

» Investor sentiment (for example, whether buying calls on ABC stock is the cool thing to do right now)

One of the questions you may run across on the Series 7 exam requires you to figure out the time value of an option premium. *Time value* has to do with how long you have until an option expires. There's no set standard for time value, such as every month until an option expires costs buyers an extra $100. However, you can assume that if two options have everything in common except for the expiration month, the one with the longer expiration will have a higher premium. Hopefully, the following equation can help keep you from getting a "pit" in your stomach:

$$P = I + T$$

In this formula, P is the premium or cost of the option, I is the intrinsic value of the option (the amount the option is in-the-money), and T is the time value of the option.

For example, here's how you find the time value for a BIF Oct 50 call option if the premium is 6 and BIF is trading at 52: Call options (the right to buy) go in-the-money when the price of the stock goes above the strike price (*call up* — see the preceding section). Because BIF is trading at 52 and the option is a 50 call option, it's two points in-the-money; therefore, the intrinsic value is 2. Because the premium is 6 and the intrinsic value is 2, the premium must include 4 as a time value:

$$P = I + T$$

$$6 = 2 + T$$

$$T = 4$$

The following question tests your knowledge of using the formula $P = I + T$.

EXAMPLE

Use the following chart to answer the next question.

Stock	Strike Price	Calls		Puts	
		July	Oct	July	Oct
LMN					
40.50	30	13	14.5	0.25	0.50
40.50	40	2.5	4.5	1.5	2.75
40.50	50	0.25	0.75	10.5	12

What is the time value of an LMN Oct 30 call?

(A) 2.5

(B) 4

(C) 6.25

(D) 9.5

The answer you're looking for is Choice (B). I threw you a curveball by giving you a chart similar to what you may see on the Series 7 exam. I hope you're able to find the premium that you need to answer the question. Most of the exhibits you get on the Series 7 are simple, and solving the problem is just a matter of locating the information you need.

Using the chart, the first column shows the price of the stock trading in the market, the second column shows the strike prices for the options, and the rest of the chart shows the premiums for the calls and puts and the expiration months. Scan the chart under the October calls, which is in the fourth column; then look for the 30 strike price, which is in the first row of data. The column and row intersect at a premium of 14.5.

Now you need to find the intrinsic value (how much the option is in-the-money). Remember that call options go in-the-money when the price of the stock is above the strike price (call up). This is a 30 call option and the price of the stock is 40.50, which is 10.5 above the strike price. Plug in the numbers, and you find that the premium includes a time value of 4:

P (premium) = I (intrinsic value) + T (time value)

$14.5 = 10.5 + T$

$T = 4$

Incorporating Standard Option Math

I'm here to make your life easier. Prep courses use several different types of charts and formulas to figure out things such as gains or losses, break-even points, maximum gain or loss, and so on. I believe that the easiest way is to use the options chart that follows. It's a simple *Money Out, Money In* chart you can use to plug in numbers. What's great about this chart is that you don't even necessarily have to understand what the heck is going on to determine the answers to most options questions. As this chapter progresses, I show you how incredibly useful the options chart can be.

Money Out	Money In

If it looks basic, it is — and that's the idea. Any time an investor spends money, you place that value in the Money Out side of the options chart, and any time an investor receives money, you place the number in the Money In side of the chart.

Buying or selling call options

The most basic options calculations involve buying or selling call or put options. Although using the options chart may not be totally necessary for the more basic calculations (such as the one that follows in the next section), working with the chart now can help you get used to the tool so you'll be ready when the Series 7 exam tests your sanity with more-complex calculations.

As you work with options charts, you may notice a pattern when determining maximum losses and gains. Table 12-1 gives you a quick reference concerning the maximum gain or maximum loss an investor faces when buying or selling call options. Notice that the buyer's loss is equal to the seller's gain (and vice versa).

TABLE 12-1 **Maximum Gains and Losses for Call Options**

Buying or Selling	Maximum Loss	Maximum Gain
Buying a call	Premium	Unlimited
Selling an uncovered call	Unlimited	Premium

TIP

The key phrase to remember when working with call options is *calls same*, which means that the premium and the strike price go on the same side of the options chart.

Buying call options

The following steps show you how to calculate the maximum loss and gain for holders of call options (which give the holder the right to buy). I also show you how to find the break-even point. Here's the order ticket for the example calculations:

Buy 1 XYZ Oct 40 call at 5

1. Find the maximum loss (maximum potential loss or maximum possible loss).

The holder of an option doesn't have to exercise it, so the most she can lose is the premium. The premium is 5, so this investor purchased the option for $500 (5 × 100 shares per option); therefore, you enter that value in the Money Out side of the options chart (think "money out of the investor's pocket"). According to the chart, the maximum loss (the most this investor can lose) is $500.

Money Out	Money In
$500	

2. Determine the maximum gain (maximum potential gain or maximum possible gain).

To calculate the maximum gain, you have to exercise the option at the strike price. The strike price is 40, so you enter $4,000 (40 strike price × 100 shares per option) under its premium (which you added to the chart when calculating maximum loss); exercising the call means buying the stock, so that's Money Out. When exercising call options, always put the multiplied strike price under its premium. (Remember *calls same:* The premium and the strike price go on the same side of the options chart.)

Money Out	Money In
$500	
$4,000	

Because you've already determined the maximum loss, look at the Money In portion of the options chart. The Money In is empty, so the maximum gain (the most money the investor can make) is unlimited.

When you see a question about the break-even point, the Series 7 examiners are asking, "At what point does this investor not have a gain or loss?" The simplest way to figure out this point for a call option is to use *call up* (remember that call options go in-the-money when the price of the stock goes above the strike price — see the section "Getting your money back: Options in-, at-, or out-of-the-money"). When using *call up*, you add the strike price to the premium:

strike price + premium = 40 + 5 = 45

For this investor, the break-even point is 45. This number makes sense because the investor paid $5 for the option, so the option has to go $5 in-the-money for the investor to recoup the amount she paid. *Note:* The break-even point is always the same for the buyer and the seller.

Selling call options

Here, I show you how to find the maximum gain and loss, as well as the break-even point, for sellers of call options. Here's the order ticket for the example calculations:

Sell 1 ZYX Oct 60 call at 2

1. **Determine the maximum gain.**

The seller makes money only if the holder fails to exercise the option or exercises it when the option is in-the-money by less than the premium received. This investor sold the option for $200 (2 × 100 shares per option); therefore, you enter that amount in the Money In side of the options chart. According to the chart, the maximum gain (the most that this investor can make) is the $200 premium received. ***Note:*** The exercised strike price of $6,000 (60 × 100 shares) doesn't come into play when determining the maximum gain in this example because the holder of the option would exercise the option only if it were in-the-money.

Money Out	Money In
	$200

2. **Find the maximum loss.**

To calculate the maximum loss, you need to exercise the option at the strike price. The strike price is 60, so you enter $6,000 (60 strike price × 100 shares per option) under its premium. The $6,000 goes in the Money In side of the options chart because this investor had to sell the stock to the holder at the strike price (60 × 100 shares). When exercising call options, always enter the multiplied strike price under its premium. (Remember *calls same:* The premium and the strike price go on the same side of the options chart.)

Money Out	Money In
	$200
	$6,000

You've already determined the maximum gain; now look at the Money Out portion of the options chart. The Money Out is empty, so the maximum loss (the most money the investor can lose) is unlimited.

When you see a question about the break-even point, the examiners are asking you, "At what point does this investor not have a gain or loss?" The simplest way to figure this out for a call option is to use *call up*. When using *call up*, you add the strike price to the premium:

$$\text{strike price} + \text{premium} = 60 + 2 = 62$$

For this investor, the break-even point is 62. This makes sense because the investor received $2 for the option, so the option has to go $2 in-the-money for this investor to lose the amount that she received for selling the option. Call options go in-the-money when the price of the stock goes above the strike price.

REMEMBER

When you're selling a call option and you don't own the stock to deliver if the option is exercised or you don't own a call option on the same stock that would be in-the-money first, your option position is considered *uncovered* or *naked*. If, however, you do own the stock for enough shares to cover the option or hold a call option on the same stock that would be in-the-money first, you're considered covered (known as a *covered call*).

Buying or selling put options

Fortunately, when you're calculating the buying or selling of put options (which give the holder the right to sell), you use the options chart in the same way but with a slight change (see the preceding section for info on call options). Instead of using *calls same* as you do with call options, you use *puts switch* — in other words, you place the premium and the strike price on opposite sides of the options chart.

Table 12-2 serves as a quick reference regarding the maximum gain or maximum loss an investor faces when buying or selling put options.

TABLE 12-2 **Maximum Gains and Losses for Put Options**

Buying or Selling	Maximum Loss	Maximum Gain
Buying a put	Premium	(strike − premium) × 100 shares
Selling an uncovered put	(strike − premium) × 100 shares	Premium

Buying put options

This section explains how to find the maximum loss, maximum gain, and the break-even point for buyers (holders) of put options. Here's the ticket order for the calculations:

Buy 1 TUV Oct 55 put at 6

1. **Find the maximum loss.**

Exercising an option is, well, optional for the holder, so buyers of put options can't lose more than the premium. Because this investor purchased the option for $600 (6 × 100 shares per option), you enter that value in the Money Out side of the options chart. The maximum loss (the most that this investor can lose) is the $600 premium paid.

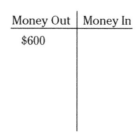

Money Out	Money In
$600	

2. Determine the maximum gain.

To find the maximum gain, you have to exercise the option at the strike price. The strike price is 55, so you enter $5,500 (55 strike price × 100 shares per option) on the opposite side of the options chart. (Remember *puts switch:* The premium and the strike price go on opposite sides of the options chart.) Exercising the option means selling the underlying stock, so that $5,500 is Money In.

Money Out	Money In
$600	$5,500

You've already determined the maximum loss; now look at the Money In portion of the options chart. Because you find $4,900 more Money In than Money Out ($5,500 – $600), the maximum gain is $4,900.

The break-even point is the security price where the investor doesn't have a gain or loss. The simplest way to figure this point out for a put option is to use *put down* (put options go in-the-money when the price of the stock goes below the strike price). When using *put down*, you subtract the premium from the strike price:

$$\text{strike price} - \text{premium} = 55 - 6 = 49$$

For this investor, the break-even point is 49. The investor paid $6 for the option, so the option has to go $6 in-the-money in order for this investor to recoup the amount that she paid. As with call options, the break-even point is always the same for the buyer and the seller.

Selling put options

The following steps show you how to calculate the maximum gain and loss for the seller of a put option. I also demonstrate calculations for the break-even point. Here's the ticket order for the example:

Sell 1 TUV Sep 30 put at 8

1. Determine the maximum gain.

The seller makes money only if the holder of the option fails to exercise it. This investor sold the option for $800 (8 × 100 shares per option); you put that number in the Money In side of the options chart. The maximum gain (the most this investor can make) is $800.

Money Out	Money In
	$800

2. **Find the maximum loss.**

To calculate the maximum loss, you have to exercise the option at the strike price. The strike price is 30, so you place $3,000 (30 strike price × 100 shares per option) on the opposite side of the options chart. (Remember *puts switch:* The premium and strike price go on opposite sides of the options chart.)

Money Out	Money In
$3,000	$800

You've already determined the maximum gain; now look at the Money Out portion of the options chart and compare it to the Money In. The maximum potential loss for this investor is the $2,200 difference between the Money Out and the Money In.

You calculate the break-even point for buying or selling puts the same way: You use *put down* (the strike price minus the premium) to figure out the break-even point:

$$\text{strike price} - \text{premium} = 30 - 8 = 22$$

For this investor, the break-even point is 22. Because this investor received $8 for the option, the option has to go $8 in-the-money for this investor to lose the amount she received for selling the option. Put options go in-the-money when the price of the stock goes below the strike price (put down).

REMEMBER

When you're selling a put option and you don't have a *short* position on that stock covering the put option or you don't own a put option on the same stock that would be in-the-money first, your option position is considered *uncovered* or *naked.* If, however, you do have a short position on the stock for enough shares to cover the option or hold a put option on the same stock that would be in-the-money first, you're considered covered (known as a covered put).

Trading options: Opening and closing transactions

Although some investors hold onto their options long enough to actually exercise them, most investors trade options the way that they trade other investments. On the Series 7, not only do you need to know the difference between opening and closing transactions, but you also have to be able to calculate the profit or loss for an investor trading options. This process is actually pretty easy when you break it down.

Putting things back where you found them: Doing opposite transactions

When distinguishing between opening and closing transactions, your key is to know whether this transaction is the first time or the second time the investor is buying or selling an option: The first time is an *opening,* and the second time is a *closing.* Regardless of whether it is an opening or closing transaction, it must be placed on the order ticket.

Here are your opening transactions:

» **Opening purchase:** An opening purchase occurs when an investor first buys a call or a put.

» **Opening sale:** An opening sale is when an investor first sells a call or a put.

If an investor already has an option position, the investor has to close that position by doing the opposite — through a closing transaction. If the investor originally purchased the option, she has to sell to close it. By contrast, if she originally sold the option, she has to purchase to close. Here are the two types of closing transactions:

» **Closing purchase:** A closing purchase occurs when an investor buys herself out of a previous option position that she sold. For example, if an investor sold an XYZ Oct 40 call (opening sale), she would have to buy an XYZ Oct 40 call to close out the position. The second transaction is a closing purchase.

» **Closing sale:** A closing sale occurs when an investor sells herself out of a previous option position that she purchased. For example, if an investor bought an ABC Sep 60 put (opening purchase), she would have to sell an ABC Sep 60 put to close out the position. The second transaction is a closing sale.

REMEMBER

When determining opening or closing transactions, whether the transactions are both calls or both puts doesn't matter.

The following question tests your knowledge of opening and closing transactions.

EXAMPLE

Mr. Dimpledell previously bought 1 XYZ Oct 65 call at 8 when the market price of XYZ was 64. XYZ is currently trading at 69, and Mr. Dimpledell decides that now would be a good time to sell the option that he previously purchased. The second option order ticket would be marked

(A) opening sale

(B) opening purchase

(C) closing sale

(D) closing purchase

The right answer is Choice (C). This is the second time that Mr. Dimpledell does something with the option that he owns; therefore, the move has to be a closing transaction, and you can immediately eliminate Choices (A) and (B). Mr. Dimpledell has to sell himself out of the position because he owns the option. The second order ticket would have to be marked closing sale.

Tricks of the options trade: Calculating gains and losses

In addition to knowing how to mark the order ticket, you have to be able to figure out an investor's gain or loss when trading options. This task isn't difficult after you master the options chart. The key thing to remember is that when an investor closes, she does the opposite of what she did before.

The following question tests your mastery of options trades.

EXAMPLE

Mrs. Rice purchased 100 shares of DPY stock at $50 per share. Two weeks later, Mrs. Rice sold 1 DPY Oct 55 call at 6. Mrs. Rice held that position for 3 months before selling the DPY stock at $52 per share and closing the DPY Oct 55 call at 4. What is Mrs. Rice's gain or loss on the transactions?

(A) $400 gain

(B) $400 loss

(C) $600 gain

(D) no gain or loss

The correct answer is Choice (A). This question introduces stock trades as well as options transactions, but that's no problem. The options chart works for questions involving actual stocks and options or just options.

When you approach the transactions one at a time, the problem-solving process is actually pretty straightforward. Mrs. Rice purchased 100 shares of DPY stock at $50 per share for a total of $5,000; therefore, you enter $5,000 in the Money Out side of the options chart. Next, she sold the DPY 55 call for a premium of 6, so you need to enter $600 (6 × 100 shares per option) on the Money In side of the chart because she received money for selling that option.

Three months later, Mrs. Rice sold the stock for $5,200 ($52 per share × 100 shares) and received money for selling the stock. Place the $5,200 in the Money In side of the options chart. When closing the option, the customer has to do the opposite of what she did before. Originally, Mrs. Rice sold the option, so to close, she has to buy the option (make a closing purchase). She purchased the option for $400 (4 × 100 shares per option), so enter $400 in the Money Out side of the options chart. All that's left for you to do is total up the two sides. Mrs. Rice has $5,800 in and $5,400 out for a gain of $400.

Money Out	Money In
$5,000	$600
$400	$5,200
$5,400	$5,800

Mastering Complex Option Calculations

You may not be happy to hear this, but some investors out there will make your life difficult. But, hey, don't be too upset, because working with these customers is how you're going to earn your six- or seven-figures-a-year salary (not including pennies). The Series 7 exam also tests your knowledge on more-complex option strategies. Of course, you can use an options chart to make your life much easier.

Long straddles and combinations

Straddles are option positions in which the investor buys a call and a put or sells a call and a put on the same underlying security with the same strike (exercise) price and the same expiration month; if the securities are the same but the strike prices and/or expiration months are different, you have a *combination* instead. What's nice is that combinations and straddles are virtually the same and the calculations are performed the same way.

This section deals with long positions, which involve purchases. (See "Short straddles and combinations" for info on sales.)

Long straddle

A *long straddle* is buying a call and a put with the same underlying stock, the same strike price, and the same expiration month. Investors who are expecting *volatility* in the underlying security purchase long straddles. These investors aren't sure which direction the stock will go, so they're covering their bases. They own a call option in case the price of the stock increases, and they own a put option in case the price of the stock decreases. Here's an example of a long straddle:

> Buy 1 DEF Oct 40 call at 6
>
> Buy 1 DEF Oct 40 put at 3

In order to have a long straddle (or combination) you must have two buys.

Long combination

A *long combination* is buying a call and a put for the same underlying stock with a different strike price and/or expiration month. As with straddles (see the preceding "Long straddle" section), an investor of a long combination is looking for a security that's volatile. The investor isn't sure which direction the security will go, so she buys a call in case the security increases in value and a put in case it decreases in value. Here's what a long combination may look like:

> Buy 1 LMN Oct 40 call at 6
>
> Buy 1 LMN Oct 30 put at 1

To distinguish a combination from a straddle, look at the expiration months and the strike (exercise) prices. If either one is different or both are different, you're dealing with a combination.

The following example tests your skill at distinguishing a straddle from a combination.

An investor who owns 1 XYZ Oct 40 call option would like to establish a long combination. Which of the following option positions would fulfill his needs?

(A) Write 1 XYZ Jan 40 put

(B) Buy 1 XZY Oct 30 put

(C) Buy 1 XYZ Oct 40 put

(D) Buy 1 XYZ Jan 30 put

The answer you're looking for is Choice (D). You can cross off Choice (A) right away because a long combination requires two purchases; Choice (A) is a sell (write), so it can't be right. You can cross off Choice (B), too, because although it looks ever so close, it involves a different security. Choice (C) would be correct if the question had indicated that the investor was looking for a straddle. A *long combination*, however, is buying a call and a put for the same security with different expiration months and/or different strike prices. Therefore, the only answer that works is Choice (D).

Try another problem to practice using the options chart (see the earlier "Incorporating Standard Option Math" section for the basics on buying and exercising options):

EXAMPLE

An investor buys 1 ABC Mar 60 call at 6 and buys 1 ABC Mar 50 put at 3. ABC subsequently increases to 68. The investor exercises the call and immediately sells the stock in the market. After the put expires unexercised, what is the investor's gain or loss?

(A) $100 gain

(B) $100 loss

(C) $500 gain

(D) $500 loss

The correct answer is Choice (B). The investor bought the call for $600 (6 × 100 shares per option), so you have to enter $600 in the Money Out section of the options chart because that was money paid from the investor's pocket. After that, the investor purchased the put for $300 (3 × 100 shares per option), so you have to enter $300 in the Money Out section of the chart. The next sentence states that the stock increased to 68, but it doesn't tell you to do anything with that yet, so you don't.

Next, you have to exercise the call option at the call strike price (always exercise at the strike price) and place the $6,000 (60 strike price × 100 shares per option) under its premium. (Remember *calls same:* The premium and strike price go on the same side of the options chart.) This investor sold the stock in the market for $6,800 (68 × 100 shares per option), which is Money In the investor's pocket. Total up each side, and you see that this investor has a loss of $100.

Money Out	Money In
$600	
$300	
$6,000	$6,800
$6,900	$6,800

TIP

When you get an option question with several steps (like the preceding one), look for the action words to tell you what to do. Action words include

>> Buys, holds, owns, longs

>> Sells, writes, shorts

>> Exercises

Every time you see an action word, think of it as a clue to remind you that you have to put something in the options chart.

Short straddles and combinations

Short positions involve selling a call and a put with the same underlying stock. In straddles, the calls and puts have the same strike price and expiration month; with combinations, one of these values may differ.

Short straddle

A *short straddle* is selling a call and a put with the same underlying stock, the same strike price, and the same expiration month. An investor who is short a straddle is looking for *stability*. Because these investors are looking for a stock that's not going to change too much in price, short straddles are considered a *neutral position*. If the stock doesn't move in price, these investors will be able to keep the premiums they received for selling the options. A short straddle may look like this:

Sell 1 GHI Oct 50 call at 9

Sell 1 GHI Oct 50 put at 2

In order to have a short straddle (or combination), you must have two sells.

REMEMBER

Short combination

A *short combination* involves selling a call and a put for the same underlying stock with a different strike price and/or expiration month. Similar to a short straddle, an investor who sells a combination has a neutral position and is looking for a security with stability. The investor is hoping the securities don't go in-the-money so the options are not exercised and she gets to keep the premiums received. A short combination may look like this:

Sell 1 QRS Dec 60 call at 4

Sell 1 QRS Mar 55 put at 3

Fortunately, for both straddles and combinations, you can calculate the maximum gain and maximum loss by just placing the premiums in the options chart. No exercising is necessary. For instance, suppose an investor has the following ticket orders:

Sell 1 TUV Jul 45 call at 6

Sell 1 TUV Jul 40 put at 3

Here's how you find the maximum potential loss and gain:

1. **Find the investor's maximum potential gain.**

This problem involves a combination because the strike prices are different. However, if it were a straddle, you'd figure out the answer the same way. Place the premiums in the options chart. The investor sold the call for $600 (6 × 100 shares per option) and the put for $300 (3 × 100 shares per option). The transactions are both *sells,* so they have to go in the Money In side of the options chart. Add the numbers, and you can see that the maximum that this investor can gain (if the options never go in-the-money) is the $900 ($600 + $300) in premiums that she received.

Money Out	Money In
	$600
	$300
	$900

2. **Determine the investor's maximum potential loss.**

With straddles and combinations, the premiums help you determine both the maximum potential gain and the maximum potential loss. After entering the premiums in the options chart, you may notice that the Money Out side of the chart is empty, so the investor's maximum potential loss is unlimited.

Break-even points for straddles and combinations

Straddles and combinations are a combination of calls and puts; therefore, you can find two break-even points (one on the way up and one on the way down). You must first add the two premiums together, because the investor either paid money twice (bought the call and bought the put) or received money twice (sold the call and sold the put). In the case cited in the preceding section, after you add the two premiums together, the total is 9 (6 + 3). Next, you use *call up* and add the combined premiums to the call strike price to get one break-even point. To get the other break-even point, use *put down* and subtract the combined premiums from the put strike price. This investor's break-even points are 31 and 54:

Combined premium: 6 + 3 = 9

Call up: Call strike + combined premium = 45 + 9 = 54

Put down: Put strike – combined premium = 40 – 9 = 31

REMEMBER

You always have two break-even points for straddles and combinations. Make sure you *call up* (add the combined premiums to the call strike price) and *put down* (subtract the combined premiums from the put strike price) to get the break-even points.

Spreads

Investors create a *spread* position by buying an option and selling an option on the same underlying security. The maximum gain or loss with a spread position is limited. Investors create spread positions to either limit their potential loss or to reduce the premium paid.

Call spread

An investor creates a *call spread* position when buying a call and selling a call on the same underlying security. Additionally, the strike prices and/or expiration months have to be different. Here's what a call spread may look like:

Buy 1 JKL Aug 50 call at 9

Sell 1 JKL Aug 60 call at 2

The following sections show you how to find the maximum gain, maximum loss, and break-even points for spreads. The process for finding the maximum gain, maximum loss, and break-even point is the same for both call spreads and put spreads. If you put the premiums in the options chart, you will see that the investor has more money out than money in. Therefore, this investor created a *debit (long) spread*.

Put spread

An investor creates a *put spread* position when buying a put and selling a put on the same underlying stock with different expiration month and/or strike prices. Here's an example of a put spread position:

Buy 1 MNO Sep 30 put at 1

Sell 1 MNO Sep 40 put at 8

When putting the premiums in the options chart, this investor will have more money in than money out, thereby creating a *credit (short) spread*. The options chart can make figuring out the particulars, such as the maximum gain, maximum loss, and break-even points easier. Here's how you find these numbers, using the preceding put spread numbers:

1. **Determine the maximum gain.**

   Begin by entering the premiums in the options chart. This investor bought the 30 put option for $100 (1 × 100 shares per option), so that $100 is Money Out of her pocket. Then this investor sold the 40 put for a premium of $800 (8 × 100 shares per option), which you enter in the Money In side of the chart because she received money for selling that option.

Money Out	Money In
$100	$800

   You end up with more Money In than Money Out; therefore, the investor's maximum potential gain is $700 ($800 in minus $100 out).

    To help you recognize a spread, notice that when you put the two premiums in the options chart, they are *spread apart* (one on either side).

2. **Find the maximum loss.**

   You already calculated the maximum gain, so next you need to exercise both options to get the maximum loss. When exercising put options, enter the strike prices (multiplied by 100 shares) on the opposite side of the chart from their premiums because puts switch (go on the opposite side of the chart from the premium). First, exercise the 30 put and enter $3,000 (30 × 100 shares per option) in the Money In side of the chart, which is opposite from the $100 premium. Next, exercise the 40 put and enter $4,000 (40 × 100 shares per option) in the Money Out side of the options chart, which is opposite its $800 premium. Total up the two sides, and you see that the maximum potential loss is $300 ($4,100 out minus $3,800 in).

Money Out	Money In
$100	$800
$4,000	$3,000
$4,100	$3,800

 Placing just the premiums in the options chart can give you the maximum potential gain or maximum potential loss but not both. To find the other answer, you must exercise both options.

Determining the break-even point for spreads

To find the break-even point, begin by finding the difference between the two premiums because you had one buy and one sell:

adjusted premium = 8 − 1 = 7

This is a put spread; therefore, you have to subtract the 7 from the higher strike price. The higher strike price is 40, so the break-even point is 33:

$$\text{break-even point (put spread)} = \text{higher strike price} - \text{adjusted premium} = 40 - 7 = 33$$

REMEMBER

For call spreads, you have to *add* the adjusted premium (after you've subtracted the smaller premium from the larger one) to the lower strike price. For put spreads, you *subtract* the adjusted premium from the higher strike price.

The following question tests your ability to determine the break-even point on spreads.

EXAMPLE

Miguel Hammer purchased 1 Apr 40 call at 9 and shorted 1 Apr 50 call at 3. What is Miguel's break-even point?

(A) 43

(B) 46

(C) 49

(D) 53

The right answer is Choice (B). First, focus on the buy and the sell. If the investor is buying one option and selling another, you should be able to recognize it as a spread. Therefore, you have to find the difference between the two premiums:

$$\text{adjusted premium} = 9 - 3 = 6$$

Next, because it's a call spread, you have to add the adjusted premium (after subtracting the smaller from the larger) to the call strike (exercise) price to get the break-even point:

$$\text{break-even point (call spread)} = 40 + 6 = 46$$

The following question tests your ability to answer a spread story question.

EXAMPLE

Mrs. Peabody purchased 1 DEF Mar 60 put at 5 and wrote 1 DEF Mar 65 put at 9 when DEF was trading at 68. Six months later, with DEF trading at 61, Mrs. Peabody's DEF Mar 65 put was exercised. Mrs. Peabody held the shares of DEF for another two months before selling them in the market for $62 per share. Mrs. Peabody's Mar 60 put expired without ever going in-the-money. What is Mrs. Peabody's gain or loss?

(A) $100 loss

(B) $100 gain

(C) $700 loss

(D) $700 gain

The answer you're looking for is Choice (B). I like to call such problems story questions because they take you on a journey, and this one is a tricky one. If you got this right, you're a master of spreads.

Begin by placing the transactions in the correct side of the options chart. Because Mrs. Peabody purchased the DEF Mar 60 put at 5, you have to enter $500 (5 × 100 shares per option) on the Money Out side of the options chart because she spent that much to purchase the option. After that, she sold a DEF Mar 65 put for 9 and received $900 (9 × 100 shares per option) Money In for selling that option. The fact that DEF was trading at 61 when the option was exercised means nothing in this question, so feel free to ignore it.

Next, you have to exercise the 65 put that Mrs. Peabody sold. Because *puts switch*, you enter the strike price (multiplied by 100 shares) in the opposite side of the options chart from its premium.

After you place the $6,500 in the Money Out section of the options chart, you have to sell the stock that Mrs. Peabody purchased when her option was exercised. She sold the stock in the market for $6,200 ($62 market price × 100 shares) and received cash for that transaction, so enter $6,200 in the Money In section of the chart. Total up the two sides, and you can see that good old Mrs. Peabody has a gain of $100.

Money Out	Money In
$500	$900
$6,500	$6,200
$7,000	$7,100

TIP

Just like other option story questions (with several things happening), enter only items in the options chart when you see action words. Remember, every time you see an action word, such as *purchased, wrote, exercised, sold,* and so on, you know that you have to enter something in the options chart.

Understanding different types of spreads

When looking at a spread position, you may be asked to determine whether it's a *vertical, horizontal,* or *diagonal* spread. The way that you can tell is by looking at the strike prices and the expiration months. If just the strike prices differ, it's called a vertical or price spread. If just the expiration months differ, it's called a horizontal or calendar spread. If both the strike prices and expiration months are different, it's called a diagonal spread.

Here is an example of a vertical (price) spread:

> Buy 1 TUV May **40** call for 6
>
> Write 1 TUV May **50** call for 2

So, for a spread, an investor is buying and selling call or put option on the same security. The preceding example shows a vertical (price) spread, as just the strike or exercise prices are different. This investor would be bullish on TUV because she's buying at the lower strike price and selling at the higher one. For this investor, you can see that if the option she purchased doesn't go in-the-money, she'll have a loss of $400 ($600 premium minus $200 premium), which makes it a debit call spread. The net premium paid is $400 ($600 minus $200), so the option purchased has to go in-the-money by over 4 (above 64) for her to be able to have a profit. Once the price of the stock goes to 50 or above, it makes no difference to this investor because every dollar gained on the option she owns will be offset by a dollar lost on the option sold.

Here is an example of a horizontal (calendar or time) spread:

> Buy 1 XYZ **May** 30 call for 4
>
> Write 1 XYZ **Aug** 30 call for 7

As with all spreads, the investor is buying and selling call or put options on the same security. The preceding example shows a horizontal (calendar or time) spread, as the exercise price is the same, but the expiration months are different. In this case, the investor already has a profit of $300 because he sold the option for 7 and purchased the option for 4 and options are for 100 shares. Therefore, it is a credit call spread. He already has a profit and therefore doesn't want the option to go in-the-money.

Here is an example of a diagonal spread:

Buy 1 LMN **May 40** call for 7

Write 1 LMN **Aug 50** call for 4

This investor is buying and selling call or put options on the same underlying security. Since both the expiration months and the exercise prices differ, the spread is considered a diagonal spread. In the preceding example, you can see that the investor has a loss, so he needs the option owned to go in-the-money by 3 (7 minus 4) to break even. Certainly if it goes higher than 43, there is a potential profit to be made; however, because the option this investor owns will expire first, he will be exposed to unlimited loss potential on the option sold.

TIP

To determine if an investor's spread position is bullish or bearish, a neat thing is that it doesn't matter whether you're dealing with call options or put options. All you need to do is look at the strike prices. If the investor purchased the option with the lower strike price and sold the one with the higher strike price (buy low, sell high) she's bullish. If the investor bought the option with the higher strike price and sold the one with the lower strike price, she's bearish.

TIP

When subtracting the premiums whether looking at call spreads or put spreads, you can determine if the investor has more money out of his pocket (debit spread) or more money in his pocket (credit spread). So for debit spreads (they can be debit call spreads or debit put spreads), the investor already has a loss, so the only way he can make money is if the options are exercised or the premium difference widens and he can close the transactions and make some money. Conversely, if the investor already has a credit spread (they can be credit call spreads or credit put spreads), he's already made the most amount of money he can, so he wants the options to expire or the premium difference to narrow so that he can close the transactions and make money.

Got it covered: Stock/option contracts

When an investor purchases or sells option contracts on securities she owns, that investor is choosing an excellent way to protect (hedge) against loss or to bring additional funds into her account, which would only be a partial hedge. The most common form is when an investor sells *covered call options.*

If an investor is selling a call option against a security that she owns, the investor is considered to be *covered.* She's covered because if the option is exercised, she has the stock to deliver.

Take the following position as an example:

Buy 100 shares of QRS at $47 per share

Sell 1 QRS Dec 55 call at 4

1. **Find this investor's maximum potential loss.**

Place the purchases and sales in the options chart. This investor purchased 100 shares of QRS stock at $47 per share for a total of $4,700. That's money spent, so enter $4,700 in the Money Out side of the options chart. Next, this investor sold 1 QRS Dec 55 call for a total premium of $400 (4 × 100 shares per option) and received money for selling that option, so you enter $400 in the Money In section of the options chart.

Money Out	Money In
$4,700	$400

This investor has more Money Out than Money In, so the investor's maximum potential loss is $4,300 ($4,700 minus $400).

2. **Determine the investor's maximum potential gain.**

   Placing the two transactions (in this case the stock purchase and the option sale) in the options chart helps you calculate the maximum gain as well as the maximum loss. To find the maximum gain, you need to exercise the option. You always exercise at the strike price, which in this case is 55. Take the $5,500 (55 × 100 shares per option) and place it under its premium. (Remember *calls same:* The exercised strike price and the premium go on the same side of the chart.) Total the two sides and you find that the Money In is $1,200 more than the Money Out, so that's the investor's maximum potential gain.

Money Out	Money In
$4,700	$400
	$5,500
$4,700	$5,900

When the investor is covered, finding the break-even point is nice and easy for stock and options. Although you can use the options chart, you really don't need to in this example case. First, look at how much the investor paid for the stock; then look at how much more she paid or received for the option. Find the difference, and you have your break-even point:

$47 stock price − $4 option premium = $43 break-even point

Because this investor paid $47 per share for the stock and received back $4 per share for selling the option, this investor would need to receive another $43 per share to break even.

REMEMBER

Here's how to find the break-even point for stock and options:

>> **If the investor purchased twice** (bought the stock and bought a *protective put* option), add the stock price and the premium.

>> **If the investor sold twice** (sold short the stock and sold an option), add the stock price and the premium.

>> **If the investor had one buy and one sell** (for example, bought the stock and sold the option or sold short the stock and bought the option), subtract the premium from the stock price.

The following example tests your knowledge on stock and option problems.

EXAMPLE

Mr. Bullwork sold short 100 shares of DIM common stock at $25 per share and bought 1 DIM Aug 30 call at 3 to hedge his position. What is Mr. Bullwork's maximum potential loss from this strategy?

(A) $300

(B) $800

(C) $2,200

(D) $2,700

The answer you're looking for is Choice (B). As always, you need to enter the initial purchase and sale into the options chart and see what you have. Your friend and client, Mr. Bullwork, sold short 100 shares of DIM common stock at $25 per share for a total of $2,500. Because Mr. Bullwork received the $2,500 for selling short, you have to put $2,500 in the Money In side of the options chart. Next, Mr. Bullwork purchased a DIM Aug 30 call to hedge (protect) his position in case the stock started increasing in value. You have to enter the $300 (3 × 100 shares per option) in the Money Out side of the options chart, because he paid money to purchase the option. Stop and take a look to see whether that calculation answers the question.

Money Out	Money In
$300	$2,500

You see more Money In at this point than Money Out, so you have a maximum gain, not a maximum loss; therefore, you have to exercise the option to get the answer you need. Make sure you exercise the option at the strike price. The strike price is 30, so enter $3,000 under its premium. (Remember *calls same:* The premium and multiplied strike price go on the same side of the chart.) Total up the two sides, and you see that the maximum potential loss for Mr. Bullwork is $800 ($3,300 minus $2,500).

Money Out	Money In
$300	$2,500
$3,000	
$3,300	$2,500

TIP

Remember that an investor who is long a particular security can buy an option on that same security to protect the position in the event that the price of the security declines or can sell an option on that same security to bring in money. For example, if an investor who is long 100 shares of DEF at 52 decides to sell a 55 call option at 4 on DEF *(covered call)* to bring some additional money (the $4 per share premium) into his account. The good part is that he lowered his break-even point to $48 ($52 per share for the stock minus $4 per share for the premium). The bad part is that he limited his upside potential for the remaining time on the option contract to $55 per share because he sold the right to have someone purchase the stock from him at $55. If this investor purchased a 50 put option at 2 *(protective put)* to limit his downside if the price of DEF starts to decrease, he just increased his break-even point from $52 to $54 ($52 per share for the stock plus $2 per share for the option).

The opposite holds true for investors who sold short. An investor who is short a particular security can purchase a call to protect himself in the event that the price of the security increases and can also sell a put on security shorted to bring some additional money into his account.

Investors who are long a stock may decide to sell a covered call on the underlying stock and purchase a protective put on the same underlying stock. This is known as a *collar*. If the cost of the premiums are equal, it is considered a *cashless collar*. Even though the cost of the trades may offset each other and now the investor has limited his downside risk, he has also limited his upside potential.

Off the charts: Multiple option contracts

Now before you start freaking out, know that working with multiple option contracts isn't that much more difficult than working with single contracts. This change is simply a matter of an investor buying two, three, four, or more of the same option contract at one time. I guide you through the steps in this section.

TIP

When you work with multiple option contracts, approach the problem as though you were dealing with only one contract. You can easily do so by taking the multiple (the number of contracts) and placing it to the side of the options chart so you don't forget it. Calculate the maximum potential loss or gain for a single contract, and then multiply that answer by the number of contracts.

The following sample calculations use this ticket order:

Buy 6 ABC Oct 40 calls at 7

Sell 6 ABC Oct 55 calls at 2

1. **Find the investor's maximum potential loss.**

Take the number of contracts (in this case it's six) and place it to the side of the options chart. Now this problem is as simple as the other options I mention in the earlier sections. In this case, you can look at the problem as though the investor is buying a call for $700 (7 × 100 shares per option), which is Money Out of the investor's pocket. Next, the investor sells (writes) the ABC Oct 55 call for $200 (2 × 100 shares per option). Because this transaction is a sale, you enter it in the Money In side of the options chart. The investor has $700 out and $200 in; therefore, the maximum loss per option is $500. Now, take a look at the multiple. Take the maximum loss and multiply it by six (six options on each side), and you end up with a maximum loss of $3,000 for this investor.

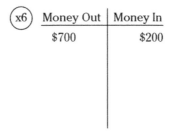

Maximum loss = $500 per option x 6 = $3,000

Note: Some option strategies include having a different number of options on each side. However, you're unlikely to be tested on these strategies on the Series 7. These strategies are covered more in the Series 4 exam (the Registered Options Principal Qualification exam).

2. Determine the investor's maximum potential gain.

When dealing with spreads, the premiums give you the maximum gain or the maximum loss but not both. Because you've already so expertly determined the investor's maximum potential loss, you need to exercise both options to get the maximum potential gain. Approach the question as if you were dealing with only one option on each side. Multiply the strike price of 40 by 100 shares per option to get $4,000. Enter $4,000 under its premium of $700. (Remember *calls same:* The premium and the strike price go on the same side of the chart.) After that, you can exercise the 55 call to get $5,500 (55 strike price × 100 shares per option). Enter $5,500 under its premium of $200 (again, following the *calls same* rule). Total up the two sides, and you have $1,000 more Money In than Money Out ($5,700 – $4,700). That value is the maximum gain for one option on each side. Because this investor has six options on each side, multiply the $1,000 by six to get $6,000 for this investor's maximum potential gain.

(x6)	Money Out	Money In
	$700	$200
	$4,000	$5,500
	$4,700	$5,700

Maximum gain = $1,000 per option x 6 = $6,000

What's nice about finding the break-even point is that it works out the same whether the investor has 1, 10, 30, or more options on either side of the market. In this case, the investor bought one option and sold the other, so you need to find the difference between the two premiums. After subtracting the two premiums, you end up with an answer of 5:

$$\text{adjusted premium} = 7 - 2 = 5$$

This is a call spread (buying a call and selling a call — see the earlier "Spreads" section), so you need to add the adjusted premium (5) to the lower strike price (40) to get the break-even point. In this case, the break-even point is 45:

$$\text{break-even point (call spread)} = 40 + 5 = 45$$

REMEMBER

Follow the same strategy for all option transactions (spreads, straddles, combinations, and so on) when dealing with multiple options: Always take the contract size and move it to the outside of the options chart when calculating the maximum gain or loss. Then multiply the gain or loss by the number of contracts.

You have to worry (and I use that term loosely) about not only multiple option contracts but also multiple options and multiples of 100 shares of stock purchases or sales. This process is a piece of cake if you follow the rules that I give you. Check out the example, which uses the following position:

Buy 400 shares of ABC common stock at $36

Buy 4 ABC Oct 30 puts at 4

1. Determine the investor's maximum potential gain.

This investor purchased 400 shares of stock and four options, which gives you a multiple of four. Take the multiple and move it to the outside of the options chart. You can then look at the problem as though the investor has only 100 shares of stock and 1 option, because you'll deal with the contract size later. First, enter the $3,600 that the investor paid for the stock ($36 × 100 shares) in the Money Out side of the options chart, because the investor spent money to purchase the stock. Next, enter the $400 that the investor paid for the option (4 × 100 shares per option) in the Money Out side of the options chart because the investor purchased the option. Because the Money In side of the chart is empty, the investor's maximum potential gain is unlimited.

(x4)	Money Out	Money In
	$3,600	
	$400	

2. **Find the investor's maximum potential loss.**

You've already determined the maximum potential gain; therefore, you need to exercise the option to get the maximum potential loss. The investor purchased a put option, so you have to enter the $3,000 (30 strike price × 100 shares per option) in the Money In side of the options chart. (Remember *puts switch:* The premium and the strike price go on opposite sides of the options chart.) Total up the two sides, and you see that you have $1,000 more Money Out than Money In, so the investor's maximum potential loss is $1,000 per option. Because this investor has four options and 400 shares, you need to multiply the $1,000 by four to get the maximum loss of $4,000.

(x4)	Money Out	Money In
	$3,600	
	$400	$3,000
	$4,000	$3,000

Maximum loss = $1,000 x 4 = $4,000

Here's how you find the investor's break-even point: In this case, the investor purchased the stock for $36 per share and the option for $4 per share. Therefore, this investor needs the price of the stock to go to $40 ($36 + $4) in order to break even:

break-even point (call spread) = 36 + 4 = 40

Spending time on LEAPS: Long-term options

LEAPS is short for Long-term Equity AnticiPation Securities. The initial expiration for most options is 9 months. LEAPS, however, can have initial expirations dates of up to 3 years and 3 months (39 months). Investors can purchase LEAPS on a large variety of stocks, ADRs, the Dow, the S&P 100, and the S&P 500. Although most options have to be paid for in full, a unique characteristic of LEAPS options is that, unlike standard options, they can be purchased on margin by an investor who comes up with 75 percent of the premium. (See the "Margin on options" section later in this chapter for more info.) As you can imagine, with all else being equal, the premium on LEAPS would be higher than those of an option with 9 months or less until expiration.

Dividends and splits, more or less

This section addresses how an option contract is adjusted for corporate actions such as a company declaring a dividend or splitting its stock (see Chapter 6 for more info on splits and dividends). I begin with the basics and move forward from there.

Stock dividends

When a company declares a stock dividend, here's what happens to option contracts:

>> The number of option contracts remains the same.

>> The strike price decreases.

>> The number of shares per option contract increases.

Please peruse the following example to see how this works out. Here, the investor's initial position is

4 ABC Sep 65 call options (100 shares per option)

If ABC declares a 5 percent stock dividend, you can find the investor's position on the *ex-dividend date* (the first day the stock trades without the dividend).

Because ABC is giving a 5 percent stock dividend, the result will be 105 shares per option instead of 100 (5 percent more shares). To find the new strike price, multiply the original 65 call options by 100 shares per option to get 6,500. Next, divide the 6,500 by the 105 shares per option to get a new strike price of 61.90 (rounded to the nearest cent). This is the new position:

4 ABC Sep 61.90 call options (105 shares per option)

WARNING

Cash dividends *do not* affect listed options. For example, suppose that an investor owns 1 ABC Oct 40 call option and ABC declares a $0.50 cash dividend. Although the price of the stock decreases by $0.50, the option still reads 1 ABC Oct 40 call.

Regular forward splits

Dealing with a regular forward split is relatively easy. In this case, you're dealing with a 2-for-1, 3-for-1, 4-for-1, and so on. I cover your approach to tackling uneven splits in the next section. In an anything-for-1 split, here's what happens:

>> The number of option contracts increases.

>> The strike price decreases.

>> The number of shares per option remains the same (normally 100).

Check out the following example, where the investor has an initial position of

2 DEF Jul 60 calls (100 shares per option)

If DEF Corporation announces a 3-for-1 split, the investor's position on the ex-dividend date is

6 DEF Jul 20 calls (100 shares per option)

In this case, the investor has three options for every one that she had before, and the strike price is 1/3 of what it was before:

$$2 \times \frac{3}{1} = \frac{6}{1} = 6 \text{ option contracts}$$

$$60 \times \frac{1}{3} = \frac{60}{3} = 20 \text{ strike price}$$

Notice how you multiply the contracts by 3/1 and the strike price by the reciprocal (1/3).

TIP

A good way to double-check your work for all dividends and splits is to multiply the number of option contracts by the strike price and then by the number of shares per option. Do the same thing after you adjust the numbers for the dividend or split. Compare the answers. You should get the same number. If you don't, you did something wrong.

Uneven and reverse splits

Uneven splits are similar to dividends in that the number of option contracts remains the same but the strike price and the number of shares per option change. Uneven splits are splits that are not *x*-for-1 (for example, 3-for-2, 4-for-3, 5-for-2, and so on). Look at the following example, where the investor has an initial position of

3 GHI Jun 50 calls (100 shares per option)

If GHI announces a 5-for-2 split, the investor's position on the ex-dividend date is

3 GHI Jun 20 calls (250 shares per option)

First, because the investor has 5 shares for every 2 that she had before, you have to multiply the shares per option by 5/2:

$$100 \text{ shares} \times \frac{5}{2} = \frac{500 \text{ shares}}{2} = 250 \text{ shares per option}$$

Next, you have to multiply the strike price by 2/5:

$$50 \text{ strike price} \times \frac{2}{5} = \frac{100}{5} = 20 \text{ new strike price}$$

To work out a reverse split (for example, 3-for-5, 2-for-3, and so forth), use the same process. Be aware that for reverse splits, the strike price increases and the shares per option decrease.

Nonequity Options

Although certainly most of the options questions you'll be dealing with on the Series 7 exam will relate to stock options, there are other options that you'll need to understand. Besides options on individual stocks, you can trade them on indexes, yields, and foreign currency.

Index options

Besides buying or selling options on an individual stock, you can also buy or sell index options. Index options allow investors to speculate on or hedge against the price movement of market or segments of the market. Like indexes themselves, index options can be broad-based or narrow-based. The main broad-based index options are the S&P 500 Index Options (SPX), the S&P 500 Volatility Market Index (VIX), and the S&P 100 Index Options (OEX). Narrow-based index options include options on the energy sector (IXE), financial sector (IXM), healthcare sector (IXV), technology sector (IXU), and so on.

Note: The Chicago Board Options Exchange (CBOE) VIX is a measure of how volatile investors believe that the S&P 500 index will be over the next 30 days. Typically, the higher the expectation of volatility, the higher the VIX premiums.

Premiums of index options

Like standard stock options, the pricing unit for index options is 100. This means that like standard stock options, you multiply the premium by 100 to get the actual cost.

Exercises in cash

Unlike regular stock options where when the option is exercised, the underlying security must be delivered, index options are settled in *cash*. This makes sense because it would be very difficult for investors to deliver a whole index. If the holder of an index call option exercises his option, he will receive the in-the-money amount multiplied by 100 based on the closing price at the *end of the trading day*, not the current value at the time of exercise.

Trading hours, settlement, and expiration dates

Narrow-based index options trade until 4:00 pm eastern time, and broad-based index options trade until 4:15 pm eastern time. Like equity options, the settlement date for index options is the next business day.

REMEMBER

Index options are either broad-based or narrow-based. So people may buy or sell index options based on how they believe the market will perform overall (broad-based) or just how a segment of the market will perform (narrow-based). In this case, the same strategy of buying calls and selling puts if you're bullish and buying puts and selling calls if you're bearish still applies. However, investors can also use index options to hedge (protect) a portfolio against a market decline. If an investor has a diverse portfolio of securities, he may decide to purchase an OEX or SPX put to protect himself in the event that the market declines. Also, an investor who has a large portfolio of healthcare sector stocks may purchase IXV put options to protect himself in the event that healthcare stocks are falling out of favor. There are even index options that only last a week *(weeklys)* that allow investors a way to trade index options based on economic news or earnings reports that may have a sudden impact on the market or a segment of the market.

TIP

You'll find that buyers and sellers of index options can incorporate most of the same strategies as equity option buyers and sellers. These strategies include covered writing, hedging, protective puts, straddles and combinations, and uncovered call or put writing.

Yield-based (interest rate) options

Yield-based (interest rate) options are based on yields instead of prices. Like index options, yield-based options are settled in cash. Yield-based options are based off of the yield of the most recently issued debt instruments such as the 13-week T-bill, the 5-year T-note, the 10-year T-note, and the 30-year T-bond. The value of the option is based on the difference between the value of the yield of the underlying debt instrument and the exercise price. For yield-based options, investors who're bullish on the yields (in other words, expecting that yields would increase) would buy yield-based calls or sell yield-based puts. Investors who're bearish on yields would buy yield-based puts or sell yield-based calls. For yield-based options, the strike price would need to be divided by 10 to determine the yield. For arguments sake, a strike price of 65 would represent a yield of 6.5 (65 strike price divided by 10). Look at the following example:

EXAMPLE

Mrs. Rice purchased an October 45 call based on the yield of a 30-year T-bond for a premium of 2.25 ($225: as with most other options, the premium gets multiplied by 100). The option expires nine months later when the settlement value is 48.50 (4.85 percent) and the call is exercised. What is Mrs. Rice's profit or loss?

To start, look to see how much the option is in-the-money (if it's out, Mrs. Rice lost her premium). In this case, the option is in-the-money by 3.5 (48.5 minus 45), so the profit would be the difference of what Mrs. Rice got at maturity, which is $350 (3.5 × 100) and what she paid ($225) for a whopping profit of $125.

TIP

Unlike regular stock options, which are exercisable *American way* (any time up until the time of expiration), yield-based options are only exercisable *European way* (only on the day of expiration). However, European-style options may still be traded up to the last trading date.

REMEMBER

There's an inverse relationship between bond yields and bond prices. So someone who is bullish on bond prices (believes they are going up) would be bearish on yields. Conversely, someone who's bearish on bond prices (believes they are going down) would be bullish on yields.

Foreign currency options

U.S. investors can purchase foreign currency options on the Australian dollar, Canadian dollar, British pound, Japanese yen, Swiss francs, and the euro. The idea behind this is that investors can speculate, or use foreign currency options to protect themselves (if they invest in foreign securities, U.S. companies with a foreign interest, or ones who get paid in foreign currency [importers and exporters]) based on what they believe is going to happen with a particular foreign currency in relation to the U.S. dollar. An investor who believes that the U.S. dollar will fall in relation to the euro might buy euro calls or sell euro puts because she is bullish on the euro compared to the U.S. dollar. Even though investors might be buying option contracts based on the euro, yen, or whatever, all exercises are settled in cash (same as index and yield-based options). Foreign currency options are actively traded on the NASDAQ OMX PHLX.

Contract sizes

Although foreign currency options used to be available to institutional or wealthy investors, the contract sizes are smaller than they used to be and now even a lot of retail investors would be able to afford them. The contract size for all foreign currency contracts except the yen is 10,000. The contract size for the yen is 1,000,000.

Strike prices and premiums

The strike prices of foreign currency options except for the yen are quoted in U.S. cents. The yen strike price is quoted in 1/100th of a U.S. cent. As with regular equity options, you have to multiply the premium by 100 to get the actual cost. So a premium of 2 means an actual cost of $200 (2 × 100). Now's where the contract size comes into play. If a euro contract is quoted with a premium of 2.5, the cost of the contract would be $250 (10,000 contract size × 0.025 quote size in pennies = $250).

Gaining Additional Option Info

To help you get a deeper understanding of options, you need to know a few additional things that you will most certainly see on the real-deal Series 7 exam. Some of these items include who issues the options, where you can get options quotations, what a ROP is, what a risk disclosure document is, and when options expire.

Clearing through the OCC

The Options Clearing Corporation (OCC) is the issuer and guarantor of all listed options. The OCC decides which options will trade and their strike prices. In addition, when an investor decides to exercise her option, it's the OCC that randomly decides which firm on the other end will be responsible for fulfilling the terms of the option.

Getting the go-ahead: Registered options principal

In order to open an options account for a client, the client must receive an ODD (covered in the next section), and you must exercise due diligence by getting the customer's investment objectives, employment status, estimated annual income, estimated net worth, estimated liquid net worth, marital status, number of dependents, age, investment experience and knowledge, and so on. In addition, the account and all transactions must be approved by a registered options principal (ROP), branch office manager, or limited principal-general securities sales supervisor. All options accounts must be approved or disapproved within ten business days. Please note that all option accounts may not be approved for all transactions — depending on the client, they may be approved for buying covered writing, uncovered writing, spreading, discretionary transactions, and so on. As with other security transactions, you must not make recommendations to customers involving options unless you have reasonable grounds to believe the option transaction(s) is/are suitable for the customer.

REMEMBER

Options are considered risky investments and are not suitable for all investors. Because of the extra risk of investing in options, all new accounts and all option order tickets must be signed by a registered options principal (ROP), which is a manager with a Series 4 license. The registered options principal determines the amount of risk that each investor can take. Certainly, sophisticated investors with a lot of money are able to handle more risk than new option investors with a limited supply of funds.

That's ODD: Options disclosure document

Because options have a risk that is greater than almost any other investment, all investors must receive an options risk disclosure document (Options Disclosure Document or ODD) and a copy of amendments (if any) prior to their first options transaction (at the time of or before the account is approved). This ODD explains to investors option terminology, strategies, potential rewards, and risks involved in investing in options, such as the chance of losing all money invested or, if selling call options, facing an unlimited maximum loss potential. In addition to the risks, the ODD must also explain tax rules related to options, transaction costs, margin requirements, a special statement for uncovered option writers, and so on.

Special statement for uncovered option writers

Because there are additional risks associated with uncovered option writing, such as the risk of losing a significant amount of money, this strategy is not suitable for all customers who have been approved for option transactions. This statement must include that (a) writing uncovered calls is an extremely risky position and the maximum potential loss is unlimited, (b) the risk associated with writing uncovered puts (although not as risky as selling uncovered calls) is still significant, (c) for combination writing (selling a call and selling a put), the maximum potential loss is unlimited, (d) if a secondary market in options becomes unavailable, writers may be required to hold their short positions until expiration. Writers of American-style options are subject to being assigned an exercise at any time until expiration. Writers of European-style options are only subject to exercise assignment at expiration of the option(s).

REMEMBER

The ODD is typically the first form of options-related communication sent to a customer. However, if any options communications are sent out prior to the delivery of an ODD, the approval of a ROP is not enough as it is with other options communications. In this case, options communications sent out prior to the ODD must be approved by either FINRA or an exchange such as the Chicago Board Options Exchange (CBOE). Approval must take place at least ten calendar days prior to the first use.

OAA: Options account agreement

Within 15 days after approval of the account by an ROP, the customer must provide proof of background and financial information used when opening the account. In addition, the customer must sign and return an options account agreement (OAA). Basically, the OAA just states that the customer has read the ODD, understands the risk associated with trading options, and will abide by the rules and regulations regarding options trading. Should anything change (such as the customers, investment objectives, or financial situation), the customer agrees to notify the firm. In the event that the OAA is not received within 15 days after approval of the account, the customer cannot open any new options positions.

Last trade, last exercise, and expiration of an option

Unlike stock certificates, options do expire after a certain period of time. In addition, investors are limited as to when they can trade and exercise an option. Here's the timeline to keep in mind:

>> **Last trade:** The last time an investor can trade an option is 4:00 p.m. Eastern Time on the business day of expiration.

>> **Last exercise:** The last time an investor can exercise an option is 5:30 p.m. Eastern Time on the business day of expiration. If an option is in-the-money by at least one point at expiration, it will be automatically exercised. A vast majority of options can be exercised any time up till expiration — this is known as *American style*. However there are also *European-style* options that can only be exercised on the expiration date. European-style options include capped index options and some foreign currency options.

>> **Option expiration:** Options expire at 11:59 p.m. Eastern Time on the third Friday of the expiration month.

Exercise and assignment

When taking the Series 7 exam, you will be expected to have a basic understanding of how options are exercised and assigned. Options are cleared through the OCC. Here's how an option is *exercised:*

When a client wants to exercise an option she owns, she contacts her broker-dealer. The broker-dealer contacts the OCC. The trade settles in two business days after the OCC is notified because when the investor is exercising an option, she is actually trading stock (the right to buy or sell stock). Stock trades settle in two business days, so exercises of options settle in two business days (trades of options settle in one business day).

The steps involved look like this:

1. Client #1 tells her broker-dealer (Broker A) to exercise the option.
2. Broker A notifies the Options Clearing Corporation.
3. The Options Clearing Corporation chooses the contra broker (the broker-dealer on the other side of the transaction — Broker B) randomly.
4. Broker B assigns (chooses the client — Client #2) either randomly, first-in-first-out (FIFO), or by any other method which is fair and reasonable. However, Broker B cannot choose the assignment based on size (the one with the most options, the one with the least options, and so on). (The firm's method of assignment must be disclosed to each option client in writing.)
5. Client #2 sends the proceeds (stock or cash) to Broker B.
6. Broker B sends the proceeds directly to Broker A. (The OCC doesn't handle stock or cash.)

So if you were to look at a flow chart, it would look something like this:

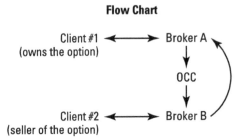

Flow Chart

Client #1 (owns the option) ⟷ Broker A

Broker A → OCC → Broker B

Client #2 (seller of the option) ⟷ Broker B

Although most exercises of options are settled by the delivery of the underlying security, there are some that are settled by the delivery of *cash*. Specifically, *index options* (options on an index of securities) and *foreign currency options* are always settled in cash. This just makes sense because investors can't be expected to deliver an entire index for index options nor be expected to deliver the underlying foreign currency for foreign currency options.

Note: No matter which way the contra broker (Broker B in this case) chooses the client, it should be fixed and it must be disclosed to options customers in writing. In addition, the contra broker must inform of the method to the exchange where the options are traded and receive approval.

Margin on options

As stated previously, with the exception of LEAPS, options cannot be purchased on margin; they must be paid for in full. LEAPS with maturities of over nine months can be purchased on margin by depositing 75 percent of the premium. All other options must be paid for in full. However, for an investor who has a margin account, buying or selling stock at the same time as buying or selling calls or puts on the same security at the same time does change the situation.

An investor buys 100 shares of HIJ on margin at 44 and writes an HIJ 45 call at 5.

The margin call for the securities purchased is $2,200 ($44 × 100 shares × 50 percent) but since the investor received $500 (5 × 100 shares per option) from selling the option, he only has to deposit $1,700 ($2,200 − $500) as a result of the two transactions. So in this case, even though the margin requirement on the stock is $2,200, the margin deposit required is only $1,700.

An investor buys 100 shares of HIJ on margin at 44 and buys an HIJ 40 put at 3.

The margin call for the securities purchased is $2,200 ($44 × 100 shares × 50 percent) but since the investor purchased the put option for $300 (3× 100 shares per option), he has to deposit $2,500 ($2,200 + $300) as a result of the two transactions. So in this case, even though the margin requirement on the stock is $2,200, the margin deposit required is $2,500.

The following example will show what happens with the margin requirement for LEAPS.

An investor buys 1 TUV Jan 40 call LEAP with a 30-month maturity at 12. The margin call for the LEAP is $900 ($12 premium × 100 shares per option × 75 percent). You should note that once the LEAP reaches nine months to maturity or less, the investor must have 100 percent of the current market value for the LEAP on deposit (100 percent maintenance requirement on options with maturities of nine months or less).

When an investor purchases stock and purchases or sells an option on the same security at the same time, the deposit required by the purchase of the stock is either decreased or increased by the amount of premium on the option depending on whether he's selling or buying. So an investor who purchased 100 shares of DIM stock at 35 in a cash account and simultaneously sold a DIM Oct 40 call (covered call) for 6 would only have to deposit $2,900 ($3,500 for the stock less the $600 received for the premium).

The margin requirement for spreads is equal to the maximum potential loss.

Taxes on options

Taxes on options are taxed as capital gains or capital losses. However, it can get a little bit tricky depending on other circumstances.

Closing transactions

Remember, this is when an investor either purchases or sells an option and then closes that option position by either selling or purchasing the same option (see "Trading options: Opening and closing transactions" earlier in this chapter). To determine the capital gain or loss, all you have to do is subtract the selling price from the purchase price and if you have more money in, it's a capital gain; more money out, it's a capital loss. Options with one year to maturity or less (most are 9 months) are taxed as short-term gains or losses. If the investor originally *purchased* a LEAP and held it for over a year before closing the position, it would be taxed as a long-term gain or loss.

Option expiration

If an option expires unexercised because it's out-of-the-money, the premium will be treated as a capital gain for the seller and capital loss for the purchaser. Since most options mature in nine months or less, the gain or loss will be short term. However for the buyer (not the seller) of a LEAP option with over one year till maturity that expires unexercised, it will be a long-term capital loss.

Option exercises

Although most investors trade their options, some do exercise. Remember, when an investor exercises an option, he has the right to purchase the stock or the right to sell the stock. What this means is that the tax situation gets a little more complicated. In cases where the investor purchases the stock, you may have to determine the cost basis (what the investor paid to purchase the security). If the investor sells the stock, you have to determine the proceeds of sale (how much the investor received from selling the security). Fortunately for you, you already calculated this when you determined the break-even point for option purchases and sales. In addition, when options are exercised, the holding period for the securities purchased begins at the time of exercise, not at the time the option was purchased or sold.

EXAMPLE

An investor buys 1 CSA Jan 40 call at 6. Four months later with CSA trading at 52, the investor exercises his call. What is the investor's cost basis for the CSA stock purchased?

Remember that the investor purchased the right to buy the stock at 40. Since he paid 6 for the premium, his cost basis per share is 46 (40 + 6) or a total of $4,600 (46 × 100 shares per option). This investor may immediately sell the stock in the market for a short-term capital gain or hold onto the stock as long as he wants. If he sells the stock above his cost basis, it's a capital gain; below his cost basis, it's a capital loss. If he holds the stock for over a year, the gain or loss will be long term.

EXAMPLE

An investor sells 1 CSA Jan 40 call at 6. Four months later with CSA trading at 52, the investor's call is exercised. What is the investor's proceeds of sale cost basis for the CSA stock sold?

I used the previous example so that you could look at it from the seller's point of view. This investor sold the right to have someone buy CSA stock from her at $40 per share. So once exercised, this investor received the $40 per share but also got to keep the $6 per share premium received. So the proceeds of sale is $46 per share (40 + 6) or a total of $4,600 (46 × 100 shares per option). (Notice that the cost basis and proceeds of sale are the same.)

Buying stock and buying puts

Some investors who purchase stock also buy puts on the same stock to hedge (protect) their position in case the stock price drops too low. Different tax situations come into play depending on when the option was purchased (same day, within the year, or over a year later).

>> **Married put:** A married put is when an investor purchases a stock and purchases a protective put on that stock the same day. In this case, the cost of the stock (on a per share basis) and the cost of the premium (on a per share basis) are added together to establish the investor's cost basis. Let's say that an investor purchased 100 shares of JKL stock at 47 and purchased a JKL 45 put option for 4 on the same day. In this case, the investors cost basis on the stock would be 51 (47 + 4). For the investor to have a gain on the position, he would have to sell his shares at a price above the cost basis. Married puts do not affect the holding period of the stock.

>> **Within the year:** Instead of the investor purchasing the stock and the put the same day, he purchases the protective put in a year or less after purchasing the stock. At the time the investor purchased the protective put, the investor had not yet established a long-term holding period (long-term being over one year). Unlike a married put where the cost basis is

increased on the stock purchased, because the stock and protective put were purchased on different days, the trades are treated as if they're separate. However, if the investor has held the stock for one year or less prior to purchasing the protective put, then the holding period starts over for tax purposes.

>> **Over one year:** If the investor purchases a protective put on stock that she's owned for over one year, she's already established a long position. As with the situation where the investor purchased the stock and protective put within a year, the stock and option are treated as two different positions. However, since this investor has already established a long position on the stock, it remains a long position and the holding period doesn't restart by her purchasing a protective put.

Some additional option rules

Yes, I know . . . even more? Don't blame me; I didn't design the test. Anyway, as with the preceding section, I think a quick perusal of the following items will give you enough of a general understanding of some of the additional rules that you should be able to pick them out of any multiple-choice questions posed on the exam.

>> **Position limits:** A number placed on the amount of option contracts that an individual, registered rep, or investors acting together can hold or write on the same side of the market (bullish or bearish) on the same security. As of now, the limit is either 25,000, 50,000, 75,000, 200,000, or 250,000 contracts on the same side of the market depending on the trading volume for the underlying options. This is subject to change but let's just say the amount will always be extraordinarily large. To see if there's a violation, long calls and short puts are added together because they're both bullish and short calls and long puts are added together because they're both bearish. As with equity options, position limits are also established for non-equity options (foreign currency options, yield-based options, and index options).

Although there are position limits on certain broad-based index options, there are no position limits on the broad-based index options (don't worry about committing them to memory): Cboe S&P 500 AM/PM Basis, Cboe S&P 500 Three-Month Realized Variance, Cboe S&P 500 Three-Month Realized Volatility, DJX, OEX, XEO, NDX, RUT, VIX, VXN, VXD, VXST, S&P 500 Dividend Index, and SPX classes.

>> **Exercise limits:** A number placed on the amount of option contracts that a person can exercise on the same side of the market (bullish or bearish) within five consecutive business days. The exercise limit is the same as the position limit. So if the position limit for a particular security is 75,000 contracts, the most a person may exercise on that security is 75,000 contracts on the same side of the market in a *five* consecutive business day period. As with equity options, exercise limits are also established for non-equity options (foreign currency options, yield-based options, and index options). Typically, the exercise limits are equal to the positions limits.

>> **Limit on uncovered short positions:** FINRA may decide to limit the amount of uncovered short positions on option contracts of a given class if deemed necessary for the protection of investors.

>> **Restrictions on option transactions and exercises:** As with the limit on uncovered short positions, FINRA may also place restrictions on option transactions or the exercise of option contracts in one or more series of options of any class when deemed necessary to help maintain a fair and orderly market.

>> **Open order on the "ex-date" (ex-dividend date):** Since the underlying stock price will be lowered due to a dividend, the OCC will adjust option contracts accordingly unless otherwise instructed by the customer.

>> **Confirmations:** Members are responsible for providing a written confirmation of each option transaction for each customer's account. The confirmation must include the type of option (call or put); the underlying security or index; the expiration month; the exercise (strike) price; the number of option contracts; the premium, trade, and settlement dates; whether it was a purchase or sale (long or short); opening or closing transaction; whether it was done on a principal or agency basis; the amount of commission; and so on. There's more on confirmations in Chapter 16 — yippee!

>> **Statements of account (account statements):** All clients must receive account statements at least monthly if there has been any trading in the account for the previous month and at least quarterly (once every three months) when there has been no trading in the previous month. The account statements must show the security and money positions, entries, interest charges, and any other charges assessed against the account. Account statements are covered in more detail in Chapter 16.

>> **Uncovered short option contracts:** Because uncovered short option contracts are the riskiest of all option contracts, member firms must create standard rules for evaluating the suitability of customers who plan on writing uncovered options.

>> **Maintenance of records:** Each member must keep a current log, index, or other file for options-related complaints. Each complaint should be easily identified and easy to retrieve if necessary. Each complaint file (hopefully there aren't many) must contain the identification of the complaint, the date the complaint was received, the name of the registered rep handling the account, a description of the complaint, any action taken (if any), and so on.

>> **Discretionary account:** As with any discretionary account in which the client gives you the right to trade his account without preapproval, it must be approved by a principal (manager). Options discretionary accounts must be approved in writing by a Registered Options Principal (ROP) or limited principal-general securities sales supervisor, and written approval must be received from the client. In addition, discretionary accounts must be reviewed frequently by an ROP. As with other discretionary accounts, there must be a reasonable basis to believe that the customer understands and can handle the risks of discretionary accounts. Each discretionary order must be marked as discretionary on the order ticket.

>> **Suitability:** Registered Representatives may not recommend any option transaction to a customer unless you believe that the transaction is suitable for the customer. Remember that you should already know the customer's investment objectives, financial information, and so on. In other words, you should not be recommending a risky option transaction for someone you deem incapable of handling the risk. Fortunately, the final call will be made by your Registered Options Principal (ROP).

>> **Supervision of accounts:** Members conducting an options business must have a written supervisory system in place to adequately address the public customer's option business. In addition, each branch office must have either a registered options principal or a limited principal-general securities sales supervisor in order to conduct options business.

>> **Adjustments:** All option contracts are subject to being adjusted according to the rules of the Options Clearing Corporation (OCC).

>> **Volume:** Trading volume is the number of contracts traded in a given period of time.

>> **Addressing of communication to customers:** No firm shall address any communications to a client who is in the care of another person unless (a) the client, within the previous 12 months, has instructed the firm in writing to send the communications to the care person, or (b) duplicate copies are sent to the client at some other address designated in writing by the client.

>> **Open Interest:** The number of option contracts that are currently open. These are option contracts that have been traded but not yet liquidated. Options can be liquidated by either exercise or an offsetting trade.

Testing Your Knowledge

Now that you've learned what you need to know about equity securities (at least as far as the Series 7 exam goes), it's time to attack some questions. Read the questions carefully so that you don't make any careless mistakes.

1. ABC Oct 70 puts are trading for 6 and ABC is currently trading at 74. What is the time value of the Oct 70 put options?

    (A) 0
    (B) 2
    (C) 4
    (D) 6

2. Which option is out-of-the-money if ABC is trading at $60 per share?

    (A) ABC May 65 put
    (B) ABC Aug 45 call
    (C) ABC Nov 80 call
    (D) ABC Dec 70 put

3. AAD Aug 35 calls are trading for 4 when AAD is at 36. What is the time value of these options?

    (A) 0
    (B) 1
    (C) 2
    (D) 3

4. Which TWO of the following are bullish options strategies?

    I. Buying calls
    II. Buying puts
    III. Writing calls
    IV. Writing puts

    (A) I and III
    (B) I and IV
    (C) II and III
    (D) II and IV

5. Melissa R. purchased an JKL May 60 call for a premium of 5. What is the maximum potential gain?

    (A) $500
    (B) $5,500
    (C) $6,500
    (D) Unlimited

6. Which of the following option positions is a long straddle?

   (A) Buying a call and selling a call
   (B) Buying a put and selling a put
   (C) Selling a call and selling a put
   (D) Buying a call and buying a put

7. Since Jim's index options are in-the-money, he would like to exercise them. Once exercised, Jim will receive

   (A) cash
   (B) 100 shares of the index
   (C) either (A) or (B)
   (D) neither (A) nor (B)

8. Declan wrote an XYZ August 30 call for 7. What is Declan's maximum potential gain?

   (A) $700
   (B) $5,300
   (C) $6,700
   (D) Unlimited

9. Ayla K. purchased 1 VMO Feb 60 put for 7 and purchased 1 VMO Feb 55 call for 2. This strategy is a

   (A) long straddle
   (B) long combination
   (C) debit spread
   (D) vertical spread

10. If an investor believes the U.S. dollar will appreciate in relation to the euro, which of the following option strategies should he choose?

    (A) Purchase U.S. dollar calls
    (B) Purchase U.S. dollar puts
    (C) Purchase euro calls
    (D) Purchase euro puts

11. An investor buys 1 TUV Aug 60 put for 7 and buys 1 TUV Aug 55 call for 2. What are the investor's break-even points?

    (A) 53 and 57
    (B) 51 and 64
    (C) 55 and 60
    (D) 46 and 69

12. Investors who own a long-straddle or long-combination position are hoping for the underlying stock to be

    (A) bullish
    (B) bearish
    (C) volatile
    (D) stable

13. An investor buys 1 LMN May 80 call and sells 1 LMN Aug 80 call. This strategy is a

    (A) vertical spread
    (B) horizontal spread
    (C) diagonal spread
    (D) long straddle

14. Place the following in order from first to last regarding the opening of an option account.

    I. The customer signs and returns the OAA
    II. A ROP approves the account
    III. The customer receives an ODD
    IV. The first trade is executed

    (A) III, II, IV, I
    (B) II, III, I, IV
    (C) IV, III, I, II
    (D) I, II, IV, III

15. Sharlene W. wishes to open an options account by purchasing 10 WXY 50 calls. Sharlene must sign an Options Account Agreement at what point?

    (A) At or prior to approval of the account
    (B) At or prior to her first transaction
    (C) Within 15 days after the approval of the account
    (D) Prior to the first account statement

16. When the OCC receives an exercise notice, it must determine which firm is responsible for exercising the option contract:

    (A) randomly
    (B) first in first out
    (C) based on size
    (D) by any method fair and reasonable

17. Which TWO of the following are TRUE regarding an investor who sold short 100 shares of DDD common stock at 35 and purchased 1 DDD Oct 40 call at 3?

    I. The maximum potential gain is $3,200
    II. The maximum potential gain is $3,800
    III. The maximum potential loss is $200
    IV. The maximum potential loss is $800

    (A) I and III
    (B) I and IV
    (C) II and III
    (D) II and IV

18. An investor is long 240,000 LMN calls. Which of the following additional positions may the investor have without violating position limits (position limit 250,000)?

(A) Long 40,000 LMN calls

(B) Long 40,000 LMN puts

(C) Short 60,000 OPQ calls

(D) Short 80,000 LMN puts

19. An investor purchased 100 shares of DEF common stock at $32 per share. 3 months later with DEF trading at $33 per share, the investor wrote 1 DEF 35 call at 4. What is the investor's break-even point?

(A) $28

(B) $29

(C) $36

(D) $37

20. An investor is long 1 ABC Oct 50 call at 9 and short 1 ABC Oct 60 call at 3. Which TWO of the following are TRUE?

I. The break-even point is 56

II. The break-even point is 62

III. The maximum potential gain is $400

IV. The maximum potential gain is unlimited

(A) I and III

(B) I and IV

(C) II and III

(D) II and IV

21. An investor buys 1 XYZ May 60 put for 6 and writes 1 XYZ May 50 put for 2. What is the investor's maximum potential gain?

(A) $200

(B) $400

(C) $600

(D) Unlimited

22. An investor writes an GHI May 40 call for 9. GHI increases to $45 just prior to expiration and the call is exercised. After the investor buys the stock in the market to meet her obligation, what is the gain or loss?

(A) $400 gain

(B) $400 loss

(C) $900 gain

(D) $900 loss

23. Sharlet R. bought 100 shares of GHI at $40 and bought 1 GHI May 40 put for 6. What is the maximum potential gain?

   (A) $600

   (B) $2,400

   (C) $3,600

   (D) Unlimited

24. An investor sells 1 XYZ May 30 put for 7. What is the break-even point?

   (A) 23

   (B) 30

   (C) 37

   (D) Cannot be determined

25. An investor sold 1 XYZ Oct 35 put at 7. 2 weeks prior to expiration with XYZ trading at 33, the investor bought 1 XYZ Oct 35 put at 3. The second transaction would be called a(n)

   (A) opening purchase

   (B) opening sale

   (C) closing purchase

   (D) closing sale

26. An investor purchased a standard option which expired out-of-the-money. How would this transaction be categorized for tax purposes?

   (A) A long-term capital loss

   (B) A short-term capital loss

   (C) An ordinary loss

   (D) Ordinary income

27. The Option Clearing Corporation sets all of the following with regard to an option contract EXCEPT the

   (A) premium

   (B) contract size

   (C) strike price

   (D) expiration date

28. If an investor believes that the S&P 500 will become bearish, which TWO of the following would be appropriate strategies?

   I. Buy SPX calls

   II. Buy SPX puts

   III. Sell SPX calls

   IV. Sell SPX puts

   (A) I and III

   (B) I and IV

   (C) II and III

   (D) II and IV

29. Which of the following is the riskiest option strategy?

    (A) Buying calls

    (B) Buying puts

    (C) Writing uncovered calls

    (D) Writing uncovered puts

30. Ayla sells 1 HIJ Nov 40 put at 6. What is Ayla's maximum potential loss on this position?

    (A) $600

    (B) $3,400

    (C) $4,600

    (D) Unlimited

Answers and Explanations

If you just read the chapter, you probably didn't find any of the questions too difficult. Because there are 30 questions, each one is worth 3.3 points.

1. **D.** The premium (P) of an option is made up of intrinsic value (I) plus time value (T). With everything else being equal, the longer the time until expiration, the higher the premium. In this case, you're dealing with a put option, and put options go in-the-money when the price of the underlying security is below the exercise (strike) price. ABC is trading at 74 and the put option exercise price is 70, so the option is not in-the-money and has no intrinsic value. So to determine the time value, use the following equation:

$$P = I + T$$
$$6 = 0 + T$$
$$T = 6$$

The premium is 6 and there is no intrinsic value, so the premium is made up of all time value.

2. **C.** For a call option to be out-of-the-money, the price of the underlying security has to be below the strike (exercise) price. For a put option to be out-of-the-money, the price of the underlying security has to be above the strike price. So out of all of the options listed, the only one that is out-of-the-money is answer (C). For answer (C) to be in-the-money, the price of ABC would have to be above the strike price of 80.

3. **D.** To determine the time value of an option, you can use the equation $P = I + T$. "P" equals the premium of the options, "I" equals the intrinsic value of the option (how much it's in-the-money), and "T" equals the time value of the option based on how much time there is until the option expires. Here's how it looks:

$$P = I + T$$
$$4 = 1 + T$$
$$T = 3$$

In this case the premium of the option is 4. The intrinsic value is 1 because the call option is 1 point in-the-money. (Call options go in-the-money when the price of the underlying security goes above the strike price). This means that the time value equals 3 (4 − 1).

4. **B.** If you're bullish on a security, you want the market price to increase. If you're bearish, you want the price to decrease. Buyers of calls and writers of puts want the price of the underlying security to increase. Buyers of puts and writers of calls want the price of the underlying security to decrease.

5. **D.** When purchasing a call option with no other positions, the maximum potential gain is unlimited. Remember, call options go in-the-money when the price of the underlying security increases in value. And because there's no limit to the price of a security, the maximum potential gain in this case is unlimited.

6. **D.** You should remember that "long" means to buy. Therefore, you can cross off answers (A), (B), and (C) right away because they all have the investor selling something. To create a long straddle, you're buying a call and buying a put with the same underlying stock, the same expiration, and the same strike price.

7. **A.** The settlement for index options is always cash.

8. **D.** When selling an option with no underlying stock position, the maximum gain is the premium received. Declan sold the option for 7, so his maximum potential gain (if the option never goes in-the-money) is $700 ($7 × 100 shares per option).

9. **B.** If an investor purchases a call and purchases a put with the same stock but different expiration dates and/or strike price, she has created a long combination.

10. **D.** If an investor believes the U.S. dollar will appreciate in value compared to the euro, an excellent strategy would be to buy U.S. dollar calls. However, since there aren't options on the U.S. dollar, the investor should purchase euro puts because he believes the euro will drop in relation to the U.S. dollar.

11. **B.** This strategy is a long combination (buy a call and buy a put on the same securities but with different expiration dates and/or strike prices). For straddles and combinations, there are two different break-even points: one on the way up and one on the way down. The first thing you have to do is add the two premiums and then call up (add the combined premiums to the call strike price) and then put down (subtract the combined premiums from the put strike price). Because this investor paid 9 (7 + 2) per share for the premiums, the break-even points are 64 (55 + 9) and 51 (60 − 9).

12. **C.** Remember, investors who are long straddles or long combinations are buying a call in case the price of the underlying stock increases in value and buying a put in case the underlying stock decreases in value. So looking at that, these investors don't care if the underlying security increases in value or decreases in value; they just want it to move enough in either direction for them to have a profit. Therefore, they are looking for volatility.

13. **B.** In this case, the strike prices are the same, and just the expiration months are different. So it is a horizontal (calendar) spread.

14. **A.** Prior to opening an options account, all customers must receive an ODD (Options Disclosure Document or an Options risk Disclosure Document). After that, a ROP (Registered Options Principal) would need to approve the account. At that point, the first options trade can be made. After the account has been approved, the customer has 15 days to sign and return the OAA (Options Account Agreement).

15. **C.** Prior to opening the account, Sharlene would have to receive an Options Disclosure Document (ODD). Once the account has been approved, Sharlene would have 15 days to sign and return the Options Account Agreement (OAA).

16. **A.** When exercising an option, the OCC (Options Clearing Corporation) chooses the brokerage firm to honor the contract randomly.

17. **B.** I would suggest that you set up an options chart to answer this question so that you're less likely to make a mistake. Check out the following setup:

Money Out	Money In	
$300	$3,500	Maximum gain = $3,200
$4,000		
$4,300	$3,500	Maximum loss = $800

The first thing to do is to put the stock and option in the chart. The investor sold the stock short for $3,500 (35 × 100 shares), so you have to put that in the Money In side of the chart. Next, the investor purchased the option fof $300 (3 × 100 shares per option), so you have to put $300 in the Money Out side of the chart. At this point, stop and take a look and you'll see that you got one answer. Since there is $3,200 more in than out ($3,500 in − $300 out), the maximum potential gain is $3,200. To get the maximum potential loss, exercise the option. It's a 40 call option, so you have to put $4,000 (40 × 100 shares per option) under its premium because *calls same* (the exercised call goes on the same side of the chart as its premium). Total up the 2 sides and you'll see that there is $800 ($4,300 − $3,500) more money out than money in, so that's your maximum potential loss.

18. **B.** Selling calls and buying puts is bearish. So the investor has 215,000 (185,000 + 30,000) bearish contracts for LMN. If the investor buys 40,000 more puts, the investor would have 255,000 bearish contracts and be in violation of OCC (Options Clearing Corporation) rules in this stock. Answer (C) is not a violation because the option is based on a different stock.

19. **A.** You don't need an options chart to answer this one. This investor purchased the stock for $32 per share and then sold the call against the same stock (covered call) for $4 per share. So since the investor purchased the stock for $32 and then got $4 per share back, the break-even point is $28 ($32 − $4).

20. **A.** This is a debit call spread. We know it's a debit spread because the investor paid more for the option purchased than he received for the option sold. To find the break-even point, begin by finding the difference between the two premiums because you had one buy and one sell:

adjusted premium $= 9 - 3 = 6$

This is a call spread; therefore, you have to add the 6 to the lower strike price. The lower strike price is 50, so the break-even point is 56:

To determine the maximum potential gain, set up an options chart:

Money Out	Money In	
$900	$300	
$5,000	$6,000	
$5,900	$6,300	Maximum gain = $400

First, put the premiums in the options chart. The investor bought the option for $900 (9 × 100 shares per option) in the Money Out side of the chart. Then put the $300 for the option sold in the Money Out side of the chart. At this point, you can see that the maximum potential loss is $600 ($900 out − $300 in). So you have to exercise both options to get the maximum gain. Because you are dealing with call options, the exercised strike prices must go underneath their premiums because *calls same*. So place the $5,000 (50 strike price × 100 shares per option) in the Money Out side of the chart. Then place the $6,000 in the Money In side of the chart. Total up the 2 sides and you'll see you have $400 more in than out, so that's the maximum potential gain.

21. C. This is a spread because the investor bought a put and sold a put. It is also a debit spread because he paid more for the option he purchased than he received for the option sold. The easiest way to figure out the maximum gain would be to set up an options chart. See the setup below:

Money Out	Money In	
$600	$200	
$5,000	$6,000	
$5,600	$6,200	Maximum gain = $600

The investor purchased the 60 put for $600 (6 × 100 shares per option), so you have to put the $600 on the Money Out portion of the chart. Next, the investor sold the 50 put option for $200 (2 × 100 shares per option), so you have to put that in the Money In portion of the chart. Stop at this point to see if that gives you the answer you need. Because you have more money out, that tells you that the maximum potential loss is $400 ($600 out – $200 in). Since you're looking for the maximum potential gain, you have to exercise both options. Put $6,000 (60 put × 100 shares per option) on the Money In side of the chart because *puts switch*, meaning that when you exercise a put, it goes on the opposite side of the chart from its premium. Next, put $5,000 (50 put × 100 shares per option) on the Money Out side of the chart. Total up the two sides and you'll see that the investor has $6,200 in and $5,600 out, which gives the investor a maximum potential gain of $600 ($6,200 in – $5,600 loss).

22. A. The best way to handle this question is to set up an options chart. Check it out:

Money Out	Money In	
$4,500	$900	
	$4,000	
$4,500	$4,900	= $400 gain

The investor wrote (sold) the GHI 40 call for 9, so you have to put the $900 (9 × 100 shares per option) received on the Money In side of the chart. Next, it said that the option was exercised. When exercising an option, always exercise at the strike price, which is 40 in this case. So you need to put $4,000 (40 strike price × 100 shares per option) on the same side as its premium because *calls same* (when exercising a call, it goes on the same side of the chart as its premium). Then the investor had to purchase the stock in the market to meet her obligation. In this case, the price of the stock was $45, so you have to put $4,500 (45 market price × 100 shares) on the Money Out side of the chart. Total up the 2 sides of the chart and you'll see that you have $400 more in than out, so that's the answer.

23. D. Although you can put this in an options chart, in this case, it's not necessary. Sharlet purchased 100 shares of GHI at $40. On that transaction alone, her maximum potential gain is unlimited because there is no limit as to how high the stock can go. She then purchased a protective put (protects her if the stock price decreases) for $6 per share. This adjusts her cost basis to $46 per share ($40 + $6) but does not limit her upside potential.

24. **A.** Certainly, "cannot be determined" is not the answer. Whether buying or selling a put option with no other positions, you can determine the break-even point by subtracting the premium from the strike price:

$$30 - 7 = 23$$

25. **C.** When the investor sold the option initially, it was an opening sale. Two weeks prior to expiration, the investor decided to close himself out of that position, so the second transaction is a closing purchase because he had to buy the option to close out the position.

26. **B.** Options are always taxed as capital gains or capital losses. Because this investor paid for an option that expired out-of-the-money, he had a loss. In order to be a long-term loss, he needed to have purchased a LEAP option with over one year until expiration. So this was a short-term capital loss.

27. **A.** The Option Clearing Corporation (OCC) sets the strike price, contract size, and expiration date for each listed option. The premium of an option is based on the market price of the security, the expiration date, and market sentiment.

28. **C.** Since the investor believes that the S&P 500 will turn bearish, it would make sense for him to peruse bearish option strategies on the S&P 500. So he should buy SPX puts and sell SPX calls.

29. **C.** Writers (sellers) of uncovered options always face more risk than buyers. Remember, when buying an option with no other position, the maximum potential loss is the premium paid. So when comparing writing uncovered puts as compared to uncovered calls, there is no unlimited maximum potential loss on puts but there is on calls, so selling uncovered calls is the riskiest option strategy.

30. **B.** You probably don't need an options chart to figure out this one, but I'll show you anyway:

Money Out	Money In	
$4,000	$600	Maximum loss = $3,400

This investor sold the 40 put option so you have to put the $600 received (6 × 100 shares per option) in the Money In side of the chart. That tells you that the maximum potential gain is $600. To determine the maximum potential loss, exercise the option. Because puts switch, you have to put the exercised option on the opposite side of the chart from its premium. After putting $4,000 out, you can see that the investor has $3,400 ($4,000 – $600) more out than in, so that's the maximum potential loss.

4
Taking Care of Your Customers and Playing by the Rules

» Understanding fundamental analysis

» Looking at the job of a technical analyst

» Taking the chapter quiz

Chapter 13

Portfolio and Securities Analysis: Examining Companies and the Market

I n terms of choosing securities, throwing darts at a list of stocks seems to have fallen out of favor. So has drawing company names out of a hat. But hey, no problem. Your psychic powers may not be the most reliable, but you still have tons of tools that can help you get a good idea of where the market's heading and how certain securities may perform.

One of your main jobs as a registered representative is to figure out the best investments for your customers. To help lead people down the path of riches, you have to analyze your customer's portfolio and the market and try to find a good fit. In many cases firms hire analysts to provide their registered reps with investment information, which helps you determine the best recommendations for each customer.

In this chapter, I cover topics relating to portfolio analysis and securities analysis. The majority of this chapter is about analyzing a customer's financial condition and seeing what happens with the money supply. Don't worry, though — I don't leave out technical and fundamental analysis; I just focus on the information that can help you get the best score on the Series 7. At the end of the chapter, I wrap it all up with a quiz that I'm sure you'll enjoy. As with most of the other chapters, you'll notice that there's a little overlap from the Securities Industry Essentials exam.

Knowing Your Customer: Portfolio Analysis

Not all investors are able to or want to take the same amount of risk, so what constitutes an excellent recommendation for one customer may be disastrous for another. When opening an account with a new customer, providing a portfolio analysis of the client's current holdings and needs and updating it as needed (due diligence) is important so you can help more effectively. When you open an account, you fill out a new account form with your customer's help (for details on the info that appears here, see Chapter 16). One important element on the form is the customer's investment objectives, which tell you how much risk the customer is able or willing to take. Of course, a customer's investment objectives aren't written in stone — they can change during his lifetime, so you also need to keep up with the customer's life changes.

Part of the know-your-customers (KYC) rule is knowing whether they're a foreign or domestic resident as well as whether they are a U.S. citizen or not, whether they're a corporate insider, and whether they are an employee of a broker-dealer or self-regulatory organization (SRO).

The Series 7 exam takes your ability to evaluate a customer's needs into consideration — so naturally, you get tested on it. The following sections explain investment objectives, what factors impact these goals, and how you can allocate assets and appropriately manage portfolios so the investments are right in line with the customer's needs.

Investment objectives

Investments aren't exactly one-size-fits-all, so asking a client about his investment objectives can be a real help. As a financial expert, you'll likely have to help clients pin down what their goals should be. I help you find out how in the next section, but for now, here are some possible investment objectives:

- » **Preservation of capital:** Investing in safe securities, such as U.S. government bonds, municipal bonds, high-rated corporate bonds, CDs, money market instruments, and so on.

- » **Current income:** Investing in securities (such as bonds, preferred stock, income funds, fixed annuities, and so on) that'll provide a steady stream of interest and/or cash dividends.

- » **Capital growth:** Investing in the common stock of relatively new companies or ones that have a high growth potential. Investors may also purchase growth funds to meet their needs. Obviously, this type of investing is riskier for investors.

- » **Total return:** Investing in a combination of stocks and bonds, looking for both growth and income.

- » **Tax advantages:** Investing in securities (such as municipal bonds, direct participation programs, retirement plans, and so on) that give tax breaks.

- » **Liquidity:** Looking to purchase securities that can be bought and sold quickly and easily. Investors looking to have access to their money quickly may purchase securities such as money market funds or T-bills.

- » **Diversification:** Investing in securities from several different companies, municipalities, and/or the U.S. government to offset the risk associated with only owning one security.

- » **Speculation:** Investing in securities with higher risk in an attempt to maximize profits if the securities move in the right direction. Investors who are speculative may purchase securities on margin, buy or sell options, invest in micro-cap stocks, and so on. This is a very risky type of investing.

- » **Trading profits:** Looking to buy and sell securities on a constant basis.

- » **Long-term or short-term:** Looking to tie up money for either a long time or a short time.

REMEMBER

When recommending securities to your customers, you need to make recommendations that are *suitable* and fit their *investment objectives*. You must have a "reasonable basis" for recommending a security to a customer. Some customers may fit into more than one category (for example, looking for diversification and liquidity), which is considered "customer-specific" suitability. And you should make recommendations based on their financial situation (income statements, balance sheets, investments, obligations, cash available for investing, and so on). This is known as "quantitative suitability." You should not be making recommendations that are beyond your customer's financial ability or comfort level. Ideally, all customers should have a diversified portfolio (meaning they own several different securities and/or types of securities). If a customer can't afford to diversify, you ought to recommend mutual funds. (For info on mutual funds and other packaged securities, check out Chapter 10.)

Note: Even though it will likely cost you a commission, there are going to be times where you are going to make recommendations to hold securities. If you feel that one of your clients is invested in securities that you believe are the right ones for them and you believe that the securities are in a position to perform well, you should probably tell them to hold their position for now, which will let your client know that you care and it'll pay off in the long run.

The following question tests your ability to answer a question about investment objectives.

EXAMPLE

Mrs. Johnson is a 60-year-old investor who is heavily invested in the market. Mrs. Johnson is looking to invest in more securities with a high degree of liquidity. Which of the following investments are you LEAST likely to recommend?

(A) DPPs

(B) Blue-chip stocks

(C) T-bills

(D) Mutual funds

The correct answer is Choice (A). Because Mrs. Johnson is looking for securities with a high degree of liquidity, you're least likely to recommend DPPs (direct participation programs), or limited partnerships, because they're the most difficult investments to get in and out of. Not only do you need to prequalify the investor, but the investor also has to be accepted by the general partner (see Chapter 11 for details). However, blue-chip stocks, T-bills, and mutual funds can all be bought and sold fairly easily.

REMEMBER

You will likely be opening *institutional accounts* as well as accounts for individual investors. However, similar rules apply. As with individual or joint accounts, recommendations to institutional investors should also fit their investment objectives. You must also make sure that the person you're dealing with who's handling the institutional account is capable of understanding the risks of particular transactions and investment strategies.

Factors that influence your customer's investment profile

If an investor is clueless about how much risk he should be taking, your job is to help your client figure it out. Think of yourself as the Sherlock Holmes of the investing world and use the information you have available, such as your client's age, whether they have a family, how much money they have, their annual income, their expenses, if they have any investments already, if they have a retirement plan, if they have kids going to college, and so on. Additionally, feel your client out to try to get an idea of how much risk they're comfortable taking.

Money, money, money: Checking out financial information

Obviously, financial factors influence future investments. To get an idea of your client's needs, you can start by looking at your customer's financial profile, which includes

>> **Your client's net worth:** The investor's current assets and liabilities, the amount of marketable securities the client owns, and whether he has any deferred assets, such as a retirement plan

>> **Money available for investing:** The client's current income and expenses, their securities holdings, their net worth, and the amount of money they have available for investments

>> **Additional background items:** Whether the investor owns a home (and mortgage info), whether they have life and/or disability insurance, their employment situation, whether they have employee stock options, their tax bracket (tax considerations), and their credit score

Money isn't everything: Considering nonfinancial influences

In addition to the customer's financial profile (see the preceding section), you need to be aware of nonfinancial considerations so you can choose appropriate investments. These considerations may include whether this customer is responsible for a family, the customer's age, the employment of other family members (for example, whether they work for a bank, broker-dealer, or insurance company), educational plans the customer has for themself or their children, and so on. Here's how such factors can affect an investor's objectives and liquidity needs:

>> **Age:** Older investors in most cases can't handle as much risk as younger investors. Older investors have a shorter *time horizon* so for most investors, holding more in fixed-income securities and less in equity securities is typically the right call.

>> **Changes in marital status:** Recently married couples may be looking for securities that provide a certain degree of safety; for instance, they may be looking to buy a house or start a family. New divorcees may face more or fewer financial responsibilities in addition to changes in income, affecting their willingness to take risk.

>> **Family responsibilities:** Investors who have a family with several dependents normally aren't as comfortable investing in more speculative securities.

>> **Education:** Parents who need to save for their kids' higher education may need to invest in securities that are not only safer but also allow for a smaller investment now with a bigger return in the future, such as zero-coupon bonds or T-STRIPS.

>> **Investment experience:** As a customer gets more used to investing, they may be willing to take more risk.

>> **Customer's risk tolerance:** Certainly not all people are created the same. Some people like to go to the casino every weekend and others refuse to even purchase lottery tickets. So, the same duplicate holds true of investors; some are going to be willing to take more risk than others and others will only want to purchase the safest of securities. Most will fall somewhere in between.

TIP

Stay updated with regard to your customers' lives. Not only does this effort make it seem like you care (which, of course, I hope you do), but it also helps you keep abreast of changing investment objectives and keep investments in line with those objectives.

Asset allocation

Asset allocation is the process of dividing an investor's portfolio among different asset classes, such as bonds, stock, and cash equivalents. The main purpose of asset allocation is to reduce risk by diversifying the investor's portfolio. Asset allocation differs from investor to investor depending on the investor's risk tolerance. For investors who aren't able to diversify their portfolio because of a lack of money available for investing, mutual funds would work well.

Strategic asset allocation

Strategic asset allocation refers to the types of investments that investor decides to hold based on his risk tolerance, investment objectives, and time horizon. Let's say an investor wants to have 60 percent invested in equity securities and 40 percent invested in bonds and cash or cash equivalents (such as money market funds) and sets up their portfolio that way. They could look at their portfolio occasionally (maybe yearly) to make sure their investments are still in line with their strategy. So, if their equity securities have been doing really well and now comprise 65 percent of their portfolio, they could sell some equity securities and purchase more fixed-income securities to bring it back in line with their original percentages. As investors get older, they typically change their portfolio to hold a higher percentage of fixed-income securities than they did when they were younger. For investors with limited resources, targeted date funds which are rebalanced for the investor as they get older would be ideal.

REMEMBER

Strategic asset allocation gives you a good starting point. If you have an aggressive investor, put a higher percentage into equity securities than the model suggests; if you have a conservative investor, put a lower percentage into equity securities.

Tactical asset allocation

Tactical asset allocation refers to rebalancing a customer's portfolio due to market conditions. For example, if the stock market is expected to do well in the short-term, you put a higher percentage into stocks. If the stock market is expected to do poorly over the short-term, you lower the percentage of stocks and purchase more fixed-income securities (bonds). Later sections in this chapter give you more info on how to analyze securities and markets.

Modern portfolio theory

The modern portfolio theory (MPT) or portfolio theory takes into account these risk measurements: alpha, beta, standard deviation, Sharpe ratio, and R-squared. Fortunately for you, you won't need to know all of them to pass the Series 7. However, if you should decide to become an investment adviser and take either the Series 65 or Series 66, you will need to know and understand them all. Decades ago, stockbrokers and the like were mainly concerned with attempting to bring in the highest returns in an investor's portfolio. However, they eventually caught on and realized that most investors are risk averse, so they had to change their thinking. The idea of the modern portfolio theory is to optimize a portfolio and maximize returns for the risk inherent in the combination of securities in the portfolio each investor is willing to take. MPT attempts to create a diversified portfolio by purchasing securities that aren't directly correlated to each other. In other words, some securities may go up while others are going down. This is obviously preferable to having all the securities go down at the same time. Hopefully, over the long haul, the value of the portfolio will be up while the risk was minimized.

Alpha

Alpha is how a security performs as compared to a certain benchmark. Let's say that a particular mutual fund somewhat mirrors the S&P 500. Now, let's say that the S&P 500 increased 10 percent over a period of time but that fund only increased 7 percent over that same period of time. Your mutual fund would have a negative alpha, which would be bad. If the fund increased more than the S&P 500 over that same period of time, the fund would have a positive alpha, which is good. Alpha can also be used for individual company stocks, such as pharmaceutical stocks. In this case, you could compare how a particular pharmaceutical stock is doing compared to all similar pharmaceutical stocks.

Beta (beta coefficient)

Beta is a measure of how volatile a stock or portfolio is in relation to the overall market (typically the S&P 500). Securities with a beta coefficient of 1 are equally volatile as the market. Securities with a beta coefficient of 0, such as a money market security, are not tied to the movement of the market.

>> If the beta = 1, the stock is equally volatile as the market

>> If the beta > 1, the stock is more volatile than the market

>> If the beta < 1, the stock is less volatile than the market

Capital Asset Pricing Model (CAPM)

Unlike the modern portfolio theory, which looks at the risk versus reward of the whole portfolio, CAPM looks at the risk versus reward of an individual security. The CAPM takes into consideration the time value of money as well as the risk. U.S. Treasury securities are considered risk-free investments believe it or not. So starting with what you'd be making on a U.S. Treasury security by way of interest, you would need to compare the risk you'd be taking on a particular security by looking at its beta coefficient and how much you'd expect to make above the return on the U.S. Treasury security. In order for a security to be worth the risk, it should meet or beat the return on a risk-free treasury security plus the risk premium (the extra return you'd expect for taking the risk).

Note: Member firms may provide *interactive investment analysis tools* to their clients. These investment analysis tools produce simulations and analysis which will help investors see the likelihood of investment outcomes if they make certain investments. However, no member may make any statement or in any way imply that FINRA approves or endorses ("FINRA does not approve or endorse") the use of the investment analysis tool or any recommendations made by the tool. If a member firm does offer an investment analysis tool, it must let customers know either in retail communication or if the tool provides a written report:

>> The criteria and methodology used and its limitations

>> That results may vary with each use and will likely vary over time

>> If applicable, the universe of securities considered in the analysis, how the tool determines which securities to select, if the tool favors certain securities and why, and so on

>> The following must be displayed: "IMPORTANT: The projections or other information generated by [name of investment analysis tool] regarding the likelihood of various investment outcomes are hypothetical in nature, do not reflect actual investment results and are not guarantees of future results."

Strategizing with portfolio management policies

In addition to all the other investment choices, investors may have a defensive investment strategy, an aggressive investment strategy, or some combination of the two. An investor who adopts a *defensive investment strategy* has safety of principal and interest as a top priority. A defensive investment strategy includes investments such as

- » Blue-chip stocks with low volatility (stocks of well-established, financially stable companies — see Chapter 6)

- » AAA rated bonds (Chapter 7)

- » U.S. government bonds (Chapter 7)

An investor who adopts an *aggressive investment strategy* is attempting to maximize gains by investing in securities with higher risk. An aggressive portfolio strategy includes

- » Investing in securities such as highly volatile stocks (Chapter 6)

- » Investing in put and/or call options (Chapter 12)

- » Investing in high-yield (junk) bonds (Chapter 7)

- » Buying securities on margin (Chapter 9)

REMEMBER

Although defensive and aggressive strategies are clearly defined, most investors have a *balanced portfolio* (aggressive/defensive), which includes securities included in both an aggressive and defensive portfolio.

Knowing Your Securities and Markets: Securities Analysis

Although most larger brokerage firms have their own analysts, you do need to know some of the basics of securities analysis to pass the Series 7. In this section, I cover investment risks that your customers face and show you the differences between technical and fundamental analysis.

Regarding risk

Investors face many risks (and hopefully many rewards) when investing in the market. You need to understand the risks because not only can this knowledge make you sound like a genius, but it can also help you score higher on the Series 7:

Systematic risk

Systematic risk is non-diversifiable or market risk. It's the risk that securities can decline due to political, social, or economic factors. Such factors can include changes in the economy, natural disasters, government policy, and so on. Examples of systematic risks are the housing crisis of 2008 and the Covid-19 pandemic of 2020. Systematic risk is a risk that could affect the whole market.

- » **Market risk:** The risk of a security or securities declining due to regular market fluctuations or negative market conditions. All securities have market risk.

- » **Interest rate risk:** The risk of bond prices declining with increasing interest rates. (Use the idea behind the seesaw from Chapter 7: When interest rates increase, outstanding bond prices decrease.) All bonds (even zero-coupon bonds) are subject to interest risk.

>> **Purchasing power (inflation) risk:** The risk that the return on the investment is less than the inflation rate. Long-term bonds and fixed annuities have high inflation risk. To address inflation risk, investors should consider buying Treasury Inflation Protected Securities (TIPS), equity securities, variable annuities, and so on.

Nonsystematic risk

Nonsystematic (unsystematic, unique, or diversifiable) risk can be eliminated through diversification. You've probably heard the expression "Don't put all your eggs in one basket." Well, the same holds true for investing. Suppose for instance that one of your customers has everything invested in DIMP Corporation common stock and DIMP files for bankruptcy, and now you have to tell your customer they've lost everything. So nonsystematic risk is more industry or firm specific.

>> **Business risk:** The risk of a corporation failing to perform up to expectations.

>> **Political (geopolitical) risk:** The risk that the value of a security could suffer due to instability or political changes in a country (for example, the nationalization of corporations).

>> **Credit risk:** The risk of default or that the principal and interest aren't paid on time. Moody's, Standard & Poor's, and Fitch are the main bond-rating companies.

>> **Regulatory (legislative) risk:** The risk that law changes will negatively affect certain securities.

>> **Reinvestment risk:** The risk that interest and dividends received will have to be reinvested at a lower rate of return. Zero-coupon bonds, T-bills, T-STRIPS, and so on have no interperiod reinvestment risk (until maturity) because they don't receive interest payments.

>> **Currency (exchange rate) risk:** The risk that an investment's value will be affected by a change in currency exchange rates. Investors who have international investments are the ones most affected by currency risk.

>> **Liquidity (marketability) risk:** The risk that the security is not easily traded without affecting the price of the security. Long-term bonds and limited partnerships have more liquidity risk.

>> **Capital risk:** The risk of losing all money invested (for options [Chapter 12] and warrants [Chapter 6]). Because options and warrants have expiration dates, purchasers may lose all money invested at expiration. To reduce capital risk, investors should buy high quality stocks or investment-grade (higher rated) bonds.

>> **Prepayment risk:** The type of risk mostly associated with real-estate investments such as mortgage-backed securities (Chapter 7). Mortgage-backed securities have an average expected life when first issued, but if mortgage interest rates decrease, more investors will refinance and the bonds will be pre-paid earlier than expected.

>> **Timing risk:** The risk of an investor buying or selling a security at the wrong time, thus failing to maximize profits.

>> **Call risk:** The risk that a corporation could call its callable bonds at a time that's not advantageous to investors. Corporations will more likely call their bonds when interest rates decrease.

TIP

On the Series 7 exam, to determine the best investment for a customer, pay close attention to the investor's risk tolerance, financial considerations, non-financial considerations, risk(s) mentioned, and so on. If the question isn't specific about the type of risk, use strategic asset allocation to determine the best answer (see the earlier "Asset allocation" section for more information).

Mitigating risk with diversification

Certainly, all investments have a certain degree of risk. Younger investors, sophisticated investors, and wealthy investors can all afford to take more risk than the average investor. However, when you are talking to your clients, you should examine their portfolio and help them make decisions that will help them mitigate their risk. You should help them invest in securities that aren't too volatile for their situation and make them aware of the potential tax ramifications of certain investments.

You've probably heard the expression, "Don't put all your eggs in one basket." Well, the same holds true for investing. Suppose for instance that one of your customers has everything invested in DIMP Corporation common stock. All of a sudden, DIMP Corporation loses a big contract or is being investigated. Your customer could be wiped out. However, if your customer had a diversified portfolio, DIMP Corporation would likely only be a small part of her investments and she wouldn't be ruined. This is the reason that having a diversified portfolio is so important.

REMEMBER

You are responsible for making sure that your clients understand the importance of having a diversified portfolio to manage risk. Investors with *securities concentration* are at risk of major losses due to having a large portion of their holdings in a single security, market segment (for example, automotive stocks) or investment class.

There are many ways to diversify:

>> **Geographical:** Investing in securities in different parts of the country or world.

>> **Buying bonds with different maturity dates:** Buying a mixture of short-term, intermediate-term, and long-term debt securities.

>> **Buying bonds with different credit ratings:** You may purchase high-yield bonds (ones with a low credit rating) with high expected returns with highly rated bonds with lower returns so that you get a mixture of high returns with the safety of the highly rated bonds.

>> **Investing in stocks from different sectors:** Often, certain sectors of the market perform better than others. By spreading your investments out among these different sectors, you can manage your risk and hopefully make a profit if one or more sector happens to be performing well. The sectors include financials, utilities, energy, healthcare, industrials, technology, and so on.

>> **Type of investment:** Investing in a mixture of different types of stocks, bonds, DPPs, real estate, options, and so on.

TIP

There are certainly many more ways to diversify a portfolio than the ones listed previously — use your imagination. In addition, they aren't mutually exclusive. Remember that mutual funds (packaged securities) and exchange-traded funds (ETFs) provide a certain amount of diversification within an individual holding. This is why smaller investors who may not be able to afford to diversify their portfolio are ideal candidates for mutual funds.

Fundamental analysis

Although most analysts use some combination of fundamental analysis and technical analysis to make their securities recommendations, both types are used for trying to predict the performance of securities in the future. For Series 7 exam purposes, you need to be able to differentiate between fundamental and technical analysis. This section discusses fundamental analysis; I cover technical analysis later in the section "Technical analysis."

Fundamental analysts perform an in-depth analysis of companies. They look at the management of a company and its financial condition (balance sheets, income statements, the industry, the company's management, earnings, and so on) and compare it to other companies in the same industry. In addition, fundamental analysts even look at the overall economy and industry conditions to determine whether an investment is good to buy.

REMEMBER

In simplest terms, fundamental analysts decide *what to buy.*

A fundamental analyst's goal is to determine the value of a particular security and decide whether it's underpriced or overpriced. If it is believed that the security is underpriced, a fundamental analyst recommends buying the security; if it is believed the security is overpriced, he recommends selling or selling the security short.

The following sections explain some of the fundamental analyst's tools of the trade and how to use them.

Balance sheet components

The *balance sheet* provides an image of a company's financial position at a given point in time. The Series 7 exam tests your ability to understand the components (see Figure 13-1) and how financial moves that the company makes (buying equipment, issuing stock, issuing bonds, paying off bonds, and so on) affect the balance sheet. In general, understanding how a balance sheet works is more important than being able to name all the components.

Assets	**Liabilities**
Current assets	Current liabilities
Fixed assets	Long-term liabilities
Intangible assets	
	Stockholder's equity (net worth)
	Par value (common)
	Par value (preferred)
	Paid-in capital
	Treasury stock
	Retained earnings

FIGURE 13-1: Components of a balance sheet.

© *John Wiley & Sons, Inc.*

REMEMBER

People call this statement a balance sheet because the assets must always balance out the liabilities plus the stockholders' equity.

Assets are items that a company owns. They include

>> **Current assets:** Owned items that are easily converted into cash within the next 12 months; included in current assets are cash, securities, accounts receivable, inventory, and any prepaid expenses (like rent or advertising).

   Note: Fundamental analysts also look at methods of inventory valuation, such as *LIFO* (last in first out) or *FIFO* (first in first out). In addition, they look at the methods of depreciation, which are either *straight line* (depreciating an equal amount each year) or *accelerated* (depreciating more in earlier years and less in later years).

- » **Fixed assets:** Owned items that aren't easily converted into cash; included are property, building(s), furniture, and equipment. Because many fixed assets wear down or become outdated over time, they can be depreciated (except for land). Therefore, accumulated depreciation is usually deducted from the fixed assets.

- » **Intangible assets:** Owned items that don't have any physical properties; included are items such as trademarks, patents, formulas, copyrights, goodwill (created when a corporation purchases or merges with another company; *goodwill* is the dollar amount paid above the fair market value to purchase that company), and so on.

Liabilities are what a company owes. They may be current or long-term:

- » **Current liabilities:** Debt obligations that are due to be paid within the next 12 months; included in current liabilities are *accounts payable* (what a company owes in bills), wages, debt securities due to mature, *notes payable* (the balance due on money borrowed), declared cash dividends, and taxes.

- » **Long-term liabilities:** Debt obligation due to be paid after 12 months; included in long-term liabilities are mortgages, bank loans, and outstanding corporate bonds.

Stockholders' equity (net worth) is the difference between the assets and the liabilities (basically, what the company is worth). This value includes

- » **Par value of the common stock:** The arbitrary amount that the company uses for bookkeeping purposes. If a company issues 1 million shares of common stock with a par value of $1, the par value on the stockholders' equity portion of the balance sheet is $1 million.

- » **Par value of the preferred stock:** The value that the company uses for bookkeeping purposes (usually $100 per share). If the company issues 10,000 shares of preferred stock, the par value on the stockholders' equity portion of the balance sheet is $1 million.

- » **Paid in capital:** The amount over par value that the company receives for issuing stock. For example, if the par value of the common stock is $1 but the company receives $7 per share, the paid in capital is $6 per share. The same theory holds true for the preferred stock.

- » **Treasury stock:** Stock that was outstanding in the market but was repurchased by the company.

- » **Retained earnings:** The percentage of net earnings the company holds after paying out dividends (if any) to its shareholders.

Balance sheet calculations

If I were to give you all the calculations that fundamental analysts derive from the balance sheet, you'd likely be cursing under your breath (or possibly out loud). The good news is that the likelihood of your having to perform these calculations on the Series 7 is remote. The most important thing for you to know is what happens to components of the balance sheet when the company makes certain transactions (sells stock or bonds, redeems bonds, and so on).

There are many tools that fundamental analysts can use to measure the financial health of a company. Fundamental analysts will compare companies based on liquidity, risk of bankruptcy, efficiency, profitability, earnings per share, competitiveness, and so on. The following balance sheet formulas help fundamental analysts measure the liquidity of a company:

Net worth of a company is pretty self-explanatory. It is determined the same way you would determine your net worth: by subtracting everything you owe from everything you own.

$$\text{Net worth (stockholder's equity)} = \text{assets} - \text{liabilities}$$

Working capital is the amount of money a company has to work with right now. The company brings in cash by issuing the bonds, which is a current asset, but doesn't have to pay off the bonds for several years, so the current liabilities remain the same. If the current assets increase and the current liabilities remain the same, the working capital increases:

$$\text{Working capital} = \text{current assets} - \text{current liabilities}$$

Current ratio is determining how many times your current assets (assets convertible into cash in a one-year period) cover your current liabilities (liabilities owed in a one-year period). Current ratios vary from industry to industry and from company to company but certainly the higher the current ratio, the healthier the company.

$$\text{Current ratio} = \frac{\text{current assets}}{\text{current liabilities}}$$

Quick or *acid-test ratio* is similar to the formula for current ratio but looks at how a company could handle its debt in a three-to-five-month period instead of a one-year period.

$$\text{Quick (acid-test) ratio} = \frac{\text{quick assets}}{\text{current liabilities}}$$

Note: Quick assets include all current assets except for inventory.

If, for instance, ABC Corp. issues 10,000 bonds at par value, you can use these formulas to figure out what'll happen to the net worth and working capital. You may not even have to plug in numbers. As far as the net worth goes, you can see that it remains unchanged. The company brings in $10 million by issuing 10,000 bonds at $1,000 par. However, because ABC has to pay off the $10 million at maturity, the liabilities go up by the same amount:

$$\text{net worth} = \text{assets} \uparrow - \text{liabilities} \uparrow$$

When a company issues bonds, assume that they're a long-term liability, not short-term, unless the question specifically states that the company is issuing short-term bonds.

The following question tests your ability to answer a balance-sheet-equation question.

DEF Corp. is in the process of buying a new $50,000 computer system. If it is paying for the computer system with available cash, what is the effect on the balance sheet?

(A) The net worth decreases and the working capital remains the same.

(B) The net worth remains the same and the working capital remains the same.

(C) The net worth decreases and the working capital decreases.

(D) The net worth remains the same and the working capital decreases.

The right answer is Choice (D). The company is exchanging one asset for another, and the overall liabilities remain the same, so the net worth of the company doesn't change. However, the company is using a current asset (cash) to purchase a fixed asset (the computer system), so the working capital (the amount of money that the company has to work with) decreases:

$$\text{net worth} = \text{assets} - \text{liabilities}$$

$$\text{working capital} \downarrow = \text{current assets} \downarrow - \text{current liabilities}$$

Take a look at the following scenarios and see whether you can determine how the balance sheet is affected. Here's what happens when a company

>> **Declares a cash dividend:** When a company declares a cash dividend, that cost becomes a current liability to the company. Because current liabilities are part of the overall liabilities owed in the net worth equation, both the net worth and the working capital decrease.

>> **Pays a cash dividend:** When the company initially declares the cash dividend, the current liabilities increase, but when the company pays that dividend, the current liabilities fall. However, the current assets also decrease because the company has to use cash to pay the dividend. If the current assets (and overall assets) decrease and the current liabilities (and overall liabilities) decrease by the same amount, the working capital and net worth both remain the same.

>> **Issues stock:** When a company issues stock, it receives cash, which is a current asset (and part of the overall assets). The company doesn't owe anything to investors, so the overall liabilities (and current liabilities) remain the same. Therefore, the net worth and working capital both increase.

TIP

When you're dealing with balance sheet equations on the Series 7 exam, write down the equations and think about the questions logically. Some possible scenarios include the following:

>> What happens if a company buys machinery for cash?

>> What happens if a company issues new debt securities?

>> What happens if a company calls its bonds?

>> What happens if a company repurchases stock?

If something is increasing, use an up arrow, and if something is decreasing, use a down arrow. Hopefully, this notation can help you solve a majority of the balance sheet problems.

Income statement components

An income statement tells you how profitable a company is right now. *Income statements* list a corporation's expenses and revenues for a specific period of time (quarterly, year-to-date, or yearly). When comparing revenues to expenses, you should be able to see the efficiency of the company and how profitable it is. I don't think you need to actually see a detailed income statement from a company, which in most cases would be much more detailed, but knowing the components of an income statement is important. Take a look at Figure 13-2 to see the way an income statement is laid out. Most of the items are self-explanatory.

Revenue/Sales
- <u>Cost of goods sold (COGS)</u>
Gross profit
- <u>Selling and general admin expenses (including depreciation)</u>
Operating income
- + Other income
- <u>Other expenses (interest expense and misc. losses)</u>
Pretax income
- <u>Income tax expense</u>
Net Income

FIGURE 13-2: Basic components of an income statement.

© John Wiley & Sons, Inc.

Financial statement calculations

Here are some additional calculations you need to know for the Series 7 that you can derive from a company's financial statements:

The following two formulas help fundamental analysts determine a company's risk of bankruptcy:

$$\text{Bond ratio} = \frac{\text{total value of bonds due after one year}}{\text{total value of bonds due after one year} + \text{equity capital}}$$

$$\text{Debt-to-equity ratio} = \frac{\text{total liabilities}}{\text{stockholders' equity}}$$

The bond ratio measures the amount of company indebtedness. Highly leveraged companies take on a lot of debt in comparison to other companies.

The following two formulas help fundamental analysts determine how efficiently a company uses its assets:

$$\text{Inventory turnover ratio} = \frac{\text{cost of goods sold}}{\text{average inventory}}$$

$$\text{Cash flow} = \text{net income} + \text{depreciation} + \text{depletion} + \text{amortization}$$

The following formulas help fundamental analysts determine a company's *profitability:*

$$\text{Margin-of-profit ratio} = \frac{\text{net income}}{\text{net sales}}$$

$$\text{Net profit ratio} = \frac{\text{net profit after tax}}{\text{net sales}}$$

As part of a company's profitability, there are a few formulas that help fundamental analysts determine the asset coverage and safety of income:

$$\text{Net asset value per bond} = \frac{\text{total assets} - \text{current liabilities}}{\text{number of bonds outstanding}}$$

$$\text{Bond interest coverage ratio} = \frac{\text{earnings before interest and taxes (EBIT)}}{\text{bond interest expense}}$$

$$\text{Book value per share} = \frac{\text{total stockholders' equity} - \text{preferred equity}}{\text{total outstanding shares}}$$

One of the major factors that could affect the market price of a stock is its earnings per share (EPS). In other words, if broken down on a per share basis, how much did the company make for each outstanding share. Obviously, the higher the better:

$$\text{EPS} = \frac{\text{net income} - \text{preferred dividends}}{\text{number of common shares outstanding}}$$

Note: If a company has convertible bonds, convertible preferred stock, warrants, and/or rights outstanding, the potential for the common stock to be diluted (that is, with more shares outstanding) is high. A calculation can also be done for *fully diluted earnings per share,* which takes into consideration the company's earnings per share if all convertible securities have been converted into common stock.

Once you've determined the EPS, you can calculate the price/earnings ratio, which compares the market price of the security to the earnings per share. In this case, the lower the P/E ratio, the better.

$$\text{Price earnings (P/E) ratio} = \frac{\text{market price}}{\text{earnings per share (EPS)}}$$

The dividend payout ratio tells analysts how much the corporation is paying out in dividends per share as compared to how much it's earning per share.

$$\text{Dividend payout ratio} = \frac{\text{annual dividends per common share}}{\text{earnings per share (EPS)}}$$

The current yield, tells analysts how much the company is paying out in dividends in comparison to the market price.

$$\text{Current yield} = \frac{\text{annual dividends}}{\text{market price}}$$

The following formula helps fundamental analysts determine the competitiveness (comparative performance) of a company:

$$\text{Return on common equity} = \frac{\text{net income}}{\text{average stockholder's equity}}$$

The following question tests your ability to answer a question on earnings per share.

EXAMPLE

Zazzoo Corp. has 1 million common shares outstanding. If Zazzoo's net income is $14 million, what are the earnings per share?

(A) $0.07

(B) $0.70

(C) $14.00

(D) Cannot be determined without knowing the preferred dividends

The answer you want is Choice (C). "Cannot be determined" is almost never the answer on the Series 7. Remember that a corporation doesn't need to issue preferred stock, only common stock. Because the question doesn't mention anything about Zazzoo having preferred stock, you can't assume that it does; the preferred dividends are equal to zero. Therefore, solving this problem is as easy as dividing the net income by the number of common shares outstanding:

$$\text{EPS} = \frac{\text{net income} - \text{preferred dividends}}{\text{no. of common shares outstanding}} = \frac{\$14,000,000 - 0}{1,000,000} = \$14.00$$

REMEMBER

You could *possibly* get a bunch of formulas relating to income statements and balance sheets on the Series 7 exam. However, the most you'll *probably* get is two. Understanding how income statements and balance sheets work is more important than remembering a bunch of formulas. If you feel that you have a handle on everything else that you need for the Series 7 exam and want to get the extra point or two by memorizing all the formulas, go for it.

Annual reports

Fundamental analysts use annual reports distributed to shareholders by most public companies to help them determine investment recommendations. Annual reports are used to help determine the company's financial position. Typically included in a company's annual report are financial data (income statements, balance sheets, footnotes), payments to the company's executives, research and development activities, future plans, subsidiary information, and so on. Besides being mailed, annual reports are typically available on the issuer's website.

Footnotes

Financial statements such as income statements and balance sheets also contain footnotes. Footnotes are added so that investors and analysts will more clearly understand how a corporation came up with its numbers. Included are the methods of depreciation, the inventory valuation used, fully diluted earnings per share (EPS), the market price of the securities, and so on. In addition, the footnotes may include items which may affect the company's performance, such as management or financial issues, management philosophy, and pending litigation. Separated out may also be specifics about the company's debt, including the amount of outstanding debt, call dates, maturity dates, interest rates, conversion privileges, assets backing the debt (if any), and so on. In addition, the footnotes may contain information regarding depreciation and/or depletion deductions (which is covered in Chapter 11).

Technical analysis

Technical analysts look at the market to identify patterns and measure indicators in an attempt to predict whether the market and/or particular securities will become or remain bullish or bearish. They look at:

>> **Trendlines:** Technical analysts can plot individual stocks, the market, or certain segments to see if there is an upward trendline or downward trendline. Even though securities may be up or down over a short period of time, when looking at a long-term trendline, technical analysts should be able to determine if they are bullish or bearish on a security, segment, or the market in general.

>> **Trading volume:** When the market trading volume is much greater than normal, a technical analyst will typically look at that as being the beginning of a bullish or bearish trend.

>> **Market sentiment:** When investors are generally feeling good about the market and the economy, that means that more people will be investing and therefore a bullish sign. However, if people are not feeling good about the market or economy, more people will be selling their securities and it would be a bearish sign.

>> **Market indices:** Market indices such as the S&P 500, Wilshire, Russell 2000, Lipper, Dow Jones, and so on, are covered in detail in the Securities Industry Essentials book. Basically, technical analysts look at different indices to help determine a pattern.

>> **Available funds:** Certainly when people have more funds available to spend, businesses do well and the market does well.

>> **Index futures:** Analysts can get an idea of how investors feel about the future of the market based on the buying or selling of index futures.

>> **New highs and lows:** When the market hits a new high, some analysts might look at that as a bearish sign and others a bullish sign depending on whether they feel there's a good reason for the market to hit a new high or not.

>> **Advance-decline ratio:** The advance-decline ratio looks at the number of stocks advancing versus the number declining. Certainly, in most instances, the more stocks advancing would be a bullish sign.

>> **Odd lot volume:** Remember, the most common unit of stock trading is 100 shares. When trades are completed for less than the normal unit of trading, it is called an odd lot. So when an investor trades 30 shares of a particular company, it is an odd lot trade. Odd lot trades are typically done by smaller, less-sophisticated investors. Smaller investors usually jump on the bandwagon a little late, so when odd lot volume is high, it is usually a bearish sign. This is known as the *Odd-Lot Theory*.

>> **Short interest:** Short interest looks at the number of short sellers as a percentage of float (number of shares publicly available for investors to buy and sell). Remember, short sellers eventually have to purchase the security they sold short. So when there are a lot of investors selling short, it may be a good time to buy.

>> **Put/call ratio:** The put/call ratio looks at the amount of investors purchasing puts as compared to purchasing calls. If more investors are purchasing calls, it's a bullish sign.

>> **Dow Jones Averages:** Mosts technical analysts believe that the Dow Jones Industrial Average (DJIA) and the Dow Jones Transportation Average (DJTA or DJT) need to be going in the same direction to confirm the future direction of the market (at least in the near term). In other words, if companies are doing well, they should be shipping out a lot of goods making the transportation average increase as well as the industrial average. This is also known as the *Dow Theory*.

Technical analysts believe that history tends to repeat itself and that past performance of securities and the market indicate its future performance.

REMEMBER

Fundamental analysts decide *what to buy,* and technical analysts decide *when to buy* (timing).

Not only do technical analysts chart the market, but they also chart individual securities. Technical analysts try to identify market patterns and patterns of particular stocks in an attempt to determine the best time to purchase or sell. Even though a stock's price may vary a lot from one day to another, when plotting out stock prices over a long period of time, the prices tend to head in a particular direction (up, down, or sideways) and create a *trendline*.

Moving averages measure the movement of stock indexes and individual stocks over a certain period of time (5 days, 10, days, 30 days, 6 months, and so on). By charting the security or index over a period of time, it helps technical analysts focus more on long-term trends rather than short-term price fluctuations.

Consolidation is occurring when a stock stays within a narrow trading range or *trading channel.* When plotted out on a graph, the trendline is moving horizontally (neither up nor down). If a stock stays within a narrow trading range for a long period of time (months or even years), it creates a *support* (bottom of the trading range) and *resistance level* (top of the trading range). For example, say that XYZ common stock has been trading between $40 and $42 per share for several months; the lower number ($40) is the support, and the higher number ($42) is the resistance. When a stock is at the top of its trading price, it is considered to be *overbought* and when it's at the bottom of its trading range, it is considered to be *oversold.*

When a stock declines below its support level or increases above its resistance level, a *breakout* is occurring. When a stock has been trading horizontally (sideways) for a long period of time, a breakout is considered significant. Breakouts are usually a sign that the stock is beginning a new downward (bearish) or upward (bullish) trend.

If a stock price is gradually moving down over a period of time, the stock's in a *downtrend*. Conversely, if the stock price is gradually moving upward over a period of time, you're looking at an *uptrend*. Here are a couple patterns technical analysts recognize as reversals of such trends:

>> **Saucer and inverted saucer:** In a saucer pattern, when the stock prices are plotted for a period of time, they make a saucer shape (gradually decreasing and then gradually increasing). A saucer pattern is a bullish sign or, to be more precise, the reversal of a bearish trend. Conversely, an inverted saucer is exactly the opposite; it's a bearish sign because it's the reversal of a bullish trend.

© John Wiley & Sons, Inc.

>> **Head and shoulders and inverted head and shoulders:** A head and shoulders pattern is formed when the price of a stock has been increasing, hits a high, and then starts decreasing. It involves three peaks, with the center peak as the highest. The two bumps in the road (one on the way up and one on the way down) are the shoulders, and the high point is the head. A head and shoulders top formation is a bearish sign because it's the reversal of a bullish trend. I also illustrate an inverted head and shoulders (also known as a head and shoulders bottom formation), which is a bullish sign because it's the reversal of a bearish trend.

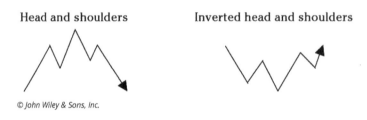

© John Wiley & Sons, Inc.

REMEMBER

The key thing to remember about these patterns is that the saucer pattern and the inverted head and shoulders pattern are bullish signs, whereas the head and shoulders and inverted saucer patterns are bearish signs.

As with individual securities, the market can also be considered overbought or oversold. The market is said to be *oversold* if a market index such as the DJIA or the S&P 500 is declining but fewer stocks are declining than advancing. If the market is oversold, it's likely a good time to buy. On the other hand, the market's *overbought* if a market index such as the DJIA or the S&P 500 is increasing but fewer stocks are advancing than declining. If the market is overbought, it's likely a good time to sell or sell short (borrow securities to sell on margin).

Showing the work: Research reports

Typically, brokerage firms send out research reports to their customers (and potential customers) with certain recommendations. Research reports are documents prepared by an analyst who is part of a brokerage or investment banking firm. As with pretty much everything on the Series 7, research reports are subject to several rules:

>> **Quiet periods:** Member firms are restricted from publishing or distributing research reports on a particular investment until at least 10 days after the initial public offering (IPO).

>> **Information barriers:** All firms must establish information barriers (firewalls) to protect analysts from any pressure they may feel from investment bankers or any other persons who may be biased in their judgment.

>> **Third-party disclosures:** Depending on the size of your firm, you may or may not have access to your own research analyst to prepare reports. A third-party research report is one in which the third party has no affiliation or contractual relationship with the distributing firm. All third-party research reports must include a disclosure unless the member firm makes nonaffiliated research available to its customers either upon request or through a website maintained by the member firm.

REMEMBER

Although not in the Series 7 outline, money supply is also something that analysts take into consideration when making investment recommendations. Money supply and how the Federal Reserve Board influences the money supply is tested on the Securities Industry Essentials (SIE) exam.

Testing Your Knowledge

Here is a quick 10-question quiz to test your understanding and test-taking ability regarding portfolio and securities analysis. Read the questions carefully so that you don't make any careless mistakes.

1. Which of the following WOULD NOT be examined by a fundamental analyst?

   (A) EPS

   (B) Balance sheets

   (C) Industry

   (D) Timing

2. For an investor who is concerned about purchasing power risk, which TWO of the following would be the best recommendations?

   I. Common stock

   II. Long-term corporate bonds

   III. Fixed annuities

   IV. Variable annuities

   (A) I and III

   (B) I and IV

   (C) II and III

   (D) II and IV

3. An inverted head and shoulder pattern indicates which of the following?

   (A) Reversal of a bullish trend

   (B) Reversal of a bearish trend

   (C) The security is consolidating

   (D) The security has broken past the resistance level

4. Which of the following are systematic risks?

    I. Currency risk

    II. Purchasing power risk

    III. Reinvestment risk

    (A) I and II

    (B) I and III

    (C) II and III

    (D) I, II, and III

5. ABC common stock has a beta of 1.4, which means

    (A) the stock is more volatile than the market

    (B) the stock is less volatile than the market

    (C) the stock is equally volatile as the market

    (D) the stock is counter cyclical

6. Which of the following securities has no reinvestment risk?

    (A) Industrial Development Revenue bonds

    (B) Treasury notes

    (C) Zero-coupon bonds

    (D) GO bonds

7. AylDec Corp. paid a cash dividend to its common stockholders. How would it affect AylDec's balance sheet?

    I. The assets would decrease

    II. The liabilities would decrease

    III. The net worth would decrease

    IV. The net worth would remain the same

    (A) I and III

    (B) II and III

    (C) I, II, and III

    (D) I, II, and IV

8. TUV Corporation has announced a $0.50 dividend to holders of record of their common stock. At the time of the announcement and prior to the dividend being paid, what happens to TUV's working capital?

    (A) It decreases

    (B) It remains the same

    (C) It increases

    (D) It's impossible to tell with the information given

9. ABC Corporation has been trading in-between $23 and $26 for quite a long period of time. $23 would be considered ABC Corporation's

    (A) support
    (B) resistance
    (C) breakpoint
    (D) none of the above

10. Use the following exhibit to answer this question:

Assets	Liabilities
Cash: $10	Accts Payable: $10
Securities: $10	Bonds Due This Year: $10
Accts Receivable: $20	Bonds Due in 10 Years: $30
Inventory: $20	
Machinery: $10	
Land: $10	

All numbers in the chart above are in millions.

What is the working capital?

    (A) $10,000,000
    (B) $20,000,000
    (C) $30,000,000
    (D) $40,000,000

Answers and Explanations

If you read the chapter recently, you probably didn't find the questions overly difficult. Because there are 10 questions, each one is worth 10 points.

1. **D.** The main function of a fundamental analyst is to help investors determine what to buy or sell based on examining items such as income statements, balance sheets, industries, management, and so on. It is the job of a technical analyst who studies the market to determine when to buy or sell.

2. **B.** Purchasing power risk is also known as inflation risk. So investors who are concerned about purchasing power risk are concerned that their investment won't keep up with the rate of inflation. Out of the choices given, common stock and variable annuities have a much better chance of keeping up with and hopefully beating the rate of inflation than long-term corporate bonds and fixed annuities.

3. **B.** A head and shoulder pattern looks how you would expect it: The head is the high point of the trend, and the two shoulders are a little lower. An inverted pattern is the same idea but only upside down. This means that the head is the lowest part of the trendline and the shoulders are the next lowest. Knowing that, an inverted head and shoulders pattern is a reversal of a bearish trend: Once it hits the head, it is showing a reversal of the downward trend, and now the security is starting to increase in value.

4. **A.** Both currency risk and purchasing power risk are systematic risks while reinvestment risk is a non-systematic risk.

5. **A.** Beta measures the volatility of a stock in relation to the market. A stock with a beta of 1 is equally volatile as the market. A stock with a beta higher than 1 (as it is in this case) is more volatile than the market. Stocks with a high beta tend to decrease in value more than the market when it's bearish and increase in value more than the market when it's bullish.

6. **C.** Reinvestment risk is the additional investment risk investors take with dividends and interest received. Zero-coupon bonds are issued at a discount, mature at par value, and don't provide interest payments along the way. Since the investor doesn't receive any additional money to invest until maturity, zero-coupon bonds have no reinvestment risk.

7. **D.** The formula for net worth is as follows:

Net worth = assets − liabilities

So certainly the assets of AylDec had to decrease because they are using cash to pay the dividend. But also remember that AylDec had to announce the dividend to shareholders before paying it, so at that point, it became a current liability on AylDec's balance sheet. So this means that the assets and liabilities reduced by the same amount because once the dividend was paid, that liability went away. Therefore, the net worth remained the same. That was definitely a tough one.

8. A. The formula for working capital is as follows:

working capital = current assets − current liabilities

Working capital is the amount of money that a corporation has to work with. Current assets are assets a company has that are easily convertible into cash within a one-year period. Current liabilities are what a company owes within a one year period. So if a company declares a cash dividend, it becomes a current liability. If the current liablities increase and the current assets remain the same, the working capital decreases.

working capital ↓ = current assets − current liabilities ↑

9. A. The support is the lower portion of the trading range and the resistance is the upper portion of the trading range.

10. D. Remember that the working capital looks at what a company owes in a one-year period subtracted from the cash a company has that can be converted into cash in a one-year period. Looking on the asset side of the exhibit, cash, securities, accounts receivable, and inventory are all current assets. This means that the current assets are

Current assets = $10,000,000 + $10,000,000 + $20,000,000 + $20,000,000 = $60,000,000

The current liabilities are accounts payable and bonds due this year:

Current liabilities = $10,000,000 + $10,000,000 = $20,000,000

This means that the working capital is

Working capital = current assets − current liabilities

Working capital = $60,000,000 − $20,000,000 = $40,000,000

» .... the primary and
secondary markets

» **Comparing stock exchanges to the over-the-counter market**

» **Looking at order qualifiers**

» **Meeting a designated market maker and looking over the books**

» **Taking the chapter quiz**

Chapter **14**

Going to Market: Orders and Trades

P art of your function as a registered rep will be to understand and explain to customers (and potential customers) how the stock market works. I designed this chapter with that in mind (along with the fact that you need to know this stuff for the Series 7, of course).

In this chapter, I cover the basics of exchanges and the over-the-counter market, along with some of the active participants who help the market run smoothly (at least most of the time). Pay particular attention to the "Talking about order types" and "Factoring in order features" sections, because you'll definitely use that information every day after you pass the Series 7 exam. At the end of this chapter, I've added a quick quiz to help you realize what you'll face when taking the real Series 7. As in the other chapters, you will notice some overlap between the material on the Securities Industry Essentials exam and the Series 7 exam.

Shopping at Primary and Secondary Markets

Depending on whether the securities are new or outstanding, they trade in either the primary or secondary market. This section deals with the differences between the two.

Buying new in the primary market

The primary market (new issue market) is broken down into two categories, depending on whether the company has ever issued securities before. A security that has never been offered or sold to the public is considered a *new issue.* When securities are sold in the primary market, a bulk of the sales proceeds go to the issuer, and the balance goes to the underwriter (who buys the securities from the issuer and sells them to the public). Here are the three types of offerings on the primary market:

>> **Initial public offering (IPO):** An IPO is the first time a company ever sells stock to the public to raise money. When a company is in the process of issuing securities for the first time, it's said to be *going public.*

>> **Primary offering:** When a company initially offers securities, it usually holds some back for future use; it later pulls those securities out of storage and sells them in a primary offering. For example, a company may be authorized to sell 2 million shares of common stock, but in its initial public offering, it may sell only 800,000. At this point, 1,200,000 new shares remain that have never been offered to the public. One year later, when the company needs to raise additional capital to build a new warehouse, it can sell some of the remaining 1,200,000 shares in a primary offering.

>> **Combined (split) offering:** This type of offering is a combination of new securities and a large block of outstanding or previously outstanding securities.

Buying used in the secondary market

When the securities are already trading in the market, the sales proceeds go to another investor instead of going to the issuer. The secondary market, also called the *aftermarket,* consists of four categories (see the following section for info on trading on exchanges versus over-the-counter markets):

>> **First market (auction market):** The first market is the trading of listed securities on the exchange floor, such as the New York Stock Exchange (NYSE).

>> **Second market (over-the-counter market):** This market is the trading of unlisted securities (securities not listed on an exchange) over-the-counter (by phone or computer).

>> **Third market:** The third market is comprised of exchange-listed securities trading over-the-counter (OTC) — traders are calling in their orders or ordering online. All NYSE, NYSE American, NYSE Arca, and most of the securities listed on other exchanges can be traded OTC.

>> **Fourth market:** The fourth market is the trading of securities between institutions without the use of a brokerage firm. Fourth-market trades are reported on Institutional Networks, or Instinet, a computerized system for institutional traders.

TIP

You're more likely to get a question on the third or fourth market than the first or second.

Making the Trade

After securities are issued publicly, they may trade on an exchange or on the over-the-counter (OTC) market.

Auctioning securities at securities exchanges

Exchanges are auction markets, where bidders and sellers get together to execute trades. I'm sure you've seen movies or TV shows featuring the New York Stock Exchange. It definitely looks very chaotic (and like it's a good place to have a heart attack or develop an ulcer). However, some sort of order is definitely there: All exchanges have a trading floor where all trades are executed. Each security listed on an exchange has its own *trading post* (location) on the floor where the auction takes place. Brokers looking to purchase shout out or make hand signals to indicate the price they're willing to spend to buy a particular security. Sellers, in turn, shout out the price they're willing to sell a security for. If buyers and sellers can come to an agreement, a trade is made.

The main exchange that the Series 7 tests you on is the New York Stock Exchange (NYSE, a.k.a. the Big Board or Exchange), but there are others, such as NYSE American (formerly the American Stock Exchange [AMEX]), NYSE Arca, NASDAQ, CBOE (Chicago Board Options Exchange), Boston Stock Exchange (formerly BSE, now NASDAQ OMX BX), and so on. *Listed securities* are ones that satisfy minimum requirements and are traded on a regional or national exchange like the NYSE. Listed securities may trade on the exchange or in the OTC market.

REMEMBER

All securities exchanges have listing requirements for companies that want to have their shares sold on the exchange, which include a minimum number of outstanding shares, a minimum stock price, a minimum net worth, a certain trading volume, and so on.

Although thousands of people may seem to be on the floor of the exchange, you don't need to be aware of too many titles. Most of the people on the floor of the exchange fall into one of three categories:

>> **Floor brokers:** These individuals act as agents in executing buy or sell orders on behalf of their firm's customers. A floor broker may also facilitate buying and selling for their firm. Floor brokers receive buy or sell orders from their firms and either transfer the orders to a designated market maker (DMM or specialist) or trade with another floor broker.

>> **Two-dollar brokers (independent brokers):** These people assist floor brokers in getting their orders executed on busy days. (By the way, they're called two-dollar brokers because many, many years ago, they used to receive $2 per trade. Commissions may have gone up a bit since then.)

>> **Designated market makers (DMMs or specialists):** These market professionals manage the auction market trading for a particular security (or for a few securities, if not actively traded). Their purpose is to maintain a "fair and orderly market" in one or more securities. A DMM can act as a broker or a dealer (trading out of their own account) to help keep trading as active as possible. An important function of a DMM is to keep track of and execute limit orders on behalf of other exchange members. For more information about a specialist, visit "Designated Market Maker and the Super Display Book (SDBK)," later in this chapter.

Under NYSE rules, only members are permitted to accept offers, make bids, or consummate transactions on the floor of the exchange. These transactions are typically handled by floor brokers or DMMs. However, firms who have a booth on the exchange may have *supervised booth clerks* process orders sent to the booth. Currently, more trading is executed electronically and less occurs on the trading floor.

Negotiating trades over-the-counter

Unlike exchanges, the OTC market is a negotiated market. Instead of yelling out bid and ask prices, traders buy and sell securities by way of telephone or computer transactions. There's no central location for trading OTC securities. Thousands of securities — both listed and unlisted — are traded this way. In fact, *unlisted securities*, which aren't listed on an exchange, can only trade OTC.

The OTC equities market is divided into NASDAQ issues (issues that meet the NASDAQ listing requirements) and non-NASDAQ issues. Non-NASDAQ issues are unlisted and trade on the Over The Counter Bulletin Board (OTCBB) or in the OTC Pink Market.

REMEMBER

U.S. government and municipal bonds trade only over-the-counter.

The NASD Automated Quotation service (NASDAQ) is the largest U.S. equities trading venue by volume. NASDAQ is an electronic quotation system that displays bid and ask prices of the most actively traded OTC stocks. Additionally, NASDAQ also includes quotes of preferred stock, convertible bonds, and warrants.

To be a market maker on NASDAQ, the dealer must have a minimum net capital requirement, be registered with FINRA, and must provide regular bid and ask prices for a security.

To make trades, people need accurate, current info on bid and ask prices. Not everyone can get the same amount of information, though. Here are the access levels of NASDAQ (the computer displays with NASDAQ information):

>> **Level I:** The most basic level of NASDAQ, this quotation screen displays up-to-the-minute inside bid and ask prices (highest bid and lowest ask prices) for several hundred OTC stocks. Level I is the computer screen that you'll most likely have on your desk when you're working as a registered rep. Level I is the most basic level of NASDAQ and includes quotes that are subject to change (*subject quotes*). Level I does not display the market makers offering to buy or sell the securities.

>> **Level II:** The second level of NASDAQ provides up-to-the-minute firm bid and ask prices (*firm quotes*) of each market maker (dealers or principals) and quote sizes for a security. Most brokerage firm *traders* use this level.

>> **Level III:** The most complete level of NASDAQ, this level not only shows the bid and ask prices of all market makers and their firm quotes, but also allows a market maker to enter and change quotes. Once a market maker enters a quote, they will appear on the system right away.

OTC market makers

Unlike exchanges where they have designated market makers, there are none in the OTC market. However, there are firms (dealers) who will make a market for particular securities and be willing to trade to and from their own inventory. If they wish to make a market in a security, they must receive FINRA's approval. OTC market makers create the inside market by offering to buy and sell securities. The inside market is the highest bid price (the most a market maker is willing to pay) for a security and the lowest ask or offer price (the most a market maker is willing to accept) for a security. In the NASDAQ system, you typically have several market makers for one security. Take a look at what happens when you have several market makers entering quotes for ABCD common stock:

Market Maker	BID	ASK
Vizzion Broker-Dealer	18.30	18.75
Silver Stanley	18.25	18.80
Utah/New Mexico Securities	18.35	19.05

By looking at this chart, you can see that there are three market makers that have entered quotes for ABCD Common stock. To determine the inside market, look at the highest bid price, which was entered by Utah/New Mexico Securities, and the lowest ask price, which was entered by Vizzzion Broker-Dealer. For ABCD, the inside market is currently 18.35–18.75. Looking at a Level I machine, you would only see the name of the security and the inside market price. If you were to give a quote to customers, you would have to let them know it's a subject quote (subject to change) because as buy and sell orders are placed, the inside market will change. Remember, if you were placing an order to buy, you would buy at the lowest ask price. If you were placing an order to sell, you would sell at the highest bid price.

Non-NASDAQ securities

Non-NASDAQ securities are OTC equity securities that don't meet the listing requirements of national securities exchanges such as NYSE or NASDAQ. Non-NASDAQ securities include warrants, ADRs, equity stocks (foreign and domestic), and DPPs. Non-NASDAQ securities can be purchased on the OTCBB or OTC Pink Market. As you can imagine, non-NASDAQ securities are among the riskiest securities available and certainly aren't suitable for all investors.

» **OTCBB:** The OTCBB is a quotation system for securities dealers for securities that don't meet the listing requirements of NASDAQ or other exchanges. Dealers who subscribe to the OTCBB can enter, update, and display quotes on individual securities on a real-time basis. Quotes may consist of bid/ask prices as well as indications of interest. There are listing requirements for a security to be sold on the OTCBB but they are quite minimal.

» **OTC Markets Group:** The OTC Markets Group used to be called Pink Sheets because firms would receive a pink sheet every so often letting them know about these low-priced securities that dealers are selling. There were no financial standards or disclosure requirements for securities listed in the Pink Sheets. However, over the years, the OTC Markets Group has expanded and now has different tiers for trading:

   OTC Best Market: The Best Market is for established U.S. and international companies. Companies listed on the Best Market must meet proper disclosure requirements, meet high financial standards, and be able to demonstrate compliance with U.S. securities laws.

   OTC Venture Market: The Venture Market is for early stage developing U.S. and international companies. Eligible companies must be current in their reporting and undertake an annual verification and certification process.

   OTC Pink: The OTC Pink (Pink Sheets) is the riskiest of all the markets and should only be considered for sophisticated investors with a high risk tolerance. There are no financial standards or disclosure requirements for companies to be listed on the OTC Pink. Companies whose securities trade on the OTC Pink include certain foreign companies with limited disclosure information, companies issuing U.S. penny stocks, distressed companies, delinquent companies, and companies not willing to provide information to investors.

REMEMBER

It is your job to attempt to get the best price for your clients when executing trades. Because there is often little price information on securities in the OTC Pink Market or the OTCBB, you may have to do a little extra work to get your client the best price. Unless there are prices quoted by at least two market makers for a particular security, you must contact a minimum of three dealers in an attempt to get your client the best price.

Consolidated Quotation Service (CQS)

The CQS is a quotation service that includes *bid* and *ask* prices of listed securities on *all markets*. For example, a security that trades on the NYSE may also trade over the counter. The price on the NYSE for that security might be quite different than the price of the security in the OTC market. The CQS allows traders to see the best bid and ask prices for a security across all markets.

Understanding the Role of a Broker-Dealer

REMEMBER

In order for a firm to be considered a broker-dealer, it must buy and sell securities from its own account and act as middleperson (middleperson?) for securities not in inventory. Here are the differences between brokers and dealers:

>> **Broker:** A firm is acting as a broker when it doesn't use its own inventory to execute a trade. A broker charges a *commission* (sales charge) for acting as a middleperson between a buyer and a seller. If a customer wants to buy a security, the broker will find a seller, and if a customer wants to sell a security, the broker will find a buyer.

If a broker has a customer who wants to sell a security and another who wants to buy the same security, the broker may cross (exchange) the securities without using the services of a dealer. This is known as an *agency cross transaction* and the trade typically takes place somewhere between the current bid and ask prices.

For Series 7 exam purposes, the term *broker* and *agent* may be used interchangeably. A registered representative is sometimes called an agent or stockbroker because they act as an intermediary between buyers and sellers.

>> **Dealer:** A firm is acting as a dealer when it uses its own inventory to execute a trade. When a dealer sells securities to a customer using its own inventory, it charges a *markup* (sales charge). When a dealer buys securities from a customer for its own inventory, it charges a *markdown* (reducing the price a customer receives by charging a sales charge). A firm becomes a dealer in the hopes that the securities it has in its own inventory will increase in price so that the dealer can benefit from the appreciation.

The terms *dealer, principal,* and *market maker* may be used interchangeably on the Series 7 exam.

Capacity refers to whether a firm is acting as a broker or dealer, and it must always be disclosed on the *confirmation* (receipt of trade). If a firm is acting as a broker, the commission always needs to be disclosed on the confirmation. However, if a firm is acting as a dealer, the markup or markdown doesn't always have to be disclosed.

REMEMBER

A firm can't act as a broker and a dealer for the same trade. In other words, charging a markup (or markdown) and a commission on the same trade is a violation. (For information on rules and regulations, see Chapter 16.)

TIP

To help you remember the differences between a broker and a dealer, think of a real-estate broker. A real-estate broker (or agent) acts as an intermediary between sellers and buyers and charges a commission, just like a stockbroker does. Conversely, a dealer like a used car dealer, sells from their own inventory, charges a markup, and buys in the hopes of making a profit on that inventory.

Firm versus subject quotes

Because market makers are buying and selling securities from their own inventory, they can make firm quotes even though those quotes may only be for a limited period of time. If a market maker enters a quote for a security and then fails to purchase or sell the stated amount of securities at the quoted price, it is a violation known as *backing away*. However, market makers may remove or change their quotes during the course of the trading day based on market conditions. When a price is not firm and is subject to confirmation by the market maker, it is considered a *subject* (nominal) quote. Subject quotes are for informational purposes only and are subject to change. For example, you could tell a customer that "ABC is currently trading at 22.00-22.25 subject."

Traders

A firm's trading department works on positioning (buying and selling securities). Traders handle the brokerage firm's inventory and execute all customers' orders. Traders must have at least a Series 7 and a Series 57 license. *Note:* A Series 57 license is required for executing transactions in equity, preferred, or convertible debt securities transacted other than on a securities exchange.

Receiving Orders from Customers

Here's where the rubber meets the road. You can receive several types of orders from customers along with numerous order qualifiers. This section explains the types of orders and how to execute them.

Recommending OTC equity securities

It is always up to you to look out for your client's best interest. Because OTC equity securities are riskier than many other securities, FINRA requires members to review financial statements and current material business information about the issuer before making a recommendation to purchase or sell short the security. In addition, the recommendation should fit into the client's investment profile and you must have a reasonable basis for making the recommendation.

Talking about order types

You can definitely expect a few questions on the Series 7 exam relating to orders. The following sections explore the order types.

Market order

A market order is one that is for immediate execution at the best price available. A majority of the orders that you'll receive will be market orders. Here are the varieties they come in:

>> **Buy order:** When an investor places a market order to buy, they're not price-specific; the investor purchases the security at the lowest ask price (the lowest price at which someone's willing to sell the security). An investor who's purchasing a security wants the price to increase (after the sale, of course) and is establishing a bullish position.

>> **Sell order:** When an investor places a market order to sell, they're not price-specific; they sell the security at the highest bid price (the highest price someone's willing to pay for the security) at the time of the trade.

>> **Selling short:** Selling short occurs when an investor sells securities they don't own. The investor is actually borrowing securities from a lender to sell. Here's how it works: Say an investor borrows 100 shares of ABC stock and sells them short at $40 per share, thus receiving $4,000. The borrower doesn't owe the lender $4,000; they owe the lender 100 shares of ABC stock. After a month or two, when ABC is trading at $20 per share, the borrower can purchase the 100 shares for $2,000 and return them to the lender, making a nice $2,000 profit (excluding commission costs). A short seller is bearish (wants the price of the security to decrease). If the price increases instead, the short seller has to buy the stock in the market at a higher price, thus losing money. All short sales *must* be executed in margin accounts. Short sales are subject to short-sale regulations under Regulation SHO (see the nearby sidebar).

> **Note:** Investors may sell short for *speculation* (believing the price of the security will decrease), *hedging* (protecting a security or several securities in the event of a market decline), or *arbitrage* (taking advantage of a price disparity on the security in different markets).

REMEMBER

When you purchase a security, the most you can lose is the amount you invest. When you're short a security, your maximum loss potential is unlimited because the price of the stock could keep climbing, in which case you'd have to spend more and more money to cover your short position. As said previously, because of the additional risk, all short sales must be executed in a margin account. Chapter 9 tells you more about margin accounts.

Stop order

A stop order is used for protection; it tries to limit how much an investor can lose. It can also be used to lock in gains. Depending on whether an investor has a long or short stock position, they may enter a buy stop order or a sell stop order:

>> **Buy stop orders:** These orders protect a short position (when an investor sells borrowed securities). A buy stop tells you to buy a security if the market price touches a particular price or higher. Investors who are short the stock make money when the price of the stock decreases; however, if the price increases, they lose money. For example, an investor who's short ABC stock currently trading at $25 could enter a buy stop order on ABC at $30. If ABC reaches $30 or more, the order is triggered and the order becomes a market order for immediate execution at the next available price.

>> **Sell stop orders:** These orders protect a long position (when an investor purchases stock); they tell you to sell a security if the market price touches a particular price or lower. Investors who are long stock make money when the price of the stock increases; if the price decreases, they lose money. For example, say an investor who is long DEF stock currently trading at $50 enters a sell stop order on ABC at $47. If DEF reaches $47 or below, the order is triggered and the order becomes a market order for immediate execution at the next available price, whether higher or lower than $47.

Limit order

A customer who's specific about the price they want to spend or receive for a security places a limit order; this order says the customer doesn't want to pay more than a certain amount or sell for less than a certain amount. Depending on whether an investor is interested in buying or selling, they can enter a buy limit or a sell limit order:

REGULATION SHO AND SHORT SALES

According to *Regulation SHO*, all order tickets must be marked as *short sale* rather than long sale, which is when a customer is selling securities they own. Additionally, all brokerage firms must establish rules to locate, borrow, and deliver securities that are to be sold short. Brokerage firms must be sure that the security can be located and delivered on the date the delivery is due before executing the short sale. In order to avoid a *fail to deliver position,* broker-dealers and customers often have a list of securities that are easy to borrow to help them expedite short sales. Broker-dealers may also have a *Hard to Borrow* list, which will tell them which securities they should avoid having customers sell short.

>> **Buy limit orders:** Investors who want to purchase a security place these orders. A buy limit order is a directive to buy a particular security at the limit price or lower. For example, suppose DEF stock is trading at $35 per share but one of your customers doesn't want to pay more than $30 per share. You could place a buy limit order at $30. If the price of DEF ever reaches $30 or less, chances are good that your customer will end up with the stock.

>> **Sell limit orders:** Investors who want to sell a security place sell limit orders. A sell limit order is a directive to sell a particular security at the limit price or higher. For example, suppose one of your customers owns LMN stock, which is currently trading at $62 per share, but they want to receive at least $70 per share if they're going to sell it. This customer could place a sell limit on LMN at $70 per share. If LMN touches or goes above $70 per share, chances are good that the stock will be sold.

Stop limit order

A *stop limit order* is a combination of a stop and limit order (see the preceding sections); it's a buy stop or sell stop order that becomes a limit order after the stop price is reached. For example, an order that reads "sell 1,000 HIJ at 41 stop, 40.75 limit" means that the sell stop order will be triggered as soon as HIJ reaches 41 or below (the stop price). If this were just a stop order, the stock would be sold on the next available trade (no matter what the price). But because this is a stop limit order, after the order is triggered, it becomes a limit order to buy at 40.75 or above (the limit price). In other words, this customer is interested in selling their stock if it drops to 41 but wants to receive at least 40.75 per share.

REMEMBER

Limit orders are something that investors want to happen (that is, buy if the price gets low enough or sell if the price gets high enough). However, there is a risk for investors placing limit orders that their order never gets executed because the market price of their security may never reach the price they want, and even if it does, there may be other limit orders in place that take precedence over theirs because they were entered earlier.

Handling limit and stop orders

REMEMBER

Because stop and limit orders are price-specific, they may or may not be executed. Additionally, even if limit orders do reach or surpass the limit price, the order may not be executed if more orders were placed ahead of the investor's.

SELLING SHORT AGAINST THE BOX

Selling short or *shorting against the box* is when an investor sells short a security that they already own. This type of sale typically happens when an investor wants to sell a security at the current price but can't get possession of their securities right away because they're traveling or whatever. By selling short against the box, the investor is locking in the price of the security because no matter which way it goes, they will be offsetting a gain or loss on the securities owned with a loss or gain on the securities sold short.

TIP

One of the exhibits that you may see on the Series 7 exam is a ticker tape. You may have to determine the price at which a limit order is executed or a stop order is triggered. When you're dealing with stop limit orders, remember that the order is first a stop order; after the stop order is triggered, it becomes a limit order. Using the BLiSS and SLoBS acronyms can help you out tremendously when you're trying to keep the prices straight:

» **BLiSS (buy limit or sell stop):** The BL stands for *buy limit,* and the SS stands for *sell stop.* All BLiSS orders are entered *at or below* the market price of the security. Another thing to remember about BLiSS orders is that they get reduced on the *ex-dividend date* (the first day a stock trades without a dividend).

The *BL* in BLiSS helps you remember that the orders are placed BeLow the market price.

» **SLoBS (sell limit or buy stop):** The SL stands for *sell limit,* and the BS stands for *buy stop.* All SLoBS orders are entered *at or above* the market price of the security. Unlike BLiSS orders, SLoBS orders remain the same on the ex-dividend date.

A good way for you to remember that SLoBS orders remain unchanged on the ex-dividend date is to remember the phrase "once a slob, always a slob."

The following question tests your understanding of trigger and execution prices.

EXAMPLE

An investor enters an order to sell MNO at 34 stop. The ticker following entry of the order is as follows: 34.75, 34.60, 34.45, 34.20, 34.10, 33.95, 34.25, 34.30, 34, 33.80

At which prices was the order triggered and executed?

(A) Triggered at 33.95 and executed at 33.80

(B) Triggered at 34.10 and executed at 33.95

(C) Triggered at 33.95 and executed at 34.25

(D) Triggered at 34.25 and executed at 33.80

The correct answer is Choice (C). The investor wants to limit losses, so they enter an order to sell if the price dips too low. The order was triggered at 33.95 and executed at 34.25. This is a sell stop order, which is a BLiSS order. BLiSS orders are triggered at or below the order price. In this case, the first transaction that was at or below 34 was 33.95, which is the trigger price. Because this is a stop order, it became a market order for immediate execution and was completed on the next trade (34.25).

The following question tests your ability to answer a stop limit question.

EXAMPLE

Julia Jingleham purchased 1,000 shares of XYZ Corp. at $45 per share. To limit her losses, a couple of weeks later, Julia places an order to sell 1,000 shares of XYZ at 43 stop 42.90 limit. The ticker following entry of the order is as follows: 43.64, 43.27, 43.30, 43.09, 42.95, 42.87, 42.85, 42.90, 42.94, 43

The order was triggered at

(A) 42.95 and executed at 42.87

(B) 42.95 and executed at 42.90

(C) 42.87 and executed at 42.94

(D) 42.87 and executed at 42.85

The right answer is Choice (B). Julia Jingleham placed this sell stop limit order to sell the stock if it drops to 43 but not sell it at less than 42.90 per share. Take care of the stop portion first, so look for where the sell stop order is triggered. Sell stop orders are BLiSS orders that are triggered at or below the stop price. The first trade that's at or below 43 is 42.95. Now that the order is triggered, it becomes a sell limit order at 42.90. Sell limit orders are SLoBS orders that are executed at or above the market price. When you move ahead from the point where it was triggered, the first trade that's at or above 42.90 is 42.90.

Factoring in order features

Besides knowing the basic types of orders (market, stop, and limit — see "Talking about order types"), you should have a handle on some additional features that may be added to the order to make your customers happy. A lot of them exist, but for the most part, the name of the order feature pretty much explains what it is:

>> **Day:** If a day order hasn't been filled by the end of the trading day, it's canceled. All price-specific orders (stop and limit) are assumed to be day orders unless marked to the contrary.

>> **Good-till-canceled (GTC):** Good-till-canceled orders are also called *open orders* because the order is kept open until executed or canceled. For example, say that an investor wants to purchase ABC stock at $30. While the price of ABC is at $35, they enter an open buy limit order for ABC at $30. If the price of ABC ever hits $30 or below, the order will likely be executed; however, if the price of ABC never hits $30 or below, the order stays open until canceled. Regardless of when an open order is placed, a designated market maker clears it out of their book at the end of April or October, and the order has to be reentered.

>> *Note:* An investor may specify that they want the order canceled next week, next month, in two months, and so on. However, the designated market maker only enters the orders as GTC, so it is up to the broker-dealer who accepted the order to cancel the order with the designated market maker on the correct date if not already executed.

>> **Not held (NH):** This order gives the broker discretion about when to execute the trade. Typically, investors use not held orders when the broker believes they can get the customer a better price later in the day.

>> Not held orders deal only with price and timing. For registered reps to choose the security, number of shares, and/or whether to buy or sell, the customer needs to open a discretionary account, which requires a written power of attorney. See Chapter 16 for details.

>> **Fill or kill (FOK):** This order instructs a floor broker either to immediately execute an entire order at the limit price or better, or to cancel it.

>> **Immediate or cancel (IOC):** These limit orders are similar to FOK orders except that the order may be partially filled. Any portion of the order that's not completed is canceled.

>> **All or none (AON):** These limit orders have to be executed either in their entirety or not at all. AON orders don't have to be filled immediately (several attempts to fill the order completely are allowed) and may be day orders or good-till-canceled orders.

>> **At the open (market-on-open):** These orders are to be executed at the security's opening price. At the open orders can be market or limit orders, but if they aren't executed at the opening price, they're canceled. These orders allow for partial execution.

>> **At the close (market-on-close):** This order is to be executed at the closing price (or as near as possible). If this order isn't completed, it's canceled. NYSE market-on-close orders must be entered before 3:40 p.m. EST to be executed at the closing price.

- >> **Do not reduce (DNR):** This order says not to reduce the price of a stop or limit order in response to a dividend. For example, say that QRS stock is currently trading at $50 on the day prior to the ex-dividend date. If QRS previously announced a $0.50 dividend, the next day's opening price would be $49.50. If a customer had placed a DNR limit order to buy 1,000 shares of QRS at $45, the order wouldn't be reduced by the $0.50 dividend.

- >> **Alternative:** The alternative order is also known as a *one cancels the other order* (OCO) or an *either/or order.* This type of order instructs the broker to execute one of two orders and then cancel the other. For example, say Mr. Smith owns stock at $60 per share. He enters a sell stop order at $55 for protection and a sell limit order at $70 in the event that the stock price increases. If one of the orders is executed, the other order is canceled immediately.

- >> **Buy minus order:** When a person enters a buy minus order it means that they only want to buy the stock below the previous sale price.

- >> **Bid wanted:** This order is an indication or notice that an investor or broker-dealer wants to sell a security at a specific price. Bid wanted is used most often when no current buyers of a security are available.

- >> **Offer wanted:** This order is an indication or notice that an investor or broker-dealer wants to buy a security at a specific price. Offer wanted is used most often when no current sellers of a security are available.

TIP

Not all exchanges accept all of the different types of order qualifiers but many broker-dealers do. So, you do need to be familiar with all order qualifier types when taking the Series 7. Fortunately, the names pretty much describe what they are. All order qualifiers must be marked on the order ticket.

Designated Market Maker and the Super Display Book (SDBK)

A *designated market maker* (also known as a specialist or DMM) is a member of a stock exchange who's responsible for maintaining a fair and orderly market on a particular security. A DMM not only maintains an inventory of stock but also posts bid and ask prices and executes trades for other broker-dealers. A DMM acts as both a broker (executing trades for others) and a dealer (buying and selling securities for their own inventory) and tries to keep trading as active as possible.

A designated market maker executes orders by priority, parity, and precedence:

- >> **Priority:** The highest bid and lowest ask prices are executed first.

- >> **Parity:** If more than one order is at the highest bid and/or lowest ask price, the order(s) that came in first is/are executed first. So, even if the limit price was hit, not all limit orders at that price are necessarily executed because other orders may have been entered first.

- >> **Precedence:** If the priority and parity are equal, larger orders are executed first.

Because DMMs are market makers in a particular security, they may guarantee a price for a floor broker on a trade of securities for a particular period of time (stopping stock). This guarantee allows the floor broker to go to the trading floor to see whether they can get a better price for their customer. In the event that they can't, they can go back to the designated market maker and do the trade for the guaranteed price. Stopping stock can only be done for public orders.

REMEMBER

A designated market maker's main function is to maintain a fair and orderly market for a particular security. A DMM can't compete with a public order; they can only narrow the gap between the bid and ask prices if it gets too wide by placing a buy or sell order in between the highest bid and lowest ask prices. DMMs use books to keep track of these orders.

Super Display Books aren't written documents like they used to be; now they've gone electronic, but they're still called *specialists' books, order books, market makers' books, display books,* or just *books.* The book receives and displays orders to DMMs and allows them to execute and then publish orders to the consolidated (ticker) tape.

Take a good look at the book in Table 14-1 to see how it works.

TABLE 14-1 Super Display Book (ABC Stock)

BID	39	ASK (OFFER)
8 Golden Sec. GTC	.00	7 Livingston Broker-Dealer STOP
7 Pride Broker-Dealer GTC	.01	
4 VizzionKlempt 14 Orlando Securities	.02	
	.03	
	.04	
6 Martin Bros. STOP GTC	.05	12 High Profit Securities GTC
	.06	6 Brown and White

When you're looking at the book, the left-hand side (under "BID") indicates bid prices that investors (potential buyers) are willing to pay for a security. The right-hand side (under "ASK") indicates the prices investors (potential sellers) are willing to accept for selling the security.

On each side of the chart are names of broker-dealers looking to buy and sell the security. The numbers to the left of the names represent how many *hundreds* of shares the investors are looking to buy or sell. For example, the "8" next to Golden Securities on the bid side represents the fact that Golden Securities is looking to buy 800 shares of ABC stock at $39 good till canceled (GTC).

REMEMBER

An SDBK keeps track of stop and limit orders. Market orders aren't kept in a book because they're for immediate execution at the best price available. Any order with the word "STOP" next to it is obviously a stop order, and all the rest are limit orders. Stop orders are *not active* when placed in a book. Stop orders are triggered (activated) at the price placed in the book but then become market orders for immediate execution at the next available price, whatever that may be. All orders in the book are day orders unless marked GTC. See "Receiving Orders from Customers" for more info on order types.

A customer entering a market order would either buy at the best ask price or sell at the best bid price.

As you can imagine, the Series 7 can ask numerous questions about a Super Display Book. No matter what the question, you need to ignore the stop orders (pretend they aren't there) because you can't be sure what price the order will be executed at, if at all. The following points are examples of information that the Series 7 may ask for. For the data, please refer to Table 14-1:

>> **Inside market:** After ignoring the stop orders, the *inside market* is the highest bid price and the lowest ask price.

In this case, the highest bid is 39.02 (VizzionKlempt and Orlando Securities) and the lowest ask is 39.05 (High Profit Securities).

>> **Size of the market:** The size of the market is the number of shares (or round lots) that are available at the best prices (highest bid and lowest ask) after you ignore the stop orders. You represent it as

shares at the highest bid price × shares at the lowest ask price

Ignoring the Martin Bros. stop, VizzionKlempt and Orlando Securities offer the highest bid at 39.02. VizzionKlempt wants 400 shares and Orlando wants 1,400, for a total of 1,800 shares. Ignoring the Livingston Broker-Dealer stop, High Profit Securities offers the lowest ask price at 39.05; High Profit wants to sell 1,200 shares. The size of the market is, therefore, 1,800 × 1,200, or 18 × 12 if given in round lots (units of 100 shares).

>> **Spread:** The *spread* is the difference between the highest bid and lowest ask (ignoring the stop orders).

In this case, the spread is $39.05 – 39.02, or $.03.

REMEMBER

The narrower the spread, the more actively traded the security. Because investors are buying at the lowest ask price and selling at the highest bid, there's a built-in loss, which is the difference between those two numbers (the spread). If you have a $2 spread between the highest bid and lowest ask, the price of the stock would have to increase by $2 in order for investors to break even (excluding commissions). As you can imagine, a security like that wouldn't garner much demand.

>> **Where a designated market maker can enter a bid for their own inventory:** Remember that a DMM can't compete with a public order. A DMM's duty is to keep trading as active as possible, so a specialist can enter a bid (or ask) in between the highest bid and lowest ask.

Using this exhibit, acceptable bids from a specialist would be 39.03 or 39.04.

REMEMBER

An SDBK is a computerized system that works during times the market is open and even when the market's closed. Members can send orders through to the system at any time. Orders that are placed off hours are either executed at the opening (if there's a matching order) or left in the book for the DMM to take care of. Any stock listed on the NYSE is eligible to be entered into the SDBK.

Adjusting orders for dividends and splits

As you can imagine, certain orders on the DMMs book would have to be adjusted due to dividends or splits. Rules for cash dividends, stock dividends, forward splits, and reverse splits are a little different.

Cash dividends

When stocks go ex-dividend, buy limit, sell stop, and sell stop limit orders in the book are reduced to reflect the cash dividend. Remember that buy limit and sell stop (BLiSS) orders are entered below the market value. So if ABC stock was paying a $.30 cash dividend, on the ex-date (the first day a stock trades without the dividend) a buy limit order for ABC common stock at 40 would be reduced to 39.70 ($40 – $.30). In addition, the market price of ABC would be decreased by the amount of the dividend. Investors who do not want their orders to be reduced by the dividend would have their order marked DNR (Do Not Reduce).

Stock dividends

Unlike cash dividends, all orders in the book are adjusted for stock dividends on the ex-dividend date. So, if there's an open order to buy 1,000 shares of ABC at 22 and there's a 10 percent stock dividend, the order will be adjusted to buy 1,100 shares of ABC at 20. If the stock dividend results in the amount of shares being something other than round lots, the odd-lot portion cannot be held in the book because the book only shows round lots. For example, if there's an open order to sell 100 shares of DEF at 60 and there's a 20 percent stock dividend, the new order in the book would be sell 100 shares of DEF at 50. Normally, you would think that the order should be sell 120 shares of DEF at 50 (20 percent more shares and the price is decreased to 50 to reflect the stock dividend), but the book only handles round lots (100-share units), so the broker dealer will have to handle the additional 20-share order.

REMEMBER

A *round lot* for stocks is typically 100 shares. Any stock trades for less than 100 shares is considered an *odd lot*. *Mixed lot* are for trades over 100 shares but with an odd lot portion included (for example, 130 shares).

Stock splits

All open orders are adjusted for stock splits. For example, if there's an open order to buy 400 shares of GHI at 60 stop and there's a 2-for-1 split, the order is changed in the book to buy 800 shares of GHI at 30 stop. Remember, for splits, take the shares and multiply them by the first number and divide by the second number. Next, to get the price, multiply it by the second number and divide it by the first number. (For more on splits, see Chapter 6.)

All open orders are canceled for reverse splits (for example, 1-for-2, 2-for-3, 3-for-5, and so on).

REMEMBER

Only orders that are placed below the market price are reduced for a cash dividend, but all orders are adjusted for stock dividends and stock splits.

Trade reporting systems

In order to help facilitate trading and the dissemination of quotes and trading activity, there are now several systems available. The following are the ones you'll have to recognize when taking the Series 7 exam:

>> **Alternative Trading System (ATS):** An ATS is a trading system that meets the definition of "exchange" but is not required to register as such. An ATS must register with the SEC and FINRA as a broker-dealer. Although an ATS is not required to register as an exchange, it's subject to FINRA rules. Examples of ATSs include ECNs and Dark Pools.

>> **Order Audit Trail System (OATS):** OATS was established by FINRA as a way of tracking trades of all NMS stocks and OTC equity securities. OATS is an automated computer system which records orders, quotes, and other trade information. OATS tracks the orders from the initial time of entry and all the way through execution or cancellation. Through OATS, FINRA is more easily able to monitor member firms.

>> **Trade Reporting and Compliance Engine (TRACE):** Like OATS, TRACE was also created by FINRA, but TRACE facilitates the over-the-counter secondary market reporting of certain fixed-income securities (mostly corporate debt securities, although certain asset-backed securities, treasuries, and CMOs are also eligible). All broker-dealers who are members of FINRA are required to report transactions in corporate bonds under SEC rules. TRACE helps make the market more transparent as trade information is released immediately to the public.

TRACE is not an execution system; it is a reporting system only. Both the buying firm and selling firm must report trades. All trades must be reported within 15 minutes. TRACE includes the trade date, the time of trade, the price, yield, quantity, and so on.

>> **Electronic Municipal Market Access (EMMA):** EMMA provides information about municipal securities. (Please see Chapter 8 for more information.)

>> **Real-Time Transaction Reporting System (RTRS):** RTRS is a web interface that allows municipal dealers to report customer and inter-dealer transactions directly to the MSRB. (Chapter 8 has more information.)

>> **Trade Reporting Facility (TRF):** TRF provides members of FINRA with a way to report transactions of certain securities when the transaction is not effected on an exchange. There are three TRFs: FINRA/NASDAQ TRF Carteret, FINRA/NASDAQ TRF Chicago, and FINRA/NYSE TRF. TRFs allow members to report trade data such as price and volume electronically after the trade has taken place. So, even though the securities could've been traded on an exchange floor, TRF is a reporting system for members when trades are negotiated between broker-dealers.

>> **OTC Reporting Facility (ORF):** The ORF works similarly to the TRF, but the ORF only reports trades of OTC securities that don't trade on NASDAQ or other exchange markets.

>> **Electronic Communications Networks (ECNs):** ECNs are quotation systems operated by banks and brokerage firms. ECNs are an Alternative Trading System (ATS). ECNs were created to allow trades to be executed with lower transaction costs and to add more liquidity. In addition, buyers and sellers remain anonymous. When institutions trade with other institutions, trades are normally executed through ECNs. ECNs are available for trading 24 hours per day and are not financially involved in transactions. ECNs are strictly electronic exchanges.

Regulation NMS (National Market System)

Regulation NMS is an SEC regulation designed to bring trading and reporting consistency to U.S. securities markets. It is designed to help improve U.S. exchanges by setting standards for displaying of quotes and access to market data. It is designed to link trading on different exchanges to make sure customers are getting the best prices.

You should be aware of the *sub-penny rule:* All equity securities quotes must be in increments of a penny. However, if the security trades for less than a dollar, the quotes may be displayed up to 1/100th of a penny.

DARK POOLS OF LIQUIDITY

Dark pools of liquidity are trades that are hidden from the public. These are large orders transacted by brokerage firms or institutions away from exchanges on crossing networks or alternative trading systems (ATS). The sizes of the trades and the identity of the trading parties within the pool are not revealed publicly. These typically large-block orders are executed in the dark pools so as not to affect public quotes or prices. Because these trades are hidden, market participants are left in the dark, and market transparency is lessened.

Trading halts: NYSE Rule 7.12 - market-wide circuit breakers (MWCB)

To keep investors from panicking when things are going the wrong way, the NYSE has put in place a way to halt trading temporarily if the market drops severely too quickly. This covers equities and options on several markets (coordinated cross-market trading halts).There are different levels put in place to halt trading if the S&P 500 Index drops too much from the previous day's closing price. During that time, the Exchange shall halt trading in all stocks and will not reopen the trading for the time periods specified below:

>> **Level 1:** A halt will occur if the S&P 500 Index declines 7 percent or more from the previous day's close.

>> **Level 2:** A halt will occur if the S&P 500 Index declines 13 percent or more from the previous day's close.

>> **Level 3:** A halt will occur if the S&P 500 Index declines 20 percent or more from the previous day's close.

If a Level 1 or Level 2 decline occurs after 9:30 a.m. EST and up to 3:25 p.m. EST (12:25 p.m. on days the Exchange closes early), the Exchange will halt trading in all stocks for a period of 15 minutes. For a Level 1 or Level 2 market decline, the Exchange will only halt trading once per trading day. If the market decline happens after 3:25 p.m. EST (12:25 p.m. on days the Exchange closes early), the Exchange will not halt trading.

If a Level 3 decline occurs any time during the trading day, the Exchange will halt trading in all stocks and options until the next trading day.

Testing Your Knowledge

Here is a quick 10-question quiz to test your knowledge of securities markets. Read the questions carefully so that you don't make any mistakes.

1. The over-the-counter market is best described as a(n)

   (A) auction market

   (B) negotiated market

   (C) centralized market

   (D) first market

2. Which of the following is a third market trade?

   (A) An exchange listed security trading over the counter

   (B) An unlisted security trading over the counter

   (C) An exchange listed security trading on an exchange

   (D) Institutional trading without using the services of a broker-dealer

3. A client enters a buy stop order for LMN at $20. After the order is entered, trades occur as follows:

19.25, 19.75, 20.13, 19.88, 20

The order was

(A) Triggered at 19.25, executed at 19.75
(B) Triggered at 20.13, executed at 19.88
(C) Triggered at 20.13, executed at 20
(D) Triggered at 19.88, executed at 20

4. Investors may sell a security short for

I. speculation
II. hedging purposes
III. arbitrage situations

(A) I and II
(B) I and III
(C) II and III
(D) I, II, and III

5. Which of the following types of orders becomes a market order as soon as a security passes a specified price?

(A) Stop
(B) Limit
(C) Market
(D) Stop limit

6. The inside market is the

(A) lowest bid price and lowest ask price
(B) lowest bid price and highest ask price
(C) highest bid price and lowest ask price
(D) highest bid price and highest ask price

7. A Designated Market Maker receives an order to buy 1,000 shares of ABC stock. Place in order from highest to lowest, what the DMM looks at to fill the order.

I. Parity
II. Precedence
III. Priority

(A) I, II, III
(B) I, III, II
(C) III, II, I
(D) III, I, II

8. Which of the following access levels of NASDAQ includes subject quotes?

   (A) Level I
   (B) Level II
   (C) Level III
   (D) Level IV

9. All of the following are reasons an investor might sell a security short EXCEPT:

   (A) for hedging purposes
   (B) to take advantage of an arbitrage situation
   (C) to have the potential for a maximum gain on the security that is unlimited
   (D) for speculation

10. If the inside market for an AAD common stock is 50.20–50.35, where can a Designated Market Maker enter an order to sell from their own inventory?

    (A) 50.20
    (B) 50.30
    (C) 50.35
    (D) 50.36 or higher

Answers and Explanations

I hope you didn't find this quiz too painful. Because there are 10 questions, each one is worth 10 points.

1. **B.** Unlike the New York Stock Exchange, which is an auction market where people yell out their bid and ask prices, the over-the-counter market is a negotiated market. Trades for the over-the-counter market take place either through phone calls or through a computerized trading system.

2. **A.** A third market trade takes place when an exchange-listed security trades over the counter.

3. **B.** This order is a buy stop order. Buy stops are SLoBS (Sell Limit and Buy Stop) orders that are triggered at or above the buy stop price, which in this case is $20. Looking at the trades, the first one at or above 20 is 20.13. Once triggered, a stop order becomes a market order for immediate execution at the next price available. So, it was triggered at 20.13 and executed at 19.88.

4. **D.** Selling short is a risky practice that allows short sellers to borrow securities to sell them in the market and then repurchase them at a later time. Short sellers are bearish, meaning that they want the price of the security to decline. Because of the risk, all short sales must be executed in a margin account. People sell short for speculation because they feel the market price of the security is going to drop. They may also do it to hedge or protect an investment they have. They may also do it for an arbitrage situation. If they're doing it for an arbitrage situation, a particular security might be trading at two different prices on different markets. In this case, they usually purchase the security on the market with the lower price and short the security on the market with the higher price.

5. **A.** Stop orders become market orders for immediate execution once the underlying security touches or passes the price on the stop order. A stop-limit order becomes a limit order once the underlying security touches or passes the stop price.

6. **C.** The inside market of a security is the highest bid price (the most an entity is willing to pay for a security) and the lowest ask (offer) price, which is the least an entity will accept for selling the security. So when investors purchase a security, they would be buying at the lowest ask price or selling at the highest bid price.

7. **D.** The first thing that's looked at is the priority, highest bid price or lowest ask price. If there is more than one seller (in the case of a buy order), at the best ask price, the seller who placed the order first (parity) will have their shares used to fill the order first. In the event that the orders came in at the same time, the seller with the largest order (precedence) will get hit first.

8. **A.** Level I machines only display the inside market (highest bid and lowest ask price) of securities. This is the type of computer access that you will most likely have when starting your career. Level II machines are the ones used by traders, and Level III machines are the ones where market makers enter their firm quotes.

9. **C.** Investors may sell a security short (borrow securities for immediate resale) for hedging purposes, speculation, or arbitrage situations. When an investor is hedging, they can sell short securities they already own to protect from a loss in the event the market declines. When selling short for speculation, the investor believes the price of the underlying security will decline so they can later repurchase the stock at a lower price. Selling short for arbitrage purposes means the security is selling at different prices on different markets. In this case, the investor would sell short the security on the market where the price is high and purchase the security on the market where the price is low. There is no unlimited maximum gain potential when selling a security short because the price of the security can only go to zero, but there is a maximum loss potential that is unlimited.

10. **B.** Remember, it is the Designated Market Maker's (DMM) job to keep trading as active as possible. If the bid and ask prices are too far apart and trading slows down, a DMM may enter an order to buy or sell securities out of their inventory in between the bid and ask prices to narrow the spread. At no point can a DMM enter a quote at the same price as a customer's order because a DMM is not allowed to compete with public orders.

Chapter **15**

Taxes and Retirement Plans: Making Sure the IRS Gets its Share

Yes, it's true what they say: The only sure things in life are death and taxes. Although taxes are an annoying necessity, investors do get tax breaks if they invest in securities for a long period of time, and you need a good understanding of the tax discounts investors receive. Additionally, the Series 7 exam tests your ability to recognize the different types of retirement plans, the specifics about each one, and the tax advantages.

In this chapter, I cover tax categories and rules, from distinguishing between types of taxes to calculating capital gains for securities received as gifts. As with the other chapters, there is some overlap between what you learned for the SIE exam and what's covered on the Series 7. And although enjoying retirement isn't quite as certain as pushing up daisies, I explain Uncle Sam's claim on the cash investors put into IRAs, 401(k)s, profit sharing, and other retirement plans. As always, you can also count on some example questions mixed in throughout the chapter and a quick quiz at the end.

TIP

As of the time of this writing, all of the tax information is correct. However, each administration likes to play with things like dividend and capital gains tax rates, income tax rates, estate tax, and so on. I would suggest that you double-check at www.irs.gov to make sure nothing has changed.

Everything in Its Place: Checking Out Tax and Income Categories

The many lines you see on tax forms clue you in to the fact that the IRS likes to break things down into categories. The following sections explain progressive and regressive taxes, as well as types of personal income.

Touring the tax categories

The supreme tax collector (the IRS) has broken down taxes into a couple categories according to the percentage individuals pay. Your mission is to understand the different tax categories and how they affect investors:

>> **Progressive taxes:** These taxes affect high-income individuals more than they affect low-income individuals; the more taxable money individuals have, the higher their income tax bracket. Progressive taxes include taxes on personal income (see the next section), gift taxes, and estate taxes (see the section "Presenting Gift and Estate Tax Rules"). The Series 7 contains more questions on progressive taxes than on regressive taxes.

>> **Regressive taxes:** These taxes affect individuals earning a lower income more than they affect people earning a higher income; everyone pays the same rate, so individuals who earn a lower income are affected more because that rate represents a higher percentage of their income. Examples of regressive taxes are payroll, sales, property, excise, gasoline, and so on.

Looking at types of income

The three main categories of income are earned, passive, and portfolio. (If you're especially interested in the details of how investments are taxed, you can find more information at www.irs.gov.) You need to distinguish among the different categories because the IRS treats them differently:

>> **Earned (active) income:** People generate this type of income from activities that they're actively involved in. Earned income includes money received from salary, bonuses, tips, commissions, and so on. Earned income is taxed at the individual's tax bracket and based on their filing status.

>> **Passive income:** This type of income comes from enterprises in which an individual isn't actively involved. Passive income includes income from limited partnerships (see Chapter 11) and rental property. When you see the words *passive income* on the Series 7 exam, immediately start thinking that the income comes from a limited partnership (DPP). Individuals can write off passive losses against any passive income to determine the net taxable income.

>> **Portfolio income:** This type of income includes interest, dividends, and capital gains derived from the sale of securities. The following section tells you more about taxes on portfolio income. Portfolio income may be taxed at the investor's tax bracket or at a lower rate, depending on the holding period.

Note: Gifts and inheritances are not considered income. For more on these sources of money, see "Presenting Gift and Estate Tax Rules" later in this chapter.

Noting Taxes on Investments

You need to understand how dividends, interest, capital gains, and capital losses affect investors. To make your life more interesting, the IRS has given tax advantages to people who hold onto investments for a long period of time, so familiarize yourself with the types of taxes that apply to investments and how investors are taxed.

Interest income

Interest income that bondholders receive may or may not be taxable, depending on the type of security or securities held:

>> **Corporate bond interest:** Interest received from corporate bonds is taxable on all levels (federal, state, and, local, where local taxes exist).

>> **Municipal bond interest:** Interest received from municipal bonds(except taxable municipals) is federally tax-free (tax-exempt interest); however, investors may be taxed on the state and local levels, depending on the issuer of the bonds (see Chapter 8).

>> **U.S. government securities interest:** Interest received from U.S. government securities, such as T-bills, T-notes, T-STRIPS, TIPS and T-bonds, is taxable on the federal level but is exempt from state and local taxes.

REMEMBER

Even though T-bills, T-STRIPS, and any other zero-coupon bonds don't generate interest payments (because the securities are issued at a discount and mature at par), the difference between the purchase price and the amount received at maturity is considered interest and is subject to taxation.

Alternative minimum tax

Congress created the alternative minimum tax (AMT) so that certain taxpayers with high income must pay a minimum tax on certain tax-preference items that taxpayers with lower income may not have to pay or may pay a lower amount. Items subject to AMT include interest on certain municipal bonds such as IDRs, certain depreciation expenses, and certain items related to owning an interest in a limited partnership.

Individuals subject to AMT must calculate (or have someone calculate for them) their taxes using the standard method and then again using AMT calculations. After the calculations are done, the individual is responsible for paying the higher of the two.

Dividends

Dividends may be in the form of cash, stock, or product. The following sections discuss dividends in cash, in stock, and from mutual funds.

Cash dividends

Qualified cash dividends received from stocks are taxed at a maximum rate of 0 percent, 15 percent, or 20 percent depending on the investor's adjusted gross income (AGI). Most investors will fall into the 15-percent range. Qualified dividends are ones in which the customer has held onto the stock for at least 61 days (91 days for preferred stock). The 61-day holding period starts 60 days prior to the *ex-dividend date* (the first day the stock trades without dividends). If the investor has held the stock for less than the 61-day holding period, the dividends are considered *nonqualified* and investors are taxed at the rate determined by their regular tax bracket.

Note: There is currently an additional net investment tax of 3.8 percent for individual investors with a modified adjusted gross income above $200,000 ($250,000 for married couples).

Stock dividends

As with cash dividends, qualified stock dividends are subject to federal taxes depending on the holder's tax bracket (current federal rates are 0 percent, 15 percent, or 20 percent). Qualified dividends are taxed at the same rate as long-term capital gains. Nonqualified (ordinary) dividends are taxed at the investor's tax bracket. (See the definition of qualified and nonqualified dividends in the preceding section, "Cash dividends.")

Dividends from mutual funds

Dividends and interest generated from securities that are held in a mutual fund portfolio are passed through to investors and are taxed as either *qualified* (see the earlier section "Cash dividends") or *nonqualified*. The type(s) of securities in the portfolio and the length of time the fund held the securities dictate how the investor is taxed. Here's how mutual fund dividends are taxed:

>> **Federally tax-free:** Municipal bond funds

>> **0, 15, or 20 percent:** Stock funds, long-term capital gains

>> **Ordinary income:** Corporate bond funds, short-term capital gains

REMEMBER

One of the great things about owning mutual funds is that they're nice enough to let you know what taxes you're going to be subject to. At the beginning of each year you will receive a statement from the mutual fund that lets you know how much you received the previous year in dividends, in short-term capital gains, and in long-term capital gains. The mutual fund also sends a copy of the statement to the IRS.

The mutual fund determines the long-term or short-term gains by its holding period, not the investors'. Also, remember that you'd be subject to capital gains tax and taxes on dividends even if the money were reinvested back into the fund.

At the sale: Capital gains and losses

Capital gains are profits made when selling a security, and *capital losses* are losses incurred when selling a security. To determine whether an investor has a capital gain or capital loss, you have to start with the investor's cost basis. The *cost basis* is used for tax purposes and includes the purchase price plus any commission (although on the Series 7 exam, the test designers usually don't throw commission into the equation). The cost basis remains the same unless it's adjusted for accretion or amortization (see "Cost basis adjustments on bonds: Accretion and amortization," later in the chapter).

REMEMBER

Accretion and amortization come into play when an investor purchases a bond at a price other than par. The bond cost basis will be adjusted toward par over the amount of time until maturity.

Incurring taxes with capital gains

An investor realizes capital gains when he sells a security at a price higher than his cost basis. Capital gains on any security (even municipal and U.S. government bonds) are fully taxed on the federal, state, and local level.

REMEMBER

A capital gain isn't realized until a security is *sold*. If the value of an investment increases, it's considered appreciation or an unrealized gain and if investor doesn't sell, the investor doesn't incur capital gains taxes. Mutual fund shareholders would be subject to taxation if the issuer sold securities held by the fund at a profit, even if the shareholder didn't sell any shares.

Capital gains are broken down into two categories, depending on the holding period of the securities:

>> **Short-term capital gains:** These gains are realized when a security is held for *one year or less.* Short-term capital gains are taxed according to the *investor's tax bracket.*

>> **Long-term capital gains:** These gains are realized when a security is held for *more than one year.* To encourage investors to buy and hold securities, long-term capital gains are currently taxed at a rate in line with cash dividends (0, 15, or 20 percent depending on the investor's adjusted gross income). (For more information on capital gains and losses, visit the Internal Revenue Service's website at www.irs.gov/taxtopics/tc409.)

Realized versus unrealized

Remember, a customer who owns a security will not *realize* a profit or loss until the security is sold. If the customer sold the security for less than the cost basis, they would have a loss; if they sold it for more than the cost basis, they would have a gain or profit. If, however, the customer purchased a security that is up in value over the cost basis but is still holding the security, it is considered an *unrealized gain* or appreciation. So the customer cannot have a gain or loss until the security is sold.

Cost valuation

If an investor purchased the same security being sold several times (monthly, yearly, or whatever), they can actually choose which securities are to be sold based on their tax situation. So let's say that Mrs. Smith purchased 100 shares of DIM common stock once every 6 months over the last 4 years. Now, Mrs. Smith sees an excellent opportunity to purchase a new penny stock but needs to sell 100 shares of her DIM common stock so that she has enough money for the purchase. If the price of DIM has been increasing over the last 4 years, she may decide to sell the first ones purchased, the ones purchased 3 years ago, the ones purchased 2 years ago, the ones purchased 6 months ago, and so on. If not specified, many firms will automatically sell the first securities purchased.

>> **FIFO (First In, First Out):** In this scenario, when an investor purchased the same security being sold several times, the first ones purchased would be the first ones sold.

>> **LIFO (Last In, First Out):** If an investor purchases the same security being sold several times, the last ones purchased would be the first ones sold.

>> **Identified Shares:** In this case, if an investor purchased the same security being sold several times, they may choose to sell the securities purchased on a certain date or several dates.

REMEMBER

You should be able to help your customers determine which of the following cost valuation scenarios would work best for them. Depending on the holding period of the securities, it could result in a long-term or short-term capital gain or loss. Also, the amount of capital gain or loss your customer would incur would be determined by which securities are being sold.

Determining the cost basis per share

The cost basis per share is what an investor paid to purchase the security plus commissions, markups, and any fees. So, certainly if the investor purchased 100 shares, you would have to divide the overall cost of the transaction by 100 to determine the cost basis per share. What can really throw a wrench into the works is when an investor exchanges convertible securities into common shares, or receives stock by way of dividend or split.

To determine the cost basis per share on a straight transaction of stock, just divide the cost basis by the number of shares purchased:

$$\text{Cost basis per share} = \frac{\text{original purchase price including fees and commission}}{\text{number of shares purchased}}$$

To calculate the cost basis per share on a security that has been converted, take a look at the following example:

EXAMPLE

Mr. Smith purchases an ABC convertible bond at an overall cost of $980 including commission and fees. Mr. Smith decides to convert his bond into ABC common stock. If the conversion price is $20, what is Mr. Smith's cost basis per share?

Assuming that the par value of the bond is $1,000, you have to get the conversion ratio:

$$\text{Conversion ratio} = \frac{\text{par}}{\text{conversion price}} = \frac{\$1,000}{\$20} = 50 \text{ shares}$$

Next, divide the overall cost by the conversion ratio to get the cost basis per share:

$$\text{Cost basis per share} = \frac{\$980}{50 \text{ shares}} = \$19.60$$

TIP

The process works the same whether dealing with convertible bonds or convertible preferred stock. Also, be careful because sometimes the conversion ratio may already be given in the question, so you'll be able to skip a step.

Next, you'll have to determine the cost basis per share on stock splits. Look at the following example. (Stock splits are covered in the Securities Industry Essentials exam.)

EXAMPLE

Mrs. Smith purchases 200 shares of ABC common stock with an overall cost of $12,400 including commission and fees. ABC declares a 2-for-1 split to shareholders of record on August 4. What is Mrs. Smith's cost basis per share after the split?

I think that the best way to handle this one is to determine the original cost basis per share prior to doing the split first:

$$\text{Cost basis per share} = \frac{\$12,400}{200 \text{ shares}} = \$62.00$$

The overall cost basis for the initial transaction is not going to change but, since the company is calling for a 2-for-1 stock split, this investor is now going to have 2 shares for every 1 that she had previously. So if the amount of shares gets doubled, the cost basis per share has to get cut in half:

$$\text{Cost basis per share after the split} = \frac{\$62}{2} = \$31.00$$

TIP

The way you determine the cost basis per share due to stock dividends is very close to the way you determine the cost basis per share on stock splits. If you'd like to see an example, you can visit Chapter 6.

REMEMBER

Securities to be delivered on a *when issued* (WI) basis have not established a dollar amount yet. So for tax purposes, it is impossible to figure out the cost basis for WI securities.

Net yield after capital gains tax

Remember, capital gains on any security (including municipal securities) is taxed. To determine the net yield after capital gains tax, you first have to determine the capital gains yield. Look at the following equation where the investor bought the security for $50 and sold it at $55:

$$\text{Capital gains yield} = \frac{\text{selling price} - \text{purchase price}}{\text{purchase price}} = \frac{\$55 - \$50}{\$50} = \frac{\$5}{\$50} = 10\%$$

Next, let's assume that the investor had held the security for over one year, so it's a long-term capital gain. If the long-term capital gain was taxed at 20 percent, what would be his net yield after capital gains tax?

Net yield after capital gains tax $= \text{capital gains yield} \times (100 - \text{capital gains tax rate})$
Net yield after capital gains tax $= 10 \times (100 - 20\%) = 10\% \times 80 = 8\%$

For this investor, even though he had a capital gains yield of 10 percent, after paying capital gains tax, his net yield was only 8 percent.

TIP

1.0 on your calculator is equal to 100%, 0.80 is equal to 80%, 0.10 is equal to 10%, and so on.

Offsetting gains with capital losses

An investor realizes a capital loss when selling a security at a value lower than the cost basis. Investors can use capital losses to offset capital gains and reduce the tax burden. As with capital gains, capital losses are also broken down into short-term and long-term:

>> **Short-term capital losses:** An investor incurs these losses when they have held the security for *one year or less*. Investors can use short-term capital losses to offset short-term capital gains.

>> **Long-term capital losses:** An investor incurs these losses when they have held the security for *more than one year*. Long-term capital losses can offset long-term capital gains.

When an investor has a net capital loss, they can write off $3,000 ($1,500 if married and filing separately) per year federally against their earned income and carry the balance forward the next year.

The following question involves capital-loss write-offs.

EXAMPLE

In a particular year, Mrs. Jones realizes $30,000 in long-term capital gains and $50,000 in long-term capital losses. How much of the capital losses would be carried forward to the following year?

(A) $3,000

(B) $17,000

(C) $20,000

(D) $30,000

The correct answer is Choice (B). Mrs. Jones has a net capital loss of $20,000 (a $50,000 loss minus the $30,000 gain). Mrs. Jones writes off $3,000 of that capital loss against her earned income and carries the additional loss of $17,000 forward to write off against any capital gains she may have the following year. In the event that Mrs. Jones doesn't have any capital gains the following year, she can still write off $3,000 of the $17,000 against any earned income and carry the remaining $14,000 forward which can be used to offset any capital gains the following year.

The wash sale rule: Adjusting the cost basis when you can't claim a loss

To keep investors from claiming a loss on securities (which an investor could use to offset gains on another investment — see the preceding section) while repurchasing substantially (or exactly) the same security, the IRS has come up with the *wash sale rule;* according to this rule, if an investor sells a security at a capital loss, the investor can't repurchase the same security or anything convertible into the same security for 30 days prior to or after the sale and be able to claim the loss. An investor doesn't end up in handcuffs for violating the wash sale rule; they simply can't claim the loss on their taxes.

However, the loss doesn't go away if investors buy the security within that window of time — investors get to adjust the cost basis of the security. For instance, if an investor were to sell 100 shares of ABC at a $2-per-share loss and purchase 100 shares of ABC within 30 days for $50 per share, the investor's new cost basis (excluding commissions) would be $52 per share (the $50 purchase price plus the $2 loss on the shares sold), thus lowering the amount of capital gains they could face on the new purchase.

The following question tests your understanding of the wash sale rule.

EXAMPLE

If Melissa sells DEF common stock at a loss on June 2, for 30 days she can't buy

   I. DEF common stock

   II. DEF warrants

   III. DEF call options

   IV. DEF preferred stock

(A) I only

(B) I and IV only

(C) I, II, and III only

(D) I, II, III, and IV

The answer you want is Choice (C). You need to remember that Melissa sold DEF at a loss; therefore, she can't buy back the same security (as in Statement I) or anything convertible into the same security (as in Statements II and III) within 30 days to avoid the wash sale rule. Warrants give an investor the right to buy stock at a fixed price (see Chapter 6), and call options give investors the right to buy securities at a fixed price (Chapter 12). However, Statement IV is okay because DEF preferred stock is a different security and is not convertible into DEF common stock (unless it's convertible preferred, which it isn't; if it were convertible, the question would have told you so). For Melissa to avoid the wash sale rule, she can't buy DEF common stock, DEF convertible preferred stock, DEF convertible bonds, DEF call options, DEF warrants, or DEF rights for 30 days. However, she can buy DEF preferred stock, DEF bonds, or DEF put options (the right to sell DEF).

Return of capital

A return of capital is not considered a dividend. This is a situation where an investor receives a portion of his money back, so he have as much at risk. A return of capital is not a taxable event because the investor is just receiving some of his invested money back that was taxed already. A return of capital will lower the investor's cost basis. A good example of return of capital is when an investor invests in mortgage-backed securities where monthly mortgage payments are passed through to the investor. A portion of the money passed through will be taxable interest and the other portion will be nontaxable return of capital.

Cost basis adjustments on bonds: Accretion and amortization

You use accretion and amortization when figuring out taxes on bonds; you simply adjust the cost of the bond toward par in the time that the bond matures. For more info on amortization and accretion, check out Chapter 7 and read on.

Accretion

When investors purchase bonds at a discount, the discount must be accreted over the life of the bond. *Accretion,* which involves adjusting the cost basis (price paid) of the bond toward par each year that the bond is held, increases both the cost basis of the bond and the reported interest income.

To determine the annual accretion, find the difference between the cost of the bond and par value; divide the result by the original number of years to maturity.

The following question tests your understanding of accretion.

EXAMPLE

Declan purchases a 5 percent corporate bond with 10 years to maturity at 80. What would Declan's annual reported income on this bond be?

(A) $20

(B) $30

(C) $50

(D) $70

The right answer is Choice (D). Declan purchased the bond at 80 ($800), and you can assume that it matures at $1,000 (par) in 10 years (you can always assume $1,000 par unless otherwise stated — see Chapter 7). You need to take the $200 difference and divide it by 10 years to get $20. Declan's reported income would be $70 ($50 interest plus $20 accretion).

TIP

Be prepared to answer questions about the annual accretion and yearly reported income and to calculate the capital gain or loss the investor would incur if selling the bond before maturity.

The following question tests your ability to figure out the capital gain or loss on a bond purchased at a discount.

EXAMPLE

Ms. Jones purchased a 7 percent DEF corporate bond at 80 with 10 years to maturity. Six years later, Ms. Jones sold the bond at 85. What is the gain or loss?

(A) $50 gain

(B) $70 loss

(C) $150 loss

(D) None of the above

The answer you're looking for is Choice (B). First, adjust the cost basis of the bond in the time the bond matures:

$$\begin{array}{c} 10 \text{ years} \\ \$800 \rightarrow \$1,000 \end{array}$$

The bond was purchased at $800 (80 percent of $1,000 par) and matures at $1,000 par in ten years. Next, take that $200 difference and divide it by the ten years to maturity:

$$\text{annual accretion} = \frac{\$200}{10 \text{ years}} = \$20$$

Then take the $20 per year accretion and multiply it by the number of years that the investor held the bond: $20 per year × 6 years = $120 total accretion

Next, add the total accretion to the purchase price of the bond to determine the investor's adjusted cost basis:

$800 original cost + $120 total accretion = $920 (adjusted cost basis)

After that, compare the adjusted cost basis to the selling price to determine the gain or loss:

$920 adjusted cost basis – $850 selling price = $70 capital loss

Ms. Jones incurred a $70 capital loss on her sale of the DEF bond, which she can use to offset capital gains on other investments (see the earlier section "Offsetting gains with capital losses").

REMEMBER

All discount bonds, *except municipal bonds purchased in the secondary market* (outstanding bonds), are accreted. If a municipal bond is purchased as an *original issue discount (OID)*, the accretion is treated as part of the tax-free interest. If an investor purchases a municipal bond in the secondary market at a discount, the bond is not accreted, but the difference between the purchase price and the selling price (or redemption price) is treated as a capital gain.

Amortization

When bonds are purchased at a premium, the premium can be amortized over the life of the bond. You amortize the bond by adjusting the cost basis of the bond toward par each year that the bond is held; amortization decreases the cost basis of the bond and decreases the reported interest income.

To find the yearly amortization, divide the difference between the purchase price and par value by the original number of years to maturity.

The following question involves annual amortization:

EXAMPLE

Mrs. Sheppard purchases a 7 percent corporate bond with 20 years to maturity at 110. If Mrs. Sheppard decides to amortize the bond, what is the annual reported income?

(A) $5

(B) $65

(C) $70

(D) $75

The correct answer is Choice (B). Because Mrs. Sheppard purchased the bond at 110 ($1,100) and you can assume that it matures at $1,000 (par) in 20 years, you need to take the $100 difference and divide it by 20 years to get $5. Mrs. Sheppard's reported income would be $65 ($70 interest minus $5 amortization).

REMEMBER

Corporate bondholders can elect to amortize their premium bonds or not; however, all *municipal bondholders must amortize their premium bonds,* whether they were purchased as a new issue or in the secondary market (outstanding).

You can use the same basic formula that you use for accretion to determine the gain or loss on an amortization problem (see the preceding section). Only the first couple steps change. You still take the difference between the purchase price and par value and divide it by the number of years until maturity, which gives you the annual amortization. Then you multiply the annual amortization by the number of years the investor held the bond. At this point, you need to subtract that amount from the purchase price instead of adding it to the purchase price to get the adjusted cost basis. Then, as you do with accretion problems, you compare the adjusted cost basis to the selling price to determine the gain or loss.

Presenting Gift and Estate Tax Rules

Fortunately, you need to know only limited information on gift and estate tax rules for the Series 7. Although some of your clients may receive a gift or inheritance of money, paintings, a car, a little red wagon, or whatever, you only need to be concerned with a gift or inheritance of securities. Both gift taxes and estate taxes are progressive taxes (the higher the tax bracket, the higher the percentage of tax paid). Additionally, the recipient is never responsible for the taxes on the gift or inheritance. The main thing that you need to focus on is the recipient's cost basis for the securities.

TIP

The inheritance of cash or securities may be referred to as a *wealth event* on the Series 7.

Gift taxes

A gift tax is a progressive tax imposed on the transfer of certain goods. In the event that a gift tax is due, it's always paid by the donor, not the recipient. For example, if someone makes a gift to a minor in a Uniform Gift to Minors Act (UGMA) account (see Chapter 16), the donor of the gift, not the minor, is responsible for any taxes due.

The IRS does allow some gift-tax loopholes. Anyone can give a gift of up to $17,000 per person per year (as of 2023) that's free from the gift tax and up to $12.92 million over the course of the gift-giver's lifetime. (See www.irs.gov/businesses/small-businesses-self-employed/estate-and-gift-taxes for more information on gifts and taxes.) Gifts between spouses aren't subject to gift taxes.

REMEMBER

To help determine capital gains or losses (see "At the sale: Capital gains and losses" earlier in this chapter), when a gift of securities is made, the recipient assumes the donor's cost basis (purchase price of the security) as long as the securities have increased in value. If the securities decrease in value after the original purchase, the recipient assumes the cost basis of the securities on the date of the gift.

The following question tests your understanding of how the cost basis carries over with gifts of securities.

EXAMPLE

Mary Johnson purchases 100 shares of LLL common stock at a price of $60 per share. She gives the securities to her son Zed when the market price is $75 per share. What is Zed's cost basis per share?

(A) $60 per share

(B) $67.50 per share

(C) $75 per share

(D) It depends on the holding period

The correct answer is Choice (A). Because LLL increased in value after the original purchase, Zed assumes his mother's cost basis.

This next question concerns the cost basis of a gift when the market price of the stock falls.

EXAMPLE

John Johnson purchased 1,000 shares of DIM Corp. common stock at $40 per share. DIM subsequently decreased in price to $30 per share, and John gave the securities to his father-in-law, Mike. Two years later, Mike sold the stock for $37 per share. What is Mike's tax situation regarding the sale of the DIM stock?

(A) $30,000

(B) $35,000

(C) $37,000

(D) $40,000

The right answer is Choice (A). Because DIM decreased from the original purchase price, Mike assumes the cost basis of the DIM stock on the date of the gift, which was $30,000 (1,000 shares × $30).

TIP

You're more likely to get a Series 7 question about a security that increases in value before it's given as a gift.

Estate taxes

Estate tax is a tax on property that is passed along to someone's estate when the person dies. Inheriting securities is a little more straightforward than receiving gifts of securities. When an individual receives securities as a result of an inheritance, he *always* assumes the fair market cost basis of the inherited securities on the date of the owner's death. Additionally, securities received by inheritance are always assigned a long-term holding characterization for tax purposes when sold.

When a person dies, estate taxes are normally paid before assets are transferred to beneficiaries. Because the estate pays the taxes on the securities, the tax liabilities aren't passed along to the beneficiaries. As of 2023, the filing of a federal estate tax return is required only for estates that involve the transfer of $12.92 million or more. For the most current estate tax information, visit www.irs.gov/businesses/small-businesses-self-employed/estate-tax.

Note: Presently there is a *unification of gift and estate taxes* rule that says a giver cannot give more than $12.92 million in gifts over his lifetime, including assets to beneficiaries upon death, without his estate being subject to additional taxes. You should be aware that $12.92 million is subject to change.

Exploring Retirement Plans

I place retirement plans in with taxes because retirement plans give investors tax advantages. When you're reviewing this section, zone in on the differences and similarities among the different types of plans. The contribution limits are important but not as important as understanding the plan specifics and who is qualified to open which type of plan.

Tax-qualified plans

The IRS may dub employee retirement plans as qualified or nonqualified. The distinction concerns whether they meet IRS and Employee Retirement Income Security Act (ERISA) standards for favorable tax treatment. A *tax-qualified plan* meets IRS standards to receive a favorable tax treatment. When you're investing in a tax-qualified plan, the contributions into the plan are made from pretax dollars and are excluded from your taxable income. Not only are contributions into the plan excluded from income, but the account also grows on a tax-deferred basis, so you aren't taxed until you withdraw money from the account at retirement. Individual Retirement Accounts (IRAs) are an example of a tax-qualified retirement plan. The two types of corporate tax-qualified retirement plans are defined contribution and defined benefit plans. These include 401(k)s, profit sharing plans, and money-purchase plans. Most corporate pension plans are tax-qualified plans.

Employee Retirement Income Security Act (ERISA)

ERISA was established by a 1974 act of Congress to cover *qualified private (corporate) pension* plans such as 401(k)s and certain union plans (not public plans for government workers). ERISA covers both defined benefit plans and defined contribution plans. The act was specifically designed to protect employees of companies by setting guidelines for fiduciaries (plan sponsors and investment advisers) to follow regarding selection of investments, eligibility, performances of duties, funding, and vesting.

>> **Participation:** If a company offers its employees a retirement plan, all full-time employees age 21 and over must be eligible after they have worked for the employer full time for at least one year.

>> **Vesting:** Vesting occurs when the money contributed to the plan goes with the employees if they leave the employer. Any money contributed by the employee is always fully vested, but the money contributed by the employer is typically not vested immediately. The contribution from the employer must be either fully vested by five years or 20 percent vested after three years if fully vested by seven years.

>> **Funding:** Contributions from the employee and employer toward the private pension plan must be segregated from the employer's other assets. The money contributed must be invested in the best interest of the employees. For defined contribution plans, employees are typically given a choice of mutual funds picked by the plan sponsor that typically cover various asset classes and are generally low cost. Employees may choose a fund or a number of funds and percentages to be invested.

>> **Account statements:** Employees must receive annual account statements and updates on plan benefits.

>> **Non-discrimination:** All employees must be treated equally and be eligible for the plan established by the employer.

Defined benefit plans

As the name implies, defined benefit plans are ones in which the employee knows how much they'll receive at retirement. These type of plans provide a fixed pre-established benefit for employees at retirement based on things such as length of employment, salary history, and so on. The benefits are not dependent on asset returns (even if the investments lose money, the defined benefit remains). So the employer assumes the investment risk. Typically, employers can contribute more to defined benefit plans than defined contribution plans and therefore the employer's tax deductions are higher. Because defined benefit plans are more complex, they are typically more costly to maintain than other plans.

All full-time employees who have worked for the employer for at least a year must be eligible. With defined benefit plans, the employer contributes most or all of the money, although some plans require employee contributions or allow voluntary employee contributions. Vesting can follow several schedules, but all full-time employees must be fully vested by seven years.

At retirement, the employee may receive either a lump-sum payment or monthly payments as established by the plan. In most cases, if the investor dies prior to receiving his expected benefits, any remaining benefits would be paid to the employee's beneficiary.

Defined contribution plans

Unlike defined benefit plans, the amount of money an investor receives at retirement will vary based on how the investments held by the plan perform. This type of plan allows for a set contribution (usually at each pay period) by employees. Defined contribution plans include 401(k) plans, 403(b) plans, employee stock ownership plans, and profit sharing plans.

TRADITIONAL 401(K) PLANS

As stated previously, a 401(k) is a corporate retirement plan. With this type of plan, employees can contribute a percentage of their salary up to a certain amount ($22,500 as of 2023) each year (as such, it's a defined contribution plan). Because it's a qualified plan, the amount contributed by the employee into the 401(k) is excluded from the employee's gross income. In addition, in most cases, the employer matches the employee's contribution up to a certain amount (for example, 25 percent, 50 percent, and so on). The account grows on a tax-deferred basis, so everything withdrawn from the account at retirement is taxable.

ROTH 401(K) PLANS

A Roth 401(k) has similarities between traditional 401(k) plans and Roth IRAs. As with a traditional 401(k), the contribution limits, which adjust yearly, are the same as well as the fact that they are both employer-sponsored plans. However, like a Roth IRA, contributions are made after taxes. So withdrawals of contributions and earnings are not taxed as long as the account has been held for at least five years and the holder is at least 59½ years old (except in cases of death or disability). Unlike Roth IRAs, required minimum distribution (RMD) rules apply.

403(B) PLANS

These are salary reduction plans for public school (elementary school, secondary school, college, and so on) employees, tax-exempt organizations, and religious organizations. These plans are also known as tax-sheltered *annuities*. As with 401(k)s, employees can elect to have a portion of their pay put into the retirement plan that's tax deferred. Like 401(k)s, the employer may match a percentage of the contributions. To be eligible, employees must be at least 21 years old and have been working for the employer for at least a year.

Stock purchase plans and stock option plans

Stock purchase plans allow investors to purchase shares of their own employer's stock at specified times usually at a discount. Employees are usually allowed to contribute anywhere between 1 percent and 10 percent of their salary. These are payroll deduction plans because the money is taken directly out of the employee's salary typically once every six months or so during the purchase period. Employees may then sell the shares in the market or hold onto them based on the unique aspects of the individual plan. Depending on how the plan is structured, it may be qualified (pre-tax contributions) or nonqualified (after-tax contributions).

Stock option plans may be offered to employees instead of stock purchase plans. In this case, the employee is given an option to purchase the company stock at a stated price over a stated time period. Typically, the option is at the money at the time of the offering, meaning that the strike price for the option is equal to the current market price of the company's stock. Usually, there's a vesting period so that employees must be employed full time by the company for a certain number of years. Unlike standard options, these options are long-term and typically expire several years later. (For more on options, visit Chapter 12.)

Profit sharing plans

Profit sharing plans are a type of defined contribution plan. Only the employer may contribute to the retirement plan. During good years, the company will contribute a specified percentage of each covered employee's salary to the plan. In years where the company has low earnings, they may skip the contributions entirely (decided by the board of directors). Contributions are tax deductible to the employer, and the money grows on a tax-deferred basis. The maximum annual contribution for 2023 is the same as the SEP-IRA (25 percent of salary up to $66,000).

REMEMBER

Because investors don't pay tax on the money initially deposited or on the earnings, the entire withdrawal from a tax-qualified plan is taxed at a rate determined by the investor's tax bracket, which is normally lower at retirement. Additionally, distributions taken before age 59½ are subject to a 10 percent tax penalty (10 percent is added to the investor's tax bracket) except in cases of death, disability, first-time home buying, educational expenses for certain family members, medical premiums for unemployed individuals, and so on.

Nonqualified plans

Obviously, a nonqualified plan is the opposite of a qualified plan. *Nonqualified plans,* such as deferred compensation plans and 457 plans, do not meet IRS and ERISA standards for favorable tax treatment. If you're investing in a nonqualified retirement plan, deposits are not tax-deductible (they're made from after-tax dollars); however, because you're dealing with a retirement plan, earnings in the plan do build up on a tax-deferred basis. People may choose to invest in nonqualified plans because either their employer doesn't have a qualified plan set up or the investment guidelines are not as strict (investors may be able to contribute more and invest in a wider choice of securities).

Deferred compensation programs

With deferred compensation programs, the employee agrees to delay receiving a portion of their salary until they retire, are terminated, are disabled, or die. Theoretically, when they retire, they would be at a lower tax bracket and would pay less in taxes later than if receiving money currently. If unfunded (not secured by specific assets safe from creditors) and the company declares bankruptcy or goes out of business, the company is not required to pay the amount of salary deferred. The employee becomes a general creditor of the company and must wait for the company to pay other debts to see if there is any cash available or assets available that can be liquidated to raise money for the compensation. The employer only receives a tax deduction once the employee is paid. Because these are nonqualified plans, the employer may discriminate and not offer the plan to all employees.

457(b) plans

457(b) are also deferred compensation plans established by state or local governments or 501(c)3 non-profit organizations. However, if a 457(b) plan is established for municipal employees, the plan must be qualified. In both cases, a person having a 457(b) plan could also have another retirement plan and make the maximum contribution into both plans. Employees may defer up to 100 percent of their compensation up to a rate determined by the IRS (indexed for inflation).

REMEMBER

Because investors have not paid tax on the money initially deposited or on the earnings, withdrawals from qualified plans are fully taxed at the rate determined by the investor's tax bracket.

IRA types and contribution limits

You'll likely be tested on a few different types of retirement plans and possibly the contribution limits. When you're looking at this section, understand the specifics of the types of plans and view the contribution limits as secondary. The contribution limits change pretty much yearly, and the Series 7 questions may not change that often. If you have a rough idea of the contribution limits, you should be okay. For updates and additional information, you can go to www.irs.gov/retirement-plans/plan-participant-employee/retirement-topics-ira-contribution-limits.

Traditional IRAs (individual retirement accounts or individual retirement arrangements)

IRAs are tax-qualified retirement plans, so deposits into the account are made from pretax dollars (they're tax-deductible). IRAs are completely funded by contributions that the *holder of the account* makes. Regardless of whether individuals are covered by a pension plan, they can still deposit money into an IRA. Here's a list of some of the key points of IRAs:

>> IRAs may be set up as *single life* (when the owner is the beneficiary of the account), *joint and last survivor* (when the sole beneficiary of the account is his or her spouse and the spouse is more than ten years younger than the owner), or *uniform lifetime* (when the spouse is not the sole beneficiary or the spouse is not more than ten years younger than the owner).

>> Permissible investments for IRAs include stocks, bonds, mutual funds, U.S. gold and silver coins, and real estate.

>> The current maximum contribution per person is $6,500 per year, with an additional catch-up contribution of $1,000 per person allowed for investors age 50 or older. Excess contributions are taxed at a rate of 6 percent until withdrawn.

>> A husband and wife can have separate accounts with a maximum contribution of $6,500 per year each, whether both are working or one is working.

>> Contributions into the IRA are fully deductible for individuals not covered by employer pension plans.

   If investors are covered by an employer pension plan, deposits into an IRA may or may not be tax-deductible. Although I think that the chances of your being tested on the values are slim, if an individual is covered by an employer pension plan and earns up to $73,000 per year ($116,000 jointly), deposits made into an IRA are fully deductible. The deductions are gradually phased out and disappear when an individual earns more than $83,000 per year ($136,000 jointly). (These numbers are as of 2023 and are typically increased each year.)

>> When an investor starts to withdraw funds from an IRA, the investor is taxed on the entire withdrawal (the amount deposited, which was not taxed, and the appreciation in value). The withdrawal is taxed as ordinary income.

>> Withdrawals can't begin before age 59½, or investors have to pay an early withdrawal penalty of 10 percent added to the investor's rate according to his tax bracket. An investor isn't subject to the 10 percent tax penalty in cases of death, disability, first-time homebuyers, and a few other exceptions. Obviously, dead retirees won't be making withdrawals, but their beneficiaries will be. In this case, the beneficiaries aren't hit with the 10 percent penalty.

>> Withdrawals must begin by April 1 of the year after the investor reaches age 73 (the required beginning date, or RBD). Investors who don't take their required minimum distribution (RMD) by that time are subject to a 25 percent tax penalty on the amount they should have withdrawn. The IRS provides minimum distribution worksheets to help you determine the amount that needs to be taken in order to avoid the penalty.

>> Deposits into IRAs are allowed up to April 15 or the filing deadline for that year (tax day) to qualify as a deduction for the previous year's taxes.

Roth IRAs

Anyone who doesn't make too much money can open a Roth IRA. The key difference between a traditional IRA and a Roth IRA is that withdrawals from a Roth IRA are tax-free. However, deposits made into the Roth IRA are not tax-deductible (made from after-tax dollars). Provided that the investor has held onto the Roth IRA for over five years and has reached age 59½, he can withdraw money from the Roth IRA without incurring any taxable income on the amount deposited or on the appreciation in the account.

REMEMBER

The maximum that an individual may contribute to a traditional IRA and Roth IRA is $6,500 per year combined (or $7,500 if over age 50).

As of 2023, investors who have an adjusted gross income of $153,000 or more per year ($228,000 if married filing jointly) can't contribute to a Roth IRA.

Simplified employee pensions (SEP-IRAs)

An SEP-IRA is a retirement vehicle designed for small business owners, self-employed individuals, and their employees. SEP-IRAs allow participants to invest money for retirement on a tax-deferred basis. Employers can make tax-deductible contributions directly to their employees' SEP-IRAs. As of 2023, the maximum employer contribution to each employee's SEP-IRA is 25 percent of the employee's compensation (salary, bonuses, and overtime) or $66,000 (subject to cost-of-living increases in the following years), whichever is less. Employees who are part of the plan may still make annual contributions to a traditional or Roth IRA.

Transfers and rollovers

Persons may decide to move their retirement account from IRA to another, from one employer's retirement plan to another, or from an employer's retirement plan to an IRA. Depending on how it's done, it would be considered either a rollover or transfer.

Transfer

A transfer is when a person decides to have his funds from one retirement plan transferred directly to another retirement plan of the same type while never taking possession of the funds. For example, let's say Mr. Smith is leaving ABC Corporation to go work for DEF Corporation. If both corporations have a 401(k), Mr. Smith can have the assets in his 401(k) moved directly from the trustee of ABC's 401(k) to the trustee of DEF's 401(k). Because Mr. Smith is not taking possession of the 401(k)'s assets, there is no limit placed on the amount of transfers that can take place in one year.

Rollover

An investor may also roll over funds received from one retirement plan into another. Using Mr. Smith again as an example, if Mr. Smith decided to take the funds from his 401(k) and deposit them into another qualified plan such as an IRA, it would be considered a rollover. Mr. Smith must roll over the money into another qualified plan within 60 days in order for it not to be taxed as a withdrawal. Rollovers may only be executed once every 12 months. With a rollover, if the check was made payable to Mr. Smith, the fund would've imposed a 20 percent withholding tax. If Mr. Smith had the check payable to the new trustee instead of his name, the withholding tax would not be imposed.

Coverdell Education Savings Accounts (Coverdell ESA)

Coverdell Education Savings Accounts (Coverdell ESA) are tax-advantaged savings accounts that allow persons to be able to make after-tax contributions of up to *$2,000 per student per year* up until the student's 18th birthday. The earnings will grow on a tax-deferred basis, and the distributions will be tax-free as long as they are used for qualified educational expenses. The money must be used by the beneficiary by her 30th birthday or the earnings will be taxed as ordinary income plus a 10 percent penalty.

Testing Your Knowledge

By this point in the book, your head is probably swimming with the amount of different questions that can be asked. Well, here's your shot at testing your ability to answer questions related to taxes and retirement plans. Read the questions carefully so that you don't make any careless mistakes.

1. All of the following are regressive taxes EXCEPT

   (A) income

   (B) sales

   (C) gasoline

   (D) alcohol

2. Declan K. purchased 1,000 shares of UPPP common stock at $40 per share. In the next 11 months, UPPP increased in value to $55 per share. How would this result for Declan be categorized?

   (A) Short-term capital gain

   (B) Long-term capital gain

   (C) Appreciation

   (D) Ordinary income

3. One of your clients has made the following transactions:

February 4th he purchased 100 shares of DIM at $40

March 15th he purchased 100 shares of DIM at $50

July 19th he sold 100 shares of DIM at $46

What is the capital gain or loss?

(A) $400 gain

(B) $400 loss

(C) $600 gain

(D) $600 loss

4. Which of the following are subject to federal taxation?

I. Cash dividends on stock

II. Interest on general obligation bonds

III. Interest on U.S. Treasury notes

IV. Capital gains on revenue bonds

(A) I and III

(B) I and III

(C) I, III, and IV

(D) I, II, III, and IV

5. In order to avoid a violation of the wash sale rule, an investor who sold a security at a loss cannot repurchase the same security nor anything convertible into the same security for at least

(A) 20 days

(B) 30 days

(C) 45 days

(D) 60 days

6. By what age must an individual begin withdrawing money from a qualified retirement plan?

(A) $59\frac{1}{2}$

(B) $70\frac{1}{2}$

(C) April 1st of the year after turning $70\frac{1}{2}$

(D) April 1st of the year after turning 73

7. Which TWO of the following are TRUE regarding Coverdell Education Savings Accounts?

I. Contributions are pre-tax.

II. Contributions are after-tax.

III. The maximum annual contribution is $2,000 per student.

IV. The maximum annual contribution is $6,500 per student.

(A) I and III

(B) I and IV

(C) II and III

(D) II and IV

8. Ms. Hudson purchased a 4-percent TUV corporate bond at 90 with 20 years to maturity. 11 years later, Ms. Hudson sold the bond at 92. What is the gain or loss?

    (A) $20 gain

    (B) $20 loss

    (C) $35 gain

    (D) $35 loss

9. Melissa purchased 1,000 shares of JKL common stock at a price of $14 per share. On her granddaughter's 18th birthday, she gives her the securities as gift. At that point, the market price of JKL is $24 per share. For tax purposes, what is her granddaughter's cost per share?

    (A) $0

    (B) $14.00

    (C) $19.00

    (D) $24.00

10. Regarding 401(k) plans, which TWO of the following are TRUE?

    I. They are defined contribution plans.

    II. They are defined benefit plans.

    III. The amount withdrawn at retirement is partially taxable.

    IV. The amount withdrawn at retirement is fully taxable.

    (A) I and III

    (B) I and IV

    (C) II and III

    (D) II and IV

Answers and Explanations

After reading this chapter, you shouldn't find any of the questions too difficult. Since there are 10 questions, each one is worth 10 points.

1. **A.** Sales, gasoline, and alcohol taxes are all regressive, meaning that all people regardless of income or net worth are taxed at the same rate. With progressive taxes, the more money you make, the higher your tax rate. Therefore, income tax is a progressive tax.

2. **C.** Had Declan sold his stock at a profit 11 months later, it would've been a short-term capital gain (1 year or less). Because the question didn't say he sold the stock, it has simply appreciated in value. Remember, there can't be a gain or loss until the security is sold.

3. **C.** Unless the client specifies that they want it done a different way, the transactions would be executed first in, first out (FIFO). This means that the first securities they purchased (the ones at $40) would be the first ones sold. Therefore, they would have a $600 gain ($4,600 selling price − $4,000 purchase price).

4. **C.** Cash dividends on common and preferred stock are taxable on all levels. Interest on U.S. government securities is taxable on the federal level but not the state level. Capital gains on all securities are taxable on all levels. However, interest on municipal bonds, such as general obligation bonds, is exempt from taxation on the federal level.

5. **B.** The wash sale rule was put in place to keep investors from claiming a loss on a security on their tax return while still holding more or less the same position. So if an investor sells a security at a loss, they cannot purchase the same security nor anything convertible into the same security for 30 days (prior or after the sale). Certainly this isn't a situation where an investor will face fines or penalties; they just won't be able to claim the loss.

6. **D.** As of January 1st, 2020, individuals must begin taking minimum distributions from their qualified retirement plans by April 1st of the year after turning 73.

7. **C.** Coverdell Education Savings Accounts (ESAs) allow contributions for students for up to $2,000 per year per student. Contributions are made from after-tax dollars but grow on a tax-deferred basis.

8. **D.** Since the bond was purchased at a discount, this is an accretion question. The first thing you have to do is adjust the cost basis towards par ($1,000) in the amount of time the bond has until maturity. This customer purchased the bond at $900 (90), and it matures in 20 years.

   20 years
   $900 → $1,000

   The difference between the purchase price and par value is $100 ($1,000 − $900). Divide the difference by the number of years until maturity to get the annual accretion.

   $$\text{annual accretion} = \frac{\$100}{20 \text{ years}} = \$5$$

Next, take the $5 per year accretion and multiply it by the number of years the customer held the bond to get the total accretion.

$5 per year $\times$ 11 years = $55 total accretion

Now, take the $55 total accretion and add it to the purchase price of $900 to determine the customer's adjusted cost basis.

$900 original cost + $55 total accretion = $955 (adjusted cost basis)

For the final step, compare the $955 adjusted cost basis to the $920 (92) selling price to determine the amount of gain or loss.

$955 adjusted cost basis − $920 selling price = $35 capital loss

9. **B.** In the case of gifted securities, if the price of the securities increased since the initial purchase, the donee (receiver of the gift) assumes the initial purchase price as a cost basis.

10. **B.** 401(k)s are corporate retirement plans. Employees decide the amount of their salary they want to contribute and typically, the employer will partially match the contribution up to a certain amount ($22,500 as of 2023). As such, they are considered defined contribution plans. The amount contributed reduces the employee's salary, so the employee's taxable income is reduced. Therefore, the employee never paid tax on the contribution or on the amount the account has appreciated in value, so withdrawals are fully taxed at the investor's tax bracket.

Chapter **16**

Rules and Regulations: No Fooling Around

First off, I'd like to apologize for having to include this chapter. Unfortunately, rules are a part of life and part of the Series 7. When you're reading this, please remember that I didn't make the rules — but I do my best to make them as easy to digest as possible. Fortunately, some of them will look familiar if you've recently taken the Securities Industry Essentials exam. Rules have become increasingly important on the Series 7 exam, especially since the Patriot Act came into the picture.

In this chapter, I cover topics related to rules and regulations. First, I help you understand who the guardians of the market are and their roles in protecting customers and enforcing rules. I also place considerable emphasis on opening, closing, transferring, and handling customers' accounts. And of course, I provide practice questions and the "Committing Other Important Rules to Memory" section to guide you on your way. At the end, I wrap it all up with a 25-question practice quiz.

The Market Watchdogs: Securities Regulatory Organizations

To keep the market running smoothly and to make sure investors aren't abused (at least too much), regulatory organizations stay on the lookout. Although you don't need to know all the minute details about each of them, you do have to know the basics.

The Securities and Exchange Commission

The Securities and Exchange Commission, or SEC, is the major watchdog of the securities industry. Congress created the SEC to regulate the market and to protect investors from fraudulent and manipulative practices. All broker-dealers who transact business with investors and other broker-dealers must register with the SEC. And that registration means something: All broker-dealers have to comply with SEC rules or face censure (an official reprimand), limits on activity, suspension or suspension of one or more associated persons (such as a registered rep or principal), a fine, and/or having their registration revoked.

REMEMBER

SEC investigations may lead to a civil (financial) complaint being filed in a federal court. The SEC may seek disgorgement (taking away) of ill-gotten gains, civil money penalties, and injunctive relief (a cease-and-desist order from the court). If the matter is criminal in nature, the investigation is conducted by the U.S. Attorney's Office and the grand jury.

Among its other numerous functions, you need to be aware that besides The Securities Act of 1933, The Securities Exchange Act of 1934, and The Trust Indenture Act of 1939, which were covered in Chapter 5, the SEC also enforces The Investment Company Act of 1940 and the Investment Advisers Act of 1940:

>> **The Investment Company Act of 1940:** This act regulates the registration requirements and the activities of investment companies.

>> **The Investment Advisers Act of 1940:** This act requires the registration of certain investment advisers with the SEC. An *investment adviser* is a person who receives a fee for giving investment advice. Any investment adviser with at least $25 million of assets under management or anyone who advises an investment company must register with the SEC. All other investment advisers have to register on the state level. The Investment Advisers Act of 1940 regulates

   ● Record-keeping responsibilities

   ● Advisory contracts

   ● Advertising rules

   ● Custody of customers' assets and funds

Self-regulatory organizations

As you can imagine, due to the unscrupulous nature of some investors and registered representatives, the SEC's job is overwhelming. Fortunately, a few self-regulatory organizations (SROs) are there to take some of the burden off of the SEC's shoulders. Although membership isn't mandatory, most broker-dealers are members of one or more SROs. SRO rules are usually stricter than those of the SEC.

The four types of SROs you need to know for the Series 7 are FINRA, MSRB, NYSE, and CBOE:

>> **The FINRA (Financial Industry Regulatory Authority):** FINRA is a self-regulatory organization that's responsible for the operation and regulation of the over-the-counter market, investment banking (the underwriting of securities), New York Stock Exchange (NYSE) trades, investment companies, limited partnerships, and so on. FINRA was created in 2007 and is a consolidation of the NASD (National Association of Securities Dealers) and the regulation and enforcement portions of the NYSE (New York Stock Exchange). FINRA is responsible for making sure that its members not only follow FINRA rules but also the rules set forth by the SEC. Additionally, FINRA is responsible for the handling of complaints against member firms and may take disciplinary action, if necessary. FINRA is also responsible for administering securities exams such as the SIE (now you know who to blame). FINRA has strict rules (as the other SROs do, I suspect) regarding filing of misleading, incomplete, or inaccurate information as to membership or registration regarding the firm's registration or registration of member associates.

>> **The Municipal Securities Rulemaking Board:** The MSRB was established to develop rules that banks and securities firms have to follow when underwriting, selling, buying, and recommending municipal securities (check out Chapter 8 for info on municipal bonds). The MSRB is subject to SEC oversight but does not enforce SEC rules.

The MSRB makes rules for firms (and representatives) who sell municipal bonds but doesn't enforce them — it leaves that up to FINRA.

>> **The New York Stock Exchange:** The NYSE is the oldest and largest stock exchange in the United States. The NYSE is responsible for listing securities, setting exchange policies, and supervising the exchange and member firms. The NYSE has the power to take disciplinary action against member firms.

>> **The Chicago Board Options Exchange:** The CBOE is an exchange that makes and enforces option exchange rules.

Although SROs may be independent, they do work together creating and enforcing rules. FINRA and NYSE can fine, suspend, censure (reprimand), and expel members. However, FINRA and the NYSE can't imprison members who violate the rules and regulations.

Look at questions with the words *guarantee* or *approve* in them very carefully. FINRA, SEC, NYSE, and so on, do *not* approve or guarantee securities. Any statement that says that they do is false. In addition, because a firm is registered with (or didn't have its registration revoked by) an SRO, it does not mean that the SRO approves of the firm, its financial standing, its business, its conduct, and so on. So member firms and their associates may not claim that they've been approved by the SEC or any SRO.

Following Protocol When Opening Accounts

The Series 7 examiners seem to be focusing more and more on the handling of customer accounts. You need to know what to do to open accounts, how to take customer orders, the rules for sending out confirmations, and so on.

Filing the facts on the new account form

When you're opening any new account for a customer, the new account form needs some basic information. Broker-dealers may, in accordance with the Patriot Act, require a customer to provide proof of identification. Getting this information is your responsibility (or the responsibility of the broker-dealer). Here's a list of the items that need to be on the new account form:

>> The name(s) and address(es) of the individual(s) who'll have access to the account as well as a trusted contact person age 18 or older (especially if the person opening the account is 65 or older). (A trusted contact person isn't mandatory but is highly encouraged.)

>> The customer's phone number.

>> Some government issued identification information (driver's license number, passport number, military ID number, and so on).

>> The customer's date of birth (the customer must be of legal age to open an account).

>> The type of account the customer is opening (cash, margin, retirement, day trading, prime brokerage, DVP/RVP, advisory or fee-based, discretionary, options, and so on).

>> The customer's Social Security number (if the customer is an individual) or tax ID number (if the customer is a business). For non-U.S. citizens: passport ID number, taxpayer ID number, alien identification card number, foreign government issued ID, residence, and photograph.

>> The customer's occupation, employer, and type of business (certain limitations are placed on customers who work for banks, broker-dealers, insurance companies, SROs, and so on).

>> Domestic or foreign residency and/or citizenship.

>> Bank references and the customer's net worth and annual income. To be considered *accredited* (sophisticated), an individual investor must be able to prove that they had an annual income of $200,000 ($300,000 combined income if married) or more for the previous two years and are expected to make at least $200,000 in the current year or have a net worth of at least $1 million excluding primary residence. ***Note:*** Accredited investors may also be banks, partnerships, corporations, nonprofit organizations, trusts, and so on. (For a complete list of who or what is considered an accredited investor, see Chapter 5.)

>> Whether the customer is an insider of a company.

>> Investment objectives (see Chapter 13).

>> The signatures of the registered representative and a principal.

REMEMBER

All the items listed should be on the new account form and you should make an effort to determine the customer's investment objectives. However, sometimes new customers may not want to provide all the information. At a bare minimum, to be able to open the account, you need the customer's name, date of birth (for individuals, not businesses), street address (not a P.O. box), and an identification number (Social Security number, tax ID number, and so on). The more information you get from the customer, the better. Besides, it helps you get to know your client better and will help you make more suitable recommendations. If anything changes (for example, a customer's address, investment objectives, place of employment, marital status, and so on), the account records need to be updated. A copy of the new account form must be sent to the client within 30 days of the account opening. The customer should review the new account form to make sure everything is accurate, including the investor's investment objectives. Account records must be updated *at least every 3 years.* Additionally, only individuals who are legally competent may open accounts.

According to FINRA Rule 2090: "Every member shall use reasonable diligence, in regard to the opening and maintenance of every account, to know (and retain) the essential facts concerning every customer and concerning the authority of each person acting on behalf of such customer."

The following question tests your ability to answer a question about opening a new account.

EXAMPLE

Which of the following people must sign a new account form?

  I. The customer

 II. The customer's spouse

III. The registered representative

IV. A principal

(A) I and II only

(B) III and IV only

(C) I and IV only

(D) I, III, and IV only

The correct answer is Choice (B). When you're opening a new account for a customer, the new account form requires only your signature and a principal's (manager's) signature. Make sure you don't assume extenuating circumstances. You need the customer's signature on a new account form only if the customer is opening a margin account. Additionally, you need the spouse's signature only if you're opening a joint account. Because the question doesn't say that the account is a margin or joint account, you can't assume that it is.

Word on the street: Numbered accounts

A *street name* or *numbered account* is an account registered in the name of the broker-dealer with an ID number. Street name accounts give the investor a certain degree of privacy and help facilitate the trading of securities (because the brokerage firm, not the customer, signs the certificates). You need to know a few rules about street name accounts for the Series 7:

>> You need a written statement from the customer attesting to the ownership of the account.

>> With the exception of margin accounts, which must remain in street name, a street name account may be changed by the customer into a regular account at any time.

>> All margin accounts must be in street name.

The Bank Secrecy Act (BSA)

The Bank Secrecy Act is also known as the Currency and Foreign Transactions Reporting Act. The BSA is a law that requires financial institutions to work with the U.S. government in cases of suspected money laundering. (Anti-Money Laundering [AML] rules were covered in detail in the Securities Industry Essential exam.) The BSA was amended due to the Patriot Act to help detect terrorist financing networks. As such, broker-dealers are required to do their part by helping to identify persons opening accounts. As part of that act, broker-dealers are required to

>> Keep records of the information used to identify the customer (via customer identification programs, or CIPs). The CIP is a program used by financial institutions to verify the identity of customers who want to conduct financial transactions.

>> Verify that a customer doesn't appear on any list of known terrorists or terrorist organizations (the U.S. Treasury keeps this list). The list that the U.S. Treasury has is maintained by the Treasury Department's Office of Foreign Assets Control (OFAC). The list contains the names of suspected terrorists, criminals, and outcast nations. Financial institutions are prohibited from doing business with any of these individuals or entities. In the event that a firm finds that one of its clients is on the list, the firm must freeze the account and inform federal law enforcement authorities. Broker-dealers must exercise extra caution when opening accounts for foreign nationals.

Closing customer accounts

In general, the customer or brokerage firm may close an account at any time. The account closure procedures are usually found in the brokerage account agreement. Included in the account agreement are terms and conditions stating how the brokerage firm may close the account at its own discretion.

Selecting the appropriate type of account

Investors can open many different types of accounts through a broker–dealer. Besides knowing a customer's investment profile (see Chapter 13), you need a basic understanding of the types of accounts for the Series 7 exam. Fortunately, most of them are pretty straightforward.

» **Pattern day traders:** Pattern day traders are investors who try to take advantage of price movements of securities that take place during the day. Specifically, pattern day traders are investors who execute *4 or more day trades within a 5-business-day period*. For customers to open a day trading account, they must deposit a *minimum of $25,000.* In addition, they must have at least $25,000 in equity in the account on any day where the customer executes a trade. Because of the additional risk involved, firms must provide a *day-trading risk disclosure statement* prior to the customer opening the day trading account and the customer must be approved for day trading by a principal (manager) of the firm. Part of the approval process includes a determination that this is an appropriate strategy for the customer (does it fit their investment objectives, trading experience, financial situation, and so on) and a signed agreement from the customer.

   Note: A *day-trading risk disclosure statement* should include information such as the following: Day trading is extremely risky; being cautious of claims of large day-trading profits; understanding securities markets; how firms operate; day trading will generate high commission costs; and day trading on margin may result in losses beyond the investment.

» **Prime brokerage:** This type of account is ideal for large retail or institutional accounts that use the services of several different broker-dealers. The customer may choose one brokerage firm (the prime broker) to combine all the information from all the accounts into one statement. Prime brokerage customers must have a minimum of $500,000 in all the accounts combined to be eligible. However, customers who also have an investment advisory account may choose to use the investment adviser as their prime broker and in that case, will only need to have $100,000 invested total in all accounts.

» **Delivery versus payment/receive versus payment (DVP/RVP):** DVP and RVP accounts are typically used for institutional clients. These transactions are settled cash on delivery (COD). In this case, securities are or cash is delivered to a bank or depository as pre-arranged by the customer. The customer or broker-dealer is responsible for contacting the bank or depository regarding each purchase or sale. The bank or depository is responsible for exchanging the cash for securities or vice versa. After the exchange, the bank forwards the money or securities to the client's broker-dealer.

» **Fee-based accounts:** For certain investors, it might be more beneficial for them to set up a fee-based account. Many firms offer fee-based accounts in which investors are charged fixed fees or a percentage of assets under management instead of charging commissions for brokerage services. Prior to recommending a fee-based account, you should take into consideration whether or not it is right for the customer considering the services provided, the cost, customer preferences, the amount of trading the customer does, and so on. These fee-based accounts may be set up for traditional brokerage accounts or accounts with investment advisory services (wrap accounts).

» **Wrap accounts:** These accounts are investment advisory accounts where broker-dealers provide clients with a host of services for a single fee. These services include asset allocation, portfolio management, trade execution, and administration.

» **Advisory accounts:** This type of account allows the investor to pay a fee (a percentage of the value of the customer's portfolio, an hourly fee, a fixed fee, and so on) for receiving investment advice. In order for you to open up an account as an investment adviser, you must be a registered investment adviser (RIA). You can become an investment adviser by passing the Series 65 or Series 66 exams along with whatever other exams you're taking like the Series 7.

Depending on the amount of client assets under management, investment advisers may have to register with the SEC as well as the states where they do business. Investment advisers with a smaller amount of client assets under management may only have to register with the state securities agency where they have their principal place of business.

Account registration types

Investors can open many different types of accounts through a broker–dealer. Besides knowing a customer's investment profile (see Chapter 13), you need a basic understanding of the types of accounts for the Series 7 exam. Fortunately, most of them are pretty straightforward.

Single and joint accounts

Some investors prefer to share; others like to go it alone. Whatever their preference, adults can open up accounts that fit their needs:

>> **Single (individual) accounts:** Naturally, this account is in the name of one person. The key thing for you to remember is that individuals may not open accounts in other people's names without written permission (power of attorney).

>> **Joint accounts:** This account is in the name of more than one person. All individuals named on the account have equal trading authority for the account. For Series 7 exam purposes, you need to be familiar with two types of joint accounts:

- **Joint tenants with rights of survivorship (JTWROS):** With this type of joint account, when a joint tenant named on the account dies, their portion of the account passes on to the surviving joint tenant. These accounts are usually set up almost exclusively for married couples. In states where community property laws exist (currently Arizona, California, Idaho, Louisiana, Nevada, New Mexico, Texas, Washington, and Wisconsin), investments acquired during the marriage are automatically presumed to be jointly owned by both spouses.

- **Joint with tenants in common (JTIC):** With this type of account, when one tenant of the account dies, their portion of the account becomes part of their estate. JTICs are usually set up for individuals who aren't related and is often set up for estate planning purposes.

- **Community property:** Community property accounts are similar to JTWROS accounts but are only for legally married couples. Certain states have community property laws which require the account to be transferred to the surviving spouse in the event of death of one of the account holders. An account designated as a community property account depends on the state where the account holders reside. For community property accounts, information must be collected about the owner and spouse.

- **Sole proprietorship:** These are business accounts opened under the name of the individual owner or their business name. The individual owner is held personally responsible for the business's debt.

The following question tests your knowledge of account types.

All the following people may open a joint account EXCEPT

(A) Two friends

(B) A husband and wife

(C) A parent and minor son

(D) Three strangers

The right choice here is (C). A joint account is an account in the name of more than one adult. Choices (A), (B), and (D) are all possible for joint accounts; however, an account opened for a minor must be a custodial account, which I discuss in the next section.

Trust accounts

Trust accounts are ones that are managed by one party (the trustee) for the benefit of another party (the beneficiary). Trustees have legal control of the assets of the trust. However, even though they have legal control over the trust's assets, the investment decisions must be in the best interests of the beneficiary. In order to open a trust account, you must have a copy of the trust agreement and proof that the trustee is legally allowed to transact business for the beneficiary. Trust accounts may be set up as revocable or irrevocable.

>> **Revocable (living) trust:** As the name implies, a revocable trust is one that can be revoked or changed by the trustee. This means that the trustee can cancel the trust, change the beneficiary, and so on. The downside is that a revocable trust still remains part of the trustee's estate. This means that it's considered part of the trustee's personal assets as far as creditors and estate taxes are concerned.

>> **Irrevocable trust:** An irrevocable trust is one that can't be changed. So, the beneficiary can't change, the terms can't change, and it can't be canceled. Once set up, the trust is no longer considered part of the trustee's estate and cannot be considered part of the trustee's personal assets and is not subject to the trustee's estate tax.

A specific type of trust account that you're most likely to see on the Series 7 exam is a custodial account. A *custodial account* is set up for a child who's too young to have their own account. A custodian (adult) makes the investment decisions for the account. Any adult can open a custodial account for a minor, so the people named on the account don't have to be related.

REMEMBER

Custodial accounts are trust accounts and may be referred to on the Series 7 exam as UGMA or UTMA accounts because they fall under the Uniform Gifts to Minors Act or Uniform Transfer to Minors Act. A *UTMA account* is an extension of the UGMA account that allows gifts in addition to cash and securities to be transferred to the minor. The additional gifts allowed are art, real estate, patents, and royalties.

Additionally, because the minor is too young to make investment decisions for themselves, some rules are specific to custodian accounts:

>> There can only be one custodian and one minor per account.

>> The minor is responsible for the taxes (the minor's Social Security number is registered for the account).

>> The account is registered in the name of the custodian for the benefit of the minor (the custodian is responsible for endorsing all certificates).

>> The account can't be held in street name (in the name of the broker-dealer with an ID number — see the earlier section "Word on the street: Numbered accounts").

>> Securities can't be traded on margin or sold short (Chapter 9 covers margin accounts).

>> Anyone may give a gift of cash or securities to the minor. The gift is irrevocable (can't be refused by the custodian).

>> If an account receives rights, the custodian can't let the rights expire. (See Chapter 6 for info on rights.) Because rights have value, a custodian can exercise or sell the rights.

Custodial accounts are for minors, so as soon as a minor reaches the age of majority, which is determined by the minor's state of residence, the custodial account is terminated and the account is transferred to a single account in the name of the (former) minor.

Discretionary accounts

Decision making can be stressful, and some investors don't want to deal with it. With a *discretionary account,* an investor can give you (the registered rep) the right to make trading decisions for the account. All discretionary accounts need prior written authorization by way of a *written power of attorney* signed by the investor, which gives trading authorization to the registered rep. As you can imagine, discretionary accounts come under extra scrutiny. All discretionary accounts must be approved by and frequently reviewed by a principal. The representative and principal must make sure that the trades fit with the customer's financial resources and investment profile. Also, the trades may not be excessive in size or frequency based on the financial resources and investment objectives of the customer.

If a customer places an order but doesn't specify the security, the number of shares or units, and/or whether the customer wants to buy or sell, you need a written power of attorney. If you don't have a written power of attorney, you can't do anything but decide when to place the order (timing). For example, suppose one of your customers calls you and says that they want to sell 100 shares of ABC common stock and you believe you can get a better price later in the day. The customer can give you verbal permission to place the order at your discretion (discretionary order). This type of order is called a *market not held order* and is usually good only for the rest of the day.

Here are some specific rules for discretionary orders that you're likely to see on the Series 7 exam:

>> Each discretionary order must be marked as *discretionary* on the order ticket.

>> As with other orders, principals must sign each order ticket.

>> A principal needs to approve each discretionary order and review discretionary accounts regularly to make sure reps don't trade excessively to generate commissions, which is called *churning.*

>> All firms dealing with discretionary accounts must maintain a written statement of supervisory procedures regarding how discretionary accounts are handled.

Don't confuse discretionary accounts with discretionary orders. Discretionary orders are ones in which customers without a discretionary account give the rep discretion as to when to place their order (price and time).

Third-party accounts

Third-party accounts are ones in which the account owner gives permission to another party to have trading authority over their account. The account holder may give permission to a family member over the age of 18, an attorney, a registered rep (like you; see the preceding section, "Discretionary accounts"), an investment adviser, and so on. For a client to give trading authority to another party, they must sign a power of attorney giving the party permission to trade their account. The power of attorney may give the party full or limited trading authority over the account.

>> **Limited Power of Attorney (limited trading authorization):** The authorized party *cannot withdraw securities or cash* without permission of the customer. The authorized party may not transfer securities or cash from the account without verbal approval of the customer. However, the authorized party may still execute trades without verbal approval of the customer.

>> **Full Power of Attorney:** There is no restriction placed on the authorized party regarding trading or transfer of assets.

>> **Durable Power of Attorney:** A regular power of attorney is terminated if the account holder becomes incapacitated (mental or physical ailment). A durable power of attorney allows the authorized party to keep handling trades in the account until the account holder dies. No matter whether the power of attorney is regular or durable, the authorized party's trading authority is terminated when the account holder dies.

REMEMBER

A *fiduciary* is anyone who can legally make decisions for another investor. Examples of fiduciaries are custodians (UGMA accounts), a registered rep having power of attorney, an executor of an estate, a trustee, guardians, and so on. Fiduciaries are responsible for choosing the investments that are in the best interests of the account holder. Many states have a *legal list* that fiduciaries can use as a guide when choosing securities. Ideally, the investments should be properly diversified and fit the investor's investment objectives. If their state does not have a legal list, fiduciaries should invest in securities that only a prudent person who's seeking reasonable income and preservation of capital would invest in.

Section 28(e)

Persons who exercise investment discretion over beneficiaries' or clients' accounts are provided a safe harbor regarding higher transaction commission paid as long as the higher commissions are substantiated by higher brokerage and research services. There was always a concern for persons handling discretionary accounts when the commission charged or paid in the account was higher than the minimum. Certainly, that would allow for the person having discretionary authority to be sued. Under SEC Rule Section 28(e), some latitude is allowed as long as the higher commissions are backed up with higher brokerage service cost and research cost.

Corporate accounts

Only incorporated businesses can open corporate accounts. If you're opening a corporate account, you need to obtain the tax ID number of the corporation, which is similar to an individual's Social Security number. Additionally, you need to obtain a copy of the *corporate resolution,* which lets you know who you should be taking trading instructions from (so you don't get a call like, "Hi, I'm Joe Blow, the janitor for XYZ Corporation, and I'd like to purchase 1,000 shares of ABC for my company").

If a corporation wants to open a margin account (accounts where it's borrowing some money from the broker-dealer to purchase securities — see Chapter 9), you also need a copy of the *corporate charter* (bylaws). The corporate charter has to allow the corporation to purchase securities on margin.

Unincorporated associations

An unincorporated association is sometimes called a voluntary organization. An unincorporated association is a group of two or more individuals who form an organization for a specific purpose (in this case, investing). If an unincorporated association has too many characteristics of a corporation, such as having a board of directors, limited liability, and so on, it may be treated and taxed at a higher rate, as if it were a corporation.

Institutional accounts

Accounts set by institutions such as banks, mutual funds, insurance companies, pension funds, hedge funds, and investment advisers are considered institutional accounts. Their role is to act as specialized investors on behalf of others.

Partnership accounts

Two or more individual owners of a business that's not set up as a corporation may set up a partnership account. All partnerships must complete a partnership agreement, which the broker-dealer has to keep on file. The *partnership agreement*, like a corporate resolution, states who has trading authorization for the account so you know whom you're supposed to be taking orders from.

REMEMBER

For corporations, partnerships, or other legal entities, the names of persons authorized to transact business on behalf of the entity must be kept on record.

Death of an account holder

When a firm becomes aware of an account holder's death, it must mark the account "deceased," cancel any open orders, and freeze the account (no trading, no money out, and so on), revoking power of attorney (if any) until receiving instructions and supporting documentation from the executor of the account holder's estate. Depending on the type of account, in order to release the assets of the account, your firm must receive a copy of the death certificate, letters testamentary, and inheritance tax waivers.

Standards and required approvals of public communications

To make sure that member firms' communications with the public are fair, balanced, and not misleading, FINRA has an Advertising Regulation Department. This department is there to ensure that broker-dealers are in compliance with the advertising rules of FINRA, the SEC, the MSRB, and SIPC. The department reviews public communications submitted by firms (voluntarily or as required). In turn, the department will provide the firms with a written review for every communication submitted.

Types of communication

There are three basic types of communication that FINRA requires that you know for the Series 7:

>> **Retail communication:** Retail investors are those investors other than institutional investors. Retail communication is any written or electronic communication that is made available or distributed to *more than 25 retail investors within any 30 calendar-day period*. This includes things like TV ads, radio ads, magazine ads, newspaper ads, billboards, and so on.

>> **Correspondence:** Correspondence is like retail communication but is sent (written or electronically) to *25 or fewer retail investors within any 30 calendar-day period*.

>> **Institutional communication:** Like retail communication and correspondence, institutional communication is any written (including electronic) communication that is made available or distributed. However, institutional communication is only to be made available or distributed to institutional clients such as banks, savings and loan associations, registered investment companies, insurance companies, registered investment advisers, government entities, employee benefit plans, FINRA member firms, persons or entities with assets of at least $50 million, and so on. Please note that inter-office communications are not considered institutional communication.

REMEMBER

As with just about everything that happens at a brokerage firm, customer communications must be approved by a qualified principal of the firm. Research reports on particular securities must be approved by a supervisory analyst who has expertise in the particular product. Testimonials (if any) must be made by a person who has the knowledge and experience to have a valid opinion.

Member firms are, in many cases, required to file retail communications with FINRA ten business days prior to first use. Members are required to keep the communications for a minimum of three years.

Seminars

As a way of drumming up business, registered reps often conduct seminars. When conducting seminars, the persons speaking must have a good knowledge of the products and services they're promoting. Information regarding the seminar, such as the sponsor, topic, the date, and location must be kept on file.

Financial exploitation of specified adults

With people living longer and the number of seniors increasing, FINRA has recently created rules to help curb or handle cases of financial exploitations of specified adults:

>> Seniors, or natural persons aged 65 or older

>> Natural persons aged 18 or older who have mental or physical impairments that render them unable to protect their own interests

For specified adults, financial institutions must obtain the information of a "Trusted Contact Person" whom they can contact regarding unusual trading activity in the account.

FINRA defines the term "financial exploitation" as

A. "the wrongful or unauthorized taking, withholding, appropriation, or use of a Specified Adult's funds or securities"; or

B. "any act or omission by a person, including through the use of a power of attorney, guardianship, or any other authority regarding a Specified Adult to:"

   a. "obtain control, through deception, intimidation or undue influence, over the Specified Adult's money, assets, or property"; or

   b. "convert the Specified Adult's money, assets, or property."

In the event that a member believes that the financial exploitation of specified adults has or may be taking place, Rule 2165 allows the member to place a temporary hold on the disbursement of the specified adult's funds or securities. If a temporary hold has been put in place, the member has up to two business days to contact all parties involved in the transaction as well as the Trusted Contact Person (unless the member believes they are involved in the exploitation) to describe the reasons for the temporary hold. The hold may last up to 15 business days while being reviewed.

The Series 7 and other FINRA exams cover topics related to protecting seniors, including

>> Firms' marketing and communications to investors aged 65 and older.

>> Information required when opening an account for a senior.

>> Any disclosures provided to senior investors.

>> Complaints filed by senior investors as well as how the firm handles the complaints.

>> Supervision of registered reps as they communicate with senior investors.

>> The suitability and types of securities marketed and sold to senior investors.

>> The training of a firm's representatives as to how they are to handle the accounts of specified adults.

FINRA recently created a helpline for seniors to provide support and assistance.

Regulation S-P

Broker-dealers, investment companies, and investment advisers must "adopt written policies and procedures that address administrative, technical, and physical safeguards for the protection of customer records and information." What this means is that members must provide a way for securing customers' non-public information. This includes things like Social Security numbers, bank account numbers, or any other personally identifiable financial information. Members must provide customers with a notice of their privacy policies. Members may disclose a customer's nonpublic information to unaffiliated third parties unless the customer opts out and chooses not to have their information shared. Members must make every effort to safeguard customers' information, including securing computers, encrypting emails, and so on. Broker-dealers must send customers a description of their privacy policies at the time the account is open and at least once a year thereafter.

Reporting requirements

Under FINRA Rule 4530, member firms must report specified events, including quarterly statistical and summary information regarding customer complaints, and copies of certain civil and criminal actions. Members must report promptly (no later than 30 days after the member knows or should've known about the event) if the member or associated person of the member

>> Has been found to have violated any securities-related or non-securities-related investment laws or standards of conduct by a U.S. or foreign regulatory organization.

>> Is the subject of a written customer complaint involving allegations of theft or misappropriation of funds or securities.

>> Is the subject of a written customer complaint involving allegations of forgery.

>> Has been named as a defendant or respondent in a proceeding brought by a U.S. or foreign regulatory body alleging a violation of rules.

>> Has been denied registration, suspended, expelled, or disciplined by a U.S. or foreign regulatory organization.

>> Is indicted, convicted of, or pleads guilty to any felony or certain misdemeanors in or outside of the U.S.

The preceding list includes firm reporting requirements under Rule 4530, but firms are required to report certain other events too. These include

>> Outside business activities (covered in the following section).

>> Private securities transactions, which are transactions outside the broker-dealer's normal business. For argument's sake, say that an associate of a firm has a client who wants to trade options, but their firm doesn't trade options because it doesn't have an options principal. In this case, with permission of their firm, they can accept the order from their client and do the trade through another firm.

>> Political contributions and consequences for exceeding dollar contribution thresholds. (See "Other violations" later in the chapter.)

>> Felonies, financial-related misdemeanors, liens, bankruptcies.

Outside business activities

While you're building your business and getting new clients, you may feel the need to make a few extra bucks working another job. If so, you must notify your brokerage firm in writing. However, you don't need to receive written permission to work the other job. Your member firm may reject or restrict your outside work if it feels there is a conflict of interest.

Accounts at other broker-dealers and financial institutions

Although you probably won't do this, persons associated with a member firm may open an account at another member firm (executing firm) with prior written permission from the employing firm. The associated person must also let the executing firm know that they are working for another member firm. Duplicate confirmations and statements must be sent to the employing firm if requested.

Trading by the Book When the Account Is Open

After you've opened a new account, you have to follow additional rules and regulations to keep working in the business. You need to know how to receive trade instructions and how to fill out an order ticket, as well as settlement and payment dates for different securities.

Filling out an order ticket

When you're working as a registered rep, completing documents such as order tickets will become second nature because you'll have them in front of you. When you're taking the Series 7, you don't have that luxury, but you still need to know the particulars about what to fill out.

Getting the particulars on paper (or in binary form)

When your customer places an order, you have to fill out an order ticket. Order tickets may be on paper or entered electronically. Regardless of how you enter the order, it needs to contain the following information:

>> The registered rep's identification number

>> The customer's account number

>> The customer's name or designation of the account

>> The description of the security (stocks, bonds, symbol, and so on)

>> The number of shares or bonds that are being purchased or sold

>> Whether the registered rep has discretionary authority over the account

>> Whether the customer is buying, selling long (selling securities that are owned), or selling short (selling borrowed securities — see Chapter 9)

- **»** For option tickets, whether the customer is buying or writing (selling), is covered or uncovered, and is opening or closing (see Chapter 12 for info on options)
- **»** Whether it's a market order, good-till-canceled (GTC) order, day order, and so on
- **»** Whether the trade is executed in a cash or margin account
- **»** Whether the trade was solicited or unsolicited
- **»** The time of the order
- **»** The execution price

Figure 16-1 shows you what standard paper order tickets may look like.

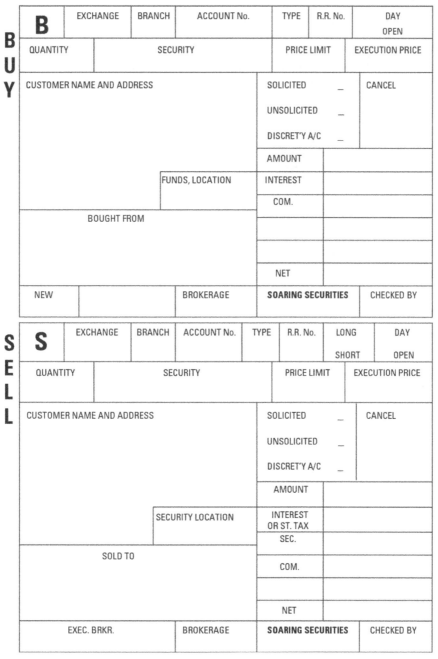

FIGURE 16-1: Buy and sell order tickets have spaces for the info you need to make a trade.

The customer's name or designation of the account cannot be changed unless authorized by a principal of the firm. If approved, the reason for the change must be documented in writing and kept on file.

Designating unsolicited trades

Normally, you'll be recommending securities in line with a customer's investment objectives. If, however, the customer requests a trade that you think is unsuitable, it's your duty to inform them about it. You don't have to reject the order (it's the customer's money, and you're in the business to generate commission). If the customer still wants to execute the trade, simply mark the order as *unsolicited*, which takes the responsibility off your shoulders.

A trip to the principal's office: Securing a signature

Principals are managers of a firm. All brokerage firms, no matter how small, must have at least one principal. When you open or trade an account, you have to bring the new account form or order ticket to a principal to sign. Principals need to approve all new accounts, all trades in accounts, and all advertisements and sales literature; they also handle all complaints (lucky break for you!). A principal doesn't have to approve a prospectus or your recommendations to your customers.

Although you'll generally bring an order ticket to a principal right after taking an order, the principal can sign the order ticket later in the day. If you're questioned about this on the Series 7 exam, you want to answer that the principal needs to approve the trade on the same day, not before or immediately after the trade.

Checking your calendar: Payment and settlement dates

Securities that investors purchase have different payment and settlement dates. Here's what you need to know:

>> **Trade date:** The day the trade is executed. An investor who buys a security owns the security as soon as the trade is executed, whether or not they have paid for the trade.

>> **Settlement date:** The day the issuer updates its records and the certificates are delivered to the buyer's brokerage firm.

>> **Payment date:** The day the buyer of the securities must pay for the trade.

Unless the question specifically asks you to follow FINRA or NYSE rules (which I doubt it will), assume the Fed regular way settlement and payment dates as they appear in Table 16-1. The FINRA and NYSE rules both require payment for securities to be made no later than the settlement date, but the Federal Reserve Board states that the payment date for corporate securities is five business days after the trade date.

Cash trades (which are same-day settlements) require payment for the securities and delivery of the securities on the same day as the trade date for all securities.

In certain cases, securities may not be able to be delivered as in the preceding chart. In these cases, the seller may specify that there's going to be a *delayed delivery*. This is also known as a *seller's option contract*. There can also be a *mutually agreed upon* date in which the buyer and seller agree on a delayed delivery date prior to or at the time of the transaction.

TABLE 16-1 Regular Way Settlement and Payment Dates

Type of Security	Settlement Date (in Business Days after the Trade Date)	Payment Date (in Business Days after the Trade Date)
Stocks, corporate bonds, and government agency securities	2 (T+2 — two business days after the trade date)	4
Municipal bonds	2 (T+2)	2
U.S. government bonds	1 (T+1)	1
Options	1 (T+1)	4

The *when, as, and if issued (when-issued transaction)* method of delivery is used for a securities issue that has been authorized and sold to investors before the certificates are ready for delivery. This method is typically used for stock splits, new issues of municipal bonds, and Treasury securities (U.S. government securities). The confirmation for when-issued securities must include a description of the security, the contract price or yield, and the trade date. The settlement date for when-issued securities can be any of the following:

» A date to be assigned

» Three business days after the securities are ready for delivery

» On the date determined by FINRA

Don't know (DK)

Occasionally, there might be a trade situation where there is some sort of discrepancy. Here are some examples: The purchasing dealer or selling dealer believed the trade was for a different number of shares. Or the trade was transacted for a different price, is not familiar with the trade at all, and so on. Sometimes, nefarious dealers will even DK a trade if the market goes in the wrong direction. DK notices are typically handled through the Automated Confirmation Transaction service (ACT), where each dealer submits their version of the trade.

Extensions

Remember, Regulation T requires that payment is due within two business days after regular way settlement for corporate securities (four business days after the trade date). In the event that a client needs an extension to pay for a trade, the purchaser's firm must request an extension from its designated examining authority (such as FINRA, NYSE, and so on). If the amount due is $1,000 or less, the broker-dealer may determine not to ask for an extension without violating Regulation T requirements. If the client cannot pay for the trade by the end of the extension time period, the broker-dealer may request another extension or sell the securities purchased (close-out transaction). If the broker-dealer decides to close out the position, the client's account will be frozen for 90 days, and the client will not be able to purchase or sell securities without having the proper amount of cash or securities in the broker-dealer's possession prior to the trade.

Confirming a trade

A *trade confirmation* (receipt of trade) is the document you send to a customer after a trade has taken place. You have to send out trade confirmations after each trade, at or before the completion of the transaction (the settlement date). Here's a list of information included in the confirmation:

» The customer's account number

» The registered rep's ID number

- » The trade date

- » Whether the customer bought (BOT), sold (SLD), or sold short

- » A description of the security purchased or sold along with its symbol

- » The number of shares of stock or the par value of bonds purchased or sold

- » The yield (if bonds) and type of yield (yield to maturity, yield to call, or current)

- » The Committee on Uniform Security Identification Procedures (CUSIP) number, a security ID number

- » The price of the security

- » The total amount paid or received, not including commission or any fees

- » The commission, which is added on purchases and subtracted on sales (if the broker-dealer purchased for or sold from its own inventory, the markdown or markup doesn't have to be disclosed)

- » The *net amount,* or the amount the customer paid or received after adding or subtracting the commission (if the investor purchased or sold bonds, the accrued interest is added or subtracted during this calculation)

- » Whether the trade was executed on a principal or agency basis (the capacity)

Note: Trade confirmations for money market funds (see Chapter 10) are not required, but certain transaction information should be included in the monthly account statement (such as purchases, sales, dividends, or distributions during the period; the date of the transaction; the identity, number and price of securities being purchased or sold; the total number of shares of such securities in the customer's account; and any remuneration [money] received or to be received in connection with the transaction).

You should recognize the items listed in this section are required for most securities trades, including municipal bonds. However, check out the "Confirmations" section in Chapter 8 for more specific rules relating to municipal securities confirmations. Trade confirmations must be sent to the client after each trade even if you have discretionary authority over the account. Confirmations may be sent to a third party, such as an investment adviser, with written consent of the client.

Although most securities are in book-entry form, the following section, "Meeting the requirements for good delivery" is currently covered on the Series 7 Exam. I assume that it will be removed at some point in the future.

Meeting the requirements for good delivery

In the securities industry, good delivery doesn't mean "in 30 minutes or it's free" (even the pizza delivery places don't promise that anymore). To constitute good delivery of certificates, the securities have to be in a certain form. The transfer agent is responsible for good delivery. Here are the general requirements:

- » They must be in good physical condition (not mutilated). Mutilated certificates must be validated by a transfer agent or other acceptable official of the issuer to be considered good delivery. Mutilated coupons must be endorsed by the issuer or commercial bank to be considered good delivery.

>> They must be endorsed by the owner whose name is registered on the certificate(s). Certificates registered in more than one name must be endorsed by all owners. As an alternative to signing on the back of the certificate(s), owners may sign a *stock or bond power.* A stock or bond power (security power) is a legal document that investors can sign instead of signing on the back of all certificates. The stock or bond power is used for the investors to transfer ownership to another person. Stock or bond powers are often easier for people to sign and also add another degree of safety because they can be sent separately from the unsigned certificates. Signing one stock or bond power represents a signature of all like securities (that is, all ABC common stock, all DEF 7% corporate bonds maturing on the same date, and so on). However, if the investor is selling more than one security, they must sign a stock or bond power for each one.

>> All customer signatures must be guaranteed by a notary or some other person acceptable to the transfer agent. The signature must exactly match the name registered on the face of the security.

>> For certificates in the names of a fiduciary, the fiduciary must provide a copy of the trust agreement or court appointment. For corporate accounts, the person signing must provide a copy of the corporate resolution giving them the authority to execute trades for the corporation.

>> For securities in the name of a deceased person, the executor or administrator of the deceased person's estate must endorse the certificate or provide a stock or bond power and have the securities transferred to the name of the estate prior to selling.

>> The exact number of shares or bonds must be delivered. Overdeliveries or underdeliveries are not good delivery.

>> The correct denomination of the certificates must be delivered.

>> If the bonds being traded have been called, they must be identified as being called when traded.

>> For municipal securities, the legal opinion must be attached unless marked "ex-legal."

And here are the requirements for good delivery of specific securities:

>> **Bearer (coupon) bonds:** These unregistered bonds must be in $1,000 or $5,000 denominations only.

REMEMBER

For a bearer bond to be in good delivery form, it must be delivered with all unpaid coupons (representing interest payments) attached in proper order. See Chapter 7 for more info on bonds.

>> **Fully registered bonds:** These bonds must be in multiples of $1,000 par value with a maximum par value on one certificate of $100,000.

>> **Stock:** Because the most easily traded unit of stock is 100 shares (a round lot), stock certificates must be in denominations of one of the following:

- Multiples of 100 shares — 100, 200, 300, 400, and so on

- Divisors of 100 shares — 1, 2, 4, 5, 10, 20, 25, 50, or 100

- Units that add up to 100 shares — 40 shares + 60 shares, 91 + 9, 80 + 15 + 5, and so on

REMEMBER

Odd lot trades (trades of less than 100 shares) or odd lot portions of orders are exempt from the good delivery rule.

The following question tests your ability to answer a good delivery question.

All of the following are considered good delivery for a 560-share order EXCEPT

(A) two 200-share certificates, one 100-share certificate, and one 60-share certificate

(B) 56 10-share certificates

(C) six 60-share certificates, five 30-share certificates, and five 10-share certificates

(D) one 400-share certificate and two 80-share certificates

The correct answer is Choice (D). Choice (A) is good because the 200-share certificates and 100-share certificates are multiples of 100 shares, and the 60-share trade (odd lot portion) is exempt. Choice (B) is good because 10 is a divisor of 100 (it goes into 100 evenly). Choice (C) is good because 60 + 30 + 10 adds up to 100, and the extra 60-share certificate is exempt because it's an odd lot portion. However, Choice (D) is bad delivery because even though the 400-share certificate is okay, the two 80-share certificates aren't good because they don't add up to 100.

Always look at the shares first to determine whether you have good delivery. I see a lot of students look at the number of certificates before they check the number of shares per certificate. The Series 7 designers want to know more about your understanding of concepts than your multiplication and addition skills, so you probably won't have to figure out the total number of shares in each answer choice — they should all add up to the number of shares in the order (in the preceding example, 560).

Rejection and reclamation

If the securities being delivered are not in good delivery form, they may be *rejected*, meaning that the buyer does not accept delivery. In the event that the buyer accepts the delivery and then finds out the securities are not in good delivery form, the order is *reclaimed*. Regardless of whether the trade was rejected or reclaimed, the seller is still obligated to sell the securities.

Fail to deliver

If the securities delivered are not in good delivery form, it is considered a *fail to deliver*. While a fail to deliver exists, the payment will not be sent to the seller. In this case, the purchasing broker-dealer may buy the securities from another source and charge the seller for any losses incurred. If a customer fails to deliver securities sold to satisfy the sale, the seller's firm must buy the securities after ten business days from the settlement date.

Due bills

As a reminder, the ex-dividend date (ex-date) is one business day before the record date. So, if an investor purchases stock that is paying a dividend prior to the ex-dividend date, they are entitled to the dividend. If the investor purchases the stock on the ex-dividend date or after, they are not entitled to the dividend. If somehow the investor who purchased the stock prior to the ex-dividend date does not receive the dividend, the purchaser's firm will send a *due bill* to the seller's firm reminding it to remit the dividend.

Book entry

Book entry (also known as "paperless securities," "digital securities," and "electronic securities") is a form of security where the investor does not receive the actual certificate. Many securities are held in book-entry form instead of physical form, which makes trading much easier. In this case, there is no transfer of actual certificates; when a trade takes place, investors receive a receipt of ownership. The Direct Registration System (DRS) allows investors to hold their securities in book-entry form with the issuer (on the issuer's records). In this case, investors receive account statements from the transfer agent or issuer. Interest and/or dividend payments, proxies, annual reports, and so on, are mailed directly to the investor from the issuer or transfer agent.

Transfer agent

The transfer agent is a person or corporation who records the names and holdings of security owners. The transfer agent *cancels old* certificates and *prints new certificates* for each trade. The transfer agent *sends* items (new certificates, dividends, proxies, and so on) to investors and is *responsible* for good delivery.

Following up with account statements

An *account statement* gives the customer information about security and money holdings as well as any transactions made in their account since the previous account statement, along with the market value at the time the statement was issued. Customers are supposed to receive account statements on a regular basis. The timing for issuing account statements should be pretty easy for you to remember.

>> **Active or inactive accounts:** Whether the securities in the account are actively traded or not traded, an account statement must be sent out at least quarterly (every three months). If the customer isn't holding any cash or securities positions at the end of the quarter, or if the account is set up solely on a DVP/RVP (Delivery vs. Payment / Receive vs. Payment) basis, no account statement needs to be sent out. In addition, a customer may consent in writing to suspend receiving account statements, which may be reinstated at any time at the request of the customer.

>> **Mutual funds:** No matter how much (or little) trading was done, a customer needs to receive an account statement semiannually (every six months).

The account statement must contain at least a description of all the client's security positions, any cash balance, and all account activity since the previous account statement.

Account activity includes purchases or sales, interest credited to or debited to the account, any miscellaneous charges or credits to the account, dividend payments received, any transfers of securities, and so on.

REMEMBER

Penny stocks (see Chapter 6) are risky securities, and it is often difficult for customers to find out current prices for certain penny stocks. Therefore, customers who own penny stocks must receive account statements *monthly* whether a penny stock trade was made during the month or not.

Keeping your dividend dates straight

When customers are purchasing securities of a company that's in the process of declaring or paying a dividend, you need to be able to tell those customers whether they're entitled to receive the dividend. Because stock transactions settle in two business days (T+2), the customers are entitled to the dividend if they purchase the securities at least two days prior to the *record date*. Here's a list of the four need-to-know dates for the Series 7 exam:

>> **Declaration date:** The day that the corporation officially announces that a dividend will be paid to shareholders. On the declaration date, the dividend amount, the record date, and the payment date will be announced.

REMEMBER

>> **Ex-dividend date (ex-date):** The first day that the stock trades without dividends. An investor purchasing the stock on the ex-dividend date isn't entitled to receive the dividend; because stock transactions take two business days to settle, the ex-dividend date is automatically one business day before the record date.

The ex-dividend date is the day that the price of the stock is reduced by the dividend amount. (Chapter 6 tells you more about dividends and related calculations.) When a stock is purchased ex-dividend (on or after the ex-dividend date), the seller is entitled to the dividend, not the buyer. Because the dividend may not be paid for up to a month, the buyer is required to sign a *due bill* indicating that the dividend belongs to the seller. In the case of a cash dividend, the due bill is in the form of a *due bill check*, which is payable on the date the dividend is paid by the issuer. In addition, if an investor buys a stock on time to receive a dividend but for some reason will not receive the certificates on time (by the record date), the seller must send a *due bill* to the buyer. A due bill states that the buyer is entitled to the rights of ownership even though they're not yet receiving the certificates.

>> **Record date:** The day the corporation inspects its records to see who gets the dividend. To receive the dividend, the investor must be listed as a stockholder in company records.

>> **Payment (payable) date:** The day that the corporation pays the dividend to eligible stockholders.

As you can see from the diagram, the buyer receives the dividend if they purchased the stock before the ex-dividend date. If the stock is purchased on or after the ex-dividend date, the seller receives the dividend.

© John Wiley & Sons, Inc.

TIP

To help you remember the sequence of dates, use the phrase *Don't Eat Rubber Pickles.* I know it sounds ridiculous, but the more ridiculous, the easier it is to remember.

REMEMBER

The board of directors must announce three dates: the declaration date, the record date, and the payment date. The ex-dividend date doesn't need to be announced because it's automatically one business day before the record date. However, mutual funds have to announce all four dates because they may set their ex-dividend date at any time (even on the record date).

The following question tests your ability to answer a dividend question.

EXAMPLE

Wedgie Corp. has just announced a $0.50 cash dividend. If the record date is Tuesday, March 9, when is the last day an investor can purchase the stock and receive the dividend?

(A) March 4

(B) March 5

(C) March 7

(D) March 8

The answer you're looking for is Choice (B). In order for an investor to purchase the stock and receive a previously declared dividend, they must purchase the stock at least one business day before the ex-dividend date. This question is a little more difficult because you have a weekend to take into consideration.

The ex-dividend date is March 8, which is one business day prior to the record date. This investor has to buy the stock before the ex-dividend date in order to receive the dividend, so they have to buy it March 5 or before (because the 6th and 7th are Saturday and Sunday). The last day an investor can purchase the stock and receive the dividend is March 5.

© John Wiley & Sons, Inc.

REMEMBER

If a stock is sold short (if the investor is selling a borrowed security), the lender of the stock sold short is entitled to receive the dividend. (See Chapter 9 for details on margin accounts.) Also, the trades in the example problems are regular way settlement (two business days after the trade date); remember that cash transactions settle on the same day as the trade date. In the case of dividends, if an investor purchases stock for cash, they receive the dividend if they purchase the stock anytime up to and including the record date.

Handling complaints

It's bound to happen sooner or later, no matter how awesome you are as a registered rep: One of your customers is going to complain about something (like unauthorized trades, guarantees, and so on). Complaints aren't considered official unless they're in writing. If necessary, FINRA wants you to follow the proper procedure for handling complaints. The following sections cover formal and informal proceedings.

Code of procedure (litigation)

The *code of procedure* is FINRA's formal procedure for handling securities-related complaints between public customers and members of the securities industry (broker-dealers, registered reps, clearing corporations, and so on). The public customer has the choice of resolving the complaint via the formal code of procedure or the informal code of arbitration (see the next section). All complaints going through code of procedure must be responded to by the firm within 25 days after receipt of the customer complaint.

In the code of procedure, the District Business Conduct Committee (DBCC) has the first jurisdiction over complaints. If the customer or member isn't satisfied with the results, they can appeal the decision to the FINRA Board of Governors. Decisions are appealable all the way to the Supreme Court.

Code of arbitration

The *code of arbitration* is an informal hearing (heard by two or three arbiters) that's primarily conducted for disputes between members of FINRA. Members include not only broker-dealers but also individuals working for member firms.

For example, if you (a registered rep) have a dispute with the broker-dealer that you're working for, you can take the broker-dealer to arbitration. If a customer has a complaint against a broker-dealer or registered rep, the customer has the choice of going through code of procedure (see the preceding section) or code of arbitration, unless the customer has given prior written consent (usually by way of the new account form) stating that they will settle disputes only through arbitration.

REMEMBER

The decisions in arbitration are binding and non-appealable, so they're less costly than court action. If a member firm or person associated with that member firm fails to comply with the terms of the arbitration (in the case of a loss) within 15 days of notification, FINRA reserves the right to suspend or cancel the firm's or person's membership.

Mediation

If an investor and/or broker-dealer are looking for a more informal way to handle disputes, they may voluntarily decide to go to mediation. Disputes settled through mediation are heard by an independent third party. Unlike arbitration, mediation is nonbinding.

REMEMBER

Not all complaints are going to end up going to arbitration, mediation, or through the court system. Sometimes, the complaints are ones of miscommunication, ones in which the customer made a mistake, a customer feels they were charged too much commission, and so on. A lot of these complaints can be handled internally without the need for progression. However, all complaints need to be kept on file along with any action taken.

Transferring accounts

If a customer wants to transfer an account, in whole or part, from one broker-dealer (the "carrying member") to another (the "receiving member"), the customer has to fill out and sign (a provable electronic signature is fine) a Transfer Initiation Form (TIF) form with the receiving member listing the securities held at the carrying member firm. Transfer instructions are then sent from the receiving member to the carrying member. Account transfers are often executed through the ACATS (Automated Customer Account Transfer Service). For members to use the ACATS service, they have to be members of the National Securities Clearing Corporation (NSCC).

Upon receipt from the customer of an authorized broker-to-broker transfer instruction form (TIF), the receiving member must immediately submit the instructions to the carrying member (done through ACATS); the carrying broker-dealer has *one business day* to either validate or take exception (for an invalid account number, wrong Social Security number, and so on) to the transfer instructions sent from the receiving member. Any exceptions must be quickly rectified by the carrying member and receiving member. After the carrying member validates the account, that dealer has *three business days* to transfer the account to the receiving member.

REMEMBER

Most account transfers are executed using the ACAT service. However, customers may, for whatever reason, choose to have the firms not use the ACAT service. Whether the ACAT service is used or not, both firms must expedite all account transfers.

Educational communication related to recruitment practices and account transfers

As you might expect, quite often when a registered rep leaves one broker-dealer to go to work at another, some of the rep's clients might decide to move their accounts too (on their own or with a little coaxing). Well, FINRA has educational communication rules that must be followed relating to client recruitment practices and account transfers.

Regardless of whether the registered rep initiates the contact with their clients or they decide to transfer the accounts to the rep's new broker-dealer, the new broker-dealer must provide the client with educational material relating to account transfers prepared by FINRA in either paper or electronic form (emailed, a hyperlink in an email, and so on).

There are some rules regarding the means and timing of delivery of the educational communications:

>> If the first contact is initiated by the client or rep in writing, the educational material must be delivered by the rep or rep's new firm to the client with their initial contact. If the contact is in electronic format, a hyperlink directly to the educational communications will suffice.

>> If the first contact is oral, the registered rep or their firm must notify the client that they will receive an educational communication that they should read prior to deciding whether to transfer assets. The educational communication must be sent within three business days of the first contact or on the day that any other documentation may have been sent to the client regarding transferring assets, whichever is sooner.

>> If a former client attempts to transfer assets to the rep's new firm without an initial contact, either by the client or rep, the new firm must deliver the educational communication to the client with the transfer approval documentation.

Note: The rules for delivery requirement of educational communications applies for a period of three months following the date the registered rep begins employment at the new firm.

Internal transfers

Occasionally, a client may want to transfer securities to another individual's account (spouse, son, daughter, and so on). In this case, all parties involved in the account transfer must approve, and a stock transfer form must be completed.

Committing Other Important Rules to Memory

Brokers and investors must follow numerous rules in order to keep themselves from facing fines or worse. In this section, I list a few of the more important rules.

The Telephone Consumer Protection Act of 1991 (Telephone Act of 1991)

To make sure that certain standards are used when calling potential customers (such as not calling them at midnight), the Telephone Act of 1991 was created. When you're dealing with *potential customers* on the phone, you need to know these rules:

>> You can't make calls before 8 a.m. or after 9 p.m. local time of the potential customer.

>> You have to give your name, company name, company address, and phone number.

>> If you get a potential customer who's tired of being called, you should place that person on a *do not call list.* Each firm must maintain its own do not call list and have the U.S. Government's National Do Not Call List available.

>> You may not send unsolicited ads by fax machine.

The Telephone Act of 1991 does not apply to existing customers (customers who have executed a trade or had a security in the firm's account in the previous 18 months) or calls from nonprofit organizations. Existing customers who want to be placed on the "do not call" list after opening an account cannot be solicited but can be updated on the status of their account.

The 5 percent markup policy

The 5 percent policy (FINRA 5 Percent Markup Policy) is more of a guideline than a rule. The policy was enacted to make sure that investors receive fair treatment and aren't charged excessively for broker-dealer services in the over-the-counter (OTC) market. The guideline says that brokerage firms shouldn't charge commissions, markups, or markdowns of more than 5 percent for standard trades.

The following trades are subject to the 5 percent markup policy:

>> **Principal (dealer) transactions:** A firm buys securities for or sells securities from its own inventory and charges a markdown or markup.

>> **Agency (broker) transactions:** A firm acts as a middleperson (broker) and charges a commission.

>> **Riskless (simultaneous) transactions:** A firm buys a security for its own inventory for immediate resale to the customer (riskless to the firm). The idea is that it is a transaction that is riskless to the dealer because they already had an order to fill. In this case, the firm is buying the security at a particular price and selling it to the customer at the same price plus a markup. The firm must disclose its capacity in the transaction. In this case, the markup charged must be disclosed.

If the securities transaction was executed on a *net* basis (one in which the firm purchased the security and sold it to a customer at a different price [not including a markup]), the member must provide disclosure and obtain consent from the customer.

>> **Proceeds transactions:** A firm sells a security and uses the money to immediately buy another security. You must treat this transaction as one trade (you can't charge on the way out and on the way in).

The 5 percent markup policy covers over-the-counter trades of outstanding (not new securities, which require a prospectus), nonexempt securities with public customers. If securities are exempt from SEC registration, such as municipal bonds, they're exempt from the 5 percent policy. Additionally, if a dealer pays $20 per share to have a security in inventory (dealer cost) and the market price is $8 per share, the dealer can't charge customers $20 per share so that it doesn't take a loss.

Under extenuating circumstances, the brokerage firm may charge more. Justifiable reasons for charging more (or less) than 5 percent include

>> Experiencing difficulty buying or selling the security because the market price is too low or too high

>> Handling a small trade — for example, if a customer placed an order for $100 worth of securities, you'd lose your shirt if you charged only 5 percent ($5); in this case, you wouldn't be out of line if you charged 100 percent (by the same token, if a customer purchased $1 million worth of securities, 5 percent [$50,000] would be considered excessive)

>> Encountering difficulty locating and purchasing a specific security

>> Incurring additional expenses involved in executing the trade

>> Dealing with odd lot trades (for details, see "Meeting the requirements for good delivery," earlier in this chapter)

>> Trading non-liquid securities

>> Executing transactions on foreign markets

Other violations

REMEMBER

You need to be aware of some violations not only for the Series 7 exam but also so you stay out of trouble. Some of the violations are more connected with broker-dealers, some with registered reps, and some with investment advisers:

>> **Commingling of funds:** Combining a customer's fully paid and margined securities or combining a firm's securities with customer securities.

>> **Interpositioning:** Having two securities dealers act as agents for the same exact trade so that two commissions are earned on one trade.

>> **Giving (or receiving) gifts:** Giving or receiving a gift of more than $100 per customer per year. Business expenses (lunch, dinner, hotel rooms, and so on) are exempt from this MSRB rule (see "Self-regulatory organizations," earlier in this chapter).

>> **Making political contributions (paying to play):** Under the Investment Advisers Act of 1940, investment advisers are prohibited from providing investment advisory services for a fee to a government client for two years after a contribution is made. This rule applies not only to the adviser, executives, and employees making contributions to certain elected officials, but also to candidates who may later be elected. In addition, investment advisers are prohibited from soliciting contributions for elected officials or candidates if the investment adviser is seeking or providing government business.

>> **Freeriding:** Allowing a customer to buy securities and immediately resell the securities without paying for the purchase.

>> **Backing away:** Failure on the part of a securities dealer to honor a firm quote.

>> **Churning:** A violation whereby a registered rep excessively trades a customer's account for the sole purpose of generating commission.

>> **Matching orders:** Illegally manipulating the price of a security to make the trading volume appear larger than it really is, such as two brokerage firms working in concert by trading the same security back and forth.

>> **Painting the tape:** Creating the illusion of trading activity due to misleading reports on the consolidated tape — for example, reporting a trade of 10,000 shares of stock as two separate trades for 5,000 shares each.

>> **Frontrunning:** A violation in which a registered rep executes a trade for themself, their firm, or a discretionary account based on knowledge of a block trade (10,000 shares or more) before the trade is reported on the ticker tape.

>> **Prearranging trades:** A prearranged trade is an illegal agreement between a registered rep and a customer to buy back a security at a fixed price.

>> **Marking the close/marking the open:** Executing a series of trades within minutes of the open or close of the market to manipulate the price of a security.

>> **Paying the media:** A violation in which brokerage firms or affiliated persons pay an employee of the media to affect the price of a security; for example, paying a TV stock expert to recommend a security that the firm has in its inventory.

>> **Spreading market rumors:** Members are prohibited from spreading false market rumors that may prompt others to either buy or sell a security. This is another form of market manipulation.

>> **Paying for referrals:** Members or persons associated with a member (for example, registered reps) are prohibited from paying cash or noncash compensation to any person except those registered with the member firm or other FINRA members. A violation occurs in the event that compensation is paid to a nonmember for locating, introducing, or referring a client.

Regulation FD

The "FD" in Regulation FD stands for *fair disclosure*. Regulation FD is an SEC rule that covers the issuer releasing material, nonpublic information. Typically, issuers will want to release certain nonpublic information to certain individuals or entities such as securities market professionals, analysts, holders of the issuer's securities, and so on. Regulation FD requires the issuer to make that information available to the public at the same time to keep persons from being able to trade on insider information. The aim of Regulation FD is to promote full and fair disclosure.

Record keeping

As you can imagine, member firms must keep certain records on file. Depending on which records they are, there are certain SEC retention requirements. The records do not necessarily need to be kept in written format; they can be kept digitally as long as they are in a non-erasable format.

Corporate or partnership documents of the member firm must be kept for the *lifetime* of the firm. The documents must contain the list of officers, partners, and/or directors of the firm. Additionally, U-4 forms of all active employees must be kept as long as the firm is in business.

The following records must be kept for a *minimum of six years:*

>> **Blotters:** Records of all trades executed by the brokerage firm for clients and for their own inventory.

>> **Ledgers:** Customer account statements, which include trade settlement dates, interest and dividends received, securities borrowed and loaned, moneys borrowed and loaned, all short and long positions, and so on.

>> **General ledgers:** A firm's financial statements, which must be updated monthly. A general ledger includes the firm's assets, liabilities, and net worth.

>> **Position record:** A record of all the securities owned by the firm and its location.

>> **Account record:** Terms and conditions of margin accounts and cash accounts.

>> **Closed accounts:** Firms must keep records of customers who've closed accounts for a minimum of six years after the account has been closed.

Note: Like FINRA rules, MSRB rules require blotters, ledgers, closed accounts, and position records to be kept for six years. However, MSRB also requires records relating to the underwriting of municipal securities, complaints (FINRA, four years), supervisory records, and gift records to be kept for six years.

The following records must be kept for a *minimum of three years:*

>> U-4 forms, U-5 forms, and fingerprints of former employees

>> Trade confirmations

>> Order tickets

>> Advertisements

>> Sales literature

>> Dividends and interest received in each account

>> Powers of attorney

>> Speeches/public appearances

>> Compliance procedure manuals

>> Gifts

>> Compensation records of associates

Note: MSRB rules require members to maintain certain records for *four years.* These include subsidiary ledgers, trades, confirmations, terms and conditions of customer accounts, checkbooks and cancelled checks, delivery of official statements, public communications, and so on.

REMEMBER

Whether the records have to be kept for three years, six years, or whatever, they have to be easily accessible for two years (FINRA and MSRB).

As you can imagine, there are strict penalties for falsification, improper maintenance, or improper retention of records. FINRA reserves the right to inspect the books, records, and accounts of all member firms and their associates. All regulatory requests by FINRA for specified books, records, or accounts should be supplied by the member firm *promptly.*

Negotiable instruments drawn from a customer's account

Members shall not submit a client's payment of a check, draft, or other form of negotiable paper drawn on a client's checking account, savings account, or similar type of account without the client's expressed written authorization. If, however, a client sends you a check with their signature on it, that is considered written authorization. In the case where a client sets up where payment for trades, services, and so on, can be withdrawn from one of their accounts, you need to keep their written authorization on file for a period of three years following the date the authorization expires.

Disclosure of control relationships

Any member controlled by or that has controlling interest in the issuer of a security must disclose that fact to a customer prior to entering into a contract with the customer who wants to purchase or sell the security. If the disclosure is not made in writing prior to the transaction, it must be sent to the customer at or prior to the completion of the transaction.

Customer protection rule

Under the Securities Exchange Act of 1934's Customer Protection Rule (Rule 15c3-3), broker-dealers must segregate customer securities and cash from the broker-dealer's securities and cash. Quite often, broker-dealers use their own securities and/or cash to execute trades. By forcing broker-dealers to segregate customers' cash and securities from the broker-dealer's transactions, it will increase the likelihood that customers' securities and cash will remain readily available to return to customers in the event of broker-dealer failure.

Networking arrangements

Members who conduct broker-dealer business on the premises of a financial institution shall

» Be clearly identified as the person conducting the broker-dealer services and shall distinguish its services from the services of the financial institution.

» Conduct its business in an area that displays the member's name.

» If possible, conduct its broker-dealer services in a location that is separate from the financial institution's retail deposit-taking activity.

» At the time of opening a customer's account, disclose in writing that the services are being provided by the broker-dealer, not the financial institution, as well as other disclosures such as the securities are not FDIC insured, the deposits are not guaranteed by the financial institution, the account is subject to investment risk, and so on.

Uniform Practice Code (UPC)

All over-the-counter securities transactions by members, except for transactions involving exempt securities, are subject to the UPC. The UPC was designed to provide a set of standards for members regarding things like trade terms, delivery of securities, payments, dividends, rights, interest, assignments, computation of interest, due bills, transfer fees, "when, as and if issued" trading, and so on. It was designed to facilitate trading and to minimize the number of disputes between member firms.

Supervision

Each member firm must establish and maintain a system to supervise each associated person in order to make sure all those persons maintain compliance with securities laws and regulations. The member firm is responsible for maintaining proper supervision of its employees. The supervision system must be written and the firm must have appropriately qualified registered principals to carry out the supervision of employees. The written procedures must also spell out procedures for reviewing the investment banking and securities business of the firm, reviewing correspondence and internal communications, reviewing customer complaints, and so on.

Testing Your Knowledge

Though I tried to make this chapter as easy as possible for you, I'm sure you found it painful. Well, here are 25 questions to test your knowledge. Read the questions carefully so that you don't make any careless mistakes.

1. Which of the following are self-regulatory organizations?

    I. FINRA

    II. MSRB

    III. SEC

    IV. NYSE

    (A) II and IV

    (B) I, II, and III

    (C) I, II, and IV

    (D) I, II, III, and IV

2. AylDec Corporation would like to open a cash account at Lightning Broker-Dealer. In order for AylDec to open the account, it would need to send Lightning a copy of its

    (A) corporate charter

    (B) corporate resolution

    (C) both (A) and (B)

    (D) neither (A) nor (B)

3. A husband and wife open up an account as joint with tenants in common. If the husband dies, what must be done with his portion of the account?

    (A) The entire account is transferred to the wife

    (B) The husband's portion of the account is transferred to his estate

    (C) The account is divided equally between the wife and the husband's estate regardless of the contribution of each

    (D) None of the above

4. Which of the following are TRUE about arbitration?

    I. Members may take non-members to arbitration

    II. Non-members may take members to arbitration

    III. Members may take members to arbitration

    IV. Decisions are final and binding

    (A) I and II

    (B) I and III

    (C) II, III, and IV

    (D) I, II, III, and IV

5. What is the settlement date for a corporate bond transaction?

   (A) 1 business day after the trade date

   (B) 2 business days after the trade date

   (C) 3 business days after the trade date

   (D) 10 business days after the trade date

6. Matching orders is

   (A) combining fully paid and margined securities for use as collateral

   (B) the illegal manipulation of a security

   (C) bringing in a third party to execute a trade

   (D) buying securities with no intention of paying for the trade

7. Bearer bonds must be delivered in denominations of

   I. $1,000

   II. $5,000

   III. $10,000

   IV. $50,000

   (A) I or II

   (B) I or III

   (C) II only

   (D) I, II, III, or IV

8. Corporate and partnership documents must be kept by a brokerage firm for

   (A) a minimum of 2 years

   (B) a minimum of 3 years

   (C) a minimum of 6 years

   (D) the lifetime of the firm

9. The return of securities previously accepted for delivery is called

   (A) a buy-in

   (B) a sell-out

   (C) reclamation

   (D) rejection

10. What is the settlement date for U.S. government bond transactions?

    (A) 1 business day after the trade date

    (B) 2 business days after the trade date

    (C) 3 business days after the trade date

    (D) The same day as the trade date

11. Alyssa H. is interested in purchasing 1,000 shares of DIM Corp. common stock. As her registered rep, you feel that the transaction is unsuitable for her. You may still take the order from her if

    (A) you obtain written approval from a principal

    (B) instructed by Alyssa to do so

    (C) you obtain written power of attorney from Alyssa

    (D) you get prior approval from FINRA

12. Investors are allowed to maintain stock or bond certificates in book entry form instead of receiving the actual certificates through

    (A) DRS

    (B) SIPC

    (C) NAC

    (D) DVP

13. Which TWO of the following are TRUE regarding a power of attorney?

    I. A durable power of attorney cancels upon mental incompetence or death of the investor

    II. A durable power of attorney only cancels upon death of the investor

    III. A regular power of attorney cancels upon mental incompetence or death of the investor

    IV. A regular power of attorney only cancels upon the death of the investor

    (A) I and III

    (B) I and IV

    (C) II and III

    (D) II and IV

14. All of the following must be included on a stock order ticket EXCEPT

    (A) the time of the order

    (B) the amount of shares

    (C) if the trade was unsolicited

    (D) the customer's signature

15. Mutual funds must send out account statements to investors at least

    (A) monthly

    (B) quarterly

    (C) semiannually

    (D) annually

16. Which of the following are subject to the FINRA 5 percent markup policy?

    I. Principal transactions

    II. Agency transactions

    III. Riskless transactions

    IV. Proceeds transactions

    (A) I and III

    (B) II, III, and IV

    (C) I, III, and IV

    (D) I, II, III, and IV

17. The ex-dividend date is _____ business day(s) before the record date.

    (A) One
    (B) Two
    (C) Three
    (D) Five

18. Broker-dealers, investment companies, and investment advisers must have written policies designed to protect customers' records and information. This falls under:

    (A) Regulation S-P
    (B) Regulation D
    (C) Regulation M
    (D) Regulation T

19. Melste Corp. has just announced a 20-cent dividend to shareholders of record. If the record date is Friday, April 12th, when is the first day an investor can purchase the stock and not receive the dividend?

    (A) Wednesday, April 10th
    (B) Thursday, April 11th
    (C) Friday, April 12th
    (D) Monday, April 15th

20. A violation in which a registered rep excessively trades a customer's account for the sole purpose of generating commissions is known as

    (A) excessive trading
    (B) frontrunning
    (C) trading ahead
    (D) churning

21. According to FINRA rules, complaints must be maintained on records of brokerage firms for at least

    (A) 2 years
    (B) 3 years
    (C) 4 years
    (D) 6 years

22. According to FINRA rules, which TWO of the following are TRUE about ACATs?

    I. When ACAT notices are received, firms have 1 business day to verify the customer's instructions
    II. When ACAT notices are received, firms have 3 business days to verify the customer's instructions
    III. Assets must be transferred within 3 business days after verification
    IV. Assets must be transferred within 4 business days after verification

    (A) I and III
    (B) I and IV
    (C) II and III
    (D) II and IV

23. What is the minimum amount of assets an investor must have to establish a prime brokerage account?

   (A) $100,000

   (B) $500,000

   (C) $1,000,000

   (D) $10,000,000

24. According to FINRA rules, what is the maximum amount of retail persons a brokerage firm may send promotions to in a 30-day period for the promotions to be considered correspondence?

   (A) 1

   (B) 10

   (C) 25

   (D) Unlimited

25. While starting your new career, you decide you want to moonlight as a bartender to help make ends meet. Who must be notified?

   I. Your brokerage firm

   II. FINRA

   III. The SEC

   (A) I only

   (B) I and II

   (C) I, II, and III

   (D) None of the above

Answers and Explanations

Congratulations if you did well on this one. Because there are 25 questions, each one is worth 4 points.

1. **C.** The SEC is a government agency. FINRA, MSRB, and the NYSE are self-regulatory organizations (SROs). SROs are unaffiliated with the government.

2. **B.** For a corporation to open a cash account at a broker-dealer, the broker-dealer would need to receive a copy of the corporation's resolution. The corporate resolution lets the broker-dealer know who has trading authority over the account. If a corporation wants to open a margin account, the broker-dealer would need to also receive a copy of the corporation's charter (bylaws), which would let them know that trading on margin is spelled out in the corporation's rules.

3. **B.** Typically a married couple open a joint with survivor account. However, in this case, the husband and wife opened a joint account with tenants in common. So, if one partner dies, their portion of the account is transferred to their estate.

4. **C.** Unless the customer signed an arbitration agreement (which you can't assume) when opening the account, the non-member decides whether a dispute goes to arbitration. So, non-members may take members to arbitration, and members may take members to arbitration, but members may *not* take non-members to arbitration. Unlike code of procedure, arbitration decisions are binding and non-appealable.

5. **B.** The settlement date for corporate stock and bond transactions is two business days after the trade date (T+2).

6. **B.** Matching orders is the trading of securities back and forth between two entities without really changing ownership. Matching orders is the illegal manipulation of a security because it makes investors believe there's a larger amount of trading on a particular security than there really is.

7. **A.** Bearer bonds must be in denominations of $1,000 or $5,000 per certificate.

8. **D.** All corporate and partnership documents must be kept for the lifetime of the firm.

9. **C.** All securities traded must be in good delivery form. In the event that a purchaser accepts securities for delivery and later finds out that they weren't in good delivery form, they'll return them and expect the delivery of new securities. This process is known as reclamation.

10. **A.** The settlement date for U.S. government bonds is one business day after the trade date (T+1).

11. **B.** If a registered rep believes a transaction is unsuitable for a customer, the registered rep may still enter the transaction if the customer says the order should be entered. In this case, the registered rep would take the order and mark the transaction unsolicited.

12. **A.** The DRS (Direct Registration System) allows investors to maintain certificates in book entry form rather than receiving physical delivery of certificates.

13. **C.** A durable power of attorney only cancels upon the death of an investor. A regular power of attorney cancels upon the death or mental incompetence of the investor.

14. **D.** The customer's signature is not required on order tickets. However, the signature of the rep who took the order and a principal must sign. Remember, most of the orders you'll be getting will be through phone calls, so the customer wouldn't be there to sign the order ticket.

15. **C.** Mutual funds must send investors account statements at least semiannually.

16. **D.** All of the choices listed are subject to the FINRA 5-percent markup policy (or 5-percent policy). This means that under normal circumstances, where you have an average-sized trade and you don't have to jump through hoops to execute the transaction, you shouldn't charge more than 5 percent to execute the trade. Now certainly, if the trade is extremely small, you would be able to charge a higher percentage so that your firm doesn't lose money. Also, if a trade is extremely large, 5 percent would be considered excessive.

17. **A.** The ex-dividend date is the first day that the purchaser of a stock will not receive a previously declared dividend. The ex-dividend date is one business day before the record date. As a reminder, Saturday and Sunday are not considered business days. So, if the record date was on Monday, the ex-dividend date would be on the previous Friday.

18. **A.** Under Regulation S-P, all broker-dealers, investment companies, and investment advisers must have written policies to protect customers' records and private information. This would include things like social security numbers, bank account numbers, and so on.

19. **B.** The first day the stock trades without the dividend is on the ex-dividend date. The ex-dividend date is one business day before the record date. In this case, the answer is Thursday, April 11.

20. **D.** Churning is a violation where a registered rep promotes excessive trading in a customer's account for the sole purpose of generating commissions.

21. **C.** According to FINRA rules, complaints must be maintained by brokerage firms on their records for at least four years. Under MSRB rules, complaints must be kept for a minimum of six years.

22. **A.** ACATs are account transfers from one brokerage firm to another. When a firm receives an ACAT notice, the firm must verify the customer's instructions within one business day and must transfer assets within three business days after verification.

23. **B.** A client must have at least $500,000 in assets available for investments to establish a prime brokerage account. However, if the account is established through an investment adviser, the requirement reduces to $100,000. Prime brokerage firms consolidate information from all brokerage accounts to provide one account statement.

24. **C.** Under FINRA rules, correspondence represents promotions sent to 25 or fewer retail persons in a 30-day period. Correspondence would not have to be approved by a principal, although record of the correspondence must be maintained by the brokerage firm for at least three years.

25. **A.** If you're moonlighting while working as a registered rep for a broker-dealer, you have to notify your firm in writing. In the event that your firm feels it's a conflict of interest, they may say no.

5
A Couple
Practice Exams

Chapter **17**
Practice Exam 1

This chapter is where you get your chance to shine like a star.

This practice exam has 125 questions in random order, just as they are in the actual Series 7 exam. Please read carefully — many test-takers make careless mistakes because they miss key words or read too quickly. Focus on the information you do need to know and ignore the information that you don't need. Read the last sentence twice to make sure you know what the question is asking.

Mark your answers on the answer sheet provided or on a separate piece of paper. You may use a basic calculator and scrap paper for notes and figuring. As you're taking the exam, be sure to circle the questions you find difficult. This step can help you determine what you really need to review.

To simulate the real exam, try to finish in 3 hours and 45 minutes or less. Please resist the urge to look at the answers and explanations as you work through the exam; save the grading for later. After you finish, check your answers (you can find the answers and detailed explanations in Chapter 18 along with an answer key at the end of that chapter). Remember, you need a score of at least 72 to pass the exam. You should thoroughly review your questions and explanations before proceeding to the next practice exam (Chapter 19).

Good luck!

Practice Exam 1 Answer Sheet

1. Ⓐ Ⓑ Ⓒ Ⓓ	26. Ⓐ Ⓑ Ⓒ Ⓓ	51. Ⓐ Ⓑ Ⓒ Ⓓ	76. Ⓐ Ⓑ Ⓒ Ⓓ	101. Ⓐ Ⓑ Ⓒ Ⓓ
2. Ⓐ Ⓑ Ⓒ Ⓓ	27. Ⓐ Ⓑ Ⓒ Ⓓ	52. Ⓐ Ⓑ Ⓒ Ⓓ	77. Ⓐ Ⓑ Ⓒ Ⓓ	102. Ⓐ Ⓑ Ⓒ Ⓓ
3. Ⓐ Ⓑ Ⓒ Ⓓ	28. Ⓐ Ⓑ Ⓒ Ⓓ	53. Ⓐ Ⓑ Ⓒ Ⓓ	78. Ⓐ Ⓑ Ⓒ Ⓓ	103. Ⓐ Ⓑ Ⓒ Ⓓ
4. Ⓐ Ⓑ Ⓒ Ⓓ	29. Ⓐ Ⓑ Ⓒ Ⓓ	54. Ⓐ Ⓑ Ⓒ Ⓓ	79. Ⓐ Ⓑ Ⓒ Ⓓ	104. Ⓐ Ⓑ Ⓒ Ⓓ
5. Ⓐ Ⓑ Ⓒ Ⓓ	30. Ⓐ Ⓑ Ⓒ Ⓓ	55. Ⓐ Ⓑ Ⓒ Ⓓ	80. Ⓐ Ⓑ Ⓒ Ⓓ	105. Ⓐ Ⓑ Ⓒ Ⓓ
6. Ⓐ Ⓑ Ⓒ Ⓓ	31. Ⓐ Ⓑ Ⓒ Ⓓ	56. Ⓐ Ⓑ Ⓒ Ⓓ	81. Ⓐ Ⓑ Ⓒ Ⓓ	106. Ⓐ Ⓑ Ⓒ Ⓓ
7. Ⓐ Ⓑ Ⓒ Ⓓ	32. Ⓐ Ⓑ Ⓒ Ⓓ	57. Ⓐ Ⓑ Ⓒ Ⓓ	82. Ⓐ Ⓑ Ⓒ Ⓓ	107. Ⓐ Ⓑ Ⓒ Ⓓ
8. Ⓐ Ⓑ Ⓒ Ⓓ	33. Ⓐ Ⓑ Ⓒ Ⓓ	58. Ⓐ Ⓑ Ⓒ Ⓓ	83. Ⓐ Ⓑ Ⓒ Ⓓ	108. Ⓐ Ⓑ Ⓒ Ⓓ
9. Ⓐ Ⓑ Ⓒ Ⓓ	34. Ⓐ Ⓑ Ⓒ Ⓓ	59. Ⓐ Ⓑ Ⓒ Ⓓ	84. Ⓐ Ⓑ Ⓒ Ⓓ	109. Ⓐ Ⓑ Ⓒ Ⓓ
10. Ⓐ Ⓑ Ⓒ Ⓓ	35. Ⓐ Ⓑ Ⓒ Ⓓ	60. Ⓐ Ⓑ Ⓒ Ⓓ	85. Ⓐ Ⓑ Ⓒ Ⓓ	110. Ⓐ Ⓑ Ⓒ Ⓓ
11. Ⓐ Ⓑ Ⓒ Ⓓ	36. Ⓐ Ⓑ Ⓒ Ⓓ	61. Ⓐ Ⓑ Ⓒ Ⓓ	86. Ⓐ Ⓑ Ⓒ Ⓓ	111. Ⓐ Ⓑ Ⓒ Ⓓ
12. Ⓐ Ⓑ Ⓒ Ⓓ	37. Ⓐ Ⓑ Ⓒ Ⓓ	62. Ⓐ Ⓑ Ⓒ Ⓓ	87. Ⓐ Ⓑ Ⓒ Ⓓ	112. Ⓐ Ⓑ Ⓒ Ⓓ
13. Ⓐ Ⓑ Ⓒ Ⓓ	38. Ⓐ Ⓑ Ⓒ Ⓓ	63. Ⓐ Ⓑ Ⓒ Ⓓ	88. Ⓐ Ⓑ Ⓒ Ⓓ	113. Ⓐ Ⓑ Ⓒ Ⓓ
14. Ⓐ Ⓑ Ⓒ Ⓓ	39. Ⓐ Ⓑ Ⓒ Ⓓ	64. Ⓐ Ⓑ Ⓒ Ⓓ	89. Ⓐ Ⓑ Ⓒ Ⓓ	114. Ⓐ Ⓑ Ⓒ Ⓓ
15. Ⓐ Ⓑ Ⓒ Ⓓ	40. Ⓐ Ⓑ Ⓒ Ⓓ	65. Ⓐ Ⓑ Ⓒ Ⓓ	90. Ⓐ Ⓑ Ⓒ Ⓓ	115. Ⓐ Ⓑ Ⓒ Ⓓ
16. Ⓐ Ⓑ Ⓒ Ⓓ	41. Ⓐ Ⓑ Ⓒ Ⓓ	66. Ⓐ Ⓑ Ⓒ Ⓓ	91. Ⓐ Ⓑ Ⓒ Ⓓ	116. Ⓐ Ⓑ Ⓒ Ⓓ
17. Ⓐ Ⓑ Ⓒ Ⓓ	42. Ⓐ Ⓑ Ⓒ Ⓓ	67. Ⓐ Ⓑ Ⓒ Ⓓ	92. Ⓐ Ⓑ Ⓒ Ⓓ	117. Ⓐ Ⓑ Ⓒ Ⓓ
18. Ⓐ Ⓑ Ⓒ Ⓓ	43. Ⓐ Ⓑ Ⓒ Ⓓ	68. Ⓐ Ⓑ Ⓒ Ⓓ	93. Ⓐ Ⓑ Ⓒ Ⓓ	118. Ⓐ Ⓑ Ⓒ Ⓓ
19. Ⓐ Ⓑ Ⓒ Ⓓ	44. Ⓐ Ⓑ Ⓒ Ⓓ	69. Ⓐ Ⓑ Ⓒ Ⓓ	94. Ⓐ Ⓑ Ⓒ Ⓓ	119. Ⓐ Ⓑ Ⓒ Ⓓ
20. Ⓐ Ⓑ Ⓒ Ⓓ	45. Ⓐ Ⓑ Ⓒ Ⓓ	70. Ⓐ Ⓑ Ⓒ Ⓓ	95. Ⓐ Ⓑ Ⓒ Ⓓ	120. Ⓐ Ⓑ Ⓒ Ⓓ
21. Ⓐ Ⓑ Ⓒ Ⓓ	46. Ⓐ Ⓑ Ⓒ Ⓓ	71. Ⓐ Ⓑ Ⓒ Ⓓ	96. Ⓐ Ⓑ Ⓒ Ⓓ	121. Ⓐ Ⓑ Ⓒ Ⓓ
22. Ⓐ Ⓑ Ⓒ Ⓓ	47. Ⓐ Ⓑ Ⓒ Ⓓ	72. Ⓐ Ⓑ Ⓒ Ⓓ	97. Ⓐ Ⓑ Ⓒ Ⓓ	122. Ⓐ Ⓑ Ⓒ Ⓓ
23. Ⓐ Ⓑ Ⓒ Ⓓ	48. Ⓐ Ⓑ Ⓒ Ⓓ	73. Ⓐ Ⓑ Ⓒ Ⓓ	98. Ⓐ Ⓑ Ⓒ Ⓓ	123. Ⓐ Ⓑ Ⓒ Ⓓ
24. Ⓐ Ⓑ Ⓒ Ⓓ	49. Ⓐ Ⓑ Ⓒ Ⓓ	74. Ⓐ Ⓑ Ⓒ Ⓓ	99. Ⓐ Ⓑ Ⓒ Ⓓ	124. Ⓐ Ⓑ Ⓒ Ⓓ
25. Ⓐ Ⓑ Ⓒ Ⓓ	50. Ⓐ Ⓑ Ⓒ Ⓓ	75. Ⓐ Ⓑ Ⓒ Ⓓ	100. Ⓐ Ⓑ Ⓒ Ⓓ	125. Ⓐ Ⓑ Ⓒ Ⓓ

TIME: 3 hours and 45 minutes for 125 questions

DIRECTIONS: Choose the correct answer to each question. Then fill in the circle on your answer sheet that corresponds to the question number and the letter indicating your choice.

1. If a bond's yield to maturity (YTM) is 6 percent, which of the following would MOST likely be refunded by the issuer?

   I. Coupon 6½ percent, maturing in 2040, callable in 2030 at 104

   II. Coupon 5½ percent, maturing in 2040, callable in 2029 at 104

   III. Coupon 5½ percent, maturing in 2040, callable in 2029 at 100

   IV. Coupon 6½ percent, maturing in 2040, callable in 2030 at 100

   (A) I and II

   (B) II and IV

   (C) II only

   (D) IV only

2. Which of the following investors have ownership positions in a corporation?

   I. Convertible bondholders

   II. Convertible preferred stockholders

   III. Common stockholders

   IV. Mortgage bondholders

   (A) II and III

   (B) I, II, III, and IV

   (C) II and IV

   (D) II only

3. Common stockholders of PXPX Corporation have which of the following rights and privileges?

   (A) The right to receive an audited financial report weekly

   (B) The right to vote for cash dividends to be paid

   (C) A residual claim to assets at dissolution

   (D) The right to vote for stock dividends to be paid

4. Which of the following types of preferred stock allows the investor to reduce inflation risk?

   (A) Cumulative

   (B) Noncumulative

   (C) Convertible

   (D) Participating

5. AylDec Corporation has been authorized to issue 20,000,000 shares of common stock. However, AylDec only issued 12,000,000 shares to the public. Six months later, AylDec repurchased 1,000,000 shares to increase the demand on their outstanding shares. How many shares of common stock does AylDec have outstanding?

   (A) 11,000,000

   (B) 12,000,000

   (C) 13,000,000

   (D) 20,000,000

6. Which of the following U.S. government securities are quoted on a discount yield basis?

   (A) Treasury bills

   (B) Treasury bonds

   (C) Treasury notes

   (D) Both A and C

7. On Wednesday, March 16, one of your customers purchases ten 6 percent Treasury bonds maturing in 2030. If the bonds pay interest on January 1 and July 1, how many days of accrued interest are added to the purchaser's price?

   (A) 75

   (B) 76

   (C) 79

   (D) 80

GO ON TO NEXT PAGE

8. Jake Hanson lives in New York and is considering purchasing a bond. He has settled on either a 5 percent municipal bond offered by New York or a 7 percent corporate bond offered by The Greenhorn Corporation, which has headquarters in New York. Jake needs some guidance and would like you to help him determine which bond will provide him with the greatest return. Which of the following information do you need to obtain before you can make the appropriate recommendation?

   (A) The business of his employer

   (B) His current tax bracket

   (C) How long he has lived in New York

   (D) His other holdings

9. An investor who is long a call option will realize a profit if exercising the option when the underlying stock price is

   (A) below the strike price minus the premium paid

   (B) above the strike price

   (C) above the strike price plus the premium paid

   (D) below the strike price

10. One of your clients is new to investing and has limited resources. Which of the following investments would you least likely recommend to this investor?

   (A) Growth funds

   (B) T-bills

   (C) Blue-chip stock

   (D) Collateralized debt obligations

11. Which of the following is required on the registration statement for a new issue?

   I. The capitalization of the issuer

   II. Complete financial statements

   III. What the money raised will be used for

   IV. The names and addresses of all of the issuer's control persons

   (A) I, II, and III

   (B) I, III, and IV

   (C) I, II, and IV

   (D) I, II, III, and IV

12. Under the Securities Act of 1933, which of the following securities must be registered with the SEC?

   (A) Closed-end funds

   (B) Variable annuities

   (C) Open-end funds

   (D) All of the above

13. Which of the following are exempt transactions?

   I. Securities issued by the U.S. government

   II. Securities issued by banks

   III. Intrastate offerings

   IV. Regulation A offerings

   (A) I and IV

   (B) III and IV

   (C) I, II, and III

   (D) I, II, III, and IV

14. A customer's confirmation must include

   I. the customer's account number

   II. whether the customer bought, sold, or sold short

   III. the price of the security

   IV. the markup, markdown, or commission

   (A) I and III

   (B) II and IV

   (C) I, III, and IV

   (D) I, II, III, and IV

15. Which of the following would qualify as management companies?

   (A) Mutual funds

   (B) Unit investment trusts

   (C) Closed-end funds

   (D) Both A and C

16. Which of the following is TRUE regarding qualified retirement plans?

   (A) Contributions are made with 100 percent pretax dollars.

   (B) Contributions are made with 100 percent after-tax dollars.

   (C) Distributions are taxable only prior to age 59½.

   (D) Distributions are subject to a 10 percent penalty.

17. Variable annuities must be registered with the

    I. Department of State

    II. State Banking Commission

    III. State Insurance Commission

    IV. Securities and Exchange Commission

    (A) I and II

    (B) I and III

    (C) I and IV

    (D) III and IV

18. All of the following items must be included on a trade confirmation EXCEPT

    (A) the customer's account number

    (B) the customer's signature

    (C) the price of the security

    (D) the commission, if the trade took place on an agency basis

19. The safeguarding of customer's non-public information is covered under

    (A) Regulation T

    (B) Regulation D

    (C) Regulation A

    (D) Regulation S-P

20. An agent's recommendations to a customer

    I. must be approved in advance by a manager

    II. must be in line with the customer's risk tolerance and investment objectives

    III. must be reviewed by a principal if they result in a trade

    IV. must be in accordance with Federal Reserve Board rules

    (A) I and IV

    (B) II and III

    (C) II, III, and IV

    (D) I and II

21. If one of your clients wants to order municipal securities that you believe to be unsuitable for their investment objectives, what should you do?

    (A) Execute the order as long as you mark the order ticket as "unsolicited."

    (B) You must refuse the order unless the client changes their investment objectives.

    (C) You must obtain the permission of the firm's compliance officer before executing the order.

    (D) You may only execute the order with prior permission of a principal of the firm.

22. Declan Jefferson bought ten municipal bonds at 105 with ten years to maturity. Three years later, he sold the bonds for 102. His tax consequence is a

    (A) $150 gain

    (B) $150 loss

    (C) $300 gain

    (D) $300 loss

23. Qualified cash dividends are currently taxed at which rates?

    I. 0 percent

    II. 10 percent

    III. 15 percent

    IV. 20 percent

    (A) I and II

    (B) I, III, and IV

    (C) III and IV

    (D) II, III, and IV

24. All broker-dealers need to maintain customer identification programs and should check the names of all new clients against

    (A) a list maintained by the SEC

    (B) a do-not-call list maintained by the firm

    (C) a list compiled by FINRA

    (D) a list of specially designated nationals (SDNs) maintained by OFAC

GO ON TO NEXT PAGE

25. Which of the following statements is NOT true of life-cycle funds?

   (A) As life-cycle funds get nearer to their target date, the portfolio holdings will be adjusted to purchase more equity securities and less fixed-income securities.

   (B) These funds are usually set up as funds of funds.

   (C) The asset allocation of the fund will be rebalanced on a regular basis to make sure that the risk/reward balance is correct given the target date of the fund.

   (D) The objective of the fund assumes that most investors cannot tolerate as much risk as they get older.

26. Mutual fund account statements must be sent out at least

   (A) monthly

   (B) quarterly

   (C) semiannually

   (D) annually

27. Which of the following securities are subject to systematic risk?

   I. common stock

   II. preferred stock

   III. municipal bonds

   (A) I and II

   (B) II and III

   (C) I and III

   (D) I, II, and III

28. Secured corporate bonds include

   I. equipment trusts

   II. income bonds

   III. mortgage bonds

   IV. debentures

   (A) I and II

   (B) I and III

   (C) III and IV

   (D) I, II, III, and IV

29. This type of municipal fund security is also know as a qualified tuition plan.

   (A) ABLE accounts

   (B) LGIPs

   (C) Section 529

   (D) TANs

30. An investor with no other position in XYZ writes 1 XYZ Aug 30 put at 2.75. If the put option is exercised when XYZ is trading at 27.50 and the investor immediately sells the stock in the market, what is their gain or loss?

   (A) $25 gain

   (B) $25 loss

   (C) $250 gain

   (D) $250 loss

31. Mrs. Smith purchases 100 shares of ABC at 35 and writes a 40 call at 5.50. If ABC stock increases to 60 and the call is exercised, Mrs. Smith has a

   (A) $2,500 gain

   (B) $3,050 loss

   (C) $2,000 loss

   (D) $1,050 gain

32. Which of the following are factors that affect the marketability of municipal GO bonds?

   I. The quality

   II. Call features

   III. The issuer's name

   IV. Credit enhancements

   (A) I and II

   (B) II and III

   (C) I, II, and III

   (D) I, II, III, and IV

33. If a customer wants to open a new account but refuses to provide some of the financial information requested by the member firm, which of the following statements is TRUE?

(A) The firm may open the account for the customer and make recommendations freely.

(B) The firm may open the account if it can determine from other sources that the customer has the financial means to handle the account.

(C) The firm may open the account and take unsolicited trades only.

(D) The firm may not accept any trades for the account until the information is received from the customer.

34. Mr. Mayvis has a margin account with a current market value of $20,250 and a debit balance of $3,000 with Regulation T at 50 percent. How much excess equity does the investor have in the account?

(A) $20,250

(B) $3,000

(C) $17,250

(D) $7,125

35. Which of the following is included in a preliminary prospectus?

I. The purpose for the funds being raised

II. Financial statements

III. A written statement in red citing that the prospectus may be amended and a final prospectus issued

IV. The final offering price

(A) I and II

(B) I, II, and III

(C) II and IV

(D) I, II, III, and IV

36. Which of the following would be considered an accredited investor?

(A) An investor that had an annual income in excess of $200,000 for at least the last three years.

(B) An investor that had an annual income in excess of $100,000 for at least the last two years.

(C) An investor that has a net worth of at least $1,000,000, excluding any equity they have in their primary residence.

(D) An investor that has a net worth in excess of $200,000.

37. A Designated Market Maker (DMM) acts as a

(A) broker and dealer

(B) broker only

(C) dealer only

(D) neither a broker nor dealer

38. The maximum potential gain for a long combination is

(A) the premiums received

(B) the average of the call strike price and put strike price multiplied by 100 shares

(C) the difference between the call strike price and the put strike price multiplied by 100 shares

(D) unlimited

39. The SEC and FINRA require customer statements to be sent out for inactive accounts at least

(A) monthly

(B) quarterly

(C) semiannually

(D) annually

40. Which of the following securities is traded on an exchange and is an entity that makes mortgage loans to developers and has a portfolio of properties?

(A) DPPs

(B) ETNs

(C) Hybrid REITs

(D) Mutual funds

GO ON TO NEXT PAGE

41. Which of the following are needed to open a margin account for a corporation?

   I. Corporate charter and resolution

   II. New account form

   III. Hypothecation agreement

   IV. Credit agreement

   (A) I and II

   (B) I and IV

   (C) III and IV

   (D) I, II, III, and IV

42. The Municipal Bond Index is

   (A) the average yield on 25 revenue bonds with 30-year maturities

   (B) the average yield on 20 selected municipal bonds with 20-year maturities

   (C) the average dollar price of 40 highly traded GO and revenue bonds

   (D) the average yield on 11 selected municipal bonds with 20-year maturities

43. Which of the following oil and gas DPPs has the highest capital appreciation potential?

   (A) Exploratory

   (B) Developmental

   (C) Income

   (D) Combination

44. Martina Martin is new to investing but has determined that her primary objective is making sure that she is prepared for retirement. Which of the following is the MOST important factor for you to consider when helping her set up her investment portfolio?

   (A) Age

   (B) Net worth

   (C) Education level

   (D) Previous investment history

45. Ayla K. has a short margin account with a market value of $30,000. What is the minimum maintenance for the account?

   (A) $7,500

   (B) $9,000

   (C) $15,000

   (D) $30,000

46. Which of the following is rated by most securities rating services?

   (A) Market risk

   (B) Investment risk

   (C) Quantity

   (D) Quality

47. Under federal law, stock CANNOT be tendered from which of the following accounts?

   (A) Short margin accounts

   (B) Margin accounts with no excess equity

   (C) Cash accounts

   (D) Long margin accounts

48. Which of the following items are required on an order ticket?

   I. The time of the order

   II. A description of the security (stocks, bonds, symbol, and so on)

   III. Whether the registered rep has discretionary authority over the account

   IV. The registered rep's identification number

   (A) I, III, and IV

   (B) I and III only

   (C) I, II, and IV

   (D) I, II, III, and IV

49. Which of the following are important factors when determining the markup or commission on a municipal bond trade?

   I. The fact that you're entitled to make a profit

   II. The difficulty of the trade

   III. The market value of the securities at the time of the trade

   (A) I and II

   (B) I and III

   (C) II and III

   (D) I, II, and III

50. When compared to statutory voting, cumulative voting provides an advantage to

    I. larger shareholders

    II. mortgage bondholders

    III. smaller shareholders

    IV. convertible bondholders

    (A) I only

    (B) II and IV

    (C) III only

    (D) II and III

51. Which of the following is NOT a benefit of investing in ADRs?

    (A) The dividends are received in U.S. currency.

    (B) The transactions are done in U.S. currency.

    (C) ADRs are subject to antifraud rules.

    (D) Currency risk is minimized.

52. CMOs are typically rated

    (A) AAA

    (B) AA

    (C) BBB

    (D) SP1

53. All of the following are types of state securities registration EXCEPT

    (A) Notification

    (B) Coordination

    (C) Qualification

    (D) Quantification

54. Declan has written a letter of complaint regarding his recent purchase of municipal bonds to his broker-dealer. Upon receipt of the complaint, the broker-dealer must first

    (A) immediately repurchase the securities at a price at or slightly above Declan's purchase price

    (B) guarantee to make the customer whole

    (C) return any markup or commission charged

    (D) accept the complaint and write down any action taken

55. An online site that provides detailed information to nonprofessional investors relating to municipal securities, including up-to-the-minute prices, is called

    (A) The Blue List

    (B) OPRA

    (C) EMMA

    (D) NASDAQ

56. Under which of the following circumstances would an investor face an unlimited maximum loss potential?

    I. Short 2 DIM Nov 40 puts

    II. Short 400 shares of DIM common stock

    III. Short 6 DIM Nov 50 uncovered calls

    IV. Short 3 DIM Nov 50 covered calls

    (A) I and II

    (B) I and III

    (C) II and III

    (D) II and IV

57. A registered representative executes the following trades for a speculative investor:

    • Buy 1 GHI May 30 call at 8

    • Sell 1 GHI May 35 call at 3

    Are these trades suitable for this investor?

    (A) It is impossible to tell with the information given.

    (B) Probably not, because the risk is not high enough for a speculative investor.

    (C) Yes, buying and selling options are always appropriate for speculative investors.

    (D) No, because it is impossible to make a profit with these positions.

GO ON TO NEXT PAGE ➤

58. Fred Freedom has held 100 shares of UPP stock for six months and decides to purchase a nine-month call on UPP. If the UPP call option expires and Fred decides to sell the UPP stock four months after the expiration of the call, what is Fred's tax position?

   (A) Short-term capital gain or long-term capital loss

   (B) Long-term capital gain or short-term capital loss

   (C) Long-term capital gain or long-term capital loss

   (D) Short-term capital gain or short-term capital loss

59. John Dow and Jane Dough, who are engaged but unmarried, want to open a new account registered as joint tenants with rights of survivorship. Which of the following should occur?

   (A) A principal of the firm should be notified immediately about the account registration so that a report can be filed with FINRA.

   (B) The agent must refuse to open the account.

   (C) The agent must notify a principal of the firm and a report must first be filed with the SEC.

   (D) The agent may open the account, but should first discuss the rules of a JTWROS account with the unmarried couple.

60. Advertisements including recommendations must include all of the following EXCEPT

   (A) If the firm is a market maker in the security being recommended

   (B) If the firm acted as an underwriter in a recent public offering of the security being recommended

   (C) If the firm participated in the selling group for a recent public offering of a security

   (D) If partners of the firm hold options or warrants to buy the security being recommended

61. If a client has a margin account with $18,000 in securities and a debit balance of $7,000, and Regulation T is 50 percent, which of the following statements is FALSE?

   (A) The account has a buying power of $4,000.

   (B) If the client withdraws any excess equity, the debit balance decreases by the amount of the withdrawal.

   (C) The account has excess equity of $2,000.

   (D) The securities held in the account most likely increased in value.

62. Which type of margin account requires a minimum equity of $25,000?

   (A) A portfolio margin account

   (B) A short account

   (C) A day-trading account

   (D) A corporate account

63. Prior to buying or selling options, a customer must first receive a(n)

   (A) ODD

   (B) OCC

   (C) margin agreement

   (D) OPRA

64. Priority, precedence, and parity rules of bids and offers dictate trading activity on the

   (A) OTC pink market

   (B) fourth market

   (C) New York Stock Exchange

   (D) OTC market

65. Who maintains a fair and orderly market on the New York Stock Exchange trading floor?

   (A) Floor brokers

   (B) Two-dollar brokers

   (C) Designated Market Makers

   (D) Order book officials

66. After an options account has been approved, the customer must sign and return a(n)

   (A) credit agreement

   (B) OCC

   (C) OAA

   (D) ODD

67. The settlement date for municipal bonds is

    (A) T+1

    (B) T+2

    (C) T+3

    (D) Up to 5 business days at the purchaser's discretion

68. Regulation SHO covers

    (A) margin requirements for municipal and U.S. government securities

    (B) the short sale of securities

    (C) margin requirements for commodities

    (D) portfolio margining rules

69. Which of the following is NOT an advantage for a customer adding REITs to their portfolio?

    (A) Having a professionally managed portfolio of real estate assets

    (B) Preferential dividend treatment

    (C) Being able to use an REIT as a potential hedge against a negative price movement in other equity securities

    (D) Liquidity

70. All of the following items would be found on the official statement of a municipal bond issue EXCEPT

    (A) the markup

    (B) a description of the issuer

    (C) the coupon rate

    (D) a legal opinion

71. Which of the following are true about the annuitization of a variable annuity?

    I. The value of the annuity units is fixed.

    II. The number of annuity units is fixed.

    III. The value of the annuity units varies.

    IV. The number of annuity units varies.

    (A) I and II

    (B) II and III

    (C) II and IV

    (D) None of the above

72. Which of the following investments requires a registered representative to obtain written verification of an investor's net worth?

    (A) Hedge funds

    (B) Variable annuities

    (C) Direct participation programs

    (D) Triple tax-free municipal bonds

73. One of your clients is interested in purchasing a stock with a beta of 1.6. You can tell them that

    (A) the stock is equally as volatile as the market

    (B) the stock is less volatile than the market

    (C) the stock is more volatile than the market

    (D) cannot be determined

74. A head and shoulders bottom formation indicates

    (A) the reversal of a bullish trend

    (B) the reversal of a bearish trend

    (C) that the stock is moving sideways

    (D) that it might be a good time to sell short

75. Michael Moneybags purchased 1,000 shares of WOW common stock at $26 per share. Six months later, WOW is trading at $60 and Michael expects a slight decline in the market price for a short period of time. However, Michael has a lot of confidence that WOW is a great company and he remains bullish on WOW's common stock overall. Providing Michael is correct in his assessment, which of the following positions would provide Michael a level of protection while still being able to generate additional income?

    (A) Sell 1,000 WOW short and purchase 10 WOW Dec 65 calls for $300 each

    (B) Buy 10 WOW straddles at 60

    (C) Sell 10 WOW Dec 65 calls for $300 each and place a 1,000-share sell-stop order for WOW at 57

    (D) Buy 10 WOW Oct 60 puts for $500 each

GO ON TO NEXT PAGE

76. One of your customers purchases 100 shares of ARGH at 44.10 and 1 OEX Sep 360 put at 4.50. A few months later, ARGH is trading at 42.55 and the OEX index is trading at 349. If your customer closes the stock position and exercises their OEX put, what is their gain?

(A) $155

(B) $495

(C) $1,100

(D) $35,395

77. All-or-none (AON) orders must be

(A) executed in their entirety immediately or the order is cancelled

(B) executed in their entirety or the order is cancelled

(C) at least partially executed immediately or the order is cancelled

(D) at least partially executed or the order is cancelled

78. To process an ACAT, a brokerage firm must be a member of the

(A) FINRA

(B) NSCC

(C) SIPC

(D) DRS

79. All of the following increase SMA in a long account EXCEPT

I. selling securities from the account

II. the purchase of additional securities in the account

III. receipt of a cash dividend

IV. a decrease in the market value of securities held in the account

(A) I and III

(B) II and IV

(C) I, III, and IV

(D) II, III, and IV

80. DEF Corporation issued stock to the public at $9 per share. If the manager's fee was $0.15 per share, the takedown was $0.50 per share, and the concession was $0.30 per share, what was the spread?

(A) $0.45

(B) $0.65

(C) $0.80

(D) $0.95

81. Which of the following customer orders are discretionary?

I. "Buy 1,000 shares of a growth company"

II. "Buy or sell 500 shares of LMN"

III. "Buy or sell as many shares of TUV as you think I can handle"

(A) I and II

(B) II and III

(C) I and III

(D) I, II, and III

82. Which of the following is true regarding dark pools of liquidity?

I. They represent pools of institutional and large retail clients.

II. They reduce the amount of transparency of information relating to securities trading.

III. Firms trading for their own inventory may be included.

IV. Trades executed by the pools are reported as exchange transactions.

(A) I and IV

(B) I, III, and IV

(C) I, II, and III

(D) II and III

83. Mutual funds must send financial statements to shareholders at least

(A) monthly

(B) bimonthly

(C) quarterly

(D) semiannually

84. Which of the following needs to be filled out on a new account form?

I. The customer's name and address

II. The customer's date of birth

III. The type of account

IV. The customer's investment objectives

(A) I and II

(B) I, II, and III

(C) I, II, and IV

(D) I, II, III, and IV

85. What is the minimum amount of assets your client must have in order to establish a prime brokerage account?

(A) $100,000

(B) $500,000

(C) $1,000,000

(D) $5,000,000

86. Investing in real-estate DPP programs can provide which of the following advantages?

I. Depreciation

II. Appreciation

III. Depletion

IV. Cash flow

(A) I and II

(B) III and IV

(C) I, II, and IV

(D) I, II, III, and IV

87. A client owns a large amount of Treasury bonds and long-term investment grade corporate bonds. Their main risk concern should be

(A) credit risk

(B) inflationary risk

(C) systematic risk

(D) timing risk

88. If LMN common stock has a $2.20 dividend, a current yield of 5.0%, a PE ratio of 6, and is trading at $44, its approximate earnings per share is

(A) $0.44

(B) $2.73

(C) $7.33

(D) $8.80

89. PE ratio equals

(A) the market price divided by the earnings per share

(B) annual dividends per common share divided by the market price

(C) annual dividends per common share divided by the earnings per share

(D) net income minus preferred dividends divided by the number of common shares outstanding

90. An investor owns the following investments:

- 50 New York 5 percent general obligation bonds maturing in 2030 and rated AA

- 50 Florida University 6.25 percent revenue bonds maturing in 2031 and rated AA

- 50 Nevada Turnpike 5.75 percent revenue bonds maturing in 2030 and rated AA

What type of diversification does this represent?

(A) Maturity

(B) Quality

(C) Quantity

(D) Geographical

91. A customer buys 1 DUD Jun 55 put at 4.50 when DUD is trading at 53.40. Just prior to expiration, the option is trading at 4.55 bid–4.65 asked. If the customer closes their position with a market order, what is the gain or loss?

(A) $5 gain

(B) $5 loss

(C) $160 gain

(D) $160 loss

92. An investor has shorted XYZ common stock at 55. XYZ common stock has recently dropped to 30, and the investor expects that the price will continue to decrease over the long term. If the investor would like to hedge against a possible increase in the price, the investor should

(A) buy an XYZ call

(B) sell an XYZ call

(C) buy an XYZ put

(D) buy an XYZ combination

GO ON TO NEXT PAGE

93. Grant Goldbarr purchased 1 ABC 60 put at 3.50 and purchased 100 shares of ABC at 62. Six months later, with ABC trading at 64, Grant closes his put for 0.75 and sells his stock at the market price. What is Grant's gain or loss as a result of these transactions?

    (A) $75 loss
    (B) $75 gain
    (C) $275 loss
    (D) $275 gain

94. If an investor buys a three-year LEAPS contract on issuance, which expires unexercised, what is the investor's tax consequence at expiration?

    (A) Short-term capital loss
    (B) Long-term capital gain
    (C) Long-term capital loss
    (D) Short-term capital gain

95. A customer, without giving written authorization, may permit a registered representative to exercise their judgment as to

    (A) whether to buy or sell
    (B) the security
    (C) the price and timing to enter the order
    (D) the number of shares

96. Which of the following are nonexempt securities?

    I. Municipal unit investment trust shares
    II. U.S. government bond fund shares
    III. Variable annuity accumulation units
    IV. Fixed annuities

    (A) I and II
    (B) III only
    (C) III and IV
    (D) I, II, and III

97. If Buddy Seagull has a limited amount of funds and wants to invest in the pharmaceutical industry but does not want to limit his investments to only one or two companies, which type of fund would be MOST suitable?

    (A) A hedge fund
    (B) A sector fund
    (C) A balanced fund
    (D) A money-market fund

98. What is the principal tax benefit for investing as a limited partner in an exploratory oil and gas drilling program?

    (A) Tax credits
    (B) Depreciation expenses
    (C) Recourse loans
    (D) Intangible drilling costs

99. One of your 60-year-old clients has a portfolio that consists of 60% invested in stocks, 30% in bonds, and 10% in cash equivalents. Using a standard strategic asset allocation model, they should:

    (A) sell some of their bonds and purchase more stocks
    (B) sell some of their stocks and purchase more bonds
    (C) sell their cash equivalents and purchase more stocks and bonds
    (D) cannot be determined with the information given

100. Ginny Gemms purchased 2 LMN 50 calls and paid a premium of 3 for each option. Ginny also purchased 2 LMN 50 puts and paid a premium of 2 for each option. At the time of purchase, LMN was trading at $50.25. Just prior to expiration, LMN was trading at $44.50, and Ginny decided to close her options for their intrinsic value. Excluding commission, Ginny had a

    (A) $50 profit
    (B) $50 loss
    (C) $100 profit
    (D) $100 loss

101. You have a new client who is in a high tax bracket and is looking for investments with a tax advantage. Which of the following securities would you LEAST likely recommend?

    (A) Municipal bonds
    (B) Collateralized mortgage obligations
    (C) Retirement plans
    (D) Direct participation programs

102. An investor wants to generate some income on a stock that they believe will remain at relatively the same price for the next year or so. Which of the following option positions would meet their goal?

(A) Buying a combination

(B) Writing a straddle

(C) Buying a call

(D) Buying a put

103. Adjustable-rate preferred stock has a dividend that adjusts according to

(A) prevailing interest rates

(B) the amount of dividend given to common stockholders

(C) the coupon rate on the issuer's bonds

(D) the rate on CMOs

104. Regulation SHO covers the

(A) resale of restricted securities

(B) short sale of securities

(C) resale of ETFs

(D) margin requirement for listed options

105. Which of the following items are found on an indenture of a bond?

I. The maturity date

II. Callable or convertible features

III. The coupon rate

IV. The name of the trustee

(A) II, III, and IV

(B) I, II, and III

(C) II and III

(D) I, II, III, and IV

106. As part of the USA Patriot Act of 2001, all financial institutions must maintain:

(A) Customer Identification Programs

(B) a fidelity bond

(C) SIPC coverage

(D) All of the above

107. Which of the following are important to investors evaluating direct participation programs?

I. The economic soundness of the program

II. The expertise of the general partner

III. The basic objectives of the program

IV. The start-up costs

(A) I, II, and III

(B) I, II, and IV

(C) II, III, and IV

(D) I, II, III, and IV

108. What is the required beginning date (RBD) for traditional IRAs?

(A) The year after the investor reaches the age of 59½

(B) The year the investor turns the age of 73

(C) April 1st of the year after the investor reaches the age of 73

(D) April 15th of the year after the investor reaches the age of 73

109. The initial maturity for Treasury Inflation Protected Securities is

(A) 2, 3, 5, 7, and 10 years

(B) 10 to 30 years

(C) 6 months to 30 years

(D) 5, 10, and 30 years

110. One of your clients is expecting to receive a lot of money over the next three years from a real estate DPP. Your client would like to shelter some of that money by investing in an oil and gas DPP. Which of the following will help your client shelter the most money?

(A) Oil and gas income

(B) Oil and gas developmental

(C) Oil and gas combination

(D) Oil and gas wildcatting

GO ON TO NEXT PAGE

111. Which of the following governmental bodies receives no revenue from ad-valorem taxes?

(A) County governments

(B) State governments

(C) School districts

(D) Local municipalities

112. According to MSRB rules, a customer confirmation must include

(A) the markup or markdown

(B) the location of the indenture

(C) the maturity date

(D) whether the trade was done on an agency or dealer basis

113. John believes that the market is about to become bearish and would like to be able to profit in the event that he is correct. Which of the following investments would meet John's needs?

I. Inverse ETFs

II. Selling SPX calls

III. High-yield bond funds

IV. Selling OEX puts

(A) I and II

(B) II and IV

(C) I, II, and III

(D) I, II, and IV

114. Ferret Enterprises pays a quarterly dividend of $0.25 per share and has an EPS of $2.50. What is the dividend payout ratio?

(A) 10 percent

(B) 40 percent

(C) 57 percent

(D) 100 percent

115. Gerry Goop purchases a new OID municipal zero-coupon for 80. If Gerry holds the bond to maturity, what is his tax consequence?

(A) $0

(B) $200 ordinary income over the time the bond is held to maturity

(C) $200 capital gain

(D) None of the above

116. Which of the following securities is/are directly backed by the U.S. government?

I. GNMA

II. FNMA

III. FHLMC

(A) I only

(B) I and II

(C) II and III

(D) I, II and III

117. Which of the following disputes must be resolved using the Code of Arbitration?

I. A dispute between a member of FINRA and a registered rep

II. A dispute between a member of FINRA and a customer

III. A dispute between two members of FINRA

IV. A dispute between a bank and a member of FINRA

(A) IV only

(B) II and IV

(C) I and III

(D) I, III, and IV

118. Duke Wallwalker purchased an LTSBR Corporation convertible bond at 95 on January 20, 2018. The bond is convertible at $40, and the investor converts his bond into stock on January 21, 2021. If the bond is trading at 104 and the common stock is trading at $42, for tax purposes, these transactions will result in

(A) a $10 gain

(B) a $10 loss

(C) a $90 gain

(D) neither a gain nor a loss

119. XYZ is currently trading at 24.10–24.25. A designated market maker in XYZ could enter a bid at which of the following prices?

(A) 24.10

(B) 24.12

(C) 24.25

(D) 24.27

120. RANs, BANs, TANs, and CLNs are issued by municipalities seeking

(A) to insure their municipal securities

(B) the approval of the SEC

(C) long-term financing

(D) short-term financing

121. If an official statement has a dated date of May 1st, but the first coupon payment is set at December 1st, it means that the first payment is a

(A) long coupon

(B) mistake printed on the official statement

(C) short coupon

(D) normal payment for a seven-month bond

122. Which of the following statements regarding municipal revenue bonds is NOT true?

(A) Revenue bonds are not subject to a debt ceiling.

(B) Revenue bonds may be issued by inter-state authorities.

(C) The maturity date of the issue will usu-ally exceed the useful life of the facility backing the bonds.

(D) Debt service is paid from revenue received from the facility backing the bonds.

123. One of your customers feels they were over-charged for a trade and sends your firm a written complaint. What must happen with regard to the complaint?

(A) The complaint must be forwarded to the SEC.

(B) The complaint must be handled by a principal.

(C) The overcharged amount in dispute must be credited to the customer's account until a decision has been reached.

(D) The complaint must be forwarded to the arbitration committee.

124. All of the following may be sources of revenue for a revenue bond EXCEPT

(A) property taxes

(B) user fees

(C) tolls

(D) airports

125. One of your clients would like to add some municipal bonds to their portfolio. Since your client has enough cash to diversify, you should let them know that some of the ways they could diversify would be

I. geographically

II. par value of certificates

III. type of bonds

IV. ratings

(A) II, III, and IV

(B) I, III, and IV

(C) I and II

(D) II and IV

DO NOT TURN THE PAGE UNTIL TOLD TO DO SO **STOP** DO NOT RETURN TO A PREVIOUS TEST

Chapter 18

Answers and Explanations to Practice Exam 1

Congratulations! If you've reached this point, you've completed the practice exam in Chapter 17. (If you haven't, flip back and take the test. You don't want to spoil all the surprises, do you?) You can stop here and review your answers. If you're going to the second exam, review this one thoroughly before proceeding.

Review, review, review. And if I haven't mentioned this yet, reviewing is definitely a good idea. Look at the questions you had problems with, retake all the questions you got wrong, and make sure you get them right the second (or third) time around. If you're short on time but just can't wait to see how you fared, you can check out the abbreviated answer key (without the explanations) at the end of this chapter. I explain how the Series 7 is scored in the section "Making the Grade," just before the answer key. But I strongly suggest you come back later and — you guessed it — review.

Wait at least a week or two before taking the same test again. Retaking the test won't help your cause if you're just memorizing the answers.

1. **D.** (Chapter 7) You have to remember to look at this question from a corporation's point of view. As a practical matter, the issuer will most likely refund the issue that will cost it the most money over the life of the issue. The first thing that an issuer would look at is the coupon rate (highest coupon first), next would be the call premium (lowest call premium first), after that, the call date (earliest call date first), and last, the maturity (longest maturity first). Following this formula leads you to Choice (D).

2. **A.** (Chapter 6) Common stockholders have equity (ownership) positions, as do preferred stockholders. However, bondholders are creditors, not owners.

3. **C.** (Chapter 6) Common stockholders of PXPX Corporation — or, for that matter, any publicly traded corporation — have a residual claim to the assets of the corporation at dissolution (meaning they're the last to get paid if any money is left). PXPX Corp. common stockholders are entitled to receive a report containing audited financial statements on a yearly, *not* weekly, basis. Finally, PXPX Corp. stockholders never get to vote on dividends to be paid (whether stock or cash); dividends are decided by the board of directors.

4. **C.** (Chapter 13) Preferred stockholders and bondholders are subject to inflation risk. Inflation risk is the risk that the fixed interest or dividend payments will become worth less over time in terms of purchasing power. By purchasing convertible preferred stock, investors may convert their preferred stock into common stock of the same corporation at any time. Common stock has a greater chance of keeping pace with inflation, which reduces the inflation risk.

5. **A.** (Chapter 5) The easiest way to figure this one out is to use the following formula:

$$\text{Outstanding} = \text{Issued} - \text{Treasury}$$
$$\text{Outstanding} = 12{,}000{,}000 - 1{,}000{,}000 = 11{,}000{,}000$$

So, to determine how many shares are outstanding in the market, look at the amount of shares the company issued, which is 12,000,000, and subtract the amount of repurchased (treasury) stock. In this case, there are still 11,000,000 shares still outstanding.

6. **A.** (Chapter 7) Treasury bills, or T-bills, are short-term U.S. government debt securities that are issued at a discount and mature at par value. Since T-bills don't make interest payments, they are issued at a discount yield basis instead of a percentage of the dollar price.

7. **A.** (Chapter 7) You have to remember that accrued interest on U.S. government bonds is calculated in actual days instead of 30-day months like corporate and municipal bonds. U.S. government bonds settle in one business day from the trade date, so the settlement date is March 17 (3/17). Next, you need to subtract the previous coupon date, which is January 1 (1/1), from the settlement date.

3/17	January +1
1/1	February –2
2 months 16 days	–1
× 30	
60 + 16 = 76 – 1 = 75 days	

Next, multiply the 2 months by 30 days to get a total of 60 days. Then add the 16 days you get after subtracting 1 day from 17 days and you have a total of 76 days (60 + 16). Because U.S. government bonds are calculated in actual days, you need to add an extra day for January (31 days in January) and subtract 2 days for February (28 days in February). After subtracting the 1 from 76, you get an answer of 75 days. *Note:* Don't add or subtract days for the settlement month (in this case March) because you didn't go through the end of the month.

8. **B.** (Chapter 8) In order to determine the best investment for Jake, you must do a taxable-equivalent yield (TEY) calculation. To accomplish this, you need to know Jake's tax bracket. Remember, the interest received from municipal bond investments is federally (and sometimes state) tax-free, and investors in higher tax brackets save more money by investing in municipal bonds when compared to other investments. The Series 7 examiners are testing you to make sure you know that the other items listed here are not relevant to the question.

9. **C.** (Chapter 12) For an investor to profit when holding a long call, the investor has to exercise the option when the market price is above the strike (exercise) price plus the premium paid.

10. **D.** (Chapter 7) Collateralized debt obligations (CDOs) are asset-backed securities backed by a pool of bonds, loans, or other debt instruments. CDOs are broken down into *tranches* (slices) of differing amounts of risks and/or maturities. Because of the complexity of these investments, they're not suitable for new or smaller investors; they're more suitable for institutional or sophisticated investors.

11. **D.** (Chapter 5) When a company decides to go public, it must file a registration statement with the SEC. The registration statement must include

>> The issuer's name and a description of its business

>> The names and addresses of all the issuer's control persons (in other words, officers, directors, and investors owning 10 percent or more of the issuer's securities)

>> What the money raised will be used for

>> The capitalization of the issuer

>> Complete financial statements

>> Whether there are any legal proceedings against the issuer

12. **D.** (Chapter 5) The securities listed in this question are all nonexempt, meaning that they all have to register with the SEC. The Securities Act of 1933 requires all new nonexempt issues of securities sold to the public to be registered. In general, exempt issues include municipal securities, U.S. government securities, bank issues, private placements, intra-state offerings, and securities issued by nonprofit organizations.

13. **B.** (Chapter 5) Remember, there's a difference between exempt securities and exempt transactions. Exempt transactions include intrastate offerings, Regulation D offerings, and Regulation A offerings. There are other securities that are exempt from registration based on who's issuing the securities. Exempt securities include: U.S. government securities, municipal bonds, securities issued by banks, public utility stocks or bonds, and so on.

14. **D.** (Chapter 16) I hope you found this question to be fairly easy. Confirmations must include pretty much all the information regarding the trade, including all the choices listed.

15. **D.** (Chapter 10) Mutual (open-end) and closed-end funds are considered management companies because they have actively managed portfolios and are defined as such according to the Investment Company Act of 1940. Because unit trusts do not have actively managed portfolios, they're not considered management companies and have their own classification.

16. A. (Chapter 15) Qualified plans under IRS laws allow investors to invest money for retirement with *pre-tax dollars* (you can write qualified plan contributions off on your taxes). In addition, earnings accumulate on a *tax-deferred* basis (the investor isn't taxed until the money is withdrawn). However, distributions (tax-deferred earnings and contributions) for which the participant receives a tax deduction are 100 percent taxable.

17. D. (Chapter 10) Tricky, tricky. The Series 7 examiners want to make sure you know that a variable annuity is derived from two separate products: an insurance contract and securities held in a separate account. Consequently, a variable annuity must be registered with the State Insurance Commission (for the insurance contract) and the Securities and Exchange Commission (for the securities held in the separate account).

18. B. (Chapter 16) The customer's signature is not required on a trade confirmation. However, the customer's account number, the registered rep's ID number, the trade date, whether the customer bought or sold, the number of shares or par value of bonds, the yield (if bonds), the CUSIP number, the price of the security, the total amount paid, the commission (if on an agency basis), and the net amount are all required on the confirmation. You can imagine how cumbersome it would be to try to get the customer's signature on each trade.

19. D. (Chapter 16) Brokerage firms, investment companies, investment advisers, and so on, must have and adopt written policies for protecting customer's records and account information, which is covered under Regulation S-P. (Think of the "S-P" as *Safeguarding Privacy*.)

20. B. (Chapter 16) Recommendations made to a customer must fit that customer's objectives and risk tolerance. A review by a principal is necessary if the recommendations result in a trade. For the Series 7 exam purposes, individual recommendations are governed by FINRA, not the FRB (Federal Reserve Board). Remember, if you're going to make your own recommendations to your customers, it is good practice, though not a rule, to run it past your principal first because they will have to sign off on the recommendation if it results in a trade.

21. A. (Chapter 16) If a registered representative believes that a customer is making an unsuitable trade, the representative may enter the order but must mark the order ticket "unsolicited." In this question, the client is making a trade that you believe is unsuitable for them, but you can still execute the trade as long as you mark the order ticket as "unsolicited," which will protect you and make your client happy.

22. B. (Chapter 15) I recommend that you set up the equation as if you're dealing with one bond and then multiply the answer by 10 at the end. Declan purchased the bonds at $1,050 (105 percent of 1,000 par) and the bonds are maturing at $1,000 par. So, as far as the IRS is concerned, Declan is losing $5 per year ($50 loss divided by 10 years) on the value of a bond. Because he sold the bonds in three years, the total amount of amortization per bond would be $15. After subtracting the $15 from the $1,050 purchase price, you see that the new cost basis is $1,035. After three years, Declan should sell the bonds for $1,035 each to break even. Because the bonds were sold for $1,020 (102 percent of 1,000 par), he had a loss of $15 per bond. Because Declan had 10 bonds, he had a capital loss of $150.

$$\$1,050 \xrightarrow{\ 10\ years\ } \$1,000$$

$50 = $5 per year amortization

$5 × 3 years = $15 total amortization

$1,050 − $15 amortization = $1,035 (new cost basis)

$1,035 (new cost basis) − $1,020 (selling price) = $15 loss per bond × 10 bonds = $150 loss.

23. B. (Chapter 15) *Qualified cash dividends* received from stocks are taxed at a maximum rate of 0 percent, 15 percent, or 20 percent depending on the investor's adjusted gross income (AGI). Non-qualified dividends are taxed at the investor's tax bracket. Please note that these rates are subject to change.

24. D. (Chapter 16) The Bank Secrecy Act establishes the U.S. Treasury Department as the regulator of anti-money-laundering programs. As such, all broker-dealers are required to have programs set up to help detect the possibility of money laundering. Broker-dealers must also review the OFAC's (Office of Foreign Asset Control's) SDN (Specially Designated Nationals) list to determine that they're not doing business with organizations or individuals that are on the list.

25. A. (Chapter 10) Life-cycle or targeted date funds are often funds of funds, which are based on an investor's age. Investors buy a life-cycle fund designed for people their age. Life-cycle funds adjust their holdings every so often so that investors are taking less risk as they get older. Because younger investors can afford to take more risk, a larger percentage of their portfolio is in equities and less is in fixed-income securities. As investors get older, they should have an increasing number of fixed-income securities and less equity securities. Life-cycle funds automatically take care of that for investors.

26. C. (Chapter 16) Mutual fund account statements must be sent out at least semiannually (once every 6 months). However, if there was any trading done in the account, a statement must be sent out that month.

27. D. (Chapter 13) Systematic risk is also known as market risk. Systematic risk is the risk that securities could decline due to negative market conditions. All securities are subject to systematic risk.

28. B. (Chapter 7) Secured bonds are ones secured with collateral. Secured corporate bonds include mortgage bonds, equipment trusts, collateral trusts, and guaranteed bonds.

29. C. (Chapter 8) Municipal fund securities include ABLE accounts, LGIPs (local government investment pools), and Section 529 plans. 529 plans are also known as qualified tuition plans because they allow money to be put aside by investors for qualified educational expenses.

30. A. (Chapter 12) The easiest way for you to see what's going on is to set up an options chart. This investor wrote (sold) the XYZ put for a premium of 2.75, so you have to put $275 (2.75 × 100 shares per option) in the "Money In" side of the chart because the investor received the money for selling the option. Next, the option was exercised, so you have to put $3,000 (the 30 strike price × 100 shares per option) in the "Money Out" side of the chart because "puts switch," meaning that the exercised option has to go on the opposite side of the chart from the premium. After that, the investor sold the 100 shares of stock in the market for $27.50 per share for a total of $2,750, which goes in the "Money In" side of the chart because the investor received money for selling the stock. Total up the two sides and you see that the investor received $3,025 and spent $3,000 for a whopping profit of $25.

Money Out	Money In
$3,000	$275
	$2,750
$3,000	$3,025

$3,025 (money in) − $3,000 (money out) = $25 gain

31. D. (Chapter 12) As with the previous question, the easiest way for you to see what's going on is to set up an options chart. Mrs. Smith purchased 100 shares of ABC at 35, so you have to put $3,500 (35 × 100 shares) in the "Money Out" side of the chart. Next, Mrs. Smith wrote (sold) an ABC call for 5.50, so you have to put $550 (5.50 × 100 shares per option) in the "Money In" side of the chart. After the stock increased, the call was exercised, so you have to put the exercised strike price of $4,000 (40 strike price × 100 shares per option) under its premium of $550 because "calls same," meaning that for call options, the premium and the exercised strike price go on the same side of the chart. Total up the two sides and you see that Mrs. Smith had a gain of $1,050.

Money Out	Money In
$3,500	$550
	$4,000
$3,500	$4,550

$4,550 (money in) − $3,500 (money out) = $1,050 gain

32. D. (Chapter 8) Factors that affect the marketability (how easy it is to buy and sell) of municipal GO (general obligation) bonds are the quality, maturity date, call features, coupon rate, block size, dollar price, issuer's name, sinking fund, and credit enhancements (typically insurance).

33. B. (Chapter 16) You will find that this is not an unusual situation. When you're opening an account for a new customer, the customer may not feel comfortable sharing all their financial information with you. However, you can still do trading in the account and make recommendations if you can determine financial information from other sources, such as D&B (Dun and Bradstreet) cards. Say, for example, that the D&B card says that the customer is the CEO of a corporation that made $5 billion last year. You can assume the customer has a lot of money, and you can certainly make recommendations that are larger in size. The recommendations you make to a customer should be suitable to their investment objectives and financial situation. If you can't determine the information from other sources, you can still make trades and recommendations that would be suitable for all investors, such as mutual funds or U.S. government securities.

34. D. (Chapter 9) Because this margin account has a debit balance, it's a long account; short accounts have a credit balance. The easiest way to deal with margin questions of this type is to set up a long margin account formula:

$$LMV - DR = EQ$$

$LMV =$ Long Market Value (the current market value of the stocks held in the account)

$DR =$ The Debit Record or Debit Balance (the amount borrowed from the broker-dealer plus any interest)

$EQ =$ Equity (the owner's portion of the account)

$$LMV - DR = EQ$$
$$\$20,250 - \$3,000 = \$17,250$$
$$\text{Reg T} \times LMV = \underline{\$10,125}$$
$$\$7,125 \ \textit{excess equality}$$

Because the LMV equals $20,250 and the DR equals $3,000, the EQ has to be $17,250. From there, you have to compare what the investor should have in equity to be at 50 percent (Regulation T) of the LMV with what is actually in equity. With Regulation T at 50 percent, which is standard, the investor should have $10,125 in EQ to be at 50 percent. However, the investor actually has $7,125 more than that, so that is the investor's excess equity.

35. **B.** (Chapter 5) A preliminary prospectus includes the purpose for the funds and financial statements. Because a preliminary prospectus (red herring) is printed before the final price is established, it may include a projected price range that is subject to change.

36. **C.** (Chapter 5) Certain purchases, such as a Regulation D private placement, may require investors to be accredited (although they have a 35 unaccredited investor exclusion). Out of the choices listed, accredited investors are ones with a net worth of at least $1 million excluding any equity they may have in their primary residence, or ones with an annual income of at least $200,000 (or $300,000 for joint accounts) for the last two (not three) years that's expected to stay at least the same for the current year.

37. **A.** (Chapter 14) DMMs (Designated Market Makers) create a trading platform for particular securities on an exchange. DMMs not only trade out of their own inventory as dealers but also execute trades for others as a broker.

38. **D.** (Chapter 12) A long combination is when an investor purchases a call and a put on the same security but with different strike prices and/or expiration months. So when an investor purchases a straddle, the maximum potential gain is unlimited on the call side.

39. **B.** (Chapter 16) Whether the account is active or inactive, the SEC and FINRA require member firms to send customer account statements at least quarterly (once every 3 months). Mutual fund statements must be sent out at least semiannually (once every 6 months).

40. **C.** (Chapter 10) Hybrid REITs (Real Estate Investment Trusts) trade on an exchange, provide mortgage loans to developers, and hold a portfolio of securities. Hybrid REITs are a combination of equity (ownership) and mortgage REITs.

41. **D.** (Chapter 9) When a corporation opens a margin account, the corporation has to provide a corporate charter, which needs to say that the corporation can buy securities on margin, and a corporate resolution, which says who has the trading authority for the account. A new account form is always needed for any type of account. The corporation also needs a hypothecation agreement, which allows the broker-dealer to hold the securities in street name so that they can be used as collateral for a loan. In addition, the corporation needs a credit agreement, which sets the terms for the loan.

42. **C.** (Chapter 8) The Municipal Bond Index is the average dollar price of 40 highly traded GO and revenue bonds with an average maturity of 20 years and a rating of "A" or better.

43. **A.** (Chapter 11) Exploratory or wildcatting programs have the highest capital appreciation potential because the drilling takes place in unproven areas. If the partnership finds oil, it paid relatively little for the land as compared to drilling in proven areas, so the capital appreciation potential is high.

44. **A.** (Chapter 13) Certainly, any information you can get about your client will help you set up a portfolio that fits the client's needs. However, because Martina's primary investment objective is making sure that she's prepared for retirement, you need to begin by looking at her age. Someone who is younger can take more risk than someone who is older.

45. B. (Chapter 9) The minimum maintenance (minimum amount of equity) required in a short margin account is 30 percent of the current or short market value.

$$\$30,000 \times 30\% = \$9,000$$

46. D. (Chapter 7) The expression "quality over quantity" applies here. Rating services are concerned with quality, defined as the issuer's (or guarantor's) default risk or ability to pay interest and principal on time. The two biggest rating services are Moody's and Standard & Poor's. The highest ratings for these rating services are Aaa and AAA, respectively.

47. A. (Chapter 9) Remember, you can't tender stock that is borrowed, and stock in a short account is borrowed stock.

48. D. (Chapter 16) All order tickets need to include the items listed in the question plus the customer's account number; the number of shares or bonds being purchased or sold; whether the customer is buying, selling, or selling short; whether the customer is covered or uncovered (option orders); whether it's a market order, good-till-canceled, and so on.

49. D. (Chapter 8) All the choices listed are important factors that can be used in determining the amount of commission, markup, or markdown charged on the purchase or sale of municipal securities.

50. C. (Chapter 6) Cumulative voting allows shareholders to aggregate (combine) their votes and vote for whomever they please. For argument's sake, if an investor owned 1,000 common shares and there were four members of the board of directors open for vote, the investor could use all 4,000 votes (1,000 shares × 4 members) for a single candidate, if desired. Cumulative voting can be used to make it easier for smaller shareholders to gain representation on the board of directors. Remember, cumulative voting doesn't give smaller shareholders more voting power, only more flexibility.

51. D. (Chapter 6) The purpose of ADRs (American Depositary Receipts) is to facilitate the trading of foreign securities in U.S. markets. ADRs carry currency risk because distributions on ADRs must be converted from foreign currency to U.S. dollars on the date of distribution. The trading price of the ADR is actually quite affected by currency fluctuation, which can devalue any dividends and/or the value of the stock.

52. A. (Chapter 7) CMOs (Collateralized Mortgage Obligations) are backed by home mortgages, which are considered to be very safe (although not as safe as in previous years), and, therefore, are generally rated AAA.

53. D. (Chapter 5) Unless exempt, securities must be registered on the state level as well as with the SEC. State registration types are notification, coordination, and qualification.

54. D. (Chapter 16) After receiving Declan's written complaint, the municipal securities broker-dealer must accept the complaint and write down any action taken to resolve the complaint. All broker-dealers should keep a complaint file for each customer and keep accurate records of any communications or actions taken regarding a complaint.

55. C. (Chapter 8) EMMA (Electronic Municipal Market Access) is a centralized online site that nonprofessional, retail investors can use to locate key information about municipal securities. Available on this site are official statements for most new municipal bond offerings and up-to-the-minute access to prices for outstanding municipal bonds.

56. **C.** (Chapter 12) You have to remember that sellers (shorters or writers) of options always face more risk than buyers; the buyer's risk is limited to the amount invested. However, sellers of put options do not face a maximum loss potential that's unlimited because put options go in-the-money when the price of the stock goes down below the strike price, and it can only go down to 0. Sellers of uncovered calls face a maximum loss potential that is unlimited because call options go in-the-money when the price of the stock goes above the strike price, and the seller has to purchase the stock at a price that could go higher and higher. Additionally, investors who short stock as in Statement II face a maximum loss potential that's unlimited because the investors have taken a bearish position and lose money when the price of the security increases, and there's nothing stopping the stock from increasing in value. Investors who have sold covered calls don't face an unlimited maximum loss potential because they have the stock to deliver if exercised.

57. **D.** (Chapter 12) These trades aren't suitable for any investor because it's impossible for the investor to make a profit. I've set up an options chart to demonstrate to you how this is so. First, put the premiums for the options in the chart. Because the investor bought the May 30 call option at 8, you have to put $800 (8 premium × 100 shares per option) in the "Money Out" side of the chart. Next, put $300 (3 premium × 100 shares per option) in the "Money In" side of the chart because the investor sold that option. Because the investor has $800 out and $300 in, you know that the investor's maximum loss potential is $500 ($800 − $300). To get the maximum gain, you have to exercise both options. Because "calls same," you have to put the exercised strike prices below their respective premiums in the chart. Place $3,000 (30 strike price × 100 shares per option) under its premium of $800 and place $3,500 (35 strike price × 100 shares per option) under its premium of $300. After that, you have to total the sides to see that because the "Money In" side and the "Money Out" side of the chart each equal $3,800, there's no way the investor can make a profit.

Money Out	Money In
$800	$300
$3,000	$3,500
$3,800	$3,800

58. **C.** (Chapter 15) Remember that short-term gains or losses are ones that take place in one year or less. The fact that Fred purchased a call option does not affect his holding period on the stock that he purchased. Because Fred has held the stock for 19 months (1 year and 7 months), the sale of the stock would be treated as a long-term capital gain or long-term capital loss.

59. **D.** (Chapter 16) No rules prohibit opening an account registered as joint tenants with rights of survivorship (JTWROS) for two unmarried persons. The registered representative should, however, take all steps to be sure that the unmarried individuals understand the resulting consequences should one party to the account die. For example, in an account registered JTWROS, if one of the engaged parties to the account (for example, John Dow) dies, the deceased party's ownership interest in the account passes to the surviving tenant (Jane Dough) rather than to the deceased party's (John Dow's) estate.

60. **D.** (Chapter 16) Advertisements that include recommendations of the firm do not need to include whether a firm acted as a selling group since selling group members have no financial risk.

61. B. (Chapter 9) Because this margin account has a debit balance, it's a long account; short accounts have a credit balance. The easiest way to deal with margin questions of this type is to set up a long margin account formula:

$$LMV - DR = EQ$$
$$LMV = \text{Long Market Value (the current market value of the stocks}$$
$$\text{held in the account)}$$
$$DR = \text{The Debit Record or Debit Balance (the amount borrowed from}$$
$$\text{the broker-dealer plus any interest)}$$
$$EQ = \text{Equity (the owner's portion of the account)}$$
$$LMV - DR = EQ$$
$$\$18,000 - \$7,000 = \$11,000$$
$$Reg\ T \times LMV = \underline{\$9,000}$$
$$\$2,000 \text{ excess equity}$$

Because the LMV equals $18,000 and the DR equals $7,000, the EQ has to be $11,000. From there, you have to compare what the investor should have in equity to be at 50 percent (Regulation T) of the LMV with what is actually in equity. With Regulation T at 50 percent, which is standard, the investor should have $9,000 in EQ to be at 50 percent. However, because the investor has $11,000 in equity, the excess equity is $2,000.

Because the account has excess equity (SMA), it has buying power. Remember, it is SMA/RT to use your buying power, which tells you that you need to divide the SMA by Regulation T to determine the buying power:

SMA/RT = SMA / Regulation T = $2,000 / 50% = $4,000

Long accounts like this one generate excess equity by the securities held in the account increasing in value.

If the investor withdraws the excess equity, they're essentially borrowing more money from the account and the debit balance increases, not decreases.

62. C. (Chapter 9) A day trading account requires an initial margin of $25,000, and the investor must keep $25,000 minimum equity in the account to keep trading. A portfolio margin account is relatively new and looks at the risk of the portfolio as a whole to determine the margin requirement. Only certain investors are able to take advantage of portfolio margin because it requires a certain degree of sophistication and a minimum equity of around $100,000.

63. A. (Chapter 12) Because of the additional risk involved when investing in options, such as the ability to lose all money invested or facing unlimited maximum loss, all investors must receive an ODD (Options risk Disclosure Document or Options Disclosure Document) prior to the first transaction. The ODD is not an advertisement; it contains the pitfalls of investing in options. After the customer receives the ODD, the ROP (Registered Options Principal) has to approve the account. Next, you can do the trade, and after that, the customer has to sign and return an OAA (Options Account Agreement) within 15 days after the account has been approved for options trading.

64. C. (Chapter 14) When several bids or offers are made at the same price at a given time on the NYSE floor, the auction rules of priority (highest bid and lowest ask first), precedence (if orders are at the same price, the one that came in first is executed first), and parity (if all else is equal, the larger order is done first) allow for the efficient execution of orders.

65. **C.** (Chapter 14) The Designated Market Maker (DMM or Specialist) is responsible for maintaining a fair and orderly market on the NYSE floor. The DMM helps keep trading as active as possible by executing trades for customers and by trading out of his own account if needed.

66. **C.** (Chapter 12) First, the customer must receive an ODD (Options risk Disclosure Document). Then the account must be approved by an ROP (Registered Options Principal). Next, a trade is executed. Finally, the customer signs and returns the OAA (Options Account Agreement). The OAA must be signed and returned within 15 days after approval of the account.

67. **B.** (Chapter 16) The settlement date for stocks, corporate bonds, and municipal bonds is T+2 (2 business days after the trade date). The settlement date is the day that the issuer updates its records and certificates are delivered to the purchaser's brokerage firm.

68. **B.** (Chapter 14) Regulation SHO covers the rules for short sales. Under SHO rules, all order tickets must be marked as short sale as compared to long sale, which is when an investor is selling securities that are owned. In addition, all brokerage firms must establish rules to locate, borrow, and deliver securities that are to be sold short. All brokerage firms must make sure that the security can be located and delivered by the delivery date prior to executing a short sale.

69. **B.** (Chapter 10) As with most other investment company products, REITs have a professionally managed portfolio. Many investors use REITs as a potential hedge against a downturn in the market because often, there is an inverse relationship between the real estate market and stock prices. In addition, REITs typically have a high degree of liquidity. However, there is no preferential dividend treatment for REITs.

70. **A.** (Chapter 8) The official statement for a municipal bond issue is similar to a prospectus for a corporate issue. The items that you find on an official statement include the offering terms, the underwriting spread, a description of the bonds, a description of the issuer, the offering price, the coupon rate, the feasibility statement, and the legal opinion.

71. **B.** (Chapter 10) When an investor of a variable annuity starts withdrawing money from the annuity, the accumulation units are converted into a fixed number of annuity units. However, the value of the annuity units varies based on the performance of the securities held in the separate account.

72. **C.** (Chapter 11) Because direct participation programs (DPPs or limited partnerships) may require limited partners to come up with additional cash beyond their initial investment, investors must provide a written verification of net worth. After the general partner signs the subscription agreement, the investor is accepted as a limited partner.

73. **C.** (Chapter 13) Beta is a measure of how volatile a stock is as compared to the market. A stock with a beta of 1 would be equally volatile as the market, meaning that if the market increased 5 percent over a given period of time, you would expect the price of your stock to increase 5 percent. If the market declines by 5 percent, you would expect the price of your stock to decline by 5 percent. If you are purchasing a stock with a beta greater than 1, it is more volatile than the market. In this case, you are dealing with a stock with a beta of 1.6, meaning that if the market increased or decreased by 10 percent over a given period of time, you would expect the price of your stock to increase 16 percent or decrease 16 percent. A stock with a beta less than 1 would be less volatile than the market.

74. B. (Chapter 13) A head and shoulders bottom formation (inverted head and shoulders formation) is a bullish sign because it means that the stock hit a bottom and is starting to reverse. In other words, a head and shoulders bottom formation is a bullish sign because it's the reversal of a bearish trend.

75. C. (Chapter 12) Because Michael owns 1,000 shares of WOW stock and wants to generate additional income, he could sell covered calls against the WOW that he owns. Additionally, by placing a sell-stop order for WOW slightly below the market price, Michael is protected against a major loss if WOW drops significantly.

76. B. (Chapter 12) The easiest way for you to see what's going on is to set up an options chart. Your customer purchased 100 shares of ARGH at 44.10, so you have to put $4,410 (44.10 × 100 shares) in the "Money Out" side of the chart. Next, your customer purchased an OEX put for 4.50, so you have to put $450 (4.50 × 100 shares per option) in the "Money Out" side of the chart. If your customer closes the stock position (to close means to do the opposite . . . if they originally bought, to close, they have to sell) for 42.55, you have to put $4,255 (42.55 stock price × 100 shares) in the "Money In" side of the chart. Then, because you're dealing with an option that settles in cash instead of delivery of the underlying security, you need to put the profit of $1,100 in the "Money In" side of the chart. To get the $1,100, you have to remember that put options go in-the-money when the price of the stock goes below the strike price, which it is by 11 (360 − 349), and options are for 100 shares. Total up the two sides, and you see that your customer has a profit of $495.

Money Out	Money In
$4,410	$4,255
$450	$1,100
$4,860	$5,355

$5,355 (money in) − $4,860 (money out) = $495 gain

77. B. (Chapter 14) Unlike fill-or-kill (FOK) orders and immediate-or-cancel (IOC) orders, all-or-none (AON) orders do not have to be executed immediately. However, like FOK orders, they must be filled entirely or the order is cancelled. AON orders remain active until they are executed or cancelled.

78. B. (Chapter 16) To process an ACAT (Automated Customer Account Transfer), a brokerage firm must be a member of the NSCC (National Securities Clearing Corporation). When a brokerage firm is a clearing firm, the firm is assuming financial responsibility if a customer does not pay for a trade or does not deliver certificates that are sold.

79. B. (Chapter 9) This question is a tough one because of the way that it's worded. I suggest that you write "increases SMA," "decreases SMA," or "doesn't change SMA" next to each possible answer before answering the question.

I. Selling securities in a margin account increases the SMA by half the amount of the sale and decreases the debit balance by half the amount of the sale (increases SMA).

II. The purchase of additional securities in a long margin account has no effect on the SMA unless using the buying power, which you can't assume (doesn't change SMA).

III. Money being deposited into the margin account by way of cash dividend or cash payment increases the SMA by the amount of the deposit (increases SMA).

IV. A decrease in the market value of the securities doesn't change the SMA. Remember, you don't lose SMA until you use it (doesn't change SMA).

Now that you have this part down, look at the question again to see what it's asking. Because this is an EXCEPT question, you're looking for the statements that do not increase the SMA, which are Statements II and IV.

80. **B.** (Chapter 5) The spread is the sum of the manager's fee ($0.15) and the takedown ($0.50): $0.15 + $0.50 = $0.65. The selling concession is paid out of the takedown and is not added to the spread equation.

81. **D.** (Chapter 14) All the Roman numeral choices listed would be considered a discretionary order and would require a written Power of Attorney signed by the customer in order to be accepted. To not need a Power of Attorney, the customer must provide or agree to the number of shares (or bonds), whether to buy or sell, and the specific security.

82. **C.** (Chapter 14) If dark pools of liquidity execute trades, the trades are reported as over-the-counter (OTC) transactions, not exchange transactions. Dark pools of liquidity represent pools of institutions, large retail clients, and firms trading for their own inventory. Since the clients and sizes of accounts remain anonymous, dark pools reduce transparency of the markets.

83. **D.** (Chapter 16) Under the Investment Company Act of 1940, mutual funds must provide semiannual (once every 6 months) reports to shareholders.

84. **D.** (Chapter 16) Actually, all the information listed needs to be on the new account form. In addition, you also need the Social Security number (or tax ID if a business), the occupation and type of business, bank references, net worth, annual income, if the customer is an insider of a company, and the signature of the registered rep and a principal.

85. **B.** (Chapter 16) Your client must have at least $500,000 in assets available for investments to establish a prime brokerage account, although if the account is established through an investment adviser, the minimum requirement only $100,000. Prime brokerage firms consolidate information from all brokerage accounts so that the client only has to receive one statement.

86. **C.** (Chapter 11) Real estate DPPs (direct participation programs — limited partnerships) provide advantages for investors such as depreciation deductions, appreciation potential, and cash flow, but not depletion. Depletion only applies to partnerships that deal in natural resources that can be depleted (used up), such as oil or gas.

87. **B.** (Chapter 13) All long-term bonds are subject to inflationary (purchasing power) risk. Inflationary risk is the risk that the return on the investment does not keep pace with inflation. To limit inflationary risk, investors should purchase stocks. Over the long haul, stocks have more than kept pace with inflation.

88. **C.** (Chapter 13) To determine a stock's earnings per share (EPS), you can divide the stock's price by the PE (price earnings) ratio.

$$EPS = \frac{\text{Stock price}}{\text{PE ratio}} = \frac{\$44}{\$6} = \$7.33$$

89. **A.** (Chapter 13) The PE (Price/Earnings) ratio is a tool that can be used by technical analysts to help determine whether a stock is overpriced or underpriced. Typically, they will compare the PE ratios of several different companies within the same industry to see if there may be a good investment opportunity. Typically, the lower the PE, the better. A company with a low PE ratio means that the earnings per share (EPS) are high as compared to its price. The equation for PE ratio is

$$\text{PE ratio} = \frac{\text{Market price}}{\text{EPS}}$$

90. **D.** (Chapter 8) Because the investor bought 50 of each bond, they were all rated AA, and they mature around the same time, you can rule out maturity, quality, and quantity as your answers. The investor's funds are an example of geographic diversification because the bonds are from a variety of issuers around the United States.

91. **A.** (Chapter 12) Although you may not need an options chart to figure out the answer to this one, creating a chart is good practice, and I think it lessens your chances of making mistakes. First, because the customer purchased the option for 4.50, you need to place $450 (4.50 × 100 shares per option) in the "Money Out" portion of the chart. Next, you have to close the option for 4.55 because you buy at the ask price and sell at the bid price. To close the option, the customer has to do the opposite of what they did originally; if they originally bought the option, as they did here, to close, they have to sell. So, you need to put $455 in the "Money In" side of the chart. Now, you can see that the customer had a $5 gain because they received $455 for selling the option and paid $450 for buying the option.

Money Out	Money In
$450	$455

92. **A.** (Chapter 12) To hedge means to protect. If the investor would like to hedge his position, they should buy a call on XYZ. Remember that the investor is short the stock and must buy XYZ back at some point to close their short position. Buying an XYZ call gives the investor the right to buy back XYZ at a fixed price, which would allow the investor to protect the position and not face an unlimited maximum loss potential.

93. **A.** (Chapter 12) The easiest way for you to see what's going on is to set up an options chart. Because Grant bought the put for 350 (3.50 × 100 shares per option) and the stock for 6,200 (62 × 100 shares), you need to put "350" and "6,200" in the "Money Out" side of the chart. Next, Grant sold the stock for $6,400 (64 × 100 shares) and closed (do the opposite — if originally you bought, to close you have to sell) the option for $75 (0.75 × 100 shares per option). So, you have to put "$6,400" and "$75" in the "Money In" side of the chart. Total up the two sides, and you see that he had a $75 loss.

Money Out	Money In
$350	$6,400
$6,200	$75
$6,550	$6,475

$6,550 (money out) − $6,475 (money in) = $75 loss

94. **C.** (Chapter 15) Options are always taxed as capital gains or capital losses. This investor purchased an option that expired worthless, and, therefore, they lost money. Because the investor held the LEAPS (Long-term Equity AnticiPation Securities) for over one year, it's taxed as a long-term capital loss. LEAPS have initial expirations of up to 39 months.

95. C. (Chapter 16) Without having discretionary authority, registered representatives may not decide on whether to buy or sell, the security to purchase or sell, or the amount of shares or dollar amount to purchase for the customer. Registered representatives may, however, without written power of attorney, choose the price or timing of an order with the customer's verbal approval.

96. D. (Chapter 5) You must distinguish a nonexempt security from an exempt security. A nonexempt security is one that is not exempt from SEC registration; in other words, it must be registered with the SEC. Variable annuities, which carry investment risk, are nonexempt securities under the Securities Act of 1933 and must be registered before public sale. Similarly, unit trusts and mutual funds are nonexempt even though the underlying securities may be exempt, such as municipals and U.S. government securities. However, a fixed annuity is an insurance product exempt from registration with the SEC. It's not considered a security because of the guaranteed payout.

97. B. (Chapter 10) A specialized or sector fund invests a minimum of 25 percent of its assets in a particular region or industry and would be the most suitable for Buddy.

98. D. (Chapter 11) Intangible drilling costs (IDCs), the costs involved in actually getting to the oil, provide a tax benefit to investors of an oil and gas exploratory (wildcatting) program. IDCs are items such as labor and surveys. IDCs are deductible expenses in the year in which they occur.

99. B. (Chapter 13) As investors age, they should start shifting more of their investments from stocks into bonds and cash equivalents such as money-market instruments. The thought is that older investors cannot afford to take as much risk. The standard asset allocation model suggests that you take 100 and subtract the person's age to determine the percentage that he should have invested in stocks. In this case, the investor is 60, so he should have 40% (100−60) invested in stocks and the balance in bonds and cash equivalents such as money market funds.

100. C. (Chapter 12) The easiest way for you to see what's going on is to set up an options chart. Ginny purchased 2 calls and 2 puts, so the first thing you should do is put the multiplier of "× 2" on the outside of the chart; this way, it's as if you're dealing with single options. Because she bought the calls for 300 each (3 × 100 shares per option) and the puts for 200 each (2 × 100 shares per option), you need to put "300" and "200" in the "Money Out" side of the chart. Next, Ginny closed her options for their intrinsic value (the in-the-money amount). Because put options go in-the-money when the price of the stock goes below the strike price, just the put option is in-the-money, not the call option. With the strike price at $44.50 and the strike price at 50, the put is 5.50 in-the-money ($50.00 − $44.50). So, you need to put $550 in the "Money In" side of the chart because Ginny closed the option (to close means to do the opposite — if you originally bought, you have to sell to close). Total up the two sides and you see that Ginny had a profit of $50 per option. Because Ginny bought 2 options, she had a profit of $100.

(x2) Money Out	Money In
$300	$550
$200	
$500	$550

$550 (money in) − $500 (money out) = $50 gain per option × 2 = $100 gain

101. **B.** (Chapter 13) CMOs (collateralized mortgage obligations) offer no tax advantages to buyers because they are taxed on all levels. However, the interest received on municipal bonds is federally tax-free and sometimes state-tax-free. In addition, retirement plans allow investors to deposit money tax-free (in most cases) and the money grows on a tax-deferred basis. DPPs (direct participation programs) allow for additional write-offs, such as depreciation and depletion, which provide for a cash flow that's greater than the net income.

102. **B.** (Chapter 12) They are trying to generate income, so they have to sell something. The only answer that has them selling something is Choice (B). Writing (selling or shorting) a straddle would allow them to generate income on a stock that's remaining stable, because they would receive the premiums for selling the straddle and be able to profit if neither the call option nor the put option that are part of the straddle go too much in-the-money.

103. **A.** (Chapter 6) Adjustable (floating rate) preferred stock receives a dividend that adjusts according to prevailing interest rates.

104. **B.** (Chapter 14) Regulation SHO covers the short sale of securities. According to Regulation SHO, all order tickets must be marked as short sale (as compared to long sale). In addition, brokerage firms must establish rules to locate, borrow, and deliver securities that are to be sold short.

105. **D.** (Chapter 7) The bond indenture (deed of trust) is the legal agreement between the issuer and investors. The bond indenture includes the maturity date, the par value, the coupon rate, any collateral securing the bond, any callable or convertible features, and the name of the trustee.

106. **A.** (Chapter 16) Under the USA Patriot Act, all financial institutions must maintain Customer Identification Programs (CIPs). It is up to the financial institution to verify the identity of any new customers, maintain records of how they verified the identity, and determine whether the new customer appears on any suspected terrorist list or terrorist organization. As part of the identification program, they must obtain the customer's name, date of birth, address (no P.O. boxes), and Social Security number.

107. **D.** (Chapter 11) All the choices listed are important to evaluate for investors of direct participation programs.

108. **C.** (Chapter 15) Withdrawals must begin by April 1 of the year after the investor turns age 73. At that point, the investor has to take a required minimum distribution (RMD), which can be determined by looking at the IRS's required minimum distribution worksheet.

109. **D.** (Chapter 7) Treasury Inflation Protected Securities (TIPS) are U.S. government bonds that pay interest payments once every 6 months. The interest payments adjust according to prevailing inflation interest rates, which means that the bond price remains more stable. TIPS have a minimum purchase price of $100 and have initial maturities of 5, 10, and 30 years.

110. **D.** (Chapter 11) An oil and gas wildcatting (exploratory) program would best suit your client's needs. Oil and gas wildcatting programs drill in unproven areas and create quite a lot of write-offs in the early years. However, if oil is hit, a wildcatting program will bring in a lot of money.

111. **B.** (Chapter 8) Remember that state governments do not collect ad-valorem (property) taxes. Ad-valorem taxes are assessed by local governments (for example, towns and counties). Generally, state governments receive the most income from income taxes and sales taxes.

112. **D.** (Chapter 16) The Series 7 examiners may try to trip you up by throwing in an irrelevant answer choice (like the date of maturity) to find out whether you know your MSRB (municipal securities rulemaking board) rules. MSRB rules require that confirmations include whether the trade was executed on a principal (dealer) or agency basis. The amount of the dealer's markup or markdown on a principal trade does not have to be disclosed, but the commission on an agency trade does need to be disclosed.

113. **A.** (Chapter 10) If John wants to profit from a possible decline in the market, he has to employ bearish strategies. Inverse ETFs (exchange-traded funds) are funds that trade on an exchange and use derivative products, such as options, to attempt to profit from a decline in the underlying securities, such as the S&P 500. Selling SPX (S&P 500) calls is a bearish strategy in which the seller profits if the underlying securities stay the same or decline in value. High-yielding bond funds (junk bond funds) are more likely to be damaged if the market declines in value, and selling OEX (S&P 100) puts is a bullish, not bearish, strategy.

114. **B.** (Chapter 13) When you're determining the dividend payout ratio, you have to remember that the formula is as follows:

$$\text{dividend payout ratio} = \frac{\text{annual dividends per common share}}{\text{EPS (earnings per share)}}$$

Because this question gives you the quarterly dividend, you need to multiply by 4 to get the annual dividend of $1.00 ($0.25 × 4).

$$\text{dividend payout ratio} = \frac{\$1.00}{\$2.50} = 40\%$$

115. **A.** (Chapter 15) Municipal original issue discount bonds must be accreted; the discount is treated as part of the investor's tax-free interest. Because these municipal discount bonds must be accreted, the cost basis is equal to the par value, and, as a tax consequence, Gerry will have no losses or gains if he holds the bond to maturity.

116. **A.** (Chapter 7) Out of all of the choices listed, the only one directly backed by the U.S. government is GNMA (a.k.a Ginnie Mae, or the Government National Mortgage Association).

117. **C.** (Chapter 16) As you can see, the one common denominator is that all the answer choices have the word "FINRA" in them, which tells you that being a FINRA member must be pretty important. The Code of Arbitration is mandatory in member-against-member disputes including a member firm and one of its registered reps. However, FINRA has no jurisdiction over banks or over disputes between nonmembers such as customers or issuers; in cases such as these, the nonmember decides whether to use arbitration or a Code of Procedure hearing to settle a dispute.

118. **D.** (Chapter 15) There are no tax consequences to Duke for converting a bond into shares of common stock. In order for Duke to have a taxable gain or loss, the shares Duke received as a result of his conversion to common stock must be sold.

119. **B.** (Chapter 14) A designated market maker (DMM) cannot compete with public orders, so Choices (A) and (C) are no good. The responsibility of a designated market maker is to keep trading as active as possible by narrowing the spread if necessary. Therefore, the only answer that works is Choice (B) because that answer is in-between the bid and ask prices.

120. **D.** (Chapter 8) Municipal short-term notes such as RANs (revenue anticipation notes), BANs (bond anticipation notes), TANs (tax anticipation notes), and CLNs (construction loan notes) are used to provide short-term (interim) financing until a permanent, long-term bond issue is floated, until tax receipts increase, or until revenue flows in.

121. **A.** (Chapter 7) You can assume that corporate and municipal bonds normally make interest payments semiannually (once every 6 months). However, because the first payment for this bond doesn't take place until 7 months after the dated date, the first payment is a long coupon. After the first payment, all additional coupon payments will be made every 6 months.

122. **C.** (Chapter 8) You need to be careful in this case because the Series 7 examiners are asking you for a false statement. The maturity of revenue bonds may be 25 to 30 years, but the facility being built by the income received from the revenue bond issue is usually expected to last a lifetime. Revenue bonds may be issued by interstate authorities, such as tolls, and the debt service (interest and principal) on the bonds is paid from revenue received from the facility backing the bonds. In addition, revenue bonds are not subject to a debt ceiling; general obligation bonds are.

123. **B.** (Chapter 16) All written complaints must be handled by a principal of the firm. All written complaints must be kept on file with the firm as well as a description of how the complaints were handled.

124. **A.** (Chapter 8) The Series 7 examiners want to make sure you can distinguish funds raised for municipal revenue bonds from those raised for general obligation bonds. Tolls, fees, airports, power plants, water, wastewater, and so forth may all be fund generators that subsidize revenue bonds. Property taxes (ad-valorem taxes) support general obligation bonds.

125. **B.** (Chapter 8) Ways to diversify in municipal bonds are geographically (buying bonds from different areas of the country), type of bonds (revenue, general obligation, notes, and so on), and ratings (AAA, AA, A, B, and so on). Buying bonds with different par values does not diversify a portfolio.

Making the Grade

Here's how the Series 7 exam is scored:

>> You get one point for each correct answer.

>> You get zero points for each incorrect answer.

A passing score is 72 percent. To calculate your grade for this exam, multiply the number of correct answers by 0.8 or divide it by 125. Whatever grade you get, make sure you round down, not up. For example, a grade of 69.6 is a 69 percent, not a 70. If you got 90 or more questions right, you're getting a passing score.

REMEMBER

The actual test contains ten additional experimental questions that don't count toward your actual score. You can't tell these questions apart from the questions that do count, so you may have to answer a few more questions right to get your 72 percent. Don't sweat it. Simply come prepared, stay focused, and do your best.

Answer Key for Practice Exam 1

1.	D	33.	B	65.	C	97.	B
2.	A	34.	D	66.	C	98.	D
3.	C	35.	B	67.	B	99.	B
4.	C	36.	C	68.	B	100.	C
5.	A	37.	A	69.	B	101.	B
6.	A	38.	D	70.	A	102.	B
7.	A	39.	B	71.	B	103.	A
8.	B	40.	C	72.	C	104.	B
9.	C	41.	D	73.	C	105.	D
10.	D	42.	C	74.	B	106.	A
11.	D	43.	A	75.	C	107.	D
12.	D	44.	A	76.	B	108.	C
13.	B	45.	B	77.	B	109.	D
14.	D	46.	D	78.	B	110.	D
15.	D	47.	A	79.	B	111.	B
16.	A	48.	D	80.	B	112.	D
17.	D	49.	D	81.	D	113.	A
18.	B	50.	C	82.	C	114.	B
19.	D	51.	D	83.	D	115.	A
20.	B	52.	A	84.	D	116.	A
21.	A	53.	D	85.	B	117.	C
22.	B	54.	D	86.	C	118.	D
23.	B	55.	C	87.	B	119.	B
24.	D	56.	C	88.	C	120.	D
25.	A	57.	D	89.	A	121.	A
26.	C	58.	C	90.	D	122.	C
27.	D	59.	D	91.	A	123.	B
28.	B	60.	D	92.	A	124.	A
29.	C	61.	B	93.	A	125.	B
30.	A	62.	C	94.	C		
31.	D	63.	A	95.	C		
32.	D	64.	C	96.	D		

Chapter **19**

Practice Exam 2

I f you've just finished Practice Exam 1 and are continuing to Practice Exam 2, please make sure that you've reviewed thoroughly the answers to the first exam and note the areas where you need to do more study. Then, give your brain a rest for a while before starting this exam. Just like Practice Exam 1, this practice exam has 125 questions. For those of you who couldn't wait to take Practice Exam 2 and bypassed Practice Exam 1, I review the test basics here.

As in the real Series 7 exam, the questions are in random order. Please read the questions carefully. You can limit your careless mistakes by focusing in on the key words. Zone in on the information you do need to know to answer the question and ignore the information that doesn't help you. I suggest reading the last sentence twice to make sure you know what the question's asking. You may use scrap paper and a basic calculator for figuring.

Mark your answers on the answer sheet provided in this chapter or on a separate piece of paper. As you're taking the exam, circle or highlight the questions that you find troublesome. After taking and grading the exam, look over the questions that you got wrong and the questions that you circled or highlighted. Review the test, retake all the questions that you circled or answered wrong, and make sure that you get them right this time. To simulate the real exam, try to finish this practice exam in three hours or less. Please resist the urge to look at the answers and explanations until you've finished the exam. You can check your answers and get detailed explanations in Chapter 20. Good luck!

Practice Exam Part 2 Answer Sheet

1. Ⓐ Ⓑ Ⓒ Ⓓ	26. Ⓐ Ⓑ Ⓒ Ⓓ	51. Ⓐ Ⓑ Ⓒ Ⓓ	76. Ⓐ Ⓑ Ⓒ Ⓓ	101. Ⓐ Ⓑ Ⓒ Ⓓ
2. Ⓐ Ⓑ Ⓒ Ⓓ	27. Ⓐ Ⓑ Ⓒ Ⓓ	52. Ⓐ Ⓑ Ⓒ Ⓓ	77. Ⓐ Ⓑ Ⓒ Ⓓ	102. Ⓐ Ⓑ Ⓒ Ⓓ
3. Ⓐ Ⓑ Ⓒ Ⓓ	28. Ⓐ Ⓑ Ⓒ Ⓓ	53. Ⓐ Ⓑ Ⓒ Ⓓ	78. Ⓐ Ⓑ Ⓒ Ⓓ	103. Ⓐ Ⓑ Ⓒ Ⓓ
4. Ⓐ Ⓑ Ⓒ Ⓓ	29. Ⓐ Ⓑ Ⓒ Ⓓ	54. Ⓐ Ⓑ Ⓒ Ⓓ	79. Ⓐ Ⓑ Ⓒ Ⓓ	104. Ⓐ Ⓑ Ⓒ Ⓓ
5. Ⓐ Ⓑ Ⓒ Ⓓ	30. Ⓐ Ⓑ Ⓒ Ⓓ	55. Ⓐ Ⓑ Ⓒ Ⓓ	80. Ⓐ Ⓑ Ⓒ Ⓓ	105. Ⓐ Ⓑ Ⓒ Ⓓ
6. Ⓐ Ⓑ Ⓒ Ⓓ	31. Ⓐ Ⓑ Ⓒ Ⓓ	56. Ⓐ Ⓑ Ⓒ Ⓓ	81. Ⓐ Ⓑ Ⓒ Ⓓ	106. Ⓐ Ⓑ Ⓒ Ⓓ
7. Ⓐ Ⓑ Ⓒ Ⓓ	32. Ⓐ Ⓑ Ⓒ Ⓓ	57. Ⓐ Ⓑ Ⓒ Ⓓ	82. Ⓐ Ⓑ Ⓒ Ⓓ	107. Ⓐ Ⓑ Ⓒ Ⓓ
8. Ⓐ Ⓑ Ⓒ Ⓓ	33. Ⓐ Ⓑ Ⓒ Ⓓ	58. Ⓐ Ⓑ Ⓒ Ⓓ	83. Ⓐ Ⓑ Ⓒ Ⓓ	108. Ⓐ Ⓑ Ⓒ Ⓓ
9. Ⓐ Ⓑ Ⓒ Ⓓ	34. Ⓐ Ⓑ Ⓒ Ⓓ	59. Ⓐ Ⓑ Ⓒ Ⓓ	84. Ⓐ Ⓑ Ⓒ Ⓓ	109. Ⓐ Ⓑ Ⓒ Ⓓ
10. Ⓐ Ⓑ Ⓒ Ⓓ	35. Ⓐ Ⓑ Ⓒ Ⓓ	60. Ⓐ Ⓑ Ⓒ Ⓓ	85. Ⓐ Ⓑ Ⓒ Ⓓ	110. Ⓐ Ⓑ Ⓒ Ⓓ
11. Ⓐ Ⓑ Ⓒ Ⓓ	36. Ⓐ Ⓑ Ⓒ Ⓓ	61. Ⓐ Ⓑ Ⓒ Ⓓ	86. Ⓐ Ⓑ Ⓒ Ⓓ	111. Ⓐ Ⓑ Ⓒ Ⓓ
12. Ⓐ Ⓑ Ⓒ Ⓓ	37. Ⓐ Ⓑ Ⓒ Ⓓ	62. Ⓐ Ⓑ Ⓒ Ⓓ	87. Ⓐ Ⓑ Ⓒ Ⓓ	112. Ⓐ Ⓑ Ⓒ Ⓓ
13. Ⓐ Ⓑ Ⓒ Ⓓ	38. Ⓐ Ⓑ Ⓒ Ⓓ	63. Ⓐ Ⓑ Ⓒ Ⓓ	88. Ⓐ Ⓑ Ⓒ Ⓓ	113. Ⓐ Ⓑ Ⓒ Ⓓ
14. Ⓐ Ⓑ Ⓒ Ⓓ	39. Ⓐ Ⓑ Ⓒ Ⓓ	64. Ⓐ Ⓑ Ⓒ Ⓓ	89. Ⓐ Ⓑ Ⓒ Ⓓ	114. Ⓐ Ⓑ Ⓒ Ⓓ
15. Ⓐ Ⓑ Ⓒ Ⓓ	40. Ⓐ Ⓑ Ⓒ Ⓓ	65. Ⓐ Ⓑ Ⓒ Ⓓ	90. Ⓐ Ⓑ Ⓒ Ⓓ	115. Ⓐ Ⓑ Ⓒ Ⓓ
16. Ⓐ Ⓑ Ⓒ Ⓓ	41. Ⓐ Ⓑ Ⓒ Ⓓ	66. Ⓐ Ⓑ Ⓒ Ⓓ	91. Ⓐ Ⓑ Ⓒ Ⓓ	116. Ⓐ Ⓑ Ⓒ Ⓓ
17. Ⓐ Ⓑ Ⓒ Ⓓ	42. Ⓐ Ⓑ Ⓒ Ⓓ	67. Ⓐ Ⓑ Ⓒ Ⓓ	92. Ⓐ Ⓑ Ⓒ Ⓓ	117. Ⓐ Ⓑ Ⓒ Ⓓ
18. Ⓐ Ⓑ Ⓒ Ⓓ	43. Ⓐ Ⓑ Ⓒ Ⓓ	68. Ⓐ Ⓑ Ⓒ Ⓓ	93. Ⓐ Ⓑ Ⓒ Ⓓ	118. Ⓐ Ⓑ Ⓒ Ⓓ
19. Ⓐ Ⓑ Ⓒ Ⓓ	44. Ⓐ Ⓑ Ⓒ Ⓓ	69. Ⓐ Ⓑ Ⓒ Ⓓ	94. Ⓐ Ⓑ Ⓒ Ⓓ	119. Ⓐ Ⓑ Ⓒ Ⓓ
20. Ⓐ Ⓑ Ⓒ Ⓓ	45. Ⓐ Ⓑ Ⓒ Ⓓ	70. Ⓐ Ⓑ Ⓒ Ⓓ	95. Ⓐ Ⓑ Ⓒ Ⓓ	120. Ⓐ Ⓑ Ⓒ Ⓓ
21. Ⓐ Ⓑ Ⓒ Ⓓ	46. Ⓐ Ⓑ Ⓒ Ⓓ	71. Ⓐ Ⓑ Ⓒ Ⓓ	96. Ⓐ Ⓑ Ⓒ Ⓓ	121. Ⓐ Ⓑ Ⓒ Ⓓ
22. Ⓐ Ⓑ Ⓒ Ⓓ	47. Ⓐ Ⓑ Ⓒ Ⓓ	72. Ⓐ Ⓑ Ⓒ Ⓓ	97. Ⓐ Ⓑ Ⓒ Ⓓ	122. Ⓐ Ⓑ Ⓒ Ⓓ
23. Ⓐ Ⓑ Ⓒ Ⓓ	48. Ⓐ Ⓑ Ⓒ Ⓓ	73. Ⓐ Ⓑ Ⓒ Ⓓ	98. Ⓐ Ⓑ Ⓒ Ⓓ	123. Ⓐ Ⓑ Ⓒ Ⓓ
24. Ⓐ Ⓑ Ⓒ Ⓓ	49. Ⓐ Ⓑ Ⓒ Ⓓ	74. Ⓐ Ⓑ Ⓒ Ⓓ	99. Ⓐ Ⓑ Ⓒ Ⓓ	124. Ⓐ Ⓑ Ⓒ Ⓓ
25. Ⓐ Ⓑ Ⓒ Ⓓ	50. Ⓐ Ⓑ Ⓒ Ⓓ	75. Ⓐ Ⓑ Ⓒ Ⓓ	100. Ⓐ Ⓑ Ⓒ Ⓓ	125. Ⓐ Ⓑ Ⓒ Ⓓ

TIME: 3 hours and 45 minutes for 125 questions

DIRECTIONS: Choose the correct answer to each question. Then fill in the circle on your answer sheet that corresponds to the question number and the letter indicating your choice.

1. Mark Schwimmer owns 2,500 shares of TP Corporation. Which of the following actions would dilute Mark's equity?

   I. Primary share offerings (registered)

   II. A stock split

   III. Payment of a stock offering

   IV. Secondary share offerings (registered)

   (A) I only

   (B) II only

   (C) I, II, and IV

   (D) I, II, III, and IV

2. What is the minimum maintenance for pattern day trading accounts?

   (A) 15% of LMV

   (B) 25% of LMV

   (C) 30% of LMV

   (D) 50% of LMV

3. All of the following are examined by a fundamental analyst EXCEPT

   (A) earnings per share

   (B) balance sheets

   (C) income statements

   (D) trendlines

4. The Trade Reporting and Compliance Engine (TRACE) promotes better market transparency by allowing trade details to be released to the investing public that purchases

   (A) corporate bonds in the OTC secondary market

   (B) warrants

   (C) CMOs

   (D) new issue primary market securities

5. Mike Smith is one of your clients. Mike is 55 years old, has a wife, two young adults going to college, and two children living at home. You have helped Mike determine his investment profile and how much risk he should be willing to take. However, Mike is hot on a particularly speculative security that doesn't fit his investment profile. Mike calls you saying he wants to purchase $20,000 worth of this security. What should you do?

   (A) Accept the order and mark it as unsolicited.

   (B) Refuse the order because it doesn't fit his investment profile.

   (C) Do nothing until talking to a principal.

   (D) Limit Mike's exposure by making sure that he doesn't purchase more than $5,000 worth of this speculative security.

6. Which TWO of the following are TRUE relating to a firm that sells securities out of its own inventory?

   I. It is acting as a broker.

   II. It is acting as a dealer.

   III. It charges a commission.

   IV. It charges a markup.

   (A) I and III

   (B) I and IV

   (C) II and III

   (D) II and IV

GO ON TO NEXT PAGE

7. Use the following exhibit to answer this question:

NY Close	Strike	Calls		Puts	
ABC		Sep	Dec	Sep	Dec
50.50	40	12	14.13	0.75	1.50
50.50	50	1	2.50	0.88	1.75
50.50	60	0.50	0.75	10	12

What is the break-even point for an investor who purchases an ABC Dec 60 put?

(A) 48

(B) 50

(C) 70

(D) 72

8. All of the following are good delivery for a trade of 930 shares EXCEPT

(A) 1 certificate for 900 shares, 1 for 30 shares

(B) 2 certificates for 400 shares each, 2 for 50 shares each, 2 for 15 shares each

(C) 4 certificates for 200 shares each, 10 for 13 shares each

(D) 4 certificates for 200 shares each, 13 for 10 shares each

9. An investor has a child who will be going to college in 15 years. Which of the following is a suitable investment?

(A) T-bills

(B) T-notes

(C) Treasury receipts

(D) Long call options

10. Which of the following statements is TRUE about revenue bonds?

(A) Their value is measured by the municipal project's capacity for generating revenue.

(B) They are secured by a mortgage-backed bond.

(C) They are a type of general obligation bond.

(D) They are subject to the statutory debt limitations of the issuing jurisdiction.

11. Which of the following is the balance sheet equation?

(A) assets = liabilities + shareholder's equity

(B) assets + liabilities = shareholder's equity

(C) shareholder's equity + assets = liabilities

(D) None of the above

12. Regarding the taxation of dividends from corporate securities, which TWO of the following are TRUE?

I. Qualified dividends are taxed at the investor's income tax rate.

II. Qualified dividends are taxed at a maximum rate of 20 percent.

III. Nonqualified dividends are taxed at the investor's tax rate.

IV. Nonqualified dividends are taxed at a maximum rate of 20 percent.

(A) I and III

(B) I and IV

(C) II and III

(D) II and IV

13. All of the following change the conditions of an option contract EXCEPT

(A) a stock split

(B) a cash dividend

(C) a stock dividend

(D) None of the above

14. Ayla Weidman owns 1,000 shares of HIT Corp. HIT issues stock with cumulative voting. What is the maximum number of votes that Ayla can cast for one candidate if there are four vacancies on the board of directors of HIT?

(A) 100

(B) 250

(C) 1,000

(D) 4,000

15. Where can an investor find the most information about a new municipal issue?

(A) In a prospectus

(B) In an official statement

(C) In a tombstone ad

(D) In a registration statement

16. Records of written customer complaints must be kept on file for at least

    (A) 2 years
    (B) 3 years
    (C) 4 years
    (D) 6 years

17. Which two of the following are true of Roth IRAs?

    I. Contributions are made from after-tax dollars.
    II. Contributions are made from pre-tax dollars.
    III. Distributions are tax-free.
    IV. Distributions are taxed on the amount above the amount of the contribution.

    (A) I and III
    (B) I and IV
    (C) II and III
    (D) II and IV

18. All of the following can validate a mutilated certificate EXCEPT

    (A) the issuer
    (B) the broker-dealer
    (C) the registrar
    (D) the paying agent

19. One of your clients wants to start adding some diversity to their portfolio by investing in mutual funds. Which of the following is the most important consideration when choosing a mutual fund?

    (A) Whether the fund is load or no-load
    (B) Management fees
    (C) Investment objectives
    (D) 12b1 fees

20. Common stockholders in a corporation can do which of the following?

    (A) Vote to elect the corporation's board of directors
    (B) Make decisions about the day-to-day dealings, such as the office supply dealer used by the corporation
    (C) Receive interest payments
    (D) Expect to be paid par value for their stock if the corporation goes out of business

21. Which of the following investments are suitable for a 21-year-old investor who has limited resources but would like to start investing on a regular basis?

    I. Growth funds
    II. Collateralized debt obligations (CDOs)
    III. Call options
    IV. Hedge funds

    (A) I only
    (B) II and IV
    (C) I, II, and III
    (D) I, III, and IV

22. Which of the following is true regarding Penny Stock Disclosure Documents?

    (A) They may be described orally prior to the customer's first transaction in penny stocks.
    (B) They must be provided to the customer in written form prior to the customer's first transaction in penny stocks.
    (C) They must be described orally and provided in written form prior to the customer's first transaction in penny stocks.
    (D) The broker-dealer must provide a link to penny stock rules on their website prior to the confirmation sent to customers after the first transaction in penny stocks.

23. Which of the following statements is TRUE regarding municipal revenue bond issues?

    (A) The bonds are backed by the issuer's unlimited taxing power.
    (B) User fees provide revenue for bondholders.
    (C) The bonds' feasibility is not dependent on the earnings potential of the facility or project.
    (D) Revenue bonds are most suitable for investors with high risk tolerance.

GO ON TO NEXT PAGE

24. Jameson and Johnson Securities sent Alyssa a confirmation of her latest trade of Johnstone Corporation common stock. Which of the following items should be on the confirmation?

I. The trade date and the settlement date

II. Whether Jameson and Johnson acted as an agent or a principal

III. The name of the security and how many shares were traded

IV. The amount of commission paid if Jameson and Johnson acted as an agent

(A) I and III

(B) I, II, and III

(C) I, III, and IV

(D) I, II, III, and IV

25. If a customer, Jessica James, gives limited power of attorney to her registered representative, which of the following is TRUE?

(A) The registered representative still needs verbal authorization from Jessica for each trade.

(B) Jessica must sign a power-of-attorney document.

(C) The registered representative must sign a power-of-attorney document.

(D) Jessica must initial each order before it is entered.

26. Which of the following is NOT a characteristic of a real estate investment trust (REIT)?

(A) Pass-through treatment of income only

(B) Pass-through treatment of income and losses

(C) At least 75 percent of the assets must be invested in real-estate-related projects.

(D) Ownership of real property without management responsibility

27. A principal is responsible for approving new accounts opened for

I. individuals

II. corporations

III. banks

IV. trusts

(A) I only

(B) I and II

(C) I, II, and III

(D) I, II, III, and IV

28. A customer of Dim Outlook Securities decides to close their account. How long after closing the account must Dim Outlook keep the customer records?

(A) 6 months

(B) 2 years

(C) 3 years

(D) 6 years

29. When a corporation declares a cash dividend, which of the following is true in relation to the corporation's balance sheet?

(A) Assets decrease.

(B) Liabilities increase.

(C) Working capital remains the same.

(D) Stockholder's equity increases.

30. George Lincoln opens a margin account and signs a loan consent, hypothecation, and credit agreement. Which of the following statements are TRUE?

I. George's stock may not be kept in street name.

II. A portion of George's stock may be pledged for a loan.

III. George will be required to pay interest on the money borrowed.

IV. George's stock must be cosigned by the broker-dealer.

(A) I and IV

(B) II and III

(C) I and II

(D) None of the above

31. Terri Hogan is a customer who wants to invest in securities. Which of the following is most likely to provide Terri with the highest dividend rate?

    (A) Straight preferred

    (B) Convertible preferred

    (C) Participating preferred

    (D) Callable preferred

32. A Regulation D private placement is

    (A) an offering of securities to no more than 35 unaccredited investors in a 1-month period

    (B) an intrastate offering

    (C) an offering of securities worth no more than $5 million in a 12-month period

    (D) a large offering of commercial paper

33. To protect investors of variable life insurance policies who become disabled, there is a rider called a(n)

    (A) disability rider

    (B) waiver of premium

    (C) early withdrawal rider

    (D) None of the above

34. As a client's investment objectives change, a registered rep should keep track of those changes so that they can rebalance the client's portfolio and make proper recommendations. Which of the following changes may affect a customer's investment objectives?

    I. Growing older

    II. Getting divorced

    III. Having triplets

    IV. Getting a higher paying job

    (A) I and III

    (B) I, II, and III

    (C) II, III, and IV

    (D) I, II, III, and IV

35. AylDec Corporation has declared a $0.40 dividend payable to shareholders of record on Thursday, September 14. What would happen to the opening price of AylDec on Wednesday, September 13?

    (A) It would be reduced by the amount of the dividend.

    (B) It would remain the same.

    (C) It would be increased by the amount of the dividend.

    (D) Cannot be determined

36. Larry Eagle is a resident of Michigan. Mr. Eagle purchased a Michigan municipal bond. What is the tax treatment of the interest that Larry earns on his Michigan bond?

    I. It is exempt from local taxes.

    II. It is exempt from state taxes.

    III. It is exempt from federal taxes.

    (A) III only

    (B) I and III

    (C) II and III

    (D) I, II, and III

37. Charges for services performed by a broker-dealer (such as collection of money due for principal, interest, or dividends; transfer or exchange of securities; safekeeping of securities; and so on) should be

    (A) considered part of the broker-dealer's business and not charged

    (B) charged at a maximum rate of 1½ percent of the customer's portfolio

    (C) charged at a maximum rate of 5 percent of the securities being held, transferred, and so on

    (D) fair and reasonable

GO ON TO NEXT PAGE

38. An investor wants to invest in a direct participation program (DPP) with a minimal amount
of risk. Which of the following are you LEAST
likely to recommend?

(A) A real-estate partnership that invests in
raw land

(B) An oil and gas developmental program

(C) An oil and gas income program

(D) An equipment leasing program

39. All the following activities are a registrar's
functions EXCEPT

(A) accounting for the number of shares
outstanding

(B) auditing the transfer agent

(C) ensuring that the outstanding shares do
not exceed the number of shares on the
corporation's books

(D) transferring shares into the name of the
new owner

40. All the following information is required on a
preliminary prospectus EXCEPT

(A) the final offering price

(B) the purpose for which the issuer is raising
the funds

(C) a statement in red lettering stating that
items on the preliminary prospectus
are subject to change before the final
prospectus is issued

(D) the issuer's history and financial status

41. Prior to opening a day trading account for a
customer, a member shall make a reasonable
effort to determine certain information about
the customer, including

(A) their investment objectives

(B) their marital status

(C) their trading experience

(D) All of the above

42. A mutual fund has an NAV of $9.60 and a POP
of $10. What is the sales charge of this fund?

(A) 2 percent

(B) 3 percent

(C) 4 percent

(D) 5 percent

43. If the FDA increases pollution standards that are
more costly for oil companies, investors who
own shares of oil company stock would most
likely see the value of their shares decline due to

(A) purchasing power risk

(B) reinvestment risk

(C) credit risk

(D) regulatory risk

44. On a competitive bid for a new municipal
underwriting, the difference between the
syndicate bid and the reoffering price is the

(A) discount price

(B) offering price

(C) spread

(D) bid price

45. While cold calling, a registered rep convinces
a customer to purchase 100 shares of MKR for
cash. On the date of that first transaction, the
signature(s) of which of the following is/are
required?

I. The registered representative

II. The customer

III. The principal

IV. The guarantor

(A) IV only

(B) I and III

(C) I, II, and III

(D) I, II, III, and IV

46. Which TWO of the following are TRUE regarding
immediate-or-cancel orders?

I. They must be executed immediately.

II. They allow for partial execution.

III. They must be executed in one attempt
immediately.

IV. They may be executed in several attempts.

(A) I and III

(B) II and IV

(C) II and III

(D) III and IV

47. All the following securities are typically sold short EXCEPT

(A) over-the-counter common stock

(B) preferred stock

(C) exchange listed stock

(D) municipal bonds

48. In an initial margin transaction, an investor purchases 100 shares of WXY at $24 per share. What is the margin call?

(A) $1,200

(B) $1,800

(C) $2,000

(D) $2,400

49. The indenture of a corporate bond includes all of the following EXCEPT

(A) the coupon rate

(B) the credit rating

(C) the name of the trustee

(D) the maturity date

50. Which of the following items can be found in the certificate of limited partnership?

I. The goals of the partnership and how long it's expected to last

II. The authority of the general partner to charge a fee for making management decisions for the partnership

III. How the profits are to be distributed

IV. The amount contributed by each partner, plus future expected investments

(A) I, II, and III

(B) II, III, and IV

(C) I, III, and IV

(D) I, II, III, and IV

51. All the following securities may pay a dividend EXCEPT

(A) warrants

(B) common stock

(C) American depositary receipts (ADRs)

(D) participating preferred stock

52. Marty Martinez wants to create a short combination using his existing option. If Marty is short 1 DEF Aug 60 call, which of the following option positions should Marty purchase or sell?

(A) Long 1 DEF Aug 70 put

(B) Long 1 DEF Aug 60 put

(C) Short 1 DEF Aug 50 put

(D) Short 1 DEF Aug 60 put

53. Which of the following is/are true of a REIT?

I. It must invest at least 75 percent of its assets in real-estate-related activities.

II. It must be organized as a trust.

III. It must distribute at least 90 percent of its net investment income.

IV. It must pass along losses to shareholders.

(A) I, II, III, and IV

(B) I, II, and III

(C) I only

(D) II and IV

54. An investor purchases 300 shares of DUD Corp. at $45 per share and purchases 3 DUD Oct 40 puts at 6. What is the customer's break-even point?

(A) 39

(B) 45

(C) 46

(D) 51

55. Under the Securities Act of 1933, which of the following securities are exempt from registration and disclosure provisions?

(A) Railroad equipment trust certificate

(B) Municipal bonds

(C) Commercial paper maturing in 270 days or less

(D) All of the above

GO ON TO NEXT PAGE

56. One of your customers is interested in investing in an oil and gas limited partnership. As their registered rep, which of the following steps are you required to take?

 I. Prescreen the customer.
 II. Determine the economic soundness of the program.
 III. Explain the risks of investing in limited partnerships.
 IV. Have your customer fill out a partnership agreement.

(A) I and III
(B) I, II, and III
(C) II, III, and IV
(D) I, II, III, and IV

57. Which of the following funds changes its balance to hold more fixed-income securities and less equity securities as the years pass?

(A) A balanced fund
(B) A hedge fund
(C) A life-cycle fund
(D) A growth fund

58. For investors interested in purchasing CMOs, which of the following tranches is considered the safest?

(A) Planned amortization class
(B) Targeted amortization class
(C) Companion
(D) Z

59. The first time a company ever issues securities is called a(n)

(A) IPO
(B) first market trade
(C) rights offering
(D) None of the above

60. A saucer formation is an indication that a security is

(A) consolidating
(B) breaking out
(C) reversing from a bullish trend
(D) reversing from a bearish trend

61. Broker-dealers may charge a

 I. commission
 II. markup
 III. markdown

(A) I only
(B) I and II
(C) II and III
(D) I, II, and III

62. Use the following exhibit to answer this question:

TUV	Strike	May	Aug.	Nov.
60.50	50	12	14.50	16
60.50	50p	a	0.50	1.25
60.50	60	2	3.25	5
60.50	60p	1.50	2.75	4

(p – put, a – not traded)

If an investor buys a TUV Nov 60 put and writes a TUV Nov 50 put, what is the maximum gain?

(A) $275
(B) $325
(C) $675
(D) $725

63. Which of the following features of a corporation would be examined by a fundamental analyst?

(A) Earnings trends
(B) Support and resistance
(C) Breadth of the market
(D) None of the above

64. Mr. Smith has an inactive account with stocks and bonds at a broker-dealer. How often is the firm required to send Mr. Smith an account statement?

(A) Once a month
(B) Once a week
(C) Once every three months
(D) Once every six months

65. Which of the following DOES NOT describe Treasury stock?

(A) It has no voting rights.

(B) It is stock that was previously authorized but is still unissued.

(C) It is issued stock that has been repurchased by the company.

(D) It does not receive dividends.

66. All of the following impact the marketing of a municipal bond issue EXCEPT

(A) the rating

(B) the interest

(C) the date of maturity

(D) the dated date

67. IRAs may be set up in all the following ways EXCEPT

(A) single life

(B) life with period certain

(C) joint and last survivor

(D) uniform lifetime

68. An investor who purchases a variable life insurance policy faces which of the following risks?

(A) The insurance company may have to increase the premium if the securities held in the separate account underperform the market.

(B) The insurance company may decrease the premium if the securities held in the separate account outperform the market.

(C) The policy may have no cash value if the securities held in the separate account perform poorly.

(D) The death benefit may fall below the minimum in the event that the securities held in the separate account underperform.

69. All of the following are nonfinancial influences that may help determine an investor's investment profile EXCEPT

(A) the investor's age

(B) the amount of marketable securities the investor owns

(C) the number of dependents

(D) investment experience

70. Which of the following is TRUE of a durable power of attorney?

(A) It would be automatically revoked in the event that the grantor is declared incompetent.

(B) It gives power of attorney to someone else in the event that an individual becomes incompetent.

(C) It gives power of attorney to someone else in the event that an individual dies.

(D) Once in place, it may not be revoked by the grantor.

71. One of your clients purchased a 4 percent ABC convertible bond yielding 5 percent and convertible at $50. If your client holds the bond until maturity, how much will they receive?

(A) $1,000

(B) $1,020

(C) $1,025

(D) $1,050

72. Barbara Billington has a margin account with a market value of $30,000 and a debit balance of $12,000. If Barbara wants to purchase an additional $10,000 of stock in this account, what amount must she deposit?

(A) $2,000

(B) $3,000

(C) $5,000

(D) $10,000

73. Ginny Goldtrain is a wealthy investor who is in the highest income bracket. Ginny is looking for an investment that would limit her tax liability and put her on equal footing with investors in lower income-tax brackets. Which of the following securities would you MOST likely recommend?

(A) High-yield bonds

(B) CMOs

(C) Municipal bonds

(D) Hedge funds

GO ON TO NEXT PAGE

74. An investor purchased 200 shares of AYLA Corp. common stock for a price of $5,000 on October 1st. The following October 1st, the investor sold the 200 shares of AYLA Corp. common stock for $6,000. The $1,000 capital gain will be

I. considered short-term

II. considered long-term

III. taxed at a maximum rate of 20 percent

IV. taxed at the investor's tax bracket

(A) I and III

(B) I and IV

(C) II and III

(D) II and IV

75. The largest source of backing for a local GO bond is

(A) property tax

(B) sales tax

(C) income tax

(D) traffic fines and parking tickets

76. Brett Overtrade is a registered representative who works for Missed Again Securities. Brett has just learned of the death of one of his customers. Which of the following actions should Brett take regarding his deceased customer's account?

I. Mark his customer's account as deceased.

II. Cancel all open orders.

III. Wait for the proper legal papers.

(A) I and II

(B) I and III

(C) II and III

(D) I, II, and III

77. The trading volume for some large institutional orders is concealed from the public. What is this called?

(A) Fourth market trades

(B) Dark pools of liquidity

(C) Third-market trades

(D) A violation

78. A Designated Market Maker is responsible for doing all of the following EXCEPT

(A) maintaining a fair and orderly market

(B) competing with public orders to keep trading as active as possible

(C) trading for their own account

(D) trading for customer accounts

79. Which of the following bonds would most likely have the highest coupon rate?

(A) DEF Corp. mortgage bonds

(B) DEF Corp. collateral trusts

(C) DEF Corp. debentures

(D) DEF Corp. equipment trusts

80. Your client, Dana Griffin, is about to retire and she wants predictable income. Which of the following would NOT be a good investment for Dana?

I. AA rated IDB

II. U.S. Treasury note

III. AA rated debenture

IV. Income bonds

(A) II only

(B) I and III

(C) II and IV

(D) IV only

81. What is the maximum loss on a debit spread?

(A) The difference between the premium paid and the premium received

(B) The difference between the two strike prices multiplied by 100, less the premium paid, plus the premium received

(C) The difference between the two strike prices multiplied by 100, less the premium paid

(D) The difference between the two strike prices multiplied by 100

82. Sal Gold is new to investing and wants to purchase a security that will provide him with current income with minimal risk. Which of the following are you LEAST likely to recommend?

   (A) An income fund

   (B) Treasury bonds

   (C) An international fund

   (D) AA rated municipal bonds

83. Which of the following is the issuer and guarantor of all listed options?

   (A) The OCC

   (B) The OAA

   (C) The ODD

   (D) The CBOE

84. If your customer, William Goate, purchases shares in a municipal bond fund, which of the following statements is TRUE?

   (A) Dividends are subject to alternative minimum tax.

   (B) Dividends are taxable to all investors.

   (C) Capital gains distributions are taxable.

   (D) Capital gains distributions are not taxable.

85. An investor opens a margin account by purchasing 1,000 shares of ABC at $15 per share and shorting 1,000 shares of DEF at $12 per share. What is the investor's margin call as a result of these transactions?

   (A) $1,500

   (B) $3,000

   (C) $13,500

   (D) $27,000

86. These municipal notes provide interim financing for a municipality that's waiting for a grant from the U.S. government.

   (A) BANs

   (B) TRANs

   (C) GANs

   (D) CLNs

87. An investor is holding 1 ABC Oct 35 call option. Which of the following option positions, if purchased by this customer, would create a long straddle?

   (A) Short 1 ABC Nov 35 call option

   (B) Short 1 ABC Oct 30 call option

   (C) Long 1 ABC Oct 40 call option

   (D) Long 1 ABC Oct 35 put option

88. Luke Landworker holds 10 XYX May 30 calls. XYX increases to $40, and he exercises the calls. Luke tells his registered rep to sell the stock immediately after purchase. If these trades are executed in a margin account, how much does Luke have to deposit?

   (A) $3,000

   (B) $30,000

   (C) $35,000

   (D) No deposit is required.

89. Regarding margin accounts, which two of the following are TRUE?

   I. Minimum maintenance on a long account is 25 percent.

   II. Minimum maintenance on a short account is 25 percent.

   III. Minimum maintenance on a long account is 30 percent.

   IV. Minimum maintenance on a short account is 30 percent.

   (A) I and II

   (B) I and IV

   (C) II and III

   (D) III and IV

GO ON TO NEXT PAGE

90. Use the following exhibit to answer this question:

Balance Sheet of ABCD Corp.	Assets	Liabilities	
Cash	$300,000	Accounts payable	$300,000
Accounts receivable	$1,500,000	Taxes payable	$250,000
Inventory	$1,200,000	Bonds maturing this year	$800,000
Goodwill	$2,000,000	Bonds maturing in 5 years	$2,000,000
Machinery	$1,500,000		
Land	$5,000,000		

What is the net worth of ABCD Corporation?

(A) $3,150,000

(B) $1,650,000

(C) $8,150,000

(D) $10,150,000

91. Which of the following is TRUE regarding standard equity options?

  I. Each standard contract represents 1,000 shares of the underlying security

  II. Each standard contract represents 100 shares of the underlying security

  III. They are exercisable European style

  IV. They are exercisable American style

(A) I and III

(B) I and IV

(C) II and III

(D) II and IV

92. One of the advantages of portfolio margin is that it allows

(A) smaller investors the opportunity to purchase securities on margin

(B) less sophisticated investors a chance to purchase securities on margin

(C) investors to avoid maintenance calls

(D) investors greater leverage

93. Which of the following statements regarding municipal bonds with call provisions is TRUE?

(A) Bonds are likely to be called when interest rates fall.

(B) Call provisions favor investors.

(C) Bonds are likely to be called when interest rates rise.

(D) Call provisions are not advantageous to issuers.

94. AylDec Corporation common stock is currently trading in the market for $22 per share. AylDec Corp. pays an annual dividend of $0.60 per share and has an earnings per share (EPS) of $4. What is the PE ratio?

(A) 4.50

(B) 5

(C) 5.50

(D) Cannot be determined

95. The Order Audit Trail System tracks the

(A) execution of an order only

(B) cancellation of an order only

(C) entire life of an order from entry to execution

(D) None of the above

96. Sam Smith sends an email to his registered rep, John Johnson, complaining about the amount of commission he was charged on his last trade. According to FINRA rules, what should John Johnson do with the complaint?

(A) Ignore it because the complaint needs to be in writing

(B) Print it out and give it to his principal

(C) Print it out and send it to FINRA

(D) Forward it to FINRA's complaint department

97. Which of the following best describes the tax status of a limited partnership?

(A) The partnership is fully taxed.

(B) All tax liability flows through to the limited partners.

(C) Any income generated is taxed as ordinary income.

(D) Any gains generated are taxed as capital gains.

98. Which of the following sequences reflects the priority of payments made when a limited partnership is liquidated?

   I. Secured creditors

   II. General creditors

   III. Limited partners

   IV. General partners

   (A) I, II, III, IV

   (B) IV, II, III, I

   (C) IV, II, I, III

   (D) I, IV, II, III

99. All of the following are types of blue-sky registration EXCEPT

   (A) registration by cooperation

   (B) registration by coordination

   (C) registration by qualification

   (D) registration by filing

100. A TUV Oct 60 call is trading for 9 when TUV is at $65. What is the time value of this option?

   (A) 0

   (B) 4

   (C) 5

   (D) 9

101. Which of the following need approval from a brokerage firm's principal?

   I. New accounts

   II. Recommendations

   III. Handling of complaints

   IV. Trades in all accounts

   (A) I and II

   (B) I, III, and IV

   (C) II, III, and IV

   (D) I, II, III, and IV

102. A quote of 1.20 bid 1.18 offered is *most* likely a quote on which of the following:

   (A) A T-bond

   (B) A T-bill

   (C) A general obligation (GO) bond

   (D) A Fannie Mae (FNMA) bond

103. Which of the following municipal bonds is backed by lease payments made by an underlying facility?

   (A) IDR

   (B) LTGO

   (C) LRB

   (D) BAB

104. If a corporation pays a cash dividend, how does it affect its balance sheet?

   I. Assets decrease

   II. Liabilities decrease

   III. Net worth decreases

   IV. Net worth remains the same

   (A) I and III

   (B) II and III

   (C) I, II, and III

   (D) I, II, and IV

105. All of the following are included on a confirmation for non-callable municipal bonds that were purchased on a yield basis EXCEPT

   (A) the purchase price

   (B) the par value

   (C) the yield to maturity

   (D) the taxable equivalent yield

106. Which of the following option positions provides an investor with potential premium income while limiting the maximum loss potential?

   (A) Debit spread

   (B) Credit spread

   (C) Long straddle or long combination

   (D) Short straddle or short combination

GO ON TO NEXT PAGE

107. A customer wants their registered representative to purchase a security that is incompatible with their investment objectives. What action should the registered representative take under FINRA rules?

(A) Enter the order and note that it was unsolicited.

(B) Enter the order only if the customer puts their request in writing.

(C) Obtain the approval of the firm's compliance officer before entering the order.

(D) The registered representative cannot enter the order.

108. All the following calculations can be determined by finding the information on a corporation's balance sheet EXCEPT

(A) working capital

(B) net worth

(C) current yield

(D) quick assets

109. Which of the following are money market securities?

(A) Commercial paper

(B) Treasury bonds

(C) American depositary receipts (ADRs)

(D) Warrants

110. Income derived from an investment in a real-estate limited partnership is termed

(A) earned income

(B) passive income

(C) portfolio income

(D) capital gains

111. ABC stock pays an annual dividend of $4, has an earnings per share of $8, and a market price of $40. What is ABC's PE ratio?

(A) 2

(B) 5

(C) 10

(D) 20

112. An investor purchases 1 TUV Sep 30 call for a premium of 4. This option will expire

(A) on the third Saturday in September

(B) on the third Friday in September

(C) on the Saturday following the third Friday in September

(D) on a date to be assigned by the CBOE

113. All of the following are true regarding limited partners EXCEPT

(A) They have access to unlimited financial information regarding the partnership.

(B) They may participate in management decisions because limited partners have a tremendous amount of risk.

(C) They may vote to terminate a partnership.

(D) They may invest in competing partnerships.

114. What is the primary objective for an individual who invests in undeveloped land?

(A) Depletion deductions

(B) Depreciation deductions

(C) Appreciation potential

(D) Tax-deferred income

115. Which of the following are true about closed-end funds?

I. They may only issue common stock.

II. They are generally listed on an exchange.

III. They have a fixed number of shares outstanding.

IV. They are redeemable.

(A) II and III

(B) I and IV

(C) I, III, and IV

(D) II, III, and IV

116. One of your wealthier clients is interested in purchasing a fund. If liquidity is high on their list of investment objectives, which of the following would be the least suitable recommendation?

(A) ETFs

(B) Inverse ETFs

(C) Hedge funds

(D) Money market funds

117. What is the maximum potential loss for an investor who sells a call option?

(A) The strike price × 100 shares

(B) The strike price × 100 shares, less the premium

(C) The strike price × 100 shares, plus the premium

(D) Unlimited

118. An investor purchased 1,000 shares of WXY at $40. If WXY announces a 5 for 4 split, what is the investor's position after the split?

(A) 1,250 WXY at $32

(B) 1,250 WXY at $50

(C) 800 WXY at $32

(D) 800 WXY at $50

119. Changes in which of the following non-financial information might change an investor's investment objectives?

I. The investor growing older

II. Getting married or divorced

III. Investment experience

IV. Family responsibilities

(A) II and IV

(B) I, II, and III

(C) I, II, and IV

(D) I, II, III, and IV

120. Which of the following ratios does not measure the liquidity of a company?

(A) Current ratio

(B) Quick ratio

(C) Ratio of cash and securities to current liabilities

(D) Debt to equity ratio

121. Which of the following is characteristic of commercial paper?

(A) It is quoted as a percent of par.

(B) It is proof of ownership of the corporation.

(C) It is issued to raise capital for a corporation.

(D) It is junior to convertible preferred stock.

122. Which of the following is true about advertising for a municipal fund security?

I. It must be approved by a principal of the firm selling the securities.

II. It must not be fraudulent.

III. It must first be approved by the MSRB.

IV. It must be approved by the state administrator in each state in which the security is to be sold.

(A) I only

(B) I and II

(C) III and IV

(D) I, II, III, and IV

123. What is the maximum contribution for a 56-year-old investor into a traditional IRA each year?

(A) $45,000

(B) $6,000

(C) $6,500

(D) $7,500

124. A mutual fund that invests only in securities within a specific industry is called a

(A) Balanced fund

(B) Growth fund

(C) Hedge fund

(D) Sector fund

125. At what time must an individual begin withdrawals from a Roth IRA?

(A) At age 59½

(B) At age 73

(C) On April 1st of the year after turning 73

(D) None of the above

Chapter 20

Answers and Explanations to Practice Exam 2

Congratulations! You've just completed Practice Exam 2 (unless you're just randomly flipping through the book). After grading both Practice Exams 1 and 2, you should have a good idea of where you stand regarding the Series 7 exam. Kudos if you did really well on both exams.

In this practice test, I decided to step it up a notch and add a few questions with exhibits. Exhibit questions aren't really any harder, but they're just different, and you need to make sure that seeing one doesn't throw you off your game.

As with the first practice exam, review all the questions that you got wrong and the ones you struggled with. Test yourself again by answering all the questions you highlighted and the questions you answered incorrectly, and make sure you get them right this time! Please give yourself a week or two before taking the same test again. Memorizing answers can give you a false sense of security, and you won't get an accurate forecast of how well you'll do on the Series 7 exam (you certainly don't want your score to be as unpredictable as the weather). I encourage you to take as many Series 7 practice exams as possible.

If you're short on time but just can't wait to see how well you did, you can check out the abbreviated answer key (without the explanations) at the end of this chapter. I explain how the Series 7 is scored in the section "Knowing the Score," just before the answer key. But I strongly suggest you come back later and do a more thorough review.

1. **A.** (Chapter 5) Another primary issue of shares would dilute Mark's ownership because new shares would be coming to the market. Don't forget that when a corporation issues stock dividends, splits its stock, or makes a secondary offering, the percent of equity does not change.

2. **B.** (Chapter 9) The minimum maintenance for pattern day trading accounts is 25% of the LMV (Long Market Value). Remember, an investor must keep at least $25,000 in equity to maintain a pattern day trading account.

3. **D.** (Chapter 13) Fundamental analysts decide what to buy and technical analysts decide when to buy (timing). A fundamental analyst would compare the earnings per share (EPS) of different companies as well as balance sheets and income statements. However, trend-lines are something that would be examined by a technical analyst.

4. **A.** (Chapter 14) The Series 7 exam tests you on your knowledge of TRACE. The trade reporting system known as TRACE is approved by FINRA for corporate bonds trading in the OTC secondary market. Therefore, Choice (A) is the correct answer. Choices (B), (C), and (D) are incorrect because warrants are not applicable to corporate bond trading, and municipal securities and asset-backed securities are specifically excluded from the TRACE reporting requirements.

5. **A.** (Chapter 16) You can accept the trade and mark it as unsolicited. Even if a customer wants to purchase a security that doesn't fit their investment profile, you can still accept it in most cases by marking it as unsolicited. I call this the CYD (cover your derriere) rule. As long as you mark the ticket as unsolicited, you save yourself some aggravation (and maybe arbitration) if Mike loses money on the deal.

6. **D.** (Chapter 14) When a securities firm buys securities for or sells securities from its own inventory, it is acting as a dealer (principal or market maker). When a dealer sells securities from its own inventory, it charges a price that includes a markup. When a dealer purchases securities for its inventory, it charges a markdown.

7. **A.** (Chapter 12) To determine the break-even point for a put option, you have to subtract the premium from the strike price of 60. To find the premium for the Dec 60 put, look under the last column. The last column is for December puts. Next, find the 60 strike price from the second column — it's in the bottom row. If you intersect the bottom row with the last column (the lower right-hand corner), you see that the premium is 12. By subtracting 12 from 60, you get a break-even point of 48. Remember, put options go in the money when the price of the underlying security decreases. In this case, the investor paid $12 per share for the option so it has to drop $12 below the $60 strike price for this investor to break even.

8. **C.** (Chapter 16) To determine good delivery, always look at the shares. The certificates must be in multiples of 100 shares (for example, 100, 200, 300, and so on), divisors of 100 shares (1, 2, 4, 5, 10, 20, 25, and 50), or shares that add up to 100 (for example, 80 + 20, 75 + 15, 60 + 30 + 10, and so on). Choice (A) is okay because 900 is a multiple of 100 and the odd lot portion (30 shares) is exempt. Choice (B) is fine because 400 is a multiple of 100, 50 is a divisor of 100, and the odd lot portion (30 shares) is exempt. Choice (D) works because 200 is a multiple of 100 and 10 is a divisor of 100. Choice (C) is the bad one (in this case, the one you're looking for) because even though 200 is a multiple of 100, 13 doesn't divide into 100 evenly.

9. **C.** (Chapter 7) T-strips or Treasury receipts are long-term zero-coupon bonds backed by the full faith and credit of the U.S. government. Zero-coupon bonds are ideal investments to plan for future events because investors don't face reinvestment risk (the additional investment risk taken with interest received). In addition, the purchase price for long-term zero-coupon bonds is comparatively low.

10. **A.** (Chapter 8) The Series 7 examiners want to see that you can distinguish revenue bonds from general obligation bonds. In this question, Choice (A) is the correct answer. Revenue bonds are backed by a project's earning capacity. Choices (B), (C), and (D) are incorrect because revenue bonds are not secured by a specific pledge of property, are not a type of general obligation bond, and are not subject to debt limitations the way that many general obligation bonds are.

11. **A.** (Chapter 13) When you look at a corporation's balance sheet, the left-hand side lists all the assets and the right-hand side lists all the liabilities plus the shareholders' equity. The left side and the right side balance out (equal the same amount of money).

12. **C.** (Chapter 15) Dividends are profits shared by corporations. Dividends can be taxed as either qualified (currently up to a maximum rate of 20 percent) or nonqualified (according to the investor's tax bracket). In order for the dividends to be qualified, the investor must have held onto the stock for at least 61 days. The 61-day holding period starts 60 days prior to the ex-dividend date. The dividend tax rate is subject to change.

13. **B.** (Chapter 12) This question is looking at how an option contract is adjusted for corporate actions. Cash dividends don't affect listed options because they don't change the amount of shares a company has outstanding. However, if a company splits its stock or gives a stock dividend, the terms of an option contract change (in other words, the more option contracts, the lower the strike price and/or the more shares per contract).

14. **D.** (Chapter 6) Ayla has a total of 4,000 votes (1,000 shares × 4 vacancies). Since HIT allows cumulative voting, Ayla can vote the shares in any way that she sees fit, even if she votes them all for one candidate. Statutory or regular voting would only have allowed Ayla to vote up to 1,000 shares for each candidate.

15. **B.** (Chapter 8) An official statement includes all relevant information about a new municipal bond. Municipal bonds don't have a prospectus, but an official statement is along the same lines. An official statement gives information about the municipal issue, such as the reason the bonds are being issued, what revenues are going to be used to pay the bonds, the issuer's payment history, and so forth. A tombstone ad is a brief advertisement that does not go into detail about the security being issued, and a registration statement is used by corporations when they are filing with the SEC.

16. **C.** (Chapter 16) Brokerage firms must keep records of written customer complaints as well as whatever action was taken for a minimum of 4 years and kept easily accessible for at least 2 years.

17. **A.** (Chapter 15) The main difference between traditional IRAs and Roth IRAs is the tax implications. Contributions to traditional IRAs are made from pretax dollars (you can write them off on your taxes), whereas contributions to Roth IRAs are made from after-tax dollars (you can't write them off on your taxes). However, distributions (withdrawals) from traditional IRAs are taxed on the amount above contribution, whereas withdrawals from Roth IRAs are tax-free. When withdrawing from a Roth IRA, neither the amount invested, which was already taxed, nor the amount the account has gone up in value (appreciation) is taxed, which is a great benefit to Roth IRA holders, especially ones in higher tax brackets.

18. **B.** (Chapter 16) Broker-dealers cannot validate mutilated certificates. Mutilated certificates must be validated by entities directly associated with the issuer. More and more issues are now in book-entry form, so this is becoming less of a problem.

19. **C.** (Chapter 10) Certainly all the choices listed are important, but the most important one is the investment objectives of the mutual fund. In other words, you need to know whether the investor is looking for a growth fund, an income fund, a municipal bond fund, an international fund, and so on. When comparing funds with the same investment objectives, all the other things, such as comparing management fees, whether the fund is load or no-load, and so on, come into play.

20. A. (Chapter 6) Common stockholders may cast votes for candidates to be members of the board of directors; therefore, Choice (A) is the correct answer. Choice (B) is incorrect because while common stockholders may vote on important issues that affect the welfare of the corporation, they do not have voting rights on the day-to-day operations of the corporation, like buying office supplies. Choice (C) is incorrect because a stockholder doesn't receive interest payments; bondholders do. Finally, Choice (D) is incorrect because a common stockholder's initial investment can be lost if a corporation fails; therefore, par value, which means little to common stockholders, is not guaranteed.

21. A. (Chapter 10) The clues in this question are that the investor is 21 years old, has limited resources, and would like to start investing on a regular basis. This investor is screaming out to be put in a mutual fund. Typically, investors of mutual funds are in it for the long haul; they're not in and out like they may be with other investments. Ideally, this investor should probably be set up on a dollar cost averaging plan whereby they invest x amount of dollars every so often (for instance, once a month). Because this investor is young, they can take a little more risk, so a growth fund would be ideal. CDOs, buying call options, and hedge funds are too risky, require too much money, and/or require a certain degree of sophistication.

22. B. (Chapter 6) Penny stock rules require that brokers must mail out a penny stock disclosure document prior to the customer's first transaction in penny stocks. This document addresses the risks involved when investing in penny stocks. Penny stocks are non-Nasdaq stocks that are sold over the counter at less than $5 per share.

23. B. (Chapter 8) The answer is Choice (B). Choices (A), (C), and (D) are incorrect. Revenue bonds are generally considered low-risk because they're issued by municipalities. The riskiest municipal bonds are IDRs (Industrial Development Revenue bonds), which are backed by a corporation, not the municipality.

24. D. (Chapter 16) When a client receives a trade confirmation (receipt of trade), the confirmation must show the trade date, settlement date, the name of the security, how many shares were traded, whether the broker-dealer acted as an agent or principal, and the amount of commission if traded on an agency basis.

25. B. (Chapter 16) The correct answer is Choice (B) because when Jessica grants her registered representative a limited power of attorney, she is the one who must sign the document. Although a principal must approve before the registered representative exercises their discretionary authority, the registered representative does not have to sign the document, and Jessica's approval of each order is not required.

26. B. (Chapter 10) Real Estate Investment Trusts pass through income earned by the real-estate investments, but not losses. Real-estate limited partnerships pass through income and losses to investors because DPPs aren't responsible for paying business taxes. Notice that "A" and "B" are in opposition to each other, so one of them has to be the false answer.

27. D. (Chapter 16) I hope this was an easy one for you. Principals must approve all new accounts and must sign all new account forms.

28. D. (Chapter 16) Broker-dealers must keep records of customer accounts at least 6 years after the customer closes their account.

29. B. (Chapter 13) When a corporation declares a cash dividend, its liabilities increase. Liabilities are something that is owed. Once a corporation declares a dividend, it must pay it, so it becomes a current liability to the corporation. The assets will remain the same until it pays the dividend, and then the assets will decrease. The working capital and stockholder's equity decrease when a corporation declares a cash dividend.

30. **B.** (Chapter 9) Because George is borrowing money through a margin account to purchase securities, he must leave the stock in the broker-dealer's safekeeping, pay interest on the loan, register the stock in street name, and agree to allow the broker-dealer to pledge the securities because he signed a loan consent agreement.

31. **D.** (Chapter 6) The Series 7 examiners want to make sure that you know the difference between the different types of securities. Both convertible preferred and participating preferred stocks tend to carry lower dividend rates because they give Terri an extra benefit, which is the right to convert to common shares at a fixed price or the right to earn more than the stated rate if the issuer has a good year and makes an extra dividend payment. Straight preferred stock has no conversion or participating features and probably carries a better rate than convertible and participating stocks. Choice (D) is the correct answer, however, callable preferred stock allows the issuer to "call" the securities away from Terri; therefore, callable preferred stock tends to pay higher rates than any of the other answer choices to offset this call risk.

32. **A.** (Chapter 5) A Regulation D offering is a provision in the Series Act of 1933 that exempts offerings sold to no more than 35 unaccredited (small) investors each year. Even though Regulation D offerings are limited to the number of small investors, the amount of money they can raise through accredited investors is not limited.

33. **B.** (Chapter 10) Variable life insurance policies often have a rider or statement of condition that allows individuals to keep their policy in force if they become disabled. This waiver of premium forgives policyholders of paying additional premiums if they become fully disabled.

34. **D.** (Chapter 16) Certainly just about anything you can think of could change a client's investment objectives. As people get older, they usually can't take as much risk. Conversely, investors who get higher-paying jobs are likely to want to take additional risk. Someone who is getting (or has gotten) divorced is likely to have less money (due to alimony payments, one person paying for the house instead of two, child support payments, and so on). Obviously, having triplets puts a financial burden on an investor (unless they get a reality show).

35. **A.** (Chapter 6) Remember, the ex-dividend date (the first day the stock trades without the dividend) is one business day before the record date. In this case, the record date is Thursday, September 14, which makes the ex-dividend date Wednesday, September 13. The opening price on the ex-dividend date is reduced by the amount of the dividend ($0.40 in this case).

36. **D.** (Chapter 8) When you purchase a municipal bond issued within your home state, the interest you receive is triple tax-free (exempt from federal, state, and local taxes). In addition, if you purchase a bond issued by a U.S. territory (such as Puerto Rico, U.S. Virgin Islands, Guam, Samoa, and Washington, D.C.), the interest is triple tax-free. However, if you purchase a bond issued by another state, the interest is exempt from federal taxes only.

37. **D.** (Chapter 16) According to FINRA, charges for services provided by broker-dealers (transfers, collection of monies, safe-keeping of securities, and so on) shall be "reasonable and not unfairly discriminatory among customers."

38. **A.** (Chapter 11) Of the choices listed, a real-estate partnership that invests in raw land is the riskiest. Partnerships that invest in raw land are considered speculative, as are oil and gas wildcatting (exploratory) programs. The risk of investing in raw land is that even though the property is purchased at a low price, developers may not be interested in that area and the partnership may be stuck with relatively worthless property.

39. D. (Chapter 16) In order to answer "ownership transfer" questions correctly on the Series 7 exam, you must be able to distinguish a registrar's functions from a transfer agent's functions. If that isn't stressful enough, you have an "except" question, which means you're looking for a false answer. As for functions, a registrar accounts for the number of shares on the corporation's books to ensure that the outstanding shares don't exceed the total number of shares on the books. The registrar also audits the transfer agent. The correct answer is Choice (D) because the transfer agent — not the registrar — records the names of stockholders, cancels old shares, and transfers shares to new owners' names.

40. A. (Chapter 5) The final offering price would not be found on the preliminary prospectus (red herring) because the price hasn't been finalized at this point. After the issuer and the syndicate manager come up with a final offering price, they place it on the final prospectus.

41. D. (Chapter 16) Day trading accounts are obviously very risky. So, customers who want to open a day trading account must receive a risk disclosure statement and the member firm shall make a reasonable effort to make sure that it is an appropriate strategy for the customer. To help determine that, the firm should determine the customer's investment objectives, investment experience, investment knowledge, financial situation, tax status, employment status, marital status, number of dependents, and age.

42. C. (Chapter 10) To determine the sales charge percentage of a fund, use the following equation:

$$\text{Sales charge} = \frac{\text{POP} - \text{NAV}}{\text{POP}} = \frac{\$10.00 - \$9.60}{\$10.00} = \frac{\$0.40}{\$10.00} = 4\%$$

The POP is the public offering price, which is the price that investors pay, including the sales charge. The NAV is the net asset value and is where the fund should be trading, excluding the sales charge.

43. D. (Chapter 13) Regulatory risk is the risk that the price of a security will decline due to new regulations placed on specific industries.

44. C. (Chapter 5) On a competitive bid for a new municipal underwriting, the difference between the bid to the issuer and the dollar price at which the underwriter reoffers the bonds to the public is the spread, which, importantly, is also the underwriter's compensation.

45. B. (Chapter 16) Remember, when a customer opens a cash account, the only signatures that are required on the date of that first transaction are that of the registered rep and a principal of the firm. However, if a customer were to open up a margin account, they'd have to sign a margin agreement prior to the first transaction.

46. C. (Chapter 14) An immediate-or-cancel (IOC) order must be attempted to be filled immediately by the firm handling the order but may be filled partially. It is a one-time order and does not allow the order to be executed in several attempts.

47. D. (Chapter 14) Although municipal bonds may be sold short, they typically aren't. The reason is that the security must be borrowed and later found to cover the short position. Because municipal bonds are usually thin issues and may not have a big national interest, they are not very liquid and, therefore, not good candidates for selling short.

48. **C.** (Chapter 9) Because this investor is opening a margin account (initial transaction), additional rules other than the 50 percent Regulation T requirement are in play. When purchasing securities for the first time, investors must pay in full, pay Regulation T (50 percent) of the transaction, or pay $2,000. If the cost is less than $2,000, the investor pays in full. If the cost is more than $2,000 but Regulation T is less than $2,000 (as it is in this case), the investor pays $2,000. If the cost of the securities is more than $2,000 and Regulation T is greater than $2,000, the investor pays the Regulation T amount.

49. **B.** (Chapter 7) The *indenture* (trust indenture or deed of trust) of a bond is a legal contract between the issuer and the trustee representing the investors. The bond indenture includes the coupon rate (nominal yield), the maturity date, the name of the trustee, collateral that may be backing the bond, and so on. However, the credit rating isn't found on the indenture because that's something that would change if the financial condition of the issuer changes.

50. **C.** (Chapter 11) The certificate of limited partnership is the legal agreement between the limited and general partners and has to be filed with the secretary of state. The certificate of limited partnership includes the name of the partnership, the partnership's primary place of business, the names and addresses of the limited and general partners, the goals of the partnership and how long it's expected to last, the amount contributed by each partner, how the profits are to be distributed, the roles of the participants, how the partnership can be dissolved, and whether a limited partner can sell or assign their interest in the partnership. The authority that allows the general partner to charge a fee for making management decisions is found in the partnership agreement.

51. **A.** (Chapter 6) The correct answer is Choice (A). Because warrants are basically long-term options to buy stock at a fixed price from the issuer, they can't pay dividends.

52. **C.** (Chapter 12) To create a short combination, Marty has to sell a call and sell a put on the same stock with different expiration months and/or strike prices. Because you need to have two sells to create a short combination, you can cross off Choices (A) and (B). The difference between a straddle and a combination is in the expiration months and the strike prices. If the expiration months are the same and the strike prices are the same, you have a straddle. If the expiration months and/or the strike prices are different, you're looking at a combination.

53. **B.** (Chapter 10) Choice (B) is the correct answer because three components are true about a REIT. As indicated by its acronym, a REIT is a Real Estate Investment Trust. REITs engage in real-estate activities and are organized as trusts. In order to qualify for favorable tax treatment, a REIT must pass through at least 90 percent of its net investment income to its shareholders. Statement IV is false because, although a REIT can pass through income to investors, it can't pass through losses.

54. **D.** (Chapter 12) The easiest way to calculate the break-even point for stock/option problems is to take a look at what's happening. This investor purchased the stock for $45 per share and then purchased the options for $6 per share. The investor paid $51 ($45 + $6) per share out of pocket, so the investor needs the stock to be at $51 per share in order to break even.

55. **D.** (Chapter 5) All the securities listed are exempt securities and are, therefore, exempt from the registration and disclosure provisions under the Securities Act of 1933.

56. B. (Chapter 11) Investors of limited partnerships bear additional risks, such as the possibility of money being tied up for a long period of time, little or no liquidity, the making of additional loans to the partnership, and so on. As a registered rep, you need to prescreen your customers to see whether they're a good match for the partnership. You should also look at the partnership and management itself to see whether they have a good track record and whether the partnership makes sense. You need to explain the risks to your customer and have your customer fill out a subscription agreement, not a partnership agreement. The subscription agreement needs to include a check, a signature giving the general partner power of attorney, financial statements, and so on.

57. C. (Chapter 10) Life-cycle funds are ideal for investors of any age. The idea behind them is that investors buy into life-cycle funds that are targeted for their age. The percentage of equities held by the fund decreases over time, whereas the percentage of fixed-income securities increases, because investors should hold a higher percentage of fixed-income securities as they age. For example, say a 45-year-old investor buys into a life-cycle fund that's targeted for investors who are currently between the ages of 44 and 47. At this particular point, the fund may have a nearly 50-50 split between equity securities and fixed-income securities. The fund rebalances every so often so that 10 years into the future, the fund may have 40 percent invested in equity securities and 60 percent invested in fixed-income securities. Ten years after that, the fund may have a 30-70 split between equity and fixed-income securities. This fund is designed to take the guesswork out of the equation for investors.

58. A. (Chapter 7) *Planned amortization class* (PAC) tranches are considered the safest of all tranches because a large portion of the prepayment and extension risk is absorbed by a companion tranche. *Targeted amortization class* (TAC) tranches are considered second in terms of safety because they're subject to additional prepayment and extension risk. Companion tranches are considered risky because the average life of a companion tranche varies greatly as interest rates change. Z tranches are basically zero-coupon tranches and are the most volatile of all tranches because they receive no payments until all the CMO tranches are retired.

59. A. (Chapter 14) An *IPO* (initial public offering) is the first time a corporation ever sells securities to the public. A first-market trade is a trade of exchange-listed securities trading on an exchange. A rights offering is when a company offers new shares to existing shareholders at a discount.

60. D. (Chapter 13) A saucer formation is similar to an inverted head and shoulders pattern in that it is a reversal of a bearish trend. However, a saucer formation is a more gradual change in direction. A saucer formation is a bullish sign, and an inverted saucer formation is a bearish sign.

61. D. (Chapter 14) Broker-dealers act as both brokers (middleperson) and dealers (selling securities out of their own inventory). When broker-dealers act as brokers, they're purchasing or selling securities for an investor through a market maker. When acting as brokers, they charge a commission. When acting as dealers, they either buy securities from investors to add to their own inventory or sell securities to investors from their own inventory. In this case, the broker-dealer charges a markup (if the customer is buying) or a markdown (if the customer is selling). So, all answer choices given are correct depending on the capacity of the trade.

62. **D.** (Chapter 12) The best way to determine the maximum gain is to set up an options chart. The first thing you need to do is find the premiums for the two options. Looking at the exhibit, you can see that the premium for the TUV Nov 60 put is 4 and the premium for the TUV Nov 50 put is 1.25. Because the investor purchased the 60 put, you have to put 400 (4 premium × 100 shares per option) on the "Money Out" side of the chart. Next, you have to put 125 (1.25 premium × 100 shares per option) on the "Money In" side of the chart because the investor sold that option. After doing that, you can see that you have $275 more in money out than money in, so that's the investor's maximum loss. To get the maximum gain, you have to exercise both options. Because "puts switch," you have to put the exercised strike price of $6,000 on the opposite side of its premium and the exercised strike price of $5,000 on the opposite side of its premium.

Money Out	Money In
$400	$125
$5,000	$6,000
$5,400	$6,125

After totaling up the two sides, you can see that the maximum gain is $725, because there's $725 more money in than out.

63. **A.** (Chapter 13) Fundamental analysts compare companies to help determine what to buy. Technical analysts examine the market to try to determine when to buy. Knowing that, fundamental analysts are definitely interested in earnings trends. Technical analysts would be interested in such things as support and resistance and the breadth of the market.

64. **C.** (Chapter 16) The broker-dealer must send out account statements at least once every three months (quarterly) for an active or inactive account. Mutual funds must send out account statements at least once every six months (semiannually).

65. **B.** (Chapter 6) If you look at Choices B and C, you will see that the answers oppose each other, so one of them has to be the answer to the question. Treasury stock is stock that was issued and subsequently repurchased by the company. Treasury stock has no voting rights and does not receive dividends.

66. **D.** (Chapter 8) Because this is an "except" question, you must find the false answer. The correct answer is Choice (D). The dated date of a bond issue is the date on which the issue begins to earn interest, which has less impact on marketing than the other answer choices.

67. **B.** (Chapter 15) IRAs may be set up as single life, joint and last survivor, or uniform lifetime. *Life with period certain* is a way to set up payout for an annuity, not an IRA. *Single life* is when the owner is the beneficiary of the account. *Joint and last survivor* is when the sole beneficiary of the account is a spouse who is more than ten years younger than the owner. *Uniform lifetime* is when the spouse is not the sole beneficiary or the spouse is not more than ten years younger than the owner.

68. **C.** (Chapter 10) Similar to variable annuities, variable life insurance policies have a separate account of securities. All variable life insurance (VLI) policies have a set premium and a minimum death benefit. However, if the securities held in the separate account perform well, the policy will build up cash value, which will increase the death benefit. If the securities held in the separate account perform poorly, there may be no cash value in the account.

69. B. (Chapter 13) Certainly, all the choices listed are important when determining a client's investment profile. However, this is an "except" question, which means that you're looking for an investment influence that is financial. The amount of marketable securities an investor owns is part of their financial profile as well as other things like net worth, money available for investing, current income, expenses, home ownership, and so on.

70. B. (Chapter 16) A durable power of attorney gives power of attorney to someone else to handle financial affairs in the event that the grantor becomes incapacitated. A durable power of attorney is unlike a regular power of attorney, which terminates in the event the grantor becomes incapacitated.

71. B. (Chapter 7) There is a lot of information in this question that was not required to come up with an answer. All you needed to know was that it is a 4 percent bond and that your client held it until maturity. The fact that it was yielding 5 percent and that it is a convertible bond is not relevant to the question. When investors hold a bond until maturity, they receive par value (usually $1,000). However, if the bond is paying interest, holders will also receive their last coupon payment at maturity. It is a 4 percent bond, so investors will receive $40 per year interest ($4 percent of $1,000 par) broken down into two $20 semiannual payments. So in this case, your client will receive $1,020 at maturity.

$1,000 par value + $20 interest = $1,020

72. A. (Chapter 9) Normally, if Barbara were purchasing $10,000 worth of stock on margin, she'd have to deposit $5,000 to meet the margin call (you can assume Regulation T is 50 percent of the purchase). First, you have to find out whether she has any excess equity in her margin account to help offset the $5,000 payment. Use the following equation:

LMV − DR = EQ

After setting up the equation, enter the market value of the securities ($30,000) under the long market value (LMV). Next, enter the $12,000 under the debit record (DR), also known as the *debit balance*. When you subtract the DR from the LMV, you come up with an equity (EQ) of $18,000. Multiply Regulation T (50 percent) by the LMV to get the amount of equity the customer needs to have in the account to be at 50 percent. This investor needs only $15,000 in equity to reach 50 percent, and this investor has $18,000, $3,000 more than necessary:

$$LMV - DR = EQ$$
$$\$30,000 - \$12,000 = \$18,000$$
$$Reg\ T \times LMV = \underline{\$15,000}$$
$$\$3,000\ \text{excess equity}$$

The $3,000 is excess equity (SMA, or special memorandum account), which she can use to help offset the margin call for the $10,000 worth of stock she wants to buy:

$5,000 margin call − $3,000 excess equity = $2,000 to deposit

73. C. (Chapter 8) The interest received on municipal bonds is federally tax-free. Because Ginny is in the highest income tax bracket, she can save more tax money by investing in municipal bonds. This strategy will put her on equal footing with other investors because neither high-income nor low-income investors have to pay taxes on the interest received from municipal bonds. Therefore, municipal bonds are more advantageous to investors in high income tax brackets.

74. B. (Chapter 15) Capital gains on securities held one year or less are considered short-term and taxed at the investor's tax bracket.

75. A. (Chapter 8) The largest backing for municipal GO (general obligation) bonds is property (*ad valorem*) taxes. The credit rating of GO bonds is highly dependent on the municipality's tax collection record, the number of people living in the municipality, property values, whether it's a limited tax GO bond or unlimited tax GO bond, and so on. Unlike revenue bonds, GO bonds typically require voter approval prior to being issued.

76. D. (Chapter 16) Upon learning about the death of a customer, a registered representative should mark the account as deceased, freeze the account (not do any trading), cancel all open orders (good-till-canceled orders), cancel all written powers of attorney, and await the proper legal papers for guidance about what to do with the account.

77. B. (Chapter 14) Believe it or not, concealing the trading volume for some orders from the public is not a violation. Sometimes large institutional investors like to keep the trading volume of some of their orders hidden from other institutional investors. This practice is called "dark pools of liquidity." They usually do this so as not to provide too much information to some of their competitors.

78. B. (Chapter 14) Designated Market Makers (DMMs) should keep trading as active as possible but *cannot* compete with public orders. To keep trading as active as possible, a DMM may place an order in-between the current bid and ask price to narrow the spread but cannot place an order for their own inventory at the same price as a customer's order.

79. C. (Chapter 7) Mortgage bonds, collateral trusts, and equipment trusts are all forms of secured bonds. Because these bonds are secured with collateral, the collateral securing the bonds is sold to satisfy the bondholders if the issuer defaults. However, debentures are not backed with collateral and are, therefore, riskier. Because more risk equals more reward, debenture holders can expect a coupon rate that's higher than that of the secured bonds.

80. D. (Chapter 7) Of the answer choices given, Choice (D) is the least preferable and, therefore, the correct answer. AA rated bonds, U.S. Treasury notes, and AA rated debentures can yield predictable income. By contrast, income bonds are issued when a corporation is coming out of bankruptcy and trying to reorganize. Therefore, income bonds only pay interest if the corporation can meet the interest payment and normally trade without accrued interest. Income bonds are not suitable for Dana because she's seeking predictable income.

81. A. (Chapter 12) You'll find that this question is actually much easier than you may have originally thought. To get the maximum loss on a debit (long) spread, all you have to do is put the premiums in the option chart to see that you have more money out than in. The difference between those two numbers is the maximum loss.

82. C. (Chapter 10) Although international funds may be okay to help diversify a portfolio and may provide current income, they're certainly the riskiest of all the choices given. International funds invest in securities outside of the investor's home country. International funds have additional risks that many other securities don't have, such as currency risk (the risk that the currency exchange rate will be bad). Also, the investor faces political risk (the risk that political changes in a country may adversely affect the price of securities). You should definitely steer this investor away from international funds.

83. A. (Chapter 12) The OCC (Options Clearing Corporation) is the issuer and guarantor of all listed options. The OCC determines which options will be traded and guarantees that option holders can always exercise their options.

84. C. (Chapter 10) Dividends that are distributed by municipal bond funds are federally tax-free, but any capital gain distribution is taxable. Choice (C) is the right answer.

85. **C.** (Chapter 9) This investor is opening a combined (long and short) margin account. The best way to deal with this is to treat each transaction separately. The investor is purchasing $15,000 ($15 × 1,000 shares) worth of ABC and shorting $12,000 ($12 × 1,000 shares of DEF). Assuming Regulation T at 50 percent, this investor would have to come up with 50 percent of each transaction.

$$\$15,000 \times 50 = \$7,500$$

$$\$12,000 \times 50 = \$6,000$$

$$\$7,500 + \$6,000 = \$13,500.$$

This investor would have to deposit $13,500 as a result of the two transactions.

86. **C.** (Chapter 8) Hopefully, the "G" in "GANs" was enough to help you get the correct answer. GANs are *grant anticipation notes,* which a municipality issues to provide temporary financing while waiting for a grant from the U.S. government.

87. **D.** (Chapter 12) "Long" means to buy, so to have a long straddle, you can't have any sells (shorts). Thus, you can cross off Choices (A) and (B). To create a long straddle, the investor needs to buy a call and buy a put with the same stock, same strike price, and same expiration date. The only answer that works is Choice (D).

88. **D.** (Chapter 9) Luke owns the calls that he's exercising. Luke exercises the options at a profit of $10 per share (less the premium) and is selling the stock immediately, so no deposit's required. It certainly wouldn't make much sense to have Luke pay $30 per share when exercising the options and then have the firm send Luke a check for $40 per share. The key here is that Luke exercised the option and sold the stock on the same day.

89. **B.** (Chapter 9) The margin requirement for both long and short margin accounts is set at 50 percent. However, the minimum maintenance for a long account is 25 percent and the minimum maintenance for a short account is 30 percent.

90. **C.** (Chapter 13) To determine the net worth (stockholder's equity) of a company, use the following equation:

net worth = assets − liabilities

net worth = $11,500,000 − $3,350,000 = $8,150,000

Remember to add all of the numbers under the Assets side of the balance sheet and subtract all of the numbers under the Liabilities side of the balance sheet.

91. **D.** (Chapter 12) Standard equity options contracts represent 100 shares of the underlying security and are exercisable at any time prior to expiration (American style).

92. **D.** (Chapter 9) *Portfolio margin* looks at the risk of an investor's portfolio as a whole when determining margin requirements. Portfolio margin allows investors greater leverage but is only available to more sophisticated investors, and those investors must keep a minimum equity in their account of around $100,000 to $150,000.

93. **A.** (Chapter 7) The correct answer is Choice (A) because issuers call bonds when interest rates are falling. Choice (B) is incorrect because after the notes are called, new bonds at the lower rate are issued to raise funds in order to call the outstanding bonds with the higher rate. Choice (D) is incorrect because municipal bond call provisions are advantageous to issuers; the call provisions reduce fixed costs by providing issuers with the ability to redeem bonds before maturity.

94. **C.** (Chapter 13) You can quickly cross off Choice (D), because this answer can be determined. To determine the price/earnings (PE) ratio, use the following formula:

$$\text{PE Ratio} = \frac{\text{market price}}{\text{EPS}} = \frac{\$22.00}{\$4.00} = 5.50$$

The answer is 5.50, Choice (C).

95. **C.** (Chapter 14) The Order Audit Trail System (OATS) is an automated computer system that tracks the life of an over-the-counter (OTC) order from entry to execution or cancellation. OATS tracks all OTC securities, including OTCBB (over-the-counter bulletin board) stocks and OTC Pink Market stocks.

96. **B.** (Chapter 16) All written complaints need to be handled by a principal and kept on file. Even though the complaint was sent via email, it's still considered a written complaint. The complaint does not need to be forwarded or sent to FINRA.

97. **B.** (Chapter 11) A partnership flows through passive gains, losses, and income to investors each year.

98. **A.** (Chapter 11) This question is actually somewhat of a logic question, and I actually put the statements in order for you. Secured creditors (loans secured with collateral) are paid first, followed by general creditors (loans not secured with collateral), then limited partners (the main investors), and lastly, the general partners.

99. **A.** (Chapter 5) All securities sold in a state must be registered in that state (also known as blue-sky registration). Coordination, qualification, and notification (filing) are all types of state registration; registration by cooperation is not. If an agent wants to sell in a state, the security, the registered rep, and the broker-dealer must be registered in that state.

100. **B.** (Chapter 12) The easiest way to figure out the answer to this question is to use the equation $P = I + T$, where

>> P = the Premium of the option

>> I = the Intrinsic value of the option (how much it is in the money)

>> T = the Time value of the option (how much the investor is paying for the time to use the option)

$P = I + T$

$9 = 5 + T$

$T = 4$

First, put the premium of 9 into the equation. Next, because the option is 5 points in-the-money (call options go in-the-money when the price of the stock goes above the strike price), insert the intrinsic value of 5 in the equation. Because the premium is 9 and the option is 5 points in-the-money, the time value is 4.

101. **B.** (Chapter 16) Principals of a firm must approve all new accounts, advertising used by the firm, handling of complaints, trades in all accounts, and so on. However, as far as the Series 7 exam goes, principals don't need to approve recommendations made by registered reps. In real life, I would get approval before making recommendations if I were you. You have to remember that principals must sign all order tickets, and if you don't clear a recommendation with them first, they may be reluctant to do so.

102. B. (Chapter 7) If you want to pass the Series 7 exam, you have to know your quotes. The correct answer is Choice (B) because it's the only discounted instrument, and discounted instruments (such as T-bills) are quoted on a discount yield basis.

103. C. (Chapter 8) LRBs (lease revenue bonds) are similar to IDRs (industrial development revenue bonds), but instead of the bonds being backed by corporations, they're backed by lease payments made by office buildings, universities, prisons, and so forth. LTGOs (limited tax general obligation bonds) are a type of GO (general obligation) bond that's backed by taxes that aren't used to back other bonds. BABs (build America bonds) are taxable municipal bonds in which the U.S. Treasury either reimburses the issuer or gives a tax credit to investors for up to 35 percent of the interest cost.

104. D. (Chapter 13) You can use logic to answer this question. When the company pays a cash dividend, it pays off some of its liabilities because the dividend was declared previously. The net worth does not change because assets (cash) and liabilities decrease by the same amount.

105. D. (Chapter 8) Remember that an "except" question is looking for a false answer. The correct answer is Choice (D). Taxable equivalent yields cannot be shown because every investor has a unique tax issue and bracket.

106. B. (Chapter 12) If the investor is looking for potential premium income, they must have sold something, so you can rule out Choice (C). Because the maximum loss potential for a short straddle or short combination is unlimited and the investor wants to limit their loss, you can cross out Choice (D). Actually, the only answer that works is a credit spread. To create a credit (short) spread, the investor sells an option that will be in-the-money first and purchases the option that will go in-the-money later. If the option never goes in-the-money, the investor gets to keep the premium of the option sold. To limit the loss, the investor purchases an option that will go in-the-money later. This position provides potential premium income and limits the maximum potential loss.

107. A. (Chapter 16) Under FINRA rules, the representative should execute the trade in accordance with the customer's request and note on the trade ticket that the order was unsolicited.

108. C. (Chapter 13) You can calculate the working capital, net worth, and quick assets by looking at a corporation's balance sheet, but you need information on the income statement to calculate the current yield.

109. A. (Chapter 7) Money market securities are a popular topic on the Series 7 exam. Remember that commercial paper, as well as negotiable certificates of deposit, are money market securities.

110. B. (Chapter 15) Any income derived from an investment in a limited partnership is termed passive. Passive gains can only be written off against passive losses. Earned income includes money made from salary, bonuses, tips, and so on. Portfolio income includes money made from interest, dividends, and capital gains made from investing in securities.

111. B. (Chapter 13) The "P" in PE ratio stands for "market Price," the "E" stands for "Earnings per share," and the word "ratio" lets you know that you need to divide. So let's set up the equation:

$$\text{PE Ratio} = \frac{\text{Market price}}{\text{EPS}} = \frac{\$40}{\$8} = 5$$

The market price is $40 and the earnings per share is $8, so that means that the PE ratio is 5.

112. **B.** (Chapter 12) Listed options expire at 11:59 p.m. EST (10:59 p.m. CST) on the third Friday of the expiration month. The last time to trade an option is 4:00 p.m. EST (3:00 p.m. CST) on the third Friday of the expiration month. The last time to exercise an option is 5:30 p.m. EST (4:30 p.m. CST) on the third Friday of the expiration month.

113. **B.** (Chapter 11) Limited partners have access to all the financial information regarding the partnership, they may vote to terminate the partnership, and they may invest in competing partnerships. However, limited partners may not make management decisions; that right is limited to the general partner(s).

114. **C.** (Chapter 11) The primary reason for investing in undeveloped land is appreciation potential. People who invest in undeveloped land either privately or by way of a real-estate DPP are hoping that their land will be of more value sometime in the near future.

115. **A.** (Chapter 10) Closed-end funds are typically listed on an exchange and have a fixed number of shares outstanding. Closed-end funds must be sold to another investor and are not redeemable. In addition, closed-end funds may issue common stock, preferred stock, and bonds.

116. **C.** (Chapter 10) ETFs (exchange-traded funds) and inverse ETFs are easily tradable and money market funds are easily redeemable, so they all have a high degree of liquidity. Hedge funds are the least liquid because they are unregulated and require a minimum holding period *(lock-up provision)* before investors can make withdrawals. Hedge funds are speculative and employ strategies unavailable to regulated investment companies. Hedge funds may purchase securities on margin, sell securities short, purchase or sell options, and so on.

117. **D.** (Chapter 12) I figured I'd give you an easy one toward the end of the test. When buying a call option, the maximum potential gain is unlimited, so an investor who's selling a call option faces an unlimited maximum potential loss.

118. **A.** (Chapter 6) After the split, stockholders are going to have 5 shares for every 4 that they had before. If the number of shares is going to increase, the price of the stock is going to decrease to make up for the additional shares. After the split, the investor should have the same overall market value of securities. Use the following equation to determine the number of shares and the stock price after a split:

$$\text{shares after the split} = \text{shares} \times \frac{A}{B}, \text{ so } 1{,}000 \times \frac{5}{4} = 1{,}250 \text{ shares}$$

$$\text{price after the split} = \text{stock price} \times \frac{B}{A}, \text{ so } \$40 \times \frac{4}{5} = \$32$$

119. **D.** (Chapter 13) Actually, all the choices listed would likely change the investor's investment objectives. Typically, as investors grow older, they will likely want to take less risk. By the same token, investing for one person or two people, as in someone getting married or divorced, would change the investment objectives. Also, as people gain investment experience, they may be open to more speculative investments or become more risk averse. Plus, you can assume that if an investor has more family responsibilities, they will want to take less risk.

120. **D.** (Chapter 13) Debt to equity ratio is the ratio of long term debt to stockholders' equity (net worth). Therefore, the debt to equity ratio of a company measures the leverage (long term debt) of a company. The other ratios mentioned are short-term ratios measuring the liquidity of a company.

121. **C.** (Chapter 7) Commercial paper is generally issued for the purpose of raising capital for a corporation. Choice (A) is incorrect because commercial instruments are not quoted as a percent of par. Choice (B) is incorrect because a commercial instrument is proof of a debt, not ownership. Choice (D) is incorrect because commercial instruments are a debt security; therefore, if a claim is filed against the issuing corporation, the commercial instrument holds a senior position to preferred stock.

122. **B.** (Chapter 16) Municipal fund securities include 529 college savings plans. All securities advertising must be approved by a principal of the firm and cannot be fraudulent (antifraud rules apply to everything). The MSRB and the states do not have to approve advertising.

123. **D.** (Chapter 15) In most instances, individuals may invest up to $6,500 per year in an IRA ($7,500 if they're age 50 or older). The maximum investment amount often changes annually, so please check the IRS website for the latest info.

124. **D.** (Chapter 10) A specialized or *sector* fund invests within a single industry or geographical area.

125. **D.** (Chapter 15) Withdrawals from a Roth IRA may begin any time after the investor reaches age 59½. However, there's no required beginning date (RBD) or required minimum distribution (RMD) for Roth IRAs like there is for other retirement plans. You need to remember that the money withdrawn from a Roth IRA is tax-free, so the IRS doesn't care when these investors take their money because it isn't getting any of it.

Knowing the Score

Here's how the Series 7 exam is scored:

>> You get one point for each correct answer.

>> You get zero points for each incorrect answer.

A passing grade is 72 percent. In other words, you need at least 90 correct answers on the whole test to get one step closer to your Nobel Prize in stockbrokerage (okay, economics). To calculate your score for this test, multiply the number of correct answers by 0.8 or divide it by 125. Whatever grade you get, make sure you round down, not up. For example, a grade of 71.2 is a 71 percent, not a 72.

Answer Key for Practice Exam 2

1.	A	33.	B	65.	B	97.	B
2.	B	34.	D	66.	D	98.	A
3.	D	35.	A	67.	B	99.	A
4.	A	36.	D	68.	C	100.	B
5.	A	37.	D	69.	B	101.	B
6.	D	38.	A	70.	B	102.	B
7.	A	39.	D	71.	B	103.	C
8.	C	40.	A	72.	A	104.	D
9.	C	41.	D	73.	C	105.	D
10.	A	42.	C	74.	B	106.	B
11.	A	43.	D	75.	A	107.	A
12.	C	44.	C	76.	D	108.	C
13.	B	45.	B	77.	B	109.	A
14.	D	46.	C	78.	B	110.	B
15.	B	47.	D	79.	C	111.	B
16.	C	48.	C	80.	D	112.	B
17.	A	49.	B	81.	A	113.	B
18.	B	50.	C	82.	C	114.	C
19.	C	51.	A	83.	A	115.	A
20.	A	52.	C	84.	C	116.	C
21.	A	53.	B	85.	C	117.	D
22.	B	54.	D	86.	C	118.	A
23.	B	55.	D	87.	D	119.	D
24.	D	56.	B	88.	D	120.	D
25.	B	57.	C	89.	B	121.	C
26.	B	58.	A	90.	C	122.	B
27.	D	59.	A	91.	D	123.	D
28.	D	60.	D	92.	D	124.	D
29.	B	61.	D	93.	A	125.	D
30.	B	62.	D	94.	C		
31.	D	63.	A	95.	C		
32.	A	64.	C	96.	B		

6

The Part of Tens

Avoid the most common traps on the Series 7 exam.

Start your career the right way with ten job-related tips.

Chapter **21**

Ten Series 7 Exam Traps to Avoid

After all the time, effort, and sacrifice you put into studying, elevating the importance of the Series 7 exam to an unrealistically high level is easy. Step back for a moment. Keep it in perspective. This situation is not life or death. If you don't pass the test the first time, the worst thing that happens is that you have to retake it.

On the other hand, getting tripped up by some trivial exam traps after you've come this far would be a shame. This chapter lists some common mistakes and gives you some last-minute advice to help you over the last hurdles that stand between you and your first million dollars as a stockbroker.

Easing Up on the Studying

Perhaps you stop studying because you're getting good scores on practice exams and your confidence is high. If you're scoring 80s on exams that you're seeing for *the first time*, shoot for 85s. If you're getting 85s, shoot for 90s. The point is that you should continue to take exams until the day before your scheduled exam day. I firmly believe that every day away from studying ultimately costs you points on your exam that you can't afford to lose.

By the same token, make sure you don't wait too long before taking the exam. If you have to wait too many weeks before you can take the exam, you lose your sense of urgency, and it's almost impossible to keep up the intense level of preparation needed for many months at a time. If you're taking a prep course before you schedule your Series 7, follow your instructor's advice as to when you should take the exam. If you're directing your own course of study, after you're passing practice exams consistently with 80s or better, take the test as soon as possible. The longer you wait to take the exam, the more likely you are to forget the key points and complex formulas. If your test date is too far in the future, you also risk falling into the "I'll study later" trap, where you think you can double your efforts later to make up for any wasted time. Overall, losing your sense of urgency leads to complacency and a lack of motivation, which probably aren't skills broker-dealers are looking for in their employees.

Assuming the Question's Intent

You glance at the question quickly and incorrectly anticipate what the exam question is really asking you. You pick the wrong answer because you were in such a rush, and you didn't see the word *except* at the end of the question. What a shame.

You don't want to fail the exam when you really know the material. Read each question carefully and look for tricky words like *except, not,* and *unless.* Then read all the answer choices before making your selection. (For more info on test-taking strategies that apply to certain question types, see Chapter 3.)

Reading into the Question

You're thinking *but what if* before you even look at the answer choices. When reviewing questions with students, I constantly get questions like "Yeah, but what if they're an insider?" or "What if they're of retirement age?" The bottom line is that you shouldn't add anything to the question that isn't there. Don't be afraid to read the question at face value and select the right answer, even if it occasionally seems too easy. Eliminate answer choices that are too much of a stretch, and remember that when two answer choices are opposites, one of them is most likely correct.

Becoming Distracted When Others Finish

Now certainly this won't happen if you're taking the test in your own home, but if you're taking it in a testing center, be aware. So, imagine that you haven't even started looking over the questions you marked for review when the woman next to you leaps from her seat, picks up her results (with a little victory dance), and makes a break for the door.

Don't let people who are taking the exam with you psych you out. If others finish ahead of you, perhaps they're members of Mensa or maybe this is the fifth time they've taken the exam — practice makes perfect. They may even be taking a totally different exam, like a nursing exam. Besides the Series 7, the testing centers also offer other securities exams with a differing amount of questions (a 65-question Series 63 exam, a 75-question Securities Industry Essentials exam, a 100-question Series 66 exam, a 130-question Series 65 exam, and so on). Keep focused and centered on taking your own exam. The only time you need to be concerned with is your own — whether you're on track.

Not Dressing for Comfort

You're trying to calculate the taxable equivalent yield on Mr. Dimwitty's GO bond, but the pencil keeps slipping out of your sweaty hand. You swear the test center has the heat cranked up to 80 degrees. Hmm. Maybe wearing your warmest wool sweater wasn't the best idea.

Dress comfortably. Don't wear a tie that's so tight it cuts off the circulation to your brain. You're under enough stress just taking the exam. Dress in layers. A t-shirt, a sweatshirt, and a jacket are great insulation against the cold. Another advantage is that you can shed layers of clothing (without ending up sitting in your underwear) if the exam room is too warm.

Forgetting to Breathe

You walk into the test center brimming with confidence. All of a sudden the exam begins, and some of the words look like they're in a foreign language. Your heart starts pounding, and you feel like you're going to pass out.

If stress becomes overwhelming, your breathing can become shallow and ineffective, which only adds to your stress level. Focus yourself before the exam by closing your eyes and taking a few deep breaths. This same process of closing your eyes and breathing deeply is a great way to calm yourself if you become stressed or anxious at any time during the exam. Now certainly, the more prepared you are, the less anxious you'll be on that important day.

Trying to Work Out Equations in Your Head Instead of Writing Them Down

While taking the exam, your memory starts to cloud and, somehow, the fact that two plus two equals five begins to make sense to you, and the only formula you can remember is that there are 12 inches in a foot.

Memorize your equations while you're studying for your Series 7 exam so you know them cold before you arrive at the test site. If your nerves are getting the best of you and clouding your memory, jotting down the more difficult equations that you want to remember as soon as you receive permission to start the exam may be helpful (this process is known as a *brain dump*). When working out complicated math problems, you have scrap paper to work with (and a basic calculator). Use them. For example, some formulas, such as those for determining the debt service coverage ratio or the value of a right (cum rights), require you to find sums and differences before you can divide. Even simple calculations, such as finding averages, can involve quite a few numbers. In problems with multiple parts, it's easy for you to accidentally skip steps, plug in the wrong numbers from the question, or forget values that you calculated along the way. Writing things out helps you keep things in place without cluttering your short-term memory.

Spending Too Much Time on One Question

To calculate the number of days of accrued interest on a T-bond, you decide to draw pictures of the calendar for the last four months. As you finish penciling the dates in those tiny boxes, you look at the clock and realize ten minutes have passed. Oops!

Not all questions have the same point value, but if you spend too much time on one question, you may lose points for many questions you didn't have time to even look at because you wasted so much time on the one that gave you trouble. If you find yourself taking too long to answer a question, take your best guess, mark it for review, and return to it later.

Changing Your Answers for the Wrong Reasons

You change an answer just because you already selected that same letter for the preceding three or four questions in a row. Just a touch of paranoia, right?

You've probably been told from the time you first started primary school not to change your answers. Trust your instincts and go with your original reaction. You have only two good reasons to change your answer:

>> You find that you initially forgot or didn't see the words *not* or *except* and you initially chose the wrong answer because you didn't see the tricky word.

>> You find that the answer choice you originally selected is not the best answer after all.

Calculating Your Final Score Prematurely

You waste valuable time concentrating on the number of questions you think you got wrong instead of focusing on the Series 7 exam questions you still have to answer.

Just read each question carefully, scrutinize the answer choices, and select the best answer. You'll find out whether you passed right after you complete the exam; it's not like you need to figure out your possible grade in advance to avoid sleepless nights until you receive your score. If you have additional time, use it to check your answers to the questions you marked for review.

Chapter **22**

Ten Ways to Start Your Career Off Right

Passing the Series 7 exam can be one of the high points in your life. You've dedicated yourself to attaining your goal, put your life (and partying) on hold while you studied, and fulfilled your commitment to long hours of studying and hard work. You're now ready to reap the rewards. As you begin your new profession, you'll encounter many new hurdles. I give you this chapter to help prepare you for what to expect and, hopefully, to maximize your chances of a long, successful career.

Win at the Numbers Game

As with any other sales job, selling securities to investors is a numbers game. Some people actually track the number of calls it takes to open a new account, but I'm not among them. There are no specific economic benchmarks; however, you may have to make 500 cold calls to get to talk to 150 people. Out of these 150 people, you may generate ten leads. Out of every ten leads, you may open up one account.

The point is that you have to pick up that phone day in and day out and make the calls. If you're making 200 to 300 phone calls per day, you're likely to open an account every few days. However, if you're making 50 phone calls a day, you'll probably open up an account every couple weeks, and unless you hook a whale (a huge investor who likes to trade), you'll have trouble paying for fuel or electricity for your new car. Remember that you're participating in a numbers game and that every "no" brings you one call closer to a "yes."

Be an Apprentice

There's no better way to hit the ground running than to have a top producer or account opener as a role model. Find the person in your firm with sales techniques that are most comfortable for you and invest as much time as possible watching how this mentor conducts themself on a daily basis.

Top producers earn the most income because they've found a way to stand out in a competitive market.

Maybe this person can take you under their wing and show you the ropes in return for leads you develop while under their supervision. You can even have a contract between you and your mentor that sets forth the agreed-upon terms for each of you for a fixed period of time.

Do Your Homework

Take time to find out as much as possible about the securities you're trying to sell. When you know what you're talking about, you inspire confidence from potential new customers. Spend some of your free time watching investing programs and reading the *Wall Street Journal* or any other trade magazines or newspapers you can get your hands on. The more you learn, the more comfortable you'll be on the phone, and the more sales you'll make.

Treat the Minnow like a Whale

More often than not, new customers don't disclose all their financial background to you. However, whether a customer has $10,000 or $10 million to invest, the money is important to them. Treat every customer as though they're the most valuable person in the world. Who knows? You may be speaking to someone with a lot of money to invest now or someone who will have a lot of money to invest in the future, or your customer may be a friend or family member of someone with substantial resources. Remember, a strong referral is a most influential lead.

Smile When You Dial

Be positive. You're going to have good days and bad days. You have to accept that as part of the business, but don't let it get you down. If you need to, take a five-minute break to gather your thoughts. If you aren't in a positive state of mind, you'll reflect that in the way you talk to existing or potential customers.

When a Security Goes the Wrong Direction, Don't Be a Stranger

You can't guarantee success, and that's okay. Savvy investors know that not every investment can end up a winner, no matter how good the situation looks in the beginning. If you recommend a security and it gets beaten down, call your customer. The customer is just waiting to hear from you. This call may be right up there with the most uncomfortable tasks you'll ever have to perform. Remember, however, that a savvy customer is most likely aware of what's going on, and your news won't be a surprise. Customers just want to be comforted and reassured that you'll be there with them — in good times and bad. Hopefully, the other seven or eight securities that you recommended are doing well.

Put In the Hours

Of course, you have to educate yourself about selling your products and cold-calling. In the beginning, be prepared to put in approximately ten hours each day. As you grow more experienced, you'll receive more leads and open more accounts in a shorter period of time, but in the beginning, you have to play the numbers game in order to earn money while you develop a more confident sales pitch.

Broaden Your Horizons

Consider obtaining other licenses to increase your skills and your ability to compete in the securities and financial industry. For example, the Series 65 or 66 (investment adviser exams) allows you to receive a fee for giving investment advice; Series 24 (the principal's license exam) allows you to manage other registered reps; and a Life, Accident, and Health Insurance license allows you to sell insurance policies and variable annuities to customers. If you take prep courses to obtain these licenses, you may also be exposed to a network of professionals who can become a source of future referrals.

Pay Yourself First

The stock market (and you with it) will have many peaks and valleys, but your own financial security doesn't have to be quite so uneven. In the peak times, put away half your earnings when you receive your big paychecks. Tell yourself that you aren't going to make a big purchase until you have a certain amount socked away (see the upcoming section on setting goals). I've seen too many new brokers go out and buy a new car, a new boat, or whatever with their first big paycheck, expecting to make that much every month. The first time they have a bad month, they're wondering how they're going to make the payments (and possibly pay the rent). Remember, stockbrokers are supposed to be good with money. Burying yourself in debt looks kind of bad.

KEEP HUNGER IN YOUR EFFORTS, NOT YOUR STOMACH

When I first began my career as a stockbroker, the sales manager at the securities firm where I worked began the staff meetings by introducing himself and stating that he'd earned $100,000 his first year in the business and spent $150,000 of it — and he considered that to be a good thing because he felt it kept him hungry! Somehow that just doesn't make sense either mathematically or logically (no matter how much your spending stimulates the economy). Some of the other trainees at the meeting were very impressed with the sales manager's suggestion, especially when he told us that he stayed hungry by spending so much more than he earned.

I remember looking at the sales manager and the other trainees who were attending this meeting and thinking, "What an idiot!" You'll get a lot of foolish suggestions along the way. If you want to stay hungry in your efforts, work hard, sock away (or invest) half your earnings, and pretend that money isn't there. Otherwise, you may be hungry for another reason — you can't afford to buy food!

Set Some Goals: The Brass Ring

Focus on your goals. Successful people have realistic short-term and long-term goals and a plan to achieve them. Whether your short-term goal is to put $5,000 away per month or to open ten new accounts, identifying what you want to do is the first step in creating a plan for your future.

What's the first thing every broker wants to do with the first big paycheck? You guessed it — buy a new car. Although that glistening Porsche or Tesla can be an awesome incentive, set yourself smaller milestones to reach prior to making a big purchase. You can break down long-term goals, such as paying for a wedding, buying a new car, or purchasing your first house, into monthly income goals after you figure out the costs involved. Take a picture of your dream car or house and put it in a frame on your desk to remind you of the reward that awaits you.

Whatever your plan is, setting your mind on what you want, defining the steps you have to take to get there, and focusing your efforts on accomplishing each goal are the essential elements of a lucrative and rewarding career. Remember, you control your destiny.

Appendix

Important Figures and Formulas

You can't bring your notes (or this Appendix) into the exam center, so be sure to squirrel the following info away in your brain and write it on the scrap paper provided *after* the test begins.

Adjust for stock splits (Chapter 6):

$$\text{Shares after the split} = \text{Shares} \times \frac{A}{B}$$

$$\text{Price after the split} = \text{Stock price} \times \frac{B}{A}$$

Determine the outstanding shares (Chapter 6):

$$\text{Outstanding shares} = \text{issued shares} - \text{Treasury stock}$$

Rights formula (Chapter 6):

$$\text{Value of a right cum rights} = \frac{M\ (\text{market price}) - S\ (\text{subscription price})}{N\ (\text{number of rights needed to purchase one share}) + 1}$$

Ex-rights formula (Chapter 6):

$$\text{Value of a right ex-rights} = \frac{M\ (\text{market price}) - S\ (\text{subscription price})}{N\ (\text{number of rights needed to purchase one share})}$$

Calculate the current yield of a stock or bond (Chapter 7):

$$\text{Current Yield} = \frac{\text{annual dividends or interest}}{\text{market price}}$$

Calculate the conversion ratio of a convertible preferred stock or convertible bond (Chapter 7):

$$\text{Conversion ratio} = \frac{\text{par value}}{\text{conversion price}}$$

Bond seesaw (Chapter 7):

Bond price   NY   CY   YTM   YTC   Bond at par

Calculate the taxable equivalent yield of a municipal bond (Chapter 8):

$$\text{Taxable equivalent yield (TEY)} = \frac{\text{municipal yield}}{100\% - \text{investor's tax bracket}}$$

Long margin account formula (Chapter 9):

Long market value (LMV) − debit record (DR) = equity (EQ)

Short margin account formula (Chapter 9):

Short market value (SMV) + equity (EQ) = credit record (CR)

Calculating the buying or shorting power (Chapter 9):

$$\text{Buying or shorting power} = \frac{\text{SMA}}{\text{Regulation T}}$$

Calculate the sales charge % of a mutual fund (Chapter 10):

$$\text{Sales charge \%} = \frac{\text{ask} - \text{bid}}{\text{ask}} = \frac{\text{POP} - \text{NAV}}{\text{POP}}$$

Calculate the public offering price of a mutual fund (Chapter 10):

$$\text{Public offering price} = \frac{\text{net asset value (NAV)}}{100\% - \text{sales charge \%}}$$

Options chart (Chapter 12):

Calculate the time value of an option (Chapter 12):

Premium (P) = intrinsic value (I) + time value (T)

Balance sheet formula (Chapter 13):

Assets = liabilities + stockholder's equity

Calculate working capital (Chapter 13):

Working capital = current assets − current liabilities

Net worth (Chapter 13):

Net worth = assets − liabilities

Price/earnings (P/E) ratio formula (Chapter 13):

$$\text{Price/earnings (P/E) ratio} = \frac{\text{market price}}{\text{EPS}}$$

Index

making phone calls, 455

obtaining other licenses, 457

putting in more hours, 457

saving half of earnings, 457

treating every customer as important, 456

cash accounts, 149

cash dividends, 75, 274, 300, 311

cash equivalents, 106

cash flow, 276

cashless collar, 234

cash trades, 346

catastrophe (calamity) clause, 119

CBOE (Chicago Board Options Exchange), 240, 289, 333

CDR (Central Registration Depository), 9, 16

Central Registration Depository (CRD), 9, 16

certificate of limited partnership, 201–202

certificates of participation (COP), 124

Cheat Sheet, 2–3

Chicago Board Options Exchange (CBOE), 240, 289, 333

churning, 339, 357

CIPs (customer identification programs), 335

Class A (front-end load) shares, 183

Class B (back-end load) shares, 183

Class C (level load) shares, 183

Class D (no load) shares, 183

CLNs (construction loan notes), 127

closed accounts, 358

closed-end funds, 173

exchange-traded funds (ETFs), 173

interval funds, 173

net asset value, 173

versus open-end (mutual) funds, 173–174

overview, 173

public offering price (POP), 173

closed-end mortgage bond, 89

closed-stem questions, 34

closing purchase (option), 223

closing sale (option), 223

closing transactions, 245

clothing, 452–453

code of arbitration, 353–354

code of procedure (litigation), 353

collar, 234

collateralized debt obligations (CDOs), 106

collateralized mortgage obligations (CMOs)

average life, 104

extension risk, 104

overview, 103

prepayment risk, 104

retail communications, 104–105

tranche types, 104–105

collaterals, 89

collateral trusts, 89

college savings plans, 115

combination (balanced) programs, 207

combinations

break-even point for, 228

long, 225

overview, 225

short, 227

combined (split) offering, 288

commercial paper

overview, 106

tax exempt, 127

commingling of funds, 38, 357

commissions, 134, 292

common stock

categories, 73

dividends

cash, 75

overview, 74–75

stock dividends, 75–76

nonvoting, 72

overview, 71–72

par value, 74, 273

penny stocks

compensation, 77

disclosure document, 77

exempt transactions, 77

overview, 76

versus preferred stock, 78

splitting, 74

stockholder's voting rights, 72–73

community property accounts, 337

companion tranches (support bonds), 104

competitive offering, 58, 121

complaints, 353–354

computer experience, lack of, 48

computerized format, 14–15

concentration, maintaining, 31

concession, 60

confirmations, 133–134, 248, 292, 347–348

conservative investors, 34

Consolidated Quotation Service (CQS), 291

consolidations, 76, 279

construction loan notes (CLNs), 127

contingent deferred sales charge (CDSC), 183

continuing disclosure agreement, 120

continuing education requirements, 16

control securities, 65–66

conversion price, 79

conversion ratio, 79, 459

convertible bonds, 99–100

convertible mortgage bonds, 41

convertible preferred stock, 79

coordination registration method, 56

COP (certificates of participation), 124

corporate accounts, 340

corporate books, 72

corporate charter, 53, 73, 340

corporate commercial paper, 106

corporate loans

bond terminology, 88

bond types, 90–91

comparing bonds, 96–100

interest, 311

practice exams for, 108–112

price and yield calculations, 91–96

secured versus unsecured bonds, 89–90

corporate resolution, 340

corporate spin-off, 76

correspondence, 341–342

cost basis per share, 313–314

cost valuation, 313

coupon rate, 88, 92

courses

attending, 20–21

class size, 21

cost of, 21

days and times, 21

instructor availability, 21

instructor's qualifications, 20–21

online, 22

recommendations for, 20

training materials, 21

training school background, 20

About the Author

After earning a high score on the Series 7 exam in the mid-1990s, **Steven M. Rice** began his career as a stockbroker for a broker dealership with offices in Nassau County, Long Island, and in New York City. In addition to his duties as a registered representative, he also gained invaluable experience about securities registration rules and regulations when he worked in the firm's compliance office. But only after Steve began tutoring others in the firm to help them pass the Series 7 did he find his true calling as an instructor. Shortly thereafter, Steve became a founding partner and educator in Empire Stockbroker Training Institute (www.empirestockbroker.com).

In addition to writing the *Series 7 Exam 2024-2025 For Dummies* and *Securities Industry Essentials Exam For Dummies,* Steve developed and designed the Empire Stockbroker Training Institute online (Series 7, Series 6, Series 63, Series 65, Series 66, Series 24, and more) exams. Steve has also co-authored a complete library of securities training manuals for classroom use and for home study, including the Series 4, Series 6, Series 7, Series 11, Series 24, Series 63, Series 65, and Series 66. Steve's popular and highly acclaimed classes, online courses, and training manuals have helped tens of thousands of people achieve their goals and begin their lucrative new careers in the securities industry.

Dedication

I dedicate this book to my beautiful wife, Melissa. Melissa was the love of my life, my inspiration, and my best friend. Sadly, my soulmate lost her eight-year battle with cancer in 2017, and there remains a hole in my heart that will never be filled. However, I carry her undying love with me every single day.

Author's Acknowledgments

A fantastic team over at John Wiley & Sons, Inc. made this book possible. I'd like to start by thanking Executive Editor Lindsay Lefevere for planning the project and setting up a great team. I would also like to sincerely thank Development Editor Colleen Diamond for all of her help making sure everything I wrote made sense, Technical Reviewer David Lambert for making sure everything written was correct, and Elizabeth McKee for her help in making sure the online testing is top notch. The whole team's attention to detail was phenomenal.

Although he passed only a few short months after my wife, I would also like to thank my dad and role model, Tom Rice, his wife Maggie, my sisters Sharlene and Sharlet, and my son Jim and his family for their love and support. I would also like to thank my grandchildren for making me smile and laugh even during the toughest of times. I feel truly blessed to have such a wonderful family.

Finally, I want to thank my wonderful wife, Melissa. No matter what was going on in her life, she always made me her top priority. I was blessed to spend every day of the last 33 years with the most loving and selfless person I've ever met. Her fearless battle with cancer was something to admire. She faced every chemo treatment and every surgery saying to me, "I'll do whatever I have to do so that no one else gets you." I spent every day trying to become the man deserving of her love. Her undying love and support helped me through the toughest times. I am eternally grateful, and I will love her forever.

Publisher's Acknowledgments

Executive Editor: Lindsay Lefevere

Development Editor: Colleen Diamond

Technical Editor: David N. Lambert

Managing Editor: Kristie Pyles

Production Editor: Mohammed Zafar Ali

Cover Image: © Yuichiro Chino/Getty Images